A/CN.4/SER.A/2006/Add.1 (Part 1)

YEARBOOK OF THE INTERNATIONAL LAW COMMISSION

2006

Volume II
Part One

Documents of the fifty-eighth session

UNITED NATIONS
New York and Geneva, 2013

NOTE

Symbols of United Nations documents are composed of capital letters combined with figures. Mention of such a symbol indicates a reference to a United Nations document.

References to the *Yearbook of the International Law Commission* are abbreviated to *Yearbook ...*, followed by the year (for example, *Yearbook ... 2006*).

The *Yearbook* for each session of the International Law Commission comprises two volumes:

Volume I: summary records of the meetings of the session;

Volume II (Part One): reports of special rapporteurs and other documents considered during the session;

Volume II (Part Two): report of the Commission to the General Assembly.

All references to these works and quotations from them relate to the final printed texts of the volumes of the *Yearbook* issued as United Nations publications.

*

* *

The reports of the special rapporteurs and other documents considered by the Commission during its fifty-eighth session, which were originally issued in mimeographed form, are reproduced in the present volume, incorporating the corrigenda issued by the Secretariat and the editorial changes required for the presentation of the final text.

A/CN.4/SER.A/2006/Add.1 (Part 1)

UNITED NATIONS PUBLICATION

Sales No.: E.11.V.12 (Part 1)
ISBN: 978-92-1-133717-4
e-ISBN: 978-92-1-055183-0

ISSN: 0082-8289

CONTENTS

ABBREVIATIONS

AOI	Arab Organization for Industrialization
CERN	European Organization for Nuclear Research
EEC	European Economic Community
FAO	Food and Agriculture Organization of the United Nations
GCIM	Global Commission on International Migration
IAEA	International Atomic Energy Agency
ICJ	International Court of Justice
ICRC	International Committee of the Red Cross
ICSID	International Centre for Settlement of Investment Disputes
IMF	International Monetary Fund
INTERPOL	International Criminal Police Organization
IOM	International Organization for Migration
ILO	International Labour Organization
ITC	International Tin Council
IUCN	International Union for Conservation of Nature
NATO	North Atlantic Treaty Organization
NGO	non-governmental organization
OAS	Organization of American States
OECD	Organization for Economic Cooperation and Development
OPCW	Organisation for the Prohibition of Chemical Weapons
PCIJ	Permanent Court of International Justice
UNCC	United Nations Compensation Commission
UNCTAD	United Nations Conference on Trade and Development
UNDP	United Nations Development Programme
UNESCO	United Nations Educational, Scientific and Cultural Organization
UNHCR	Office of the United Nations High Commissioner for Refugees
WHO	World Health Organization
WIPO	World Intellectual Property Organization
WTO	World Trade Organization

*

* *

BYBIL	*British Year Book of International Law*
I.C.J. Pleadings	ICJ, *Pleadings, Oral Arguments, Documents*
I.C.J. Reports	ICJ, *Reports of Judgments, Advisory Opinions and Orders*
ILM	*International Legal Materials* (Washington, D.C.)
ILR	*International Law Reports* (United Kingdom)
LGDJ	Librairie générale de droit et de jurisprudence (Paris)
P.C.I.J., Series A	PCIJ, *Collection of Judgments* (Nos. 1–24: up to and including 1930)
P.C.I.J., Series B	PCIJ, *Judgments, Orders and Advisory Opinions* (Nos. 1–18: up to and including 1930)
P.C.I.J., Series A/B	PCIJ, *Collection of Advisory Opinions* (Nos. 40–80: beginning in 1931)
P.C.I.J., Series C	PCIJ, *Pleadings, Oral Arguments, Documents* (Nos. 52–88: beginning in 1931)
RGDIP	*Revue Générale de Droit International Public* (Paris)
UNRIAA	United Nations, *Reports of International Arbitral Awards*

*

* *

In the present volume, the "International Tribunal for the Former Yugoslavia" refers to the International Tribunal for the Prosecution of Persons Responsible for Serious Violations of International Humanitarian Law Committed in the Territory of the Former Yugoslavia since 1991; and the "International Tribunal for Rwanda" refers to the International Criminal Tribunal for the Prosecution of Persons Responsible for Genocide and Other Serious Violations of International Humanitarian Law Committed in the Territory of Rwanda and Rwandan Citizens Responsible for Genocide and Other Such Violations Committed in the Territory of Neighbouring States between 1 January and 31 December 1994.

*

* *

NOTE CONCERNING QUOTATIONS

In quotations, words or passages in italics followed by an asterisk were not italicized in the original text.

Unless otherwise indicated, quotations from works in languages other than English have been translated by the Secretariat.

*

* *

The Internet address of the International Law Commission is **www.un.org/law/ilc/**.

FILLING OF CASUAL VACANCIES IN THE COMMISSION (ARTICLE 11 OF THE STATUTE)

[Agenda item 1]

DOCUMENT A/CN.4/563

Note by the Secretariat

[*Original: English*]
[*30 January 2006*]

1. Following the election of Mr. Bernardo Sepúlveda to ICJ on 7 November 2005 and his subsequent resignation from the Commission, one seat on the Commission has fallen vacant.

2. In this case, article 11 of the statute of the Commission is applicable. It prescribes that:

> In the case of a casual vacancy, the Commission itself shall fill the vacancy having due regard to the provisions contained in articles 2 and 8 of this statute.

Article 2 reads:

> 1. The Commission shall consist of thirty-four members who shall be persons of recognized competence in international law.
>
> 2. No two members of the Commission shall be nationals of the same State.
>
> 3. In case of dual nationality a candidate shall be deemed to be a national of the State in which he ordinarily exercises civil and political rights.

Article 8 reads:

> At the election the electors shall bear in mind that the persons to be elected to the Commission should individually possess the qualifications required and that in the Commission as a whole representation of the main forms of civilization and of the principal legal systems of the world should be assured.

3. The term of the member to be elected by the Commission will expire at the end of 2006.

DIPLOMATIC PROTECTION

[Agenda item 2]

DOCUMENT A/CN.4/567

Seventh report on diplomatic protection, by Mr. John Dugard, Special Rapporteur

[Original: English]
[7 March 2006]

CONTENTS

Multilateral instruments cited in the present report

	Source
Treaty of Peace between the Allied and Associated Powers and Germany (Treaty of Versailles) (Versailles, 28 June 1919)	*British and Foreign State Papers*, 1919, vol. CXII (London, HM Stationery Office, 1922), p. 1.
Convention relating to the Status of Refugees (Geneva, 28 July 1951)	United Nations, *Treaty Series*, vol. 189, No. 2545, p. 137.
Treaty establishing the European Community (Rome, 25 March 1957), incorporating the amendments made by the Treaty of Nice of 26 February 2001	*Ibid.*, vol. 294, No. 4300, p. 3. See also Consolidated version of the Treaty on European Union, *Official Journal of the European Communities*, vol. 45, No. C 325 (24 December 2002).
Convention on the High Seas (Geneva, 29 April 1958)	*Ibid.*, vol. 450, No. 6465, p. 11.
Vienna Convention on Diplomatic Relations (Vienna, 18 April 1961)	*Ibid.*, vol. 500, No. 7310, p. 95.
Vienna Convention on Consular Relations (Vienna, 24 April 1963)	*Ibid.*, vol. 596, No. 8638, p. 261.
Optional Protocol to the Vienna Convention on Consular Relations concerning the Compulsory Settlement of Disputes (Vienna, 24 April 1963)	*Ibid.*, No. 8640, p. 487.
Vienna Convention on the Law of Treaties (Vienna, 23 May 1969)	*Ibid.*, vol. 1155, No. 18232, p. 331.
Convention on the Elimination of All Forms of Discrimination against Women (New York, 18 December 1979)	*Ibid.*, vol. 1249, No. 20378, p. 13.
United Nations Convention on the Law of the Sea (Montego Bay, 10 December 1982)	United Nations, *Treaty Series*, vol. 1833, No. 31363, p. 3.
Treaty establishing a Constitution for Europe (Rome, 29 October 2004)	*Official Journal of the European Union*, vol. 47, No. C 310 (16 December 2004), p. 1.

Works cited in the present report (which do not appear in the annex)

AMERASINGHE, C. F.

"The local remedies rule in appropriate perspective", *Heidelberg Journal of International Law*, vol. 36, 1976, pp. 727–759.

AMERICAN LAW INSTITUTE

Restatement of the Law Third: Foreign Relations Law of the United States. Vol. 2. St. Paul, Minn., American Law Institute, 1987.

BARBER, Nick

"Citizenship, nationalism and the European Union", *European Law Review* (London), vol. 27, 2002, pp. 241–259.

BEDERMAN, David J.

"Interim report on 'lump sum agreements and diplomatic protection'", *Report of the Seventieth Conference held in New Delhi, 26 April 2002*. London, International Law Association, 2002, pp. 230–258.

BERLIA, Georges

"Contribution à l'étude de la nature de la protection diplomatique", *Annuaire français de droit international* (Paris), vol. III, 1957, pp. 63–72.

BOLLECKER-STERN, Brigitte

Le préjudice dans la théorie de la responsabilité internationale. Paris, Pedone, 1973. 382 p.

BORCHARD, Edwin M.

The Diplomatic Protection of Citizens Abroad or the Law of International Claims. New York, Banks Law Publishing Co., 1919. 988 p.

"Protection diplomatique des nationaux à l'étranger", *Annuaire de l'Institut de Droit International*, Cambridge session, July 1931, vol. I, pp. 256–435.

"The protection of citizens abroad and change of original nationality", *Yale Law Journal*, vol. XX, No. 4, January 1934, pp. 359–392.

BROWNLIE, Ian

Principles of Public International Law. 6th ed. Oxford, Oxford University Press, 2003.

CARREAU, Dominique

Droit International. 7th ed. Paris, Pedone, 2001. 688 p.

DENZA, Eileen

Diplomatic Law: A Commentary on the Vienna Convention on Diplomatic Relations. 2nd ed. Oxford, Clarendon Press, 1998. 451 p.

DUBOUIS, Louis

"La distinction entre le droit de l'État réclamant et le droit du ressortissant dans la protection diplomatique (à propos de l'arrêt rendu par la Cour de cassation le 14 juin 1977)", *Revue critique de droit international privé* (Paris), 1978, pp. 615–640.

DUNN, Frederick Sherwood

The Protection of Nationals: A Study in the Application of International Law. Baltimore, Johns Hopkins Press, 1932. 228 p.

FELLER, A. H.

The Mexican Claims Commissions, 1923–1934: A Study in the Law and Procedure of International Tribunals. New York, Macmillan, 1935. 572 p.

GARCÍA-AMADOR, F. V., Louis B. SOHN and R. R. BAXTER

Recent Codification of the Law of State Responsibility for Injuries to Aliens. Dobbs Ferry, New York, Oceana, 1974. 402 p.

GECK, Wilhelm Karl

"Diplomatic protection", *in* Rudolf Bernhardt, ed., *Encyclopedia of Public International Law*. Vol. 1. Amsterdam, Elsevier, 1992, pp. 1045–1067.

HACKWORTH, Green Haywood

Digest of International Law. Vol. V. Washington, D.C., United States Government Printing Office, 1943. 851 p.

HURST, Sir Cecil J. B.

"Nationality of claims", *British Year Book of International Law*, 1926, vol. 7, pp. 163–182.

JENNINGS, Sir Robert and Sir Arthur WATTS, eds.

Oppenheim's International Law. 9th ed. Vol. I. *Peace.* Introduction and part 1. Harlow, Longman, 1992.

LEE, Luke T.

Consular Law and Practice. 2nd ed. Oxford, Clarendon Press, 1991. 739 p.

LILLICH, Richard B.

"The United States–Hungarian Claims Agreement of 1973", *American Journal of International Law* (Washington, D.C.), vol. 69, 1975.

LILLICH, Richard B. and Burns H. WESTON

International Claims: Their Settlement by Lump Sum Agreements. Charlottesville, University Press of Virginia, 1975.

MOORE, John Bassett

A Digest of International Law. Vol. VI. Washington, D.C., Government Printing Office, 1906.

MUMMERY, David R.

"The content of the duty to exhaust local judicial remedies", *American Journal of International Law* (Washington, D.C.), vol. 58, 1964, pp. 389–414.

NIELSEN, Fred K.

American and British Claims Arbitration: under the Special Agreement concluded between the United States and Great Britain (18 August 1910). Washington, D.C., Government Printing Office, 1926.

RALSTON, Jackson H.

The Law and Procedure of International Tribunals. Rev. ed. Stanford University, California, Stanford University Press, 1926. 512 p.

SCHWARZENBERGER, Georg

International Law. 3rd ed. Vol. 1. London, Stevens, 1957.

SHAW, Malcolm N.

International Law. 5th ed. Cambridge, Cambridge University Press, 2003. 1288 p.

SIMPSON, J. L. and Hazel FOX

International Arbitration: Law and Practice. London, Stevens, 1959. 330 p.

STEIN, Torsten

"Interim report on 'diplomatic protection under the European Union Treaty'", *Report of the Seventieth Conference held in New Delhi, 2–6 April 2002.* London, International Law Association, 2002, pp. 277–289.

WHITEMAN, Marjorie M.

Digest of International Law. Vol. 8. Washington, D.C., United States Government Printing Office, 1967.

ZOUREK, Jaroslav

"Some theoretical problems of consular law", *Journal du droit international* (Paris), vol. 90, No. 1, 1963, pp. 4–67.

Introduction[1]

1. The International Law Commission completed the first reading of a set of 19 draft articles on diplomatic protection at its fifty-sixth session, held in 2004.[2] The Commission subsequently decided, in accordance with articles 16 and 21 of its statute, to transmit the draft articles, through the Secretary-General, to Governments for comments and observations, with the request that such comments and observations be submitted to the Secretary-General by 1 January 2006. By a note dated 19 October 2004, the Secretariat invited Governments to submit their written comments by 1 January 2006. As at 26 January 2006, written comments had been received from the following 11 States: Austria, El Salvador, Guatemala, Mexico, Morocco, the Netherlands, Norway, on behalf of the Nordic countries (Denmark, Finland, Iceland, Norway and Sweden), Panama, Qatar, United States of America and Uzbekistan.[3]

[1] The Special Rapporteur wishes to acknowledge, with gratitude, the assistance of Annemarieke Künzli, PhD fellow at the University of Leiden, the Netherlands, and Alex Smithyman, formerly of New York University and presently of Chen Palmer, Wellington, New Zealand, who served as an intern to the Special Rapporteur in 2005.

[2] See *Yearbook ... 2004*, vol. II (Part Two), pp. 18 *et seq.*, para. 59. The draft articles with commentaries thereto are reproduced in paragraph 60.

[3] These comments, as well as those of Belgium, Italy and the United Kingdom of Great Britain and Northern Ireland, appear in document A/CN.4/561 and Add.1–2, reproduced in the present volume. Those of Kuwait are also reproduced in the present volume (document A/CN.4/575).

2. Since 2000, when the first draft articles on diplomatic protection were approved by the Commission, there has been a steady flow of books (both monographs and new editions of general treatises) and scholarly articles on diplomatic protection, with particular reference to the work of the Commission. A bibliography of these writings appears in the annex to the present report.

3. Many of the post-2000 publications deal with the nature of diplomatic protection and consider the question whether diplomatic protection is a procedure for the protection of the individual's human rights or a mechanism for the protection of the interest of the State exercising diplomatic protection. Some of them seriously question the validity of the rule in the *Mavrommatis Palestine Concessions* case that:

> By taking up the case of one of its subjects and by resorting to diplomatic action or international judicial proceedings on his behalf, a State is in reality asserting its own rights—its right to ensure, in the person of its subjects, respect for the rules of international law.[4]

Such critics correctly argue that several of the requirements for the exercise of diplomatic protection—such as the continuous nationality rule, the exhaustion of local remedies and the assessment of damages—indicate that the claim is in reality that of the individual and not of the

[4] *Mavrommatis Palestine Concessions, Judgment No. 2, 1924, P.C.I.J., Series A, No. 2*, p. 12.

State. This argument, however, fails to take into account the distinction between primary and secondary rules of international law, a distinction which is fundamental to the present draft articles. The individual has a right not to be tortured or not to be deprived of his or her property without compensation. These rights clearly are not the rights of a State. These rights of the individual, the violation of which may give rise to the exercise of diplomatic protection by his or her national State, belong to the field of primary rules of international law. However, the right of the State to exercise diplomatic protection in response to the violation of such a primary rule of international law by espousing the claim is a secondary rule of international law.[5] As the international legal personality of the individual is incomplete, owing to the limited capacity of the individual to assert his or her rights, the fiction inherent in the *Mavrommatis Palestine Concessions* case is the means employed by international law—a secondary rule—to enforce the primary rule, which protects the undoubted right of the individual. In the light of the fact that the draft articles are premised on the soundness (if not accuracy) of the *Mavrommatis* rule (see, in particular, article 1), little purpose would be served by an examination of criticisms of the rule at this stage. The writings in question do, however, serve to emphasize that diplomatic protection is an instrument which allows the State to become involved in the protection of the individual and that the ultimate goal of diplomatic protection is the protection of the human rights of the individual. In this sense, diplomatic protection and human rights law complement each other.[6] This notion is strongly endorsed by the Netherlands, which urges the Commission to pay closer attention to the position of the individual in the formulation of its draft articles.[7]

[5] See Dominicé, "La prétention de la personne privée dans le système de la responsabilité internationale des Etats"; and "Regard actuel sur la protection diplomatique".

[6] See Condorelli, "L'évolution du champ d'application de la protection diplomatique"; Flauss, "Vers un aggiornamento des conditions d'exercice de la protection diplomatique"; Kooijmans, "Is the right to diplomatic protection a human right?"; Feria Tinta, "Due process and the right to life in the context of the Vienna Convention on Consular Relations: arguing the *LaGrand* case"; and Pinto, "De la protection diplomatique à la protection des droits de l'homme".

[7] A/CN.4/561 and Add.1–2 (see footnote 3 above), general remarks.

4. Some of the literature is critical of decisions of the Commission not to include certain proposals. For instance, criticisms have been directed at the Commission for failing to impose a duty on States to exercise diplomatic protection by way of progressive development.[8] As these matters cannot, and should not, be reopened for discussion at second reading, they are not considered in the present report.

5. Several scholarly reviews deal critically with the language or content of particular provisions in the draft articles. They are considered in the course of the re-examination of such provisions, as are the comments of States.

6. No attempt is made in the present report to draft articles dealing with matters that will need to be included if the draft articles are translated into treaty form, such as signature, ratification and dispute settlement. In this respect, the precedent of the draft articles on responsibility of States for internationally wrongful acts is followed. The fate of the present draft articles is closely bound up with that of the draft articles on responsibility of States for internationally wrongful acts.[9] If a decision is taken to translate the latter into treaty form, it is probable and desirable that the present draft articles be incorporated into any such treaty. If, on the other hand, the draft articles on State responsibility retain their present status as a restatement of the law, it seems inevitable that the present draft articles will serve the same purpose.

7. The present report will examine the draft articles approved by the Commission at first reading in the context of comments, criticisms and suggestions made by Governments and scholars in respect of those articles. Where necessary, an amended or new provision will be proposed to take the place of the previous draft article. Only one major innovation will be proposed. Some members of the Commission, some States and some academic writers have called upon the Commission to include a provision dealing with the payment to a national of compensation received in respect of injury to that national by the State of nationality. A proposal to that effect is included after the examination of the 19 draft articles.

[8] Milano, "Diplomatic protection and human rights before the International Court of Justice: re-fashioning tradition?", pp. 94–97; and Kooijmans, *loc. cit.*

[9] *Yearbook ... 2001*, vol. II (Part Two), p. 26, para. 76.

Chapter I

Consideration of draft articles

A. Article 1

Definition and scope

Diplomatic protection consists of resort to diplomatic action or other means of peaceful settlement by a State adopting in its own right the cause of its national in respect of an injury to that national arising from an internationally wrongful act of another State.

8. The comments on article 1 fall into three categories: those calling for clarity in language or changes to the text; those suggesting additions to the commentary; and those calling for a clear distinction to be made between diplomatic protection and consular assistance. The third category is certainly the most important and will be fully considered. Other comments and suggestions may be more easily disposed of.

9. Uzbekistan suggests that the draft articles include a provision indicating the sense in which terms such as "nationality of a legal person", "incorporation" and "damage to property" are used.[10] It also objects to the use of the term "nationality" in respect of legal persons, on the

[10] A/CN.4/561 and Add.1–2 (see footnote 3 above), other comments and suggestions. The full comment from Uzbekistan makes the nature of its suggestion clearer.

ground that nationality is an attribute of natural and not legal persons.[11] This calls for two comments. First, definitions are dangerous and often create more problems than they solve.[12] It is wiser to explain the meaning of terms in the context of each rule—which the draft articles attempt to do. Secondly, in law the term "nationality" is used so frequently in respect of legal persons that it is impossible to discard this usage.

10. The Netherlands suggests that it should be made clear that article 1 includes stateless persons and refugees within the meaning of article 8.[13] It is proposed that this suggestion be accepted by an amendment to the text.

11. Guatemala has proposed an addition to paragraph (7) of the commentary on article 1 to make it clear that diplomats and consuls may benefit from diplomatic protection where they act outside their official capacities.[14] This will be done.

12. Article 1 makes it clear that "an internationally wrongful act of another State" is a requirement for diplomatic protection. This does not preclude a State from taking steps to protect its nationals before a wrongful act has occurred, but such measures do not qualify as diplomatic protection.[15] The Netherlands has wisely suggested that this matter be clarified in the commentary.[16]

13. The commentary should also make it clear that the reference to "national" in article 1 includes the protection of groups of nationals—as suggested by Condorelli.[17]

14. Several States have suggested that article 1 and its commentary provide greater clarity on the meaning of the terms "diplomatic action" and "other means of peaceful settlement" and that a clear distinction be drawn between diplomatic protection and consular assistance.[18] Academic writings have made the same point. This matter therefore requires careful consideration.

Diplomatic protection and consular assistance

15. International law recognizes two kinds of protection that States may exercise on behalf of their nationals: consular assistance and diplomatic protection.[19] There are, however, fundamental differences between the two; and a persistent subject of debate and controversy is the question of which activities by Governments fall under diplomatic protection and which actions do not. This debate is fuelled by an equally persistent misunderstanding of the definition of the term "action" for the purpose of diplomatic protection, resulting in actions being mistakenly classified as an exercise of consular assistance. The problem is not so much what constitutes consular assistance, but the definition of action for the purpose of diplomatic protection to the exclusion of consular assistance.

16. Diplomatic protection is often considered to involve judicial proceedings. Interventions outside the judicial process on behalf of nationals are sometimes not regarded as constituting diplomatic protection, but instead as falling under consular assistance. This, however, is too narrow a view of diplomatic protection. Any intervention, including negotiation, at inter-State level on behalf of a national *vis-à-vis* a foreign State should be classified as diplomatic protection (and not as consular assistance), provided that the general requirements of diplomatic protection have been met—i.e. that there has been a violation of international law for which the respondent State can be held responsible, that local remedies have been exhausted and that the individual concerned has the nationality of the acting State. That such a broad view of "action" in the context of diplomatic protection is warranted is supported by doctrine[20] and both international[21] and national[22] judicial decisions. Article 1 and its commentary give clear support to such a broad interpretation of diplomatic action. Article 1 provides that diplomatic protection comprises "resort to diplomatic action or other means of peaceful settlement" and paragraph (5) of the commentary states that:

> "Diplomatic action" covers all the lawful procedures employed by a State to inform another State of its views and concerns, including protest, request for an inquiry or for negotiations aimed at the settlement of disputes. "Other means of peaceful settlement" embraces all forms of lawful dispute settlement, from negotiation, mediation and conciliation to arbitral and judicial dispute settlement. [23]

[11] *Ibid.*, comments on draft article 1.

[12] "[A] definition … often creates more problems than it solves"—Lord Reid in *Brutus* v. *Cozens*, *Weekly Law Reports* (1972), vol. 3, pp. 525–526.

[13] A/CN.4/561 and Add.1–2 (see footnote 3 above), comments on draft article 1.

[14] *Ibid.*

[15] This view is disputed by Condorelli, "L'évolution du champ d'application …", p. 7.

[16] A/CN.4/561 and Add.1–2 (see footnote 3 above), comments on draft article 1.

[17] "L'évolution du champ d'application …", pp. 6–7.

[18] A/CN.4/561 and Add.1–2 (see footnote 3 above), comments on draft article 1 (Austria, the Netherlands and Panama), and general remarks (El Salvador).

[19] Another source of confusion concerns diplomatic representation and diplomatic protection. They are, however, very different in nature for, as Warbrick and McGoldrick state: "Diplomatic representations cover a wide range of communications from one government to another, in which one expresses its disapproval about some action or inaction of the other. They do not necessarily impute unlawful conduct to the other State"—a requirement for the exercise of diplomatic protection ("Current developments: public international law", p. 724).

[20] Borchard, *The Diplomatic Protection of Citizens Abroad or the Law of International Claims*, p. 439; Dunn, *The Protection of Nationals*, pp. 18–19; Condorelli, "L'evolution du champ d'application …", pp. 5–6.

[21] In the *Mavrommatis Palestine Concessions* case, PCIJ declared that States are allowed to take up the case of a national "by resorting to diplomatic action *or** international judicial proceedings on his behalf" (see footnote 4 above). See also *Panevezys-Saldutiskis Railway, Judgment, 1939, P.C.I.J., Series A/B, No. 76*, p. 16; *Nottebohm, Second Phase, Judgment, I.C.J. Reports 1955*, p. 24; and *Reparation for Injuries Suffered in the Service of the United Nations, Advisory Opinion, I.C.J. Reports 1949*, p. 177.

[22] In the *Rudolf Hess* case, for instance, the Federal Constitutional Court considered that diplomatic démarches by the Government of the Federal Republic of Germany were proof that the Government had fulfilled its obligations under the German Constitution, which grants a right to diplomatic protection to German citizens (ILR vol. 90 (1992), p. 396). See also *Kaunda and others* v. *President of the Republic of South Africa and Others*, *South African Law Reports* (2005 (4)), p. 235; and ILM, vol. 44 (January 2005), p. 173.

[23] *Yearbook ... 2004*, vol. II (Part Two), p. 21, para. 60.

It is difficult to draft a more comprehensive provision and commentary on the meaning of diplomatic "action" in the context of diplomatic protection. It is therefore suggested that the present draft article should not be rephrased. The provision does not, however, expressly exclude consular assistance, and this is a matter that requires further attention.

17. Unfortunately, neither government officials nor legal scholars[24] distinguish clearly between diplomatic protection and consular assistance. There are, however, three structural differences which should act as a guide to the distinction between the two institutions. First, the limited nature of consular functions provided for in the Vienna Convention on Consular Relations (hereinafter the 1963 Vienna Convention) compared with the less limited function of diplomats contained in the Vienna Convention on Diplomatic Relations; secondly, the difference in level of representation between consular assistance and diplomatic protection; and thirdly, the preventive nature of consular assistance as opposed to the remedial nature of diplomatic protection. Consuls are seriously limited in respect of the action they may take to protect their nationals by article 55, paragraph 1 of the 1963 Vienna Convention, which provides that consuls "have a duty not to interfere in the internal affairs of that State". This means, according to Shaw, that: "They have a particular role in assisting nationals in distress with regard to, for example, finding lawyers, visiting prisons and contacting local authorities, but they are unable to intervene in the judicial process or internal affairs of the receiving state or give legal advice or investigate a crime."[25] This means that consuls are permitted to represent the interests of the national but not the interests of the State in the protection of the national. This is a matter for the diplomatic branch. There is another element of distinction between diplomatic protection and consular assistance. Consular assistance has a largely preventive nature and takes place before local remedies have been exhausted or before a violation of international law has occurred. This allows for consular assistance to be simultaneously less formal and more acceptable to the host State.[26] Consular assistance is primarily concerned with the protection of the rights of the individual and requires the consent of the individual concerned.[27] Indeed, as stipulated in article 36, paragraph 1 (*b*), of the 1963 Vienna Convention, consular assistance will only be provided if the individual concerned so requests. A diplomatic démarche on the other hand, is designed to bring the matter to the international, or inter-State, level and can ultimately result in international litigation. Moreover, the individual concerned cannot prevent his national State from taking up the claim or from continuing procedures in the exercise of diplomatic protection.

18. The *LaGrand* and *Avena* cases[28] require special mention in this connection as they involved both consular assistance and diplomatic protection. In these cases Germany and Mexico, respectively, filed a case against the United States for violation of the 1963 Vienna Convention in their own right and in their right to exercise diplomatic protection, as their nationals had individually suffered from non-compliance with the Convention. The merits of the cases before ICJ thus concerned the exercise of consular assistance while the mechanism utilized to bring the claim was, in both cases, the exercise of diplomatic protection. In *LaGrand* ICJ accepted Germany's claim (partly) as an exercise of its right to diplomatic protection and established that both the State of Germany and the German nationals had suffered from lack of consular assistance.[29] However, in the case of Mexico, the Court decided otherwise and determined that the violations of the Convention constituted a direct injury to Mexico with the result that diplomatic protection was not necessary as an instrument for bringing the claim. The *LaGrand* case is particularly important. The claim Germany presented before ICJ was based on the failure by the United States to notify without delay the LaGrands of their right to consular assistance and to inform the German authorities of the arrest and detention of two German nationals, both obligations deriving from article 36, paragraph 1, of the Convention. Germany argued that it would have been able through the exercise of consular assistance to provide adequate legal assistance and relevant information which, in its turn, perhaps, would have prevented the LaGrands from being sentenced to death.[30] The claim was presented both in Germany's own right and in its right to exercise diplomatic protection on behalf of its nationals.[31] The United States contested Germany's claim under diplomatic protection and tried to convince the Court that Germany was confusing diplomatic protection and consular assistance and that the Court should therefore declare the claim inadmissible. It argued that the Convention does not deal with diplomatic protection, but only with consular assistance. In addition, it was claimed that, contrary to the argument of Germany, the Convention did not protect individual rights and therefore the exercise of diplomatic protection should not be accepted.[32]

The Court rejected the objections presented by the United States and decided that it had jurisdiction to entertain the claim based on both direct and indirect injury. It stated clearly that the general jurisdiction clause under the Optional Protocol to the Vienna Convention on Consular Relations concerning the Compulsory Settlement of Disputes would "not prevent a State party to a treaty, which creates individual rights, from taking up the case of one of its nationals and instituting international judicial proceedings on behalf of that national".[33] The Court clearly distinguished between consular assistance and diplomatic protection, accepting that individual rights arising under a treaty on consular relations could be claimed through the vehicle of diplomatic protection.[34] Diplomatic protection is a mechanism that may be resorted to after an internationally wrongful act has occurred, causing injury

[24] See Denza, *Diplomatic Law: A Commentary on the Vienna Convention on Diplomatic Relations*, p. 33; and Lee, *Consular Law and Practice* pp. 138, 148–151, 155 and 167. See generally on this subject, Künzli, "Exercising diplomatic protection: the fine line between litigation, démarches and consular assistance".

[25] Shaw, *International Law*, p. 688.

[26] See Caflisch, "La pratique suisse de la protection diplomatique", p. 77.

[27] Zourek, "Some theoretical problems of consular law", p. 55.

[28] *LaGrand (Germany* v. *United States of America), Judgment, I.C.J. Reports 2001*, p. 466, and *Avena and Other Mexican Nationals (Mexico* v. *United States of America), Judgment, I.C.J. Reports 2004*, p. 12.

[29] See *I.C.J. Reports 2001* (footnote 28 above), p. 494, para. 77.

[30] *Ibid.*, p. 491, para. 71.

[31] *Ibid.*, p. 481, para. 38, and p. 489, para. 65.

[32] *Ibid.*, p. 482, para. 40.

[33] *Ibid.*, p. 483, para. 42; see also Spiermann, "The *LaGrand* case and the individual as a subject of international law".

[34] *I.C.J. Reports 2001* (see footnote 28 above), pp. 492–494, paras. 75–77.

to an alien. Since the non-compliance with the 1963 Vienna Convention by the United States gave rise to injury to the German nationals as a result of the violation of their individual rights under that Convention, Germany had invoked the proper procedure to claim redress for the injury.

19. A particular source of confusion of diplomatic protection and consular assistance is article I–10 of the Treaty establishing a Constitution for Europe (hereinafter the Constitution), which corresponds to article 46 of the Charter of fundamental rights of the European Union[35] and article 20 of the Treaty establishing the European Community. The article provides in paragraph 2 (*c*) that:

> Citizens of the Union ... shall have ... the right to enjoy, in the territory of a third country in which the Member State of which they are nationals is not represented, the protection of the diplomatic and consular authorities of any Member State on the same conditions as the nationals of that State.[36]

At first sight, the provision may seem non-controversial. It is an expression of the principle of non-discrimination, which is fundamental to the European Union. Since discrimination on the ground of nationality is prohibited within the Union, it is not surprising that Union citizens should also receive equal protection outside the Union. However, by providing for both consular assistance and diplomatic protection, the provision disregards the fundamental differences between these two mechanisms. In addition, it is particularly problematic in the light of the criteria for diplomatic protection.

The principal objection to this provision is that it offends the principle of *pacta tertii nec nocent nec prosunt*. The European treaties are treaties under international law and therefore are governed by article 34 of the Vienna Convention on the Law of Treaties, which provides that treaties are only applicable between the parties to a treaty and are not binding on third States. Thus, any provision contained in a European Union treaty, charter or constitution is not binding upon States that are not members of the Union. Third States are not bound to respect any of the provisions contained in treaties and conventions in force within the Union and are not obliged to—and with respect to diplomatic protection are unlikely to—accept protection by States that are not the State of nationality of an individual Union citizen.[37]

A "citizen" of the European Union is not a national of all member States of the Union, which means that Union citizenship does not fulfil the requirement of nationality of claims for the purpose of diplomatic protection. The Union treaty provisions purporting to confer the right to diplomatic protection on all Union citizens by all member States of the Union is therefore flawed—unless it is interpreted as applicable to consular assistance only. It is submitted that this is indeed its intention.[38] Although consular assistance is usually exercised only on behalf of a national, international law does not prohibit the rendering of consular assistance to nationals of another State. Since consular assistance is not an exercise in the protection of the rights of a State nor an espousal of a claim, the nationality criterion is not required to be applied as strictly as in the case of diplomatic protection. There is therefore no necessity for a legal interest through the bond of nationality.

20. In theory, the distinction between diplomatic protection and consular assistance is clear. The former is an inter-State intervention conducted by diplomatic officials or government representatives attached to the foreign ministry which occurs when a national is injured by an internationally wrongful act committed by another State, and the national has exhausted local remedies. It is an intervention designed to remedy an international wrong, which may take many forms, including protest, negotiation and judicial dispute settlement. Consular assistance, on the other hand, involves assistance rendered to nationals (and possible non-nationals) who find themselves in difficulties in a foreign State by career consuls or honorary consuls not engaged in political representation. Such assistance is preventive in the sense that it aims to prevent the commission of an international wrong. The national is provided with consular advice and legal assistance to ensure that he receives a fair trial (if he is charged with a criminal offence) or to protect his personal or proprietary interests in the host State. Despite the clear theoretical distinction between the two institutions there are overlaps (as illustrated by *LaGrand* and *Avena*) and failures to distinguish the two (as shown by the European Union treaties). In these circumstances, it might be wise to make it clear in article 1 that the Commission is aware of the distinction and wishes it to be maintained. The commentary will also address this issue.

21. It is proposed that article 1 be amended to read:

"1. Diplomatic protection consists of resort to diplomatic action or other means of peaceful settlement by a State adopting in its own right the cause of its national *or a person referred to in article 8* in respect of an injury to that national *or person* arising from an internationally wrongful act of another State.

"2. *Diplomatic protection shall not be interpreted to include the exercise of consular assistance in accordance with international law.*"

B. Article 2

Right to exercise diplomatic protection

A State has the right to exercise diplomatic protection in accordance with the present draft articles.

22. There are few comments on this provision. The Netherlands suggests that paragraph (3) of the commentary be deleted or clarified.[39] It does indeed seem to be superfluous and should be deleted.

---

[35] *Official Journal of the European Union*, vol. 43, No. C 364 (18 December 2000), p. 19.

[36] Although the Constitution has not (yet) entered into force and thus is not yet a binding document, this is the most recent document in which the right to diplomatic protection is provided for. It should be borne in mind that this provision is literally the same as the provision in the Treaty establishing the European Community, which of course is binding upon European Union member States.

[37] See Storost, *Diplomatischer Schutz durch EG und EU?*, pp. 148–149.

[38] Stein, "Interim report on 'diplomatic protection under the European Union Treaty'", pp. 278, 283–284.

[39] A/CN.4/561 and Add.1–2 (see footnote 3 above), comments on draft article 2.

23. Paragraph (2) of the commentary states that the State has a right to exercise diplomatic protection but is under no duty to do so. This issue has been the subject of several national decisions since the Commission decided not to impose a duty on States to exercise diplomatic protection: *Abbasi and another* v. *Secretary of State for Foreign and Commonwealth Affairs and another*;[40] *Kaunda and Others* v. *President of the Republic of South Africa and Others*;[41] and *Van Zyl and Others* v. *Government of the Republic of South Africa and Others*.[42] These decisions, which give some support to the existence of duty to exercise diplomatic protection under national law, should be considered in the commentary.

24. In a general comment on the draft articles, Austria states:

> It seems that the Commission concentrated only on one aspect of diplomatic protection, namely as a right of a State to make certain claims in the interest of its nationals. This right is, however, balanced by the corresponding obligation of the other States to accept such claims by a State. The legal regime on diplomatic protection also stipulates under which conditions a State has to accept such interventions by another State. Such a view undoubtedly sheds some new light on that legal regime and reveals different aspects of it, which the text of the Commission does not sufficiently take into account.[43]

It is suggested that article 2 is the appropriate place to provide for recognition of such a duty on the part of States. Article 2 might therefore be amended to read:

"1. A State has the right to exercise diplomatic protection in accordance with the present draft articles.

"2. *A State is under an obligation to accept a claim of diplomatic protection made in accordance with the present draft articles.*"

C. Article 3

Protection by the State of nationality

1. The State entitled to exercise diplomatic protection is the State of nationality.

2. Notwithstanding paragraph 1, diplomatic protection may be exercised in respect of a non-national in accordance with draft article 8.

25. The Netherlands proposes that the provision be formulated to read: "The State of nationality is the State entitled to exercise diplomatic protection." How this places "greater emphasis on the perspective of the individual",[44] as suggested by the Netherlands, is difficult to understand. But it is a more elegant formulation than the present article 3 and should be adopted.

26. The Netherlands also states, without any explanation, that this provision is to be seen in the light of developments relating to European citizenship. As explained above, there is a distinction between European "citizenship" and nationality of member States. In directive 2004/38/EC,[45] the concept of European Union citizenship is defined. Although the directive primarily concerns movement and residence of individuals eligible for Union citizenship *within* the Union, some of its provisions are relevant to the question of protection *outside* the Union. While it is stipulated in the preamble (point (3)) that "Union citizenship should be the fundamental status of nationals of the Member States when they exercise their right of free movement and residence", the operative part defines a Union citizen as "any person having the nationality of a Member State" (art. 2 (1)), nationality thus being a prerequisite for Union citizenship. In the Constitution it is stated in article I–10, paragraph 1, that "[c]itizenship of the Union shall be additional to national citizenship and shall not replace it".[46] These provisions clearly demonstrate that citizenship cannot be equated with nationality and that Union citizenship should not be interpreted to negate the nationality of individual States, or the power of Union member States to determine their own nationality laws and criteria for naturalization. In these circumstances, it is difficult to see how Union citizenship can have any bearing on nationality.

27. It is proposed that article 3 should be amended to read:

"1. *The State of nationality is the State entitled to exercise diplomatic protection.*

"2. Notwithstanding paragraph 1, diplomatic protection may be exercised in respect of a non-national in accordance with article 8."

D. Article 4

State of nationality of a natural person

For the purposes of diplomatic protection of natural persons, a State of nationality means a State whose nationality the individual sought to be protected has acquired by birth, descent, succession of States, naturalization or in any other manner, not inconsistent with international law.

28. Article 4 has been criticized on the ground that it fails to make it clear that nationality is determined by internal, national law—provided it is not inconsistent with international law.[47] The Commission clearly believed that

[40] [2002] EWCA Civ 1598; [2002] All ER (D) 70 (Nov); ILM, vol. 42, No. 2 (March 2003), p. 358.

[41] See footnote 22 above.

[42] Judgment of 20 July 2005, case No. 20320/2002 [2005] 4 All SA 96 (T).

[43] A/CN.4/561 and Add.1–2 (see footnote 3 above), general remarks.

[44] *Ibid.*, comments on draft article 3.

[45] Directive 2004/38/EC of the European Parliament and of the Council of 29 April 2004 on the right of citizens of the Union and their family members to move and reside freely within the territory of the Member States, *Official Journal of the European Union*, vol. 47, No. L 158 (30 April 2004), pp. 77–123.

[46] See Barber, "Citizenship, nationalism and the European Union", who states that "European citizenship was intended to complement, and not to replace, national citizenship" (p. 241).

[47] See the comment by Uzbekistan, A/CN.4/561 and Add.1–2 (see footnote 3 above), comments on draft article 4. Santulli suggests that the article be reformulated as follows: "A State of nationality means a State whose nationality the individual [sought to be protected] has acquired in good faith in accordance with its internal law." ("Travaux de la Commission du droit international" (2001), p. 371).

this was implicit in the formulation of the provision and placed this beyond all doubt in paragraph (1) of the commentary. This may, however, be made clear in article 4 itself.

29. Austria objects to the formulation of article 4 on the ground that "nationality is not acquired by State succession but as a consequence of State succession",[48] and suggests that it should be reformulated accordingly.

30. In order to meet these criticisms, article 4 might be reformulated to read:

"For the purposes of diplomatic protection of natural persons, a State of nationality means a State whose nationality the individual sought to be protected has acquired by birth, descent *or naturalization, or as a consequence of the succession of States, or in any other manner recognized by the law of that State, provided it is not inconsistent with international law.*"

E. Article 5

Continuous nationality of a natural person

1. A State is entitled to exercise diplomatic protection in respect of a person who was its national at the time of the injury and is a national at the date of the official presentation of the claim.

2. Notwithstanding paragraph 1, a State may exercise diplomatic protection in respect of a person who is its national at the date of the official presentation of the claim but was not a national at the time of the injury, provided that the person has lost his or her former nationality and has acquired, for a reason unrelated to the bringing of the claim, the nationality of that State in a manner not inconsistent with international law.

3. Diplomatic protection shall not be exercised by the present State of nationality in respect of a person against a former State of nationality of that person for an injury incurred when that person was a national of the former State of nationality and not of the present State of nationality.

31. Article 5 has elicited the most comments and criticisms from States. The main points of criticism relate to the *dies ad quem* (official presentation of the claim) and to paragraph 2. These will be fully examined. However, there are a number of drafting suggestions that should be dealt with first.

32. Austria objects to the phrase "bringing of the claim" in paragraph 2 on the ground that it suggests a judicial procedure, and is thus more limited than the forms of diplomatic protection described in article 1.[49] It is suggested that the commentary make it clear that such limitation is not intended—if paragraph 2 is retained.

33. The Netherlands suggests that "shall" in paragraph 3 be replaced with "may" because this accords more with the discretionary nature of diplomatic protection.[50] In English, "may not" is not more discretionary than "shall not", so this suggestion should not be accepted. The Netherlands also suggests, in order to bring article 5, paragraph 3, into line with other provisions, that the word "incurred" be replaced with "caused". This seems wise.

34. The United States suggests the insertion of the word "only" in the first line of paragraph 1—"A State is entitled to exercise diplomatic protection *only** in respect of ..."—to make it clear that the paragraph intends to limit the right to diplomatic protection found in articles 2 and 3 to claims by persons who meet the continuous nationality requirement.[51] It is recommended that this suggestion be followed.

35. Several States have raised objections to paragraph 2.[52] The most helpful criticism comes from the United States, which argues that the main purpose of paragraph 2 is to protect a person whose nationality has changed as a result of succession. It questions whether laws mandate a change of nationality in the case of marriage and adoption. Indeed, it might have added that the prohibition on the automatic change of nationality of women in the case of marriage contained in the Convention on the Elimination of All Forms of Discrimination against Women[53] reduces still further the likelihood of such changes taking place. The United States believes that the right of diplomatic protection passes in State succession, and the right to diplomatically protect in this situation should not be viewed as an exception to the general requirement. Accordingly it suggests that the issue should be addressed through the addition of a reference to the "predecessor State" in article 5, paragraph 1. It is recommended that this proposal be adopted.

36. There is virtually no State practice to support a requirement that nationality be retained continuously from the time of injury to the date of presentation or resolution of the claim.[54] Yet, as the United States points out,[55] it is incongruous to draft a rule on continuous nationality that fails to take account of the period between the *dies a quo* and *dies ad quem*. It is suggested that article 5, paragraph 1, be adjusted accordingly. This may be an exercise in progressive development but it seems to be one that is justified.

37. The most controversial aspect of the continuous nationality rule concerns the *dies ad quem*—the final date or stage of the proceedings at which the injured individual must still be a national. The Commission has chosen, on the basis of its reading of State practice, the date of the official presentation of the claim. This position

[48] A/CN.4/561 and Add.1–2 (see footnote 3 above), comments on draft article 4.

[49] *Ibid.*, comments on draft article 5.

[50] *Ibid.*

[51] *Ibid.*

[52] *Ibid.* (El Salvador, Qatar and the United States).

[53] Art. 9, para. 1.

[54] See *Yearbook ... 2000*, vol. II (Part One), document A/CN.4/506 and Add.1, pp. 243–244, paras. 200–205.

[55] A/CN.4/561 and Add.1–2 (see footnote 3 above), comments on draft article 5.

is supported by several States.[56] On the other hand, it is strongly opposed by the United States which argues for the date of the resolution of the claim, that is, the making of the award.[57]

38. The United States relies largely on the decision of an ICSID arbitral tribunal in the *Loewen* case, which held that:

> In international law parlance, there must be continuous national identity from the date of the events giving rise to the claim, which date is known as the *dies a quo*, through the date of the resolution of the claim, which date is known as the *dies ad quem*.[58]

This decision, it argues, is supported by a number of other arbitral decisions and claims presented through diplomatic channels in which the person on whose behalf the claim was presented changed his/her nationality *after* the claim was officially presented, but before the final resolution of the claim. In each of these cases, the international claim was dismissed or withdrawn when it became known that the claim was being asserted on behalf of a national of a State other than the claimant State. The United States claims that these cases reflect a consistent State practice amounting to a customary rule. Moreover, as a policy matter this rule is preferable, as it avoids a situation where the respondent State owes the claimant State for an injury to a person who is no longer the legal concern of that State.

39. Academic opinion is not helpful on this subject. Some writers favour the date of presentation,[59] while others support the date of the resolution of the claim.[60] Most, however, acknowledge that the *dies ad quem* is uncertain on the ground that there is support for both positions.[61] State practice is equally unhelpful, as treaties differ in their formulation of the *dies ad quem*.[62] Although the Conference for the Codification of International Law (The Hague, 1930) is often cited in support of the date of the award,[63] it must be recalled that this "support" is based on a survey of State opinion only, and that of the 20 States that responded to the survey, eight rejected continuous nationality as a rule, three abstained and nine voted in favour (including the United Kingdom of Great Britain and Northern Ireland and four of its dominions)![64]

40. Judicial decisions on this subject are also too uncertain to provide evidence of a rule of customary international law. In large part the divergences of judicial opinion may be ascribed to the divergences in treaties regulating such claims. As Umpire Parker stated in *Administrative Decision No. V*:

> When the majority decisions in these cases come to be analyzed, it is clear that they were in each case controlled by the language of the particular protocol governing the tribunal deciding them, which language limited their jurisdiction to claims possessing the nationality of the nation asserting them not only in origin but continuously—in some instances to the date of the *filing* of the claim, in others to the date of its *presentation* to the tribunal, in others to the date of the *judgment* rendered, and in still others to the date of the *settlement*. This lack of uniformity with respect to the period of continuity of nationality required for jurisdictional purposes results from each case being controlled by the language of the particular convention governing.[65]

In these circumstances, it is not surprising that some decisions favour the date of presentation,[66] some favour the date of the award,[67] and others are inconclusive.[68] Significantly, many of the decisions in favour of the date of the resolution of the claim, and on which the United States relies, involve instances in which the national changed his/her nationality after the presentation of the claim and before the award to that of the respondent State. In such a case it could hardly be expected that the claim would succeed, as the respondent State would then be paying compensation to another State in respect of an injury to its own national![69] This was the case with *Ebenezer*

[56] *Ibid.*, Austria, the Netherlands and Norway, on behalf of the Nordic countries.

[57] *Ibid.*

[58] *The Loewen Group Inc.* v. *United States of America*, case No. ARB(AF)/98/3, Award (26 June 2003), *ICSID Reports*, vol. 7, p. 485, para. 225; see also ILM, vol. 42, No. 4 (July 2003), p. 811.

[59] Borchard, *op. cit.*, p. 666.

[60] Jennings and Watts, *Oppenheim's International Law*, p. 512; Hurst, "Nationality of claims", p. 163; García-Amador, Sohn and Baxter, *Recent Codification of the Law of State Responsibility for Injuries to Aliens*, p. 82.

[61] *Oppenheim's* (Jennings and Watts, *op. cit.*, p. 512, footnote 6) qualifies support for the date of the award by stating that in some cases the date of presentation of the claim will suffice. See also Schwarzenberger, *International Law, p.* 597; Brownlie, *Principles of Public International Law*, p. 461; Feller, *The Mexican Claims Commissions, 1923–1934*, pp. 86 and 96–97; separate opinion of Judge Jessup, *Barcelona Traction, Light and Power Company, Limited, Second Phase, Judgment, I.C.J. Reports 1970*, pp. 202–203; Borchard, "The protection of citizens abroad and change of original nationality", pp. 377–378; and "Protection diplomatique des nationaux à l'étranger", pp. 256 and 284; Hurst, *loc. cit.*, pp. 179–180; Duchesne, "The continuous-nationality-of-claims principle: its historical development and current relevance to investor-State investment disputes", pp. 799–802; and Paulsson, *Denial of Justice in International Law*, p. 183.

[62] See the comment of Umpire Parker in *Administrative Decision No. V* (31 October 1924), UNRIAA, vol. VII (Sales No. 1956.V.5), p. 143. See also Ralston, *The Law and Procedure of International Tribunals*, pp. 164–165; and Hackworth, *Digest of International Law*, pp. 807–808.

[63] See *Minnie Stevens Eschauzier (Great Britain)* v. *United Mexican States* (24 June 1931), UNRIAA (Sales No. 1952.V.3), vol. V, pp. 210–211.

[64] For a history of this survey of opinion, see Duchesne, *loc. cit.*, pp. 794–797.

[65] *Administrative Decision No. V* (see footnote 62 above).

[66] Case of *Captain W. H. Gleadell* (Great Britain *v.* Mexico), UNRIAA, vol. V (Sales No. 1952.V.3), p. 44; also reported in Hackworth, *op. cit.*, p. 805; case of *F. W. Flack* (Great Britain *v.* Mexico), UNRIAA (see above), p. 61; also reported in Feller, *op. cit.*, p. 96.

[67] *Minnie Stevens Eschauzier* (see footnote 63 above), p. 207; *Benchiton* case, *Affaire des biens britanniques au Maroc espagnol (Spain* v. *Great Britain)* (1 May 1925), UNRIAA, vol. II (Sales No. 1949.V.1), p. 615 (translation in *Annual Digest of Public International Law Cases, years 1923 to 1924* (London, Longmans, Green, 1933), p. 189); case of *María Guadalupe* (unpublished), reported in Feller, *op. cit.*, p. 97; *Loewen* case (see footnote 58 above).

[68] *Exors. of F. Lederer (deceased)* v. *German Government*, *Recueil des Décisions des Tribunaux Arbitraux Mixtes institués par les Traités de Paix*, vol. III (Paris, Sirey, 1924), p. 762 (largely a question of treaty interpretation); *F. H. Redward and Others (Great Britain)* v. *United States (Hawaiian Claims)* (10 November 1925), UNRIAA, vol. VI (Sales No. 1955.V.3); also reported in Nielsen, *American and British Claims Arbitration*, p. 30 (claims withdrawn); *Chopin*, UNRIAA, vol. X (Sales No. 1955.V.3), p. 68; and *French and American Claims Commission, 1880–1884*, vol. 60, Records of Claims (claim withdrawn); case of *Maud T. de Gennes* reported in Ralston, *op. cit.*, p. 165; *Kren Claim*, ILR, vol. 20 (1953), p. 234.

[69] See the comment to this effect by the United States Supreme Court in *Burthe* v. *Denis*, 133 U.S. 514 (1890), pp. 520–521.

Barstow,[70] the claim of the executors of *F. Lederer*,[71] the *Hawaiian Claims*,[72] *Chopin*,[73] *Gribble*[74] and, of course, *Loewen*.[75]

41. The United States relies largely on the decision in *Loewen*; but this decision—on this aspect of the case—is seriously flawed. While most of the decision is carefully reasoned and researched (for instance on local remedies), the crucial issue before the tribunal, that of the *dies ad quem*, is disposed of in a manner which gives no indication that the tribunal applied its mind to the matter at all. It simply asserts, without any examination whatsoever of authority (despite the fact that counsel referred the tribunal to the relevant authorities), that under customary international law "there must be continuous national identity from the date of the events giving rise to the claim ... through the date of the resolution of the claim."[76] The tribunal notes that "the International Law Commission issued a report which proposed eliminating the continuous nationality rule even in cases of diplomatic protection"; that "[t]he report itself met with criticism in many quarters"; and that the Commission "is far from approving any recodification based on the report".[77] Had the tribunal read the report,[78] it would have been aware of the dispute over the *dies ad quem*, which features prominently in the report. Moreover, had it, before giving judgement on 26 June 2003, enquired about the work of the Commission on this subject, it would have learned that in 2002 the Commission had adopted a draft article on continuous nationality which gives approval to the date of the official presentation of the claim as the *dies ad quem*.[79] But it made no attempt to do so. Had the tribunal taken the trouble to find out about the controversy surrounding the *dies ad quem* in continuous nationality, it is not unlikely that it would have sought to fashion a more restrictive rule and one that took account of the facts before it—namely a rule that confined itself to making it impossible for a State to present a claim on behalf of a national where that national, subsequent to the filing of the claim, had acquired the nationality of the respondent State.

42. *Loewen* has, rightly, been vigorously criticized. Paulsson states that:

> The tribunal's treatment of the continuous nationality issue, considering its outcome-determinative effect, was startling in its succinctness.[80]
>
> There is nothing in the award to indicate that the arbitrators had considered the special addendum on "continuous nationality and the transferability of claims" prepared by the ILC's rapporteur on diplomatic protection, Professor Dugard, in early 2000. They wrote only that Loewen had *contended* such a report had been issued, and had encountered some criticism. But anyone who reads the Report would see that Dugard's extensive review of the authorities led him to conclude that there was no established rule in this area. The *dies ad quem* requirement which commended itself to the *Loewen* arbitrators was perhaps the least plausible of a long series of alternative candidates.[18]
>
> [18] ... These included: (i) the date on which a government endorses the claim of a national; (ii) the date of initial diplomatic negotiations; (iii) the date of filing the claim; (iv) the date of signature of the treaty referring to the relevant forum; (v) the date of ratification of said treaty; (vi) the date of its entry into force; (vii) the date of presentation of the claim ...; (viii) the date of conclusion of the oral hearings; (ix) the date of judgment (i.e. the *Loewen* solution); and (x) the most extreme, the date of settlement.
>
> Without any indication of being aware of it, the *Loewen* arbitrators adopted the reasoning in the case of *Minnie Stevens Eschauzier* (*Great Britain* v. *US*), 24 June 1931, V RIAA 207; whose claim was rejected because she lost her British nationality by marriage to an American between the date of conclusion of the oral hearing and the judgment. As the Umpire (Edwin P. Parker) noted in the far more influential *Administrative Decision No. V* (*US* v. *Germany*), 31 October 1924, VII RIAA 119: (A) the acquisition of nationality transfers allegiance but does not transport existing state obligations and, (B) at any rate, most of the decisions depend on the *lex specialis* of the relevant treaty and therefore do not reflect a general principle; 'it may well be doubted whether the alleged rule [of continuous nationality] has received such universal recognition as to justify the broad statement that it is an established rule of international law'.[81]

Duchesne, in similar vein, contends that "there is good reason to discount the weight" of *Loewen*. He continues:

> Whatever other reaction the *Loewen* tribunal's decision might invite, its discussion of the continuous-nationality "rule" was, if not cursory, then at least conclusory ... the tribunal's discussion of the continuous-nationality issue simply asserts the existence of a "rule" without citation or even discussion. The tribunal goes so far as to assert: "There is only limited dispute as to the history of the requirement of continuous nationality to the end of any international proceeding." But ... even those authorities who support treating continuous nationality as a "rule" have acknowledged that there is much confusion, and little consensus, concerning the point to which original nationality must be maintained. The *Loewen* tribunal's failure to acknowledge, much less deal with, the contrary authority, particularly after substantial briefing by the disputing parties and a full oral hearing on the issue, strongly suggests that ... it approached the issue with a preconceived notion of customary international law and felt little need to put that notion to the test of careful examination.[82]

In these circumstances, it is small wonder that the Netherlands "considers that it is not clear whether the *Loewen* case truly reflects the law as it currently stands".[83]

43. In the light of the uncertainty surrounding the *dies ad quem* the Commission is required to make a choice between the date of the official presentation of the claim and the date of the resolution of the claim. The authorities are inconclusive and the response of States, while small, favours the date of the presentation of the claim. In these circumstances, the Commission must be guided by principle and policy in the exercise of its choice. Principle supports the date of the presentation of the claim, as this most favours the interests of the individual. So too does policy, if policy is equated with fairness. Many years may pass between the presentation of a claim and its final resolution and it is unfair to deny the individual the right to change nationality, through marriage or naturalization,

[70] See Hackworth, *op. cit.*, p. 805.

[71] See footnote 68 above.

[72] *Ibid.*

[73] *Ibid.*

[74] See the Report of Robert S. Hale, Esq., *Papers relating to the Treaty of Washington*, vol. VI (Washington, D.C., Government Printing Office, 1874), p. 14.

[75] See footnote 58 above.

[76] *Ibid.*

[77] *Ibid.*, para. 236.

[78] See footnote 54 above.

[79] *Yearbook ... 2002*, vol. II (Part Two), p. 67, para. 280.

[80] Paulsson, "Continuous nationality in *Loewen*", p. 214.

[81] Paulsson, *Denial of Justice in International Law*, pp. 183–184.

[82] Duchesne, *loc. cit.*, pp. 808–809. The reader should be aware that the author was involved in the *Loewen* case.

[83] A/CN.4/561 and Add.1–2 (see footnote 3 above), comments on draft article 5.

during this period. Moreover, the date of presentation is significant as it is the date on which the State of nationality shows its clear intention to exercise diplomatic protection—a fact that was hitherto uncertain. Perhaps the strongest statement on policy is to be found in the *Minnie Stevens Eschauzier* case (on which the United States relies for its position):

> It might be argued that international jurisdiction would be rendered considerably more complicated if the tribunal had to take into account changes supervening during the period between the filing of the claim and the date of the award. Those changes may be numerous and may even annul one another. Naturalizations may be applied for, and obtained, and may be voluntarily lost. Marriages may be concluded and dissolved. In a majority of cases, changes in identity or nationality will escape the knowledge of the tribunal, and often of the Agents as well. It will be extremely difficult, even when possible, to ascertain whether at the time of the decision all personal elements continue to be identical to those which existed when the claim was presented. Jurisdiction would undoubtedly be simplified if the date of filing were accepted as decisive, without any of the events that may very frequently occur subsequently to that date, having to be traced up to the date of rendering judgment.
>
> It can therefore not be a matter for surprise that both *Borchard* (pages 664 and 666), and *Ralston* (section 293), state that a long course of arbitral decisions has established that a claim must have remained continuously in the hands of a citizen of the claimant Government, until the *time of its presentation*.[84]

44. Different policy considerations apply where the national on whose behalf the claim is brought acquires the nationality of the respondent State after the presentation of the claim as occurred in *Loewen* and many of the cases on which the United States relies. In such circumstances, fairness dictates that the date of the award be selected as *dies ad quem*, as the contrary position would, in the words of *Loewen*, "produce a result so unjust that it could be sustained only by irrefutable logic or compelling precedent, and neither exists".[85]

45. It is therefore proposed that the Commission retain the official date of presentation of the claim as the *dies ad quem* for the continuous nationality rule, but that an exception be made for the case in which the national on whose behalf the claim is brought acquires the nationality of the respondent State after the presentation of the claim. Here the date of the resolution of the claim is the *dies ad quem*.

46. It may be argued that article 5, paragraph 3, is superfluous in the light of the discarding of article 5, paragraph 2. On the other hand, it is suggested that it may have relevance in the case of change of nationality arising from the succession of States. For this reason it is retained.

47. It is proposed that article 5 should read:

"1. A State is entitled to exercise diplomatic protection *only* in respect of a person *who was a national of that State, or any predecessor State, continuously from the date of injury to the date of the official presentation of the claim.*

"2. *A State is not entitled to exercise diplomatic protection in respect of a person who acquires the nationality of the State against which the claim is brought after the presentation of the claim.*

"3. Diplomatic protection *may* not be exercised by the present State of nationality in respect of a person against a former State of nationality of that person for an injury *caused* when that person was a national of the former State of nationality and not of the present State of nationality."

F. Article 6

Multiple nationality and claim against a third State

1. Any State of which a dual or multiple national is a national may exercise diplomatic protection in respect of that national against a State of which that individual is not a national.

2. Two or more States of nationality may jointly exercise diplomatic protection in respect of a dual or multiple national.

48. Austria comments that there is no need for paragraph 2 "as there is certainly no doubt that two or more States may jointly act when exercising the right of diplomatic protection". Even if such a clause is omitted "the State to which the claim is presented must accept such a joint démarche".[86] Austria warns that this paragraph will inevitably raise difficult questions about how joint actions are to be conducted or which State is to enjoy priority in bringing a claim. The correctness of its warning is borne out by the comments made by El Salvador, Guatemala, Qatar and Uzbekistan.[87] In these circumstances, it seems best to retain only paragraph 1 of article 6.

G. Article 7

Multiple nationality and claim against a State of nationality

A State of nationality may not exercise diplomatic protection in respect of a person against a State of which that person is also a national unless the nationality of the former State is predominant, both at the time of the injury and at the date of the official presentation of the claim.

49. This provision has elicited little criticism from either scholars[88] or States. Austria and Norway (on behalf of the Nordic States) welcome it.[89] Whereas some States question it as a rule of customary international law,[90] Norway states that it "constitutes a codification of existing customary international law".[91] Some States insist on clarification of the term "predominant",[92] which is explained in the commentary, while Morocco prefers the term "effective" to "predominant".[93] The Commission has, however,

---

[84] UNRIAA (see footnote 63 above), p. 209.

[85] ILM, vol. 42, No. 4 (July 2003), p. 848, para. 232.

[86] A/CN.4/561 and Add.1–2 (see footnote 3 above), comments on draft article 6.

[87] *Ibid.*

[88] See Santulli, "Travaux de la Commission ..." (2001), pp. 369–378.

[89] A/CN.4/561 and Add.1–2 (see footnote 3 above), comments on draft article 7.

[90] *Ibid.*, Qatar and possibly Morocco.

[91] *Ibid.*

[92] *Ibid.*, El Salvador and Uzbekistan.

[93] *Ibid.*

made it clear, in the commentary, that it prefers the term "predominant" as it conveys the element of relativity and indicates that the individual has stronger ties with one State rather than another.[94]

It is suggested that article 7 be retained in its present form.

H. Article 8

Stateless persons and refugees

1. A State may exercise diplomatic protection in respect of a stateless person who, at the time of the injury and at the date of the official presentation of the claim, is lawfully and habitually resident in that State.

2. A State may exercise diplomatic protection in respect of a person who is recognized as a refugee by that State when that person, at the time of the injury and at the date of the official presentation of the claim, is lawfully and habitually resident in that State.

3. Paragraph 2 does not apply in respect of an injury caused by an internationally wrongful act of the State of nationality of the refugee.

50. There is general support, of varying degrees, for article 8, which is a clear exercise in progressive development.[95] As it is progressive development, it is wise to be cautious, perhaps strict, in prescribing conditions for the exercise of diplomatic protection. Thus it is recommended that the Commission should not follow the suggestion of Austria that a refugee qualify for diplomatic protection if, after recognition as a refugee in one European State, he/she assumes lawful residence in another European State.[96] For the same reason, it is recommended that the Nordic proposal[97] that "lawful and habitual residence" as a requirement be replaced with "lawfully stay" not be followed. Conversely, Uzbekistan's proposal[98] that lawful and permanent residence be required goes too far in the other direction and should not be accepted.

51. There is a dispute over the Commission's decision to adopt a flexible approach to the meaning of "refugee" and not to confine it to refugees as defined in the Convention relating to the Status of Refugees.[99] Austria argues that one cannot expect a respondent State to accept a claim for diplomatic protection on behalf of a person characterized as a refugee by the claimant State without strict regard for the international definition.[100] The Nordic States, on the other hand, argue "that a State may exercise diplomatic protection on behalf of persons fulfilling the requirements of territorial connection to the State exercising diplomatic protection, and which in that State's judgement clearly is in need of protection without necessarily formally qualifying for status as a refugee".[101] Although this matter concerns the commentary rather than the formulation of article 8, it is an important matter of principle. The Nordic States see the subject entirely from the perspective of the claimant State, while Austria, wisely, warns that the respondent State may refuse to recognize the right of a State to exercise diplomatic protection on behalf of a refugee who does not strictly qualify as a refugee. The Special Rapporteur would appreciate guidance on this subject from the Commission.

I. Article 9

State of nationality of a corporation

For the purposes of diplomatic protection of corporations, the State of nationality means the State under whose law the corporation was formed and in whose territory it has its registered office or the seat of its management or some similar connection.

52. The comments on the provision raise two important issues. First, the final phrase "or some similar connection" may be interpreted as requiring a genuine link between the corporation and the State exercising diplomatic protection. Secondly, there is the problem of the corporation "formed" (incorporated) in one State but with a registered office in another State. Which State may exercise diplomatic protection?

53. In its commentary on article 9, the Commission states that

> [T]he registered office, seat of management "or ... some similar connection" should not ... be seen as forms of a genuine link ...
>
> The phrase "or ... some similar connection" must be read in the context of the "registered office or the seat of its management", in accordance with the *ejusdem generis* rule of interpretation, which requires a general phrase of this kind to be interpreted narrowly to accord with the phrases that precede it. This means that the phrase is to have no life of its own. It must refer to some connection similar to that of "registered office" or "seat of management".[102]

Despite this explanation, it seems certain that the phrase "or some similar connection" will be construed as requiring some form of genuine link. This is demonstrated by the comments of Austria, the Netherlands and Qatar.[103] It is recommended that the phrase be deleted, as no amount of explaining in the commentary will succeed in preventing it from being read as synonymous with the requirement of a genuine link.

---

[94] *Yearbook ... 2004*, vol. II (Part Two), p. 27, para. (5) of the commentary to draft article 7.

[95] The United States requests (A/CN.4/561 and Add.1–2 (see footnote 3 above), other comments and suggestions) that it be made clear that this is an exercise in progressive development. This is done in paragraph (2) of the commentary to draft article 8 (*Yearbook ... 2004*, vol. II (Part Two), p. 28).

[96] A/CN.4/561 and Add.1–2 (see footnote 3 above), comments on draft article 8.

[97] *Ibid.*

[98] *Ibid.* Uzbekistan's other suggestion that "and has been granted asylum" be added after "as a refugee" in paragraph 2 is unnecessary to consider, as this issue is already covered by the requirement of recognition as a refugee contained in that paragraph.

[99] See *Yearbook ... 2004*, vol. II (Part Two), pp. 28–29, para. (8) of the commentary to draft article 8.

[100] A/CN.4/561 and Add.1–2 (see footnote 3 above), comments on draft article 8. See also the comments of El Salvador and Qatar (*ibid.*).

[101] *Ibid.*

[102] *Yearbook ... 2004*, vol. II (Part Two), p. 30, paras. (5)–(6).

[103] A/CN.4/561 and Add.1–2 (see footnote 3 above), comments on draft article 9.

54. Several States raise the question of whether a State may be diplomatically protected if it has its registered office in a State other than that in which it is formed (incorporated).[104] This is a fair question, as the present language of article 9 suggests that only the State in which the corporation is formed *and* in whose territory it has "its registered office or the seat of its management or some similar connection" may exercise diplomatic protection. This interpretation is confirmed by the fact that article 9 speaks of "*the** State of nationality" and paragraph (7) of the commentary states that: "This language is used to avoid any suggestion that a corporation might have dual nationality".[105] This is an error that must be rectified. As the Netherlands rightly points out,[106] corporations are often formed in more than one State and have registered offices in more than one State. This is a fact of commercial life that cannot be ignored or wished away. It is suggested that article 9 requires a substantial revision; and it is suggested that Guatemala's proposal might provide the solution.[107] This would require recognition of the possibility of dual nationality of corporations and adoption of the test of "closest connection", "effective nationality" or "predominant nationality" (to accord with article 7) as an indication of which State may exercise diplomatic protection. (Guatemala's suggestion that it should be made clear that the term "corporation" means "limited liability company" is already taken care of in paragraph (2) of the commentary.)

55. It is proposed that article 9 be amended to read:

"1. A State is entitled to exercise diplomatic protection in respect of an injury to a corporation which has the nationality of that State.

"2. For the purposes of diplomatic protection of corporations, a corporation has the nationality of the State under whose law the corporation was formed or in whose territory it has its registered office or the seat of its management.

"3. When two States are entitled to exercise diplomatic protection in terms of paragraph 2, the State whose nationality is predominant shall exercise that protection."

J. Article 10

Continuous nationality of a corporation

1. A State is entitled to exercise diplomatic protection in respect of a corporation which was its national at the time of the injury and is its national at the date of the official presentation of the claim.

2. Notwithstanding paragraph 1, a State continues to be entitled to exercise diplomatic protection in respect of a corporation which was its national at the time of the injury and which, as the result of the injury, has ceased to exist according to the law of that State.

56. The continuous nationality rule has already been dealt with exhaustively in respect of article 5. It is therefore unnecessary to rehearse the arguments in favour of amending paragraph 1 to include the words "only" and "continuously" and to provide for the case of the predecessor State.[108] Nor is it necessary to repeat the arguments in favour of retaining the date of the official presentation of the claim as the *dies ad quem* except where the national sought to be protected acquires the nationality of the respondent State after the presentation of the claim.

57. The United States, however, objects to paragraph 2 of article 10,[109] arguing that the protection of extinct corporations should not be an exception to the rule of continuous nationality. It claims that:

> [A] State may continue to exercise protection with respect to the claims of a corporation so long as the corporation retains a legal personality, which can be as bare as the right to sue or be sued under municipal law. Many municipal systems allow for corporations to continue to raise and defend claims that arose during corporate life for a finite period of time after dissolution, meaning that legal personality persists until that period expires. Thus, the problem of espousing claims of extinct corporations would arise infrequently, as the vast majority of claims can be considered while the corporation maintains a legal personality.[110]

It adds that sound policy considerations in municipal law allow the legal personality of corporations to lapse: "Municipal survival and corporate wind-up statutes include a finite wind-up period to allow those involved with a corporation to obtain the benefits of finality, knowing that after the wind-up period has ended claims for and against the corporation will cease."[111] In support of its argument, the United States refers to laws in Canada, France, the United Kingdom and the United States, which allow corporations to sue and be sued for several years following dissolution.

58. Unfortunately, the Unites States fails to consider the concerns raised in this connection by judges (notably the American judge, Judge Jessup in *Barcelona Traction*[112]), tribunals and scholars, referred to in the commentary and the fourth report on diplomatic protection.[113] In the light of the failure to refute (or even to consider) these authorities, and in the absence of a wider comparative survey of corporate law and practice to establish that many legal systems allow corporations to sue and be sued following dissolution, the inclination of the Special Rapporteur is to retain paragraph 2, albeit *ex abundanti cautela*.

59. The revised article 10 should therefore read:

---

[104] *Ibid.* (El Salvador, Guatemala, Morocco and the Netherlands.)

[105] *Yearbook ... 2004*, vol. II (Part Two), p. 30.

[106] A/CN.4/561 and Add.1–2 (see footnote 3 above), comments on draft article 9.

[107] *Ibid.*

[108] *Ibid.* The concerns of Austria (*ibid.*, comment on draft article 10) that article 10 does not provide for the case of State succession are met by the inclusion of reference to the "predecessor State".

[109] *Ibid.*

[110] *Ibid.*

[111] *Ibid.*

[112] *I.C.J. Reports 1970* (see footnote 61 above), p. 193. See also the opinions of Judges Gros (p. 277), Sir Gerald Fitzmaurice (pp. 101–102) and Riphagen (p. 345).

[113] *Yearbook ... 2004*, vol. II (Part Two), p. 31, para. (4) of the commentary to draft article 10, footnotes 106–108; and *Yearbook ... 2003*, vol. II (Part One), document A/CN.4/530 and Add.1, pp. 23–26, paras. 93–105.

"1. A State is entitled to exercise diplomatic protection *only* in respect of a corporation *that was a national of that State, or any predecessor State, continuously from the date* of injury to the date of the official presentation of the claim.

"2. *A State is not entitled to exercise diplomatic protection in respect of a corporation that acquires the nationality of the State against which the claim is brought after the presentation of the claim.*

"3. Notwithstanding paragraph 1, a State continues to be entitled to exercise diplomatic protection in respect of a corporation which was its national at the time of the injury and which, as the result of the injury, has ceased to exist according to the law of that State."

K. Article 11

Protection of shareholders

The State of nationality of the shareholders in a corporation shall not be entitled to exercise diplomatic protection on behalf of such shareholders in the case of an injury to the corporation unless:

(*a*) The corporation has ceased to exist according to the law of the State of incorporation for a reason unrelated to the injury; or

(*b*) The corporation had, at the time of the injury, the nationality of the State alleged to be responsible for causing injury, and incorporation under the law of the latter State was required by it as a precondition for doing business there.

60. Article 11 (*a*), seeks to give effect to the *dictum* in *Barcelona Traction* in which ICJ acknowledged the existence of an exception to the general rule that only the State of incorporation may protect a corporation (and its shareholders) where the company has ceased to exist.[114] The Commission restricted the scope of this exception by requiring that the corporation must have ceased to exist "for a reason unrelated to the injury". Austria rightly points out that this restriction "makes very little sense, since the State where the company is terminated differs from the injuring State".[115] The Special Rapporteur shares this view and suggests that this phrase be deleted.

61. Austria's further suggestion that article 11 (*a*), be amended to read "State of nationality" instead of "State of incorporation"[116] cannot be accepted, as it is intended to emphasize that the law of the State of incorporation is to govern. This will usually be the same as the State of nationality but need not always be so in the light of the proposed revision of article 9.

62. The United States proposes that article 11 (*a*) be deleted "because it creates the anomalous situation of granting States of shareholders a greater right to espouse claims of a corporation than the State of incorporation itself".[117] It states that the commentary provides no justification for such an exception. However, the United States fails to consider the reasoning of ICJ in *Barcelona Traction* in favour of such an exception.[118] Article 11 aims to codify the law as set out in *Barcelona Traction*, for which it has been congratulated by other States.[119] In these circumstances, it is suggested that article 11 (*a*) be retained, subject to the deletion suggested by Austria.

63. The United States objects to article 11 (*b*) on grounds of law and public policy. As to the law, it argues that the cases on which the Commission relies as evidence for this exception are based on

> a special agreement between two States granting a right to shareholders to claim compensation, or an agreement between the injuring State and its national corporation granting compensation to the shareholders. As a result of those agreements, the above-mentioned cases provide little support for the existence of a customary international law rule allowing States to espouse claims of shareholders against the State of incorporation where incorporation was mandated for doing business in the State.[120]

On the subject of policy, the United States claims:

> [T]his exception would create a regime where shareholders of corporations incorporated in a State have greater rights to seek diplomatic protection of their claims in that State than shareholders of foreign-owned corporations, who would have to rely on the corporation's State to pursue claims. It is not clear that such a result is just.[121]

64. The Special Rapporteur finds himself unable to agree with the above criticisms for the following reasons:

(*a*) The fact that the cases relied on for this exception are based on special agreements does not deprive them of value in the law-formation process. The twin requirements for the creation of a customary rule are *usus* and *opinio juris*. The settlement of claims by special agreement between the State of incorporation and the State of nationality of the shareholders provides evidence both of State practice (*usus*) and of a sense of obligation on the part of the respondent State to settle the claim (*opinio juris*);

(*b*) The United States fails to consider the wealth of judicial opinion in favour of such an exception, for example, the separate opinions of Judges Wellington Koo,[122] Jessup,[123] Tanaka[124] and Sir Gerald Fitzmaurice[125] in *Barcelona Traction*. Nor does it consider whether the *ELSI* case[126] lends support to the exception as suggested

[114] *I.C.J. Reports 1970* (see footnote 61 above), pp. 40–41, paras. 64–68.

[115] A/CN.4/561 and Add.1–2 (see footnote 3 above), comments on draft article 11 (*a*).

[116] *Ibid.*

[117] *Ibid.*

[118] *I.C.J. Reports 1970* (see footnote 61 above), pp. 40–41, paras. 64–68.

[119] A/CN.4/561 and Add.1–2 (see footnote 3 above), comments on draft article 11 (Nordic countries) and on 11 (*b*) (the Netherlands).

[120] *Ibid.*, comments on draft article 11 (*b*).

[121] *Ibid.*

[122] *Barcelona Traction, Light and Power Company, Limited, Preliminary Objections, Judgment, I.C.J. Reports 1964*, p. 58, para. 20.

[123] *I.C.J. Reports 1970* (see footnote 61 above), pp. 191–193.

[124] *Ibid.*, p. 134.

[125] *Ibid.*, pp. 72–75.

[126] *Elettronica Sicula S.p.A. (ELSI), Judgment, I.C.J Reports 1989*, p. 15.

in the commentary[127] and in the fourth report on diplomatic protection;[128]

(*c*) Although doctrine is divided on this subject, there is considerable support for the proposed exception;

(*d*) Draft articles 9, 11 and 12 seek to codify the law expounded by ICJ in *Barcelona Traction*. This exception is part of the principles on this subject expounded by the Court;

(*e*) The United States submission is, possibly, weakest in respect of policy. As Norway states (on behalf of the Nordic countries):

> A State should not be allowed to require foreign interests to incorporate under local law as a condition for doing business in that State and then plead such incorporation as the justification for rejecting the exercise of diplomatic protection from the State of nationality of the foreign interests.[129]

This echoes the reply of the United Kingdom to the argument of Mexico in *Mexican Eagle* that a State (*in casu* the United Kingdom) might not intervene on behalf of its shareholders in a Mexican company:

> If the doctrine were admitted that a Government can first make the operation of foreign interests in its territories depend upon their incorporation under local law, and then plead such incorporation as the justification for rejecting foreign diplomatic intervention, it is clear that the means would never be wanting whereby foreign Governments could be prevented from exercising their undoubted right under international law to protect the commercial interests of their nationals abroad.[130]

A company compelled to incorporate in a State as a precondition for doing business there has been described as a "Calvo corporation", as incorporation protects the host State as firmly as the Calvo clause. Hence the comment of the Netherlands that "the State of nationality of the shareholder in cases of Calvo corporation would be entitled to exercise diplomatic protection".[131] Policy considerations of this kind are more powerful than those raised by the United States;

(*f*) A final weakness in the United States position is that it makes no attempt to distinguish between corporations that freely and voluntarily incorporate in a State and those that are compelled to incorporate in such State as a result of law or political pressure. This distinction, which is central to article 11 (*b*),[132] is not considered by the United States.

65. The Special Rapporteur has been guided in his formulation of the present draft articles largely by State practice, judicial decisions and general principles. On article 11 (*b*), he has been strongly influenced in favour of such an exception by United States practice (*Delagoa Bay Railway Co.*,[133] *El Triunfo*[134]), judicial decisions involving the United States (*ELSI* case[135]), judicial opinion (Judge Jessup in *Barcelona Traction*[136]) and general principles (opposition to Calvo clause and "Calvo corporation"). He therefore finds it strange that the United States should denounce an exception which is so strongly supported by American authority. In summary, it is suggested that the reasons advanced for the deletion of article 11 (*b*) are unconvincing and that it should be retained.

66. The Nordic States object to the requirement in article 11 (*b*) that, in order to succeed in the exception it must be shown that incorporation "under the law" of the wrongdoing State was required as a precondition for doing business there. It suggests that "[t]here are … as a part of the progressive development of international law, good reasons to extend this exception also to cases where the requirement of incorporation is not a formal one, but follows from pressure of an informal or political nature on the foreign interests".[137] The Nordic countries suggest that this matter be dealt with in the commentary. It is, however, recommended that it be dealt with in the text of article 11 (*b*) itself. In most instances, the Government will place political pressure on foreign investors to incorporate in the host States without the backing of local law. Inevitably such pressure will be as effective as the letter of the law.

67. Suggestions by the Netherlands[138] in favour of consistency of language and by Austria[139] for an explanation of the meaning of "injury" in the context of article 11 (*b*), in the commentary, should be acceded to.

68. It is proposed that article 11 be revised to read:

"The State of nationality of the shareholders in a corporation shall not be entitled to exercise diplomatic protection on behalf of such shareholders in the case of an injury to the corporation unless:

"(*a*) The corporation has ceased to exist according to the law of the State of incorporation [for a reason unrelated to the injury]; or

"(*b*) The corporation had, at the time of the injury, the nationality of the State alleged to be responsible for causing *the* injury, and incorporation [under the law of the latter State] was required by it as a precondition for doing business there."

L. Article 12

Direct injury to shareholders

To the extent that an internationally wrongful act of a State causes direct injury to the rights of shareholders as such, as distinct from those of the corporation

[127] *Yearbook ... 2004*, vol. II (Part Two), pp. 33–34, para. (10) of the commentary to draft article 11.

[128] *Yearbook ... 2003* (see footnote 113 above), p. 21, paras. 81–82.

[129] A/CN.4/561 and Add.1–2 (see footnote 3 above), comments on draft article 11 (*b*).

[130] Whiteman, *Digest of International Law*, pp. 1273–1274.

[131] A/CN.4/561 and Add.1–2 (see footnote 3 above), comments on draft article 11 (*b*).

[132] See *Yearbook ... 2004*, vol. II (Part Two), p. 33, para. (8) of the commentary to draft article 11.

[133] Moore, *Digest of International Law*, p. 647.

[134] *El Triunfo Company*, decisions of 2 and 8 May 1902, UNRIAA, vol. XV (Sales No. 1966.V.3), p. 467.

[135] See footnote 126 above.

[136] *I.C.J. Reports 1970* (see footnote 61 above), pp. 191–193.

[137] A/CN.4/561 and Add.1–2 (see footnote 3 above), comments on article 11 (*b*).

[138] *Ibid.*

[139] *Ibid.*

itself, the State of nationality of any such shareholders is entitled to exercise diplomatic protection in respect of its nationals.

69. The United States suggests that this provision is superfluous, as the rights of shareholders are already covered by articles 2–3.[140] This is correct. However, if the draft articles are to codify fully the principles expounded in *Barcelona Traction*,[141] it should be retained. A further advantage of retaining it is that the commentary to this provision ensures that the commentaries—and the draft articles on the protection of corporations and shareholders—provide a comprehensive picture of the law on this aspect of diplomatic protection. The Special Rapporteur makes no recommendation to the Commission on this subject, but expresses a mild preference for retention.

M. Article 13

Other legal persons

The principles contained in draft articles 9 and 10 in respect of corporations shall be applicable, as appropriate, to the diplomatic protection of other legal persons.

70. Article 13 is intended to extend the principles relating to the diplomatic protection of corporations to other legal persons. It is not intended that such other legal persons include natural persons.[142] On the other hand, as pointed out by Guatemala,[143] legal persons or companies other than corporations (that is profit-making enterprises with limited liability whose capital is represented by shares) may have shareholders who are liable for the company's debts up to but not exceeding the level of their equity contribution. The principles covered in articles 11–12 are applicable to them. Consequently, the reference to articles 9–10 should be extended to include articles 9–12. The Special Rapporteur fails to understand why the independence of non-governmental organizations would be compromised by diplomatic protection, as suggested by Qatar.[144]

71. Article 13 should therefore be revised to read:

"The principles contained in draft articles *9 to 12* in respect of corporations shall be applicable, as appropriate, to the diplomatic protection of other legal persons."

N. Article 14

Exhaustion of local remedies

1. A State may not bring an international claim in respect of an injury to a national or other person referred to in draft article 8 before the injured person has, subject to draft article 16, exhausted all local remedies.

2. "Local remedies" means legal remedies which are open to an injured person before the judicial or administrative courts or bodies, whether ordinary or special, of the State alleged to be responsible for the injury.

72. Apart from suggestions relating to the redrafting of the commentary by the Netherlands,[145] the only comment affecting article 14, paragraph 1, is raised by the United States. It points out that in the *ELSI* case ICJ "acknowledged that a claim could be exhausted for international law purposes when the essence of the claim was considered by municipal tribunals, irrespective of whether the same person or entity pursuing the municipal claim was being diplomatically protected".[146] It accordingly suggests that paragraph 1 be reformulated to exclude the requirement that the injured person be the party exhausting local remedies. The Special Rapporteur is indebted to the United States for this helpful suggestion which is accordingly recommended to the Commission.

73. The Netherlands has suggested a minor amendment to paragraph 2 to bring it into line with article 11 (*b*).[147]

74. It is proposed that article 14 be revised to read:

"1. *A State may not bring an international claim in respect of an injury to a national or other person referred to in draft article 8 before local remedies have been exhausted, subject to draft article 16.*

"2. 'Local remedies' means legal remedies which are open to an injured person before the judicial or administrative courts or bodies, whether ordinary or special, of the State alleged to be responsible for *causing* the injury."

O. Article 15

Category of claims

Local remedies shall be exhausted where an international claim, or request for a declaratory judgement related to the claim, is brought preponderantly on the basis of an injury to a national or other person referred to in draft article 8.

75. The ICJ decision in *Avena*[148] adds considerably to the law on the distinction between direct and indirect injuries in the context of the exhaustion of local remedies rule, but it does not affect the validity of the formulation of the principle contained in article 15. Obviously, it will require discussion in the commentary. Austria raises a question about the title of article 15.[149] "Mixed claims" might be a more appropriate title. No change is recommended to article 15 itself.

[140] *Ibid.*, comments on draft article 12.

[141] *I.C.J. Reports 1970* (see footnote 61 above), p. 36, paras. 46–47.

[142] See the suggestion to this effect by El Salvador (A/CN.4/561 and Add.1–2 (see footnote 3 above), comments on draft article 13.

[143] *Ibid.*

[144] *Ibid.*

[145] *Ibid.*, comments on draft article 14.

[146] *Ibid.*, paragraph 1. For the position under human rights treaties, see Schermers, "Exhaustion of domestic remedies", pp. 954–958.

[147] A/CN.4/561 and Add.1–2 (see footnote 3 above), comments on draft article 11 (*b*).

[148] *I.C.J. Reports 2004* (see footnote 28 above), particularly pp. 35–36, para. 40. See also the separate opinions of Judges Parra-Aranguren (pp. 90–91, paras. 27–28) and Vereshchetin (pp. 81–83, paras. 7–11). See further Künzli, "Case concerning Mexican nationals"; and Milano, *loc. cit.*, pp. 128–130.

[149] A/CN.4/561 and Add.1–2 (see footnote 3 above), comments on draft article 15.

P. Article 16

Exceptions to the local remedies rule

Local remedies do not need to be exhausted where:

(*a*) The local remedies provide no reasonable possibility of effective redress;

(*b*) There is undue delay in the remedial process which is attributable to the State alleged to be responsible;

(*c*) There is no relevant connection between the injured person and the State alleged to be responsible or the circumstances of the case otherwise make the exhaustion of local remedies unreasonable;

(*d*) The State alleged to be responsible has waived the requirement that local remedies be exhausted.

76. Mexico makes two general comments on article 16.[150] First, it draws attention to the exception to the exhaustion of local remedies rule in the case of a likely repetition of the injury. Although this exception receives separate attention by Amerasinghe[151] it seems to be covered by subparagraph (*a*) and will be dealt with in the commentary to subparagraph (*a*). Mexico also proposes that a provision be included on the burden of proof in respect of the local remedies rule. It will be recalled that the Commission decided not to include such a provision.[152] It may, however, be wise to deal with this matter in the commentary.

1. Subparagraph (*a*)

77. It will be recalled that when the Commission debated subparagraph (*a*) it had three options before it: obvious futility; no reasonable prospect of success; and no reasonable possibility of effective redress.[153] It showed a preference for the third option, which now features in subparagraph (*a*). The United States[154] calls upon the Commission to reconsider its decision and to adopt the futility rule on the ground that it more accurately reflects customary international law[155] and is supported by policy considerations which require that "in all but the most extreme circumstances a State has the opportunity to rectify within its own legal system violations of international law".[156] The United States therefore proposes the following provision:

> Local remedies do not need to be exhausted where the local remedies are obviously futile or manifestly ineffective. Exhaustion of local remedies is not obviously futile or manifestly ineffective where a forum was reasonably available to provide effective redress.[157]

While the Special Rapporteur does not favour the reopening of issues that have already been decided, it must be recalled that the futility rule did enjoy some support in the Commission. It is therefore suggested that the Commission reconsider this matter. However, it should be aware of the arguments raised against the futility rule referred to in the commentary[158] and the third report on diplomatic protection).[159] As shown in the third report, the "obvious futility" test, first expounded in the *Finnish Ships Arbitration*,[160] was not followed in the *ELSI* case,[161] and has been criticized by writers.[162] The main objection to this test is that it suggests that the ineffectiveness of the local remedy must be *ex facie* immediately apparent. In order to overcome this, Sir Hersch Lauterpacht suggested introducing the element of reasonableness into the test, which allows a court to examine whether, in the circumstances of the particular case, an effective remedy was a "reasonable possibility".[163] This was the text preferred by the Commission in 2002 and one that is still advocated by the Special Rapporteur.

78. Should the Commission decide not to accept the proposal of the United States, it should consider the Austrian proposal to insert the word "available" into subparagraph (*a*) to bring it into line with article 44[164] of the draft articles on responsibility of States for internationally wrongful acts.[165]

2. Subparagraph (*c*)

79. Two very different proposals are made in respect of subparagraph (*c*). Austria proposes that the first part of the paragraph be dropped and that it be confined to the situation where the circumstances of the case make the exhaustion of local remedies unreasonable.[166] The United States, on the other hand, proposes that only the first part of the paragraph be retained and that it be rewritten to provide:

> Local remedies do not need to be exhausted where there is no relevant connection between the injured person and the State alleged to be responsible.[167]

---

[150] *Ibid.*, comments on draft article 16.

[151] *Local Remedies in International Law*, p. 212.

[152] *Yearbook ... 2002*, vol. II (Part Two), p. 64, para. 252.

[153] *Ibid.*, p. 56, para. 178.

[154] A/CN.4/561 and Add.1–2 (see footnote 3 above), comments on draft article 16 (*a*).

[155] See Amerasinghe, *op. cit.*, p. 206: "[T]he test is obvious futility or manifest ineffectiveness, not the absence of a reasonable prospect of success or the improbability of success, which are both less strict tests."

[156] A/CN.4/561 and Add.1–2 (see footnote 3 above), comments on draft article 16 (*a*).

[157] *Ibid.*

[158] *Yearbook ... 2004*, vol. II (Part Two), pp. 38–39, paras. (2)–(3) of the commentary to draft article 16.

[159] *Yearbook ... 2002*, vol. II (Part One), document A/CN.4/523 and Add.1, pp. 56–61, paras. 18–45.

[160] *Claim of Finnish shipowners against Great Britain in respect of the use of certain Finnish vessels during the war* (1934), UNRIAA, vol. III (Sales No. 1949.V.2), p. 1504.

[161] *I.C.J. Reports 1989* (see footnote 126 above), pp. 46–47, paras. 59 and 62.

[162] Amerasinghe, "The local remedies rule in appropriate perspective", p. 752; Simpson and Fox, *International Arbitration: Law and Practice* p. 114; Mummery, "The content of the duty to exhaust local judicial remedies", p. 401.

[163] *Certain Norwegian Loans, Judgment, I.C.J. Reports 1957*, p. 39.

[164] A/CN.4/561 and Add.1–2 (see footnote 3 above), comments on draft article 16 (*a*).

[165] Article 44 reads:

"The responsibility of a State may not be invoked if:

...

(*b*) the claim is one to which the exhaustion of local remedies applies and any available and effective remedy has not been exhausted."

(*Yearbook ... 2001*, vol. II (Part Two), p. 29).

[166] A/CN.4/561 and Add.1–2 (see footnote 3 above), comments on draft article 16 (*c*).

[167] *Ibid.*

The Special Rapporteur agrees with the proposal of the United States. The main purpose of subparagraph (*c*) was to provide for an exception to the local remedies rule where the injured person has no voluntary connection with the State alleged to be responsible for the injury—as in the case of cross-border pollution or straying aircraft.[168] Some members of the Commission then raised other situations in which it might not be necessary to exhaust local remedies, such as denial of entry to the territory of the respondent State or prohibitive costs.[169] The second part of subparagraph (*c*) was adopted to cater for such situations. However, as the United States points out, such situations are already covered by subparagraph (*a*). It is therefore proposed that the United States proposal be adopted, subject to the insertion of a phrase that makes it clear that the relevant connection must be absent at the moment of injury, as proposed by Austria.[170]

3. SUBPARAGRAPH (*d*)

80. Subparagraph (*d*) does not distinguish between express and implied waivers. The commentary does, however, make it clear that waiver may be implied where the intention to waive local remedies is clear.[171] This commentary will be redrafted to take account of Guatemala's helpful suggestion on this subject.[172]

81. It is proposed that article 16 be considered in the following form:

"Local remedies do not need to be exhausted where:

"EITHER

"(*a*) The local remedies provide no reasonable possibility of *available and* effective redress;

"OR

"(*a*) *The local remedies are obviously futile or manifestly ineffective. Exhaustion of local remedies is not obviously futile or manifestly ineffective where a forum was reasonably available to provide effective redress*;

"(*b*) There is undue delay in the remedial process which is attributable to the State alleged to be responsible;

"(*c*) *There was no relevant connection between the injured person and the State alleged to be responsible at the time of the injury*;

"(*d*) The State alleged to be responsible has waived the requirement that local remedies be exhausted."

[168] The United States suggests that the commentary elaborate further on the absence of a relevant connection in the case of overflight (*ibid.*).

[169] See *Yearbook ... 2004*, vol. II (Part Two), p. 41, para. (11) of the commentary to draft article 16, for further examples.

[170] A/CN.4/561 and Add.1–2 (see footnote 3 above), comments on draft article 16 (*c*).

[171] See *Yearbook ... 2004*, vol. II (Part Two), p. 41, para. (16) of the commentary to draft article 16. For this reason there is no need to include an express provision on implied waiver, as suggested by Uzbekistan in A/CN.4/561 and Add.1–2 (see footnote 3 above), comments on part four.

[172] A/CN.4/561 and Add.1–2 (see footnote 3 above), comments on draft article 16 (*d*).

Q. Articles 17 and 18

Article 17

Actions or procedures other than diplomatic protection

The present draft articles are without prejudice to the rights of States, natural persons or other entities to resort under international law to actions or procedures other than diplomatic protection to secure redress for injury suffered as a result of an internationally wrongful act.

Article 18

Special treaty provisions

The present draft articles do not apply where, and to the extent that, they are inconsistent with special treaty provisions, including those concerning the settlement of disputes between corporations or shareholders of a corporation and States.

82. Uzbekistan proposes that the heading to this part should be "Other provisions" rather than "Miscellaneous provisions".[173] This should be considered.

83. As proposals have been made for the merger of articles 17 and 18,[174] these two provisions will be considered together. Articles 17 and 18 serve the same purpose: to make it clear that the present draft articles do not affect, nor are they directly affected by, other procedures or mechanisms, under customary international law or treaty law, which provide methods for the assertion of rights or the settlement of claims. At first blush it might seem wise to merge the two provisions. Indeed, the fifth report on diplomatic protection recommended such a merger in an article that read:

> These articles are without prejudice to the rights of States or persons to invoke procedures other than diplomatic protection to secure redress for injury suffered as a result of an internationally wrongful act [that might also give rise to a claim for diplomatic protection by the State of nationality of the injured person].[175]

However, it seems, on reflection, that in the light of the very different interests that articles 17 and 18 seek to serve, that the wisest course would be to retain two separate provisions.

84. Article 17 is essentially designed to ensure that the institution of diplomatic protection does not interfere with or obstruct the protection of human rights by other means. The Commission acknowledges that diplomatic protection is but one means for the protection of human rights, and a very limited one, seeing that it is confined to the protection of the human rights of nationals. Other procedures for the protection of human rights are not limited in this respect. Human rights treaties confer rights and grant remedies to all humans whose human rights

[173] *Ibid.*, comments on part four.

[174] El Salvador (*ibid.*, comments on draft article 18) and Qatar (*ibid.*, comments on draft article 17). See also the Netherlands (*ibid.*, other comments and suggestions).

[175] *Yearbook ... 2004*, vol. II (Part One), document A/CN.4/538, chap. IV.B, p. 55.

are violated, irrespective of nationality. Moreover, new developments in international law allow a State to protect—by protest, negotiation, arbitration and judicial proceedings[176]—both nationals and non-nationals subjected to the violation of human rights norms (with the status of *jus cogens*[177] or which qualify as obligations *erga omnes*[178]) in foreign countries.[179] This was recently emphasized by Judge Simma in the case concerning Armed Activities on the Territory of the Congo (*Democratic Republic of the Congo* v. *Uganda*),[180] in which he held that developments of this kind in international law would have made it possible for Uganda to protect both nationals and non-nationals whose human rights were threatened by the army of the Democratic Republic of the Congo at Kinshasa airport.

85. Unfortunately the purpose of article 17 has not been fully understood. Milano has interpreted the relationship between the 2001 articles on responsibility of States for internationally wrongful acts and the 2004 draft articles on diplomatic protection to mean that the right of a State to intervene under article 48, paragraph 1 (*b*), of the articles on responsibility of States for internationally wrongful acts on behalf of non-nationals whose *jus cogens* rights have been violated is limited by the draft articles on diplomatic protection, which require proof of nationality.[181] He reaches this conclusion by interpreting article 48 to be subject to article 44, which provides that the responsibility of a State may not be invoked if "the claim is not brought in accordance with any applicable rule relating to the nationality of claims", as now elaborated upon in the draft articles on diplomatic protection. This leads him to conclude that "under the law of State responsibility the mechanisms of diplomatic protection are accorded pre-eminence over those of human rights law, even when the injury to the individual is caused by a violation of his or her human rights".[182] He adds that:

> [F]rom a joint reading of the 2001 Articles on Responsibility and the 2004 Draft Articles on Diplomatic Protection, the room left for the enforcement of *erga omnes* human rights obligations beyond the traditional mechanisms of diplomatic protection appears to be minimal.[183]

86. Article 17 must dispel doubts of this kind by making it clear that the draft articles are in no way intended to obstruct other procedures for the protection of human rights. This purpose can best be served by a separate provision, like article 17. However it seems, judging by Milano's paper,[184] that it has not achieved this result. In these circumstances, it might be necessary to redraft article 17 to make its purpose ever clearer—though to the Special Rapporteur it seems difficult to make this intention clearer. Perhaps this might be achieved by the proposed reformulation offered by the Netherlands?

> The rights of States, natural persons or other entities to resort to actions or procedures other than diplomatic protection to secure redress for injury suffered as a result of an internationally wrongful act are not affected by the present draft articles.[185]

87. It is therefore proposed that article 17 be retained as a separate provision and that it read:

"EITHER

"The present draft articles are without prejudice to the rights of the States, natural persons or other entities to resort [under international law?[186]] to actions or procedures other than diplomatic protection to secure redress for injury suffered as a result of an internationally wrongful act.

"OR

"*The right of States, natural persons or other entities to resort to actions or procedures other than diplomatic protection to secure redress for injury suffered as a result of an internationally wrongful act, are not affected by the present draft articles.*"

88. The intention of article 18 is to make it clear that the draft articles do not interfere with bilateral and multilateral investment treaties that may include different rules relating to the treatment of both individual and corporate investors. As these treaties differ substantially both in substance and form from those contemplated in article 17, it is wise to deal separately with these treaties.

89. Both Austria and Morocco object to the drafting of article 18, particularly in respect of the phrase "special treaty provisions".[187] Morocco, correctly, points out that the Vienna Convention on the Law of Treaties does not recognize the concept of "special treaties". It therefore suggests, and the Special Rapporteur recommends, that it be reformulated to read:

"The present draft articles do not apply where, and to the extent that, they are inconsistent with *special regimes provided for under bilateral and multilateral treaties regarding the protection of investments.*"

---

[176] Subject, of course, to the existence of a jurisdictional link. But this qualification is equally applicable to diplomatic protection.

[177] See articles 40, 41 and 48 of the draft articles on responsibility of States for internationally wrongful acts, *Yearbook ... 2001*, vol. II (Part Two), pp. 29–30.

[178] *I.C.J. Reports 1970* (see footnote 61 above), p. 32.

[179] See further on this subject, Gaja, "Is a State specially affected when its nationals' human rights are infringed?"; and "Droits des États et droits des individus dans le cadre de la protection diplomatique"; Condorelli, "L'évolution du champ d'application ..."; and Forcese, "Shelter from the storm: rethinking diplomatic protection of dual nationals in modern international law", pp. 497–498.

[180] *Armed Activities on the Territory of the Congo (Democratic Republic of the Congo* v. *Uganda), Judgment, I.C.J. Reports 2005*, separate opinion of Judge Simma, pp. 339–350, paras. 17–41. See also the dissenting opinion of Judge *ad hoc* Kateka, *ibid.*, p. 381, para. 69.

[181] Milano, *loc. cit.*, pp. 103–108.

[182] *Ibid.*, p. 106.

[183] *Ibid.*, p. 107. Milano suggests that the odd relation between article 44 and article 48 may have been caused by an oversight on the part of the Commission to specify that article 44 applies only to claims of diplomatic protection and not to article 48. Perhaps he is right!

[184] *Ibid.* Milano remains unconvinced by article 17.

[185] A/CN.4/561 and Add.1–2 (see footnote 3 above), comments on draft article 17.

[186] The Netherlands suggests the deletion of this phrase on the ground that the right of States to submit an *amicus curiae* brief in domestic proceedings, as the European Union has done in United States legal cases, must remain unchanged (*ibid.*).

[187] *Ibid.*, comments on draft article 18.

R. Article 19

Ships' crews

The right of the State of nationality of the members of the crew of a ship to exercise diplomatic protection on their behalf is not affected by the right of the State of nationality of a ship to seek redress on behalf of such crew members, irrespective of their nationality, when they have been injured in the course of an injury to the vessel resulting from an internationally wrongful act.

90. Most States that have submitted comments have responded positively to article 19,[188] but have made a number of suggestions. Austria points out that the condition attached to the flag State's exercise of protection might be construed as being applicable to the right of the State of nationality of the crew members to exercise diplomatic protection. This may be overcome by splitting the provision into two sentences, as proposed below. Mexico asks the Commission to resolve the question of competing claims. The Commission has resisted this course in respect of claims by dual nationals and it would seem equally unwise or unnecessary to do it here. The Netherlands proposes that article 19 be incorporated into article 8, as they appear to belong together. This is, however, not correct. Article 8 deals with the extension of diplomatic protection to stateless persons and refugees, while article 19 recognizes the right of the State of nationality of a ship to seek redress on behalf of crew members, but not to exercise diplomatic protection.

91. The United States finds no fault with the principles expounded in article 19. However, it argues that as the right of the flag State to seek redress on behalf of crew members falls outside the field of diplomatic protection, it should not be included.[189] This issue should be considered by the Commission. On the other hand, it should be recalled that the Commission decided to include article 19 because the protection offered by the flag State is analogous to that of diplomatic protection, as recognized by the International Tribunal for the Law of the Sea in the *M/V "Saiga" (No.2)* case,[190] and policy demands that both methods of protection be reaffirmed because ships crews are vulnerable and require all the protection they can get.[191]

92. It is proposed that, if the Commission elects to retain article 19, it should do so in its present form. Alternatively it might split the provision into two sentences to meet Austria's criticism. In this form it might read:

> "The State of nationality of the members of the crew of a ship has the right to exercise diplomatic protection on their behalf. The State of nationality of a ship [The flag State?] may [similarly?] seek redress on behalf of crew members, irrespective of their nationality, when they have been injured in the course of an injury to the vessel resulting from an internationally wrongful act."

The Special Rapporteur prefers the original text, as he doubts whether it is open to the interpretation placed on it by Austria.

[188] *Ibid.*, comments on draft article 19: Austria, Mexico, the Netherlands and Norway (on behalf of the Nordic countries).

[189] *Ibid.*

[190] *M/V "Saiga" (No. 2)* case (*Saint Vincent and the Grenadines* v. *Guinea*), *Judgment*, *ITLOS Reports* 1999, vol. 3, paras. 103–107.

[191] See *Yearbook ... 2004*, vol. II (Part Two), pp. 43–44, commentary to draft article 19.

Chapter II

The right of the injured national to receive compensation

93. The present draft articles cover only the nationality of claims and the exhaustion of local remedies. They do not deal with the primary rules of diplomatic protection, that is, the rules governing the treatment of aliens. Nor do they deal with the consequences of diplomatic protection. The limited confine of the draft articles has been debated and approved by the Commission at both its fifty-sixth and fifty-seventh sessions, in 2004 and 2005. The decision not to deal with the consequences of diplomatic protection can be justified on the ground that the articles on responsibility of States for internationally wrongful acts, together with their comprehensive commentary, cover most aspects of this subject.[192] Nevertheless, there is one aspect of the consequences of diplomatic protection that is not considered in the articles on responsibility of States for internationally wrongful acts, namely, the question whether there is an obligation on the successful claimant State to pay over any compensation it may have received to the injured national. The draft articles have been criticized on the ground that they have missed the opportunity to recognize such a rule, albeit by way of progressive development.[193] Speaking in the Sixth Committee on 24 October 2005, the French delegate stated that the reasons given by the Special Rapporteur as to why it was not necessary to deal with the consequences of diplomatic protection were not fully convincing. Even if diplomatic protection constituted an exception with regard to the general law on responsibility, the question whether a State was under an obligation to pay over to an injured individual money that it had received by way of compensation for a claim based on diplomatic protection was fundamental.[194]

A similar point was made by Austria in its comments to the Commission:

> A further issue that deserves particular consideration is the problem of the relation between the individual whose rights are protected and the State exercising the right to diplomatic protection. It could be considered to address also the problem of the result of the exercise of diplomatic protection and the access of the individual to such a result.

[192] *Yearbook ... 2001*, vol. II (Part Two), pp. 87–110, arts. 28–39.

[193] Milano, *loc. cit.*, p. 108. See also Gaja, "Droits des États ...", p. 69.

[194] See *Official Records of the General Assembly, Sixtieth Session, Sixth Committee*, 11th meeting, para. 73.

Of course, on the one hand, one could argue that this is a matter of the relation between a State and its nationals; on the other hand, however, it should be ensured that the injured individual in whose interest the claim was raised will benefit from the exercise of diplomatic protection.[195]

On reflection, the Special Rapporteur believes that the Commission should consider this issue, even at the eleventh hour.

94. The rule in the *Mavrommatis Palestine Concessions* case would seem to dictate that a claimant State has absolute discretion in the disbursement of any compensation it may receive in a claim brought on behalf of an injured national. If, as the rule claims, "By taking up the case of one of its subjects … a State is in reality asserting its own rights" and becomes the "sole claimant",[196] it is difficult to argue, as a matter of logic, that any restraints are placed on the State, in the interests of the individual, in the settlement of the claim or the payment of any compensation received. As the State has "complete freedom of action",[197] it is not required to press for the full damages suffered by the injured national. Instead it may agree to a partial settlement, which often happens. This means that in practice the individual may receive as little as 10 per cent of the value of the claim.[198] In the Franco-Russian accord concluded in 1998, 99 per cent of the pecuniary rights of the natural and legal persons were conceded.[199] In 1994, the High Court of Justice of Madrid dismissed the complaint of a national relating to the conclusion of a lump-sum agreement between Morocco and Spain, holding that international practice permits the giving of indemnities less than the amount of damage.[200]

95. The Commission has accepted the rule in the *Mavrommatis Palestine Concessions* case as the foundation for its draft articles. Out of deference to this decision it rejected a proposal that a State be obliged to exercise diplomatic protection to a national injured as a result of the violation of a norm of *jus cogens*. On the other hand, the logic of *Mavrommatis* does not always prevail. Both the continuous nationality rule and the exhaustion of local remedies requirement undermine the logic of *Mavrommatis,* as they show that an injury to a national does not automatically confer on the claimant State a right to diplomatic protection. Nor is *Mavrommatis* logically and consistently applied in respect of the assessment of the damages claimed, as compensation is generally calculated on the basis of the injury suffered by the individual. This was acknowledged by PCIJ in the *Factory at Chorzów* case[201] and is now said to be a rule of customary international law.[202] The anomaly of the legal situation was recognized by Judge Morelli in *Barcelona Traction* when he stated:

International reparation is always owed to the State and not to the private person, even in the case of compensation and despite the fact that the amount of compensation must be determined on the basis of the damage suffered by the private person.[203]

If the damage suffered is to be "determined on the basis of the damage suffered by the private person", it seems that the claimant State is obliged to consult with the injured individual on this matter, which shows that the State does not have complete freedom of action in the making of a claim.

96. State practice is contradictory on this subject. While judicial decisions, both international and national, emphasize that the injured national has no right to claim any compensation received by the State, other national mechanisms suggest that States acknowledge that there is some obligation on them to disburse compensation received to the injured national.

97. In *Administrative Decision No. V,* the United States–German Mixed Claims Commission affirmed the wide discretion of the State:

In exercising such control [the nation] is governed not only by the interest of the particular claimant but by the larger interests of the whole people of the nation and must exercise an untrammeled discretion in determining when and how the claim will be presented and pressed, or withdrawn or compromised, and the private owner will be bound by the action taken. *Even if payment is made to the espousing nation in pursuance of an award, it has complete control over the fund so paid to and held by it and may, to prevent fraud, correct a mistake, or protect the national honor, at its election return the fund to the nation paying it or otherwise dispose of it**.[204]

National courts have adopted a similar position.[205]

(a) *United Kingdom*

In the *Civilian War Claimants* case,[206] the claimants petitioned the Crown for a share of the reparations paid to the United Kingdom Government by Germany pursuant to the Treaty of Versailles for damage done during the First World War. It was held that when the Crown was negotiating a treaty with another Head of State, it was inconsistent with its sovereign position that it should act as trustee or agent for its nationals unless it expressly declared that

[195] A/CN.4/561 and Add.1–2 (see footnote 3 above), general remarks.

[196] See footnote 4 above.

[197] In the *Barcelona Traction* case ICJ declared:

"The State must be viewed as the sole judge to decide whether its protection will be granted, to what extent it is granted, and when it will cease. It retains in this respect a discretionary power the exercise of which may be determined by considerations of a political or other nature, unrelated to the particular case. Since the claim of the State is not identical with that of the individual or corporate person whose cause is exposued, the State enjoys *complete freedom of action**."

(*I.C.J. Reports 1970* (see footnote 61 above), p. 44)

[198] Geck, "Diplomatic protection", p. 1058; Bederman, "Interim report on 'lump sum agreements and diplomatic protection'"; Lillich, "The United States-Hungarian Claims Agreement of 1973"; Lillich and Weston, *International Claims: Their Settlement by Lump Sum Agreements*.

[199] Carreau, *Droit International*, p. 462, para. 1118.

[200] Pastor Ridruejo, "La pratique espagnole de la protection diplomatique", p. 112.

[201] *Factory at Chorzow, Merits, Judgment No. 13, 1928, P.C.I.J., Series A, No. 17*, p. 28: "The damage suffered by an individual is never therefore identical in kind with that which will be suffered by a State; it can only afford a convenient scale for the calculation of the reparation due to the State." Dubouis has commented on this *dictum* in "La distinction entre le droit de l'État réclamant et le droit du ressortissant dans la protection diplomatique (à propos de l'arrêt rendu par la Cour de cassation le 14 juin 1977)", p. 624.

[202] Bollecker-Stern, *Le préjudice dans la théorie de la responsabilité internationale*, p. 98.

[203] *I.C.J. Reports 1970* (see footnote 61 above), p. 223.

[204] *Administrative Decision No. V* (see footnote 62 above), p. 152.

[205] See Jennings and Watts, *op. cit.*, p. 539.

[206] *Civilian War Claimants Association* v. *The King*, House of Lords, *Law Reports* (1932), p. 14. See also *Rustomjee* v. *The Queen* (1876) 1 Q.B.D., p. 487.

it was so acting. There was nothing in the treaty to suggest this. Rather, the treaty left it to the Governments, as between themselves and their nationals, to determine how that money was to be distributed. This decision was recently affirmed in *Lonrho Exports Ltd* v. *Export Credits Guarantee Department*.[207]

(b) *United States*

As a matter of United States law: "The money received from a foreign government as a result of an international award, or in settlement, belongs to the United States",[208] and the distribution of indemnities is left to the goodwill of Congress:

> By cases decided by the Supreme Court of the United States, it seems to have been established that funds received from foreign governments in settlement of claims of American citizens are national funds of the United States; that no claimant has as a matter of strict legal right any lien on funds obtained; and that Congress is not under any legal obligation to pay any claim out of the proceeds of a fund, although undoubtedly there is a *moral** obligation on the Government to remit funds to persons who have suffered losses.[209]

(c) *France*

In France diplomatic protection remains an *acte du gouvernement*—the last bastion of the non-rule of law—and the procedures for the attribution of indemnities have traditionally remained unsusceptible to judicial oversight.[210]

98. Despite the above assertions of the absolute right of a State to distribute compensation received as it pleases, it is not uncommon to find statements that the normal practice of a State in such a case is to pay money received to the injured individual. Geck, for example, argues that: "The claimant State usually forwards to the injured individuals the damages paid by the defendant State."[211] The commentary to the draft convention on the international responsibility of States for injuries to aliens, prepared by Harvard Law School, is to the same effect: "[T]he normal practice of transfer by the claimant State to the individual claimant of any reparation which it secures ..."[212] In order to understand statements of this kind it is necessary to examine the steps that States have taken to limit their discretion.

99. Beginning in the 1950s, States started to introduce judicial review of compensation awards. France, the United Kingdom and the United States set up commissions for the distribution of lump-sum awards received from Eastern European States after the Second World War. This phenomenon was a consequence of the large number of claimants competing for a share in vastly inferior returns of the cumulative value of confiscated or nationalized private property. The distribution of the indemnity became a particularly delicate affair and it became judicious to create specialized agencies for this purpose. Each State designed a different procedure.

(a) *United States*

After the Second World War, several bloc settlement agreements led to the creation in 1949 of the International Claims Commission under the International Claims Settlement Act of 1949, to deal with the distribution of lump-sum agreements concluded with Yugoslavia and later Panama, and other popular democracies which had engaged in nationalizations. It was renamed Foreign Claims Settlement Commission of the United States in 1982. Its function is to distribute funds received from foreign Governments among the various claimants, after considering each claim separately and deciding on its validity and the amount due to each claimant on the basis first, of the particular accord at issue and secondly, applying "applicable principles of international law, justice and equity".[213] The Commission is quasi-judicial in nature. There is no appeal from its decisions. There is a standing

---

[207] *All England Law Reports* [1996] 4 All ER, p. 687:

"(3) When the Crown espouses claims (e.g. of nationals who are creditors of foreign states or nationals) and affords diplomatic protection (e.g. by the negotiation of a treaty providing for payment to the Crown for distribution to its nationals), under international law the Crown is maintaining its own right in its own name to such protection of its nationals …

"(4) (Subject to (5) below) in concluding and performing the obligations under such a treaty, the Crown does not act as agent or trustee for the nationals; and irrespective of the terms of the treaty and (as it seems to me) the characterisation of the payments by the treaty, payments made to the United Kingdom pursuant to such treaties are received by the Crown in a sovereign capacity and form the absolute property of the State …

…

"(6) The entitlement of the Crown to retain the payments made to it is not, as a matter of English law, affected by the terms of the treaty or whatever the treaty may provide regarding their distribution. Nor can the terms of the treaty affect or qualify the sovereign character of the Crown's receipt of such payments … The Crown has under English law no legal or equitable, but at best a mere moral, obligation to fulfil those terms. If the Crown fails to do so, the only remedies lie in Parliament or (at the instance of the foreign government) in international law proceedings …

"(7) The Crown in distributing any payments received pursuant to a treaty may determine the character to be borne by the payments it makes and earmark such payments."

[208] American Law Institute, *Restatement of the Law Third: Foreign Relations Law of the United States*, para. 902, pp. 348–349.

[209] *Distribution of Aslop Award by the Secretary of State* (1912), opinion of J. Reuben Clark, Solicitor for the Department of State, cited in Hackworth, *op. cit.*, p. 766.

[210] Bollecker-Stern, *op. cit.*, p. 108.

[211] Geck, *loc. cit.*, p. 1057.

[212] García-Amador, Sohn and Baxter, *op. cit.*, p. 151. In *Administrative Decision No. V*, the umpire of the United States–German Mixed Claims Commission, established under the agreement of 10 August 1922, said:

> "But where a demand is made on behalf of a designated national, and an award and payment is made on that specific demand, the fund so paid is not a national fund in the sense that the title vests in the nation receiving it entirely free from any obligation to account to the private claimant, on whose behalf the claim was asserted and paid and who is the real owner thereof. Broad and misleading statements susceptible of this construction are found in cases where lump-sum awards and payments have been made to the demanding nation covering numerous claims put forward by it and where the tribunal making the award did not undertake to adjudicate each claim or to allocate any specified amount to any designated claim. It is not believed that any case can be cited in which an award has been made by an international tribunal in favor of the demanding nation on behalf of its designated national in which the nation receiving payment of such award has, in the absence of fraud or mistake, hesitated to account to the national designated, or those claiming under him, for the full amount of the award received. So far as the United States is concerned it would seem that the Congress has treated funds paid the nation in satisfaction of specific claims as held 'in trust for citizens of the United States or others'."

(*Administrative Decision No. V* (see footnote 62 above), p. 152)

[213] *Restatement of the Law Third* (see footnote 208 above), pp. 228–229, para. 713.

appropriation for the distribution of funds received by the United States from a foreign government. Thus, although the money received from settlements is money belonging to the Government of the United States, Congress has usually provided for payment to private claimants, especially to those whose claims are settled in accordance with decisions of the special United States claims commission dividing a lump-sum settlement.[214]

(b) *United Kingdom*[215]

The British Foreign Compensation Commission was established by the Foreign Compensation Act of 1950 with a view to distributing indemnities as a result of the accords concluded with Czechoslovakia, Poland and Yugoslavia. The Commission functions like an ordinary tribunal, applying domestic law. The law to be applied is determined by Orders in Council, which in turn often mirror the terms of the accord in question. There is no appeal from their decisions.

(c) *France*[216]

In France, the system works on an *ad hoc* basis with a commission for the distribution of indemnities created for each of the accords executed, starting in 1951. A commission to deal with the creditors in the Russian loans debacle spanning from the Russian Tsarist era, was established as recently as 1998.[217] There is no general right of appeal. Although not specified, the tendency of the commissions is to apply international law, both treaty law and customary law.

100. Not too much significance can be attached to these developments, as they reflect national legal institutions.[218] Despite this, some writers insist that they have had an impact on international law.[219]

101. Further evidence of the erosion of the State's discretion is to be found in the decisions of arbitration tribunals which prescribe how the award is to be divided.[220] Moreover, in 1994 the European Court of Human Rights decided in *Beaumartin* v. *France*[221] that an international agreement making provision for compensation could give rise to an enforceable right on the part of the injured persons to compensation.

102. Although there is some support for curtailing the absolute right of the State to withhold payment of compensation received to the injured national in national legislation, judicial decisions and doctrine, it can hardly be argued that this constitutes a settled practice or that there is any sense of obligation on the part of States which has limited their freedom of disposal. Public policy, equity and respect for human rights may all support the curtailment of the State's discretion in the disbursement of compensation, but this does not constitute a rule of customary international law.

103. It is suggested, in these circumstances, that the Commission seriously consider adopting a provision on this subject as an exercise in progressive development. The present draft articles contain little progressive development. Indeed, a number of respondent States have criticized them on this ground. To adopt a provision on this subject would be to remove one of the major inequities of diplomatic protection. The following proposal is placed before the Commission:

"1. In quantifying its claim for diplomatic protection a State shall have regard to the material and moral consequences of the injury suffered by the national in respect of whom it exercises diplomatic protection. [To this end it shall consult with the injured national.]"

Comment: To a large extent this provision simply codifies existing practice.

"2. When a State receives compensation in full or partial fulfilment of a claim arising out of diplomatic protection it shall [should] transfer that sum to the national in respect of whom it has brought the claim [after deduction of the costs incurred in bringing the claim]."

Comment: The Commission may prefer to use the word "should" rather than "shall" in paragraph 2. This would create an imperfect obligation for States. Such a course is known to international law. For example, article 3 of the Convention on the High Seas provided that: "In order to enjoy the freedom of the seas on equal terms with coastal States, States having no sea-coast *should** have free access to the sea." (Article 125 of the United Nations Convention on the Law of the Sea states that: "Land-locked States *shall** have the right of access to and from the sea.")

---

[214] *Ibid.*, p. 349, para. 902.

[215] Berlia, "Contribution à l'étude de la nature de la protection diplomatique", pp. 66–68.

[216] *Ibid.*

[217] Carreau, *op. cit.*, pp. 484–485, para. 1172.

[218] *Ibid.*, p. 485, para. 1173; opinion of J. Reuben Clark (see footnote 209 above), p. 763.

[219] See, for instance, Berlia, *loc. cit.*, p. 70.

[220] Bollecker-Stern, *op. cit.*, p. 109.

[221] European Court of Human Rights, *Series A: Judgments and Decisions*, vol. 296, case of *Beaumartin* v. *France*, judgment of 24 November 1994, p. 50. See also on the jurisprudence of the Court, Flauss, "Contentieux européen des droits de l'homme et protection diplomatique", pp. 829–830.

Annex

POST-2000 BIBLIOGRAPHY ON DIPLOMATIC PROTECTION

Books

AMERASINGHE, Chittharanjan Felix

Local Remedies in International Law. 2nd ed. Cambridge, Cambridge University Press, 2004. 445 p.

FLAUSS, Jean-François, ed.

La protection diplomatique: mutations contemporaines et pratiques nationales. Brussels, Bruylant, 2003.

PAULSSON, Jan

Denial of Justice in International Law. Cambridge, Cambridge University Press, 2005. 279 p.

STOROST, Christian

Diplomatischer Schutz durch EG und EU? Berlin, Duncker & Humblot, 2005. 300 p.

TIBURCIO, Carmen

The Human Rights of Aliens under International and Comparative Law. The Hague, Martinus Nijhoff, 2001. 318 p.

Articles

CAFLISCH, Lucius

"La pratique suisse de la protection diplomatique", *in* Jean-François Flauss, ed., *La protection diplomatique: mutations contemporaines et pratiques nationales.* Brussels, Bruylant, 2003, pp. 73–86.

CONDORELLI, Luigi

"L'évolution du champ d'application de la protection diplomatique", *in* Jean-François Flauss, ed., *La protection diplomatique: mutations contemporaines et pratiques nationales.* Brussels, Bruylant, 2003, pp. 3–28.

"La protection diplomatique et l'évolution de son domaine d'application actuelle", *Rivista di Diritto Internazionale*, vol. LXXXVI, 2003, pp. 5–26.

DEEN-RACSMÁNY, Zsuzsanna

"Diplomatic protection and the *LaGrand* case", *Leiden Journal of International Law*, vol. 15, 2002, pp. 87–103.

DOMINICÉ, Christian

"La prétention de la personne privée dans le système de la responsabilité internationale des États", *Studi di Diritto Internazionale in Onore di Gaetano Arangio-Ruiz.* Naples, Editoriale Scientifica, 2004, pp. 729–745.

"Regard actuel sur la protection diplomatique", Liber Amicorum *Claude Reymond: Autour de l'arbitrage.* Paris, Éditions du Juris-Classeur, 2004, pp. 73–81.

"L'arrêt AVENA et le sort judiciaire des droits individuels", *in* Jürgen Bröhmer and others, eds., *Internationale Gemeinschaft und Menschenrechte: Festschrift für Georg Ress.* Carl Heymanns, 2005, pp. 55–62.

DUCHESNE, Matthew S.

"The continuous-nationality-of-claims principle: its historical development and current relevance to investor-State investment disputes", *George Washington International Law Review*, vol. 36, No. 4, 2004, pp. 783–815.

DUGARD, John

"Diplomatic protection and human rights: the draft articles of the International Law Commission", *Australian Year Book of International Law* (Canberra), vol. 24, 2005, pp. 75–91.

ERASMUS, Gerhard and Lyle DAVIDSON

"Do South Africans have a right to diplomatic protection?", *South African Yearbook of International Law*, vol. 25, 2000, pp. 113–130.

FERIA TINTA, Monica

"Due process and the right to life in the context of the Vienna Convention on Consular Relations: arguing the *LaGrand* case", *European Journal of International Law*, vol. 12, 2001, pp. 363–366.

FERRARI BRAVO, Luigi

"La pratique italienne de la protection diplomatique", *in* Jean-François Flauss, ed., *La protection diplomatique: mutations contemporaines et pratiques nationales.* Brussels, Bruylant, 2003, pp. 87–91.

FLAUSS, Jean-François

"Protection diplomatique et protection internationale des droits de l'homme", *Swiss Review of International and European Law*, vol. 13, 2003, pp. 1–37.

"Vers un aggiornamento des conditions d'exercice de la protection diplomatique?", *in* Jean-François Flauss, ed., *La protection diplomatique: mutations contemporaines et pratiques nationales.* Brussels, Bruylant, 2003, pp. 29–62.

"Contentieux européen des droits de l'homme et protection diplomatique", *Libertés, Justice, Tolérance: Mélanges en hommage au Doyen Gérard Cohen-Jonathan.* Vol. I. Brussels, Bruylant, 2004, pp. 813–838.

"Le contentieux des décisions de refus d'exercice de la protection diplomatique: à propos de l'arrêt du Tribunal fédéral suisse du 2 juillet 2004, Groupement X c./Conseil fédéral (1re Cour civile)", RGDIP, vol. CIX, 2005, pp. 407–419.

FORCESE, Craig

"Shelter from the storm: rethinking diplomatic protection of dual nationals in modern international law", *George Washington International Law Review*, vol. 37, No. 2, 2005, pp. 469–500.

GAJA, Giorgio

"Droits des États et droits des individus dans le cadre de la protection diplomatique", *in* Jean-François Flauss, ed., *La protection diplomatique: mutations contemporaines et pratiques nationales.* Brussels, Bruylant, 2003, pp. 63–69.

"Is a State specially affected when its nationals' human rights are infringed?", *in* Lal Chand Vorah and others, eds., *Man's Inhumanity to Man: Essays on International Law in Honour of Antonio Cassese.* The Hague, Kluwer, 2003, pp. 373–382.

HOPKINS, Kevin

"Diplomatic protection and the South African Constitution: does a South African citizen have an enforceable constitutional claim against the government?", *SA Public Law*, vol. 16, Nos. 1–2, 2001, pp. 387–395.

IOVANE, Massimo

"The activity of the International Law Commission during its 55th session", *Italian Yearbook of International Law*, vol. XIII, 2003, pp. 171–188.

KOOIJMANS, Pieter H.

"Is the right to diplomatic protection a human right?", *Studi di Diritto Internazionale in Onore di Gaetano Arangio-Ruiz.* Naples, Editoriale Scientifica, 2004, pp. 1975–1984.

KÜNZLI, Annemarieke

"Case concerning Mexican nationals", *Leiden Journal of International Law*, vol. 18, 2005, pp. 49–64.

"Exercising diplomatic protection: the fine line between litigation, démarches and consular assistance", *Heidelberg Journal of International Law*, vol. 66, 2006, pp. 321–350.

MALENOVSKY, Jiri

"La pratique de la protection diplomatique dans les P.E.C.O., en République Tchèque en particulier", *in* Jean-François Flauss, ed., *La protection diplomatique: mutations contemporaines et pratiques nationales*. Brussels, Bruylant, 2003, pp. 93–107.

MILANO, Enrico

"Diplomatic protection and human rights before the International Court of Justice: re-fashioning tradition?", *Netherlands Yearbook of International Law*, vol. XXXV, 2004, pp. 85–142.

PASTOR RIDRUEJO, José

"La pratique espagnole de la protection diplomatique", *in* Jean-François Flauss, ed., *La protection diplomatique: mutations contemporaines et pratiques nationales*. Brussels, Bruylant, 2003, pp. 109–113.

PAULSSON, Jan

"Continuous nationality in *Loewen*", *Arbitration International*, vol. 20, No. 2, 2004, pp. 213–215.

PELLET, Alain

"'Human rightism' and international law", *Italian Yearbook of International Law*, vol. X, 2000, pp. 3–16.

PINTO, Mónica

"De la protection diplomatique à la protection des droits de l'homme", RGDIP, vol. CVI, 2002, pp. 513–547.

PUISSOCHET, Jean-Pierre

"La pratique française de la protection diplomatique", *in* Jean-François Flauss, ed., *La protection diplomatique: mutations contemporaines et pratiques nationales*. Brussels, Bruylant, 2003, pp. 115–120.

RESS, Georg

"La pratique allemande de la protection diplomatique", *in* Jean-François Flauss, ed., *La protection diplomatique: mutations contemporaines et pratiques nationales*. Brussels, Bruylant, 2003, pp. 121–151.

SANTULLI, Carlo

"Travaux de la Commission du droit international", *Annuaire français de droit international* (Paris), vol. XLVI, 2000, pp. 424–427; vol. XLVII, 2001, pp. 369–378; vol. XLVIII, 2002, pp. 561–564; vol. XLIX, 2003, pp. 442–446.

"Entre protection diplomatique et action directe—la représentation: éléments épars du statut international des sujets internes", *Colloque du Mans: Le Sujet en Droit International*. Paris, Pedone, 2005, pp. 85–98.

SCHERMERS, Henry G.

"Exhaustion of domestic remedies", *in* Nisuke Ando and others, eds., Liber Amicorum: *Judge Shigeru Oda*. Vol. 2. The Hague, Kluwer, 2002, pp. 947–975.

SPIERMANN, Ole

"The *LaGrand* case and the individual as a subject of international law", *Austrian Journal of Public and International Law*, vol. 58, 2003, pp. 197–221.

STOROST, Christian

"Der Fall Abbasi: Wegbereiter eines gemeineuropäischen Anspruchs auf diplomatischen Schutz?", *Archiv des Völkerrechts*, vol. 42, 2004, pp. 411–424.

WARBRICK, Colin and Dominic MCGOLDRICK, eds.

"Current developments: public international law", *International and Comparative Law Quarterly*, vol. 51, part 3, July 2002, pp. 723–733.

WITTICH, Stephan

"Direct injury and the incidence of the local remedies rule", *Austrian Review of International and European Law*, vol. 5, 2000, pp. 121–187.

ZIECK, Marjoleine

"Codification of the law on diplomatic protection: the first eight draft articles", *Leiden Journal of International Law*, vol. 14, 2001, pp. 209–232.

DOCUMENT A/CN.4/561 and Add. 1–2

Comments and observations received from Governments

[*Original: Arabic/English/French/Spanish/Russian*]
[*27 January, 3 and 12 April 2006*]

CONTENTS

Multilateral instruments cited in the present report

	Source
Convention on Certain Questions relating to the Conflict of Nationality Laws (The Hague, 12 April 1930)	League of Nations, *Treaty Series*, vol. CLXXIX, No. 4137, p. 89.
Convention relating to the Status of Refugees (Geneva, 28 July 1951)	United Nations, *Treaty Series*, vol. 189, No. 2545, p. 137.
Protocol relating to the Status of Refugees (New York, 31 January 1967)	*Ibid.*, vol. 606, No. 8791, p. 267.
Treaty establishing the European Community (Rome, 25 March 1957), incorporating the amendments made by the Treaty of Nice of 26 February 2001	Consolidated version of the Treaty on European Union, *Official Journal of the European Communities*, C325, vol. 45 (24 December 2002).
Vienna Convention on Diplomatic Relations (Vienna, 18 April 1961)	United Nations, *Treaty Series*, vol. 500, No. 7310, p. 95.
Vienna Convention on Consular Relations (Vienna, 24 April 1963)	*Ibid.*, vol. 596, No. 8638, p. 261.
International Covenant on Civil and Political Rights (New York, 16 December 1966)	*Ibid.*, vol. 999, No. 14668, p. 171.
Vienna Convention on the Law of Treaties (Vienna, 23 May 1969)	*Ibid.*, vol. 1155, No. 18232, p. 331.
United Nations Convention on the Law of the Sea (Montego Bay, 10 December 1982)	*Ibid.*, vol. 1833, No. 31363, p. 397.
Treaty on European Union (Maastricht, 7 February 1992)	United Nations, *Treaty Series*, vol. 1757, No. 30615, p. 3.

Works cited in the present report

AMERASINGHE, Chittharanjan Felix

Local Remedies in International Law. 2nd ed. Cambridge, Cambridge University Press, 2004. 445 p.

AMERICAN LAW INSTITUTE

Restatement of the Law Third: Foreign Relations Law of the United States. Vol. 2. St. Paul, Minn., American Law Institute, 1987.

BORCHARD, Edwin M.

The Diplomatic Protection of Citizens Abroad or the Law of International Claims. New York, Banks Law Publishing Co., 1919. 988 p.

BROWNLIE, Ian

Principles of Public International Law. 6th ed. Oxford, Oxford University Press, 2003.

FELLER, A. H.

The Mexican Claims Commissions, 1923–1934: A Study in the Law and Procedure of International Tribunals. New York, Macmillan, 1935. 572 p.

FLETCHER, William Meade

Fletcher Cyclopedia of the Law of Private Corporations. Rev. vol. by Jennifer L. Berger and Carol A. Jones. Vol. 16A. West, Thomson, 2003.

GARCÍA-AMADOR, F. V., Louis B. SOHN and R. R. BAXTER

Recent Codification of the Law of State Responsibility for Injuries to Aliens. Dobbs Ferry, New York, Oceana, 1974. 402 p.

GROSSFELD, Bernhard

"Management and control of marketable share companies", *in* Alfred Conard and Detlev Vagts, eds., *International Encyclopedia of Comparative Law*. Vol. XIII: *Business and Private Organizations*. Tübingen, Mohr Siebeck, 1973.

HACKWORTH, Green Haywood

Digest of International Law. Vol. V. Washington, D.C., United States Government Printing Office, 1943. 851 p.

JENNINGS, Sir Robert and Sir Arthur WATTS, eds.

Oppenheim's International Law. 9th ed. Vol I: Peace. Introduction and part 1. Harlow, Longman, 1992. 554 p.

JONES, Mervyn

"Claims on behalf of nationals who are shareholders in foreign companies", *British Year Book of International Law*, 1949, vol. 26.

LA PRADELLE, A. DE and Jacques POLITIS

Recueil des arbitrages internationaux. Vol. III. Paris, Éditions Internationales, 1954.

MOORE, John Bassett

History and Digest of the International Arbitrations to which the United States has been a Party. Vol. II. Washington, D.C., Government Printing Office, 1898.

A Digest of International Law. Vol. VI. Washington, D.C., Government Printing Office, 1906.

NIELSEN, Fred K.

American and British Claims Arbitration: under the Special Agreement concluded between the United States and Great Britain (18 August 1910). Washington, D.C., Government Printing Office, 1926.

RALSTON, Jackson H.

The Law and Procedure of International Tribunals. Rev. ed. Stanford University, California, Stanford University Press, 1926. 512 p.

SCHWARZENBERGER, Georg

International Law. Vol. I: *International Law as applied by International Courts and Tribunals.* 2nd ed. London, Stevens, 1949.

SINCLAIR, I. M.

"Nationalityof claims: British practice", *British Year Book of International Law*, 1950, vol. 27, pp. 125–144.

WHITEMAN, Marjorie M.

Digest of International Law. Vol. 8. Washington, D.C., United States Government Printing Office, 1967.

Introduction

1. The International Law Commission completed the first reading of a set of 19 draft articles on diplomatic protection at its fifty-sixth session, held in 2004.[1] The Commission subsequently decided, in accordance with articles 16 and 21 of its statute, to transmit the draft articles, through the Secretary-General, to Governments for comments and observations, with the request that such comments and observations be submitted to the Secretary-General by 1 January 2006. By a note dated 19 October 2004, the Secretariat invited Governments to submit their written comments by 1 January 2006.

2. On 2 December 2004, the General Assembly adopted resolution 59/41, entitled "Report of the International Law Commission on the work of its fifty-sixth session", which, *inter alia*, drew the attention of Governments to the importance for the Commission of having their views, in particular, on the draft articles and commentary on diplomatic protection. The Assembly again drew the attention of Governments to the matter in its resolution 60/22 of 23 November 2005.

3. As at 12 April 2006, written comments had been received from the following 14 States: Austria, Belgium, El Salvador, Guatemala, Italy, Mexico, Morocco, the Netherlands, Norway (on behalf of the Nordic countries Denmark, Finland, Iceland, Norway and Sweden), Panama, Qatar, the United Kingdom of Great Britain and Northern Ireland, the United States of America and Uzbekistan. Their comments are reproduced below, on an article-by-article basis.

[1] See *Yearbook ... 2004*, vol. II (Part Two), p. 18, para. 59. The articles, along with commentary, are reproduced in paragraph 60, pp. 20 *et seq.*

Comments and observations received from Governments

General remarks

Austria

1. The law of diplomatic protection is undoubtedly a classical topic of international law that lends itself to codification. It meets with all the conditions that are decisive for a useful work in this regard. Of course, it could be asked to what extent this legal regime still plays a major role in international law in view of the emergence of the system of human rights. However, as practice reveals, even in recent cases before ICJ it is still of major importance for the protection of individuals.

2. Austria appreciates that the Commission boiled down the draft articles to basic rules and concentrated on the secondary norms regarding diplomatic protection; any other approach, such as the attempt to define the breaches of substantive law, would have faced insurmountable difficulties. Consequently, Austria favours the exclusion of any draft article on denial of justice since that is a matter of primary law. The obligation to exhaust local remedies must be distinguished from the State's obligation to offer access to its courts. Likewise, Austria concurs with the Commission that the draft articles neither address the issue of the Calvo clause nor the clean hands doctrine. Both clauses seem to suffer from the absence of general acceptability.

3. It seems that the Commission concentrated only on one aspect of diplomatic protection, namely as a right of a State to make certain claims in the interest of its nationals. That right is, however, balanced by the corresponding obligation of the other States to accept such claims by aState. The legal regime on diplomatic protection also stipulates under which conditions a State has to accept such interventions by another State. Such a view undoubtedly sheds some new light on that legal regime and reveals different aspects of it, which the text of the Commission does not sufficiently take into account.

4. It could further be asked whether other issues should also have been included under the topic, such as the right of international organizations to exercise diplomatic protection, in particular in view of the draft article on the relevant right of the flag State of a vessel. Originally, Austria favoured such a broadening of the topic. However, international organizations still pose major problems with respect to their legal structure, as can be seen in the context of the responsibility of international organizations. For that reason, it seems better to put the focus on States alone in order to achieve a manageable legal regime. Nevertheless, this restriction should not be understood as a denial of the necessity to eventually embark on the problem of international organizations which perform an increasing role in international relations even with respect to the protection of individuals.

5. A further issue that deserves particular consideration is the problem of the relation between the individual whose rights are protected and the State exercising the right to diplomatic protection. Addressing the problem of the result of the exercise of diplomatic protection and the access of the individual to such a result could also be considered. Of course, on the one hand, it could be argued that this is a matter of the relation between a State and its nationals; on the other hand, however, it should be ensured that the injured individual in whose interest the claim was raised will benefit from the exercise of diplomatic protection.

Belgium

Belgium would like to point out that it views diplomatic protection, in respect of which the Commission adopted on first reading, a very useful set of draft articles, as one of a series of mechanisms for the protection of human rights and fundamental freedoms emanating from international treaty law and customary international law, several of which provide for the right of any State to intervene in respect of any individual (including a non-national) whose rights have been violated.

El Salvador

1. El Salvador considers that a clear distinction should be drawn between the scope of the diplomatic protection envisaged in the draft articles and the protection referred to in the Vienna Convention on Diplomatic Relations and the Vienna Convention on Consular Relations. Otherwise, since the Commission is engaged in the codification and progressive development of international law in this area, El Salvador believes that it would be necessary to take due account of the relevant provisions of the Vienna Convention on Diplomatic Relations and the Vienna Convention on Consular Relations, particularly the provisions of article 36 of the latter Convention, which refers to the consular protection to be afforded to a national detained in another State, guaranteeing, moreover, that such nationals shall be granted due process. That provision is of such importance that it has elicited advisory opinions both from inter-American bodies, such as advisory opinion OC–16/99 of the Inter-American Court of Human Rights,[2] and from universal organs, such as the ICJ judgment in the case concerning *Avena and Other Mexican Nationals*.[3]

2. El Salvador raises the above points because, according to the definition of diplomatic protection proposed in draft article 1, such protection is limited to cases in which a State in its own right adopts the cause of a national and exercises diplomatic protection in accordance with the draft articles in question, which could be interpreted to mean that some consular functions under the Vienna Convention on Consular Relations would be excluded, since there are situations in which the State does not adopt in its own right the cause of a national.

3. In view of the above, El Salvador believes it is important to bear in mind that, at the international level, the concept of diplomatic protection should be distinguished from other concepts of international law that relate to the protection of individuals, particularly in the field of human rights, which imposes precise obligations on States, namely, *jus cogens* and *erga omnes*.

Italy

Italy congratulates the Commission for its work, and endorses the approach adopted by the Commission in formulating the draft articles.

Mexico

1. As Mexico has noted on previous occasions, diplomatic protection is a key, high-priority concern in Mexico's foreign policy. Mexico has, accordingly, followed with much interest the development of the Commission's draft articles. Although, in broad terms, it finds the draft articles acceptable, Mexico wishes to highlight several points in relation to draft articles 9, 14, 16 and 19 (see below).

2. Mexico wishes to reiterate its comments on the subject of the clean hands doctrine in the light of the present draft articles on diplomatic protection. As the Commission establishes in draft article 1, diplomatic protection consists of resort to diplomatic action or other means of peaceful settlement by a State adopting in its own right the cause of its national in respect of an injury to that national arising from an internationally wrongful act of another State.

3. In that context, Mexico considers that if an individual is or is presumed to be responsible for reprehensible conduct abroad, his State of nationality might, on account of that unfortunate circumstance, decide not to resort to the exercise of diplomatic protection. Nevertheless, this is by no means the same as saying that "clean hands" is a *sine qua non* for a State's exercise of diplomatic protection. For that reason, Mexico welcomes the Commission's decision to withdraw this topic from the draft articles.

Netherlands

1. The Netherlands generally supports the draft articles and thus applauds the work of the Commission to date.

---

[2] The Right to Information on Consular Assistance in the Framework of the Guarantees of the Due Process of Law, Advisory Opinion OC–16/99, Inter-American Court of Human Rights, Series A, No. 16 (1999).

[3] *Avena and Other Mexican Nationals (Mexico* v. *United States of America), Judgment, I.C.J. Reports 2004*, p. 38, paras. 45–47.

2. The Netherlands notes that in his first report, the Special Rapporteur of the Commission, Mr. John Dugard, had already included diplomatic protection within the context of the protection of human rights when he wrote "diplomatic protection remains an important weapon in the arsenal of human rights protection".[4] The Special Rapporteur also wrote in his fifth report that "the customary international law rules on diplomatic protection that have evolved over several centuries, and the more recent principles governing the protection of human rights, complement each other and, ultimately, serve a common goal—the protection of human rights".[5] The Netherlands fully endorses this position as expressed by the Special Rapporteur.

3. Seen from the above perspective, the Netherlands regrets that such complementarity of diplomatic protection has not been thoroughly elaborated either in the draft articles or in the commentary. The formulation of some of the draft articles is consonant with current protection of human rights and other developments in international law. The Netherlands considers that the draft articles as they now stand do not provide sufficient elements of or scope for progressive development. Several of the proposals by the Netherlands for the text of the draft articles—draft article 3 for instance—are rooted in the general approach outlined here.

4. The Netherlands hopes that further discussion will prompt the Commission to pay closer attention to the position of the individual.

5. The Netherlands endorses the conclusions of the Special Rapporteur in regard to the clean hands doctrine.

Norway, on behalf of the Nordic countries (Denmark, Finland, Iceland, Norway and Sweden)

1. The complete set of draft articles meets the general satisfaction of the Nordic countries.

2. The Nordic countries support the chosen approach, on the basis of the main premise that States have a right, not a duty, to exercise diplomatic protection. Moreover, they emphasize that principles and rules of diplomatic protection are without prejudice to the law of consular protection and other applicable rules of international law, including those pertaining to the law of the sea.

3. Furthermore, the Nordic countries take note of the view of the majority of the members of the Commission with regard to the clean hands doctrine and share the view that the doctrine should not be included in the draft articles.

Panama

1. Panama believes that the draft articles have fully encompassed in their provisions the issues that have traditionally been covered by the topic of diplomatic protection as a mechanism designed to secure redress for an injury to the national of a State. The draft articles deal in detail with the rules governing the nationality of claims and the exhaustion of local remedies.

2. Panama accordingly supports the focus of the draft in that it codifies customary rules regarding the conditions for the exercise of diplomatic protection in the most traditional and classical sense. It clearly, for this reason, leaves outside its scope functional and other types of protection, which are provided for by other rules, institutions and procedures.

3. Panama agrees with the Commission that the general provisions of the draft articles should maintain the distinction between primary rules and secondary rules, with the latter governing the circumstances in which diplomatic protection may be exercised and the preconditions for its exercise. Panama therefore believes that the aim of the draft is not to address the question of the effects of diplomatic protection and that for this reason it sets aside the application of rules on reparation.

United Kingdom of Great Britain and Northern Ireland

1. The United Kingdom reiterates its support for the work of the Commission on diplomatic protection. There exists a large body of well-established State practice on much of the subject matter of the draft articles.

2. The United Kingdom agrees with the Commission's decision that the present review of diplomatic protection is not an appropriate situation for any review of the functional protection to be accorded to international organizations. The draft articles are intended to be without prejudice to any rights a State may have to exercise consular protection in respect of its nationals abroad; however, the United Kingdom believes that this should be made clearer either in the draft articles themselves or at least in the commentary.

Uzbekistan

1. Uzbekistan believes that the draft articles on diplomatic protection legalize the long-standing and rather widespread practice of "political lobbying" for property and other interests under foreign jurisdiction. The draft articles are based on the principle that local remedies must be exhausted before diplomatic protection may be exercised by a State. In that respect, Uzbekistan considers the draft articles on diplomatic protection as a means of harmonizing existing practice currently carried out on an individual basis.

2. It is necessary to define clearly in the draft articles the rights, obligations and responsibilities of States parties with respect to the exercise of diplomatic protection in the case of an injury arising from a wrongful act of another State.

---

[4] *Yearbook ... 2000*, vol. II (Part One), document A/CN.4/506 and Add.1, p. 215, para. 32.

[5] *Yearbook ... 2004*, vol. II (Part One), document A/CN.4/538, p. 54, para. 37.

Part One

GENERAL PROVISIONS

Draft article 1. Definition and scope

Austria

The gist of draft article 1 is acceptable. However, even though "diplomatic action" does not seem to have a generally accepted meaning, it is necessary to clarify that certain acts, such as protective measures by consulates, do not fall under this term.

Belgium

Draft article 1 defines diplomatic protection as action by a State adopting in its own right the cause of its national "in respect of an injury to that national arising from an internationally wrongful act of another State". This is a very broad interpretation of diplomatic protection. Belgium proposes that the end of the phrase should read as follows: "in respect of an injury to that national arising from an internationally wrongful act of another State whose international responsibility is therefore formally called into question." This clarification enables States to resort to informal procedures which do not fall within the strict framework of diplomatic protection.

Guatemala

With regard to paragraph (7) of the commentary to draft article 1, it is clear that the rules on diplomatic protection are not applicable in cases where a State in whose territory a diplomatic or consular agent exercises his or her functions fails to comply with the obligations relating to such persons incumbent upon it pursuant to the relevant articles of the Vienna Convention on Diplomatic Relations and the Vienna Convention on Consular Relations. The above is confirmed by the last sentence of paragraph (4) of the commentary to draft article 15. However, in the view of Guatemala, diplomatic protection should be applicable to injury caused by that State to such persons outside the exercise of their functions and the application of the aforementioned draft articles. Guatemala is of the opinion that diplomatic protection should, for example, be applicable to the expropriation without compensation of property personally owned by a diplomatic official in the country to which he or she is accredited.

Italy

1. Italy believes that draft article 1, in giving a definition of the concept of "diplomatic protection" and of its scope of application, adopts a wording which is too traditional, especially when it speaks of a State "adopting in its own right the cause of its national". The wording implies not only that the right of diplomatic protection belongs only to the State exercising such protection, but also that the right that has been violated by the internationally wrongful act belongs only to the same State. However, the latter concept is no longer accurate in current international law. ICJ, in the *LaGrand* case[6] and in *Avena and Other Mexican Nationals*,[7] has established that the breach of international norms on treatment of aliens may produce both the violation of a right of the national State and the violation of a right of the individual. The same conclusion has been reached by the Inter-American Court of Human Rights, in its advisory opinion OC–16/99.[8]

2. Therefore Italy suggests that draft article 1 be modified in order to codify more clearly current international law. The new wording (which has been extracted from the *Avena* case, para. 40) could be the following:

"Diplomatic protection consists of resort to diplomatic action or other means of peaceful settlement by a State claiming to have suffered the violation of its own rights and the rights of its national in respect of an injury to that national arising from an internationally wrongful act of another State."

It should be noted that this wording leaves unchanged the basic concept according to which the right to exercise diplomatic protection belongs to the State.

Netherlands

1. The draft article excludes consular assistance. This exception should perhaps be explicitly indicated in the commentary.

2. The draft articles differentiate between "diplomatic action" and "other means of peaceful settlement". It is not always clear whether a draft article relates to one or both of these. The Netherlands suggests that the commentary indicate that several draft articles relate only to "other means of peaceful settlement".

3. Under paragraph (2) of the commentary to draft article 1, a "wrongful act" must have occurred before diplomatic protection can be exercised. The commentary might state that, outside the framework of these draft articles, a State naturally has many other options for taking the necessary steps to protect its subjects before a "wrongful act" has actually occurred.

4. The Netherlands considers that the term "its national" is too restrictive because the scope of the draft articles is widened in later ones. Accordingly, a sentence should be added to the commentary which makes it clear that draft article 1 is not intended to exclude draft article 8.

---

[6] *LaGrand (Germany* v. *United States of America), Judgment, I.C.J. Reports 2001*, p. 494, para. 77.

[7] *Avena and Other Mexican Nationals (Mexico* v. *United States of America), Judgment, I.C.J. Reports 2004*, p. 35, para. 40. See also ILM, vol. 43 (2004), p. 581.

[8] The Right to Information on Consular Assistance in the Framework of the Guarantees of the Due Process of Law, Advisory Opinion OC–16/99, Inter-American Court of Human Rights, Series A, No. 16 (1999), paras. 80–84.

Panama

With regard to who has the right to exercise diplomatic protection and the possibility of doing so, Panama feels it is important to make it clear that this right belongs to States and that, accordingly, the State's legal interest in exercising diplomatic protection stems from the bond of nationality between the State and the person injured through the wrongful act of another State. Consequently, Panama considers it appropriate to incorporate into draft article 1 the provision describing the legitimate and peaceful measures that may be adopted by the State when it resorts to diplomatic protection and the distinction maintained in the provision between the two procedures, namely, diplomatic action and other means of peaceful settlement.

Uzbekistan

The term "nationality of a legal person" is used in draft article 1 [Russian text], which is unacceptable, as nationality is an attribute of natural, not legal, persons. Nations are a historically developed form of community of persons with a common language, national character and distinct culture. In this respect, it seems appropriate to change the term "nationality of a legal person" to "State of origin of a legal person", meaning the State where the legal person is established.

Draft article 2. Right to exercise diplomatic protection

Austria

Although the structure of diplomatic protection as a right of a State has always been discussed—as it is only a fiction that the State is injured through its nationals—draft article 2 raises no major concerns. It reflects the long-standing practice in this regard.

El Salvador

(*See General remarks above.*)

Italy

1. Italy believes that the exercise of diplomatic protection is, as a rule, a right that belongs only to the State and that international law does not provide either for a right of the injured individual to obtain diplomatic protection from its State or for a corresponding duty upon that State. However, an exception to that rule would be appropriate in some particular and very limited circumstances, from the perspective of the progressive development of international law, when the protection of fundamental values pertaining to the dignity of the human being and recognized by the international community as a whole is at stake.

2. The Special Rapporteur, Mr. John Dugard, following the above approach, provided for a similar exception in cases of breach of *jus cogens* norms. By contrast, Italy maintains that a more precise and more limited exception should be included in draft article 2 under the following conditions: (*a*) in the case of grave violations of fundamental human rights and, more precisely, with respect to the right to life, the prohibition of torture and inhuman or degrading treatment or punishment, the prohibition of slavery and the prohibition of racial discrimination; and (*b*) if, in addition, following those violations it is impossible for the individual victim to resort to international judicial or quasi-judicial organs able to afford reparation. When the two cumulative conditions are present, the national State should have the duty to exercise diplomatic protection in favour of the injured individual and the subsidiary duty to provide, in favour of the individual, for an effective domestic remedy against its own refusal.

3. In the above-mentioned exceptional circumstances, the fact that certain international primary rules on human rights (which surely have the nature of *jus cogens*) also confer individual rights and the fact that their breach (which entails a very serious form of State responsibility) also violates individual rights cannot but have an impact on the secondary rules concerning diplomatic protection, by affecting the relationship between the national State and the injured individual. It should also be considered that, in those exceptional and residuary circumstances, diplomatic protection is the only remedy available for the individual, so that its denial by the national State would impair those fundamental principles on the dignity of the human being that the entire international community strongly intends to protect.

4. Therefore, Italy suggests that two paragraphs be added to article 2, which could be worded in the following way:

"2. Notwithstanding paragraph 1, a State has a legal duty to exercise diplomatic protection on behalf of the injured person upon request:

"(*a*) If the injury results from a grave breach, attributable to another State, of an international obligation of essential importance for safeguarding the human being, such as protection of the right to life, the prohibition of torture or of inhumane or degrading treatment or punishment, and the prohibition of slavery and racial discrimination.

"(*b*) If, in addition, the injured person is unable to bring a claim for such an injury before a competent international court or tribunal or quasi-judicial authority.

"3. In the cases set out in paragraph 2, States are obliged to provide in their municipal law for the enforcement of the individual right to diplomatic protection before a competent domestic court or other independent national authority."

Netherlands

Paragraph (3) of the commentary to draft article 2 states that "[t]he right of a State to exercise diplomatic protection may only be carried out within the parameters of the present articles". Exactly what these parameters are is unclear. The Netherlands believes that, in view of the wording of draft article 2, paragraph (3) should be either deleted or clarified.

United Kingdom of Great Britain and Northern Ireland

The United Kingdom welcomes the Commission's characterization of diplomatic protection as a right of the State that the State is under no obligation to exercise. It agrees that every State retains the discretion, subject to its internal laws, as to how this right of diplomatic protection is exercised, if at all. That there is no duty to do so is also made clear in the commentaries to draft articles 2, 3 and 8.

PART TWO

NATIONALITY

Morocco

With regard to the draft articles dealing with the question of nationality, it would be advisable for the Commission to take State practice in that area into account when considering these draft articles at the second reading.

CHAPTER I. GENERAL PRINCIPLES

Draft article 3. Protection by the State of nationality

Austria

Draft article 3, which sets out the fundamental rule of the requirement of the bond of nationality between the injured person and the State exercising diplomatic protection and reflects a basic understanding, raises no major problems.

Netherlands

1. The Netherlands proposes that paragraph 1 be reformulated to read as follows: "The State of nationality is the State entitled to exercise diplomatic protection." This places greater emphasis on the perspective of the individual.

2. In addition, it is important to see draft article 3 in the light of European citizenship (that is, of the European Union). There is currently no reason to be more specific on this point, but future developments cannot be predicted.

(*See also General remarks above.*)

United Kingdom of Great Britain and Northern Ireland

Draft article 3 reaffirms the customary international law rule that the State entitled to exercise diplomatic protection is the State of nationality of the injured person. However, the United Kingdom does not agree that the exception to this rule in article 3, paragraph 2, discussed further in relation to article 8, reflects customary international law.

(*See also comments on draft article 2 above.*)

CHAPTER II. NATURAL PERSONS

Draft article 4. State of nationality of a natural person

Austria

1. Draft article 4 must be understood *cum grano salis* since nationality is not acquired by State succession but as a consequence of State succession. As a rule, nationality is acquired through the law of the respective State. This law can use as a decisive criterion for the acquisition of nationality one of the facts enumerated in this draft article. In the case of State succession, different criteria could be applied in order to grant nationality, as can be seen from the work of the Commission in this regard. It is therefore proposed to reformulate draft article 4 accordingly.

2. In this context, Austria would like to refer to a problem that does not seem to be addressed in the draft articles. In recent times, the practice has evolved that States delegate their right to exercise diplomatic and consular protection to other States. The best example of this practice is article 8*c* of the Treaty on European Union[9] according to which a European Union member State other than the national State may exercise such protection if the national State is not represented in the receiving State. Of course, it could be argued that this is not a case of genuine diplomatic protection; it would, however, certainly fall within the purview of the definition of draft article 1 as it is worded now. As a consequence, either it must be clarified that such protection is not addressed by the draft articles, or they would also have to address this problem. At the moment, the draft articles give no clear guidance in this respect.

Belgium

Belgium observes that the draft articles do not require the effective nationality of the claimant State or States, although, pursuant to draft article 7, the nationality of the claimant State must predominate over the accused State in the case of a claim against the State of nationality. While Belgium notes the progress made in this area, particularly with regard to the judgment in the *Nottebohm* case,[10] it fears an increase in "nationality shopping". In order to minimize that risk, the commentary could refer to the right of the accused State to challenge the exercise of diplomatic protection where there is no genuine link of nationality, it being understood that the burden of proof lies with that State.

(*See also comments on draft article 7 below.*)

El Salvador

The principles on nationality enshrined in the doctrine of private international law need to be taken into account, as there is a need to establish the relationship to both the positive and negative conflicts of nationality that arise from persons having dual or multiple nationalities or having no nationality. El Salvador therefore believes that draft article 4 should distinguish between nationality by birth, whether by *jus soli* or *jus sanguini*, and acquired nationality, as the latter refers to naturalization.

---

[9] Subsequently included as article 20 in the Consolidated Version of the Treaty establishing the European Community.

[10] *Nottebohm, Second Phase, Judgment, I.C.J. Reports 1955*, p. 4.

Qatar

The draft article is not only clear, but extremely explicit, in that it affirms the absolute right of States to determine, in accordance with their domestic law, who qualifies for their nationality. This is consistent with the position enunciated in international law that "[i]t is for each State to determine under its own law who are its nationals".[11]

United Kingdom of Great Britain and Northern Ireland

Draft article 4 contains the generally accepted bases for conferment of nationality in international law. The United Kingdom agrees with the implication of draft article 4 that it is primarily for the State of nationality to determine which individuals it considers to be its nationals in accordance with its own domestic law. Its own rules applying to international claims (see the annex to the present report) require that the injured party must be a United Kingdom national if the United Kingdom is to present a claim on his or her behalf. However, the United Kingdom does not require an additional "effective link" between the claimant and the State of nationality. It supports the Commission's conclusion that ICJ in the *Nottebohm* case[12] did not intend to establish a rule of general application and that the requirement for an effective or genuine link cannot readily be applied in other situations.

Uzbekistan

Draft article 4 indicates the means of acquiring nationality, with the stipulation that those means must be consistent with international law. It seems necessary to point out that the procedures for obtaining nationality are established by national, not international, law and that the means of acquiring it must therefore be consistent with the domestic law of the State in question. These comments relate to draft article 5, paragraph 2.

Draft article 5. Continuous nationality

Austria

With respect to draft article 5, Austria concurs with the general substance of the draft provision. Nevertheless, it must be kept in mind that it could sometimes be difficult to prove that nationality was acquired in a manner not inconsistent with international law. The wording of this draft article suffers from a certain inconsistency with the definition contained in draft article 1: whereas draft article 5 speaks of "bringing a claim", which indicates a rather formal and even judicial procedure, draft article 1 gives diplomatic protection a broader meaning, also encompassing acts other than merely the bringing of a claim. Harmonization would be useful.

Belgium

1. With regard to paragraph 1, and, more specifically, the open question of whether or not nationality has to be retained between injury and presentation of the claim, Belgium takes the view that a lack of continuous nationality does not have any bearing on the right to exercise diplomatic protection provided that the nationality existed at the time of the injury and that it exists (again) when the claim is presented.

2. Furthermore, Belgium regrets the fact that the question of the relationships between State succession and diplomatic protection was not addressed, even in the commentary to draft articles 5 and 7. Two situations should be discussed:

(*a*) Cases in which the predecessor State wishes to exercise diplomatic protection in respect of one of its nationals who has involuntarily acquired the nationality of the successor State without having lost the nationality of the predecessor State, provided that the nationality of the predecessor State is predominant;

(*b*) Cases in which the successor State wishes to exercise diplomatic protection in respect of one of its nationals who has involuntarily retained the nationality of the predecessor State provided that the nationality of the successor State is predominant.

El Salvador

Although draft article 5 does refer to the basic rule of continuous nationality, El Salvador is somewhat concerned by paragraph 2. It believes that change of nationality should be addressed in more precise terms in order to ensure that there is no deviation from the basic rule set forth in paragraph 1 of this draft article.

Guatemala

(*See comments on draft article 8 below.*)

Netherlands

1. The Netherlands endorses the regulation proposed in this draft article because it attempts to protect the position of the individual. The Netherlands has studied the question of whether the decision of the International Centre for Settlement of Investment Disputes (ICSID) in the *Loewen* case is a reason to amend draft article 5. Paragraph 225 of the *Loewen* decision reads as follows:

> Claimant TLGI [The Loewen Group Inc.] urges that since it had the requisite nationality at the time the claim arose, and, antedate the time that the claim was submitted, it is of no consequence that the present real party in interest—the beneficiary of the claim—is an American citizen. Both as a matter of historical and current international precedent, this argument must fail. In international law parlance, there must be continuous national identity from the date of the events giving rise to the claim, which date is known as the *dies a quo*, through the date of the resolution of the claim, which date is known as the *dies ad quem*.[13]

2. The Netherlands, however, considers that it is not clear whether the *Loewen* case truly reflects the law as it currently stands. Moreover, application of that rule would have undesirable consequences in cases involving a third

---

[11] Convention on Certain Questions relating to the Conflict of Nationality Laws, art. 1.

[12] *Nottebohm, Second Phase, Judgment, I.C.J. Reports 1955*, p. 4.

[13] *The Loewen Group Inc.* v. *United States of America, ICSID Reports*, vol. 7 (Cambridge, Grotius, 2005), p. 485. See also ILM, vol. 42 (2003), p. 847.

country. The following hypothetical situation can serve as an example: Luxembourg undertakes action against an individual of Dutch nationality, which causes injury to that individual. The Netherlands then decides to exercise diplomatic protection, but before the court or arbiter can issue a judgement, the person loses Dutch nationality and acquires German nationality. Application of the *Loewen* criteria would mean that neither the Netherlands nor Germany could then exercise "full" diplomatic protection.

3. It would be preferable to replace the words "shall not be exercised" in paragraph 3 with "may not be exercised" because "may not" is more in line with the discretionary authority of the State in respect of exercise of diplomatic protection. In addition, "may not" also appears in draft articles 7 and 14. For the rest, "injury caused" is used in the other draft articles and not "injury incurred" as here. Consistency in language is recommended.

Norway, on behalf of the Nordic countries (Denmark, Finland, Iceland, Norway and Sweden)

In draft article 5, a requirement for the exercise of diplomatic protection is continuous nationality. An issue is whether this requirement should apply until the resolution of the dispute or the date of an award or a judgement, and not only until the time of the official presentation of the claim. In practice, however, it can be very difficult to fix the exact point in time of resolution of the dispute. Therefore, the Nordic countries support the chosen approach of the Commission, whereby a State may exercise diplomatic protection in respect of a person who was its national at the time of the injury and is a national at the date of the official presentation of the claim.

Qatar

1. Qatar supports the continuous nationality rule that a State is entitled to exercise diplomatic protection in respect of a person who was its national from the time of the injury up to the date of the official presentation or at most until the adjudication of the claim. However, the paucity of cases in which a person can change his or her nationality in such circumstances cannot be used as justification for draft article 5, paragraph 2, since the fact that a case is rare does not preclude the application of the legal principle to all cases, especially those envisaged during the elaboration of the draft articles.

2. Qatar is stressing this point because it would like to prevent individuals from attempting to change their nationality to that of a State with greater international influence. The adoption of the principle of continuous nationality would close off this option, enhancing the credibility of the rules on the implementation of the principle of diplomatic protection.

United Kingdom of Great Britain and Northern Ireland

1. Draft article 5, paragraph 1, is consistent with customary international law in that it requires the claimant to be a national at the date of injury and at the date of presentation of the claim. The United Kingdom's claims rules (see the annex to the present report) require the individual to be a national continuously from the date of injury up to the date of presentation of the claim; however, in practice it has been sufficient to prove nationality at the date of the injury and at the date of presentation of the claim.

2. Draft article 5, paragraph 2, would represent a change in existing customary international law provisions. The United Kingdom's own claims rules (see the annex to the present report) allow it to take up the claim of a national who ceases to be or becomes a national after the date of the injury. Where the United Kingdom decides to bring a claim in such circumstances, it will normally only be brought in concert with the State of former or subsequent nationality. The United Kingdom believes that it is important to maintain the rule on continuous nationality of claims so as to preclude claimants changing their nationality to that of a State which may be more likely to bring a claim on his or her behalf. The United Kingdom therefore welcomes the inclusion of the requirements of loss of nationality and acquisition of nationality for reasons unrelated to the claim in draft article 5, paragraph 2, as being necessary to protect against potential manipulation of claims rules by future claimants.

United States of America

1. Draft article 5, paragraph 1, would require that a person be a national of a State at the date of injury and the date of official presentation of the claim for that State to exercise diplomatic protection in respect to the national's claim. The commentary accompanying the draft article explains that the date of injury will normally coincide with the date on which the injurious act occurs. The commentary also states that "the date of presentation of the claim is that on which the first official or formal demand is made by the State exercising diplomatic protection".[14] The article as drafted would leave open the question of whether nationality must be maintained continuously between the period the claim arose and the date on which the claim was brought.

2. Draft article 5, paragraph 2, would create an exception to the continuous nationality rule where the person seeking diplomatic protection has lost his former nationality, has acquired a new nationality for reasons unrelated to the claim, and has acquired the new nationality in a manner not inconsistent with international law. Draft article 5, paragraph 3, then would limit this exception by not permitting claims against the former State of nationality where the injury was suffered while the person was still a national of that former State. The draft commentary explains that these rules are designed to allow for claims on behalf of individuals who lost their nationality through State succession, adoption or marriage.

3. Draft article 10, paragraph 1, would require that a corporation be a national of a State exercising diplomatic protection at both the "time of the injury" and the "date of the official presentation of the claim". This draft article also would leave open the question of whether nationality must be maintained continuously between the period the claim arose and the date on which the claim was brought.

[14] *Yearbook ... 2004*, vol. II (Part Two), p. 24, para. (4) of the commentary to article 5.

4. The United States believes that these draft articles do not accurately reflect customary international law and are not drafted in a manner most tailored for the goals sought to be advanced by the draft articles. It strongly urges, therefore, that draft article 5, paragraph 1, be changed to state:

"A State is entitled to exercise diplomatic protection only in respect of a person who was a national of that State, or any predecessor State, continuously from the date of injury through the date of resolution of the claim."

Likewise, draft article 10, paragraph 1, should state:

"A State is entitled to exercise diplomatic protection only in respect of a corporation that was a national of that State, or any predecessor State, continuously from the date of injury through the date of resolution of the claim."

5. These suggested revisions differ from the Commission's draft in four important respects, as explained below. First, the word "only" is proposed to be added to both proposed draft articles to clarify that these articles limit the scope of diplomatic protection to only those claims where the national in question satisfies the continuous nationality requirement. Secondly, the end date for the period of continuous nationality requirement should be described as the "date of resolution of the claim" to bring the draft in line with customary international law. Thirdly, nationality should be required continuously between the date of the events giving rise to the claim and the date of resolution of the claim in order to create consistency between the draft and traditional formulations of the rule. Fourthly, it is proposed that the effect of a change in nationality brought about by the succession of one State by another should be addressed simply and directly by recognizing that the right to assert diplomatic protection also passes by State succession, thereby obviating the need for draft article 5, paragraph 2, in that respect; there is an insufficient basis to venture into the other areas addressed by draft article 5, paragraph 2, to warrant retaining it. The concerns that prompt these suggestions are addressed more fully below.

6. First, draft articles 5, paragraph 1, and 10, paragraph 1, intend to limit the right of diplomatic protection found in draft articles 2–3 to claims held by persons who meet the continuous nationality requirement. The addition of the word "only" is necessary to achieve that goal, as without that word it is not clear that these articles are meant to limit the scope of draft articles 2–3.

7. Secondly, the United States questions the end point for the nationality requirement used in draft articles 5 and 10. The draft commentary states that while there may be a requirement of nationality to the date of resolution, "the paucity of such cases in practice"[15] led to the adoption of "date of presentation of the claim"[16] as the end point for the nationality requirement. The United States is aware, however, of eight specific instances in the context of arbitral decisions and claims presented through diplomatic channels in which the effect of a change in nationality between the presentation and the resolution of the claim was raised and addressed.[17] In each of those instances, the nationality of the claimant or the person on whose behalf the claim was presented changed after the date the claim was officially presented to the respondent State but before the claim's final resolution.[18] In each of the cases, the international claim was dismissed or withdrawn when it became known that the claim was now being asserted on behalf of a national of a State other than the claimant State. The arbitral tribunal in the *Loewen* case most recently affirmed this principle, stating: "In international law parlance, there must be continuous national identity from the date of the events giving rise to the claim ... through the date of the resolution of the claim."[19]

---

[15] *Yearbook ... 2004*, vol. II (Part Two), p. 24, para. (5) of the commentary on article 5.

[16] *Ibid.*

[17] See Hackworth, *Digest of International Law*, vol. V, p. 805, where American claimant Ebenezer Barstow died after his claim was presented to the government of Japan, and the United States declined to continue to espouse the claim because the deceased's wife, who was the new owner of the claim, was Japanese; *Minnie Stevens Eschauzier (Great Britain)* v. *United Mexican States* (24 June 1931), UNRIAA (Sales No. 1952.V.3), vol. V, p. 207, dismissing the claim by a former British national who became a United States citizen by marriage after filing the claim; *María Guadalupe* (unpublished) (Franco-Mexican Commission 1931), discussed in Feller, *The Mexican Claims Commissions, 1923–1934: A Study in the Law and Procedure of International Tribunals*, p. 97 (tribunal denied claim where French nationality was lost "not only subsequent to the filing but also after the specific claim had been listed as receivable in the Supplementary French–Mexican Convention of 1930"); *Benchiton* case, *Affaire des biens britanniques au Maroc espagnol (Spain* v. *Great Britain)* (1 May 1925), UNRIAA, vol. II (Sales No. 1949.V.1), p. 706 (claim denied where claimant lost protected status after first British démarche to Spain concerning claim: "the claim must remain national up to the time of the judgment, or at least up to the time of the termination of the argument relating thereto") (translation in *Annual Digest of Public International Law Cases, years 1923 to 1924* (London, Longmans, Green, 1933), p. 189); *Exors. of F. Lederer (deceased)* v. *German Government*, *Recueil des Décisions des Tribunaux Arbitraux Mixtes institués par les Traités de Paix*, vol. III (Paris, Sirey, 1924), pp. 762 and 765 (Anglo-German Mixed Arbitral Tribunal 1923) (where after notification of claim British claimant died leaving German beneficiaries, claim refused: to allow such relief would "be inconsistent with the meaning of the Treaty, for it would lead in effect to payments ... by Germany to German nationals" (p. 770); *F. H. Redward and Others (Great Britain)* v. *United States (Hawaiian Claims)* (10 November 1925), UNRIAA, vol. VI (Sales No. 1955.V.3); also reported in Nielsen, *American and British Claims Arbitration*. In the *Hawaiian Claims* case before the Arbitral Tribunal (Great Britain–United States), the British Government voluntarily withdrew three claims, "the claimants having acquired American nationality" (*ibid.*, p. 30) during the fourteen years between the date the claims were first filed and the date the memorial was submitted; *Chopin*, UNRIAA, vol. X (Sales No. 1955.V.3), p. 68 (*French and American Claims Commission, 1880–1884*, vol. 60, Records of Claims (claim formally presented by France through diplomatic channels on 30 August 1864, withdrawn by 24 May 1883 motion to dismiss claim as to one beneficiary who had since become a United States national by marriage); Report of Robert S. Hale, Esq., *Papers relating to the Treaty of Washington*, vol. VI (Washington, D.C., Government Printing Office, 1874), p. 14 (report of agent before the American–British Claims Commission that the commission was unanimous that the claimant in the *Gribble* case lacked standing as a British subject because he "had filed his declaration of intention [to seek United States citizenship] ... before the presentation of his memorial, had subsequently, and pending his claim before the commission, completed his naturalization, and was at the time of the submission of his cause a citizen of the United States").

[18] While most of the examples provided involve cases where the national being protected became a national of the respondent State, in at least one case the national became a citizen of a third State. In *Minnie Stevens Eschauzier*, the United Kingdom brought a claim against Mexico, but had the claim dismissed when the national being protected became a United States citizen after the claim's presentation, but prior to its resolution (see footnote 17 above).

[19] *The Loewen Group Inc.* v. *United States of America, ICSID Reports*, vol. 7 (Cambridge, Grotius, 2005), p. 485, para. 225. See also ILM, vol. 42 (2003), p. 847.

8. These cases evidence a clear customary international law rule. In each of these cases, the dismissal or withdrawal of the claims reflected a sense of legal obligation. In each case decided by an arbitral tribunal, the issue was governed by customary international law rather than the specific terms of a treaty. In each case where the claim was withdrawn, it was withdrawn against the interest of the claimant State in receiving compensation from the respondent State for an act it alleged to be internationally wrongful. These cases, in short, reflect consistent State practice. Moreover, as a policy matter this rule is preferable, as it avoids a situation where the respondent State owes the claimant State for an injury to a person that is no longer the legal concern of that State. Draft article 5, paragraph 1, and draft article 10, paragraph 1, should be modified to reflect this rule of international law.

9. Thirdly, the United States believes that draft article 5, paragraph 1, should be modified to require nationality to be maintained continuously from the date of injury through to the date of resolution. While the United States acknowledges the Commission's concern that there has been limited practice applying this rule, its proposal is based upon the customary wording of the continuous nationality requirement made by most scholars and international adjudicatory bodies. As noted above, the tribunal in the *Loewen* case defined the nationality requirement as one of "*continuous** national identity from the date of the events giving rise to the claim ... through the date of the resolution of the claim".[20] In addition to consistency with practice, great dissonance would be created by crafting a continuous nationality requirement and then not requiring continuity of nationality as part of the requirement. The United States therefore urges the Commission to bring draft article 5, paragraph 1, into line with customary descriptions of the rule made by scholars and tribunals.

10. Finally, the United States is cognizant of the issue posed with respect to the requirement of continuous nationality by State succession, which does result in a change in designated nationality. However, the United States believes that the right of diplomatic protection passes in State succession, and the right to diplomatically protect in this situation should not be viewed as an exception to the general requirement. As a result, it proposes deletion of draft article 5, paragraph 2. Rather, the United States believes that the issue can best be addressed through the addition of a reference to the "predecessor State" in draft article 5, paragraph 1, and draft article 10, paragraph 1. This proposal makes clear that there is no interruption of continuous nationality created by State succession, as the successor State retains the right to assert protection with respect to the claims of its citizens that were citizens of the predecessor State, provided all other requirements are met. Retention of what is now draft article 5, paragraph 3, ensures that a successor State cannot espouse a claim of a citizen against his former State of nationality.

11. While the proposed modification to draft article 5, paragraph 1, addresses problems posed by State succession, deleting draft article 5, paragraph 2, leaves unaddressed diplomatic protection of claims of persons whose citizenship has compulsorily changed due to adoption or marriage. The United States questions the factual predicate for this provision since the commentary does not cite any laws mandating loss of citizenship upon marriage to or adoption by a foreigner. In addition, draft article 5, paragraph 2, is in tension with the theoretical underpinnings of diplomatic protection. That paragraph would allow a State to exercise diplomatic protection in respect of an injury suffered when the person who suffered the injury was a national of another State, and thus where the injury in question was one that had an impact only on the international law rights of that other State. This is in contrast to State succession where the new State has succeeded to the international law rights and obligations of the predecessor State and thus is deemed to have had its rights under international law infringed. For the above reasons the United States proposes the deletion of paragraph 2. The proposal by the United States would retain the right of newly created States to exercise diplomatic protection on behalf of their citizens, while avoiding permitting States to exercise diplomatic protection over injuries suffered by other States.

Uzbekistan

(*See comments to draft article 4 above.*)

In draft articles 5 and 10, it is proposed to establish in respect of nationals or legal persons a requirement of affiliation with the State presenting the claim, at the time of the injury and at the time a decision on the violation of rights is rendered; that would allow the rights of such parties to be clearly protected.

Draft article 6. Multiple nationality and claim against a third State

Austria

Whereas paragraph 1 of draft article 6 does not arouse special comments, paragraph 2 requires further comment. In the view of Austria, there is no need of such a provision as there is certainly no doubt that two or more States may jointly act when exercising the right of diplomatic protection. Even if such a clause as that contained in paragraph 2 is lacking, the State to which the claim is presented must accept such a joint démarche. The real problem lies in the possibility that two States may exercise the right of diplomatic protection in a different manner. The commentary deliberately leaves the issue open because of its complexity; in the view of Austria, however, it would be the particular task of the Commission to address even more complicated issues and to provide a solution for

[20] *Ibid.* The panel in *Loewen* is far from the only tribunal or scholar to use this formulation. For example, Brownlie states that the continuous nationality rule requires that a person whose claim is being protected be a national of the claimant State "continuously and without interruption" from date of injury to date of resolution (*Principles of Public International Law*, p. 483). Likewise, García-Amador, Sohn and Baxter state that "the predominant opinion both in diplomatic practice and in international case-law" requires that "the injured person was its national at the moment when the damage was caused and *retains** its nationality until the claim is decided" (*Recent Codification of the Law of State Responsibility for Injuries to Aliens*, p. 82). See also Ralston, *The Law and Procedure of International Tribunals*, pp. 188–189 (criticizing the French-American Claims Commission for failing to apply the continuous nationality rule where France asserted claim on behalf of a national who became American and then French again during the period in which the claim was pending).

them once the Commission refers to the possibility of multiple diplomatic protections. Otherwise, it would be better not to address the issue of joint diplomatic protection since this reference automatically raises the questions just mentioned.

Belgium

(*See comments on draft articles 4 above and 7 below.*)

El Salvador

El Salvador believes that the text should take account of the rules of private international law on dual and multiple nationality, which provide that States must honour the nationality which is effectively being used. This also relates to the international jurisprudence of ICJ in the *Nottebohm* case, which established the precedent of "effective nationality".[21]

Guatemala

With regard to the last part of paragraph (4) of the commentary on draft article 6, it would be interesting to receive some clarification regarding the "general principles" referred to: what are they or where can they be found?

Qatar

1. Qatar considers that it might be useful to review paragraph 2 in order to make it clearer, so that it either identifies one State as having the right of protection, or lays down criteria to avert any problems that could arise from the filing of separate claims by two or more States. In this regard, Qatar proposes the following:

"(*a*) That the two States of nationality agree to file a joint claim;

"(*b*) That the two States of nationality agree that one of them shall file the claim;

"(*c*) That the predominant [effective] nationality be the one that is taken into consideration."

2. This approach is in line with that taken by Mr. F. V. García Amador in his third report on international responsibility submitted to the Commission, where he stated that: "In cases of dual or multiple nationality, the right to bring a claim shall be exercisable only by the State with which the alien has the stronger and more genuine legal and other ties."[22]

United Kingdom of Great Britain and Northern Ireland

Draft article 6 provides that where there is dual nationality either State may exercise the right of diplomatic protection against any State other than the other State of nationality. This provision may extend beyond existing customary international law. The United Kingdom may take up the claim of an individual who is a dual national, although in certain circumstances it may be appropriate for the claim to be taken in concert with the other State or States of nationality or to be taken solely by the other State of nationality. The proposed rule differs from the United Kingdom's own treaty obligations, including article 5 of the Convention on Certain Questions relating to the Conflict of Nationality Laws, which allows the State with which the individual is most closely connected to bring the claim. Although not indicative as to the circumstances in which the United Kingdom will exercise diplomatic protection, it will normally only extend consular protection to a dual national in a third State where the individual is travelling using travel documents issued by the United Kingdom.

Uzbekistan

1. Draft article 6, paragraph 1, should be worded as follows:

"The State with which a dual or multiple national is most closely connected may exercise diplomatic protection in respect of that national against a State of which that individual is not a national."

2. Such wording would help to avoid duplication of effort by the States of which the person is a national aimed at protecting his or her rights.

Draft article 7. Multiple nationality and claim against a State of nationality

Austria

In draft article 7, the Commission has opted for a progressive view in the case of dual nationality. Although that view is inconsistent with the suppression of the requirement of a genuine link in draft article 3, Austria is nevertheless in favour of this draft provision.

Belgium

Belgium considers that the predominant nationality requirement cannot be satisfied merely by providing proof of its bona fide acquisition, as the commentary on the draft articles appears to suggest by referring to the practice of the United Nations Compensation Commission, which was established by the Security Council to provide for compensation for damages caused by Iraq's occupation of Kuwait. Belgium takes the view that the practice of that Commission is justified by specific considerations that should not be applied wholesale to diplomatic protection. The reference to this practice does not therefore seem appropriate.

(*See comments on draft articles 4–5 above.*)

El Salvador

El Salvador has certain observations to make regarding the scope of predominant nationality (effective nationality). In its view, this is a very broad term which may give rise to very subjective interpretations.

[21] *Nottebohm, Second Phase, Judgment, I.C.J. Reports 1955*, p. 22.

[22] *Yearbook ... 1958*, vol. II, document A/CN.4/111, p. 61, art. 21, para. 4.

Italy

1. Italy, with regard to the possibility of a State exercising diplomatic protection against another State, suggests the reintroduction of the genuine link criterion instead of that of the predominant nationality. The genuine and effective link criterion appears more in conformity with the elements outlined by the international jurisprudence.[23]

2. For the above reasons, Italy suggests that the final text of draft article 7 could be the following:

"A State of nationality may exercise diplomatic protection in respect of a person against a State of which that person is also a national if there is a genuine link between that person and the former State, both at the time of the injury and at the date of the official presentation of the claim."

Morocco

1. Draft article 7 raises the question of predominant nationality, but does not clearly specify the criteria used to distinguish predominant nationality from nationality pure and simple. Furthermore, this sort of hierarchy among nationalities compromises to some extent the sovereign equality of States, which is an immutable principle of both customary law and codified law.

2. It would therefore be more prudent in this case to refer to the concept of effective nationality as described in the *Nottebohm* case[24] rather than the concept of predominant nationality, which is not defined in international law, and remains a subjective and ambiguous formulation. This approach would at least have the merit of not challenging the principle of the sovereign equality of States and is, moreover, enshrined in international law.

Norway, on behalf of the Nordic countries (Denmark, Finland, Iceland, Norway and Sweden)

The Nordic countries strongly support the approach of the Commission in draft article 7. In the case of multiple nationality, the State of nationality that is "predominant" both at the time of the injury and at the date of the official presentation of the claim should be entitled to exercise diplomatic protection against another State of nationality of the person concerned. In the view of the Nordic countries, draft article 7 constitutes a codification of existing customary international law. It should be added, for the sake of full clarity, that this rule has no bearing on possibilities to provide consular assistance, which are not governed by the law pertaining to diplomatic protection.

Qatar

In the view of Qatar, draft article 7 diverges somewhat from the traditional notion of diplomatic protection, which is essentially exercised by the State of nationality against a foreign State that has committed a breach of international law. Qatar also believes that the criterion of predominant nationality is inappropriate in this case, since the two or more States of nationality of the person concerned would have equal legal standing.

United Kingdom of Great Britain and Northern Ireland

Draft article 7 sets out a general rule of international law that a State will not support the claim of a dual national against another State of nationality. The United Kingdom will not normally take up the claim of a national if the respondent State is the State of second nationality. However, exceptionally, it may take up the claim of a person against another State of nationality where the respondent State has, in the circumstances leading to the injury, treated that person as a British national. However, the United Kingdom considers that the test for "predominant nationality" included in draft article 7 requires further clarification.

Uzbekistan

Draft article 7 uses the phrase "the nationality of the former State is predominant". It is not clear in which cases nationality may be predominant. Evidently, there is a need to take into account that the predominance of one nationality or another depends on the extent to which a national is connected with one State or another (place of residence, work and so on).

Draft article 8. Stateless persons and refugees

Austria

1. In the light of the increasing number of refugees, draft article 8 is of particular importance. With regard to stateless persons, the requirement of lawful and habitual residence sets a relatively high standard, but is certainly needed in order to prevent abuse of such rights.

2. As to the refugees addressed in paragraph 2, it may be asked whether the conditions for the exercise of diplomatic protection are not too restrictive since not only lawful and habitual residence in the State exercising the right of diplomatic protection is required, but also recognition by that State of the person as a refugee. It is conceivable for such a person to be lawfully resident in a State different from the one that has granted refugee status; this situation could occur within the European Union. In such a case, the refugee would not enjoy any diplomatic protection. It could therefore be asked whether that State would be entitled to exercise diplomatic protection where the person is lawfully and habitually resident once this person has been granted refugee status.

3. Contrary to the commentary to draft article 8, Austria proceeds from the assumption that the term "refugee" used in this draft provision is that of the Convention relating to the Status of Refugees. A State cannot be expected to attach two different meanings to that term.

---

[23] See the ICJ decision of 6 April 1955 in *Nottebohm, Second Phase, Judgment, I.C.J. Reports 1955*, pp. 25–26; the decision of the Italian–United States Conciliation Commission in the *Mergé* claim (10 June 1955), UNRIAA, vol. XIV (Sales No. 65.V.4), pp. 246–247, also in ILR (year 1955), p. 455. See also the awards of the Iran–United States Claims Tribunal of 29 March 1983 in case No. 157, *Nasser Esphahanian* v. *Bank Tejarat, Iran–United States Claims Tribunal Reports*, vol. 2 (Cambridge, Grotius, 1984), pp. 166 *et. seq.*, and in case No. 211, *Ataollah Golpira* v. *The Government of the Islamic Republic of Iran*, *ibid.*, pp. 174–175.

[24] *Nottebohm, Second Phase, Judgment, I.C.J. Reports 1955*, p. 22.

It must also be borne in mind that the legal effect of the right to exercise diplomatic protection consists in the duty of the other State to accept a claim made under this legal title. An open meaning of the term "refugee", as the commentary suggests, would certainly cause problems since the State to which the claims are addressed would depend on the definition of the term "refugee" by the claimant State. It is therefore advisable to modify the commentary accordingly.

Belgium

1. Belgium is of the opinion that the concept of "refugee" should have the meaning assigned to it by international law.

2. With regard to paragraph 3 and in keeping with its comment on draft article 1, Belgium considers that, if the broad interpretation of diplomatic protection is to be retained, this paragraph should be deleted in order to allow for certain informal remedies against the State of nationality of the refugee. Otherwise, paragraph 3 creates an unjustified distinction between refugees in the State of residence and nationals of that State. In addition, the State whose protection is requested remains free to decide whether or not to grant it.

El Salvador

The scope of the term "refugees" used here goes far beyond that which is provided for in the Convention relating to the Status of Refugees and its Protocol, which is the universally accepted definition. Although El Salvador does not oppose this usage, it should be carefully considered, as it would constitute a new definition which would need to be introduced and made compatible with the Convention.

Guatemala

With regard to paragraphs 1–2 of draft article 8, Guatemala takes the view that an exception should be made to the continuous nationality rule established in draft article 5, paragraph 1, in respect of a stateless person or a refugee protected by virtue of paragraphs 1–2 of draft article 8 if, between the time of the injury and the date of the official presentation of the claim, that person, without being covered by draft article 5, paragraph 2, acquires the nationality of the protecting State.

Morocco

Although the provision is not part of customary international law or codified international law, but rather represents progressive development of the law, it raises no real difficulty given that, on a practical level, the status of that category of persons is of limited duration.

Netherlands

Draft article 8 is one of the few progressive elements in the draft articles. The Netherlands considers this draft article to be a step in the right direction and appreciates the arguments given by the Commission in paragraph (7) of the commentary.

Norway, on behalf of the Nordic countries (Denmark, Finland, Iceland, Norway and Sweden)

1. The Nordic countries are particularly pleased that the Commission has drafted a provision on diplomatic protection on behalf of stateless persons and refugees in certain cases. Draft article 8 deviates from earlier opinions to the effect that a State should exercise diplomatic protection only on behalf of its nationals. It is highly important to be able to offer diplomatic protection to these vulnerable categories of persons.

2. The Nordic countries support the element of flexibility that appears in the commentary to draft article 8, where it follows that the term "refugee" is not necessarily limited to those persons who fall within the definitions in the Convention relating to the Status of Refugees and its Protocol. The commentary leaves it up to a State to "extend diplomatic protection to any person that it considered and treated as a refugee".[25] It is the position of the Nordic countries that a State may exercise diplomatic protection on behalf of persons fulfilling the requirements of territorial connection to the State exercising diplomatic protection, and who in that State's judgement clearly are in need of protection without necessarily formally qualifying for status as a refugee.

3. A particular question may be raised with regard to the suggested temporal requirement for the exercise of diplomatic protection in that the stateless person or refugee concerned must have lawful and habitual residence in the State exercising diplomatic protection at the time of the injury and at the date of the official presentation of the claim. Such a requirement would, in the view of the Nordic countries, appear to set an excessively high threshold. In many cases where there is a need of effective diplomatic protection, the injury will in fact have occurred prior to the entry of the person concerned into the territory of the State exercising diplomatic protection.

4. Thus, the Nordic countries would suggest a consideration of an adjustment of the suggested criteria. Rather than criteria of "lawful and habitual residence" in draft article 8 criteria of "lawful stay" might be considered. This is the exact wording used in article 28 of the Convention relating to the Status of Refugees with regard to the issuing of travel documents to refugees.

Panama

Panama believes that within the traditional system of diplomatic protection, draft article 8, in particular, on diplomatic protection for stateless persons and refugees, is not only relevant and justified, but also contributes effectively to the progressive development of international law. Indeed, the adoption of the same norm of protection for both stateless persons and refugees, for which the connecting factor is those persons' lawful and habitual residence in a given State—provided that other additional requirements (family ties, centre of interests, occupational activity and the like) indicating a genuine link between the individual and the State are met—is the appropriate solution for both categories of persons.

[25] *Yearbook ... 2004*, vol. II (Part Two), p. 28–29, para. (8) of the commentary to article 8.

Qatar

Paragraph 2 restricts the granting of legal status to a refugee by the protecting State without taking account of how the term "refugee" is defined under international law. Recently, there have been large waves of migration for a variety of reasons, and Qatar considers that this paragraph should be studied more closely with a view to establishing objective criteria for the protection of refugees in accordance with international norms.

United Kingdom of Great Britain and Northern Ireland

In relation to draft article 8, the protection of stateless persons and refugees is not a matter which the United Kingdom regards as falling within the scope of the concept of diplomatic protection as that is understood in current international law. The United Kingdom considers that the provisions of draft article 8 are *lex ferenda*. Whether the United Kingdom would exceptionally, for example on humanitarian grounds, be prepared to make representations or take other action on behalf of stateless persons or refugees would depend on the circumstances of the case and would be in its own discretion, but it would not *sensu stricto* be an exercise of diplomatic protection. In any event, any such representations would not be conclusive or indicative of the status of the individual as a refugee or national of the United Kingdom or the prospect of such status being granted.

(*See comments on draft articles 2–3 above and 15 below.*)

United States of America

(*See Other comments and suggestions, below.*)

Uzbekistan

1. In paragraphs 1–2, the term "lawfully and habitually resident in that State" should be replaced by "lawfully and permanently resident in that State". In those paragraphs, the phrase "habitually resident" may be interpreted in two ways: either as customarily resident or as permanently resident. Uzbekistan therefore proposes that it should read "permanently resident".

2. In paragraph 2, the words "and has been granted asylum" should be added after the words "as a refugee".

Chapter III. Legal persons

Draft article 9. State of nationality of a corporation

Austria

1. Draft article 9 raises major problems by requiring the fulfilment of two conditions: the registered office on the one hand and the seat of the management or some similar connection on the other. Such a requirement for the existence of two criteria would certainly deprive some corporations of diplomatic protection. Nevertheless, as the commentary indicates, the two criteria are those to which ICJ referred in its judgment on the *Barcelona Traction* case.[26] However, it is interesting to note that the Commission referred, in this context, to some sort of genuine link in conformity with the ruling of ICJ in the *Barcelona Traction* case whereas in the case of natural persons no such link is required, contrary to the *Nottebohm* case.[27]

2. It must nevertheless be emphasized that in certain situations to which ICJ also referred, other criteria, such as that of control over the corporation, could apply: according to draft article 18 such exceptions necessarily need a conventional base as a *lex specialis*. It could be asked whether the *lex specialis* rule should be confined only to treaties or could also be based on customary international law, as it is imaginable that a State considers itself entitled to apply the concept of control in its claims against a State, if both States use this concept of control in their established practice in order to determine the nationality of corporations. Austria would therefore suggest softening the rigidity of this rule reflected in draft article 9.

El Salvador

El Salvador wishes to know what would happen in the case of a corporation which establishes its registered office or headquarters in a State other than the State in which it was incorporated. Would there be no possibility of diplomatic protection for such corporations?

Guatemala

1. Draft article 9 appears too elliptical. This can be rectified by dividing it into two paragraphs, the first of which would be paragraph 1 of the text of draft article 17 that appears in footnote 71 of the report of the Commission on its fifty-fifth session.[28] The second paragraph would be a slightly modified version of the current text of draft article 9.

2. If the above proposal is accepted, draft article 9 would read as follows:

"1. A State is entitled to exercise diplomatic protection in respect of an injury to a corporation which has the nationality of that State.

"2. For the purposes of diplomatic protection of corporations, a corporation has the nationality of the State under whose law the corporation was formed and in whose territory it has its registered office or the seat of its management or some similar connection."

3. However, there is a problem with paragraph 2 above. The problem arises when, as commonly occurs, a corporation has its registered office or the seat of its management or some similar connection in one State, but was formed under the law of another State. In this case, it would seem that no State can exercise diplomatic protection in respect of the corporation. The difficulty could be resolved by replacing the "and" in paragraph 2 with "or". However, if that change is made in the hypothetical case considered,

---

[26] *Barcelona Traction, Light and Power Company, Limited, Second Phase, Judgment, I.C.J. Reports 1970*, p. 3.

[27] *Nottebohm, Second Phase, Judgment, I.C.J. Reports 1955*, p. 4.

[28] *Yearbook ... 2003*, vol. II (Part Two), p. 25, para. 70.

two States would be entitled to exercise diplomatic protection. To resolve this new problem, a new third paragraph should be added, which would read as follows:

"3. Whenever the application of paragraph 2 means that two States are entitled to exercise diplomatic protection, the State with which the corporation has, overall, the closest connection shall exercise that protection."

4. At first sight, the other issues of concern to Guatemala in relation to corporations appear to be merely linguistic, but, in reality, they go deeper.

5. Anyone with even the most rudimentary knowledge of Anglo-American law knows that under that system the term "corporation" does not apply only to what in French and Spanish are called, respectively, *société anonyme* and *sociedad anónima*, a term found in the original French version of the ICJ judgment in the *Barcelona Traction* case[29] and which corresponds, in the English version of the judgment, to the term "limited company whose capital is represented by shares".

6. However, Guatemala is inclined to believe that the word "corporation" in the English version of the draft articles does not cause problems. It is clear that, in that version, that term has the meaning most commonly assigned to it in English-speaking countries, that is, limited company. However, it might be as well to include in the English version of the final text a footnote indicating that in that version the word "corporation" should be understood to mean "limited company whose capital is represented by shares".

7. Nevertheless, with regard to the French and Spanish versions of draft articles 9–12 inclusive, Guatemala is of the opinion that, if those articles are to correspond with the English text, the words "*société*" and "*sociedad*" should be replaced by "*société anonyme*" and "*sociedad anónima*" respectively.

Italy

1. Italy doubts that the granting of nationality to a corporation for the purposes of diplomatic protection should be subject both to the place of incorporation and to the place of the registered office (*siège social*, in the French text) or to the place of its management or some similar connection. It is true that the ICJ decision in the *Barcelona Traction* case[30]—a decision that is the unique precedent to which the Commission refers—takes into account simultaneously the two connecting factors. However, the Court was dealing with a case wherein the two connecting factors coincided in fact. Moreover, the Court also held that "in the particular field of the diplomatic protection of corporate entities, no absolute test of the 'genuine connection' has found general acceptance".[31] Aside from *Barcelona Traction*, what worries Italy is the case wherein a corporation is incorporated in one State and then transfers its registered office or management office to another State. The case is not a theoretical one. For instance, article 8 of Council of the European Union regulation of 8 October 2001 ((EC) No. 2157/2001), on the statute for a European company,[32] deals exactly with such a case. It is difficult to imagine what the Court would have decided in 1970 had it been confronted with a corporation availing itself of the possibilities addressed by article 8 of the European Community regulation!

2. There is no doubt that if the incorporation takes place in a State different from the one to which the corporation is attached on the basis of the other connecting factors envisaged by draft article 9, the simultaneous application of the criterion of the State of incorporation and the other criteria results in the lack of any diplomatic protection. From the comments to draft article 9, it is not clear to what extent the Commission has considered this possibility. In any case, Italy suggests that, in order to fill such a gap, draft article 9 should not consider the place of incorporation for the purpose of diplomatic protection; rather, one among the other connecting factors envisaged by draft article 9 should be considered. Although this may lead to a situation in which more than one State is considered for the purpose of diplomatic protection, it should be preferred to one in which no State can be considered as the State of nationality. Obviously, coordination among different States of nationality could be achieved by applying the criteria envisaged by draft article 6 for natural persons.

Mexico

Mexico recognizes, in reading the text, that the comments it has contributed in the past few years concerning the determination of the nationality of corporations for purposes of the exercise of diplomatic protection have been taken into account by the Commission.

Morocco

As it is worded, the draft article uses the (specified) criteria to determine the State of nationality of the corporation. It should nevertheless be noted that the draft article does not specify which State has the right to exercise diplomatic protection with respect to a corporation formed in one State which has had its registered office transferred to another State.

Netherlands

1. The Netherlands considers that the Commission should research the draft article more thoroughly and that taking into account comparative corporate law and current economic developments would be useful. As the draft article now stands, it excludes the possibility of corporations having dual nationality. In this respect, the Commission's attention may be drawn to corporations with dual nationality in the Netherlands like Fortis and Unilever.

2. The Netherlands suggests deleting the expression "or some similar connection" because it is too vague. The

[29] *Barcelona Traction, Light and Power Company, Limited, Second Phase, Judgment, I.C.J. Reports 1970*, p. 37, para. 50.

[30] *Ibid*, p. 42, para. 70.

[31] *Ibid.*

[32] *Official Journal of the European Communities*, No. L 294 (10 November 2001), p. 4.

criteria used in the *Barcelona Traction* case[33] have already been sufficiently adapted in this draft article to fit into different national legal systems. Adding this criterion only creates confusion.

Qatar

1. Qatar considers, as a matter of principle, that any corporation established under the law of a State must register and have the seat of its management in that State in order for that State to exercise the right of diplomatic protection of said corporation. The draft article is therefore both logical and practical, and obviates, as far as possible, the need to explore the issue of a multiple nationality of corporations.

2. The phrase "or some similar connection" at the end of the draft article is vague, and could be open to interpretation in the future. It might be preferable, therefore, to consider deleting that phrase or replacing it with one that is more precise.

United Kingdom of Great Britain and Northern Ireland

Draft article 9 appears to introduce a new requirement for the exercise of diplomatic protection on behalf of a corporation: the existence of another connecting factor, additional to the place of incorporation. No such requirement exists under customary international law. ICJ in the *Barcelona Traction* case found that customary international law did not require a "genuine connection"[34] between the State and the corporation for the State to exercise diplomatic protection in respect of the corporation. Moreover, the United Kingdom concurs that the concept of "genuine connection" advanced by ICJ in relation to natural persons in the *Nottebohm* case[35] has no application in the realm of diplomatic protection of corporations. In determining whether to exercise the right of diplomatic protection, the United Kingdom may consider whether the company has in fact a real and substantial relationship with the United Kingdom. However, this is as a matter of policy and not the result of any legal requirement.

Uzbekistan

The term "State of nationality of a corporation" should be replaced by "State of origin of a corporation", and a definition of that concept should be inserted in a draft article entitled "Use of terms" (see other comments and suggestions below). Draft article 10 and draft article 11 (*b*), require the same changes.

Draft article 10. Continuous nationality of a corporation

Austria

With respect to draft article 10, the commentary characterizes the case of State succession as one that does not need to be addressed because of its exceptional nature. Recent developments, however, have proved a need for regulation similar to that concerning natural persons. Austria cannot see a reason why in the case of companies no regulation is sought whereas in that of natural persons such a situation is covered. In regard to the application of the continuity rule to corporations in the situation of State succession, the following problems could arise: in most cases of State succession, the internal legal order of the predecessor State continues to exist as the law of the newly established State. Hence, corporations incorporated under the law of the predecessor State simply continue to exist under the laws of the new State. However, at the same time, the corporations acquire a new nationality. In such circumstances, the existing wording of draft article 10 could result in the loss of the benefit of diplomatic protection.

Netherlands

The comments on draft article 5 above also apply to draft article 10.

Norway, on behalf of the Nordic countries (Denmark, Finland, Iceland, Norway and Sweden)

Consistent with the view (expressed in relation to draft article 5 (see above)), the Nordic countries support the approach taken by the Commission when applying the same solution in draft article 10 also with regard to corporations. The exception in draft article 10, paragraph 2, whereby a State may continue to exercise diplomatic protection in respect of a corporation which was its national at the time of the injury and which, as the result of the injury has ceased to exist, appears to be sound.

United Kingdom of Great Britain and Northern Ireland

With regard to protection in situations where a corporation has ceased to exist, as provided for in draft articles 10, paragraph 2, and 11 (*a*), the United Kingdom sees little basis for distinguishing the State which may exercise protection in terms of whether the corporation has ceased to exist as a result of the injury. In general, where a company has ceased to exist for whatever reason, the State of incorporation may have little incentive to protect the capital of shareholders that are not its nationals, while the State of nationality of the shareholders will usually have a stronger interest in doing so.

United States of America

(*With respect to paragraph 1, see comments to draft article 5 above.*)

1. The commentary accompanying the draft articles acknowledges that the rule in paragraph 2 does not reflect customary international law, but rather is an attempt to address difficulties that may arise when the continuous nationality rule is applied to extinct corporations. However, the commentary does not provide a basis for assessing the likelihood these difficulties would arise, leaving an insufficient policy basis for draft article 10.

2. The United States disagrees with the Commission that the diplomatic protection of extinct corporations requires

[33] *Barcelona Traction, Light and Power Company, Limited, Second Phase, Judgment, I.C.J. Reports 1970*, p. 42, para. 70.

[34] *Ibid.*

[35] *Nottebohm, Second Phase, Judgment, I.C.J. Reports 1955*, p. 23.

an exception to the continuous nationality rule. To begin with, a State may continue to exercise protection with respect to the claims of a corporation so long as the corporation retains a legal personality, which can be as bare as the right to sue or be sued under municipal law.[36] Many municipal systems allow for corporations to continue to raise and defend claims that arose during corporate life for a finite period of time after dissolution, meaning that legal personality persists until that period expires.[37] Thus, the problem of espousing claims of extinct corporations would arise infrequently, as the vast majority of claims can be considered while the corporation maintains a legal personality.

3. After the corporation ceases to exist, however, there is a salient policy reason that may oppose the exception proposed. The exception ignores the municipal law policy reasons for allowing the legal personality of corporations to lapse. Municipal survival and corporate wind-up statutes include a finite wind-up period to allow those involved with a corporation to obtain the benefits of finality, knowing that after the wind-up period has ended claims for and against the corporation will cease.[38] Draft article 10, paragraph 2, threatens to undermine this finality, and the resource allocation decisions that accompany it, by allowing for claims involving the corporation to persist indefinitely after the life of the corporation has ended.

Uzbekistan

(*See comments to draft articles 5 and 9 above.*)

[36] ICJ explained in *Barcelona Traction* that the company there had not "ceased to exist" because it remained free to exercise its legal rights in Spanish courts, its financial problems notwithstanding. As the Court stated, "a precarious financial situation cannot be equated with the demise of the corporate entity ... the company's status in law is alone relevant" (*Barcelona Traction, Light and Power Company, Limited, Second Phase, Judgment, I.C.J Reports 1970*, p. 41, para. 66).

[37] In most jurisdictions in the United States, for example, corporations may sue and be sued for up to three years after dissolution (Model Business Corporation Law, chap. 14.07 (2002)); see also the Delaware Code, Title 8: Corporations, chap. 278 (2005) (three-year period for claims after corporate dissolution). The Model Business Corporation Act and the Delaware Code are considered the reference codes for United States corporation law. Other States allow claims that arose during the life of the corporation for periods ranging from two years after dissolution to forever, subject to the statute of limitation for the claim. See 2005 Illinois Code-805 ILCS 5/ Business Corporation Act of 1983, sect. 12.80 (claims for or against corporation that arose prior to dissolution may be pursued for up to five years after dissolution); New York Business Corporation Law, para. 1006 (*a*) (4) (any claims for or against corporation that arose prior to dissolution enforceable with no time limit); Pennsylvania Consolidated Statutes, part 15, para. 1979 (two-year limit to claims for or against corporations after dissolution). Other nations have similar laws to address the legal personality of a corporation following dissolution. In the United Kingdom, corporations may sue or be sued for up to two years after dissolution with court permission (Companies Act 1985 (c. 6), sect. 651). In Canada, court permission is also required before a dissolved corporation may sue or be sued, although no time period appears to limit that right (Canada Business Corporations Act, R.S.C. 1985, chap. C–44, para. 209). The French Commercial Code permits claims to be considered for and against corporations for up to three years after dissolution (art. L.231-1–237-31).

[38] It is for this reason that, at least in the United States, claims that remain unresolved during the corporate wind-up period are generally abated when that period ends (Fletcher, *Fletcher Cyclopedia of the Law of Private Corporations*, para. 8144.40).

Draft article 11. Protection of shareholders

Norway, on behalf of the Nordic countries (Denmark, Finland, Iceland, Norway and Sweden)

1. With regard to the exercise of diplomatic protection on behalf of shareholders, the Nordic countries are content that the Commission has ensured overall consistency with the case law of ICJ, based on the *Barcelona Traction* case.[39]

2. The ICJ judgment of 1970 strikes a fair balance between the interests of the company and the interests of the shareholders, and enhances legal clarity. The Nordic countries agree against overturning the basic rule that diplomatic protection on behalf of a company primarily be made by the State of nationality of the company. Moreover, inability to claim protection from their own government is perhaps one of the commercial risks that shareholders undertake when buying shares in foreign companies.

United Kingdom of Great Britain and Northern Ireland

1. The United Kingdom broadly supports draft articles 11–12 regulating the protection of shareholders in a corporation. As reflected in the views of the majority in the *Barcelona Traction* case,[40] international law recognizes two exceptions to the general rule that the State of nationality of a shareholder does not possess a separate right to exercise diplomatic protection: first, when the corporation is defunct; and secondly, where the State of incorporation itself causes the injury.

2. Draft article 11 contemplates the possibility that multiple claims may emerge based on the existence of shareholders of several nationalities, thus entitling several States to exercise diplomatic protection. Where the United Kingdom may be entitled to make such a claim, it would, as a matter of practice rather than law, normally seek to do so in concert with other States. It may also refrain from making representations unless the States whose nationals hold the bulk of the share capital will support the United Kingdom in making representations. More generally, the United Kingdom urges the Commission to give greater consideration to situations involving multiple claims, including the need to coordinate claims.

3. Draft article 11 is restricted to the interests of a shareholder in the corporation, based on the clear intention of ICJ that the decision in the *Barcelona Traction* case was to apply only to corporations with limited liability whose capital was represented by shares. Consideration should be given to the interests of a corporation's investors other than its shareholders, such as debenture holders, nominees and trustees. The United Kingdom's claims rules (see the annex to the present report) permit the United Kingdom to intervene where a United Kingdom national has an interest in a company, whether as a shareholder or otherwise.

[39] *Barcelona Traction, Light and Power Company, Limited, Second Phase, Judgment, I.C.J Reports 1970*, p. 3.

[40] *Ibid.*

Subparagraph (a)

Austria

As to draft article 11 (*a*), it may be asked why the wording only refers to "State of incorporation" instead of nationality, as is done in the other relevant draft articles taking into account the double criteria required for nationality. The effect of this paragraph is very broad, since its wording addresses situations where a company has the nationality of State A and is terminated in that State "according to the law of the State of incorporation", but is injured by State B. If shareholders of the company have the nationality of States C and D, which could give rise to a multiplicity of claims, the restriction of "a reason unrelated to the injury" makes very little sense, since the State where the company is terminated differs from the injuring State. This clause is useful only if this provision is meant also to address corporations that were the national of the injuring State at the time of the injury and that, as a result of the injury, have ceased to exist according to the law of that State. In order to be as clear as necessary, Austria suggests formulating the two issues in two separate paragraphs.

El Salvador

With regard to draft article 11 (*a*), which addresses the case of the protection of shareholders when the corporation has ceased to exist according to the law of the State of incorporation for a reason unrelated to the injury, but does not provide for the case of shareholders of a corporation that ceases to exist as a result of the injury, it would appear that the more the rights of shareholders are injured, the less their States of nationality can exercise diplomatic protection.

Norway, on behalf of the Nordic countries (Denmark, Finland, Iceland, Norway and Sweden)

The Nordic countries support, at the same time, the exceptions suggested in draft article 11 (*a*)–(*b*).

United Kingdom of Great Britain and Northern Ireland

As the United Kingdom has observed, it agrees that the State of nationality of a shareholder may intervene on behalf of the shareholder where the corporation is defunct. However, the United Kingdom is concerned that the requirement that the claim be unrelated to the reason that the corporation has been rendered defunct narrows unduly the exception acknowledged in the *Barcelona Traction* case. The right of the State of nationality of the shareholders should not be contingent upon why or how the corporation ceased to exist.[41]

(*See comments on draft article 10 above.*)

United States of America

The United States strongly urges the Commission to delete draft article 11 (*a*), because it creates the anomalous situation of granting States of shareholders a greater right to espouse claims of a corporation than the State of incorporation itself. At least under United States law, shareholders do not have any right to assert the expired rights of a dissolved corporation,[42] because the corporation is the primary vehicle for protecting its own rights. It is for that reason that ICJ in *Barcelona Traction*[43] held that the State of incorporation should exercise diplomatic protection with respect to injuries to the corporation. The commentary provides no justification for creating a category of claims where States of shareholders can espouse corporate claims and the State of incorporation cannot. Owing to this rule's inconsistency with basic corporate law principles, it should be deleted. Doing so would in no way infringe upon the right of States of shareholders to espouse claims for the direct injuries suffered by shareholders, of course, which is permitted by draft articles 2–3.

Subparagraph (b)

Austria

Draft article 11 (*b*), raises the question of the injury since it is not clear which kind of injury is meant in this context, in particular, whether it should be understood in the sense of draft article 1 that speaks of "injury to that national arising from an internationally wrongful act of another State". Read in conjunction with the introductory phrase, it becomes clear that the injury referred to in draft article 11 (*b*) must be inflicted upon the company. Since the company, however, has the nationality of the State causing "injury", this injury could hardly be one "arising from an internationally wrongful act of another State". The commentary does not provide an answer to this question; in order to remove any doubts on this issue, it would be advisable to clarify this issue in the commentary.

Belgium

Belgium takes the view that the restrictive condition imposed on the diplomatic protection of shareholders, whereby the incorporation of the corporation under the law of the State responsible for causing injury is required by the latter as a precondition for doing business there, does not reflect a rule of customary international law. This condition should therefore be removed.

Netherlands

1. The draft article seems to have stirred controversy in the Sixth Committee. The Commission has attempted to codify the two exceptions as formulated in the *Barcelona Traction* case.[44] The Netherlands agrees with the

---

[41] *Barcelona Traction, Light and Power Company, Limited, Second Phase, Judgment, I.C.J. Reports 1970*, p. 3.

[42] Fletcher, *op. cit.*, para. 8144.40, describing how United States law does not permit shareholders to raise expired rights of a dissolved corporation. The United States is generally one of the more permissive States regarding shareholder actions on behalf of the corporation, suggesting other States may not permit shareholder suits to enforce the rights of deceased corporations either. See Grossfeld, "Management and control of marketable share companies", p. 107, explaining that the United States is generally more favourable than other States towards representative suits by shareholders.

[43] *Barcelona Traction, Light and Power Company, Limited, Second Phase, Judgment, I.C.J. Reports 1970*, p. 3.

[44] *Ibid.*

Commission that the State of nationality of the shareholder in cases of Calvo corporation would be entitled to exercise diplomatic protection.

2. Subparagraph (*b*) reads "alleged to be responsible for causing injury". In draft article 14, paragraph 2, the wording is different: "alleged to be responsible for the injury". The wording of the draft articles should be consistent.

Norway, on behalf of the Nordic countries (Denmark, Finland, Iceland, Norway and Sweden)

(*See comment to subparagraph* (a) *above.*)

1. A State should not be allowed to require foreign interests to incorporate under local law as a condition for doing business in that State and then plead such incorporation as the justification for rejecting the exercise of diplomatic protection from the State of nationality of the foreign interests.

2. According to the commentary to draft article 11 (*b*), this exception applies to cases where the requirement of incorporation under local law as a precondition for doing business is a formal requirement contained in the local legislation. There are, however, as a part of the progressive development of international law, good reasons to extend this exception also to cases where the requirement of incorporation is not a formal one, but follows from pressure of an informal or political nature on the foreign interests. The Nordic countries suggest that the existing wording of draft article 11 (*b*), "was required by it as a precondition for doing business there" should also cover such requirements of an informal nature. This should then be reflected in the commentary to draft article 11 (*b*).

United Kingdom of Great Britain and Northern Ireland

The United Kingdom considers that the right of the State of nationality of the shareholders to exercise protection should be allowed irrespective of the reasons for incorporation in the State of incorporation. For example, its own claims rules (see the annex to the present report) provide that where a British national is a shareholder in a corporation incorporated elsewhere and the State of incorporation injures the corporation, the United Kingdom may intervene to protect the interests of the British shareholder. Thus, in the view of the United Kingdom, draft article 11 (*b*), is unduly restrictive.

United States of America

1. The United States has serious concerns about draft article 11 (*b*). As it has previously explained to the Commission, the proposed exception lacks support in customary international law. In all of the cases provided by the Commission as evidence for the exception, there was in fact a special agreement between two States granting a right to shareholders to claim compensation, or an agreement between the injuring State and its national corporation granting compensation to the shareholders.[45] As a result of those agreements, the above-mentioned cases provide little support for the existence of a customary international law rule allowing States to espouse claims of shareholders against the State of incorporation where incorporation was mandated for doing business in the State. Likewise, ICJ in *Barcelona Traction*[46] had no occasion to consider the validity of the exception, as the injuring State in that case was not the State of incorporation.

2. Without this customary international law support, the United States has concerns about whether there is a sound public policy basis for this exception. As it has previously stated, this exception would create a regime where shareholders of corporations incorporated in a State have greater rights to seek diplomatic protection of their claims in that State than shareholders of foreign-owned corporations, who would have to rely on the corporation's State to pursue claims. It is not clear that such a result is just.

Uzbekistan

(*See comment to draft article 9 above.*)

Draft article 12. Direct injury to shareholders

United Kingdom of Great Britain and Northern Ireland

(*See comments on draft article 11 above.*)

United States of America

The United States believes that draft article 12 would codify customary international law by stating that the State of nationality of shareholders is entitled to exercise diplomatic protection on behalf of shareholders where they have suffered direct losses. That statement is superfluous here. Draft articles 2–3 would clarify that a State has the right to exercise diplomatic protection in respect to claims of its nationals where the other requirements of the draft articles are met. Since shareholders are nationals, like all others, there is no reason to adopt a separate article to note that their claims are permissible. Rather, if the Commission feels it is necessary, the commentary to draft articles 2–3 should include a statement that shareholders too are nationals whose injuries are eligible for diplomatic protection.

Draft article 13. Other legal persons

Austria

Austria emphasizes the importance of draft article 13 in view of the existence of different kinds of legal persons under Austrian national law.

---

[45] *Delagoa Bay Railway Co.* (Moore, *A Digest of International Law*, p. 647), resolved through agreement between Portugal, the United Kingdom and the United States, to refer to the international arbitration question of compensation owed United Kingdom and United States shareholders due to Portuguese expropriation of a Portuguese company; *Mexican Eagle* (*El Aguila*) (Whiteman, *Digest of International Law*, p. 1274, dispute between Mexico and the United Kingdom over Mexican nationalization of oil fields owned by Mexican corporations controlled by British interests resolved through settlement between Mexico and the company; *Romano-Americana* (Hackworth, *op. cit.*, p. 844), dispute settled by Romanian offer to pay Romanian oil company compensation for assets seized; *El Triunfo Company* (1902) UNRIAA, vol. XV (Sales No. 1966.V.3), p. 467 (protocol between El Salvador and the United States agreed to refer to international arbitration question of compensation owed United States shareholders for El Salvadoran expropriation of assets of El Salvadoran company).

[46] *Barcelona Traction, Light and Power Company, Limited, Second Phase, Judgment, I.C.J. Reports 1970*, p. 3.

El Salvador

El Salvador would recommend that the draft article should also include a reference, where applicable, to draft articles 11–12, since those other legal persons might also be natural persons comparable to shareholders.

Guatemala

1. In civil law systems, there exists a type of hybrid commercial company halfway between the corporation or limited company—whose capital is represented by shares that mark the limits of its shareholders' liability and are freely transferable—and the partnership, whose shareholders are fully liable for the company's debts and cannot easily transfer their portion of its assets. This intermediate type of commercial corporation is the limited liability company—*société à responsabilité limitée* in French and *Gesellschaft mit beschräenkter Haftung* in German. The shareholders of companies of this type, which apparently also exist in at least some countries governed by common law systems under the name of limited liability companies, are similar to the stockholders of corporations or limited companies in that they are liable for the company's debts up to but not exceeding the level of their equity contribution. However, the capital of the limited liability company is not represented by shares of stocks.

2. There is no doubt that the limited liability company falls within the scope of draft article 13, and consequently draft articles 9–10 are applicable to it, as appropriate. However, from a literal standpoint, draft articles 11–12 are not applicable, because they are not mentioned in draft article 13. Nevertheless, Guatemala takes the view that draft articles 11–12 should be applicable to limited liability companies and their shareholders.

3. Accordingly, in draft article 13, "9 and 10" should be replaced by "9 through 12 inclusive" and, in paragraph (4) of the commentary to draft article 13, explicit mention should be made of the limited liability company. It would thus be clear that, for the purposes of draft articles 11–12, shareholders of a limited liability company would be equivalent to shareholders of a corporation or limited company.

Netherlands

The words "engaged in worthy causes" in paragraph (4) of the commentary are unnecessary and should be deleted. The Netherlands believes that the discretionary authority of the State to exercise diplomatic protection provides sufficient scope.

Qatar

Qatar should like to draw the Commission's attention to the fact that the distinguishing feature of non-governmental human rights organizations, which would be covered by draft article 13, is independence. Qatar fears that the exercise of the right of diplomatic protection by the State of such an organization could undermine that independence, adversely affecting the organization's relations with its international milieu.

United Kingdom of Great Britain and Northern Ireland

The United Kingdom considers this to be a proposal for the development of the law relating to diplomatic protection, since accepted principles of customary international law are currently restricted to consideration of the nationality of corporations. Many forms of entity are not currently considered to have separate legal personality within the United Kingdom legal system. The previous practice of the United Kingdom, at least in relation to firms, partnerships and associations, has been to base nationality on the nationality of the individuals or partners creating the legal entity. The United Kingdom supports clarification of the law in this area, but considers that further clarification, perhaps in the commentary, would assist.

Part Three

LOCAL REMEDIES

Draft article 14. Exhaustion of local remedies

Mexico

Mexico is particularly interested in the application of the exhaustion of local remedies rule. To ensure the correct application of that rule, it is essential that the exceptions to it should be codified. As already noted in its comments on the Commission's reports since 2003, Mexico is in general agreement with the formulation of both the rule and the exceptions to it in the draft articles currently under review.

Netherlands

1. The Netherlands suggests inserting the following passage in the commentary:

"No prior exhaustion of local remedies is required for diplomatic action stopping short of bringing an international claim. *See Restatement (Third) of the Foreign Relations Law of the United States (1987)*, paragraph 703, comment *d*: 'The individual's failure to exhaust [domestic] remedies is not an obstacle to informal intercession by a state on behalf of an individual'."

2. The Netherlands also believes that the commentary must make clear whether any distinction is intended between "rule" and "principle".

3. Finally, the Netherlands notes that the commentary is inconsistent in respect of "claim". Paragraph (3) is somewhat confusing. When read in conjunction with paragraph (5) of the commentary to draft article 1, and paragraph (6) of the commentary to draft article 5, it is

unclear whether "claim" must be understood as referring only to a formal claim.

Paragraph 1

Austria

(*See General remarks above.*)

United States of America

1. Draft article 14, paragraph 1, states that an international claim cannot be brought for an injury suffered by a national unless "the injured person has, subject to draft article 16, exhausted all local remedies". In the commentary accompanying draft article 14, the Commission explains that the article seeks to capture the exhaustion rule provided in the *ELSI* case, which requires that for a "claim to be admissible, it is sufficient if the essence of the claim has been brought before the competent tribunals and pursued as far as permitted by local law and procedures, and without success".[47]

2. The United States agrees that the ICJ decision in *ELSI* correctly captures the customary international law exhaustion requirement. The United States believes, however, that draft article 14, paragraph 1, should be revised to state:

"A State may not bring an international claim in respect of an injury to a national or other person referred to in draft article 8 before local remedies have been exhausted, subject to draft article 16."

3. This formulation is a better expression of customary international law than the current draft article because, consistent with *ELSI*, it permits an entity other than the "injured person" to satisfy the exhaustion requirement so long as the essence of the claim was exhausted in a municipal court. In *ELSI*, the United States brought a claim against Italy alleging that Italy had violated the Treaty of friendship, commerce and navigation[48] between Italy and the United States through its requisition of the *ELSI* plant and assets. It was undisputed that *ELSI*, a wholly owned Italian subsidiary of Raytheon and Machlett, United States corporations, had challenged the legality of Italy's seizure of its plant and assets in an Italian court, without ultimate success. As a preliminary matter, however, Italy argued that the United States could not assert a claim on behalf of Raytheon and Machlett because those American companies had not challenged the seizure separately in Italian courts, alleging that the seizure was a violation of the Treaty.

4. ICJ rejected the suggestion by Italy that the *ELSI* suit could not satisfy the exhaustion of the local remedies requirement. The Court noted that the substance of the claim brought by *ELSI*, challenging the legality of the requisition given its causal link to the *ELSI* bankruptcy, was the same as that brought by the United States to ICJ. Under those circumstances, the Court held that "the [exhaustion of] local remedies rule does not, indeed cannot, require that a claim be presented to the municipal courts in a form, and with arguments, suited to an international tribunal, applying different law to different parties".[49] In other words, the Court acknowledged that a claim could be exhausted for international law purposes when the essence of the claim was considered by municipal tribunals, irrespective of whether the same person or entity pursuing the municipal claim was being diplomatically protected.[50] The proposed reformulation better expresses the holding in *ELSI* by removing a requirement that the "injured person", who is, presumably, the subject of diplomatic protection, be the party exhausting local remedies.

Uzbekistan

1. In accordance with draft article 14, the exercise of the right of a natural or legal person to protection from the State requires the "exhaustion" of local remedies and, that being the case, it would take a certain length of time for the person to receive protection, taking into account the different legal procedures in individual countries. That in turn might lead to a reduction in the effectiveness of diplomatic protection.

2. There is a need to indicate means of securing protection besides the "exhaustion" of local remedies and to amend draft article 16 accordingly.

Paragraph 2

Austria

Austria understands the meaning of draft article 14 in a sense that excludes the resort to the international courts or tribunals for the protection of human rights and fundamental freedoms from the definition of "local remedies". Consequently, it is not excluded that a State exercise its right to diplomatic protection simultaneously with the institution of proceedings by an individual against that State before the European Court of Human Rights. That situation can be explained by recognizing that there would be two different disputes that could be addressed in two different forums.

Mexico

1. Mexico cannot pass over in silence the definition of the term "local remedies" included by the Commission in paragraph 2 of draft article 14. It covers both judicial and administrative remedies open to an injured person before the courts, whether ordinary or special, of the State alleged to be responsible for the injury.

2. Mexico is pleased to observe in this regard that the Commission has taken into account the ICJ judgment in

---

[47] *Elettronica Sicula S.p.A. (ELSI), Judgment, I.C.J. Reports 1989*, p. 46, para. 59.

[48] Signed in Rome on 2 February 1948 (United Nations, *Treaty Series*, vol. 79, No. 1040, p. 171).

[49] See footnote 47 above.

[50] Indeed it was in *ELSI*. The Court did consider whether Italian law afforded the American companies a unique remedy not available to ELSI that they were obligated to exhaust. The Court concluded that Italy did not prove the existence of any such remedy, and thus held that remedies were exhausted, allowing the Court to proceed to the merits (*ibid.*, pp. 46–48, paras. 60–63).

the *Avena* case,[51] in paragraph (6) of its commentary on draft article 14 concerning the exhaustion of local remedies. As the Commission states, while it is true that administrative remedies must also be exhausted, this applies only to those that may result in redress. The injured person is not required to petition the executive power of the State where he exhausts local remedies to grant him relief through the exercise of discretionary powers, since local remedies do not include remedies as of grace, such as executive clemency or a request for a pardon.

Uzbekistan

1. It seems necessary to insert draft article 14, paragraph 2, in a draft article entitled "Use of terms" (see other comments and suggestions below) in order to define the concept of "local remedies".

2. This paragraph also needs revision. To make the text clearer the following wording could be used:

"'Local remedies' means legal remedies which are open to an injured person. This may include recourse to judicial or administrative courts or ordinary or special bodies of the State alleged to be responsible for the injury."

Draft article 15. Category of claims

Austria

1. Austria wonders whether the title of this provision corresponds to the substance of the draft article since the gist of this draft article is connected with so-called mixed claims and the question whether a State claims direct injury where no exhaustion of local remedies is required or indirect injury where the exhaustion is required. The recent ICJ decision in the *Avena* case[52] has clearly exposed the problem of this distinction. That judgment only highlights the necessity for a rule as is contained in this draft article.

2. In its oral comments in the Sixth Committee, Austria asked whether a specific reference to a "request for a declaratory judgement" should be maintained in this draft article since the sole decisive criterion in this context was whether or not there was a direct injury to the State. The introduction of a possible further criterion would only create confusion. The text of the draft provision seemed to suggest that a "request for a declaratory judgement" was to be distinguished from any other "international claim". However, in view of the extensive explanation in the commentary, Austria no longer raises this issue.

United Kingdom of Great Britain and Northern Ireland

The United Kingdom supports the adoption of the preponderance test since it agrees that the emphasis should be on the nature of the injury suffered. However, to the extent that draft article 15 refers to claims on behalf of non-nationals as provided for in draft article 8, the United Kingdom reiterates its previous comments in relation to that article that the right to bring a claim on behalf of a non-national is not reflected in customary international law.

Draft article 16. Exceptions to the local remedies rule

El Salvador

Although El Salvador agrees with the substance of the draft article, it believes that the wording is complicated in some places and vague in others, and might lead to confusion between its various provisions. El Salvador therefore considers that clearer and more precise wording would help present the exceptions to the rule more effectively.

Mexico

(*See comments on draft article 14 above.*)

1. With regard to the exceptions to the local remedies rule, Mexico considers that there is an exception that has not been covered by any of the four subparagraphs in draft article 16. It applies to cases in which it is not necessary to exhaust local remedies in situations if there will be a repetition of the injury.[53] This exception is based on the futility of exhausting local remedies if there is a definite possibility that the act that caused the injury may be repeated.

2. Mexico considers it important to stipulate in the draft articles that it is the responsibility of the respondent State to prove that local remedies have not been exhausted by specifying the remedies that still remain open to the claimant. In the event that it can be shown that there are still local remedies to which recourse can be had, the burden of proof as to the existence of some exception to the requirement that local remedies must be exhausted will be on the claimant.[54]

Uzbekistan

(*See comment on draft article 14, paragraph 1, above.*)

Subparagraph (a)

Austria

Austria understands draft article 16 (*a*), as referring also to the availability of local remedies, similar to the wording adopted by the Commission in article 44 (*b*) of the articles on responsibility of States for internationally wrongful acts[55] (that is, "any available and effective local remedy"). For the sake of terminological conformity with those articles it would seem sensible to use the same wording here.

Italy

1. Italy believes that the first exception to the local remedies rule, which is also the most important one, is phrased too summarily and restrictively.

2. First, it should be considered that international practice and case law have, over time, developed a series of exceptions, namely the "non-existence", "inaccessibility",

[51] *Avena and Other Mexican Nationals (Mexico* v. *United States of America), Judgment, I.C.J. Reports 2004*, p. 12.

[52] *Ibid.*

[53] See Amerasinghe, *Local Remedies in International Law*, p. 206.

[54] See Jennings and Watts, *Oppenheim's International Law*, p. 526.

[55] *Yearbook ... 2001*, vol. II (Part Two), p. 29, para. 76.

"ineffectiveness" and "inadequacy" of local remedies. These are four specific, precise and autonomous concepts, and it is very difficult to take account of all of them within the so-called criterion of the "futility rule" or within a similar criterion, such as that used in draft article 16 (*a*) ("no reasonable possibility of effective redress"). Actually, the wording in subparagraph (*a*) does not include all the above-mentioned exceptions, but rather deals with a slightly different problem: that is, to find the most suitable test or interpretative criterion to evaluate concretely, each time, the futility of local remedies, especially from the point of view of their ineffectiveness. Therefore, the wording of subparagraph (*a*) is too vague, uncertain and generic, and it risks not covering all the above-mentioned exceptions, to the detriment of the individual victim. Italy suggests modifying subparagraph (*a*) in the following way:

"The local remedies are inexistent or inaccessible or ineffective or inadequate."

3. Secondly, if the Commission does not accept the above-mentioned suggestion and prefers to maintain a single and comprehensive expression, Italy believes that the present wording of subparagraph (*a*) is too restrictive, considering the most recent developments of the local remedies rule not only in the field of diplomatic protection in the strict sense, but also in the field of human rights. In fact, practice is moving towards a more flexible interpretative criterion, which would be better expressed by the wording: "The local remedies offer no reasonable prospect of success." This wording had been taken into consideration, but then unfortunately rejected, by the Special Rapporteur, Mr. John Dugard. However, Italy is of the view that the present wording of subparagraph (*a*) goes against the trend of international practice and risks making more rigid, and less favourable to individuals, the future application of the local remedies rule.

Qatar

1. Qatar views the exceptions set out in subparagraphs (*a*), (*b*) and (*c*) of draft article 16 as being so broad and vague as potentially to render draft article 14 inoperative. They will also contribute to violations of the rule on the exhaustion of local remedies, which is a necessary condition for exercising the right of diplomatic protection. Moreover, these exceptions might lead to differing and conflicting international legal rulings being issued, since the courts would have to examine each case on its own merits in order to determine whether or not local remedies had been exhausted, having no explicit criterion to rely on to determine whether the exceptions set down in draft article 16 apply.

2. Qatar considers that the exceptions might be acceptable when cases relating directly to fundamental human rights and freedoms are being considered.

United Kingdom of Great Britain and Northern Ireland

Draft article 16 (*a*), elaborates further the notion of an "effective" remedy, with the Commission attempting to resolve the appropriate formulation for when a remedy will be ineffective. In selecting the option of "no reasonable possibility of effective redress", the Commission has developed existing principles. The United Kingdom would interpret this provision as not placing a claimant under an obligation to pursue an appeal to a higher court where it can be established on the facts that such an appeal would have no effect. Similarly, a claimant should not be required to exhaust justice in a State where there is no justice to exhaust. The United Kingdom also considers that obstruction or prejudice to a claimant in the process of exhausting domestic remedies may amount to a denial of justice to that claimant, and it reserves the right to intervene on behalf of a claimant who is a British national to secure redress for such injustice. Subject to these comments, the United Kingdom generally supports the Commission's development of this area of diplomatic protection.

United States of America

1. In the commentary accompanying draft article 16, the Commission explains that it considered three different standards before arriving at the "reasonable possibility of effective redress" standard. The Commission rejected an "obvious futility" standard on grounds that it set "too high a threshold" for proving futility. Likewise the Commission dismissed the European Commission of Human Rights standard of "no reasonable prospect of success"[56] because it would have allowed claimants to bypass local remedies in too many instances. Instead, the Commission believes that its proffered standard splits the difference and is consistent with international practice.

2. The United States respectfully disagrees with the Commission's conclusion that the obvious futility standard sets "too high a threshold" for proving futility. Properly understood, the United States believes it sets a bar that both respects State sovereignty and is consistent with customary international law. The United States believes that this draft article should state:

"Local remedies do not need to be exhausted where the local remedies are obviously futile or manifestly ineffective. Exhaustion of local remedies is not obviously futile or manifestly ineffective where a forum was reasonably available to provide effective redress."

3. Under applicable customary international law principles, a claimant may establish that he need not exhaust local remedies only in the most limited circumstances. It is not enough that a claimant demonstrate that the possibility of success is low or that further appeals are difficult or costly. Rather, for a State to be held liable without exhaustion of local remedies, "the test is obvious futility or manifest ineffectiveness, not the absence of a reasonable prospect of success or the improbability of success, which are both less strict tests."[57] Under draft article 16 (*a*), the

[56] *Yearbook ... 2004*, vol. II (Part Two), p. 38–39, para. (3) of the commentary to article 16.

[57] Amerasinghe, *op. cit.*, p. 206. See also, for example, *Claim of Finnish shipowners against Great Britain in respect of the use of certain Finnish vessels during the war* (1934), UNRIAA, vol. III (Sales No. 1949.V.2), p. 1504 (rule excusing exhaustion is "most strictly construed, and if substantial right of appeal existed, failure to prosecute an appeal operated as a bar to relief"); and Borchard, *The Diplomatic Protection of Citizens Abroad or the Law of International Claims*, p. 824

focus of the futility inquiry would be on whether redress is possible, thereby steering consideration towards the possibility of a successful outcome, which Amerasinghe notes is incorrect under international law. Moreover, the assessment of whether a successful outcome is possible is an extremely difficult undertaking. By contrast, the second sentence of the proposed alternative formulation focuses on whether there is a forum reasonably capable of providing redress. Doing so recognizes that the proper test of futility is whether the municipal court system itself is reasonably capable of providing relief. Thus, the focus should be on the availability of a suitable forum rather than on the likelihood of success in that forum.

4. Moreover, as a policy matter the United States believes the formulation above is preferable to the draft article. The purpose of the local remedies rule is to ensure that a State has the opportunity to address within its own legal system violations of international law.[58] Most, if not all, States have legal systems that have this self-correcting capacity. Under those circumstances, respect for State sovereignty demands that a claimant take advantage of the State's legal system as a condition precedent to invocation of State responsibility for a breach of international law. The formulation advocated by the United States, in addition to being consistent with international law, has the advantage of ensuring that in all but the most extreme circumstances a State has the opportunity to rectify within its own legal system violations of international law. By contrast, the draft article allows claimants to move claims of alleged breaches of international law to international forums before this corrective process is complete, thereby undermining State sovereignty as well as development of the rule of law in municipal judicial systems.

Uzbekistan

It is necessary to specify which national or international body would define the "reasonableness" or "unreasonableness" of resorting to local remedies.

Subparagraph (b)

Italy

Italy believes that not only undue delay in the remedial process, but also the denial of justice itself should be included in subparagraph (*b*). In fact, international practice shows that there is an exception to the local remedies rule when (at any stage during the remedial process) local courts refuse to render justice[59] or do not have the necessary independence,[60] or give a manifestly unjust judgement or a *mala fide* judgement, or violate the fundamental procedural rights of the individual.[61] By contrast, the exception of denial of justice cannot be easily inferred from article 16 (*a*). Therefore, subparagraph (*b*) should be modified in the following way:

"There has been a denial of justice or there is undue delay in the remedial process which is attributable to the State alleged to be responsible."

Qatar

(*See comments to subparagraph* (a) *above.*)

United Kingdom of Great Britain and Northern Ireland

The United Kingdom supports draft article 16 (*b*), as a codification of the existing rule regarding undue delay.

Subparagraph (c)

Austria

Although Austria supports the limitation to diplomatic protection in subparagraph (*c*) it would, nevertheless, prefer a more elaborated definition of the particular circumstance of the absence of a relevant connection. It is also not clear when the lack of relevant connection must be given: it could be imagined that a person at the moment of the injury was present in the State where it suffered the injury, but then left the territory. Could, in such a circumstance, the State whose nationality the person possesses benefit from the exception spelled out in subparagraph (*c*), or was the relevant connection given as required for the need to exhaust local remedies? The wording of the subparagraph does not provide a clear answer. Unless it is made clear that it is at the moment of injury when the relevant connection must be absent, it could be proposed to link the absence of a relevant connection with "reasonableness" so that no exhaustion would be required only if there were no relevant connection between the injured person and the State alleged to be responsible and the exhaustion of local remedies would be unreasonable. In view of such an approach it could also be suggested to drop the first part of this subparagraph and confine the subparagraph to the situation where the circumstances of the case make the exhaustion of local remedies unreasonable. The commentary could then exemplify this situation by a reference to the absence of a relevant connection. However, that solution would exclude a misuse of this subparagraph by a person that suffered an injury and simply leaves the State allegedly responsible in order to circumvent the need for exhaustion of local remedies. The individual could then easily deprive the State allegedly responsible of the possibility to remedy the injury through its own procedures. Taking into account the basic objective of the rule of exhaustion of local remedies, namely to give the State an opportunity to make up for the injury, it is certainly necessary to preclude such an abuse.

("A claimant is not ... relieved from exhausting his local remedies by alleging his inability, through poverty, to meet the expenses involved; his ignorance of his right of appeal; the fact that he acted on the advice of counsel; or a pretended impossibility or uselessness of action before the local courts.").

[58] See *Interhandel, Preliminary Objections), I.C.J. Reports 1959*, p. 27.

[59] *Cotesworth & Powell* case, in Moore, *History and Digest of the International Arbitrations to which the United States has been a Party*, p. 2050.

[60] *Robert E. Brown (United States)* v. *Great Britain*, UNRIAA, vol. VI (Sales No. 1955.V.3), pp. 124 *et. seq.*; *Don Pacifico* case, Moore, *A Digest of International Law*, p. 853; *Panevezys-Saldutiskis Railway, P.C.I.J., Series C, No. 86*, p. 195; *I.C.J. Pleadings, Aerial Incident of 27 July 1955* (Israel *v.* Bulgaria; United States of America *v.* Bulgaria; United Kingdom *v.* Bulgaria), p. 327.

[61] *Salem* case (Egypt, United States) (8 June 1932), UNRIAA, vol. II (Sales No. 1949.V.1), p. 1202; *B. E. Chattin (United States)* v. *United Mexican States* (23 July 1927), *ibid.*, vol. IV (Sales No. 1951.V.1), pp. 288 *et. seq.*

Italy

1. Italy thinks that the provision in subparagraph (*c*) should be separated into two different paragraphs, since it deals with two different exceptions to the local remedies rule: (*a*) "[t]here is no relevant connection between the injured person and the State alleged to be responsible"; and (*b*) "the circumstances of the case ... make the exhaustion of local remedies unreasonable". There are no meaningful connections between the two exceptions. Moreover, according to the present wording, it is not clear whether the lack of relevant connections works by itself as an exception, or whether it works only when it makes unreasonable the exhaustion of local remedies (as could perhaps be inferred from paragraph (7) of the commentary to draft article 16).

2. That being said, Italy believes that the second abovementioned exception (that relating to the circumstances of the case) should be phrased in a more extensive and, at the same time, more precise way, both by explicitly adopting the well-known terminology of "special circumstances"[62] and by expressly listing in draft article 16 (or at least in the commentary) the most important "special circumstances" that can be inferred from international practice.

3. The terminology of "special circumstances" can be found in the practice existing in the field of diplomatic protection in a strict sense and even more often in the field of human rights. Moreover, the practice of both fields allows one to single out the main special circumstances, of an objective and a subjective character, which makes it extremely difficult for the injured individual to exhaust local remedies. They are (*a*) serious and objective difficulties of practical or spatial character;[63] (*b*) situations of danger, risks of reprisals or serious damages and exorbitant judicial costs;[64] (*c*) general conditions of dysfunctioning of the system of administration of justice or of instability of the whole governmental machinery;[65] (*d*) unlawful legislative measures or administrative practices;[66] and (*e*) situations of grave and systematic human rights violations.[67] The last three circumstances are the most important and relevant in recent practice.

[62] *Yearbook ... 2002*, vol. II (Part One), document A/CN.4/523 and Add.1, p. 72, art. 15, para. 2.

[63] *John W. Carmalt*, in La Pradelle and Politis, *Recueil des arbitrages internationaux*, p. 126; *M. S. Perry*, *ibid.*, p. 127; *I.C.J. Pleadings, Nottebohm*, Vol. I (Liechtenstein *v.* Guatemala), p. 416.

[64] *Neptune*, in Schwarzenberger, *International Law*, p. 244; and in La Pradelle and Politis, *op. cit.*, pp. 139 *et seq.*; *Nottebohm* (see footnote 63 above), p. 408.

[65] *Akdivar and Others* v. *Turkey*, European Court of Human Rights, *Reports of Judgments and Decisions 1996–IV*, p. 1211, para. 69; *Aksoy* v. *Turkey*, *ibid.*, pp. 2276–2277, paras. 52–57; *Godínez Cruz* case, Inter-American Court of Human Rights, Series C, No. 5 (1989), para. 58; and others.

[66] *Donnelly and others* v. *the United Kingdom*, Council of Europe, *Yearbook of the European Convention on Human Rights* (1976), p. 146; *Akdivar* (see footnote 65 above), p. 1210, para. 67; *Velásquez Rodríguez*, Inter-American Court of Human Rights, Series C, No. 4 (1988), para. 68; and others.

[67] *Dermit Barbato* v. *Uruguay*, decision of 21 October 1982, *Official Records of the General Assembly, Thirty-eighth Session, Supplement No. 40* (A/38/40), annex IX, p. 124; *Free Legal Assistance Group* v. *Zaïre*, African Commission on Human and Peoples' Rights, *International Human Rights Reports* (1997), p. 92; *Amnesty International* v. *Sudan*, *ibid.* (2001), p. 261; and others.

4. However, Italy notes that draft article 16 (*c*), as it is presently phrased, gives only a marginal and residual importance to this exception. This is confirmed also by the commentary, which is very concise and which, by citing as examples only a few circumstances, neglects the most important ones.

5. Instead, Italy assigns great importance to this exception and believes that the insertion in the draft of an explicit and autonomous exception concerning the "special circumstances", followed by an exemplifying list that also takes into account the recent practice in the field of human rights, would make a remarkable contribution to the progressive development of international law with regard to the exceptions to the local remedies rule.

Netherlands

The Netherlands considers that the commentary in paragraph (11) should be adopted so that the draft article covers both "legal denial" and "factual denial".

Qatar

(*See comments on subparagraph* (a) *above.*)

United Kingdom of Great Britain and Northern Ireland

The United Kingdom considers that draft article 16 (*c*) represents a proposal for the progressive development of existing customary international law which, at present, contains no need for a voluntary link or territorial connection, or provision for hardship. The United Kingdom suggests that greater clarification is needed, particularly in respect of the required "relevant connection".

United States of America

1. Draft article 16 (*c*) would allow a claimant to avoid exhaustion of local remedies either where there is "no relevant connection" between the injured person and the injuring State or where exhaustion of local remedies is "unreasonable". The commentary accompanying the draft article explains that the former exception is designed to address the situation where a claimant did not intend to interact with the respondent State, but is nonetheless injured by an action of that State. The classic examples provided are that of cross-border pollution and straying aircraft. The latter exception is, according to the commentary, an attempt to allow for case-by-case exceptions to the local remedies rule where its application appears "unreasonable".

2. The United States agrees that an exception in this area is warranted where there is no relevant connection between the injured person and the injuring State. It, however, proposes that the "unreasonable" component be eliminated to avoid vagueness and excessive breadth. The United States urges that draft article 16 (*c*) be rewritten to state:

"Local remedies do not need to be exhausted where there is no relevant connection between the injured person and the State alleged to be responsible."

3. The revision proposed by the United States eliminates the clause providing an exception to the exhaustion of local remedies rule where "the circumstances of the case otherwise make the exhaustion of local remedies unreasonable". That exception is not supported by customary international law or sound public policy concerns. The United States believes that the formulation in subparagraph (*c*) is vague and introduces too much uncertainty to the application of the exhaustion of local remedies rule. The exceptions provided in the rest of draft article 16 accurately encompass the situations where the exhaustion requirement should not be applied, including those listed in paragraph (11) of the commentary. A lack of factual access to the courts, criminal obstruction of the judicial process and prohibitive cost could all render a remedy "obviously futile", thereby excusing the exhaustion of local remedies requirement pursuant to draft article 16 (*a*). Thus, no further open-ended exceptions are necessary here.

4. The United States also believes that the commentary should be clarified to indicate that overflight alone over the territory of a State does not constitute a "relevant connection" requiring exhaustion of local remedies. While the commentary is clear that aircraft that stray into the airspace of a State have no "relevant connection" with the State, the United States believes that where an aircraft merely flies over a State as part of its planned flight path, no "relevant connection" has been established. The requirement of exhaustion is too burdensome in such circumstances, given the remote link between the injured person and injuring State. By contrast, a merchant trucking goods through a State en route elsewhere does have a more tangible link with the State, including the benefit of using local courts in the through-State to protect his property. Under those circumstances, a "relevant connection"—here, commercial and territorial—has been established, thus mandating exhaustion of local remedies.

Subparagraph (d)

Guatemala

1. The principle that a State must expressly waive a right is well established in customary international law. However, paragraphs (12), (15), (16) and (17) of the commentary on draft article 16 raise a number of questions concerning the applicability of the principle to waivers of a State's right to require the exhaustion of local remedies.

2. Nevertheless, it should be pointed out that in many, if not most, cases, the above-mentioned problem will not be a problem at all. Where an arbitration agreement is concluded to resolve an already existing dispute in a case in which, under normal circumstances, the rule of exhaustion of local remedies would be applicable to one of the two States parties, it cannot be said that the State has waived, expressly or tacitly, its right to such exhaustion. In fact, something completely different has happened: a rule of customary international law, namely, that requiring the exhaustion of local remedies, has, by virtue of the principle that exceptional circumstances prevail over normal circumstances, been superseded by contradictory provisions contained in a treaty. The mere fact that the waiver is essentially unilateral illustrates that it is incorrect to talk of a waiver in such cases. When treaties provide for the settlement by arbitration of future disputes in matters in which, under normal circumstances, local remedies must be exhausted, such treaties are interpreted in order to determine whether or not they prescribe the inapplicability of the relevant rule. If it is found that one of those treaties does impose such inapplicability, it cannot, by the same token, be concluded that the local remedies rule has been waived.

Morocco

Morocco proposes to delete subparagraph (*d*) on the grounds that the provision would diverge from an important principle of international law and, moreover, has no practical significance.

Qatar

The exception in subparagraph (*d*) is acceptable since it is consistent with general principles of law.

United Kingdom of Great Britain and Northern Ireland

Draft article 16 (*d*), providing for waiver of the requirement that local remedies be exhausted, requires further consideration. Waiver of such a fundamental requirement of customary international law should be express; to allow waiver to be implied in the absence of an express intention to do so is contrary to the current position in international law. Any rule on waivers adopted must be strictly interpreted since it also protects interests other than those of the State waiving the requirement. The Commission may also wish to consider whether there could ever be a waiver in the face of an express treaty obligation to exhaust domestic remedies.

Uzbekistan

The following phrase should be added after the word "exhausted": "or its actions or inaction are tantamount to a waiver."

Part Four

MISCELLANEOUS PROVISIONS

Uzbekistan

Part four should be called "Other provisions" rather than "Miscellaneous provisions".

Draft article 17. Actions or procedures other than diplomatic protection

Austria

Draft article 17 protects other legal devices through which the rights of individuals can be ensured. This could lead to a duplication of proceedings in different forums with the possibility of divergent decisions. However, that risk has to be accepted in the interest of effective protection of the rights of individuals.

El Salvador

The fact should be taken into account that diplomatic protection exists for cases where the State adopts in its own right the cause of one of its nationals, not the right of nationals for their State to exercise diplomatic protection on their behalf as a result of injury caused by another State. Diplomatic protection cannot therefore be placed at the same level as the existing protection measures provided for in international human rights law. El Salvador therefore believes that the wording of draft article 17 should reflect this point.

Italy

1. The article includes a savings clause allowing the State, or the person to be protected, to resort to actions or procedures other than diplomatic protection under international law. The commentary (para. (4)) reports, among such procedures, those envisaged in the various international conventions on human rights, or those aimed at creating mechanisms to protect investments. Also in the commentary (para. (6), last sentence), the Commission warns that even in the case in which the State avails itself of an alternative procedure, it will still be able to exert its right to the diplomatic protection of its national.

2. Italy underlines the importance of the last part of paragraph 6 of the commentary. However, its opinion is that such part can be improved and made more specific and that the specification should be included in the text of draft article 17. Indeed, when an alternative procedure—whether resorted to by the State or by the individual to be protected—entails a binding decision adopted by a fully independent and impartial judge, the right to exert diplomatic protection should no longer exist. There should be no ground to exert the diplomatic action in such a case, since the action undertaken warrants a more secure elimination of the consequences of any wrongful act that might have been committed. Such outcome would not arise when the alternative procedure is undertaken before an institution (for instance the Human Rights Committee, established under article 28 of the International Covenant on Civil and Political Rights) that is not competent to make binding decisions. In this case, the State cannot be forced to give up its right to exert diplomatic protection, given that the offending State, whose offence has been ascertained by the institution, is not obliged to comply with such decision nor suffer its consequences.

3. Therefore Italy suggests that an approach be adopted in draft article 17 allowing for diplomatic protection and alternative procedures to be coordinated on the basis of the aforementioned criterion. Italy is aware that the Commission has rejected a proposal of one of its members aimed at considering remedies on human rights matters as being *lex specialis* with respect to the rules on diplomatic protection (see commentary, para. (7)), and acknowledges that in reference to any alternative remedy, such a proposal would certainly be excessive. However, Italy considers such a proposal more than reasonable if it refers only to the above-mentioned narrower category of jurisdictional remedies.

Netherlands

1. The words "under international law" should be deleted. The Netherlands is of the opinion that the right to, *inter alia*, submit an *amicus curiae* brief in domestic proceedings, as the European Union has done in American legal cases, must remain unchanged.

2. The Netherlands also suggests that draft article 17, like draft article 19, should be amended as follows:

"The rights of States, natural persons or other entities to resort to actions or procedures other than diplomatic protection to secure redress for injury suffered as a result of an internationally wrongful act are not affected by the present draft articles."

Qatar

1. There is no need to reaffirm the right of States, natural persons or other entities to resort under international law to actions or procedures other than diplomatic protection to secure redress for injury suffered as a result of an internationally wrongful act, since this is already considered an inalienable right of States and individuals under the rules of international law.

2. If draft article 17 refers to the right of States and individuals to invoke international human rights conventions, then it adds nothing new either. In any event, the fact that States and individuals can resort to international human rights law offers more safeguards than diplomatic protection, because the former is based on appropriate and flexible legal principles that help and enable individuals to exercise their rights when their fundamental rights and freedoms are violated.

3. On the basis of the foregoing, Qatar concurs with the view that draft articles 17 and 18 should be merged, and proposes that the resulting draft article should read as follows:

"The present draft articles do not apply where, and to the extent that, they are inconsistent with special treaty provisions concerning the settlement of disputes between corporations or shareholders of a corporation and States."

United Kingdom of Great Britain and Northern Ireland

The United Kingdom supports draft article 17 to the extent that it protects existing rights under human rights and other instruments and principles of customary international law. The United Kingdom suggests that further consideration be given to the likelihood of several claims arising in different forums.

(See comments on draft article 18 below.)

Uzbekistan

The provisions of draft article 17 should be inserted in a draft article entitled "Use of terms" (see Other comments and suggestions, below) in order to define the term "other means of peaceful settlement" (as per draft article 1).

Draft article 18. Special treaty provisions

Austria

Austria refers to its comments made in connection with draft article 4 concerning nationality. It cannot be excluded that some of the provisions, such as those relating to the issue of nationality, could be replaced by bilateral or regional customary law. It is therefore suggested only to refer to *lex specialis* or simply to "special rules of international law" as was done in the *lex specialis* provision in the framework of the articles on responsibility of States for internationally wrongful acts (art. 55).[68]

El Salvador

El Salvador believes that the draft article reflects an idea similar to that contained in draft article 17, and would therefore be in favour of combining them into a single draft article.

Morocco

1. The formulation of the draft article gives rise to ambiguities on two fronts. First, [French text] Morocco does not know what "il est incompatible" refers to. If the phrase refers to "présents articles", it should be recast in the plural.

2. Secondly, the draft article refers to special treaties, implying that there are ordinary treaties and special treaties. Nevertheless, in international law, in particular in the Vienna Convention on the Law of Treaties, there is no mention of "special treaties". Accordingly, one might either refer to special rules, as was done for the responsibility of States and the responsibility of international organizations, or amend the latter part of the sentence to read: "inconsistent with special regimes provided for under bilateral and multilateral treaties regarding the protection of investments."

[68] *Yearbook ... 2001*, vol. II (Part Two), p. 30.

Qatar

(See the comments on draft article 17 above.)

United Kingdom of Great Britain and Northern Ireland

The United Kingdom approves of the relocation of draft article 18 to the end of the draft articles and considers it an improvement upon previous versions. It considers that clarification in the commentary of the relationship between draft article 18 and draft article 17, which also potentially applies to investment treaties, would be helpful.

Draft article 19. Ships' crews

Austria

The idea underlying draft article 19 is certainly confirmed by practice. The structure of the draft article, however, should be reconsidered since the present wording could lead to unintended results. It could be asked whether the right of the State of nationality of crew members to exercise diplomatic protection is affected if the condition expressed in the last part of the phrase is not met. That result is certainly not intended. It is therefore suggested first to stress the right of both categories of States to exercise diplomatic protection and then to state that the right of the one State does not affect the right of the other.

Belgium

Belgium takes the view that, as part of a gradually evolving process and in view of the growth of air transport and the increasingly multinational character of cabin crews, an extension of this provision to cover aircraft cabin crews is justified.

Mexico

1. With regard to draft article 19 concerning ships' crews, Mexico recognizes that the Commission's codification appropriately reflects international law and practice in this sphere. Likewise, it notes with satisfaction that the Mexican delegation's comments on this particular topic in recent years have been taken into account and incorporated by the Commission in this work.

2. The capacity of the State of nationality to exercise diplomatic protection and the right of the flag State to seek redress on behalf of the ship's crew undoubtedly represent a fundamental development towards ensuring full respect for the human rights of ships' crews. However, paragraph (8) of the commentary on draft article 19 does not resolve the issue of competing claims if both States should seek redress.

3. For the above reason, Mexico requests the Commission to study this hypothesis so that it may then incorporate in the draft articles or the commentary on draft article 19 a reference that will resolve the issue of dual reparation by the offending State.

Netherlands

(*See the comments on draft article 17 above.*)

The Netherlands recommends that the draft article be incorporated into draft article 8. This is more consistent with the structure of the draft articles.

Norway, on behalf of the Nordic countries (Denmark, Finland, Iceland, Norway and Sweden)

The Nordic countries fully support the approach in draft article 19, whereby the right to exercise of diplomatic protection by the flag State does not exclude the same right to be exercised by the State of nationality of the members of the crew of a ship and vice versa. This is a very important principle. This solution means that important protective measures established by the law of the sea are consequently not undermined.

United Kingdom of Great Britain and Northern Ireland

The amendments to draft article 19 reflect the decision in the *Saiga* case.[69] Like the Commission, the United Kingdom recognizes the existence of practical considerations supporting the bringing of claims by the flag State in the context of the United Nations Convention on the Law of the Sea. To the extent that this article is controversial in that it may develop existing customary international law, the United Kingdom considers that the article could be omitted from the present draft articles on diplomatic protection since it does not relate to the exercise of diplomatic protection as currently understood in international law.

United States of America

1. Draft article 19 would affirm the right of the State of nationality of ship crew members to exercise diplomatic protection on behalf of its nationals without derogating from the right of the State of the nationality of the ship to seek redress on behalf of crew members irrespective of their nationality when they have been injured through an international wrong to the ship. The commentary accompanying the draft article notes that international law is inconclusive on the question of whether a State can extend protection to non-national crewmen, but concludes that international jurisprudence leans towards recognition of a right of redress. The commentary is careful to note that this right to seek redress is not diplomatic protection, but explains that the right closely resembles such protection.

2. The United States welcomes the commentary's clarification that draft article 19 would not intend to confer a right of diplomatic protection to the State of nationality of a ship for non-national crew members. As the United States explained in its May 2003 comments,[70] there is great uncertainty as to whether customary international law allows the State of nationality of a ship to protect crew members from a third State.

3. However, given the fact that the Commission now clearly recognizes in its commentary that this provision does not concern diplomatic protection, the United States believes the draft article is outside the scope of the present project and should be omitted. General Assembly resolution 51/160 of 16 December 1996, inviting this project, asked the Commission to consider "diplomatic protection" alone. Consistent with that mandate, a working group of the Commission reported to the forty-ninth session of the Commission that the draft articles would be limited to "diplomatic protection *stricto sensu*".[71] Given that the draft articles were intended to codify rules of diplomatic protection alone, extension of the project into rights of States to seek redress for crew members risks creating confusion about the scope of the draft articles as a whole and, thus, is unwarranted. Rather, this issue is better left to other international law instruments, such as the United Nations Convention on the Law of the Sea.

4. The commentary to draft article 19 also states that a purpose of the article is to affirm that the State of nationality of a ship's crew member can espouse his claim. While the United States agrees that this principle is customary international law, its statement here is superfluous. Draft articles 2–3 would clarify that a State has the right to exercise diplomatic protection in respect of claims of its nationals where the other requirements of the draft articles are met. Since crew members are nationals, like all others, there is no reason to adopt a separate draft article to note that their claims are cognizable. Rather, if the Commission feels it is necessary, the commentary to draft articles 2–3 should include a statement that crew members too are nationals whose injuries are subject to diplomatic protection.

Other comments and suggestions

Netherlands

1. In chapter IV of the fifth report of the Special Rapporteur are two proposed "savings clauses" that might be alternatives to draft articles 17–18. The first proposal, an alternative for draft article 17, reads:

> *Article 26*
>
> These articles are without prejudice to the right that a State other than a State entitled to exercise diplomatic protection or an individual may have as a result of an internationally wrongful act.[72]

The Netherlands considers that this draft article can be supported.

2. The second proposal includes alternative wording for draft article 21 that merges draft articles 17 and 18 into one:

> These articles are without prejudice to the rights of States or persons to invoke procedures other than diplomatic protection to secure redress for injury suffered as a result of an internationally wrongful act [that might also give rise to a claim for diplomatic protection by the State of nationality of the injured person].[73]

---

[69] *M/V "Saiga" case* (No. 2) (*Saint Vincent and the Grenadines* v. *Guinea*), *Judgment, ITLOS Reports 1999*, p. 10.

[70] On file with the Codification Division, United Nations, New York.

[71] *Yearbook ... 1997*, vol. II (Part Two), p. 60, para. 176.

[72] *Yearbook ... 2004*, vol. II (Part One), document A/CN.4/538, chap. IV.A, p. 54.

[73] *Ibid.*, chap. IV.B, p. 55.

The Netherlands considers that this "omnibus savings clause"[74] can also be supported.

3. The sixth report on diplomatic protection[75] deals with the "clean hands" doctrine. The Netherlands endorses the conclusions of the Special Rapporteur.

United States of America

1. The United States has not been in a position to review every assertion, footnote and citation provided in the commentaries. Its review of the commentaries has uncovered, however, numerous instances where cases or treatises appear to be cited for propositions that they do not support. The United States urges the Commission to review carefully the accuracy of the commentaries and characterizations of the materials cited therein.

2. The United States would like to request that the Commission make clear in the commentaries which draft articles it considers progressive development of the law, as opposed to codification of customary international law. For example, while the United States does not find draft article 8 objectionable, it is clearly a progressive development of the law and should be characterized as such.

[74] *Ibid.*, para. 42.

[75] *Yearbook ... 2005*, vol. II (Part One), document A/CN.4/546, p. 1.

Uzbekistan

In the view of Uzbekistan, it is necessary to provide an explanation, in a separate draft article entitled "Use of terms", of the following terms used in the draft articles: "nationality of a legal person" [Russian text]; "nationality of a corporation"; "incorporation"; "State of incorporation"; "personal injury"; "damage to property"; "damage to personal non-property rights"; and the like.

Comments on final form

Norway, on behalf of the Nordic countries (Denmark, Finland, Iceland, Norway and Sweden)

The Nordic countries believe that there is merit in proceeding rather swiftly to the adoption of the draft articles on second reading. Moreover, the Nordic countries do also believe that the provisions on diplomatic protection should, in a relatively short time, be adopted in the form of a convention. This would enhance legal clarity and predictability in this important field of law.

Annex

UNITED KINGDOM OF GREAT BRITAIN AND NORTHERN IRELAND RULES APPLYING TO INTERNATIONAL CLAIMS

1. Basis of the rules

The UK's rules and the comments have appeared in a number of published works, for example, the *International and Comparative Law Quarterly*, vol. 37 (1988), pp. 1006–1008. These rules are based on general principles of customary international law.

It may sometimes be permissible and appropriate to make informal representations even where the strict application of the following rules would bar the presentation of a formal claim.

The rules do not deal with the more complex question of what conduct on the part of a State amounts to a breach of international law for which it is responsible. This is covered more fully in chapter 4.

2. Rules regarding nationality of claimant

Rule I

HMG [Her Majesty's Government] will not take up the claim unless the claimant is a United Kingdom national and was so at the date of the injury.

Comment

International law requires that for a claim to be sustainable, the claimant must be a national of the State which is presenting the claim, both at the time when the injury occurred and continuously thereafter up to the date of formal presentation of the claim. In practice, however, it has hitherto been sufficient to prove nationality at the date of the injury and of presentation of the claim (see "Nationality of claims: British practice" by I. M. Sinclair, *British Year Book of International Law*, 1950, vol. 27, pp. 125–144).

The term "United Kingdom national" includes:

(*a*) All British nationals who fall into one of the following categories under the British Nationality Act 1981 (or one of the corresponding categories under earlier legislation):

(i) British citizens

(ii) British Dependent Territories citizens

(iii) British Nationals (Overseas)

(iv) British Overseas citizens

(v) British subjects under Part IV of the Act

(vi) British protected persons;

(*b*) Companies incorporated under the law of the United Kingdom or of any territory for which the United Kingdom is internationally responsible.

Rule II

Where the claimant has become or ceases to be a UK national after the date of the injury, HMG may in an appropriate case take up the claim in concert with the government of the country of his former subsequent nationality.

Rule III

Where the claimant is a dual national, HMG may take up his claim (although in certain circumstances it may be appropriate for HMG to do so jointly with the other government entitled to do so). HMG will not normally take up the claim of a UK national if the respondent State is the State of his second nationality, but may do so if the respondent State has, in the circumstances which gave rise to the injury, treated the claimant as a UK national.

Rule IV

HMG may take up the claim of a corporation or other juridical person which is created and regulated by the law of the United Kingdom or of any territory for which HMG are internationally responsible.

Comment

This rule rests on the principle that a juridical person (such as a company, corporation or other association having a legal personality distinct from its members) has the nationality of that country whose law has formally created it, which regulates its constitution and under whose law it can be wound up or dissolved. This principle was endorsed by the International Court of Justice in the *Barcelona Traction* case (Belgium *v.* Spain) in 1970. Certain States determine nationality of a corporation by different tests: in place of central administration (*siège social*) or the place of effective control (to determine which, the residence of the majority of shareholders as well as of the directors may be taken into account). The Court however said that no one of these tests of "genuine connection" has found general international acceptance.

In determining whether to exercise its right of protection, HMG may consider whether the company has in fact a real and substantial connection with the United Kingdom. (This question and other points arising from rules IV–VI are discussed further in Mervyn Jones' paper "Claims on behalf of nationals who are shareholders in foreign companies", *British Year Book of International Law*, 1949, vol. 26, p. 225.)

Rule V

Where a UK national has an interest, as a shareholder or otherwise, in a company incorporated in another State, and that company is injured by the acts of a third State, HMG may normally take up the claim only in concert with the government of the State in which the company is incorporated. Exceptionally, as where the company is defunct, there may be independent intervention.

Rule VI

Where a UK national has an interest, as a shareholder or otherwise, in a company incorporated in another State and of which it is therefore a national, and that State injures the company, HMG may intervene to protect the interests of that UK national.

Comment

In some cases the State of incorporation of a company does not possess the primary national interest in the company. A company may be created for reasons of legal or economic advantage under the law of one State though nearly all the capital is owned by nationals of another. In such circumstances, the States in which the company is incorporated may have little interest in protecting it, while the State to which the nationals who own the capital belong has considerable interest in so doing. In the *Barcelona Traction* case, the International Court of Justice denied the existence under customary international law of an inherent right for the national State of shareholders in a foreign country to exercise diplomatic protection. However, the majority of the Court accepted the existence of a right to protect shareholders in the two cases described in rules V and VI (when the company is defunct, and where the State in which the company is incorporated, although theoretically the legal protector of the company, itself causes injury to the company).

Where the capital in a foreign company is owned in various proportions by nationals of several States, including the United Kingdom, it is unusual for HMG to make representations unless the States whose nationals hold the bulk of the capital will support them in making representations.

Rule VII

HMG will not normally take over and formally espouse a claim of a UK national against another State until all the legal remedies, if any, available to him/her in the State concerned have been exhausted.

Comment

Failure to exhaust any local remedies will not constitute a bar to a claim if it is clearly established that in the circumstances of the case an appeal to a higher municipal tribunal would have had no effect. Nor is a claimant against another State required to exhaust justice in that State if there is no justice to exhaust.

Rule VIII

If, in exhausting any municipal remedies, the claimant has met with prejudice or obstruction, which are a denial of justice, HMG may intervene on his behalf to secure redress of injustice.

Rule IX

HMG will not take up a claim if there has been undue delay in its presentation to them unless the delay results from causes outside the control of the claimant, but no time limits are fixed and they are subject to equitable rather than legal definition.

3. Rule regarding remedies under a treaty

Rule X

Where an express provision in any treaty is inconsistent with one or more of rules I to IX, the terms of the treaty will, to the extent of the inconsistency, prevail. In case of ambiguity, the terms of any treaty or international agreement will be interpreted according to these rules and other rules of international law.

4. Rule regarding devolution of claims

Rule XI

Where the claimant has died since the date of injury to him or his property, his personal representatives may seek to obtain relief or compensation for the injury on behalf of his estate. Such a claim is not to be confused with a claim by a dependant of a deceased person for damages for his death.

Comment

Where the personal representatives are of a different nationality from that of the original claimant, the rules set out above would probably be applied as if it were a single claimant who had changed his/her national status.

DOCUMENT A/CN.4/575

Comments and observations received from Governments

[Original: Arabic/English]
[18 August 2006]

CONTENTS

Introduction

1. In a communication dated 1 August 2006, Kuwait transmitted a set of comments and observations on the draft articles and commentaries on diplomatic protection, adopted by the International Law Commission, on first reading, at its fifty-sixth session, in 2004.[1] The Commission did not have the opportunity to consider the comments and observations, as they were received after the adoption of the draft articles on second reading.

[1] See *Yearbook ... 2004*, vol. II (Part Two), p. 18, para. 59. The draft articles are reproduced in paragraph 60, pages 20 *et seq.*

Comments and observations received from Governments

Kuwait

A. The legal nature of diplomatic protection

2. Whenever an ordinary individual is unable to obtain his rights, he induces the State to which he belongs by virtue of his nationality to take up his defence and institute legal action against the State that is at the origin of the internationally wrongful act. Such intervention on the part of the State is known under the rules of State responsibility as "diplomatic protection of nationals abroad".

3. Such intervention transforms a conflict between an individual and a State into a dispute between sovereign States and removes the individual from the realm of the dispute. He has to wait for the judgement to be rendered in his case at the international level, so that his State may turn over to him what it has obtained in the way of compensation from the State bearing the international responsibility. His State itself, moreover, has been harmed as a result of the insult to its national.

4. Kuwait therefore concludes that diplomatic protection is part of State responsibility, i.e. one of its main topics, and also an international instrument for the protection of human rights against violations involving a wrongful act by another State or, as decided by the Commission, diplomatic protection is simply one means of protecting human rights (para. 84 of the seventh report on diplomatic protection (A/CN.4/567)).[2]

[2] Reproduced in the present volume.

1. Waiver of diplomatic protection

5. On the basis of the considerations referred to in paragraphs 2–4 above, an individual does not have the right to waive the right of his State to protect him, for in such a case he would be waiving a right that is possessed not by him but rather by his State. Furthermore, what is involved here is a human right that has been violated by another State through a wrongful act on its part. Such rights are inalienable and therefore not subject to waiver. Moreover, they belong to *jus cogens*, which cannot be derogated from by agreement.

2. Discretionary right of States to exercise diplomatic protection

6. During its discussion of draft article 2, the Commission decided not to impose any obligation on States to exercise diplomatic protection, in application of the rule taken from international case law that the exercise of such protection is a right of the State, whence it may make use or not make use of that right.

3. Exhaustion of local remedies

7. Exhaustion of local remedies by the injured person as a precondition for the exercise of diplomatic protection is a constant and firmly established rule of customary international law, as affirmed and decided by ICJ in the *Interhandel* case of 1959.[3]

8. This rule rests on two considerations, the first of which is respect for the sovereignty of the foreign State in whose territory the individual is living, his subjection to the national jurisdiction of that State and the assumption that such jurisdiction is unbiased and neutral. The second consideration can be summed up in the granting of an opportunity to the State which committed the act to remedy it by the State's own methods and within the framework of its domestic law.

9. The Commission has dealt with this requirement, which is governed by draft articles 14–16.

4. Nationality requirement

10. Established State practice requires that a nationality link should exist between the individual and the State at two points in time at least: the first is the time of occurrence of the internationally wrongful act and the coming into being of the injury, and the second, the date of official presentation of the claim for protection, either by the diplomatic channel or by way of international jurisdiction.

11. Exhaustive discussions among States are taking place within the Commission regarding continuity of nationality (draft articles 3–10 deal with the question of the existence of nationality, article 5 dealing specifically with continuous nationality) as a fundamental condition for a State's exercise of diplomatic protection.

12. The most controversial aspects of the continuity of nationality rule pertain to the final date on which the person having suffered the injury must still be a national and to whether, in that regard, it is the date of official presentation of the claim or the date of the final decision on the claim and the rendering of the related judgement that must be taken into account.

13. A look at the international position on the matter shows that a number of States support the first approach, favouring continuous nationality up to the date on which the claim is presented internationally, whereas there is strong objection to this view on the part of the United States of America, which considers it necessary for nationality to continue to the date of the resolution of the claim.

14. The United States relies heavily on the decision of the arbitral tribunal of the International Centre for the Settlement of Investment Disputes (ICSID) in the *Loewen* case, which ruled that in the language of international law, "there must be continuous national identity from the date of the events giving rise to the claim",[4] which is the date known by the expression "the time of the occurrence of the injury", "through the date of the resolution of the claim", which is known as the "final date".

5. Paragraphs 35–46 of the seventh report on diplomatic protection

15. Whatever the opinion may be concerning the said award, on which the United States has relied in its position that nationality must continue until the date of resolution of the international claim for diplomatic protection, Kuwait views that position as appropriate and in keeping with legal and practical criteria and sees the wisdom of diplomatic protection itself.

16. Indeed, it is neither acceptable nor reasonable for a State to continue to shower its diplomatic protection on someone who has lost the nationality to which he belonged, not to mention the fact that diplomatic protection, as Kuwait has stated, rests on two considerations, namely the right of the State and the right of the person offended against by the internationally wrongful act. In the event that the latter's nationality ends, the right of the State to continue its diplomatic protection ceases, for the person is no longer its national. What is more, such protection represents an international claim forbidden to individuals by virtue of the fact that they are not international persons, who alone have the right to institute proceedings of that kind.

17. As to the argument that such continuity is not necessary, on the grounds that the new State to which the injured person will belong will exercise diplomatic protection on his behalf, this does not weaken, but rather strengthens, the view that continuity of nationality is necessary, if one considers that the new State will resume the prosecution of the international action for diplomatic protection. The matter is different during the period between the injured person's loss of the nationality of his original State and his acquisition of the nationality of another State. Such is also the case when the new State fails to afford diplomatic protection to an injured person who has acquired its citizenship, inasmuch as the exercise of the right of diplomatic

[3] *Interhandel, Preliminary Objections, Judgment, I.C.J. Reports 1959*, p. 6.

[4] *The Loewen Group Inc.* v. *United States of America, ICSID Reports*, vol. 7 (Cambridge, Grotius, 2005), p. 485, para. 225.

protection—as previously pointed out—is a discretionary right of the State, i.e. one that it may, at its option, either exercise or refrain from exercising.

18. With regard to the above presentation and examination of the legal nature of diplomatic protection, it is Kuwait's intention—in addition to making its contribution to this international effort—that these principles should have an impact on the draft articles being prepared by the Commission.

B. Draft articles

19. The proposed draft includes 19 articles whereby the Commission, at its fifty-eighth session in 2006, regulated some aspects of diplomatic protection in international law, namely nationality and the exhaustion of local remedies. It did not, however, take up the primary rules of diplomatic protection, i.e. the rules governing the treatment of aliens; nor did it deal with the consequences arising from diplomatic protection, such as the question of determining whether there is an obligation on the successful claimant State to pay over any compensation it may have received in respect of the claim to the injured national. This is a question that is taken up in the concluding part of the seventh report on diplomatic protection.[5]

20. Kuwait will now take up the draft articles in succession, in accordance with the following points:

1. Article 1

21. Paragraph 1 of the proposed amended version of the article defines "diplomatic protection". Paragraph 2 refers to the distinction between diplomatic protection and consular assistance, stating that the former should not be interpreted as including the exercise of the latter, based on the considerations propounded in the seventh report on diplomatic protection, i.e. correct theoretical and practical considerations to which Kuwait refers the reader in the interest of conciseness and to avoid repetition.

2. Article 2

22. The text of this article, after being amended, affirms the right of the State to exercise diplomatic protection in accordance with the provisions of the draft articles.

23. In this regard, Kuwait refers the reader to the observations it made above concerning the State's right to exercise such protection as one of the aspects of the legal nature of diplomatic protection.

3. Articles 3–8

24. These articles govern the provision of protection by the State of nationality to natural persons, including multiple nationals, as well as to stateless persons and refugees.

25. Kuwait considers that article 4 should be redrafted to include the expression "determined by the law of the State", inasmuch as questions of nationality still belong exclusively to States.

[5] See footnote 2 above.

26. Concerning the continuous nationality rule (art. 5), Kuwait refers the reader to the remarks made above in that regard, in connection with the discussion of the legal nature of diplomatic protection.

27. Apart from these points, Kuwait agrees with the said draft articles drawn up by the Commission.

4. Articles 9–10

28. Draft articles 9 and 10 govern aspects of diplomatic protection for legal persons relating respectively to the State of nationality of a corporation and continuous nationality of a corporation.

(a) *Article 9. State of nationality of a corporation*

29. Kuwait agrees with the wording of article 9 following the proposed amendment of its second paragraph and the deletion of the phrase "or some similar connection" appearing at the end of the paragraph, so that it reads as follows:

"For the purposes of diplomatic protection of corporations, the State of nationality means the State under whose law the corporation was formed and in whose territory it has its registered office or the seat of its management"

on the grounds that the said phrase, if included in the paragraph, would open the door wide to various interpretations and give rise to confusion regarding its construction, apart from being obscure and lacking precision.

(b) *Article 10. Continuous nationality of a corporation*

30. The wording of paragraph 2 of this article (para. 3 of revised article 10) reads as follows:

> Notwithstanding paragraph 1, a State continues to be entitled to exercise diplomatic protection in respect of a corporation which was its national at the time of the injury and which, as the result of the injury, has ceased to exist according to the law of that State.[6]

31. The word "exist", included in the text, may be imprecise and give rise to numerous difficulties and problems of interpretation inasmuch as established practice has it, according to the rules in force in most (civilized) States regarding the continued existence of corporations or the cessation thereof, that the corporation's legal personality continues to exist even after the corporation's dissolution—either by consent or by decree—until the satisfaction of all creditors' claims, either in full or, in the case of insufficient assets, in part, and in accordance with the details laid out in the legal rules governing the liquidation of corporations.

32. Kuwait therefore proposes amending the phrase "and which, as the result of the injury, has ceased to exist according to the law of that State" to read "and which, as the result of the injury, no longer has legal personality and has been totally liquidated, according to the law of that State".

[6] *Yearbook ... 2004*, vol. II (Part Two), p. 30, para. 60.

5. Article 11

33. With regard to the phrase "The corporation has ceased to exist", which appears in the text both before and after revision, Kuwait refers the reader to its previous comments concerning the existence of the corporation and proposes that the text be redrafted, with the phrase "The corporation has been liquidated and its legal personality has lapsed" substituted for the aforementioned existing phrase.

6. Article 18

34. Kuwait proposes substituting the phrase "bilateral and multilateral treaties" for the phrase "special treaty provisions", with a view to clearly defining the meaning and in accordance with the notion of treaties.

7. The right of the injured national to receive compensation adjudged

35. The established principle on which international practice used to be based required that international reparation for injury was always owed to the State and not to the individual, even in the case of compensation and despite the fact that the amount of compensation must be determined on the basis of the damage suffered by the individual. In modern times, however, this principle has come under examination in many States, which acknowledge that there is some obligation on them to disburse compensation received to the injured national and that the injured individual in whose interest the claim was raised should benefit from the exercise of diplomatic protection.

36. Considerations of equity and respect for human rights have compelled the Commission seriously to contemplate adopting a provision on this subject as an exercise in progressive development and thus removing one of the major sources of inequity of diplomatic protection. It has thus drafted language, with which Kuwait agrees, calling for the transfer of the sum turned over to it by way of compensation for the injury in fulfilment of a claim arising out of diplomatic protection to the national in respect of whom it has brought the claim, after deduction of the costs incurred by the State in so doing.

INTERNATIONAL LIABILITY FOR INJURIOUS CONSEQUENCES ARISING OUT OF ACTS NOT PROHIBITED BY INTERNATIONAL LAW (INTERNATIONAL LIABILITY IN CASE OF LOSS FROM TRANSBOUNDARY HARM ARISING OUT OF HAZARDOUS ACTIVITIES)

[Agenda item 3]

DOCUMENT A/CN.4/566

Third report on the legal regime for the allocation of loss in case of transboundary harm arising out of hazardous activities, by Mr. Pemmaraju Sreenivasa Rao, Special Rapporteur*

[*Original: English*]
[*7 May 2006*]

CONTENTS

* The Special Rapporteur wishes to express his thanks to the Max Planck Institute for Comparative Public Law and International Law, Heidelberg, Germany, for hosting him for the purpose of preparing the present report. He is also grateful to Ms. Dinah Shelton of the George Washington University Law School, Washington, D.C., for getting her students to write memorandums on laws and practice of various countries focusing on matters under consideration. The Special Rapporteur also wishes to acknowledge with thanks the research support provided by Mr. Ilias Plakokefalos of Athens University Law School, Greece, during the preparation of the present report.

Multilateral instruments cited in the present report

	Source
Treaty establishing the European Community (Rome, 25 March 1957), incorporating the amendments made by the Treaty of Nice of 26 February 2001	Consolidated version of the Treaty on European Union. *Official Journal of the European Communities*, vol. 45, No. C 325 (24 December 2002), p. 33.
Convention on the High Seas (Geneva, 29 April 1958)	United Nations, *Treaty Series*, vol. 450, No. 6465, p. 11.
The Antarctic Treaty (Washington, D.C., 1 December 1959)	*Ibid.*, vol. 402, No. 5778, p. 71.
Protocol on Environmental Protection to the Antarctic Treaty (Madrid, 4 October 1991)	Final Report of the Eleventh Antarctic Treaty Special Consultative Meeting, chap. III, p. 111. See also ILM, vol. XXX, No. 6 (November 1991), p. 1461.
Annex VI to the Protocol on Environmental Protection to the Antarctic Treaty: Liability Arising from Environmental Emergencies (Stockholm, 17 June 2005)	Antarctic Treaty Consultative Meeting, Final Report of the Twenty-Eighth Meeting, chap. II A, p. 63. See also ILM, vol. 45 (2006), p. 5.
1968 Brussels Convention on jurisdiction and the enforcement of judgments in civil and commercial matters (Brussels, 27 September 1968)	*Official Journal of the European Communities*, vol. 15, No. L 299 (31 December 1972), p. 32.
United Nations Convention on the Law of the Sea (Montego Bay, 10 December 1982)	United Nations, *Treaty Series*, vol. 1833, No. 31363, p. 3.
Convention on jurisdiction and the enforcement of judgments in civil and commercial matters (Lugano, 16 September 1988)	*Official Journal of the European Communities*, vol. 31, No. L 319 (25 November 1988), p. 9.
International Convention on oil pollution preparedness, response and cooperation, 1990 (London, 30 November 1990)	United Nations, *Treaty Series*, vol. 1891, No. 32194, p. 51.
Convention on the Transboundary Effects of Industrial Accidents (Helsinki, 17 March 1992)	*Ibid.*, vol. 2105, No. 36605, p. 457.
Rotterdam Convention on the Prior Informed Consent Procedure for Certain Hazardous Chemicals and Pesticides in International Trade (Rotterdam, 10 September 1998)	*Ibid.*, vol. 2244, No. 39973, p. 337.
Cartagena Protocol on Biosafety to the Convention on Biological Diversity (Montreal, 29 January 2000)	*Ibid.*, vol. 2226, No. 30619, p. 208.

Works cited in the present report

AUSTIN, Jay E. and Carl E. BRUCH

"The Kosovo conflict: a case study of unresolved issues", *in* Jay E. Austin and Carl E. Bruch, eds., *The Environmental Consequences of War: Legal, Economic, and Scientific Perspectives*. Cambridge, Cambridge University Press, 2000, pp. 647–664.

BAR, Christian VON

"Environmental damage in private international law", *Collected Courses of The Hague Academy of International Law, 1997*. The Hague, Martinus Nijhoff, 1999. Vol. 268, pp. 291–411.

BAXTER, R. R.

"Multilateral treaties as evidence of customary international law", *British Year Book of International Law*, 1965–1966, vol. 41, pp. 275–300.

"Treaties and custom", *Collected Courses of The Hague Academy of International Law*, 1970–I. Leiden, Sijthoff, 1971. Vol. 129, pp. 25–105.

BERNASCONI, Christophe and Gerrit BETLEM

"Transnational enforcement of environmental law: second report", *Report of the Seventy-first Conference held in Berlin, 16–21 August 2004*. London, International Law Association, 2004, pp. 896–933.

BIRNIE, P. W. and A. E. BOYLE

International Law and the Environment. 2nd ed. Oxford, Oxford University Press, 2002. 798 p.

BOEHMER-CHRISTIANSEN, Sonja

"The precautionary principle in Germany: enabling government", *in* Tim O'Riordan and James Cameron, eds., *Interpreting the Precautionary Principle*. London, Earthscan, 1994, pp. 31–60.

BOUTILLON, Sonia

"The precautionary principle: development of an international standard", Michigan Journal of International Law (Ann Arbor), vol. 23, No. 2, winter 2002, pp. 429–469.

BOYLE, A. E.

"Globalising environmental liability: the interplay of national and international law", *Journal of Environmental Law*, vol. 17, No. 1, 2005, pp. 3–26.

BRIGGS, Herbert W.

The International Law Commission. Ithaca, New York, Cornell University Press, 1965. 380 p.

BROWNLIE, Ian

Principles of Public International Law. 6th ed. Oxford, Oxford University Press, 2003. 742 p.

CASSESE, Antonio

International Law. 2nd ed. Oxford, Oxford University Press, 2005. 558 p.

CHARNEY, Jonathan I.

"Third State remedies for environmental damage to the world's common spaces", *in* Francesco Francioni and Tullio Scovazzi, eds., *International Responsibility for Environmental Harm*. London, Graham & Trotman, 1991, pp. 149–177.

CRAWFORD, James

The International Law Commission's Articles on State Responsibility: Introduction, Text and Commentaries. Cambridge, Cambridge University Press, 2002. 387 p.

CUPERUS, K. W. and A. E. BOYLE

"Articles on private law remedies for transboundary damage in international watercourses", *Report of the Sixty-seventh Conference of the International Law Association held at Helsinki, 12–17 August 1996*. London, International Law Association, 1996, pp. 403–411.

DAILLIER, Patrick and Alain PELLET

Droit international public. 7th ed. Paris, LGDJ, 2002. 1510 p.

DUPUY, Pierre-Marie

"La contribution du principe de non-discrimination à l'élaboration du droit international de l'environnement", *Revue québécoise de droit international*, vol. 7, No. 2, 1991–1992, pp. 135–144.

FREESTONE, David

"The road from Rio: international environmental law after the Earth Summit", *Journal of Environmental Law*, vol. 6, 1994, pp. 193–218.

INTERNATIONAL UNION FOR CONSERVATION OF NATURE (IUCN)

"Guidelines for applying the precautionary principle: biodiversity conservation and NCM management", *Environmental Policy and Law*, vol. 35, No. 6, December 2005, pp. 274–275.

KAMMERHOFER, Jörg

"Uncertainty in the formal sources of international law: customary international law and some of its problems", *European Journal of International Law*, vol. 15, No. 3, June 2004, pp. 523–553.

KISS, Alexandre and Dinah SHELTON

International Environmental Law. 3rd ed. Ardsley, New York, Transnational, 2004. 837 p.

KOESTER, Veit

"Global environmental agreements: drafting, formulation and character", *Environmental Policy and Law*, vol. 35, No. 4–5, October 2005, pp. 170–183.

LAMMERS, J. G.

Pollution of International Watercourses: A Search for Substantive Rules and Principles of Law. Boston, Martinus Nijhoff, 1984. 724 p.

LARSSON, Marie-Louise

The Law of Environmental Damage. Liability and Reparation. The Hague, Kluwer, 1999. 681 p.

LEFEBER, René

Transboundary Environmental Interference and the Origin of State Liability. The Hague, Kluwer, 1996. 365 p.

LEIGH, Kathy

"Liability for damage to the global commons", *Australian Year Book of International Law*, vol. 14, 1993, pp. 129–156.

MAHIOU, Ahmed

"Rapport général", Société Française pour le Droit International, *Colloque d'Aix-en-Provence: la codification du droit international*. Paris, Pedone, 1999, pp. 11–65.

MCINTYRE, Owen and Thomas MOSEDALE

"The precautionary principle as a norm of customary international law", *Journal of Environmental Law*, vol. 9, No. 2, 1997, pp. 221–241.

OKOWA, Phoebe N.

State Responsibility for Transboundary Air Pollution in International Law. Oxford, Oxford University Press, 2000. 285 p.

"Procedural obligations in international environmental agreements", *British Year Book of International Law*, 1996, vol. 67, pp. 275–336.

REID, Elspeth

"Liability for dangerous activities: a comparative analysis", *International and Comparative Law Quarterly* (London), vol. 48, 1999, pp. 731–756.

REST, Alfred

"Need for an international court for the environment? Underdeveloped legal protection for the individual in transnational litigation", *Environmental Policy and Law*, vol. 24, No. 4, 1994, pp. 173–187.

SADELEER, Nicolas DE

Environmental Principles: From Political Slogans to Legal Rules. Translated by Susan Leubuscher. Oxford, Oxford University Press, 2005.

SAND, Peter H.

"Compensation for environmental damage from the 1991 Gulf war", *Environmental Policy and Law*, vol. 35, No. 6, December 2005, pp. 244–249.

SANDS, Philippe

Principles of International Environmental Law. 2nd ed. Cambridge, Cambridge University Press, 2003. 1116 p.

SCHACHTER, Oscar

"International law in theory and practice: general course in public international law", *Collected Courses of The Hague Academy of International Law*, 1982–V. Dordrecht, Martinus Nijhoff, 1985. Vol. 178, pp. 9–395.

SHAW, Malcolm N.

International Law. 5th ed. Cambridge, Cambridge University Press, 2003.

SINCLAIR, Sir Ian

The International Law Commission. Cambridge, Grotius, 1987. 177 p.

SMETS, Henri

"Le principe de non-discrimination en matière de protection de l'environnement", *Revue européenne de droit de l'environnement*, No. 1, 2000, pp. 3–33.

STOLL, Peter-Tobias

"Transboundary pollution", *in* Fred L. Morrison and Rüdiger Wolfrum, eds., *International, Regional and National Environmental Law*. The Hague, Kluwer, 2000, pp. 169–200.

WOLFRUM, Rüdiger

"Purposes and principles of international environmental law", *German Yearbook of International Law*, vol. 33, 1990, pp. 308–330.

"International environmental law: purposes, principles and means of ensuring compliance", *in* Fred L. Morrison and Rüdiger Wolfrum, eds., *International, Regional and National Environmental Law*. The Hague, Kluwer, 2000, pp. 3–70.

XUE, Hanqin

Transboundary Damage in International Law. Cambridge, Cambridge University Press, 2003. 368 p.

Introduction

1. At its fifty-sixth session, in 2004, the International Law Commission adopted, on first reading, the draft principles on the allocation of loss in the case of transboundary harm arising out of hazardous activities.[1] In paragraph 3 of resolutions 59/41 of 2 December 2004 and 60/22 of 23 November 2005, the General Assembly drew the attention of Governments to the importance, for the Commission, of having their views on the draft principles. On the whole, the draft principles were well received by delegations participating in the debate on the report of the Commission in the Sixth Committee during the fifty-ninth session of the General Assembly in 2004. Delight was expressed that the Commission was able to produce the draft principles expeditiously, within one year of the Assembly noting the importance of the Commission completing the remaining portion of its mandate under the agenda item "International liability for injurious consequences arising out of acts not prohibited by international law".[2] It will be recalled that at its fifty-sixth session, in 2001, the General Assembly, while expressing its appreciation for the valuable work done on the issue of prevention,[3] requested the Commission to resume its work on the liability aspects, bearing in mind the interrelationship between prevention and liability and taking into account the developments in international law and comments by Governments.[4] In addition to the comments in the Sixth Committee, some Governments also offered written comments on the draft principles of allocation that the Commission finalized in its first reading in 2004.[5]

2. In the present report, the Special Rapporteur analyses the issues that ought to be addressed by the Commission on second reading of the draft principles on the allocation of loss in the case of transboundary harm arising out of hazardous activities, in the light of comments and observations by Governments. In some instances, specific drafting suggestions were offered by Governments. Such suggestions are not part of the present report. The Commission, within the context of its Drafting Committee, will no doubt consider them at the appropriate time.

[1] *Yearbook ... 2004*, vol. II (Part Two), pp. 65–66, para. 175.

[2] See the statement of the Netherlands, *Official Records of the General Assembly, Fifty-ninth Session, Sixth Committee*, 17th meeting, para. 47.

[3] For the text of the draft articles on prevention of transboundary harm from hazardous activities, see *Yearbook ... 2001*, vol. II (Part Two), p. 146, para. 97.

[4] General Assembly resolution 56/82 of 12 December 2001, para. 3.

[5] A/CN.4/562 and Add.1 (reproduced in the present volume).

CHAPTER I

Comments and observations of Governments on the draft principles on the allocation of loss in the case of transboundary harm arising out of hazardous activities

A. Significant trends

3. The following trends appear discernible from an analysis of the comments and observations of Governments in their written responses and in statements in the Sixth Committee on the draft principles on the allocation of loss in the case of transboundary harm arising out of hazardous activities:

(*a*) Generally, States welcome the basic approach of the Commission that the draft should be general and residual, leaving flexibility to States to fashion specific liability regimes for particular sectors of activity, taking into consideration relevant peculiar circumstances;[6]

(*b*) There exists a wide acknowledgement of the approach of attaching primary liability to the operator of the activity, that is, the person who is in command or control in the management of the risk at the time the incident giving rise to transboundary damage takes place;[7]

(*c*) Given the nature of activities contemplated for inclusion within the scope of the draft, namely, hazardous activities, there is support for strict liability of the operator. It is understood that such liability is also limited. Further, there would be exceptions to the liability of the operator. However, such exceptions must be few.[8] Within such a scheme, suggestions were made for the inclusion of a rebuttable presumption of causal connection between the hazardous activity and the transboundary damage. Thus the burden of proof will be on the operator to prove that he is not liable;[9]

(*d*) Considering that the preferred operator's liability is strict but limited, there was also support for the possibility for supplementary funding from different sources to allocate loss and to minimize as far as possible the burden on the victims of transboundary damage to bear the

[6] See the topical summary of the discussion held in the Sixth Committee of the General Assembly during its fifty-ninth session (A/CN.4/549/Add.1), para. 58. Germany, however, doubted the value of the flexible approach as the regime suggested by the Commission, in its view, would not be self-executing (*Official Records of the General Assembly, Fifty-ninth Session, Sixth Committee*, 18th meeting, para. 4).

[7] A/CN.4/549/Add.1 (see footnote 6 above), para. 63. See also the written comments of Pakistan in A/CN.4/562 and Add.1 (reproduced in the present volume), sect. A, and Uzbekistan, *ibid.* The United Kingdom of Great Britain and Northern Ireland in written comments, while strongly supporting the operator's liability and the polluter pays principle, opposed imposition of liability, even secondary or residual liability, on the State (*ibid.*).

[8] See the comments of Austria, *Official Records of the General Assembly, Fifty-ninth Session, Sixth Committee*, 18th meeting, para. 55. The United Kingdom, however, suggested that the strict liability regime be proposed in less rigid terms and it felt that it may not be applicable across the board to all hazardous activities (A/CN.4/562 and Add.1, reproduced in the present volume).

[9] See the written comments of Mexico (A/CN.4/562 and Add.1, sect. C, reproduced in the present volume).

loss, due to such limited liability. In this regard, it was envisaged that the State of origin would participate in any such supplementary funding scheme.[10] Recalling the duties of the State of origin to ensure that any hazardous activity within its territory or areas under its exclusive jurisdiction and control is conducted with its prior authorization, and that such prior authorization should be conditioned upon the operator employing best means and efforts possible to manage the risk of transboundary harm, it is asserted that the operator should further be required to have the necessary financial means to meet claims of compensation in case of transboundary damage. It is suggested that this could be secured by the operator acquiring suitable insurance or through appropriate bank and other financial guarantees;[11]

(*e*) The importance of access to remedies was also highlighted; the State of origin and the other States concerned should allow victims of transboundary damage access to judicial and other administrative forums to pursue their claims of compensation without any discrimination and seek such remedies as are available to national victims of the same damage.[12] There is some support for the establishment of some minimum standards by way of remedies to be made available and of compensation to all victims of damage arising from the hazardous activity, and requiring States to provide the same within their national legislation.[13] In other words, it is regarded as no longer acceptable under international law for a State to authorize a hazardous activity within its territory with a risk of causing transboundary harm and not have legislation in place which guarantees suitable remedies and compensation in case of an incident causing transboundary damage. This obligation of the State, however, is treated, according to one view, as a best effort obligation, without prejudice to the particular circumstances of the country or countries concerned;[14]

(*f*) The broad definition of damage to include damage to persons, property and environment *per se* within the national jurisdiction also elicited favourable comments.[15] Suggestions were also made to include damage to global commons beyond national jurisdiction, perhaps to the extent that damage to such areas is directly traceable to the hazardous activity in question.[16] However, regarding the question of standing to sue in case of damage to the environment *per se*, the type of claims that would be admissible including claims concerning the "no-use value" are, in the opinion of some Governments, unresolved matters and perhaps best left for a separate examination or regulated by national legislation;[17]

(*g*) There was also support for principles 5 (response measures), 7 (development of specific international regimes) and 8 (implementation).[18]

4. To conclude, it seems to the Special Rapporteur that there was general endorsement of the policy considerations on the basis of which the Commission had already adopted the draft principles on the allocation of loss in the case of transboundary harm arising out of hazardous activities on first reading. Some disagreements or differences of view, however, still exist on the form in which these principles could be cast. One group of States viewed it as imperative that these principles be expressed in the form of draft articles and in as prescriptive a form as possible. On the other hand, another group of States felt that

---

[10] A/CN.4/549/Add.1 (see footnote 6 above), paras. 66, 68, 90 and 91. See also the comments of Portugal (*Official Records of the General Assembly, Fifty-ninth Session, Sixth Committee*, 19th meeting, para. 15), the Russian Federation (*ibid.*, para. 64), Mexico (*ibid.*, 25th meeting, para. 48) and Sierra Leone (*ibid.*, para. 52). The United Kingdom noted, however, that imposing any residual liability on the State would be problematic (*ibid.*, 18th meeting, para. 36). Kenya thought that the role of the State should be more limited and the commentary should make it clear that the State of origin is not required to set aside funds (*ibid.*, 20th meeting, para. 18).

[11] Statement of Germany (*Official Records of the General Assembly, Fifty-ninth Session, Sixth Committee*, 18th meeting, para. 5). The United Kingdom noted that securing insurance and other financial guarantees is not an easy matter and that this requirement should not be imposed in a rigid manner (A/CN.4/562 and Add.1 (reproduced in the present volume)).

[12] The United Kingdom felt that the matter of access to national administrative and judicial remedies in respect of claims concerning transboundary damage is governed by private international law and should be subject to such principles (A/CN.4/562 and Add.1 (reproduced in the present volume)).

[13] Statement of the Netherlands (*Official Records of the General Assembly, Fifty-ninth Session, Sixth Committee*, 17th meeting, para. 49). See also the written comments of the Netherlands (A/CN.4/562 and Add.1 (reproduced in the present volume), sect. E).

[14] See the statement of India (*Official Records of the General Assembly, Fifty-ninth Session, Sixth Committee*, 18th meeting, para. 11). See also A/CN.4/562 and Add.1 (reproduced in the present volume), sect. E.

[15] The inclusion of the environment *per se* in the definition of damage in principle 2 was objected to by a few delegations on the ground that environmental loss referred to principle 2 (*a*) (iii) could not be easily quantified in monetary terms, and that there would be difficulties in establishing *locus standi* as well as in establishing a causal connection between the activity in question and the environmental damage (see A/CN.4/549/Add.1 (footnote 6 above), para. 77). But these are not unresolvable problems. See below and also *Yearbook ... 2004*, vol. II (Part Two), p. 74, para. (12) of the commentary to principle 2.

[16] See the statements of Italy (*Official Records of the General Assembly, Fifty-ninth Session, Sixth Committee*, 17th meeting, para. 85) and New Zealand (*ibid.*, para. 89). See also the written comments of the Netherlands (A/CN.4/562 and Add.1 (reproduced in the present volume), sect. D).

[17] See A/CN.4/549/Add.1 (footnote 6 above), paras. 76–77. See also the statements of China (*Official Records of the General Assembly, Fifty-ninth Session, Sixth Committee*, 17th meeting, para. 69), India (*ibid.*, 18th meeting, para. 10) and the Russian Federation (*ibid.*, 19th meeting, para. 62). The United Kingdom felt that, given the complexities involved in the question of standing and the quantification of damage to the environment *per se*, they should be better explained in the commentary. It was also of the view that State claims concerning such damage should be left outside the scope of the draft principles, and these should be confined only to claims of private parties (A/CN.4/562 and Add.1 (reproduced in the present volume).

[18] A/CN.4/549/Add.1 (see footnote 6 above), para. 65. See also the written comments of the Czech Republic, Mexico, the Netherlands, the United States of America and Uzbekistan (A/CN.4/562 and Add.1 (reproduced in the present volume, sect. F). According to these comments, while the basic thrust of the draft principles is acceptable, they may be improved or the points at issue may be better clarified and some specific suggestions have also been made. The United Kingdom noted, with respect to principle 5, that the draft principle is not clear enough on the basis of the duty of States to take response measures; further, principle 4 should have a requirement imposing a duty on the operator to take remedial action, as did European directive 2004/35/CE on environmental liability with regard to the prevention and remedying of environmental damage [*Official Journal of the European Communities*, No. L 143, vol. 47 (30 April 2004), p. 56]; with respect to principle 7, that it is important to encourage non-binding instruments both as between States and as between non-State entities, as agreement on binding instruments is not always easy; and with respect to principle 8, that the matter of implementation is a domestic matter and should not be part of the draft principles (A/CN.4/562 and Add.1 (see above)).

the form adopted, on first reading, should be maintained; the draft principles could provide necessary guidance to States in negotiating treaties or agreements on specific sectors of activity or covering particular areas in which such activities may take place. Any other form, according to this view, would be inconsistent with the general and residual approach that the Commission has adopted and which States in general also endorsed. The matter of form on which the Commission reserved its position at the time it adopted the draft principles on first reading thus remains to be considered before the Commission concludes its second and final reading. The Special Rapporteur addresses this matter in chapter III of the present report.

B. Clarifications on some issues raised

5. In their comments, States also sought other clarifications. For example, some delegations questioned the decision of the Commission to bring the regime proposed into play only in the case of significant damage.[19] Moreover, whereas the draft principles on the allocation of loss in the case of transboundary harm arising out of hazardous activities deal with hazardous activities within its scope, the view was expressed that it would be useful to have an illustrative list of these activities in the commentaries.[20] It was also suggested that the scope of the draft principles be broadened to include liability for transboundary harm caused to neutral States in case of war between two or more States; liability arising from hazardous activity engaged in by terrorists and liability arising from storage of water in dams.[21] Other clarifications sought related to the definition of terms, particularly the broad definition of damage; the relationship between the draft articles on responsibility for internationally wrongful acts[22] and the right of a State to sue as a victim for damage done to public property; methods and means by which prompt and adequate compensation could be achieved; and the role of the "polluter pays" and precautionary principles. One viewpoint desired that the regime proposed not result in a multiplicity of claims,[23] and such multiplicity of claims could be the result of claims of compensation for the same cause of action against the operator and the State in the same jurisdiction or claims against the State in one jurisdiction and against the operator in another jurisdiction or against the operator in multiple jurisdictions at the same time. Another viewpoint sought clarification of the status of the draft principles and felt that the exercise of the Commission went beyond codification and progressive development in the traditional sense.[24] It was pointed out that the draft principles were "clearly innovative and aspirational in character and not descriptive of current law or State practice".[25]

6. The Special Rapporteur considers it appropriate to dispose of some of these matters in the following paragraphs.

1. Question of threshold

7. Starting first with the point made that no threshold should be prescribed in the case of transboundary damage even if such threshold is considered useful and necessary for the purpose of the draft articles on prevention of transboundary harm from hazardous activities, it suffices to note that this matter has been discussed at various stages in the consideration of the topic, particularly before it was divided into two parts, prevention and liability, and at all stages a threshold was considered necessary.[26] In this connection, it must be observed that, with the possible exception of radioactive contamination, States in their mutual relations tolerate some measure of pollution and it is generally perceived that such pollution becomes actionable only if it is significant.[27] While the threshold of "significant" has gained currency and acceptance in the context of the topic of international liability, it is clear that it "denotes factual and objective criteria and involves a value judgement which depends on the circumstances of a particular case and the period in which such determination is made".[28] Thus, a deprivation which is considered to be significant at one time or in one region may not necessarily be considered to be so at another time or in another region. The matter of specifying a threshold is therefore a matter of policy that has received considerable support within the Commission throughout the consideration of the topic. Further, the point that bears repeating is that the threshold is designed to prevent frivolous or

---

[19] See the written comments of the Netherlands (A/CN.4/562 and Add.1 (reproduced in the present volume), sect. C). The Nordic countries also objected to the use of the threshold "significant" in defining damage coming within the scope of the draft articles (*Official Records of the General Assembly, Fifty-ninth Session, Sixth Committee*, 17th meeting, para. 95; see also A/CN.4/549/Add.1 (footnote 6 above), para. 73). See further the written comments of Pakistan (A/CN.4/562 and Add.1, sect. A). The United Kingdom, on the other hand, suggested that the threshold be raised to "serious harm" and to only a foreseeable serious harm (*ibid.*).

[20] See the written comments of Pakistan (A/CN.4/562 and Add.1 (reproduced in the present volume), sect. A).

[21] *Ibid.*

[22] *Yearbook ... 2001*, vol. II (Part Two), p. 26.

[23] See the written comments of the Czech Republic and the United Kingdom (A/CN.4/562 and Add.1 (reproduced in the present volume), sect. A.) as well as the statement of the United Kingdom (*Official Records of the General Assembly, Fifty-ninth Session, Sixth Committee*, 18th meeting, para. 35).

[24] See the statement of the United Kingdom (*Official Records of the General Assembly, Fifty-ninth Session, Sixth Committee*, 18th meeting, para. 34). See also A/CN.4/549/Add.1 (footnote 6 above), para. 62.

[25] Written comment of the United States (A/CN.4/562 and Add.1 (reproduced in the present volume), sect. A).

[26] See *Yearbook ... 1998*, vol. II (Part One), document A/CN.4/487 and Add.1, pp. 195–197, paras. 87–98. While Mr. Robert Quentin-Baxter proposed a higher threshold of "substantial transboundary harm" (*ibid.*, para. 90), draft article 2 (*a*), provisionally adopted in 1994, suggested a lower threshold, "significant harm" (*ibid.*, para. 94), which the Working Group of the Commission approved in 1996 (*ibid.*, para. 95). It was then clarified that the concept of "significant harm" refers to more than "detectable" or "appreciable" harm, but to less than "serious" or "substantial" harm. Further, it was defined to mean a harm that is not *de minimis,* or that is not negligible (*ibid.*, para. 97, footnote 140). It was further suggested that given the fact that the topic is dealing with activities that are not prohibited by international law, the threshold could not be placed any lower than that (*ibid.*).

[27] See Okowa, *State Responsibility for Transboundary Air Pollution in International Law*, p. 176. Lefeber, in *Transboundary Environmental Interference and the Origin of State Liability*, pp. 86–89, notes the need felt for a threshold and examines the rationale for and the possible ways of explaining the meaning of the threshold of "significant harm". See also Lammers, *Pollution of International Watercourses*, pp. 346–347, and Wolfrum, "Purposes and principles of international environmental law", p. 311. See also the United Nations Economic Commission for Europe Guidelines on responsibility and liability regarding transboundary water pollution (ENVWA/R.45 of 20 November 1990, annex).

[28] *Yearbook ... 1998* (see footnote 26 above), p. 197, para. 98.

vexatious claims and is defined so as to allow practically all claims that involve more than a negligible amount of damage. In view of this, there appears no strong reason to reverse the approach adopted by the Commission with respect to maintaining the threshold of "significant" in respect of the liability aspects of the topic.

8. A separate point is also made that prescribing a threshold might be in violation of the principle of non-discrimination. This point is made on the assumption that nationals of States of origin would stand to be compensated even for trivial damage, while the victims of transboundary damage would be entitled to compensation only in the case of significant damage. This might be more of a theoretical than a present or practical problem in the absence of any evidence in State practice. In any event, international law does tolerate certain forms of discrimination in treatment between nationals and foreigners. To the extent that treatment conforms to the minimum standard of treatment sanctioned by international law, which in this case is the principle of compensation for significant transboundary damage, it may be argued that there is no violation of the principle of non-discrimination if, under national law, nationals are given the right to claim compensation even without having to suffer significant damage.[29] Under a different perspective, it cannot be ruled out that a State may even grant foreigners the same treatment as it provides to its nationals, both as a matter of the application of the principle of non-discrimination and by choosing to apply to foreign victims a better standard than is required or mandated by international law.[30]

2. Clarification on list of activities falling within the scope of the topic

9. Secondly, on the need to specify a list of activities which may be considered as coming within the scope of the draft principles, it is appropriate to refer to paragraph (3) of the commentary to draft principle 1.[31] The matter of specifying a list of activities was carefully considered by the Commission and it decided against it. It is clarified that it is difficult to capture various elements that constitute risk-bearing activities, risk being "primarily a function of the application of particular technology, the specific context and the manner of operation".[32]

3. Expansion of the scope of the topic

10. Thirdly, one may consider the possibility of broadening the scope of the draft principles to include liability arising from the conduct of war on account of damage caused to neutral States, "hazardous activity caused by terrorist activity" and "[t]ransboundary damage caused by any benign activity, such as the storage of water in dams".[33] It has to be recalled that from the very beginning the topic was conceived to address only "activities not prohibited by international law", and activities wrongful *per se* were excluded.[34] It covers activities which involve a risk of causing significant harm by virtue of their physical consequences. In 1996, before the draft articles on prevention of transboundary harm from hazardous activities were adopted, the Working Group of the Commission recognized that the outcome would embrace activities with a continuing operation and effect.[35] As noted in the commentary to draft principle 4, the operator's liability is exonerated where damage is the result of an act of war. In several instruments liability is excepted where damage occurs as a result of an act of armed conflict, hostilities, civil war or insurrection. Under some national legislation acts of terrorism also exonerate liability.[36] On the other hand, it has been the understanding that a reservoir which is perfectly safe could become dangerous as a result of an earthquake, and consequently the continued operation of such a reservoir would be an activity involving risk. Storage of water in dams could therefore be a risk-bearing activity and may be considered as covered within the draft principles, unless excluded by the parties to a convention or a treaty which also governs the same subject matter, in case of a dispute.

---

[29] Brownlie observed in a different context but commenting on the standard of national treatment that

> "[a]ccess to the courts may be maintained, but with modified rules in ancillary matters: thus an alien may not have access to legal aid and may have to give security for costs. More general variations may of course be created by treaty. The various standards of treatment commonly employed are as follows: those of reciprocity, the open door, good neighbourliness, and of identical, national, most-favoured-nation, equitable, and preferential treatment."

(*Principles of Public International Law*, p. 502).

Schachter, "International law in theory and practice: general course in public international law", p. 321, notes that

> "[w]hile equality of treatment is a laudable norm it does not justify international liability for State action based on conditions of transnational business and the economic policies of the States concerned". On the other hand, he believed that "the non-discrimination principle should require liability and preventive measures by States that sustain discrimination based on social prejudice or that act against foreign nationals in retaliation for policies of their governments".

[30] It may also be noted that international law as a result of the highly developed law of human rights provides certain minimum standards of treatment for foreigners in national jurisdictions, without discrimination between nationals and foreigners and treating them all as individuals deserving of protection of their human rights (see Cassese, *International Law*, p. 122, and Shaw, *International Law*, p. 736.

[31] *Yearbook ... 2004*, vol. II (Part Two), p. 69.

[32] *Ibid.* See also, however, footnote 366 (*ibid.*), for a reference to conventions which specify the type of activities that could come within the scope of the draft principles.

[33] Written comments of Pakistan (A/CN.4/562 and Add.1 (reproduced in the present volume), sect. A).

[34] Briefly, it may be noted that if damage occurred as a result of the act of a State party to a conflict considered to have engaged in use of force in violation of the prohibition contained in customary law, such as was held to be the case with the Iraqi invasion of Kuwait, it is responsible for the damage. On the other hand, in the case of a State which is engaged in the conflict in rightful exercise of self-defence, there could be a cause of action for compensation if it violated applicable laws of war. But the problem is that claims concerning conflict usually remain unresolved with no possible determinations to be made as to wrongfulness of the use of force involved and the legality when any particular target is destroyed. For an interesting analysis, see Austin and Bruch, "The Kosovo conflict: a case study of unresolved issues".

[35] *Yearbook ... 1996*, vol. II (Part Two), annex I, pp. 106–107, para. (23) of the commentary to article 1. See also *Yearbook ... 1998* (footnote 26 above), p. 198, para. 111 (*c*), and *Yearbook ... 2001*, vol. II (Part Two), p. 146, art. 2 (*a*) of the draft articles on prevention, specifying only activities with a "[r]isk of causing significant transboundary harm" as coming within its scope.

[36] *Yearbook ... 2004*, vol. II (Part Two), pp. 84–85, para. (27) of the commentary to principle 4. See also *Yearbook ... 2004*, vol. II (Part One), document A/CN.4/543, p. 85. See further Annex VI to the Protocol on Environmental Protection to the Antarctic Treaty.

4. Damage to the environment *per se* and claims of compensation for damage to "non-use" values

11. Draft principle 2 defines damage, and damage to the environment *per se* is included along with damage to persons and property in paragraph (*a*). In paragraph (*b*), environment is broadly defined to encompass "characteristic aspects of the landscape". It must be noted that the definition refers only to the environment within national jurisdiction and control, and excludes the environment as it pertains to global commons.

12. Three different sets of issues were highlighted in the observations made by Governments concerning the environment. First, it has been noted that the definition of environment in draft principle 2 did not include damage to global commons.[37] It may be recalled that the Special Rapporteur recommended that damage to global commons should be addressed within the scheme of the draft principles insofar as it can be traced and linked to the hazardous activities coming within the scope of the draft articles on prevention of transboundary harm from hazardous activities.[38] However, the Commission, on the basis of the recommendation of the Working Group set up at the fifty-sixth session in 2004,[39] decided to exclude issues concerning global commons. While it was recognized that such issues were important, it was considered best to deal with global commons separately because it raised its own peculiar problems in relation to standing to sue, proper forum, applicable law and quantification of damage.[40] The Special Rapporteur is convinced that these issues cannot properly be analysed within the economy of the present draft principles, where the focus is transboundary harm within the territories of the States concerned and involving their nationals and resources.

13. Secondly, some Governments viewed the definition of environment to be broad. It has to be acknowledged that the world community has come to recognize the value of the environment and the need to be ever vigilant and assess, on a continuous basis, the adverse impact of various human activities on the environment. In adopting a holistic definition of environment, the Commission was guided by the ICJ dictum in the case concerning the *Gabčíkovo-Nagymaros Project*.[41] Besides, several recently concluded conventions on the subject have dealt with the concept of harm to the environment.[42] As a minimum, damage to the environment relates to claims involving reasonable measures of response and restoration,[43] including clean-up costs and compensation for damage arising from impairment of environment insofar as it resulted in loss of income directly deriving from an economic interest in any use of the environment.[44] Given contemporary concern for the environment, the Special Rapporteur is of the view that the definition of environment is best cast in broader terms in a liability regime which is general and residual to "attenuate any limitation imposed under liability regimes on the remedial responses acceptable".[45]

14. Thirdly, recognizing the value of the approach adopted by the Commission, some Governments expressed their wish to go even further to include and make admissible claims against "non-use value" of the environment. There is some support for this claim from the Commission itself: it adopted its draft articles on responsibility of States for internationally wrongful acts, even though it is admitted that such damage is difficult to quantify.[46] The recent decisions of UNCC, in opting for a broad interpretation of the term "environmental damage" are a pointer of developments to come. In the case of the F-4 category of environmental and public health claims, the UNCC F-4 Panel allowed claims for compensation for damage to natural resources without commercial value (so-called pure environmental damage) and also claims where there was only a temporary loss of resource use during the period prior to full restoration.[47] The broader definition of environment in the context of the draft principles on the allocation of loss in the case of transboundary harm arising out of hazardous activities opens possibilities for further developments of the law in the liability aspects.

---

[37] A/CN.4/549/Add.1 (see footnote 6 above), para. 61. See also statements by Mexico (*Official Records of the General Assembly, Fifty-ninth Session, Sixth Committee*, 25th meeting, para. 47) and New Zealand (*ibid*., 17th meeting, para. 89) and comments by the Netherlands (A/CN.4/562 and Add.1 (reproduced in the present volume), sect. D, p. 95).

[38] See *Yearbook ... 2004*, vol. II (Part One), document A/CN.4/540, p. 73, para. 36 (8).

[39] See A/CN.4/L.661 and Corr.1, para. 2.

[40] On the difficulties surrounding the issue of damage to the global commons, such as standing and the proper legal basis for a claim, see Charney, "Third State remedies for environmental damage to the world's common spaces", p. 150; Xue, *Transboundary Damage in International Law*, pp. 236–269; Leigh, "Liability for damage to the global commons".

[41] *Gabčíkovo-Nagymaros Project (Hungary/Slovakia), Judgment, I.C.J. Reports 1997*, pp. 77–78, para. 140. See also *Yearbook ... 2004*, vol. II (Part Two), p. 75, para. (15) of the commentary to principle 2.

[42] *Yearbook ... 2004*, vol. II (Part Two), p. 74, para. (13) of the commentary to principle 2, and footnote 400.

[43] In respect of restoration, the point is well accepted that it should aim at recreating the conditions existing prior to the occurrence of damage. Where that is not possible, costs incurred to introduce, where appropriate, elements of equivalent value are admissible (*ibid*., para. (19) of the commentary to principle 2). For sanctioning of three compensation projects (for loss of rangeland and habitats Jordan received US$ 160 million, for shoreline preserves Kuwait received US$ 8 million and Saudi Arabia US$ 46 million) by way of replacing ecological services that were irreversibly lost in the wake of the 1991 Gulf war (see UNCC, Report and recommendations made by the Panel of Commissioners concerning the fifth instalment of "F4" claims (S/AC.26/2005/10), technical annexes, cited in Sand, "Compensation for environmental damage from the 1991 Gulf war", p. 249, note 41).

[44] See *Yearbook ... 2004*, vol. II (Part Two), pp.75–76, paras. (18)–(21) of the commentary to principle 2.

[45] *Ibid*., p. 75, para. (16).

[46] See *Yearbook ... 2001*, vol. II (Part Two), p. 101, para. (15) of the commentary to article 36: "[E]nvironmental damage will often extend beyond that which can be readily quantified in terms of clean-up costs or property devaluation. Damage to such environmental values (biodiversity, amenity, etc.—sometimes referred to as 'non-use values') is, as a matter of principle, no less real and compensable than damage to property, though it may be difficult to quantify." See also Crawford, *The International Law Commission's Articles on State Responsibility: Introduction, Text and Commentaries)*, p. 223.

[47] See S/AC.26/2005/10 (footnote 43 above). See also Sand, *loc. cit.*, p. 247. Set out in five instalment reports, the awards recommended by the F-4 Panel and approved without change by the UNCC Governing Council add up to US$ 5.26 billion, "the largest amount of compensation ever awarded in the history of international environmental law" (*ibid*., p. 245). See also the UNCC Guidelines for the follow-up programme for environmental awards (S/AC.26/Dec.258 (2005), annex), also in *Environmental Policy and Law*, vol. 35, No. 6 (December 2005), pp. 276–281.

5. Multiplicity of claims

15. Multiplicity of claims may be envisaged in a number of scenarios. In one instance, claims may be filed by a plaintiff for the damage suffered in one jurisdiction, against the State of origin for failing to discharge its obligations of due diligence and against the operator for causing the transboundary damage. The two underlying assumptions are that there is failure to observe duties of due diligence on the part of the State of origin and that failure to observe duties of due diligence did not come to the notice and could not be relied upon by the affected States and individuals until damage actually occurred.[48] Normally, if such failure had been noticed before the damage occurred, representations could have been made to the State by other concerned States and natural or legal persons to press it to perform the obligations it owed to them under international law. Most of the obligations of due diligence incorporated in the draft articles on prevention of transboundary harm from hazardous activities are regarded as part of customary law[49] and non-performance of any one or more of them would preclude the State of origin from asserting that the harm did not occur for want of due diligence.[50] In such a situation, State responsibility and liability of the operator would provide a basis for the claims. To the extent that there may be claims involving the same cause of action against the State and the operator, the case of multiplicity of claims is a real possibility. While State responsibility claims could lie between States, operator liability could engage the victims of damage *qua* natural and legal persons as plaintiffs and the operator as the respondent. Whether the claims against the State should be entertained after exhausting the claims against the operator, sometimes given the limits of liability set, or as a separate and independent charge, is a matter of debate and perhaps could also be determined by the circumstances of the case.

16. Such a multiplicity of claims, however, can be handled by courts first by clubbing them, and sorting out the responsibility of the State on one hand and the liability of the operator on the other. To the extent that no direct causal link could be established between the State responsibility and the damage, the State may be required to express apology and give guarantees of performance. To the extent that there is material damage due to its non-performance, the State would have to compensate the loss suffered by the plaintiffs. As for the operator, he would be liable for the damage caused within the limits of his liability. In any case, the compensation to be received by the victims on both these accounts could not be more than the actual quantum of loss suffered by them as assessed by the courts.

17. In another scenario, multiplicity of claims arises from the fact of filing different claims for the same damage involving the same plaintiff in different jurisdictions. Here, there is a need to prevent legal action from proceeding at the same time in different jurisdictions. The 1968 Brussels Convention on jurisdiction and the enforcement of judgments in civil and commercial matters provides one set of solutions. This set of solutions has been generally endorsed in a more recently proposed 2001 draft convention on jurisdiction and foreign judgments in civil and commercial matters, submitted to the first part of the Diplomatic Conference held at The Hague.[51] While postulating priority for the jurisdiction of the Contracting Party in which the defendant is domiciled,[52] in the case of an environmental tort claim an alternative ground of jurisdiction is provided. This is the forum of the State where an act or omission causing injury took place or before the courts of the State where the damage arose.[53] Thus, the claimant is provided with a choice as to the forum which he or she deems most appropriate for him or her. The provision of such a choice is considered to be based on "a trend now firmly established in both international Conventions on international jurisdiction and in national systems".[54]

18. In the matter of choice for transboundary victims between the law of the State of origin[55] and the law of the State of the victim,[56] there is considerable support for the principle that the law that is most favourable to the victim should be applied. The "most favourable law principle", according to the authors of the second report on transnational enforcement of environmental law to the Conference of the International Law Association (Berlin, 2004), is adopted in several jurisdictions in Europe, Tunisia and Venezuela, and possibly even in China.[57] Several authors and even those who do not normally favour this principle in all transboundary tort cases favour it in transfrontier pollution matters.[58] However, United States law appears to favour the law of the place which has the "most significant relationship" with the event and the parties.[59] In

[48] If the failure to observe the obligations of due diligence by the State of origin had come to the notice of the concerned States or persons and if they did not press for the observance of those obligations within a reasonable period of time, whether State responsibility could still be engaged later at the stage of consideration of claims of compensation is a matter of doubt. There is authority to say that in such cases the individuals and the States concerned would be estopped from raising issues of State responsibility (see Okowa, *op. cit.*, pp. 169–170).

[49] See Birnie and Boyle, *International Law and the Environment*, p. 113.

[50] Okowa, *op. cit.*, p. 169.

[51] Hague Conference on Private International Law, Summary of the outcome of the discussion in Commission II of the first part of the Diplomatic Conference (6–20 June 2001), prepared by the Permanent Bureau and the Co-reporters.

[52] This is based on the principle, which promotes the policy that the defendant is best able to defend himself or itself in the courts of the State in which he or it is domiciled. This is justified on the ground that the force of a judgement is directed against the defendant. However, while the domicile of the natural person is left to be determined by the law of each State, the case of the nationality of the legal persons or the corporation is not so well defined. The 1968 Brussels Convention and the parallel 1988 Convention on jurisdiction and the enforcement of judgments in civil and commercial matters "leave the determination of the domicile to the law that is determined by the law of conflict of laws as administered by the courts of the State where the claim is filed" (Bar, "Environmental damage in private international law", p. 336).

[53] See Bernasconi and Betlem, "Transnational enforcement of environmental law", p. 900. A defence against the ground of jurisdiction is, however, admissible if it can be established that damage in the State, not being the State of origin, is not foreseeable.

[54] *Ibid.*, p. 899.

[55] *Ibid.*, p. 914. Austria, Denmark, Finland, Japan and Sweden adopt the law of the place of the dangerous activity (*lex loci actus*).

[56] *Ibid.*, France, Romania, Spain, Turkey, the United Kingdom, and most recently, the Netherlands adopted the law of the place of the damage (*lex damni*). Quebec in Canada has similar legislation.

[57] *Ibid.*, p. 911.

[58] *Ibid.*

[59] *Ibid.*, pp. 914–915. Under rule 145, paragraph (2), of the Restatement of the Law, Second, Conflict of Laws, issued in 1971, "contacts" to be taken into account are the place of damage, the place where the act that gave rise to the damage was committed, the domicile, residence, nationality, place of incorporation, and place of business of the parties, and the place where any relationship between the parties is centred.

spite of the lack of total uniformity in national laws and practice, it appears to be a sound policy to adopt the "most favourable law principle" as it has the advantage of raising the level of protection to the environment and provide some sort of incentive for the operator to engage in better maintenance of his or her installation.[60]

6. Legal status of the draft principles

19. On the legal status of the draft principles, while few States have expressed their position, some delegations favour casting the draft principles in the form of draft articles. This implies a readiness to accept some or most of the principles, at a minimum, as *de lege ferenda*, as evidence of consistent State practice. Clearly, some other delegations would like to treat the draft principles as purely aspirational.

20. There are obvious difficulties in identifying the legal status of the draft principles. First, in their very nature, authoritative assertions cannot be made convincingly that a principle is part of general international law merely on the basis that it has been adopted repeatedly by States as agreed provisions in texts of treaties. The difficulty would arise, for example, if the treaties concluded have not come into force or do not have any chance of coming into force. Even if they are in force, on the face of it and without more,[61] they could at best be treated as mere expressions of bilateral and multilateral accommodation and as such applicable only as between the parties to the treaties concerned. Hence, they cannot be regarded by themselves as giving rise to a general principle of international law.

21. In the case of customary law, the problem of showing consistent and uniform practice of States is itself very complicated, principally because of lack of agreement on what constitutes relevant practice. The burden of proving *opinio juris* accompanying such State practice is even more complicated, for States do not normally announce their intentions when they follow a certain practice. Assessment of *opinio juris* therefore involves subjective analysis at two levels: the level at which the State itself has to make a judgement before electing to follow what it perceives to be a consistent and uniform practice and the level of the decision-maker/observer, regarding whether States are indeed following that practice out of a conviction that it is mandatory and not merely because they find the practice convenient or expedient to follow. This makes the assessment of customary law with respect to any one principle that much more difficult.[62] Aside from the difficulties noted, as a matter of practice, despite its mandate under article 15 of its statute, the Commission does not normally differentiate the recommendations it adopts into those that belong to the codification of existing international law on the one hand and to the progressive development of law on the other.[63]

22. In spite of the difficulties inherent in any exercise concerning the assessment of the legal status of the draft principles, the legal value of the principles, which found repeated assertion in different national legislations and treaty formulations as evidence of a predominant trend in international law endorsing some common policy preferences, cannot be underestimated.[64] The presumption in favour of *opinio juris* is strong when States choose to repeat certain formulations while rejecting other possible formulations, when they are open to be adopted, because the formulation chosen has already found wide acceptance among States. It has been pointed out that the Commission did not shy away from codifying customary principles of the law of the sea on the basis of uniform national legislation and comments of States.[65] It has also been noted that there is legal value to the effort of the Commission when it "consolidate[s] developments in a particular area of law, making them part of the *droit acquis*".[66]

---

[60] *Ibid.*, p. 912.

[61] While acknowledging the difficulties inherent in looking at treaties as conclusive evidence of customary law, Baxter pointed out that each one of the multilateral and bilateral treaties "must be weighed in the balance with other evidence of customary law before the true rule of international law may be ascertained". According to him:

> "The task is easiest in the case of the law-declaring treaty, such as a codification treaty ... Even the draft of a treaty or a treaty which has been signed but has not yet entered into force will have its influence ... The amount of deliberation that has gone into the text, the number of participants in the process of establishing the text of the treaty, and above all, the fact that it represents, relative to the rest of the evidence of the law, a clear and uniform statement of the law commend it to non-parties. It is evidence that is *easy* to use."

(Baxter, "Treaties and custom", pp. 99–100)

[62] See Daillier and Pellet, *Droit international public*, pp. 334–336. See also Kammerhofer, "Uncertainty in the formal sources of international law: customary international law and some of its problems".

[63] See generally, Sinclair, *The International Law Commission*, p. 7. There was extensive discussion on the basic mandate of the Commission stated in article 1 of its statute: the object of promoting progressive development of (primarily public) international law and its codification. It is understood from the beginning of its work that a strict distinction between progressive development and codification cannot be maintained either for the purpose of choosing the methods of procedures of work or for formatting its final recommendations. It is even more difficult, as the experience of the Commission showed, to neatly separate its conclusions into those that belong to one category or the other. Sinclair noted that "the Commission, at a fairly early stage in its labours, more or less abandoned the attempt to maintain a clear distinction between projects involving 'progressive development' and projects involving 'codification'". Briggs (*The International Law Commission*, p. 140) pointed out that by the time of its 1956 report in "preparing its rules on the law of the sea, the Commission has become convinced that, in this domain at any rate, the distinction established in the statute between these two activities [codification and development] can hardly be maintained" (*Yearbook ... 1956*, vol. II, document A/3159, p. 255, para. 26)). See also Mahiou, "Rapport général", p. 19.

[64] A/CN.4/543 (see footnote 36 above), para. 6, makes a pertinent point in this regard: "The study has not ignored the difficulties of evaluating a particular instance as 'evidence' of State practice. Different policies may motivate the conclusion of treaties or decisions. Some may be compromises or accommodations for extraneous reasons. But repeated instances of State practice, when they follow and promote similar policies, may create expectations about the authoritativeness of those policies in future behaviour. Even though some of the policies may not have been explicitly stated in connection with the relevant events, or may purposely and explicitly have been left undecided, continuous similar behaviour may lead to the creation of a customary norm. Regardless of whether the materials examined here have been established as customary law, they demonstrate a trend in expectations and may contribute to the clarification of policies concerning some detailed principles of liability relevant to the topic. Practice also demonstrates ways in which competing principles, such as 'State sovereignty' and 'domestic jurisdiction', are to be reconciled with the new norms." See also Baxter, "Multilateral treaties as evidence of customary international law", p. 291, where he noted the legal value of the Convention on the High Seas, as a source of law for those States that had not yet become parties to it.

[65] Brownlie, *op. cit.*, p. 384. This happened according to the author in the case of the law of the sea, where the Commission relied mostly on national legislation and comments of Governments.

[66] View of Mr. James Crawford quoted in Boyle, "Globalising environmental liability: the interplay of national and international law", p. 19.

Chapter II

Review of some of the salient features of the draft principles

23. The draft principles on the allocation of loss in the case of transboundary harm arising out of hazardous activities, adopted by the Commission on first reading in 2004, are the result of careful assessments of trends concerning developments on the topic over a long period of time. The strength of the policy they represent and their legal value have been the subject of repeated discussion within the Commission and widely endorsed conclusions have provided the basis for their formulation. Some of the salient provisions have also received recognition as general rules of international law, even if that status is reserved to some of them at some high level of generality and no uniformity in State practice can yet be deduced with regard to the implementation of specific elements associated with the general concepts. At this point it may be instructive to review some of the salient features of the draft principles and their legal status in the light of State practice, judicial decisions and the views of commentators.

A. Precautionary approach or principle

24. This is, for example, the case with the "precautionary approach" adopted as principle 15 of the Rio Declaration on Environment and Development.[67] Some States treat this as a principle, whereas global agreements refer to it as precautionary measures. The difference in the use of terminology is not important, even though it is used with different nuances.[68] This is a principle or approach which States are required to respect in the implementation of their due diligence obligations, incorporated in the draft articles on prevention of transboundary harm arising out of hazardous activities, authorized to take place within the territory or under control of the State of origin. Even though it is a principle which essentially arose out of European practice,[69] as a principle or approach of prudent management of economic development and exploitation of natural resources and biodiversity consistent with environmental protection, it is embraced worldwide.[70] Its significance and legal status may be explained thus:

> Although it is still evolving, the precautionary principle appears as a standard of international law at the doctrinal level as well as in practice ... but dissent remains on either end of the spectrum [the European and the United States], considering the principle as a guideline or claiming its binding force.
>
> ...
>
> Key elements of such a regime would be following objective risk assessment procedures, defining a socially acceptable level of risk, continuing scientific research and reexamining the precautionary measures as information becomes available. The issue of burden of proof remains perhaps the most controversial aspect of the precautionary principle as reversing the burden of proof is often considered the foremost expression of the principle.
>
> ...
>
> It is important that the status of the principle as a standard is not necessarily a step on the way to the creation of a rule. The fact that a treaty makes it a rule to use precaution does not alter the nature of precaution as a standard. The reference to reasonableness in domestic law, for example, derives its force from being a standard of judgment and cannot become a hard line rule. International standards operate in a similar way. The precautionary principle will therefore gain its legal value from being refined by negotiators and interpreted by adjudicators rather than being turned into a traditional rule.[71]

25. A set of guidelines has been developed to help policymakers and decision makers to apply the precautionary principle. These guidelines urge that, while best available information, which may be obtained from multiple "independent and publicly accountable institutions without conflict of interest",[72] may be used in arriving at decisions, all social and economic costs and benefits of the application of the principle of precaution must be kept in view. As noted by a learned commentator, debate about the legal status of the principle or approach is to a certain extent too simplistic, and the reality is that judicial tribunals and policymakers are paying attention to the principle and applying it to particular contexts with significant effect.[73]

[67] *Report of the United Nations Conference on Environment and Development, Rio de Janeiro, 3–14 June 1992*, vol. I, *Resolutions Adopted by the Conference* (United Nations publication, Sales No. E.93.I.8 and corrigendum), resolution I, annex I.

[68] According to Sands, the language of principle 15 of the Rio Declaration now attracts "broad support" (*Principles of International Environmental Law*, p. 279). See also generally Sadeleer, *Environmental Principles: From Political Slogans to Legal Rules*, pp. 91–223).

[69] In fact it was an approach that was first adopted in German law: see Boehmer-Christiansen, "The precautionary principle in Germany: enabling government". Article 174, paragraph 2, of the Treaty establishing the European Community provides that Community policy on the environment "shall be based on the precautionary principle and on the principles that preventive action should be taken". It has been endorsed by the European Court of Justice in case C–180/96 R, *United Kingdom of Great Britain and Northern Ireland* v. *Commission of the European Communities*, order of the Court of 12 July 1996, *European Court Reports 1996*, p. I–3903, and in case T–76/96 R, *The National Farmers' Union and Others* v. *Commission of the European Communities*, order of the President of the Court of First Instance of 13 July 1996, *ibid.*, p. II–815. The precautionary principle has been endorsed by almost all international instruments on the environment since 1992 (see Kiss and Shelton, *International Environmental Law*, p. 207).

[70] ICJ did not pronounce on the matter in the *Gabčíkovo-Nagymaros Project* case (see footnote 41 above), even though Hungary raised it and Judge Weeramantry referred to it with approval in his dissenting opinion (see Birnie and Boyle, *op. cit.*, p. 118).

[71] Boutillon, "The precautionary principle: development of an international standard", pp. 468–469. A similar, yet not identical, view is expressed by McIntyre and Mosedale, who assert that "the precautionary principle is, therefore, a 'tool for decision-making in a situation of scientific uncertainty', which effectively 'changes the role of scientific data'" ("The precautionary principle as a norm of customary international law", p. 222). The view that the principle reflects customary law has been expressed by Sands, *op. cit.*, p. 279.

[72] IUCN, "Guidelines for applying the precautionary principle: biodiversity conservation and NRM management", a joint initiative of Fauna & Flora International, IUCN, Resource Africa and TRAFFIC, p. 274.

[73] For the application of the principle in the Indian context, see *A. P. Pollution Control Board* v. *M. V. Nayudu*, India, Supreme Court Cases (2001), No. 2, p. 62. The issue involved was whether a hazardous industry should be allowed to continue in the face of a possible contamination of underground water from the effluents of the plant. The High Court of Andhra Pradesh relied on the expert evidence of

(*Continued on next page.*)

26. Thus, the growing role of the precautionary principle in the context of application of the draft principles on the allocation of loss in the case of transboundary harm arising out of hazardous activities, during the process of occurrence of transboundary damage and after the damage has taken place, remains to be seen. It is clear that during the process of occurrence of harm, the State of origin has the duty to ensure and if necessary undertake, on its own or in cooperation with the operator and other competent organizations concerned, all appropriate response measures to mitigate the effects of harm. In this effort, the best available technology is required to be used. Wolfrum regards this as a duty directly connected with the application of the precautionary principle or approach.[74] The principle or approach, as already noted, has important implications in the context of making, and deciding on, claims for compensation or as part of remedies that should be available to victims. For example, one remedy is the suspension or closure of the activity once damage has occurred or even when threatened according to the best, but quite possibly not definitive, scientific evidence available, until it is cleared once again as environmentally sound. Accordingly, in making or deciding on the claims, particularly claims for the closure or suspension of a hazardous operation in progress, the principle of precaution appears to bear upon the standard of proof required and on reversing the burden of proof.[75]

B. Polluter pays principle: strict and limited operator's liability

27. There is a strong case to assert that, under customary international law, the operator's[76] liability for damage arising from ultrahazardous activities is strict but limited. The operator's liability gained ground for several reasons and principally on the basis of the belief that one who creates high risks seeking economic benefit must bear the burden of any adverse consequences of controlling the activity. This also came to be called in broad terms the polluter pays principle. While the polluter pays principle itself cannot be termed as having acquired the status of a general principle of international law,[77] the operator's liability for

(Footnote 73 continued.)

the industry and allowed its operation. On an appeal, the Supreme Court, having obtained scientific evidence from wider sources and independent expert bodies, reversed the High Court permission and stopped the operation of the industry, because the scientific evidence indicated a greater possibility of underground water contamination with nickel deposits being released by the effluents of the plant. The Law Commission of India noted that the precautionary principle clearly applied here and that with "more data and by application of better scientific procedures, or better technology, more accurate conclusions can always be arrived at" ("One hundred eighty sixth report on proposal to constitute environment courts" (September 2003), p. 18, available at http://lawcommissionofindia.nic.in/reports.htm).

[74] On the requirement of best available technology, Wolfrum noted that it is closely associated with the precautionary principle ("International environmental law: purposes, principles and means of ensuring compliance", p. 15). It is also suggested that the term "available" means that "states are responsible for applying only those technological advances that have already been marketed, as opposed to every new development in pollution control" (Stoll, "Transboundary pollution", p. 182).

[75] See, for an understanding of the application of the precautionary principle, Freestone, "The road from Rio: international environmental law after the Earth Summit", p. 211. For a mention of some instances of suspension, see Birnie and Boyle, *op. cit.*, p. 118. The International Tribunal for the Law of the Sea suspended further exploitation of bluefin tuna in the face of scientific uncertainty surrounding the conservation of tuna stocks pending the resolution of the dispute (see *Southern Bluefin Tuna cases (New Zealand* v. *Japan; Australia* v. *Japan), Provisional Measures, Order of 29 August 1999, ITLOS Reports 1999,* p. 280). For closure of activity, see the *A. P. Pollution Control Board* case (footnote 73 above). Sadeleer notes that the "precautionary principle should shed new light on the duty of care … and … lessen the severity of having to prove causation" (*op. cit.*, p. 212).

[76] The draft principles envisage the definition of "operator" in functional terms in functional terms, based on the factual determination of who has use, control and direction of the object at the relevant time. Such a definition is generally in conformity with notions prevailing in French law. See Reid, "Liability for dangerous activities: a comparative analysis", p. 755. More generally, it is pointed out that while "[n]o basic definition of the operator generally applied has been developed … recognition has been gained for the notion that by operator is meant one in actual, legal or economic control of the polluting activity" (Larsson, *The Law of Environmental Damage: Liability and Reparation*, p. 401). It should be clear, however, that the term operator would not include employees who work in or are in control of the activity at the relevant time. See Annex VI to the Protocol on Environmental Protection to the Antarctic Treaty: Liability Arising from Environmental Emergencies, art. 2 (*c*), which States that "'[o]perator' means any natural or juridical person, whether governmental or non-governmental, which organises activities to be carried out in the Antarctic Treaty area. An operator does not include a natural person who is an employee, contractor, subcontractor, or agent of, or who is in the service of, a natural or juridical person, whether governmental or non-governmental, which organises activities to be carried out in the Antarctic Treaty area, and does not include a juridical person that is a contractor or subcontractor acting on behalf of a State operator". The definition of "operator" employed in principle 2 (*e*) of the draft adopted by the Commission in 2004 is a functional one. For this and for an illustration of the definitions on "operator" employed in some conventions, see *Yearbook ... 2004*, vol. II (Part Two), pp. 76–77, paras. (26)–(29) of the commentary to principle 2.

[77] Wolfrum notes that: "Although the International Convention on Oil Pollution Preparedness, Response and Co-operation, 1990 and the Convention on the Transboundary Effects of Industrial Accidents both refer in their Preambles to the polluter-pays principle as being a 'general principle of international environmental law', such view is not sustained in light of the United States' practice and also in light of the uncertainties about its scope and consequences." ("International environmental law …", p. 19). See generally Sadeleer, *op. cit.*, pp. 21–60. However, the polluter pays principle has been endorsed or is being endorsed in different national jurisdictions with varying effect. The Indian Supreme Court in *Vellore Citizens Welfare Forum* v. *Union of India* (*All India Reporter 1996*, vol. 83, Supreme Court Section, p. 2715), ruled that the precautionary principle, the polluter pays principle and the new burden of proof, supported by articles 21, 47, 48A, and 51A(g) of the Constitution of India, have become part of the environmental law of the country (see report of the Law Commission of India (footnote 73 above), p. 36). Multiple provincial statutes of Canada regarding liability for environmental damage and subsequent remediation recognize the principle. In Spain, the Spanish courts have relied on the *cujus est commodum ejus debet esse incommodum* principle, that is, the person who derives a benefit from an activity must also pay for resulting damage, to impose liability on persons for damage caused by mines, waste, damage as result of loss of water, and toxic gas. In Japan, with regard to pollution caused by mining activities and marine pollution, the polluter pays to clean up the contamination to the commons and to restore the victim's property to its pre-damage state. The French legal system endorsed the polluter pays principle in various forms. In *Epoux Vullion* v. *Société Immobilière Vernet-Christophe*, JCP 1971.II.16781, France's Cour de Cassation held that "the owner's right to enjoy his property in the most absolute manner not prohibited by law or regulation is subject to his obligation not to cause damage to the property of anyone else which exceeds the normal incommodities of neighbourhood". The Swedish Environmental Code, adopted in 1998, which came into force on 1 January 1999, makes the party who is liable, to a reasonable extent, for pollution to pay for investigations of possible pollution, clean-up and mitigation of damage. The test of reasonableness is determined with reference to (*a*) the length of time elapsed since the pollution occurred; (*b*) environmental risk involved; (*c*) the operator's contribution. Ireland enacted statutes to integrate, into domestic law, international treaties imposing strict liability for oil and hazardous waste spills by ships. It is also preparing to implement European directive 2004/35/CE (see footnote 18 above), which will become effective by 2007, and which imposed strict liability and the polluter pays principle for environmental harm. Irish courts have already begun to rely upon the polluter pays principle. In Brazil, strict liability is becoming a standard for damage caused by activities which are hazardous or those that harm

ultrahazardous activities could be said to have acquired that status.[78] The case for strict liability for ultrahazardous or abnormally dangerous activities was held to be the most proper technique under both common and civil law to enable victims of dangerous and ultrahazardous activities to recover compensation without having to establish proof of fault on the basis of what is often detailed technical evidence,[79] which, in turn, would require on the part of victims a complete understanding of the complicated and complex operation or activity. The case for strict liability is strengthened when the risk has been introduced unilaterally by the defendant.[80] However, in the case of damage arising from hazardous activities, it is fair to designate strict but limited liability of the operator at the international level as a measure of progressive development of law.[81]

28. The point, however, should be made that in transforming the concept of strict liability from a domestic, national context—where it is well established but with all the differences associated with its invocation and application in different jurisdictions—into an international standard, its ingredients should be carefully defined while keeping its basic objective in view, that is, to make the person liable, without any proof of fault, for having created a risk by engaging in a dangerous or hazardous activity. Such a definition is necessary, not only to capture the most positive elements of the concept of strict liability as they are obtained in different jurisdictions, and thus to make the international standard widely acceptable, but also to ensure that the adopted standard truly serves the cause of the victims exposed to dangerous activities, thus facilitating prompt and effective remedies.

29. This can be approached in different ways,[82] for example, by adopting a proper definition of damage as has been done in the case of draft principle 1, which defines damage as damage to person, property and environment. Secondly, while designating strict liability as the standard for invoking liability, it may be specified that it is meant to include all damage foreseeable in its most generalized form and knowledge of the extent of the potential danger is not a prerequisite of liability. Further, it may be noted as part of application of the rule that it is not open to the operator to plead exemption from the liability on the ground that the use involved is a natural one and it is sufficient if the use posed a risk of harm to the others.

30. Strict liability, of course, allows some defences and international treaties, and national legislation which regulate the concept provide for a variety of exceptions.[83] However, in order to highlight the role that the polluter pays principle could play in the general scheme of the draft principles on the allocation of loss in the case of transboundary harm arising out of hazardous activities, it may be opportune to designate the minimum of such exceptions, namely, act of armed conflict, hostilities, civil war or insurrection, act of God or nature and the act of a third party—including the acts of victims (or contributory negligence).[84]

C. Notable obligations of State

31. State liability for transboundary damage for either ultrahazardous activities or hazardous activities does not appear to have support even as a measure of progressive development of law. However, a general principle of international law has clearly emerged, requiring the State to

---

or have a risk of causing harm to the environment. Intent need not be proved. Under the National Environmental Management Act (No. 107 of 1998), of South Africa, strict liability is imposed on operators who may cause, have caused or are causing significant pollution, degradation or environmental harm. Singapore provides strict liability for criminal offences and imposes obligations of clean-up on polluters without the need for any intentional or negligent behaviour.

Note: the information concerning different national laws and practice is based on memorandums on national laws prepared by the students of the environmental law class of Ms. Dinah Shelton, George Washington University Law School, Washington, D.C., for presentation to and on file with the Special Rapporteur. See also A/CN.4/543 (footnote 36 above).

[78] In A/CN.4/543, the Secretariat of the Commission, after reviewing national legislation and practice at the domestic level concerning the operation of abnormally dangerous activities or ultrahazardous activities, concluded that:

> "The above review of domestic law indicates that strict liability, as a legal concept, now appears to have been accepted by most legal systems. The extent of activities subject to strict liability may differ; in some countries it is more limited than in others. The legal basis for strict liability also varies from 'presumed fault' to the notion of 'risk', or 'dangerous activity involved', etc. However, it is evident that strict liability is a principle common to a sizeable number of countries with different legal systems which have had the common experience of having to regulate activities to which this principle is relevant. While States may differ as to the particular application of this principle, their understanding and formulation of it are substantially similar. Strict liability is also increasingly employed in legislation concerning protection of the environment."

(*Yearbook ... 2004* (see footnote 36 above), p. 111, para. 112).

[79] See Reid, *loc. cit.*, p. 756. See also A/CN.4/543 (footnote 36 above), p. 97, para. 23.

[80] See also A/CN.4/543 (footnote 36 above) for an interesting review of the concept of liability in civil and common law.

[81] Consider the hesitation exhibited by the Working Group of the Commission on international liability for injurious consequences arising out of acts not prohibited by international law in 1996 in designating damage arising from all activities covered within the scope of the draft principles subject to the regime of strict liability. It may be recalled that the Commission noted that the concepts of strict and absolute liability which "are familiar and developed in the domestic law in many States and in relation to certain [ultrahazardous] activities in international law ... have not yet been fully developed in international law, in respect to a larger group of activities such as those covered by article 1" (*Yearbook ... 1996*, vol. II (Part Two), annex I, para. (1) of the general commentary to chapter III). In arriving at this conclusion the Working Group had the benefit of the survey prepared by the Secretariat on liability regimes (*Yearbook ... 1995*, vol. II (Part One), p. 61, document A/CN.4/471).

[82] In making the following suggestions, the Special Rapporteur is guided by the helpful observations of Reid, *loc. cit.*, pp. 741–743. See also chapter I B of the useful survey of liability regimes prepared by the Secretariat (A/CN.4/543 (footnote 36 above), paras. 29–260. The Indian Supreme Court, in *M. C. Mehta and another* v. *Union of India and others*, *All India Reporter 1987*, vol. 74, Supreme Court Section, p. 1086 (the Oleum gas leak case), held that in the case of hazardous activities, exceptions which could be pleaded to avoid absolute or strict liability, such as unforeseeable damage and natural use, were not available (see the report of the Law Commission of India (footnote 73 above), p. 30).

[83] See A/CN.4/543 (footnote 36 above).

[84] Terrorist acts are included in the most recent liability instrument: Annex VI to the Protocol on Environmental Protection to the Antarctic Treaty: Liability Arising from Environmental Emergencies. Article 8, paragraph 1, of Annex VI, which deals with exemptions from liability, reads as follows:

> "An operator shall not be liable pursuant to Article 6 if it proves that the environmental emergency was caused by:
>
> (*a*) an act or omission necessary to protect human life or safety;
>
> (*b*) an event constituting in the circumstances of Antarctica a natural disaster of an exceptional character, which could not have been reasonably foreseen, either generally or in the particular case, provided all reasonable preventative measures have been taken that are designed to reduce the risk of environmental emergencies and their potential adverse impact;
>
> (*c*) an act of terrorism; or
>
> (*d*) an act of belligerency against the activities of the operator."

perform the obligation of due diligence both at the stage of authorization of hazardous activities[85] and in monitoring the activities in progress after authorization and extending into the phase when damage might actually materialize, in spite of best efforts to prevent same. ICJ, in the case concerning the *Gabčíkovo-Nagymaros Project*, noted the need, and it might be said the obligation, for continuous monitoring of hazardous activities as a result of "awareness of the vulnerability of the environment and the recognition that environmental risks have to be assessed on a continuous basis".[86]

32. These obligations in customary law carry with them some ancillary duties as well. An extension of this obligation for the purpose of the present draft principles is the duty of the State concerned to be ever vigilant and be ready to prevent the damage as far as possible, and when damage indeed takes place, to mitigate the effects of damage with the best available technology.[87] States are therefore obliged to develop, by way of response measures, necessary contingency preparedness and employ the best means at their disposal once the emergency arises, consistent with the contemporary knowledge of risks and technical, technological and financial means available to manage them. The State is also under an obligation in customary law to notify all States concerned in case of any emergency arising from the operation of the activity in question when the spread of transboundary damage is imminent or is a fact.[88] Once notified, there is also an obligation under customary law upon the States affected to take all appropriate and reasonable measures to mitigate the damage to which they are exposed.[89] It is clear that the duty of care expected of a State in this regard is the duty associated with good governance. Nevertheless, it must be borne in mind, given the wide divergence of social and economic conditions obtaining among States, as principle 11 of the Rio Declaration[90] notes so aptly, that standards applied by some countries may be inappropriate and of unwarranted economic and social cost to other countries, in particular developing countries.[91]

D. Principle of non-discrimination and minimum standards

33. The principle of non-discrimination is referred to in paragraph 3 of draft principle 6 and provides that States should ensure no less prompt, adequate and effective remedies to transboundary victims than those available to its nationals. That principle could thus be seen to be referring to both procedural and substantive requirements. The first requirement, which is essentially a procedural one, means that the State of origin should grant access to justice to the residents of the affected State on the same basis as it does for its own nationals. This is a requirement which is gaining increasing acceptance in State practice.[92] The second, the substantive aspect of the requirement of non-discrimination, on the other hand, raises more difficult issues concerning its precise content and lacks similar consensus.[93] It is suggested that as long as the same substantive level of remedies is provided to transboundary victims as that made available to nationals, the requirements of the principle should be treated as fully complied with.

---

[85] Closely associated with the duty of prior authorization is the duty to conduct an environmental impact assessment (EIA). See Xue, *op. cit.*, p. 166. Okowa notes at least five types of ancillary duties associated with the obligation to conduct an EIA. One of them is that the nature of the activity as well as its likely consequences must be clearly articulated and communicated to the States likely to be affected. However, she noted that with the exception of a few conventions, it is widely provided that the State proposing the activity is the sole determinant of the likelihood or seriousness of adverse impact. None of the treaties under consideration permit third States to propose additional or different assessments if they are dissatisfied with those put forward by the State of origin. See Okowa, "Procedural obligations in international environmental agreements", pp. 282–285. On the content of an EIA, *ibid.*, p. 282, footnote 25, and p. 286.

[86] *I.C.J. Reports 1997* (see footnote 41 above), p. 68, para. 112.

[87] *Ibid*, p. 78, para. 140. ICJ stated that it was mindful that in the field of environmental protection vigilance and prevention were required on account of the often irreversible character of damage to the environment and of the limitations inherent in the very mechanism of reparation of this type of damage. On the requirement of best available technology, see footnote 74 above.

[88] Okowa, *op. cit.*, p. 170, who thoroughly analysed the various components of the due diligence obligations, including their legal status, is very positive about the duty of the State of origin to notify all States concerned in case of an emergency situation of the dangers to which they have been exposed.

[89] In the *Gabčíkovo-Nagymaros Project* case (see footnote 41 above), in defence of variant C it implemented on the river Danube appropriating nearly 80 to 90 per cent of the water of the river, in the face of Hungary's refusal to abide by the terms of the treaty concluded between Czechoslovakia and Hungary in 1977, Slovakia argued that: "It is a general principle of international law that a party injured by the non-performance of another contract party must seek to mitigate the damage he has sustained." (*I.C.J. Reports 1997*, p. 55, para. 80). ICJ, referring to this principle, noted that "[i]t would follow from such a principle that an injured State which has failed to take the necessary measures to limit the damage sustained would not be entitled to claim compensation for that damage which could have been avoided" (*ibid.*) The Court observed that: "[W]hile this principle might thus provide a basis for the calculation of damages, it could not, on the other hand, justify an otherwise wrongful act." (*Ibid.*) It is a different matter that the Court found the implementation of variant C as a wrongful act and hence did not go further to examine the principle of the duty of the affected States to mitigate the effects of damage to which they are exposed. The very willingness of the Court to consider any failure in this regard as an important factor in the computation of damages to which those States would eventually be entitled amounts to an important recognition under general international law of the duty imposed on States affected by transboundary harm to mitigate the damage to the best extent they can.

[90] See footnote 67 above.

[91] For a note on some of the general rules of international law applicable to the discharge of the duties of due diligence, see Stoll, *loc. cit.*, pp. 180–183, and for the need to apply the standard of due diligence with due regard for the economic and social factors affecting States, pp. 181–182. For a suggestion that "[i]f the State community wishes to enhance the technology used, there is the possibility of doing so by transferring the appropriate conservation or preventive technology to the States which have no access thereto for economic or other reasons", see Wolfrum, "International environmental law …", pp. 15–16.

[92] See Kiss and Shelton, *op. cit.*, pp. 201–203, and Birnie and Boyle, *op. cit.*, pp. 269–270. According to the procedural aspect of non-discrimination, some requirements of the procedural laws of the State of origin should be removed; among them are, as Cuperus and Boyle note, "security for costs from foreign plaintiffs, the denial of legal aid to such plaintiffs, and the rule found in various forms in certain jurisdictions that deny jurisdiction over actions involving foreign land" ("Articles on private law remedies for transboundary damage in international watercourses", p. 408).

[93] Birnie and Boyle note that insofar as it is possible to review State practice on such a disparate topic as equal access, it is not easy to point to any clear picture (*op. cit.*, pp. 271–274). On the limitations of the non-discrimination rule, *ibid*, pp. 274–275. See also Xue, *op. cit.*, pp. 106–107. See further Kiss and Shelton, *op. cit.*, pp. 201–203; Birnie and Boyle, *op. cit.*, pp. 269–270; and Dupuy, "La contribution du principe de non-discrimination à l'élaboration du droit international de l'environnement". For the view that the principle of non-discrimination has become a principle of general international law, see Smets, "Le principe de non-discrimination en matière de protection de l'environnement".

34. Viewed thus, as paragraph (7) of the commentary to draft principle 6 notes, "[f]or all its disadvantages, in providing access to information, and in ensuring appropriate cooperation between relevant courts and national authorities across national boundaries, the principle does go beyond the requirement that States meet a minimum standard of effectiveness in the availability of remedies for transboundary claimants".[94] As the same commentary notes, the disadvantage remains that principle 6, paragraph 3, does not, and given the economy of the draft, cannot "alleviate or resolve problems concerning choice of law", which are a significant factor and at the moment an "obstacle" to the delivery of "prompt, adequate and effective judicial recourse and remedies to victims".[95] States, with the assistance of the appropriate professional bodies, must continue to strive both bilaterally and multilaterally to alleviate these problems.

35. In some regions, the content of minimum standards is continually being improved. However, to achieve such minimum standards at the global level there has to be a greater economic, social and political integration of values among different States and across regions in the world.[96] Thus, while absolute equality cannot be ensured in all jurisdictions by way of global common minimum standards, it should still be possible to suggest that the principle of non-discrimination does assume that suitable remedies and adequate compensation would be available to nationals in the first instance in case of any damage arising from hazardous activities and that the same remedies and levels of compensation would be available to the transboundary victims as well.

E. Ensuring prompt and adequate compensation

36. Draft principle 3 refers to prompt and adequate compensation as the main objective of the draft principles. The standard of promptness and adequacy, which is observed to be the most significant contribution of the scheme adopted by the Commission in 2004, is a standard that has support in the *Trail Smelter* case,[97] principle 10 of the Rio Declaration[98], article 235, paragraph 2, of the United Nations Convention on the Law of the Sea, article 2, paragraph (1), of the draft articles on remedies for transboundary damage in international watercourses, prepared by the International Law Association in 1996,[99] and in human rights law precedents.[100]

37. In this connection, it should be clarified that "promptness" refers to the procedures that would govern access to justice and rendering necessary decisions in accordance with the law of the land determining the compensation payable in a given case. This is also a necessary criterion to be emphasized in view of the fact that litigation in domestic courts involving claims of compensation could be costly and protracted over several years. To render access to justice more widespread, efficient and prompt, suggestions have been made to establish special national or international environmental courts.[101] On the other hand, "adequate" compensation could refer to any number of things.[102] For example, the lump-sum amount of compensation agreed upon as a result of negotiations between the operator or the State of origin and the victims or other States concerned following the consolidation of claims of all the victims of harm is an adequate compensation. Compensation awarded by a court as a result of the litigation entertained in its jurisdiction is adequate as long as the requirement of due process of law is met. In any case, as long as compensation awarded is not arbitrary or grossly disproportionate to the damage actually suffered, even if less than full it can be regarded as adequate. In other words, adequacy is not intended to denote "sufficiency".

---

[94] *Yearbook ... 2004*, vol. II (Part Two), p. 88.

[95] *Ibid.*, para. (8) of the commentary to principle 6.

[96] Xue , *op. cit.*, makes the point well when she notes first that "[d]amage recovery is not a matter merely concerning judicial justice, but an economic issue requiring resource allocation" (p. 107), and secondly, that "[e]ven within an ecological system, where each and every portion of the resources is physically interrelated, national boundaries cannot simply be overlooked, since different political, economic, and social systems exist within them" (p. 108).

[97] UNRIAA, vol. III (Sales No. 1949.V.2), p. 1905.

[98] See footnote 67 above.

[99] Cuperus and Boyle, *loc. cit.*, p. 405.

[100] For helpful guidance on the strength of the principle of prompt and adequate compensation, see Boyle, *loc. cit.*, p. 18.

[101] See Rest, "Need for an international court for the environment? Underdeveloped legal protection for the individual in transnational litigation". At the national level, the Law Commission of India made a very persuasive case for the establishment of national environmental courts in India (see footnote 73 above). Access to justice, particularly in environmental matters, is an essential facet of article 21 of the Constitution of India. Australia and New Zealand already have environmental courts.

[102] For an exhaustive enumeration of the implementation of the principle of prompt, adequate and effective compensation in practice, see Lefeber, *op. cit.*, pp. 229–311.

Chapter III

Final form of the draft principles

38. It must first be observed that, although the projects on prevention and on allocation of loss in case of damage (including liability) were conceived originally as integral, they have actually proceeded substantively at two different levels. The draft articles on prevention of transboundary harm for hazardous activities were developed with a wide consensus on the content, which received ever growing acceptance in State practice and even more importantly, recognition in judicial decisions around the world. On the other hand, the draft principles on the allocation of loss in the case of transboundary harm arising out of hazardous activities are built upon some general principles on which wide consensus exists. For example, the basic objective of the draft principles, the obligation to provide prompt and adequate compensation to victims of transboundary damage, is well accepted in State practice and national judicial decisions, and some commentators treat it as a general principle of international law. Accordingly, at least one commentator suggested that the Commission should consider changing the language in draft principle 4, paragraph 1 and draft principle 6, paragraphs 1 and 3, from a mere recommendatory form to a more prescriptive one by replacing the word "should" with

the word "shall" if the progress of the Commission on this important subject is not to be reduced to a mere "illusion".[103]

39. However, concerning the complex of associated obligations which are equally important for giving full effect to the basic obligation, it appears time is needed for them to gain judicial recognition and affirmation in State practice. The obligations of conduct and the due diligence obligations which the draft principles suggest that the State should bear to give full effect to the principle of prompt and adequate compensation to the victims of transboundary damage arising out of hazardous activities, in contrast to the obligations of due diligence imposed upon the State in the context of prevention, require greater and more uniform acceptance in the practice of States. They also await confirmation by judicial decisions around the world, as these are still few and far between. By way of illustration the following principles may be referred to in this regard: the obligation of a State to arrange for a wider net of funds, including the obligation to participate in such a fund to meet the claims of compensation when they cannot be met by the operator either because of the limited liability accepted in the law of the land or of insolvency; the obligation of a State to ensure, and the obligation of the operator to obtain, adequate levels of insurance cover for the risk-bearing hazardous operation;[104] the duty of a State to install a level of contingency preparedness and to possess a technical and economic capacity proportional to the risk of the operation; and the further duties of a State not only to monitor technologically complex operations, but also to institute effective response measures in case of an incident; and the duty to move beyond the basic principle of non-discrimination and provide for administrative and judicial remedies and compensation consistent with certain minimum standards on which there is not yet any sufficient clarity or consensus.

40. It is not difficult to see why the international consensus is slow in coming. There are differences in legal systems and among the practices of States even when they have similar legal systems. The difficulties inherent in any exercise of harmonization at the global level are also obvious. Political realities, priorities of development and the resource constraints of developing countries are other factors. These points are borne out by a survey of the legal status of the principles noted above and in the previous reports and as part of conclusions reached by the Special Rapporteur in his second report on the legal regime for the allocation of loss in case of transboundary harm arising out of hazardous activities.[105]

41. It may also be recalled that in the past the Commission discussed the matter of the form in which the end product of the present subject matter could be adopted. While one suggestion was to adopt it in the form of a "framework arrangement" without drafting primary rules, another suggestion was to adopt it as guidelines to assist States in giving more positive content to the basic duty of cooperation. "In the event", notes Sinclair, "no final decision was taken on the form of eventual end-product, although it emerges from the debate that the topic might not yield to the treatment the Commission usually applies to the drafting of articles for eventual incorporation in a convention".[106]

42. There is value in couching the entire end product in a more prescriptive form, only if it is possible and feasible.[107] Equally, it cannot be denied that there is value in casting the end product in the form of draft principles when that is the best course available for lack of a better alternative.[108] The commentary to the draft principles noted this when it stated that:

> On balance, the Commission concluded that the draft principles would have the advantage of not requiring a potentially unachievable harmonization of national laws and legal systems. It is also of the view that the goal of widespread acceptance of the substantive provisions is more likely to be met if they are cast as recommended draft principles.[109]

43. Such widespread consensus and the inherent merits of the principles themselves would have utility for judges and statesmen to give them effect in the domestic and international arena. This might pave the way for eventual codification of international law on the subject by international agreement.

44. Given this reality, it seems appropriate, in the view of the Special Rapporteur, to confirm that the end product of the topic on allocation of loss be cast in the form of draft principles. However, the Commission may give some serious consideration to reflecting the basic obligation on the duty to pay compensation and the right to seek remedies in language that is more prescriptive.

---

[103] Boyle, *loc. cit.*, p. 19.

[104] In the context of the European Union negotiations on the liability for environment, it is said that agreement on the directive was reached after nearly 15 years, and one of the last issues holding up the agreement was the issue concerning insurance. The compromise was to make the requirement of insurance optional and not mandatory (see "EU agrees to make polluters pay for environmental damage", *Agence France Presse* (21 February 2004), cited in the Swedish national law memorandum prepared by students of the George Washington University Law School (see footnote 77 above), p. 17, on file with the Special Rapporteur.

[105] *Yearbook ... 2004*, vol. II (Part One), document A/CN.4/540, p. 75, para. 36, conclusion (10).

[106] Sinclair, *op. cit.*, p. 38.

[107] It is stated that: "Concrete obligations (actions and specific measures) tend to be more stringent and rigorous, and monitoring of compliance with concrete obligations is *ceteris paribus* considerably easier than doing it with regard to other categories of obligations. In addition, concrete obligations have a potential for preventing disputes, especially if obligations are at the same time implicitly or automatically constituting direct rights for Parties, such as obligations relating to transboundary activities (*e.g.*, the 1998 Rotterdam Convention on the Prior Informed Consent Procedure for Hazardous Chemicals and Pesticides in International Trade (PIC Convention) and the [Cartagena Protocol on Biosafety] CPB)" (Koester, "Global environmental agreements: drafting, formulation and character", p. 170). However, most multilateral environmental agreements are a good example of "the art of the possible", because they are adopted by consensus. The process has been described as a strong tendency to seek the "lowest common denominator", and "in even more pessimistic ways". But the fact is "that countries desire to become parties and therefore promote provisions with which they will be able to comply, assessing to that end not only to what extent, for example, amendments of national legislation are needed, but also to what extent they are feasible, their economic consequences, etc. Considerations like this can hardly be criticised" (*ibid.*).

[108] "[I]t has been observed that 'soft' law instruments provide for many advantages such as willingness to adopt clear (and ambitious) commitments, which are more effective because they are more easily translated into specific actions and more readily reviewed and evaluated. Research has also demonstrated that the influence of 'soft' law instruments on behaviour can be very positive, and that the 'benefits of non-binding instruments due to several reasons often [are] most evident when applied in tandem with legally binding measures'. So 'soft' law instruments can be a means to further effectiveness.

Furthermore, such instruments can improve compliance and serve as tools for preventing disputes to the extent they provide clarity about the detailed and precise content of commitments under the treaty." (*Ibid.*, p. 174)

[109] *Yearbook ... 2004*, vol. II (Part Two), p. 68, para. (14) of the general commentary.

Chapter IV

Relationship between the draft principles and the draft articles on prevention

45. The question then arises as to the relationship between the draft articles on prevention of transboundary harm from hazardous activities, which are awaiting further action in the General Assembly, and the draft principles on the allocation of loss in the case of transboundary harm arising out of hazardous activities. It is suggested that it may be feasible for the General Assembly to adopt the draft articles on prevention. Indeed, in 2001 the Commission recommended to the General Assembly the elaboration by the Assembly of a convention on the basis of the draft articles on prevention. As appropriate, this may be done in a review within a working group of the Sixth Committee. Such a review may consider including some elements of liability in the draft articles on prevention in the form of a draft article on liability to endorse the obligation of States to ensure effective judicial access and remedies and prompt and adequate compensation to victims of transboundary damage. The same draft article could note that this basic obligation should be achieved keeping in view the draft principles on allocation of loss which the Commission may wish to finalize in the second and final reading. These draft principles could be annexed in a separate part of any accompanying resolution.

46. The other possibility is to treat the prevention and liability aspects, although interrelated, entirely separately. Two separate resolutions may be adopted by the General Assembly, endorsing and adopting the draft articles on prevention of transboundary harm from hazardous activities on the one hand, and draft principles on the allocation of loss in the case of transboundary harm arising out of hazardous activities on the other. The Commission could suggest these possibilities to the Assembly. Eventually, this is essentially a matter for the Assembly to decide after due consideration of the matter.

DOCUMENT A/CN.4/562 and Add.1

Comments and observations received from Governments

[Original: Arabic, English, French, Russian, Spanish]
[27 January and 12 April 2006]

CONTENTS

Multilateral instruments cited in the present report

	Source
Vienna Convention on civil liability for nuclear damage (Vienna, 21 May 1963)	United Nations, *Treaty Series*, vol. 1063, No. 16197, p. 265.
Convention on international liability for damage caused by space objects (London, Moscow and Washington, D.C., 29 March 1972)	*Ibid.*, vol. 961, No. 13810, p. 187.
United Nations Convention on the Law of the Sea (Montego Bay, 10 December 1982)	*Ibid.*, vol. 1833, No. 31363, p. 3.
Basel Convention on the control of transboundary movements of hazardous wastes and their disposal (Basel, 22 March 1989)	*Ibid.*, vol. 1673, No. 28911, p. 57.
Protocol on liability and compensation for damage resulting from the transboundary movements of hazardous wastes and their disposal (Basel, 10 December 1999)	UNEP/CHW.5/29, annex III.
Convention on the Protection and Use of Transboundary Watercourses and International Lakes (Helsinki, 17 March 1992)	United Nations, *Treaty Series*, vol. 1936, No. 33207, p. 269.
Protocol on Civil Liability and Compensation for Damage Caused by the Transboundary Effects of Industrial Accidents on Transboundary Waters to the 1992 Convention on the Protection and Use of Transboundary Watercourses and International Lakes and to the 1992 Convention on the Transboundary Effects of Industrial Accidents (Kiev, 21 May 2003)	ECE/MP.WAT/11–ECE/CP.TEIA/9.
Convention on Civil Liability for Damage Resulting from Activities Dangerous to the Environment (Lugano, 21 June 1993)	Council of Europe, *European Treaty Series*, No. 150. See also ILM, vol. XXXII (1993), p. 1230.
Convention on the Law of the Non-navigational Uses of International Watercourses (New York, 21 May 1997)	*Official Records of the General Assembly, Fifty-first Session, Supplement No. 49*, vol. III, resolution 51/229, annex.
Annex VI to the Protocol on Environmental Protection to the Antarctic Treaty: Liability Arising from Environmental Emergencies (Stockholm, 17 June 2005)	Antartic Treaty Consultative Meeting, Final Report of the Twenty-Eighth Meeting, chap. II A, p. 63. See also ILM, vol. 45 (2006), p. 5.

Introduction

1. At its fifty-sixth session, in 2004, the International Law Commission adopted, on first reading, draft principles on the allocation of loss in the case of transboundary harm arising out of hazardous activities.[1] In paragraphs 29–30 of the report, the Commission stated that it would welcome comments and observations from Governments on all aspects of the draft principles and the commentaries to those principles, including in particular on the final form. In paragraph 173 of its report, the Commission decided, in accordance with articles 16 and 21 of its statute, to request the Secretary-General to transmit the draft principles to Governments for comments and observations, requesting also that such comments and observations be submitted to the Secretary-General by 1 January 2006. The Secretary-General transmitted a circular note to that effect on 24 October 2004. In paragraph 3 of its resolutions 59/41 of 2 December 2004 and 60/22 of 23 November 2005, the General Assembly drew the attention of Governments to the importance, for the Commission, of having their views on the draft principles.

2. As at 12 April 2006, replies had been received from the following States: the Czech Republic, Lebanon, Mexico, the Netherlands, Pakistan, the Syrian Arab Republic, the United Kingdom of Great Britain and Northern Ireland, the United States of America and Uzbekistan. The replies have been organized thematically, starting with general comments and continuing on a principle-by-principle basis.

[1] *Yearbook ... 2004*, vol. II (Part Two), pp. 65 *et seq.*, para. 175.

Comments and observations received from Governments

A. *General comments*

Czech Republic

The draft principles on the allocation of loss in the case of transboundary harm arising out of hazardous activities are a promising tool for the progressive development of international law. However, according to the Czech Republic the present version poses some problems. Of course, other problems may yet arise as the text of the instrument develops towards its final version. The Czech Republic would like to take a closer look at the following three issues, which are discussed further below, with respect to principles 2, 3, 4 and 6: (*a*) the broad definition of "damage", including damage caused to the environment in principle 2; (*b*) the proposed solution for "prompt and adequate compensation" in principles 3–4; and (*c*) the proposed solution for "international and domestic remedies" in principle 6.

Lebanon[2]

The Commission, meeting at the United Nations Office at Geneva at its fifty-sixth session in 2004, was composed of 34 experts in international law representing the world's various continents. Lebanon did not, in fact, find the text of the draft principles on the allocation of loss in the case of transboundary harm arising out of hazardous activities to contain anything contrary to the laws and regulations on which Lebanon is founded.

Mexico

1. Mexico attaches great importance to the topic. The Commission's efforts will result in the strengthening of existing rules on international environmental damage, to which States committed themselves in the Rio Declaration on Environment and Development.[3]

2. With regard to the substance of the draft in question, Mexico wishes to make the following comments:

(*a*) In general, Mexico agrees with the substantive aspects of the draft. With respect to its scope, Mexico agrees that a regime of a general and residual character should be established;

(*b*) Mexico agrees with the Commission that the type of liability that would arise out of environmental damage under the draft principles should be strict liability rather than absolute liability;

(*c*) Mexico firmly believes that the crux of the Commission's work on this subject is the principle that an innocent victim should not be left to bear loss as a result of transboundary harm. Mexico welcomes the fact that the Commission's work is directed towards a regime that provides for prompt and adequate compensation for innocent victims. As the Commission itself points out, this approach is consistent with principles 13 and 16 of the Rio Declaration.

Netherlands

1. The Netherlands would observe that the introduction of the draft principles by the Commission promotes an important new idea in international law, namely the existence of an obligation on States to regulate compensation in the event of transboundary harm arising from hazardous activities that are not in themselves unlawful. Examples include both large-scale industrial activity that is directly hazardous (toxic discharges and the like) and activities such as those creating air pollution that can in

[2] The preambular parts of the response prepared by the Legislative and Consultation Panel of the Ministry of Justice of Lebanon, which substantially reproduced the text of the eight draft principles, have been omitted and are available for consultation in the Codification Division of the Office of Legal Affairs.

[3] *Report of the United Nations Conference on Environment and Development, Rio de Janeiro, 3–14 June 1992*, vol. I, *Resolutions Adopted by the Conference* (United Nations publication, Sales No. E.93.I.8 and corrigendum), resolution 1, annex I.

the long term cause harm across a State's boundaries. Moreover, the principles stipulate not only that States are liable to pay compensation to one another, but they also explicitly recognize the right of individual victims to claim compensation, although individuals are not granted specific legal remedies.

2. The principles represent an extension of the classical rules of State responsibility in which responsibility must always be based on a wrongful act. If a victim cannot prove that the harm suffered arose from a wrongful act, there can be no question of compensation (*ubi jus, ibi remedium*: only the violation of a right creates entitlement to a remedy). The principles, however, no longer apply this doctrine absolutely. The harmful activities are not wrongful and need not be prohibited by law. However, against this right to perform what are often economically significant hazardous activities, the principles place the obligation on States—individually and collectively—to ensure "prompt and adequate" compensation for damage caused.

3. The Netherlands concludes that the principles constitute a significant contribution to the development of international law, because they include such progressive elements as the recognition that there are hazardous activities which are not unlawful, but which impose a responsibility on States which undertake and/or permit them. Given the continuing increase in—and the economic significance of—such activities, the importance to society of the growing acceptance of that principle speaks for itself. In this way, States can be made more conscious of their responsibilities in regard to hazardous activities—enacting legislation, monitoring compliance, punishing non-compliance and so on—and more compensation can be provided for victims, while economic development driven by the activity in question still remains possible.

4. Another positive factor is that the Commission argues that victims of transboundary damage should be compensated as far as possible and that States have, and should accept, a responsibility to do so.

5. Given the position taken by States, the Netherlands is pleasantly surprised that such an agreement on the principles could be reached within the Commission, although it still takes the view that a remedy should be available to individual victims. The Netherlands would also observe that the commentary contained in the Commission's report[4] really goes no further than annotating the principles.

Pakistan

1. The draft principles are very general and potentially have a very wide scope. An example of this is the "significant" threshold in draft principles 1–2. In addition, very broad definitions of "damage" and "environment" have been given in draft principle 2. It is therefore felt that there is dire need to re-examine the draft principles with an aim to define different aspects clearly and to be more specific.

2. The draft principles are basically designed for hazardous activities, but at no stage have the hazardous activities been specified, nor have any examples been elaborated in the commentaries provided, except nuclear fallout. It is therefore felt that there is a need to define the list of activities that fall under this law. In addition, transboundary harm caused to a neutral State in case of war between two or more States has not been touched upon in the draft principles. Therefore, it is suggested that the scope of "liability" be broadened and that the States responsible for such activity be included.

3. Any hazardous activity caused by terrorist activity could be included in the principles. Transboundary damage caused by any benign activity, such as the storage of water in dams, could also be covered in the draft principles.

4. Damage or loss caused by hazardous activities should be compensated by the "operator" and not by the State in which he or she operates. Therefore, alternative B concerning principle 4 (Prompt and adequate compensation), as proposed by the Special Rapporteur, is supported.[5]

5. International judicial legislation is required in the case of a dispute which arises between operators and States and which may be a part of the principles. To address such cases, an international compensatory authority could be established to provide efficient compensation to victims.

6. There should be a monitoring set-up to measure and study pollution generated by different countries. The data should conform with international quality and standards.

7. A third-party institution could be provided for arbitration, as the draft principles do not address situations in which the operator or entity fails or refuses to pay compensation to the victims.

8. Safeguards could be provided for lower riparian States to protect them from transboundary hazardous activities through river system flows from neighbouring States. The risk of significant transboundary harm from their physical consequences should not be ignored.

9. Likewise, an increased level of greenhouse and other hazardous gases attributed to enhanced industrial activities in neighbouring countries or to pollution of the sea in coastal areas owing to shipping activities would need a stronger and more effective national and international legal framework for compensation for the damages emanating therefrom, not otherwise prohibited by extant international laws.

Syrian Arab Republic

1. Owing to the need to establish the legislative, administrative and regulative measures necessary to implement such principles, draft principles 4–8 should be clearer and should be reformulated.

[4] *Yearbook ... 2004*, vol. II (Part Two), pp. 66 *et seq*., para 176.

[5] See *Yearbook ... 2004*, vol. II (Part Two), pp. 63–64, footnote 351.

2. Research in the field of treaties recognizes the need for measures to implement the principles. However, it is also recognized that national legislatures are the bodies entitled to enact such measures.

United Kingdom of Great Britain and Northern Ireland

1. The United Kingdom commends the Commission and its Special Rapporteur for their work on the draft principles on the allocation of loss in the case of transboundary harm arising out of hazardous activities.

2. The United Kingdom notes that the Commission has provisionally reached the conclusion that the draft principles should be adopted in a non-binding form. The United Kingdom firmly takes the same view. As the Commission has observed, the generality and the residual nature of the draft principles suggest that they are not suitable for codification or progressive development in the form of a legally binding instrument. The United Kingdom also considers that there are a number of respects elaborated below in which the draft principles do not represent the current state of the law and which the United Kingdom considers are too broadly stated to constitute a desirable direction for the *lex ferenda.*

3. The United Kingdom notes that the draft principles, though addressed to States at the international level, are primarily concerned with the provision of civil remedies in their own national legal systems in respect of the victims of transboundary harm from hazardous activities. The premise of the commentary, which the United Kingdom would support, appears to be that as the draft principles are not legally binding and concern the development of civil liability at the national level, their contravention would not give rise to State responsibility.

4. Nevertheless, the commentary does suggest that where a State is in breach of its obligations concerning the prevention of harm, there may be a claim under the international law of State responsibility "in addition to" claims for compensation envisaged by the draft principles. The United Kingdom would therefore request that the Commission consider a little further what relationship there may be between claims for State responsibility in respect of obligations of prevention and civil claims envisaged by the draft principles. For example, it may be helpful to consider how overlapping claims might be coordinated so as to ensure that double recovery is not possible.

United States of America

1. Recalling that the draft principles are distinct from and without prejudice to the work of the Commission on the topic of State responsibility in that they address the question of "liability" in instances where harm results from an act or omission that involves no violation of an international law duty, the United States wishes to state clearly that, in its view, the draft principles are clearly innovative and aspirational in character and not descriptive of current law or State practice.

2. That said, the Commission has crafted a framework that might help guide States in the circumstances the Commission identifies in the report of its fifty-sixth session. Specifically, the report of the Commission states that the principles are "intended to contribute to the further development of international law in this field *both by providing appropriate guidance to States in respect of hazardous activities not covered by specific agreements and by indicating the matters that should be dealt with in such agreements**".[6]

3. With respect to the matter of guidance related to hazardous activities not covered by international agreements, the United States wishes to note a number of aspects of the Commission's draft principles that may bear particular consideration by States in specific contexts: (*a*) the principles carefully address their scope of application, that is, the scope is limited to specific activities involving a risk of causing significant transboundary harm through their physical consequences and to damage caused in the territory or other places under the jurisdiction or control of States; (*b*) the principles do not presuppose that it is only the "operator" of an activity who should be liable in any given context; and (*c*) the principles recognize that there might be specific conditions, limitations or exceptions to liability.

4. With respect to indicating the matters that should be dealt with in international agreements relating to hazardous activities, the United States believes that the Commission's work is helpful in highlighting many of the important questions that must be addressed by States involved in crafting any specific liability regime related to hazardous activities, for example: (*a*) what type of damage can be compensated? Direct economic damages to plaintiffs only? Environmental damages? (*b*) is there a particular threshold at which damage entails liability, for example, significant damage or exceptional damage? (*c*) what types of remedies should be available? (*d*) will there be a financial limit on liability? (*e*) how will causation be established? (*f*) who is liable under the regime? Private operators? Private persons other than operators? States? (*g*) what is the standard for liability: absolute, strict, other? (*h*) what defences are available in the case of strict and fault-based regimes: armed conflict, act of nature, compliance with public permit? (*i*) what is the forum for liability claims? (*j*) is the liability regime exclusive, default, supplemental? and (*k*) will the regime apply retroactively or prospectively only? If prospectively, is this from the date of the act or omission or the date when damage becomes known?

Uzbekistan

1. There has long been a need to develop and adopt a single international convention of the United Nations on the international liability of States for harm arising out of hazardous activities.

2. The draft principles have been discussed by the international community at length. Uzbekistan believes that the principles treat transboundary harm in a sufficiently fair manner, address the issue of compensation and provide local remedies for victims. Nevertheless, Uzbekistan believes that it would make sense to incorporate in principle 4, on prompt and adequate compensation, alternative B proposed by the Special Rapporteur,[7] as it imposes

[6] *Yearbook ... 2004*, vol. II (Part Two), p. 67, para. (6) of the general commentary.

[7] See *Yearbook ... 2004*, vol. II (Part Two), pp. 63–64, footnote 351.

a large share of liability on the operator of the hazardous activity rather than on the State. Other rules are more easily specified in bilateral or regional agreements.

3. It is necessary to define in the draft principles which body will assess the transboundary harm and which currency will be used, taking into account that each State has a different national currency.

B. Preamble

Netherlands

1. In the opinion of the Netherlands, the core of the principles can be found in the fifth preambular paragraph: "prompt and adequate compensation" must be provided as far as possible for victims of incidents that cause transboundary harm or loss. With respect to judicial proceedings, the Netherlands observes that provision should be made for the possibility that States could be held liable as operators (see the Vienna Convention on civil liability for nuclear damage).

2. The fifth preambular paragraph uses the qualifying phrase "as far as possible", a limitation that does not appear anywhere else in the principles. The Netherlands takes the view that this phrase should be deleted.

C. Principle 1—Scope of application

Netherlands

1. The Netherlands observes that the use of the adjective "significant" to qualify "transboundary harm" raises the threshold for applying the principles (see also principle 2). The Netherlands is aware that the word "significant" appears in the draft articles on prevention of transboundary harm from hazardous activities.[8] However, the obligations in the principles should not be equated with those in the draft articles. The latter apply between States only, whereas the principles are concerned with providing a remedy for individual victims as well.

2. In this connection, the Netherlands refers to the Vienna Convention on civil liability for nuclear damage. For the allocation of loss, that Convention does not require the harm incurred to be significant. This is related to the concept of strict liability used in the Convention. Nor do other liability regimes apply a similar threshold. It is true that the Convention on Civil Liability for Damage Resulting from Activities Dangerous to the Environment refers to "tolerable levels"[9] of environmental impact, and Annex VI to the Protocol on Environmental Protection to the Antarctic Treaty limits liability in the event of response action to environmental emergencies, but neither represents a typical form of civil liability.

3. The Netherlands is of the opinion that the non-discrimination principle does not allow for any difference in the treatment of foreign and domestic victims of harm caused by the same activity: the aim of the principles is to ensure that, while foreign victims do not have to show that they suffered significant damage and are compensated only for such damage, victims within the State's boundaries are not subject to the same burden of proof and are compensated for all the harm suffered.

4. The Netherlands further observes that any assessment of whether harm is "significant" is time-related and hence restrictive when it comes to the right to compensation. Harm suffered in the past might well have been acceptable according to the views prevailing at the time or might not even have been noticed. However, advances in understanding, for example of environmental impacts, may reveal later that the harm was indeed significant. Nonetheless, compensation can be paid only if, according to the current state of scientific knowledge, it can be predicted that significant harm could be caused by the hazardous activity in question. With respect to the "significant" threshold, it should also be noted that activities will generally be hazardous each time they are performed. However, a hazard may also lie concealed in the repetition of activities, each of which is individually acceptable but which can cumulatively cause significant harm. It becomes even more difficult to recover compensation for harm that does not come to light until much later, because shorter limitation periods are often applied in respect of strict liability than in respect of general liability.

5. The Netherlands concludes that the restriction implicit in "significant" makes it all the more important for the principle of non-discrimination enshrined in principle 8, paragraph 2, to be given greater prominence and to be moved up the list of principles.

United Kingdom of Great Britain and Northern Ireland

1. Draft principle 1 sets out in very broad terms the scope of application of the draft principles. The key elements appear to be that there is (*a*) transboundary damage; (*b*) caused by activities not prohibited by international law; (*c*) which involve a risk of causing significant transboundary harm. The United Kingdom considers that the first element (transboundary damage) should be more precisely correlative to the third element; that is, that the damage which occurs should be of the same nature as the risks adverted to in the third element; that is, that it should be foreseeable.

2. The United Kingdom notes that the draft principles are applicable in cases where the transboundary damage reaches the threshold of "significant" harm. While it recognizes that this threshold has been adopted in certain other agreements (including, for example, the Convention on the Law of the Non-navigational Uses of International Watercourses (General Assembly resolution 51/229 of 21 May 1997)), the United Kingdom notes that there is still relatively little practice in which it has been given further definition. The United Kingdom has some concern that, in the context of such a potentially broadly applicable regime as the present draft principles, the threshold of significant harm may be too vague a standard and may run the danger of setting the threshold too low. The United Kingdom would ask the Commission to consider further whether a clearer and higher threshold, such as "serious" harm, would be more appropriate.

---

[8] See *Yearbook ... 2001*, vol. II (Part Two), p. 146, para. 97.

[9] Art. 8 (*d*).

D. *Principle 2—Use of terms*

Czech Republic

1. Draft principle 2 defines "damage" as "significant damage caused to persons, property or the environment". The definition is very broad as it includes the following, according to the draft:

(i) Loss of life or personal injury;

(ii) Loss of, or damage to, property, including property which forms part of the cultural heritage;

(iii) Loss or damage by impairment of the environment;

(iv) The costs of reasonable measures of reinstatement of the property, or environment, including natural resources;

(v) The costs of reasonable response measures.[10]

2. It should be admitted, and the Commission does so, that there have been hesitations as to whether to accept liability for damage caused to the environment *per se* in cases where no damage is caused to persons or property. The Commission eventually noted that the situation was changing continuously and apparently opted for the path of progressive development of law. It noted that, in the case of damage caused to natural resources or to the environment, there existed a right to compensation for the cost of reasonable prevention, restoration and reinstatement measures (of course, the question remains which measures can be called "reasonable"). Such progressive development towards broader definition of compensable damage should not be *a priori* rejected. The risk of abuse might arise only in connection with substantive and procedural conditions of compensation.[11]

Mexico

Mexico recognizes the Commission's wisdom in including the concept of damage to the environment *per se*. This underlines the importance of environmental protection for the international community at all times, with an emphasis on allocating liability for the damage caused and for the consequences of it. It is true that assessing the cost of environmental damage presents difficulties, and Mexico therefore suggests that the Commission should encourage States, in commenting on the draft principles, to explore this question further, including the concept of non-use value.

Netherlands

1. In the interests of better protection of victims, the Netherlands supports the fairly wide definition of "damage" used in principle 2, including not only personal injury and damage to property, but also other financial loss and environmental damage.

2. The Netherlands observes that it will be no simple matter to approach value determination objectively and scientifically, especially in relation to environmental damage. By way of illustration, consider the rhetorical question of the financial value to be placed on the extermination of the dodo.

3. The Netherlands notes that the global commons (such as the open sea) are not covered by the principles, in which "transboundary" means "across the boundary of another State". To fall within the scope of the principles, damage must be caused in the territory of a State or in places under the jurisdiction or control of a State, in line with the Commission's draft articles on prevention of transboundary harm from hazardous activities.[12] As with the draft articles, the Netherlands believes this lack of coverage to be an omission.

4. In the opinion of the Netherlands, it would have been better if the terms "State of origin", "State likely to be affected" and "States concerned" used in the commentary of the Commission on the draft principle[13] had been included in principle 2 in the interest of more uniform definitions, given the connection between the terms used and the scope of application of the principles.

5. On the definition of "Environment" in paragraph (*b*) as including "natural resources", it may be remarked that the term "natural resources" generally has very functional, economic connotations. In this case, however, "natural resources" is—rightly—being used more comprehensively. The definition encompasses not only the individual factors, but also the interaction between them.

6. Following paragraph (*e*), which defines "Operator", the Netherlands proposes adding paragraph (*f*), as follows: "'Person' means any natural or legal person", to ensure that the principles apply to both natural and legal persons or to a combination of the two. This proposal is particularly relevant to the imposition of liability.

United Kingdom of Great Britain and Northern Ireland

The United Kingdom notes that draft principle 2 (*a*) (iii) includes the possibility of loss or damage to the environment *per se* being within the scope of the draft principles. In the view of the United Kingdom, liability for the protection of the environment *per se* is a relatively recent concept, on which practice is confined to a few, very specific contexts. The United Kingdom considers that it raises some complex questions that are not fully addressed in the draft principles and the commentary. For example, the commentary suggests that it is primarily public authorities and perhaps certain public interest groups that have standing to bring such claims. However, in the view of the United Kingdom, this may raise questions as to whether a civil liability regime is an appropriate means to consider questions of the broad public interest. Further, on the question of quantification of such loss, the commentary offers little guidance. The United Kingdom would urge the Commission therefore to consider the preceding and other relevant matters in more detail in the commentary.

[10] *Yearbook ... 2004*, vol. II (Part Two), p. 65, para. 175.

[11] See also paragraph 176 (*ibid.*), pp. 87–88, commentary to principle 6.

[12] *Yearbook ... 2001*, vol. II (Part Two), p. 146, para. 97.

[13] See Yearbook ... 2004, vol. II (Part Two), p. 76, para. (23) of the commentary to principle 2.

Uzbekistan

1. It is necessary to determine whether the terms used in principle 2 are consistent with the definitions given in the international instruments currently in force: the Convention on international liability for damage caused by space objects; the Basel Convention on the control of transboundary movements of hazardous wastes and their disposal; the Declaration of the United Nations Conference on the Human Environment;[14] and the Rio Declaration on Environment and Development.[15]

2. For example, the definition of the term "damage" in the draft principles does not include the destruction of or damage to State property and property of legal persons. That omission must be corrected. There is also a need to define more specifically the concept of "transboundary damage".

3. The concept of the "environment" must be more clearly worded to cover both the natural environment and the human environment.

4. Uzbekistan considers it advisable to define the concept of "damage to property" in principle 2 (*a*) (ii). The level of damage to property that might be considered "significant damage" is also not clear from the text of the draft principle.

5. The level of loss or damage that might be considered "damage to the environment", that is, the degree of harm reflected in the impairment of natural resources or of the environment, should be defined in draft principle 2 (*b*).

6. Principle 2 (*a*) (iv), would be better put, in the view of Uzbekistan, as follows: "Expenditures on measures actually taken for reinstatement of the property or natural resources or environment."

E. Principle 3—Objective

Principle 4—Prompt and adequate compensation

Czech Republic

1. With regard to the objectives of the document, the Czech Republic's position is that rather than restricting the scope of the definition of damage it seems better to balance out the progressive development of law by refining it, especially as concerns conditions for compensation, relationships between individual claims and restrictions imposed on them, so that the total compensation does not eventually exceed the overall cost of damage.

2. Principles 3 and 4, which should be read in conjunction with each other as well as in conjunction with the preamble, provide for "prompt and adequate compensation" to all victims of transboundary damage; they may be natural or legal persons, but also States. It is obvious that in the case of damage caused to the environment *per se* (i.e. not to any individual person or property), States will be the entities entitled to sue. Indeed, in practice it is usually the State that bears the costs of sanitation and restoration measures. However, instead of providing for the international liability of States, the draft principles establish a general compensation regime for all, based probably on the principle of no-fault liability arising from civil law.

3. According to the draft principles, the State assumes no direct obligation to compensate for the damage, but only undertakes to set up, within its internal legislation, a functioning system to ensure "prompt and adequate compensation" to all entitled, that is, injured entities, if the damage was caused by activities located within the State's territory or otherwise under its jurisdiction or control. The liable entity (entitled to be sued) would, as a rule, be the operator of the hazardous activity, but it might also be the person exercising control at the moment of the accident leading to the damage, or another person most capable of providing compensation. However, this departure from the principle of "concentrated liability" (which normally prevails in special treaties) means that the injured party would be entitled to claim compensation from more than one entity. That may pose a problem if the relationship between the entities is not specified in detail (joint liability, warranty, complementarity, and the like).

4. The draft principles clearly declare (in particular in the preamble) that States are responsible for infringements of their obligations of prevention under international law. The emphasis on the primary liability of the operator does not relieve the State from its responsibility. In other words, there is no relief from liability of the State for an unlawful activity, that is, for being in infringement of its primary obligations. Prevention is, of course, one of those obligations, and the State is liable in case of its neglect. But the primary obligation of the State is also to ensure "prompt and adequate compensation" at a national level. In this respect, the State also risks being held liable for an internationally unlawful activity if it does not secure the injured party's right to compensation according to prescribed parameters. Such liability would probably consist, typically and predominantly, in compensation for damages, provided in the form of financial compensation where restitution is not possible.

5. From the point of view of international law, all this is only a logical consequence of the solution that was chosen. It is not necessarily a problem if, at the same time, there are rules regulating the relationship between the compensation paid as a consequence of the State's liability and the compensation paid by the operator, by a third party or in some cases even by the State (directly or indirectly). Since there is no rule stating that the former excludes (or proportionally reduces) the latter, there is no way to avoid multiple claims and parallel payment of compensation for the same damage (in the sense of material damage). This may involve large amounts of money that could eventually directly or indirectly burden the State budget.

[14] *Report of the United Nations Conference on the Human Environment, Stockholm, 5–16 June 1972* (United Nations publication, Sales No. E.73.II.A.14 and corrigendum), part one, chap. I.

[15] *Report of the United Nations Conference on Environment and Development, Rio de Janeiro, 3–14 June 1992*, vol. I, *Resolutions Adopted by the Conference* (United Nations publication, Sales No. E.93.I.8 and corrigendum), resolution 1, annex I.

Mexico

1. Mexico is pleased to note that the liability regime for activities included within the scope of the draft allocates liability primarily to the operator and that such liability is to be so imposed without proof of fault being required. Mexico believes that the correct way to proceed is to impose strict liability on the operator. That is consistent with international instruments in the area of civil liability and with the nature of hazardous activities.

2. Mexico believes that having to prove a causal connection would pose an excessive burden on innocent victims of such harm. In that regard, it considers that the emerging principles of international law, such as the polluter pays principle and the precautionary principle, should be extended to the procedural aspects, so that the burden of proof of a causal connection would not reside with the innocent victim. This could be achieved by allowing for presumption of causality and stipulating that the defendant must prove that no causal connection exists between the activity in question and the damage. Mexico recommends that the Commission consider including this possibility in paragraphs (24) or (25) of the commentary to draft principle 4.[16]

Netherlands

1. The Netherlands endorses the objective of the principles as expressed in principle 3, namely ensuring prompt and adequate compensation for transboundary damage. This is the core of the principles.

2. The Netherlands would observe that principle 1 should be read in combination with principle 3. The principles are about transboundary incidents for which prompt and adequate compensation must be provided. In the Netherlands's opinion, "adequate" means, at least, that the compensation given to victims in other countries should equal that given to victims in the State where the activity originated. The non-discrimination principle is a minimum standard, but is not sufficient in all cases. Not all legal systems are equally developed. Since the rationale behind the principles is to compensate victims as well as possible, "prompt and adequate compensation" must sometimes mean more than the mere application of the non-discrimination principle and must also meet objective, absolute, minimum standards. In other words, "prompt and adequate compensation" should mean "compensation not less than national treatment, whichever is more favourable to the victim", as is also clear from principle 8, paragraph 2.

3. The Netherlands believes that the implementation of principle 4 depends on implementation at the national level being non-discriminatory. States should take the "necessary measures" referred to in principle 4, paragraph 1, at national level. The Netherlands would also observe that the phrase "necessary measures to ensure that prompt and adequate compensation" is not preceded by a definite article and is not determined in any other way, for example by a word such as "all". The Netherlands is in favour of some such determiner.

4. The Netherlands agrees that proof of fault should not be required, as stated in principle 4, paragraph 2, since strict liability applies here. Nevertheless, it is appropriate to issue a warning at the same time: the restrictions that accompany strict liability also apply. They relate, for example, to the level of compensation possible and the time limit on claiming compensation. The internationally accepted restrictions imposed by international regimes already in force, such as damage caused by acts of war, also apply. However, the Netherlands takes the view that those restrictions cannot and must not go so far as to compromise the main objective, namely prompt and adequate compensation.

5. With regard to the question of what party should most appropriately be held liable, the Netherlands would observe that the operator is not always in the best position to accept liability. Sometimes it would be more appropriate to opt for the party or parties best placed to accept the risk and actually to provide compensation, as was done in the Protocol on liability and compensation for damage resulting from the transboundary movements of hazardous wastes and their disposal.[17] From the point of view of victims, it is best if a single entity can be held liable. From an environmental point of view, it is even more clear-cut: it should be the entity that can exert the most effective influence on the risk. Since the principles are aimed at States, thus forming a general framework, the Netherlands concludes that specific agreements and/or treaties are required in practice to regulate the imposition of liability satisfactorily.

6. The Netherlands agrees with the far-reaching restrictions placed on the limitations and exceptions to liability in principle 4, paragraph 2. However, the Netherlands would observe that the exceptions referred to in the Commission's commentary are not or are no longer used in the nuclear liability conventions.[18]

7. Where principle 4, paragraphs 2–3, refer to "the operator or, where appropriate, other person or entity", the Netherlands proposes that this wording should be replaced by "the operator and any other person", since these terms are clearly defined in principle 2 (*e*) ("operator") and the proposed paragraph (*f*) of principle 2 ("person" means any natural or legal person). Owners or suppliers could thus be held liable in addition to operators, as intended by principle 4, paragraph 2.

8. The Netherlands agrees with principle 4, paragraph 5. The obligation to make effective provision to cover any remaining liability on the part of the State is a progressive element that is very welcome from the point of view of victim protection. There is, however, no need to draw all the funds required for this purpose from the public purse: a fund could be established from resources provided by the operators.

---

[16] *Yearbook ... 2004*, vol. II (Part Two), p. 84.

[17] See also *Yearbook ... 2004*, vol. II (Part Two), p. 82, para. (12) of the commentary to principle 4.

[18] *Ibid.*, pp. 84–85, para. (27): "Liability is excepted if, despite taking all appropriate measures, the damage was the result of (*a*) an act of armed conflict, hostilities, civil war or insurrection; or (*b*) the result of a natural phenomenon of exceptional, inevitable, unforeseeable and irresistible character; or (*c*) wholly the result of compliance with a compulsory measure of a public authority in the State of injury; or (*d*) wholly the result of the wrongful intentional conduct of a third party." page 85, See also paragraphs (28)–(29).

9. The Netherlands proposes that the words "additional financial resources are allocated" in principle 4, paragraph 5, be replaced by "additional financial resources are available". After all, those resources need not all be taken from the public purse, and the words "are available" echo the usage of principle 4, paragraph 1.

Pakistan

1. Principle 4, paragraph 2, provides for the imposition of liability on the operator or entity without proof of fault. Such liability should be subjected to a thorough external investigation before fixing the operator's liability.

2. To ensure additional availability of funds in cases of insufficient compensation, the proposed funding mechanism may be linked with one of the existing funding mechanisms, such as that established for the United Nations Convention on the Law of the Sea or other similar conventions.

United Kingdom of Great Britain and Northern Ireland

1. The United Kingdom recognizes that the objective of the draft principles set out in draft principle 3, namely that victims of transboundary damage should receive prompt and adequate compensation, broadly reflects principle 13 of the Rio Declaration on Environment and Development.[19]

2. However, the United Kingdom believes that the inclusion of States within the category of victims of transboundary damage is not appropriate. The inclusion of claims by States would, in its view, take the draft principles beyond a civil liability scheme for implementation in national law. The United Kingdom would not support any attempt to transpose the rules on civil liability contained in the present draft principles which concern civil claims primarily between private parties before national courts, in order that they might be applied to claims made by States as a matter of public international law.

3. While the United Kingdom believes that it is important to set out the principles according to which compensation is payable, it has some concerns about the current formulation of draft principle 4. In the first place, the United Kingdom considers that the polluter pays principle ought to be the guiding principle in this respect, and is surprised not to see more explicit reference to it in the text of principle 4. In particular, paragraphs 2–3 are not as clear as they might be in this respect when they refer to "the operator or, where appropriate, other person or entity".

4. Draft principle 4, paragraph 2, appears to require the imposition of strict liability, without need for proof of fault. The United Kingdom accepts that in a number of particular fields, for example certain ultrahazardous activities, no-fault liability may have a role to play. The United Kingdom has accepted a number of specific international agreements where this is so, and at the level of national law additional schemes imposing strict liability in certain matters are in place where this is appropriate. In the view of the United Kingdom, therefore, the draft principles should be more flexible on this point, that is, endorsing the imposition of strict liability where it is appropriate, rather than its imposition across the board.

5. In relation to draft principle 4, paragraph 3, concerning the requirement of compulsory insurance or other financial security for operators, the United Kingdom believes that the requirement is set out too rigidly at present. The availability of insurance for environmental matters should not be overestimated, and the additional burdens on industry that insurance or financial security schemes of a compulsory nature may represent should not be underestimated. A general requirement in respect of compulsory insurance or compulsory maintenance of financial security may therefore result in an unacceptably heavy burden on industry, and therefore the United Kingdom cannot support the proposal.

6. The United Kingdom is concerned that draft principle 4, paragraph 5, suggests that there may be a degree of residual liability on the State to ensure that adequate financial resources are available to meet the costs of compensation. The United Kingdom notes that it is not clear whether the reference is to the State of the victim or to the State in which the hazardous activity takes place. However, and in either event, the United Kingdom does not believe that such residual liability of the State represents the current state of international law. Nor does it believe that the imposition of residual liability of the State in this respect is appropriate, not least since it once again risks confusing principles applicable to claims in civil liability with those applicable to claims between States in public international law.

7. Finally, in relation to the remedial provisions in draft principle 4, the United Kingdom notes that there is no reference to the possibility of a requirement that the operator must take remedial action in respect of environmental damage. In that respect, it notes the provisions of directive 2004/35/CE of the European Parliament and of the Council of 21 April 2004 on environmental liability with regard to the prevention and remedying of environmental damage,[20] which includes the provision that the competent authorities of the State may require an operator actually to take remedial measures. While such provisions may be beyond the scope of a classic civil liability scheme, in the view of the United Kingdom, in certain cases compensation alone, without the possibility of requiring that action be taken by the operator to remedy the damage, may be insufficient. The United Kingdom would therefore ask the Commission to give further thought to this issue.

Uzbekistan

The title of principle 3 does not reflect its content. It would be better to call it "Objectives of the principles" and move it to the beginning of the draft principles.

[19] *Report of the United Nations Conference on Environment and Development, Rio de Janeiro, 3–14 June 1992*, vol. I, *Resolutions Adopted by the Conference* (United Nations publication, Sales No. E.93.I.8 and corrigendum), resolution 1, annex I.

[20] *Official Journal of the European Communities*, No. L 143, vol. 47 (30 April 2004), p. 56.

F. *Principle 5—Response measures*

Netherlands

Principle 5 forms a bridge between the draft articles on prevention of transboundary harm from hazardous activities[21] and the principles. Moreover, from a methodological point of view, principle 5 does not in fact concern—or concerns only in part—the matters that the principles are supposed to regulate,[22] for the objective of the principles is to allocate costs for harm already incurred. In contrast, principle 5 is about avoiding further damage and paying for measures to that end. However, given the practical connection between compensation for damage done and the prevention of further damage, it is good that principles 5 and 7 were included. It must be borne in mind here that operators must be genuinely capable of restricting the damage if they are to be assigned any meaningful task.

United Kingdom of Great Britain and Northern Ireland

The United Kingdom notes that draft principle 5 appears to be directed to response measures that the State should take. Again it is not clear whether the principle envisages action to be taken by the State in which the hazardous activity takes place or by the State of the victim. It is also not clear whether the Commission is proposing a legal duty on the State to take response measures nor, if so, whether it is a duty that is intended to be owed to its nationals as a matter of national law or a duty that is intended to be owed as between States at the level of international law.

G. *Principle 6—International and domestic remedies*

Czech Republic

1. Problems that are not fully solved by substantive law (inadequate regulation of the conditions of compensation) may still be addressed at the procedural level by forbidding a repeated or parallel suit for damages. The solution of international and domestic remedies proposed in principle 6 is even more vague than the substantive regulation of liability. According to the draft principle, the States should only ensure the remedies, whether in the form of international procedures (i.e. arbitration, global compensation) or at the level of domestic administrative and judicial mechanisms. Obviously, this is only a framework regulation, details being left to special treaties. However, the problem is that the State should at least enable access by injured foreigners to its domestic procedures on a non-discriminatory basis. Nevertheless, the draft principle does not regulate the choice of a forum, and probably allows for free choice in this respect (or "forum shopping"). In addition, there may exist international mechanisms allowing for an expeditious settlement of claims (which the draft supports). This implies that instead of the traditional diplomatic protection, conditional on exhaustion of diplomatic remedies, prompt arbitration should be made possible.

2. Like the substantive law, which fails to regulate the relationship between parallel compensation claims, the procedural rules fail to regulate the relationship between suits brought in more than one national or even international institution. There is no doubt that the proposed framework principles are primarily designed to protect the victim, that is, to ensure prompt and adequate compensation for damage. However, some examples taken from other fields of international law, such as disputes concerning the protection of international investments, show that even a well-meant regulation can turn against the State that adopted it. Where there are multiple treaty regimes regulating compensation and related procedures, there is also a risk of multiple suits being brought against different entities, including the State, or against one entity in different forums.

3. In order to ensure legal certainty for defendants (but also of plaintiffs), it would be appropriate to respect, also in international instruments, the general principles of its litispendence (*lis pendens*) and of *res judicata*. International treaties on human rights may serve as a model, since they do not allow a complaint to be lodged with more than one international controlling body (for example, the European Court of Human Rights, the Human Rights Committee, and so on).

4. According to the Czech Republic, the issue of procedural remedies (at the international as well as national levels) and their interrelationship needs further elaboration.

Netherlands

1. The Netherlands would point out that the non-discrimination principle has—rightly—been incorporated in principle 6 as well, in connection with legal procedures. It would also stress the need for effective remedies, as referred to in principle 6, paragraph 3.

2. The Netherlands believes it conceivable that the question could be asked whether, if a State failed to fulfil its obligations under the prevention articles, this would give rise to aggravated liability or at least whether it could be argued that the liability is greater than if no obligation had been violated. However, the Netherlands concludes that the principles are intended solely to ensure compensation for harm actually suffered and not to impose punitive damages.

3. The Netherlands advises the Commission to include choice of forum and recognition of judgements in principle 6. Although those matters are discussed in the commentary, no conclusions are drawn regarding the content of principle 6.

4. As to the exclusive choice of forum made by the Commission, the Netherlands observes that from the victims' point of view it would at first sight seem advisable, unlike the Commission, to allow for a choice of forum to be

---

[21] *Yearbook ... 2001*, vol. II (Part Two), p. 146, para. 97.

[22] This also applies to principle 7, paragraph 1:

"States should cooperate in the development of appropriate international agreements on a global, regional or bilateral basis in order to make arrangements regarding the prevention and response measures to be followed in respect of particular categories of hazardous activities as well as the compensation and financial security measures to be taken."

(*Yearbook ... 2004*, vol. II (Part Two), p. 66, para. 175)

made.[23] However, this could mean that an unwise choice is made and the victim is faced with a *forum non conveniens*. The eventual choice was therefore that proceedings should take place in the country where the damage was caused. The Netherlands supports that decision. Practical experience teaches that the treaties that provide for exclusive liability (oil damage and nuclear damage) are the only ones in the category that work well. It should also be remembered that if funds were available to several uncoordinated forums, it could obviously cause problems. Accordingly, effective victim protection does not necessarily mean that more than one remedy is available. The Lugano Convention and the Basel and Kiev Protocols,[24] however, do provide for a choice of forum. Opting exclusively for the State where the damage was caused is also the simplest option from the point of view of enforcement of judgements.

United Kingdom of Great Britain and Northern Ireland

In relation to draft principle 6, the United Kingdom has some concerns about the apparent breadth of the provision which suggests that States should provide domestic remedies to victims of transboundary damage. In relation to draft principle 6, paragraph 1, it is not clear upon which State the proposed requirement to provide appropriate procedures to victims might fall, that is, the State of the victim or the State in which the hazardous activity takes place. Indeed, the commentary suggests that the proposed duty falls on "all States".[25] This may be contrasted with draft principle 6, paragraph 3, which the commentary suggests is aimed primarily at the State of origin of the damage (i.e. the State in which the hazardous activity takes place). Such cases may raise complex questions of private international law, and the United Kingdom cannot be certain that administrative and/or judicial procedures would necessarily be available to victims in all of the circumstances potentially covered in draft principle 6. The United Kingdom believes that the provisions of draft principle 6 should be qualified to the extent that they are compatible with accepted principles of private international law in the forum State.

H. Principle 7—Development of specific international regimes

Netherlands

1. The Netherlands would observe that the provisions in the draft articles on prevention of transboundary harm from hazardous activities relating to the settlement of disputes[26] cannot be employed here: in the draft articles, disputes are about whether or not damage could have been prevented. Further, the Netherlands would like to point out the importance of coordinating liability where prevention and compensation regimes either fail or do not exist.

2. The Netherlands stresses that regimes must be effective and appropriate. It is not simply a question of concluding more treaties: rather, there should be better treaties with better implementation.

United Kingdom of Great Britain and Northern Ireland

The United Kingdom notes that draft principle 7, which encourages States to develop international agreements on prevention and compensation, also reflects principle 13 of the Rio Declaration on Environment and Development.[27] Nevertheless, as the Special Rapporteur has observed in his earlier work on the topic, experience suggests that legally binding liability regimes at the international level are complex and time-consuming to negotiate and that in many cases they have met with little success. The United Kingdom therefore urges the Commission to redraft principle 7 in a more flexible form, recognizing that a range of international instruments and/or other arrangements may be developed as appropriate. They may include formal international agreements where appropriate as well as non-binding arrangements between States and binding or non-binding arrangements between private actors, such as industry-wide agreements or codes of practice.

United States of America

The United States observes that draft principle 7 encourages States to cooperate in the development of appropriate international agreements. Without prejudice to States' sovereign discretion to pursue such agreements and what they should contain, the United States would emphasize that the contexts in which specific liability regimes might be developed vary widely (for example, such negotiations might concern quite distinct industrial sectors), and it should be recognized that the approaches chosen may differ accordingly. In accordance with this, the view of the United States is that international regulation in the area of liability ought to proceed in careful negotiations concerned with particular topics (for example, oil pollution, hazardous wastes) or with particular regions (for example, the recently concluded negotiations of Annex VI to the Protocol on Environmental Protection to the Antarctic Treaty addressing liability arising from environmental emergencies). The United States believes that it is only in specific contexts that States can appropriately consider the kinds of matters that the Commission has rightly suggested need to be addressed in any liability regime.

I. Principle 8—Implementation

Mexico

An important aspect of draft principle 8 is the Commission's express reference to the need for States to adopt measures to incorporate the principles, thereby strengthening their implementation and, as a result, reinforcing protection of the environment.

[23] See *Yearbook ... 2004*, vol. II (Part Two), p. 88, para. (8) of the commentary to principle 6.

[24] Convention on Civil Liability for Damage Resulting from Activities Dangerous to the Environment; Protocol on liability and compensation for damage resulting from the transboundary movements of hazardous wastes and their disposal; Protocol on Civil Liability and Compensation for Damage Caused by the Transboundary Effects of Industrial Accidents on Transboundary Waters to the 1992 Convention on the Protection and Use of Transboundary Watercourses and International Lakes and to the 1992 Convention on the Transboundary Effects of Industrial Accidents.

[25] *Yearbook ... 2004*, vol. II (Part Two), p. 87, para. (1) of the commentary to principle 6.

[26] *Yearbook ... 2001*, vol. II (Part Two), pp. 147–148, para. 97.

[27] *Report of the United Nations Conference on Environment and Development, Rio de Janeiro, 3–14 June 1992*, vol. I, *Resolutions Adopted by the Conference* (United Nations publication, Sales No. E.93.I.8 and corrigendum), resolution 1, annex I.

Netherlands

1. The Netherlands would like to emphasize the importance of principle 8, paragraph 2, and point out its connection with article 15 of the draft articles on prevention of transboundary harm from hazardous activities,[28] although clearly the latter is concerned with damage that already exists, such as oil discharged from a ship that has foundered, where the only concern is to minimize the pollution damage, for example, to the coast (see also principle 5 and article 16 of the draft articles[29]).

2. Whereas the wording of principle 8, paragraph 3, is "States should cooperate with each other to implement the present draft principles consistent with their obligations under international law", the preamble uses the more peremptory word "shall" ("States shall be responsible for infringements of their obligations of prevention under international law"). The Netherlands definitely prefers the latter.

United Kingdom of Great Britain and Northern Ireland

The United Kingdom considers that draft principle 8 on implementation is miscast in an instrument of this nature, which is more appropriately viewed as guidance for national policymakers rather than as a series of obligations requiring implementation.

Uzbekistan

1. The title of principle 8, "Implementation", should be expanded, as follows: "Measures to be taken by the State to implement the provisions of the principles."

2. Uzbekistan believes that it would be advisable to reflect in paragraph 2 the list of relevant factors in the principle of non-discrimination, taking into account the provisions of the Universal Declaration of Human Rights,[30] of 10 December 1948, particularly with respect to race, colour, sex, language, religion, political or other opinion, national or social origin, property, birth or other status.

J. Final form

Mexico

1. The drafting should stress the legal obligation attaching to the activities regulated here; therefore the provisions of the instrument should be drafted in the form of rules (in articles) and not merely as principles. It must be recalled that the purpose of the draft is not only to develop international law, but to codify rules applicable to those situations in which damage is caused by acts not prohibited by international law.

2. Moreover, Mexico recalls that, in paragraph 3 of its resolution 56/82 of 12 December 2001, the General Assembly stated that, in its work on that topic, the Commission should bear in mind the interrelationship between prevention and liability. Accordingly, the same treatment should be given to the provisions on liability as to those on prevention.

3. Mexico still has doubts about the use of the term "allocation of loss" in the title of the subtopic since one of the main functions of the liability regime is to provide compensation for damage and not just to distribute "loss". Moreover, the term used would appear to create a legal regime for damage compensation different from the rules derived from the legal principle of "polluter pays". However, Mexico recognizes that the title is a secondary issue, provided the draft takes the form of articles rather than principles.

4. If the Commission decides that the provisions should continue to take the form of principles, as at present, Mexico considers it essential to reformulate some of them (in particular, principles 4–8) so that they are prescriptive rather than hortatory in nature. Therefore, Mexico would recommend replacing the word "should" by the word "shall" in the draft (see, for example, principles 4–8).

5. Mexico believes that the Commission should seize the opportunity, as it considers this very important topic, to establish a clear, fair and prescriptive set of rules with the ultimate aim of protecting the global environment and ensuring that the "polluter pays". To provide prescriptive rules on prevention of damage, but not on compensation in the event of accidents, would undoubtedly result in an unbalanced and inequitable treatment of the topic, which would not contribute to the legal certainty being sought.

Netherlands

1. The Commission has said that it will examine the question of the final form to be taken by the instrument during the second reading of the principles. If the Commission plans to draft a framework agreement, the Netherlands believes that this would mean further negotiations on principles 4–8 and that the Commission would have to make some additions, particularly on dispute settlement and the reconciliation of the draft articles on the prevention of transboundary harm from hazardous activities with other international instruments.

2. The Netherlands hopes that as many States as possible take an active part in the further discussion of the principles, in the formal discussion of this part of the Commission's report to the Sixth Committee as well as elsewhere. The Netherlands hopes that the Commission's report will inspire bilateral, regional and other multilateral agreements and provisions on transboundary harm caused by hazardous activities.

United States of America

In the light of the fact that the Commission reserved the right to return to the question of final form during the second reading of the draft principles, the United States wishes to record its strong agreement with the Commission that the principles are more likely to gain widespread acceptance in their current form than they would were they not recommendatory.[31] Such acceptance is also more likely in the light of the decision to avoid controversial assertions not necessary for the exercise, such as general assertions regarding precaution, "polluter pays", or the global commons.

---

[28] *Yearbook ... 2001*, vol. II (Part Two), p. 147.

[29] *Ibid.*

[30] General Assembly resolution 217 A (III).

[31] *Yearbook ... 2004*, vol. II (Part Two), p. 68, para. 176, general commentary, para. (14).

RESPONSIBILITY OF INTERNATIONAL ORGANIZATIONS*

[Agenda item 4]

DOCUMENT A/CN.4/564 and Add. 1–2

Fourth report on responsibility of international organizations, by Mr. Giorgio Gaja, Special Rapporteur

[Original: English]
[28 February, 12 and 20 April 2006]

CONTENTS

Multilateral instruments cited in the present report

	Source
Inter-American Treaty of Reciprocal Assistance (Rio de Janeiro, 2 September 1947)	United Nations, *Treaty Series*, vol. 21, No. 324, p. 77.
North Atlantic Treaty (Washington, D.C., 4 April 1949)	*Ibid.*, vol. 34, No. 541, p. 243.
Convention for the Protection of Human Rights and Fundamental Freedoms (European Convention on Human Rights) (Rome, 4 November 1950)	*Ibid.*, vol. 213, No. 2889, p. 221.

* The Special Rapporteur gratefully acknowledges the assistance given for the preparation of this report by Stefano Dorigo (PhD candidate, University of Pisa, Italy), Paolo Palchetti (Associate Professor, University of Macerata, Italy) and Antonios Tzanakopoulos (LLM, New York University).

	Source
Treaty on the Non-Proliferation of Nuclear Weapons (London, Moscow and Washington, D.C., 1 July 1968)	*Ibid.*, vol. 729, No. 10485, p. 161.
Vienna Convention on the Law of Treaties (Vienna, 23 May 1969)	*Ibid.*, vol. 1155, No. 18232, p. 331.
Convention on international liability for damage caused by space objects (London, Moscow, Washington, D.C., 29 March 1972)	*Ibid.*, vol. 961, No. 13810, p. 187.
United Nations Convention on contracts for the international sale of goods (Vienna, 11 April 1980)	*Ibid.*, vol. 1489, No. 25567, p. 58.
Sixth International Tin Agreement (Geneva, 26 June 1981)	*Ibid.*, vol. 1282, No. 21139, p. 205.
Constitutive Act of the African Union (Lomé, 11 July 2000)	*Ibid.*, vol. 2158, No. 37733, p. 3.
Treaty establishing the European Community (Rome, 25 March 1957), incorporating the amendments made by the Treaty of Nice of 26 February 2001	Consolidated version of the Treaty on European Union, *Official Journal of the European Communities*, No. C 325, vol. 45 (24 December 2002), p. 33.
International Cocoa Agreement, 2001 (Geneva, 13 March 2001)	UNCTAD (TD/COCOA.9/7 and Corr.1).

Works cited in the present report

ABASS, Ademola

“Consent precluding State responsibility: a critical analysis”, *International and Comparative Law Quarterly*, vol. 53, part 1, January 2004, pp. 211–225.

ADAM, H.-T.

Les organismes internationaux spécialisés: contribution à la théorie générale des établissements publics internationaux. Paris, LGDJ, 1965. 338 p.

AMERASINGHE, C. F.

“Liability to third parties of member States of international organizations: practice, principle and judicial precedent”, *American Journal of International Law* (Washington, D.C.), vol. 85, 1991, pp. 259–280.

AMRALLAH, Borhan

“The international responsibility of the United Nations for activities carried out by U.N. peace-keeping forces”, *Revue égyptienne de droit international* (Cairo), vol. 32, 1976, pp. 57–82.

ARSANJANI, Mahnoush H.

“Claims against international organizations: *quis custodiet ipsos custodes*”, *Yale Journal of World Public Order*, vol. 7, No. 2, Spring 1981, pp. 131–176.

BROWNLIE, Ian

Principles of Public International Law. 6th ed. Oxford, Oxford University Press, 2003. 742 p.

“The responsibility of States for the acts of international organizations”, *in* Maurizio Ragazzi, ed., *International Responsibility Today: Essays in Memory of Oscar Schachter*. Leiden, Martinus Nijhoff, 2005, pp. 355–362.

COX, Katherine E.

“Beyond self-defense: United Nations peacekeeping operations & the use of force”, *Denver Journal of International Law and Policy*, vol. 27, No. 2, spring 1999, p. 239–273.

DI BLASE, Antonietta

“Sulla responsabilità internazionale per attività dell’ONU”, *Rivista di diritto internazionale*, vol. LVII, No. 2, 1974, pp. 250–280.

FRULLI, Micaela

“Le operazioni di peacekeeping delle Nazioni Unite e l’uso della forza”, *Rivista di diritto internazionale*, vol. LXXXIV, No. 2, 2001, pp. 347–392.

GALICKI, Zdzislaw

“Liability of international organizations for space activities”, *Polish Yearbook of International Law*, vol. V, 1972–1973, pp. 199–207.

GATTINI, Andrea

“Smoking/no smoking: some remarks on the current place of fault in the ILC draft articles on State responsibility”, *European Journal of International Law*, vol. 10, No. 2, 1999, pp. 397–404.

GINTHER, Konrad

Die völkerrechtliche Verantwortlichkeit internationaler Organisationen gegenüber Drittstaaten. Vienna, Springer-Verlag, 1969. 202 p.

HARTWIG, Matthias

Die Haftung der Mitgliedstaaten für Internationale Organisationen (Responsibility of Member States for International Organizations). Berlin, Springer-Verlag, 1993. 371 p. (Thesis, University of Heidelberg, 1991)

HERDEGEN, Matthias

“The insolvency of international organizations and the legal position of creditors: some observations in the light of the International Tin Council crisis”, *Netherlands International Law Review*, vol. XXXV, issue 2, 1988, pp. 135–144.

HIGGINS, Rosalyn

“The legal consequences for member states of the non-fulfilment by international organizations of their obligations toward third parties: provisional report”, Institute of International Law, *Yearbook*, vol. 66, part I, session of Lisbon, 1995, preparatory works.

HIRSCH, Moshe

The Responsibility of International Organizations Toward Third Parties: Some Basic Principles. Dordrecht, Martinus Nijhoff, 1995. 222 p. (Legal aspects of international organization, vol. 20)

HOFFMANN, Gerhard

“Der Durchgriff auf die Mitgliedstaaten internationaler Organisationen für deren Schulden”, *Neue juristische Wochenschrift*, vol. 41, No. 10, March 1988, pp. 585–590.

JOHNSTONE, Ian

“The plea of ‘necessity’ in international legal discourse: humanitarian intervention and counter-terrorism”, *Columbia Journal of Transnational Law*, vol. 43, No. 2, 2005, pp. 337–388.

KIRSCH, Philippe, ed.

"Canadian practice in international law: at the Department of Foreign Affairs in 1995–96", *Canadian Yearbook of International Law*, vol. XXXIV, 1996, pp. 387–416.

KLEIN, Pierre

La responsabilité des organisations internationales dans les ordres juridiques internes et en droit des gens. Brussels, Bruylant, 1998.

LAMBERTI ZANARDI, Pierluigi

La legittima difesa nel diritto internazionale. Milan, Giuffrè, 1972. 313 p.

LOWE, Vaughan

"Precluding wrongfulness or responsibility: a plea for excuses", *European Journal of International Law*, vol. 10, No. 2, 1999, pp. 405–411.

MÜNCH, Ingo von

Das völkerrechtliche Delikt in der modernen Entwicklung der Völkerrechtsgemeinschaft. Frankfurt am Main, Keppler, 1963. 356 p.

PELLET, Alain

"L'imputabilité d'éventuels actes illicites: responsabilité de l'OTAN ou des États membres", *in* Christian Tomuschat, ed., *Kosovo and the International Community: A Legal Assessment*. The Hague, Kluwer, 2002, pp. 193–202.

PERNICE, Ingolf

"Die Haftung internationaler Organisationen und ihrer Mitglieder", *Archiv des Völkerrechts*, vol. 26, 1988, pp. 406–433.

PITSCHAS, Christian

Die völkerrechtliche Verantwortlichkeit der Europäischen Gemeinschaft und ihrer Mitgliedstaaten: Zugleich ein Beitrag zu den völkerrechtlichen Kompetenzen der Europäischen Gemeinschaft. Berlin, Duncker & Humblot, 2001. 302 p.

RITTER, Jean-Pierre

"La protection diplomatique à l'égard d'une organisation internationale", *Annuaire français de droit international*, vol. VIII, 1962, pp. 427–456.

SADURSKA, Romana and C. M. CHINKIN

"The collapse of the International Tin Council: a case of State responsibility?", *Virginia Journal of International Law*, vol. 30, No. 4, summer 1990, pp. 845–890.

SALMON, Jean

"Les accords Spaak–U Thant du 20 février 1965", *Annuaire français de droit international* (Paris), vol. XI, 1965, pp. 468–497.

"Les circonstances excluant l'illicéité", *in* Prosper Weil, ed., *Responsabilité internationale*. Paris, Pedone, 1987, pp. 89–225.

SAPIENZA, ROSARIO

"Considerazioni sulle attività di assistenza e monitoraggio elettorale dell'ONU", *Rivista di diritto internazionale*, vol. LXXXVIII, No. 3, 2005, pp. 647–666.

SANDS, Philippe and Pierre KLEIN

Bowett's Law of International Institutions. 5th ed. London, Sweet & Maxwell, 2001.

SAROOSHI, Dan

International Organizations and their Exercise of Sovereign Powers. Oxford, Oxford University Press, 2005. 151 p.

SCHERMERS, Henry G.

"Liability of international organizations", *Leiden Journal of International Law*, vol. 1, No. 1, May 1988, pp. 3–14.

SCHMALENBACH, Kirsten

Die Haftung Internationaler Organisationen im Rahmen von Militäreinsätzen und Territorialverwaltungen. Frankfurt am Main, Peter Lang, 2004.

SEIDL-HOHENVELDERN, Ignaz

"Die völkerrechtliche Haftung für Handlungen internationaler Organisationen im Verhältnis zu Nichtmitgliedstaaten", *Österreichische Zeitschrift für öffentliches Recht* (Vienna), vol. XI, Nos. 3–4, 1961, pp. 497–506.

Corporations in and under International Law. Cambridge, Grotius, 1987. 138 p. (Hersch Lauterpacht Memorial Lecture Series)

"Liability of member States for acts or omissions of an international organization", *in* Sabine Schlemmer-Schulte & Ko-Yung Tung, eds., Liber Amicorum *Ibrahim F. I. Shihata: International Finance and Development Law*. The Hague, Kluwer, 2001, pp. 727–739.

SHIHATA, Ibrahim F. I.

"Role of law in economic development: the legal problems of international public ventures", *Revue égyptienne de droit international*, vol. 25, 1969, pp. 119–128.

SHRAGA, Daphna

"UN peacekeeping operations: applicability of international humanitarian law and responsibility for operations-related damage", *American Journal of International Law* (Washington, D.C.), vol. 94, No. 2, April 2000, pp. 406–412.

STEIN, Torsten

"Kosovo and the international community—the attribution of possible internationally wrongful acts: responsibility of NATO or of its member States", *in* Christian Tomuschat, ed., *Kosovo and the International Community: A Legal Assessment*. The Hague, Kluwer, 2002, pp. 181–192.

TALLON, Denis

"Article 79", *in* C. M. Bianca and M. J. Bonell, *Commentary on the International Sales Law: The 1980 Vienna Sales Convention*. Milan, Giuffrè, 1987, pp. 572–595.

WENCKSTERN, Manfred

"Die Haftung der Mitgliedstaaten für internationale Organisationen", *Rabels Zeitschrift für ausländisches und internationales Privatrecht*, vol. 61, 1997, pp. 93–114.

ZEMANEK, Karl

"The legal consequences for member States of the non-fulfilment by international organizations of their obligations toward third parties: *réponses et observations des membres de la Commission*", Institute of International Law, *Yearbook*, vol. 66, part I, session of Lisbon, 1995, preparatory works, pp. 325–330.

ZWANENBURG, Marten

Accountability of Peace Support Operations. Leiden, Martinus Nijhoff, 2005. 363 p. (International Humanitarian Law Series, vol. 9)

Introduction

1. At its fifty-fifth, fifty-sixth and fifty-seventh sessions, in 2003, 2004 and 2005, the International Law Commission provisionally adopted 16 draft articles on the topic "Responsibility of international organizations".[1] These draft articles have been divided into four chapters, with the following headings: "Introduction" (arts. 1–3), "Attribution of conduct to an international organization" (arts. 4–7), "Breach of an international obligation" (arts. 8–11) and "Responsibility of an international organization in connection with the act of a State or another international organization" (arts. 12–16).

2. The draft articles so far adopted and the questions raised by the Commission have elicited a certain number of comments from States (mainly in the debates in the Sixth Committee) and from international organizations. After the publication of the comments in writing which were referred to in previous reports, some further comments were collected in document A/CN.4/556.[2] More recent comments in writing were received, before the submission of the present report, from Belgium, INTERPOL, the Organization for the Prohibition of Chemical Weapons (OPCW) and the World Bank.

3. Views which have been expressed on issues that the Commission has yet to discuss will be examined in the present report, while comments relating to draft articles already adopted by the Commission will be considered when the Commission revises the current draft articles.

4. In chapter I of the present report, circumstances precluding wrongfulness are addressed, while in chapter II, responsibility of a State in connection with the act of an international organization is considered.

[1] The text of the draft articles heretofore provisionally adopted is reproduced in *Yearbook ...2005*, vol. II (Part Two), pp. 40–42, para. 205.

[2] *Yearbook ... 2005*, vol. II (Part One), p. 27, Comments and observations received from Governments and international organizations.

Chapter I

Circumstances precluding wrongfulness

A. General remarks

5. As in previous reports, the present analysis follows the general pattern that was adopted in the articles on responsibility of States for internationally wrongful acts. Part one, chapter V, of those articles contains eight articles under the heading "Circumstances precluding wrongfulness".[3] Part one, chapter V, of the current draft articles is intended to have the same heading.

6. A few commentators noted that the articles on responsibility of States for internationally wrongful acts in part one, chapter V, group some heterogeneous circumstances and, in particular, do not make a distinction between causes of justification and excuses.[4] If that distinction were made, the first category would group circumstances which radically exclude wrongfulness, while the other circumstances would have a more limited effect and only exceptionally provide a shield against responsibility. A distinction on the suggested lines may have some relevance with regard to the question of proof. However, a cause of justification cannot appropriately be ranged among the circumstances precluding wrongfulness, because it would rule out any breach of an international obligation. Thus, the suggested distinction was not used in the articles on State responsibility. While the commentary does use both terms, "justification" and "excuse", for describing circumstances precluding wrongfulness,[5] according to the commentary on article 20:

> [A] distinction must be drawn between consent in relation to a particular situation or a particular course of conduct, and consent in relation to the underlying obligation itself.[6]

Only the first type of consent was considered as a circumstance precluding wrongfulness. It seems preferable for the Commission to adopt the same approach in the present draft articles, because the question of responsibility of international organizations presents no special feature in this regard.

7. The same reason of coherence with the approach taken with regard to State responsibility suggests that the present draft articles should not introduce circumstances precluding wrongfulness that were not so characterized in the articles on responsibility of States for internationally wrongful acts, but would apply in the same way with regard to States and international organizations.

8. One case in point is that of an international organization acting under coercion. Coherence with the text on State responsibility makes it preferable not to list this case among the circumstances precluding wrongfulness,[7] although article 14 (*a*) of the current draft suggests that

[3] *Yearbook ... 2001*, vol. II (Part Two), pp. 27–28, para. 76.

[4] Lowe, "Precluding wrongfulness or responsibility: a plea for excuses", p. 405; Gattini, "Smoking/no smoking: some remarks on the current place of fault in the ILC draft articles on State responsibility", p. 401; Johnstone, "The plea of 'necessity' in international legal discourse: humanitarian intervention and counter-terrorism", pp. 349–356.

[5] For instance, in the commentary concerning the introduction to chapter V (*Yearbook ... 2001*, vol. II (Part Two), p. 71, para. (2)).

[6] *Ibid.*, pp. 72–73, para. (2).

[7] The Russian Federation held that coercion by a State or an international organization could give rise to a circumstance precluding wrongfulness (*Official Records of the General Assembly, Sixtieth Session, Sixth Committee*, 12th meeting, para. 70). The inclusion of duress as a circumstance precluding wrongfulness in the articles on responsibility of States for internationally wrongful acts had been advocated in the Commission by Mr. John Dugard (*Yearbook ... 1999*, vol. I, 2592nd meeting, p. 178, paras. 22–23). Sarooshi, *International Organizations and their Exercise of Sovereign Powers*, p. 51, considered that a possible circumstance precluding wrongfulness would exist when an international "organization has in good faith sought to exercise its constitutional control to prevent the commission of an unlawful act but the control by a State over the organization has in any case caused the

a coerced State or international organization would be excused from international responsibility when it considers that:

The act would, but for the coercion, be an internationally wrongful act of the coerced State or international organization.[8]

Apart from the fact that the subparagraph above refers to an international organization alongside a State, the text is identical to article 18 (*a*) on responsibility of States for internationally wrongful acts. Moreover, the latter provision implicitly envisages coercion as a circumstance precluding wrongfulness, although the articles on State responsibility do not list this case specifically.[9] A differentiation in this respect of the current draft articles from the articles on State responsibility would be unwarranted.

B. Consent

9. Consent is the first among the circumstances precluding wrongfulness that is mentioned. The commentary on the relevant provision (art. 20) explains that this "reflects the basic international law principle of consent".[10] That principle applies to States as well as to international organizations.

10. An international organization may express consent with regard to conduct of a State or an international organization. Consent given by an organization to a State falls outside the present draft articles, because in that case consent would preclude the responsibility of the State. What needs to be considered here is consent given to the commission of an act by an international organization.

11. Like States, international organizations perform several functions which would give rise to international responsibility if they were not consented to by a State or an international organization. The most frequent relevant case is consent given by the State on whose territory the organization exercises its functions.

12. Requests for verification of the electoral process by an international organization represent relatively frequent examples of consent given by States to an organization so that it may exercise functions that would otherwise interfere with national sovereignty.[11]

13. One recent example of consent given by a State both to an international organization and to several States is provided by the deployment of the Aceh Monitoring Mission in Indonesia. This mission was sent on 15 September 2005, following an official invitation addressed by the Government of Indonesia to the European Union, five contributing countries of the Association of Southeast Asian Nations (Brunei Darussalam, Malaysia, the Philippines, Singapore and Thailand), Norway and Switzerland.[12]

14. There does not appear to be any reason for distinguishing the conditions under which consent represents a circumstance precluding wrongfulness for States and the conditions applying to international organizations. It is therefore expedient to make only the necessary textual alterations to article 20 on responsibility of States for internationally wrongful acts.[13] On the basis of the foregoing remarks, the following text is proposed:

"Article 17. Consent

"Valid consent by a State or an international organization to the commission of a given act by another international organization precludes the wrongfulness of that act in relation to that State or the former organization to the extent that the act remains within the limits of that consent."

C. Self-defence

15. While Article 51 of the Charter of the United Nations refers to self-defence only with regard to an armed attack on a State, it is far from inconceivable that an international organization may find itself in the same situation as a State. This was taken for granted in a memorandum by the Office of Legal Affairs to the Senior Political Adviser to the Secretary-General, which stated that:

[T]he use of force in self-defence is an inherent right of United Nations forces exercised to preserve a collective and individual defence.[14]

It would indeed be odd if an international organization could not lawfully respond—not necessarily through the use of force[15]—if it were made the object of an armed attack.[16]

16. The view had been expressed that, when the United Nations force in the Congo reacted against attacks by Belgian mercenaries, the United Nations could invoke

commission of the act". The following chapter will be the more appropriate place to discuss the view expressed in a statement by Belarus, that

"[i]n certain situations, it would be appropriate to absolve international organizations of responsibility for internationally wrongful acts and to provide instead for the collective responsibility of member States, particularly with regard to international organizations with limited resources and a small membership, where each member State had a high level of control over the organization's activities."

(*Official Records of the General Assembly* (see above), para. 52)

[8] *Yearbook ... 2005*, vol. II (Part Two), p. 41, para. 205.

[9] *Yearbook ... 2001*, vol. II (Part Two), p. 27.

[10] *Ibid.*, p. 72, para. (1).

[11] With regard to the role of consent in relation to the function of verifying an electoral process, see the report of the Secretary-General on enhancing the effectiveness of the principle of periodic and genuine elections (A/49/675), para. 16. A recent survey was made by Sapienza, "Considerazioni sulle attività di assistenza e monitoraggio elettorale dell'ONU".

[12] A reference to the invitation by the Government of Indonesia, which had been made on 12 July 2005, may be found in paragraph (3) of the Council Joint Action 2005/643/CFSP of 9 September 2005 on the European Union Monitoring Mission in Aceh (Indonesia), *Official Journal of the European Union* (10 September 2005), No. L 234, p. 13.

[13] *Yearbook ... 2001*, vol. II (Part Two), p. 72.

[14] *United Nations Juridical Yearbook, 1993* (United Nations publication, Sales No. E.97.V.13), p. 372, para. 6 of a memorandum dated 19 July 1993.

[15] This point was made by Salmon, "Les circonstances excluant l'illicéité", p. 169.

[16] Among the writers who held that self-defence is invocable by the United Nations and other international organizations when they are the object of an armed attack, see Arsanjani, "Claims against international organizations: *quis custodiet ipsos custodes*", p. 176; Klein, *La responsabilité des organisations internationales dans les ordres juridiques internes et en droit des gens*, p. 421; Schmalenbach, *Die Haftung Internationaler Organisationen im Rahmen von Militäreinsätzen und Territorialverwaltungen*, pp. 264–265; and Zwanenburg, *Accountability of Peace Support Operations*, p. 16.

self-defence and hence did not engage its international responsibility.[17] In relation to the United Nations Protection Force, a memorandum from the Legal Bureau of the Department of Foreign Affairs and International Trade of Canada held that:

> "Self-defence" could very well include the defence of the safe areas and of the civilian population in those areas.[18]

17. Reference to self-defence has often been made in texts establishing the mandate of peacekeeping forces. For instance, with regard to the United Nations Peacekeeping Force in Cyprus (UNFICYP), the Secretary-General stated:

> Troops of UNFICYP shall not take the initiative in the use of armed force. The use of armed force is permissible only in self-defence.[19]

The actual meaning of self-defence in mandates relating to peacekeeping and peace-enforcement forces has widened over time. The Secretary-General had originally held:

> A reasonable definition seems to have been established in the case of UNEF [United Nations Emergency Force], where the rule is applied that men engaged in the operation may never take the initiative in the use of armed force, but are entitled to respond with force to an attack with arms, including attempts to use force to make them withdraw from positions which they occupy under orders from the Commander, acting under the authority of the Assembly and within the scope of its resolutions.[20]

According to a recent assessment, which was made by the High-level Panel on Threats, Challenges and Change:

> [T]he right to use force in self-defence ... is widely understood to extend to "defence of the mission".[21]

While the mandates of peacekeeping and peace-enforcement forces vary, references to self-defence confirm that self-defence constitutes a circumstance precluding wrongfulness. This conclusion is not affected by the fact that the provisions in question appear to envisage a reaction against attacks that are directed against United Nations forces mainly by entities other than States and international organizations.[22] No distinction is made according to the source of the armed attack.

18. The invocability of self-defence should not be limited to the United Nations. Some other organizations deploy military forces or are involved in the administration of territories. The relevance of self-defence as a circumstance precluding wrongfulness of an act taken by an international organization depends on the conditions under which self-defence is admissible. The wider the concept of armed attack, the more likely it is that self-defence could apply to an international organization engaging in military operations. In this context, it may be recalled that, in its judgement in the case concerning *Oil Platforms*, ICJ said that:

> The Court does not exclude the possibility that the mining of a single military vessel might be sufficient to bring into play the "inherent right of self-defence".[23]

19. Article 21 on responsibility of States for internationally wrongful acts does not specify the conditions under which self-defence is invocable otherwise than by requiring that the measure of self-defence be "lawful" and "taken in conformity with the Charter of the United Nations".[24] It is clearly preferable to follow the same approach in the current draft articles. This implies that the text of the draft articles should not address the question of the invocability of self-defence by an international organization in case of an armed attack against one of its members. It may, however, be useful to raise this question here and consider whether something should be said in the commentary on the draft articles. The question arises because several organizations were established for the purpose of facilitating collective self-defence on the part of their members. Although the provisions of most treaties establishing those organizations only refer to the use of force by member States and not by the organization concerned,[25] it may have been understood that member States would act through the organization or even that the organization would respond directly.[26]

20. In any case, the invocability of self-defence as a circumstance precluding wrongfulness of an act of an international organization appears to be sufficiently important to warrant the inclusion of a specific draft article.[27] This could be written following closely the text of article 21 on responsibility of States for internationally wrongful acts.[28] The draft article would then read:

---

[17] This view was expressed by Salmon, "Les accords Spaak–U Thant du 20 février 1965", p. 482.

[18] Kirsch, "Canadian practice in international law: at the Department of Foreign Affairs in 1995–96", p. 389.

[19] S/5653 (11 April 1964), para. 16.

[20] *Official Records of the General Assembly, Thirteenth Session, Annexes*, agenda item 65, document A/3943 (9 October 1958), para. 179.

[21] A more secure world—our shared responsibility: report of the High-level Panel on Threats, Challenges and Change (A/59/565), para. 213. Recent surveys of the evolution of the role of self-defence in peacekeeping and peace-enforcement operations were provided by Cox, "Beyond self-defense: United Nations peacekeeping operations & the use of force", and by Frulli, "Le operazioni di *peacekeeping* delle Nazioni Unite e l'uso della forza", p. 347.

[22] This aspect was stressed by Lamberti Zanardi, *La legittima difesa nel diritto internazionale*, pp. 298–299, and by Klein, *op. cit.*, p. 421.

[23] *Oil Platforms (Islamic Republic of Iran* v. *United States of America), Judgment, I.C.J. Reports 2003*, p. 195, para. 72.

[24] *Yearbook ... 2001*, vol. II (Part Two), p. 27.

[25] For example, the first paragraph of article 5 of the North Atlantic Treaty reads as follows:

> "The Parties agree that an armed attack against one or more of them in Europe or North America shall be considered an attack against them all; and consequently they agree that, if such an armed attack occurs, each of them, in exercise of the right of individual or collective self-defense recognized by Article 51 of the Charter of the United Nations, will assist the Party or Parties so attacked by taking forthwith, individually and in concert with the other Parties, such action as it deems necessary, including the use of armed force, to restore and maintain the security of the North Atlantic area."

Article 3 of the Inter-American Treaty of Reciprocal Assistance was written from a similar perspective.

[26] This approach is reflected in the language of texts such as Security Council resolution 770 (1992), para. 2, in which the Council requested States to "take nationally or through regional agencies or arrangements all measures necessary to facilitate" the delivery of humanitarian assistance in Bosnia and Herzegovina.

[27] While noting that "[c]ertain difficulties" would occur "if an attempt were made to apply certain circumstances precluding wrongfulness, such as self-defence, to international organizations" (*Official Records of the General Assembly, Sixtieth Session, Sixth Committee*, 12th meeting, para. 70), the Russian Federation did not rule out that self-defence could be one of those circumstances.

[28] *Yearbook ... 2001*, vol. II (Part Two), p. 27.

"Article 18. Self-defence

"The wrongfulness of an act of an international organization is precluded if the act constitutes a lawful measure of self-defence taken in conformity with the Charter of the United Nations."

D. Countermeasures in respect of an internationally wrongful act

21. In the articles on responsibility of States for internationally wrongful acts, countermeasures are considered in article 22 and in part three, chapter II (arts. 49–54).[29] While the latter articles consider the conditions under which States may take countermeasures, the purpose of article 22 is simply to say that:

> The wrongfulness of an act of a State not in conformity with an international obligation towards another State is precluded if and to the extent that the act constitutes a countermeasure taken against the latter State in accordance with chapter II of Part Three.[30]

22. A similar approach could be taken with regard to international organizations, provided that the possibility that organizations may take countermeasures is not categorically ruled out. This would be an unlikely conclusion, since a substantial body of literature which analysed practice relating to the admissibility of countermeasures by international organizations shows that the fact that international organizations may in certain cases take countermeasures is not contested.[31] This finding would suggest that a provision concerning countermeasures should be included, at least within brackets, among the draft articles on circumstances precluding wrongfulness.

23. Should an international organization fail to comply with an obligation under international law towards another organization, for instance because it does not supply a certain product and, moreover, does not make reparation for its wrongful act, the question would be raised whether, and under what conditions, the injured organization could resort to countermeasures in order to ensure compliance with the primary obligation or with the obligation to make reparation. The examination of the conditions under which an organization is entitled to resort to countermeasures against another organization could be deferred to a later stage: to the time when the Commission considers the implementation of the international responsibility of an international organization.

24. Further questions that arise in this context concern the resort to countermeasures by an international organization against a State and the reverse case of countermeasures taken by a State against an organization. These two cases are connected, because it seems difficult to admit that a State could use countermeasures against an organization without at the same time admitting that the latter could do likewise. A decision on whether these questions should also be addressed in the current draft articles will best be taken in the course of a study of the implementation of international responsibility.

25. It would be difficult to draft the text of an article concerning countermeasures as circumstances precluding wrongfulness of acts of international organizations without knowing whether the question of countermeasures taken by an organization against a State will eventually be addressed in the draft articles. One option would be to leave the text of the article provisionally blank. As an alternative, a text could be written, part of which would be placed within brackets. The provision could then be drafted on the lines of article 22 on responsibility of States for internationally wrongful acts.[32] However, given the fact that it would make little sense to include a reference to conditions that have yet to be analysed, countermeasures could be provisionally qualified as "lawful". The draft article in its two suggested alternatives would read as follows:

"Article 19. Countermeasures

"Alternative A

"...

"Alternative B

"The wrongfulness of an act of an international organization not in conformity with an international obligation towards another international organization [or a State] is precluded if and to the extent that the act constitutes a lawful countermeasure taken against the latter organization [or the State]."

E. *Force majeure*

26. Legal systems generally consider that responsibility cannot be incurred in case of *force majeure* or similar circumstances, which may be defined as frustration, impracticability, *imprévision* or supervening impossibility.[33] The variety of approaches taken by national legal systems prompted the use of neutral terms in a treaty of uniform law like the United Nations Convention on contracts for the international sale of goods. Article 79, paragraph (1), of this Convention provides that:

> A party is not liable for a failure to perform any of his obligations if he proves that the failure was due to an impediment beyond his control and that he could not reasonably be expected to have taken the impediment into account at the time of the conclusion of the contract or to have avoided or overcome it or its consequences.

27. With regard to international law in its relation to States, a definition of *force majeure* and the pertinent conditions is to be found in article 23 on responsibility of States for internationally wrongful acts.[34] There would be little reason for holding that the same conditions do not apply to international organizations.

28. Some instances of practice, although limited, may be found concerning *force majeure* with regard to international organizations. Certain agreements concluded by international organizations provide examples to that effect. For instance, article XII, paragraph 6, of the

[29] *Ibid.*, p. 30.

[30] *Ibid.*, p. 27.

[31] See Klein, *op. cit.*, pp. 396–409.

[32] *Yearbook ... 2001*, vol. II (Part Two), p. 27.

[33] See, for example, Tallon, "Article 79", pp. 573–575.

[34] See footnote 32 above.

Executing Agency Agreement between UNDP and WHO stated that:

> In the event of *force majeure* or other similar conditions or events which prevent the successful execution of a Project by the Executing Agency, the Executing Agency shall promptly notify the UNDP of such occurrence and may, in consultation with the UNDP, withdraw from execution of the Project. In case of such withdrawal, and unless the Parties agree otherwise, the Executing Agency shall be reimbursed the actual costs incurred up to the effective date of the withdrawal.[35]

Although this paragraph concerns withdrawal from the Agreement, it implicitly considers that non-compliance with an obligation under the Agreement because of *force majeure* does not constitute a breach of the Agreement.

29. *Force majeure* has been invoked by international organizations in order to exclude wrongfulness of conduct in proceedings before international administrative tribunals. In Judgment No. 24, *Fernando Hernández de Agüero* v. *Secretary General of the Organization of American States*, the OAS Administrative Tribunal rejected the plea of *force majeure*, which had been made in order to justify termination of an official's contract:

> The Tribunal considers that in the present case there is no *force majeure* that would have made it impossible for the General Secretariat to fulfill the fixed-term contract, since it is much-explored law that by *force majeure* is meant an irresistible happening of nature.[36]

Although the Tribunal rejected the plea, it clearly recognized the invocability of *force majeure*.

30. A similar approach was taken by the ILO Administrative Tribunal in its Judgment No. 664, in the *Barthl* case. The Tribunal found that *force majeure* was relevant to an employment contract and said:

> *Force majeure* is an unforeseeable occurrence, beyond the control and independent of the will of the parties, which unavoidably frustrates their common intent.[37]

It is immaterial that in the case in hand *force majeure* had been invoked by the employee against the international organization instead of by the organization.

31. INTERPOL pointed to the relevance of financial distress that, in circumstances beyond an organization's control, may affect the ability of an organization to comply with its obligations:

> Unlike States and other territorial entities, generally international organizations do not possess jurisdiction over tax, and cannot therefore generate their own income. International organizations are dependent on the financial contributions of the participating countries. Should it happen that a significant number of countries fail to pay their contributions, a situation may arise in which an organization would not be able to meet its financial obligations. As proved by the demise of the International Tin Council, unlike the case of States, insufficient funding can be a life-threatening situation for an international organization. This issue demands special attention in the codification and progressive development of the law of responsibility of international organizations, either under the heading, *force majeure* or "necessity", or in an arrangement for dealing with the insolvency of international organizations.[38]

Financial distress might constitute an instance of *force majeure* that the organization concerned could invoke in order to exclude wrongfulness of its failure to comply with an international obligation. The fact that the situation of *force majeure* may be due to the conduct of the organization's member States would not prevent the organization, as a separate entity, from availing itself of that situation. Non-compliance by the organization would raise the question, to be discussed in the following part, whether member States incur responsibility.

32. Taking article 23 on responsibility of States for internationally wrongful acts[39] as a model for a provision concerning the invocability of *force majeure* by an international organization, the following text may be proposed:

"*Article 20. Force majeure*

"1. The wrongfulness of an act of an international organization not in conformity with an international obligation of that organization is precluded if the act is due to *force majeure*, that is, the occurrence of an irresistible force or of an unforeseen event, beyond the control of the organization, making it materially impossible in the circumstances to perform the obligation.

"2. Paragraph 1 does not apply if:

"(*a*) the situation of *force majeure* is due, either alone or in combination with other factors, to the conduct of the organization invoking it; or

"(*b*) the organization has assumed the risk of that situation occurring."

F. Distress

33. Article 24 on responsibility of States for internationally wrongful acts[40] considers that distress constitutes a circumstance precluding wrongfulness when "the author of the act in question has no other reasonable way ... of saving the author's life or the lives of other persons entrusted to the author's care". Instances in which distress was invoked in order to preclude the wrongfulness of an act of a State are rare. It is therefore not surprising that known practice does not offer examples of the invocation of distress by an international organization in a similar

---

[35] UNDP and WHO Executing Agency Agreement (New York, 17 September 1992 and Geneva, 19 October 1992), United Nations, *Treaty Series*, vol. 1691, No. 1066, p. 325.

[36] Para. 3 of the judgement, made on 16 November 1976. The text is available at www.oas.org. In a letter dated 8 January 2003 to the Secretary of the Commission, OAS noted that:

> "The majority of claims presented to the OAS Administrative Tribunal allege violations of the OAS General Standards, other resolutions of the OAS General Assembly, violations of rules promulgated by the Secretary General pursuant to his authority under the OAS Charter, and violations of rules established by the Tribunal itself in its jurisprudence. Those standards and rules, having been adopted by duly constituted international authorities, all constitute international law. Thus, the complaints claiming violations of those norms and rules may be characterized as alleging violations of international law."

(*Yearbook ... 2004*, vol. II (Part One), document A/CN.4/545, sect. I.5, para. 3)

[37] Para. 3 of the judgement, made on 19 June 1985, available at www.ilo.org.

[38] Letter dated 9 February 2005 from the INTERPOL General Counsel to the Secretary of the Commission (see *Yearbook ... 2005*, vol. II (Part One), document A/CN.4/556, sect. M.2, p. 49). Footnotes have been omitted in the quotation.

[39] *Yearbook ... 2001*, vol. II (Part Two), p. 27.

[40] *Ibid.*

situation. However, there does not seem to be any reason for not applying the same circumstance precluding wrongfulness to an international organization, should the wrongful act of an organization be caused by the attempt of an organ or agent of that organization to save the organ's or agent's life or the lives of other persons entrusted to the organ's or agent's care.[41] There is also no reason for suggesting that different rules should apply to States and international organizations.

34. Thus, a draft article based on the wording of article 24 on responsibility of States for internationally wrongful acts[42] is suggested here:

"*Article 21. Distress*

"1. The wrongfulness of an act of an international organization not in conformity with an international obligation of that organization is precluded if the author of the act in question has no other reasonable way, in a situation of distress, of saving the author's life or the lives of other persons entrusted to the author's care.

"2. Paragraph 1 does not apply if:

"(*a*) the situation of distress is due, either alone or in combination with other factors, to the conduct of the organization invoking it; or

"(*b*) the act in question is likely to create a comparable or greater peril."

G. Necessity

35. Necessity is probably the most controversial circumstance precluding wrongfulness. It has almost always been considered only in relation to States. It is true, as was noted by IMF,[43] that in the *Gabčíkovo-Nagymaros Project* case ICJ did not specifically refer to States when it said that:

[T]he state of necessity is a ground recognized by customary international law for precluding the wrongfulness of an act not in conformity with an international obligation.[44]

However, if this passage is taken in the context of the facts of the case and of the full quotation of the draft article on necessity adopted by the Commission on first reading, it is clear that the Court only considered the relations between States. It would thus be difficult to agree with the IMF comment to the effect that:

[T]he quoted observation could be used to lend support to the proposition that necessity might preclude the wrongfulness of acts of international organizations.[45]

36. Little can be deduced from the fact that some agreements concluded by certain international organizations allow for non-compliance with international obligations in case of serious troubles or difficulties.[46] This practice, which is not widespread, is not sufficiently indicative of the fact that an international organization could invoke necessity as an excuse for non-compliance as a matter of general international law.

37. A more significant element of practice is given by statements that assert that United Nations forces may invoke "operational necessity" or "military necessity".[47] In his report on financing of the United Nations peacekeeping operations, the Secretary-General held that:

The liability of the Organization for property loss and damage caused by United Nations forces in the ordinary operation of the force is subject to the exception of "operational necessity", that is, where damage results from necessary actions taken by a peacekeeping force in the course of carrying out its operations in pursuance of its mandates.[48]

In this perspective, operational necessity would seem to render interference with private property lawful. In other cases, what is invoked is "military necessity", for instance, in a memorandum prepared by the Office of Legal Affairs in relation to the occupation by the United Nations Operation in Somalia II (UNOSOM II) of a compound in Mogadishu:

If it is established ... that occupation of the compound by hostile factions would have exposed UNOSOM II to serious threat so that effective protection to "the personnel, installations and equipments of United Nations and its agencies, ICRC as well as NGOs" ... could not have been assured without UNOSOM II taking physical possession of the compound, the occupation thereof may be considered as an act of military necessity to ensure the achievement of the objectives laid down in Security Council resolution 814 (1993).

From this perspective, the occupation of the compound may be considered legal.[49]

38. A reference to the invocability of necessity by an international organization was made by the ILO Administrative Tribunal in its Judgment No. 2183, in the *T.D.-N.* v. *CERN* case. This case concerned access to the electronic account of an employee who was on leave. The Tribunal said that:

[I]n the event that access to an e-mail account becomes necessary for reasons of urgency or because of the prolonged absence of the account holder, it must be possible for organisations to open the account using appropriate technical safeguards. That state of necessity, justifying access to data which may be confidential, must be assessed with the utmost care.[50]

---

[41] Klein, *op. cit.*, pp. 415–416, gives as a hypothetical example the unauthorized crossing of a border by UNHCR agents in order to save some refugees under the protection of the organization from the effects of the bombing of a refugee camp.

[42] See footnote 39 above.

[43] Letter dated 1 April 2005 from the IMF General Counsel to the Secretary of the Commission (see *Yearbook ... 2005*, vol. II (Part One), document A/CN.4/556, sect. M.3, p. 49).

[44] *Gabčíkovo-Nagymaros Project (Hungary/Slovakia), Judgment, I.C.J. Reports 1997*, p. 40, para. 51.

[45] See footnote 43 above.

[46] Klein, *op. cit.*, pp. 417–419, referred to some cooperation agreements that were concluded by the European Economic Community with certain non-member States. The same agreements were referred to in a statement by Belgium (*Official Records of the General Assembly, Fifty-ninth Session, Sixth Committee*, 22nd meeting, para. 77).

[47] For the distinction between the two concepts, see Shraga, "UN peacekeeping operations: applicability of international humanitarian law and responsibility for operations-related damage", pp. 410–411. The wide scope given to "military necessity" has raised some criticism. See Sands and Klein, *Bowett's Law of International Institutions*, p. 520, footnote 64.

[48] A/51/389, para. 13.

[49] *United Nations Juridical Yearbook, 1994* (United Nations publication, Sales No. E.00.V.8), p. 405.

[50] Para. 19 of the judgement, made on 3 February 2003. The Registry's translation from the original French is available at www.ilo.org.

While this passage specifically concerns relations between an international organization and its employees, the Tribunal's statement is of a more general character and conveys the view that an organization may invoke necessity as a circumstance precluding wrongfulness.[51]

39. Even if practice is scarce, as was noted by INTERPOL:

> [N]ecessity does not pertain to those areas of international law that, by their nature, are patently inapplicable to international organizations.[52]

The invocability of necessity by international organizations was also advocated by the European Commission,[53] IMF,[54] WIPO[55] and the World Bank.[56] Although comments made in the Sixth Committee in reply to a question raised by the International Law Commission were divided, the majority of the views expressed by States were in favour of including necessity among the circumstances precluding wrongfulness.[57] Statements that were negative mainly stressed the lack of relevant practice, the risk of abuse or the need to provide stricter conditions than those applying to States. The latter concern could be met by taking into account the specific features of international organizations when stating the conditions of invocability of necessity.

40. When considering necessity as a circumstance precluding wrongfulness, article 25 on responsibility of States for internationally wrongful acts requires that the act "is the only way for the State to safeguard an essential interest against a grave and imminent peril".[58] In its judgment in the *Gabčíkovo-Nagymaros Project* case, ICJ also stressed the requirement that there be a threat to an "'essential interest' of the State which is the author of the act conflicting with one of its international obligations".[59] In its commentary on article 25, the Commission notes that:

> The extent to which a given interest is "essential" depends on all the circumstances, and cannot be prejudged. It extends to particular interests of the State and its people, as well as of the international community as a whole.[60]

41. As IMF observed:

> It is unclear whether international organizations could claim "essential interests" similar to those of States, in order to invoke the defence of necessity.[61]

While a State may be considered as entitled to protect an essential interest that is either its own or that of the international community, the scope of interests for which an international organization may invoke necessity cannot be as wide. One cannot assimilate, for instance, the State's interest in surviving with that of an international organization in not being extinguished. Nor are international organizations in the same position as States with regard to the protection of essential interests of the international community.

42. For international organizations, the essential interest in question has to be related to the functions that are entrusted to the organization concerned. According to the World Bank:

> As international organizations have a separate legal personality from that of their member States, and are therefore separate legal subjects, it cannot be denied, *a priori*, that they too have essential interests to safeguard in accordance with their constituent instruments.[62]

Similarly, IMF held that:

> [T]he application of necessity to an international organization would also need to be related to the organization's purposes and functions.[63]

As was pointed out by the European Commission:

> [A]n environmental international organization may possibly invoke "environmental necessity" in a comparable situation where States would be allowed to do so, provided that
>
> ... It needs to protect an essential interest enshrined in its Constitution as a core function and reason of its very existence.[64]

43. The foregoing remarks lead to the consideration that international organizations may invoke necessity only if the grave peril[65] affects an interest that the organization

[51] In a letter of 31 January 2006 to the Secretary of the Commission, INTERPOL "noted that although the Tribunal utilized the term 'state of necessity', it could be argued that the test set forth in article 16 (*a*) of the Commission's articles on responsibility of States for internationally wrongful acts was not met" (A/CN.4/568 and Add.1, sect. J.3, para. 6, reproduced in the present volume).

[52] Letter dated 9 February 2005 from the INTERPOL General Counsel to the Secretary of the Commission (see *Yearbook ... 2005*, vol. II (Part One), document A/CN.4/556, sect. M.2, p. 49).

[53] Letter dated 18 March 2005 from the European Commission to the Legal Counsel of the United Nations (see *Yearbook ... 2005*, vol. II (Part One), document A/CN.4/556, sect. M.1, p 48).

[54] Letter dated 1 April 2005 from IMF to the Legal Counsel of the United Nations (see *Yearbook ... 2005*, vol. II (Part One), document A/CN.4/556, sect. M.3, p. 49).

[55] Letter dated 19 January 2005 from the WIPO Legal Counsel to the Legal Counsel of the United Nations (see *Yearbook ... 2005*, vol. II (Part One), document A/CN.4/556, sect. M.5, p. 50).

[56] Letter dated 31 January 2006 from the Senior Vice President and General Counsel of the World Bank to the Secretary of the Commission (see A/CN.4/568 and Add.1, sect. K.11, para. 6, reproduced in the present volume).

[57] Statements clearly in favour were made by France (*Official Records of the General Assembly, Fifty-ninth Session, Sixth Committee*, 22nd meeting, para. 12), Austria (*ibid.*, para. 23), Denmark, on behalf of the Nordic countries, Finland, Iceland, Norway and Sweden (*ibid.*, para. 65), Belgium (*ibid.*, para. 76), the Russian Federation (*ibid.*, 23rd meeting, para. 23) and Cuba (*ibid.*, para. 25). A tentatively favourable position was taken also by Spain (*ibid.*, 22nd meeting, para. 49). The contrary view was expressed in statements by Germany (*ibid.*, 21st meeting, para. 22), China (*ibid.*, para. 42), Poland (*ibid.*, 22nd meeting, para. 2), Belarus (*ibid.*, para. 45) and Greece (*ibid.*, 23rd meeting, para. 43). Tentatively negative positions were taken by Singapore (*ibid.*, 22nd meeting, para. 57) and New Zealand (*ibid.*, 23rd meeting, para. 10).

[58] *Yearbook ... 2001*, vol. II (Part Two), p. 28.

[59] *I.C.J. Reports 1997* (see footnote 44 above), p. 40, para. 52. In *Legal Consequences of the Construction of a Wall in the Occupied Palestinian Territory, Advisory Opinion, I.C.J. Reports 2004*, p. 195, para. 140, the Court referred again to the requirement of an "essential interest" by quoting article 25, paragraph 1 (*a*), of the articles on State responsibility.

[60] *Yearbook ... 2001*, vol. II (Part Two), p. 83, para. (15).

[61] See footnote 54 above.

[62] See footnote 56 above.

[63] See footnote 54 above.

[64] See footnote 53 above.

[65] The delegate of Singapore "wondered whether there was a common understanding of what constituted such a peril to an international organization" (*Official Records of the General Assembly, Fifty-ninth Session, Sixth Committee*, 22nd meeting, para. 57). It could be observed that the peril in question would have to affect the essential interest, but not necessarily the organization.

has the function to protect. Reference only to the constituent instrument may be too restrictive. As ICJ pointed out in its advisory opinion on the *Legality of the Use by a State of Nuclear Weapons in Armed Conflict*:

> The powers conferred on international organizations are normally the subject of an express statement in their constituent instruments. Nevertheless, the necessities of international life may point to the need for organizations, in order to achieve their objectives, to possess subsidiary powers which are not expressly provided for in the basic instruments which govern their activities. It is generally accepted that international organizations can exercise such powers, known as "implied" powers.[66]

44. Should an international organization be established with the objective of protecting an interest of the international community, the organization could invoke necessity in case of grave peril to that interest. This would also seem to apply in the case of non-universal organizations, since they would do so because they have been established for that purpose by their members, which, according to the definition in draft article 2,[67] are States or at least include States. As, according to article 25 on responsibility of States for internationally wrongful acts,[68] States could invoke necessity for protecting an essential interest of the international community individually, the same should apply to the organization of which they are members.

45. According to article 25 on responsibility of States for internationally wrongful acts, the act for which necessity is invoked should not "impair an essential interest of the State or States towards which the obligation exists, or of the international community as a whole".[69] In a draft article concerning the invocability of necessity by an international organization, it would not be necessary to add a reference to the impairment of an essential interest of another international organization. No more than in the case of the invocation by States, the essential interest of another organization could be protected only to the extent that it coincides with those of one or more States or of the international community.

46. Under aspects that have not been discussed above, there is no reason for departing from the model provided by article 25 on responsibility of States for internationally wrongful acts.[70] The following text is therefore suggested:

"*Article 22. Necessity*

"1. Necessity may not be invoked by an international organization as a ground for precluding the wrongfulness of an act not in conformity with an international obligation of that organization unless the act:

"(*a*) is the only means for the organization to safeguard against a grave and imminent peril an essential interest that the organization has the function to protect; and

"(*b*) does not seriously impair an essential interest of the State or States towards which the obligation exists, or of the international community as a whole.

"2. In any case, necessity may not be invoked by an international organization as a ground for precluding wrongfulness if:

"(*a*) the international obligation in question excludes the possibility of invoking necessity; or

"(*b*) the organization has contributed to the situation of necessity."

H. Compliance with peremptory norms

47. Part one, chapter V, of the articles on responsibility of States for internationally wrongful acts contains a "without prejudice"[71] provision which refers to all the circumstances precluding wrongfulness. The purpose of this provision is to state that an act, which would otherwise not be considered wrongful, would be so held if it was "not in conformity with an obligation arising under a peremptory norm of general international law".[72] In principle, peremptory norms bind international organizations in the same way as States. However, the application of certain peremptory norms with regard to international organizations may raise some problems.

48. The main problems relate to the prohibition of the use of force, which is widely recognized as a prohibition deriving from a peremptory norm. While a State may validly consent to a specific intervention by another State,[73] a general consent given to another State that would allow the latter State to intervene militarily on its own initiative would have to be taken as inconsistent with the peremptory norm. It is clear that no breach of that norm occurs because of the fact that the United Nations has been given the power to use force under Chapter VII of the Charter of the United Nations. On the contrary, the attribution to a regional organization of certain powers of military intervention could be viewed as contravening the peremptory norm. However, a different view could be held with regard to regional organizations which are given the power to use force if that power represents an element of political integration among the member States.[74]

49. While the application of a "without prejudice" provision concerning peremptory norms may present some special features, the general statement that is contained in article 26 on responsibility of States for internationally

[66] *Legality of the Use by a State of Nuclear Weapons in Armed Conflict, Advisory Opinion, I.C.J. Reports 1996*, p. 79, para. 25.

[67] *Yearbook ... 2005*, vol. II (Part Two), p. 40, para. 205.

[68] *Yearbook ... 2001*, vol. II (Part Two), p. 28.

[69] *Ibid.*

[70] *Ibid.*

[71] *Ibid.*, art. 27.

[72] *Ibid.*, art. 26.

[73] The view that "consensual intervention can preclude the operation of Article 26" on responsibility of States for internationally wrongful acts was expressed by Abass, "Consent precluding State responsibility: a critical analysis", p. 224.

[74] One may consider under this perspective article 4 (*h*) of the Constitutive Act of the African Union, which provides for "[t]he right of the Union to intervene in a Member State pursuant to a decision of the Assembly in respect of grave circumstances, namely war crimes, genocide and crimes against humanity". An additional, or possibly alternative, explanation could be that the power of an organization to intervene in those circumstances would not be considered as prohibited by a peremptory norm.

wrongful acts[75] could be reproduced here by simply inserting the term "international organization" instead of "State":

"*Article 23. Compliance with peremptory norms*

"Nothing in this chapter precludes the wrongfulness of any act of an international organization which is not in conformity with an obligation arising under a peremptory norm of general international law."

I. Consequences of invoking a circumstance precluding wrongfulness

50. The substance of what is stated in article 27 (*a*) on responsibility of States for internationally wrongful acts could hardly be contested and certainly also applies to international organizations. The text runs as follows:

> The invocation of a circumstance precluding wrongfulness in accordance with this chapter is without prejudice to:
>
> (*a*) compliance with the obligation in question, if and to the extent that the circumstance precluding wrongfulness no longer exists.[76]

Although this text emphasizes the element of time,[77] what is said about compliance also concerns all the other dimensions of the circumstance. It is clear that a circumstance may preclude wrongfulness only insofar as it goes. In fact, the provision does not leave any question unprejudiced. It simply conveys the meaning that, beyond the reach of the relevant circumstance, wrongfulness of the act is not affected.

[75] *Yearbook ... 2001*, vol. II (Part Two), p. 28.

[76] *Ibid.*

[77] This temporal element may have been emphasized because ICJ in its judgment in the *Gabčíkovo-Nagymaros Project* case had said that "[a]s soon as the state of necessity ceases to exist, the duty to comply with treaty obligations revives" (*I.C.J. Reports 1997* (see footnote 43 above), p. 63, para. 101).

51. The question of compensation, which is referred to under article 27 (*b*), is left unprejudiced in the articles on responsibility of States for internationally wrongful acts because it is not covered. It would be difficult to set a general rule concerning compensation for losses caused by an act that would be wrongful, but for the presence of a certain circumstance. In any event, no responsibility for an internationally wrongful act would arise. The distinction between justifications and excuses would not provide decisive elements for resolving the question whether compensation is due.[78] For instance, consent to a certain act may or may not imply a waiver to any claim relating to losses.

52. Since the position of international organizations is identical to that of States with regard to the matters covered by article 27 on responsibility of States for internationally wrongful acts,[79] the preferable course is to reproduce the text in the current draft articles, although the wording of subparagraph (*a*) could be improved by referring more generally to all the elements of the circumstance and not only to the temporal element. The following text is proposed:

"*Article 24. Consequences of invoking a circumstance precluding wrongfulness*

"The invocation of a circumstance precluding wrongfulness in accordance with this chapter is without prejudice to:

"(*a*) compliance with the obligation in question, if and to the extent that the circumstance precluding wrongfulness no longer exists;

"(*b*) the question of compensation for any material loss caused by the act in question."

[78] The need to distinguish between justification and excuses for this purpose was upheld by Lowe, *loc. cit.*, p. 410; and Johnstone, *loc. cit.*, p. 354.

[79] See footnote 75 above.

Chapter II

Responsibility of a State in connection with the act of an international organization

A. General remarks

53. According to article 1, paragraph 2, of the current draft articles:

> The present draft articles also apply to the international responsibility of a State for the internationally wrongful act of an international organization.[80]

As the related commentary explains,[81] the inclusion of this subject within the scope of the current draft articles is intended to fill a gap that was deliberately left in the articles on responsibility of States for internationally wrongful acts. Article 57 of the latter articles stated that they were "without prejudice to any question of the responsibility under international law of an international organization, or of any State for the conduct of an international organization".[82]

54. Not all the questions that may affect the responsibility of a State in connection with the conduct of an international organization should be examined in the present context. For instance, questions relating to attribution of conduct to a State have already been covered in the articles on responsibility of States for internationally wrongful acts. It would clearly be preferable not to consider them here again. Thus, if an issue arises as to whether a certain conduct is to be attributed to a State or to an international organization or to both, the current articles will provide criteria only for settling the question as to whether that conduct is to be attributed to an international organization, while the articles on State responsibility

[80] *Yearbook ... 2005*, vol. II (Part Two), p. 40, para. 205.

[81] *Yearbook ... 2003*, vol. II (Part Two), p. 19, para. (7).

[82] *Yearbook ... 2001*, vol. II (Part Two), p. 30.

will say whether that same conduct is to be attributed or not to a State.

55. The pattern set by the articles on responsibility of States for internationally wrongful acts does not provide a chapter in which one could appropriately include questions concerning State responsibility in connection with the act of an international organization. In the current draft a new chapter has to be envisaged for this purpose. The placing of this chapter in part one of the draft would have the advantage of addressing those questions in the same part that already deals with similar issues, relating to the reverse case of the responsibility of an international organization in connection with the act of a State.[83] If the option here suggested is taken, the heading of part one, which currently reads, "The internationally wrongful act of an international organization" may have to be modified as a consequence of including some provisions concerning the responsibility of States in that part.

56. Most of the questions to be considered in the new chapter relate to cases in which the responsibility of a State may arise in connection with a wrongful act of an international organization. However, in certain cases the act of the organization is not necessarily wrongful. This also occurs with regard to matters considered in chapter IV of the current draft articles, which also covers the case of a State or an international organization coercing another entity into committing what would be, but for the coercion, an internationally wrongful act.

57. With regard to questions of the responsibility, if any, of States as members of an international organization for the wrongful act of the latter, the conclusions to be reached in relation to States would probably apply also to entities other than States that may also be members of the same organization. Should the draft articles to be adopted in this regard cover the latter members as well, the new chapter would extend beyond questions of responsibility of a State in connection with the act of an international organization. This could be done by referring to "members" instead of "States" in the relevant provisions; however, the current draft cannot also deal with the question of responsibility of entities other than States or international organizations. Insofar as members of an international organization other than States are themselves international organizations, another option could be to refer only to States in all the provisions of the new chapter and to write some specific, albeit parallel, provisions with regard to international organizations as members of other international organizations. The latter provisions could then be included in chapter IV. The current title of that chapter, which reads, "Responsibility of an international organization in connection with the act of a State or another international organization",[84] is wide enough to cover the said provisions as well.

B. Aid or assistance, direction and control, and coercion by a State in the commission of an internationally wrongful act of an international organization

58. Part one, chapter IV, of the articles on responsibility of States for internationally wrongful acts[85] only covers cases of States that aid or assist another State in the commission of an internationally wrongful act, or direct and control another State in the commission of such an act, or else coerce another State to commit an act that would, but for the coercion, be an internationally wrongful act. It would be difficult to find reasons for ruling out that States may act similarly with regard to international organizations. It would likewise be difficult to assume that different rules should apply when, for instance, on the one hand, a State assists another State in the commission of an internationally wrongful act, such as the unlawful use of force, and, on the other hand, a State assists an international organization in doing the same.[86]

59. One could apply by analogy to the case of assistance given by a State to an international organization in the commission of an internationally wrongful act a rule which is in substance identical to the one that was expressed in chapter IV on responsibility of States for internationally wrongful acts with regard to the relations between States. The same goes for all the other cases mentioned in that chapter. However, it seems preferable to include in the current draft certain rules that are specifically designed to cover the case in which a State assists an organization in the commission of an internationally wrongful act and the other cases envisaged in chapter IV on State responsibility. This solution, although largely repetitive, would contribute to clarity. Moreover, if the draft includes a chapter on responsibility of a State in connection with the act of an international organization, it would be odd if no mention were made of the case of aid or assistance, or of direction and control by a State in the commission of an internationally wrongful act by an international organization. Nor would the reason for omitting the case of coercion by a State on an organization be easily understood.

60. In its report to the General Assembly in 2005,[87] the Commission raised the question of whether provisions on aid or assistance, direction and control, and coercion by a State should be included in the current draft. The great majority of the comments expressed by States in the Sixth Committee gave an affirmative reply to this question.[88]

[83] *Yearbook ... 2005*, vol. II (Part Two), p. 40–42, para. 205.

[84] *Ibid.*

[85] *Yearbook ... 2001*, vol. II (Part Two), p. 27.

[86] Several authors held, sometimes implicitly, that similar rules should apply to the relations between a State and another State and to those between a State and an international organization. Amrallah, "The international responsibility of the United Nations for activities carried out by U.N. peace-keeping forces", p. 69, held that "the host state may bear international responsibility—in addition to the U.N. responsibility—for unlawful acts of the U.N. force if it commits an act of complicity in the aforesaid unlawful act, i.e., to instigate or facilitate its committal". Klein, *op. cit.*, pp. 468–469, referred to the case of a State putting its own territory at the disposal of an international organization in order to allow that organization to commit a breach of an international obligation. Sands and Klein, *op. cit.*, p. 524, and Sarooshi, *op. cit.*, pp. 63 and 104, considered the case of aid or assistance by a State in the commission of an internationally wrongful act by an international organization. Hirsch, *The Responsibility of International Organizations Toward Third Parties: Some Basic Principles*, p. 171, referred to cases in which "a single member state has in fact complete, or almost complete, control over the activities of the organization".

[87] *Yearbook ... 2005*, vol. II (Part Two), p. 13, para. 26.

[88] Statements by China (*Official Records of the General Assembly, Sixtieth Session, Sixth Committee*, 11th meeting, para. 52), Austria (*ibid.*, para. 64), the Republic of Korea (*ibid.*, para. 86), Italy (*ibid.*, 12th meeting, para. 4), Belarus (*ibid.*, paras. 49–50), the Russian Federation (*ibid.*, para. 71), Romania (*ibid.*, para. 77), Hungary (*ibid.*, 13th meeting, para. 8), Denmark, on behalf of the Nordic countries, Finland, Iceland, Norway and Sweden (*ibid.*, para. 20), the Libyan Arab Jamahiriya (*ibid.*, 19th meeting, para. 11) and Algeria (*ibid.*, 20th meeting, para. 60).

The few States that were not favourable to the inclusion of provisions on these issues, accepted the idea of a "reference clause" to the corresponding provisions on responsibility of States for internationally wrongful acts[89] or suggested a savings clause, with a reference in the commentary.[90] While INTERPOL held that the current draft would not be "the right place" to deal with the case of a State "aiding and assisting or directing and controlling an international organization in the commission of an internationally wrongful act",[91] and the European Commission considered that the "existing rules on State responsibility may well be applied by analogy when a State does not aid or assist another State but an international organization to commit an international wrongful act".[92] OPCW and WHO expressed a view favourable to including provisions that are parallel to those contained in the articles on State responsibility.[93]

61. Some criticism of a general nature has been voiced with regard to articles 16–18 on responsibility of States for internationally wrongful acts and to the parallel provisions of the current draft which consider aid or assistance, direction and control, and coercion on the part of an international organization.[94] Without going into the merits of that criticism, the need for coherence both with the articles on State responsibility and with those already included in the current draft suggests that, at the present stage, the wording of the model articles be modified only to the extent that is necessary to identify the cases that the proposed draft articles are intended to cover.

62. The State that aids or assists, or directs and controls, or coerces an international organization may or may not be a member State. Should it be a member State, the relevant conduct could not simply consist in participating in the decision-making process of the organization according to the pertinent rules of the organization. The influence which may amount to aid or assistance, direction and control, or coercion, has to be used by the State as a legal entity that is separate from the organization. This is not to say that, when acting within an organ of an international organization, a State may not commit an internationally wrongful act, or that, because of its conduct as a member, a State could not incur responsibility for an internationally wrongful act of the organization. The latter question will be considered later in the present report.[95]

63. Given the fact that, with regard to aid or assistance, direction and control, and coercion, there is no reason for distinguishing between the relations between a State and an international organization, on the one hand, and the relations between States, on the other, the articles to be drafted should closely follow the text of articles 16–18 on responsibility of States for internationally wrongful acts. The headings need to be slightly modified in order to distinguish them from those which have been used in articles 12–14 of the current draft.[96] Article 19 on State responsibility contains a savings clause[97] which is not necessary to replicate in the present context. The following texts are suggested:

"Article 25. Aid or assistance by a State in the commission of an internationally wrongful act by an international organization

"A State which aids or assists an international organization in the commission of an internationally wrongful act by the latter is internationally responsible for doing so if:

"(*a*) that State does so with knowledge of the circumstances of the internationally wrongful act; and

"(*b*) the act would be internationally wrongful if committed by that State.

"Article 26. Direction and control exercised by a State over the commission of an internationally wrongful act by an international organization

"A State which directs and controls an international organization in the commission of an internationally wrongful act by the latter is internationally responsible for that act if:

"(*a*) that State does so with knowledge of the circumstances of the internationally wrongful act; and

"(*b*) the act would be internationally wrongful if committed by that State.

"Article 27. Coercion of an international organization by a State

"A State which coerces an international organization to commit an act is internationally responsible for that act if:

"(*a*) the act would, but for the coercion, be an internationally wrongful act of that international organization; and

"(*b*) that State does so with knowledge of the circumstances of the act."

---

[89] Spain stated that: "It might be sufficient to include a reference clause that would ensure the application, *mutatis mutandis*, of the rules already established under the articles on Responsibility of States for Internationally Wrongful Acts." (*Ibid.* 13th meeting, para. 53)

[90] According to the statement made by France, "[a] saving clause accompanied by a commentary should be sufficient" (*ibid.*, 11th meeting, para. 80). Israel held that "it might be appropriate to make some reference ... in the commentary" (*ibid.*, 16th meeting, para. 57).

[91] See footnote 52 above.

[92] A.CN.4/568 and Add.1, sect. L.1 (reproduced in the present volume at p. 125), letter of 3 February 2006 from the Director General of the Legal Service of the European Commission to the Legal Counsel of the United Nations.

[93] *Ibid.*, pp. 127–128, letters of 30 January 2006 from the OPCW Legal Adviser , and 21 February 2006 from the WHO Legal Counsel to the Legal Counsel of the United Nations.

[94] Statement by Israel (*Official Records of the General Assembly, Sixtieth Session, Sixth Committee*, 16th meeting, paras. 55–56). The criticism concerned the appropriateness "to limit a State's responsibility in situations of aid or assistance only to cases in which the act would be internationally wrongful if committed by that State".

[95] Sect. D below, p. 119.

[96] *Yearbook ... 2005*, vol. II (Part Two), p. 41, para. 205.

[97] Article 19 on the responsibility of States for internationally wrongful acts reads as follows: "This chapter is without prejudice to the international responsibility, under other provisions of these articles, of the State which commits the act in question, or of any other State". (*Yearbook ... 2001*, vol. II (Part Two), p. 27)

C. Use by a State that is a member of an international organization of the separate personality of that organization

64. Article 15 of the current draft concerns the case in which an international organization takes a decision binding its members or makes a recommendation or gives an authorization to members for the commission of an act that implies a circumvention, on the part of that organization, of one of its international obligations.[98] In this type of case the organization refrains from acting directly. It apparently does not infringe any of its obligations, but achieves the same result, taking advantage of the separate legal personality of its members for avoiding compliance. While article 15 elicited a variety of comments in the Sixth Committee,[99] most, if not all, of these comments did not query the basic assumption that an international organization may incur international responsibility because of what it requires member States to do.

65. In the Sixth Committee the delegation of Ireland noted that article 15 "did not cover the situation where the act of the member State would not have incurred international responsibility if committed by the international organization".[100] The delegation of Switzerland added that "States should not be able to hide behind the conduct of the international organization".[101] While chapter IV of the draft was not the appropriate place for considering the problem from the angle of the responsibility of member States, it is indeed reasonable to also envisage in the draft the reverse situation in which a State may incur international responsibility because, in order to avoid compliance with one of its international obligations, it requires an international organization to act in its stead. In the latter case the entity that makes use of the separate legal personality of another entity is a State.

66. The case examined in article 15 and the reverse case now under consideration acquire practical importance when the entity which is required to act could do so without committing a breach of one of its international obligations and its conduct would therefore be lawful. One example could be that of a State that is a party to a treaty which forbids the development of certain weapons and that indirectly acquires control of those weapons by making use of an international organization which is not bound by the treaty.

67. The role that a member State may have within the organs of an international organization would not justify attribution of responsibility to the State for the conduct of the organization: this would be tantamount to denying the separate legal personality of the organization. Should the obligation also cover conduct that the State may take as the member of an international organization, responsibility, if any, of the State in this context would be for breach of an international obligation through its own conduct, not for what the organization did. Example can be taken of the obligation of not acquiring nuclear weapons that non-nuclear States have under the Treaty on the Non-Proliferation of Nuclear Weapons. This type of obligation would then appear to include the prohibition for a State party to the Treaty to contribute to the acquisition of nuclear weapons by an international organization of which the State was a member. Should, on the contrary, the obligation under a treaty be regarded as not covering conduct that States parties take as members of an organization, the conduct of a State within the organization would not as such cause responsibility of the State to arise. The responsibility of a State party to the treaty could be asserted only if it was held respon-sible for achieving, through the organization, a result that the treaty precludes.

68. While the case envisaged in article 15 and the reverse case under discussion here bear some similarities, it would be difficult to give weight to the same factors that article 15 considers relevant when examining the question of the international responsibility of a State for the conduct of an international organization. For instance, it is not inconceivable, but it is unlikely, that a State be entitled to take a decision binding an organization or even to influence the conduct of the organization through a recommendation. The most likely case that may be relevant under the present perspective is that of a State acquiring certain international obligations with regard to some of its functions and then transferring those functions to an international organization. To return to the example of the non-proliferation of nuclear weapons, States that are bound by the Treaty on the Non-Proliferation of Nuclear Weapons could be held responsible if they established an international organization that acquired or developed nuclear weapons.

69. The European Court of Human Rights considered in some judgements the question as to whether States that are members of an international organization incurred responsibility for a breach of an obligation under the Convention for the Protection of Human Rights and Fundamental Freedoms (European Convention on Human Rights) when those States had transferred certain sovereign functions to that organization. In *Waite and Kennedy* v. *Germany* the Court examined the question as to whether the right of access to justice had been unduly impaired by a State that granted immunity to the European Space Agency in relation to claims concerning employment. The Court said that:

> [W]here States establish international organisations in order to pursue or strengthen their cooperation in certain fields of activities, and where they attribute to these organisations certain competences and accord them immunities, there may be implications as to the protection of fundamental rights. It would be incompatible with the purpose and object of the Convention, however, if the Contracting States were thereby

---

[98] *Yearbook ... 2005*, vol. II (Part Two), pp. 41–42, para. 205.

[99] Statements by Ireland (*Official Records of the General Assembly, Sixtieth Session, Sixth Committee*, 11th meeting, paras. 33–37), China (*ibid.*, para. 51), Austria (*ibid.*, paras. 61–62), France (*ibid.*, para. 79), Japan (*ibid.*, 12th meeting, para. 7), the Netherlands (*ibid.*, paras. 15–18), the United States (*ibid.*, paras. 26–28), Portugal (*ibid.*, para. 35), Belarus (*ibid.*, para. 50), the Russian Federation (*ibid.*, paras. 68–69), Guatemala (*ibid.*, para. 105), Hungary (*ibid.*, 13th meeting, para. 7), Denmark, on behalf of the Nordic countries, Finland, Iceland, Norway and Sweden (*ibid.*, para. 19), Greece (*ibid.*, paras. 26–28), Germany (*ibid.*, para. 34), Switzerland (*ibid.*, para. 45), Spain (*ibid.*, para. 52), Poland (*ibid.*, para. 59) and India (*ibid.*, 18th meeting, para. 60). Comments on this question were also expressed by the observer for the European Commission (*ibid.*, 12th meeting, paras. 13–14).

[100] *Ibid.*, 11th meeting, para. 33.

[101] *Ibid.*, 13th meeting, para. 45.

absolved from their responsibility under the Convention in relation to the field of activity covered by such attribution.[102]

The Court nevertheless concluded that, although access to German courts was precluded by the immunity given to the relevant organization, "the essence" of the applicants' "right to a court" under the Convention was not impaired, in view of the "alternative means of legal process available" to them.[103]

70. In *Bosphorus Hava Yollary Turizm ve Ticaret Anonim Sirketi* v. *Ireland*, the European Court of Human Rights took a similar approach, but made the criterion of equivalence more general. The application related to a State measure which had been taken for implementing an obligation stemming from a regulation of the European Community. The Court reiterated its view that a State could not free itself from its obligations under the European Convention on Human Rights by transferring functions to an international organization, because:

absolving Contracting States completely from their Convention responsibility in the areas covered by such a transfer would be incompatible with the purpose and object of the Convention; the guarantees of the Convention could be limited or excluded at will, thereby depriving it of its peremptory character and undermining the practical and effective nature of its safeguards ... The State is considered to retain Convention liability in respect of treaty commitments subsequent to the entry into force of the Convention.[104]

The Court held that what was required from States parties to the Convention was that the relevant organization protected "fundamental rights, as regards both the substantive guarantees offered and the mechanisms controlling their observance, in a manner which can be considered at least equivalent to that for which the Convention provides".[105] If, as in the case in hand, an equivalent protection was granted, the State did not incur responsibility.

71. It is noteworthy that the Commission of the European Communities had taken the same view before the European Court of Human Rights when it said in its written observations in *Senator Lines GmbH* v. *Fifteen member States of the European Union* that:

While it may be true as a matter of principle that signatories to the Convention may not evade their obligations by transferring powers to independent international organizations, it does not follow that they can be held liable for the actions of those organizations in individual cases. In order to comply with their obligations under the Convention it is sufficient that they ensure the institution of an equivalent level of protection of fundamental rights within the organization in question.[106]

72. There is a significant body of literature which advocates the responsibility of member States when they "abuse the separate personality in order to commit illegal acts, or in order to evade their legal obligations".[107] As one author put it: "States should be prevented from creating an artifice with the intention of avoiding consequences which they would have to bear were they to carry out the activity, which they have assigned to the international organization, individually."[108] The emphasis is on the case of States establishing an international organization and entrusting it with functions in respect of which they are bound by obligations under international law while the organization is not so bound.[109] As the case of avoidance of compliance with international obligations by transferring functions to an international organization is the same as the one that was envisaged in the instances of practice referred to in the previous paragraphs, it seems preferable to write a draft article that addresses that case. This option would not rule out other cases being treated in a similar way, by resorting to analogy.

73. In draft article 15 the verb "to circumvent" is used in order to describe the case in which an international organization incurs responsibility for avoiding compliance with one of its international obligations by adopting "a decision binding a member State or international organization to commit an act that would be internationally wrongful if committed by the former organization".[110] The term "circumvention" received some criticism in the Sixth Committee,[111] mainly because it appeared to be unclear, although the commentary attempted to explain that term, indicating in particular that no "specific intention of circumventing" was required.[112] In view of this criticism, it would be preferable to use different wording in the present context. A change of terminology does not raise

[102] European Court of Human Rights, *Reports of Judgments and Decisions* (1999–I), *Waite and Kennedy* v. *Germany*, judgment of 18 February 1999 (Strasbourg, Council of Europe), p. 410, para. 67. A similar passage is contained in the judgment of the same day in *Beer and Regan* v. *Germany*, *European Human Rights Reports*, vol. 33 (London, Sweet & Maxwell, 2001), p. 78, para. 57. A more succinct version is in the judgment, again of the same day, in *Matthews* v. *the United Kingdom*, *Reports of Judgments* ... (see above), p. 265, para. 32. The passage quoted in the text reflects the view that the European Commission of Human Rights had expressed in its decision of 9 February 1990 in *M. & Co.* v. *the Federal Republic of Germany*, *Decisions and Reports*, vol. 64, p. 145.

[103] *Reports of Judgments* ... (see footnote 102 above), p. 412, para. 73.

[104] European Court of Human Rights, judgment of 30 June 2005, *Reports of Judgments and Decisions* (2005–VI) (Strasbourg, Council of Europe), pp. 157–158, para. 154.

[105] *Ibid.*, p. 158, para. 155.

[106] Observations dated 1 March 2001 (JURM (2000) 4030), para. 25. The Court did not address the question in its judgement in the case.

[107] Hirsch, *op. cit.*, p. 195.

[108] Zemanek, "The legal consequences for member States of the non-fulfilment by international organizations of their obligations toward third parties: *réponses et observations des membres de la Commission*", p. 329.

[109] Münch, *Das völkerrechtliche Delikt in der modernen Entwicklung der völkerrechtsgemeinschaft*, p. 269, linked the responsibility of member States of an international organization to circumvention of their obligations through the use of the separate legal personality of that organization. Seidl-Hohenveldern, *Corporations in and under International Law*, p. 121, maintained that: "Just as a State cannot escape its responsibility under international law by entrusting to another legal person the fulfilment of its international obligations, the partner States of a common inter-State enterprise are jointly and severally responsible in international law for the acts of the enterprise". Similar views were expressed with regard to the relations between member States and international organizations by Di Blase, "Sulla responsabilità internazionale per attività dell'ONU", pp. 271–276; Sands and Klein, *op. cit.*, p. 524; and Sarooshi, *op. cit.*, p. 64. After examining the dictum of the European Court of Human Rights in *Waite and Kennedy* v. *Germany* mentioned above (para. 69), Brownlie, "The responsibility of States for the acts of international organizations", p. 361, noted that: "Whilst the context is that of human rights, the principle invoked would seem to be general in its application."

[110] *Yearbook ... 2005*, vol. II (Part Two), pp. 41–42, para. 205. The text refers to paragraph 1; the same verb was used in paragraph 2, which considers the case in which an international organization authorizes a member, or recommends to a member, "to commit an act that would be internationally wrongful if committed" by that organization.

[111] See statements by the observer for the European Commission (*Official Records of the General Assembly, Sixtieth Session, Sixth Committee*, 12th meeting, paras. 13–14), the Netherlands (*ibid.*, paras. 15–18), the United States (*ibid.*, paras. 26–28), Guatemala (*ibid.*, para. 105), Hungary (*ibid.*, 13th meeting, para. 7) and Greece (*ibid.*, paras. 26–28).

[112] *Yearbook ... 2005*, vol. II (Part Two), p. 47, para. 206, para. (4) of the commentary to article 15.

questions of coherency in relation to article 15 because, as has been noted above, the cases in which an international organization would incur responsibility according to that article are different from those that are relevant for the draft article under discussion here.

74. While responsibility of members of an international organization may concern entities other than States, for the reasons expressed in paragraph 57 above, the draft that is here proposed only refers to States. Practice and literature point to the requirement that the act that implies avoidance of the international obligation should actually occur. Although, as has been noted above, the practical relevance of this case depends on the fact that the international organization is not bound by the obligation, this is certainly not a requirement and it may be preferable to say as much, as has been done in draft article 15, paragraph 3. The suggested heading attempts to follow the style of those of the previous draft articles in the chapter. The following text is therefore suggested:

"Article 28. Use by a State that is a member of an international organization of the separate personality of that organization

"1. A State that is a member of an international organization incurs international responsibility if:

"(*a*) it avoids compliance with an international obligation relating to certain functions by transferring those functions to that organization; and

"(*b*) the organization commits an act that, if taken by that State, would have implied non-compliance with that obligation.

"2. Paragraph 1 applies whether or not the act in question is internationally wrongful for the international organization."

D. Question of the responsibility of members of an international organization when that organization is responsible

75. Two affairs have highlighted the question of whether States that are members of an international organization incur responsibility because they are members of an organization which commits an internationally wrongful act. Both affairs led to a number of judgements by municipal courts, one of them also to some arbitral awards. Although in neither instance was the focus on whether member States were responsible under international law, several remarks were made on this question; moreover, certain considerations of a general nature that were made in those decisions also appear to be relevant to issues of international responsibility.

76. The first case had its origin in a request for arbitration which was made by Westland Helicopters Ltd. against the Arab Organization for Industrialization (AOI) and the four States members of that organization (Egypt, Qatar, Saudi Arabia and the United Arab Emirates). The request was based on an arbitration clause in a contract that had been concluded between the company and AOI. The arbitration tribunal examined in an interim award the question of its own competence and that of the liability of the four member States for the acts of the organization. This award deserves relatively long quotations as it tried to make a case for the responsibility of member States. The tribunal's main points in this regard were the following:

> A widespread theory, deriving moreover from Roman law ("*Si quid universitati debetur, singulis non debetur, nec quod debet universitas singuli debent*") Dig. 3, 4, 7, 1), excludes cumulative liability of a legal person and of the individuals which constitute it, these latter being party to none of the legal relations of the legal person. This notion, which could be deemed "strict", cannot however be applied in the present case ... [T]he designation of an organization as "legal person" and the attribution of an independent existence do not provide any basis for a conclusion as to whether or not those who compose it are bound by obligations undertaken by it.[113]

> In default by the four States of formal exclusion of their liability, third parties which have contracted with the AOI could legitimately count on their liability. This rule flows from general principles of law and from good faith.[114]

> [T]he four States, in forming the AOI, did not intend wholly to disappear behind it, but rather to participate in the AOI as "members with liability".[115]

> [O]ne must admit that in reality, in the circumstances of this case, the AOI is one with the States. At the same time as establishing the AOI, the Treaty set up the Higher Committee ("joint Ministerial Higher Committee") composed of the competent Ministers of the four States, charged with the responsibility not only to approve the Basic Statute, and to set up a provisional Directorate, but furthermore to direct the general policy of the AOI, and Article 23 of the Basic Statute describes this Committee as the "dominating authority". There could be no clearer demonstration of this identification of the States with the AOI, especially since Article 56 of the Statute specifies that in case of disagreement within the Committee, reference should be made to the Kings, Princes and Presidents of the States.[116]

After referring to the circumstances in which the agreement between AOI and the company had been concluded and noting that the member States "could not help but be aware of the implications of their actions",[117] the arbitral tribunal concluded:

> If it is true that the four States are bound by the obligations entered into by the AOI, these four States are equally bound by the arbitration clause concluded by the AOI, since the obligations under substantive law cannot be dissociated from those which exist on the procedural level.[118]

The tribunal made a brief reference to international law when it put forward some "considerations of equity":

> Equity, in common with the principles of international law, allows the corporate veil to be lifted, in order to protect third parties against an abuse which would be to their detriment (International Court of Justice, 5 February 1970, *Barcelona Traction*).[119]

77. The arbitral award was set aside by the Court of Justice of Geneva at the request of Egypt and in relation to

[113] *Westland Helicopters Ltd.* v. *Arab Organization for Industrialization*, interim award of 5 March 1984, quoted from the English translation published in *International Law Reports*, vol. 80 (1989), p. 612.

[114] *Ibid*., p. 613.

[115] *Ibid*., p. 614.

[116] *Ibid*., pp. 614–615.

[117] *Ibid*., p. 615.

[118] *Ibid*.

[119] *Ibid*., p. 616.

that State only.[120] In finding that the arbitral tribunal was incompetent, the Court dissented from

the conclusion of the Arbitral Tribunal that the AOI is in some way a general partnership (*société en nom collectif*) which the four States did not intend to hide behind but agreed to take part in as "members with liability" (*membres responsables*). It is not clear what legal grounds the Arbitral Tribunal has for accepting that the AOI is a legal entity under international law and then assimilating it to a corporation under private law, recognized by national legislations and subject to the rules of these legislations.[121]

Westland Helicopters unsuccessfully appealed against this judgement to the Federal Supreme Court of Switzerland. The Court confirmed that the arbitration clause did not bind Egypt and said:

The predominant role played by [the member] States and the fact that the supreme authority of the AOI is a Higher Committee composed of ministers cannot undermine the independence and personality of the Organization, nor lead to the conclusion that when organs of the AOI deal with third parties they *ipso facto* bind the founding States.

... The fact that the AOI's status derives from public international law does not cause any attenuation of its independence *vis-à-vis* its founding States.[122]

78. A new arbitration panel considered the issue of the liability of AOI and the three member States which had not challenged the interim award. The tribunal found that:

The States' responsibility in each individual case can be assessed only on the basis of the acts constituting the joint organization when construed also in accordance with the behaviour of the founder States.[123]

The tribunal concluded that member States had not intended to exclude their liability and that the special circumstances of the case "invited the trust of third parties contracting with the Organization as to its ability to cope with its commitments because of the constant support of the member states".[124] However, it appears that the final award was given only against AOI.[125]

79. The second affair which caused an in-depth discussion of the responsibility of member States originated in the failure of the International Tin Council (ITC) to fulfil its obligations under several contracts. In one of the cases before the English High Court, the plaintiffs sued the United Kingdom Department of Trade and Industry, 22 foreign States and the European Economic Community (EEC).[126] After referring to the interim arbitral award examined above and to an EEC regulation, Justice Staughton said:

There is thus material on which one could conclude that, both in the domestic law of some countries and in public international law, the fact that an association is a legal person is not inconsistent with its members being liable to creditors for its obligations.[127]

However, he added:

As it is, I reach no conclusion as to whether legal personality of an association is or is not, in international law, inconsistent with the members being liable for its obligations to third parties.[128]

He concluded instead that, according to English law, members were not liable. One of the arguments ran as follows:

It seems to me that the view of Parliament ... was that in international law legal personality necessarily meant that the members of an organization were not liable for its obligations.[129]

In a parallel case in the High Court, Justice Millett took the same approach and held that, if the member States were "to be criticised, it is not for their failure to pay the creditors directly, but for their failure to put the ITC in funds to discharge the obligations they allowed it to incur".[130]

80. The two judgements given in the High Court were the subject of appeals, which were decided jointly. In the Court of Appeal one of the majority opinions was Lord Kerr's. He noted that the legal problems arising in the case would require an "analysis on the plane of public international law and of the relationship between international law and the domestic law" of England.[131] On the first aspect he said that:

The preponderant view of the relatively few international jurists to whose writings we were referred, since we were told that there are no others, appears to be in favour of international organisations being treated in international law as "mixed" entities, rather than bodies corporate. But their views, however learned, are based on their personal opinions; and in many cases they are expressed with a degree of understandable uncertainty. As yet there is clearly no settled jurisprudence about these aspects of international organisations.

... There is no other source from which the position in international law can be deduced with any confidence.[132]

Lord Kerr held that:

[I]t may well be that if an international association were to default upon an obligation to a state or association of states or to another international organisation, then the regime of secondary liability on the part of its members would apply as a matter of international law. But it does not by any means follow that any similar acceptance of obligations by the members can be assumed within the framework of municipal systems of law.[133]

---

[120] *Ibid.*, judgment of 23 October 1987, p. 622.

[121] *Ibid.*, p. 643.

[122] *Ibid.*, judgment of 19 July 1988, p. 658. The original French texts of the judgements of the Court of Justice of Geneva and of the Swiss Federal Court can be found in *Revue de l'arbitrage*, No. 3 (July–September 1989), pp. 515 and 525, respectively.

[123] Para. 56 of the award of 21 July 1991, as quoted by Higgins, "The legal consequences for member states of the non-fulfilment by international organizations of their obligations toward third parties: provisional report", p. 393.

[124] *Ibid.*, pp. 393–394.

[125] The text of the final award, which was given on 28 June 1993, was not published. The award was referred to in the judgement of the High Court, England, of 3 August 1994, *Westland Helicopters Ltd.* v. *Arab Organization for Industrialization, International Law Reports*, vol. 108 (1998), p. 567.

[126] *J. H. Rayner (Mincing Lane) Ltd.* v. *Department of Trade and Industry and Others* (24 June 1987), *International Law Reports*, vol. 77 (1988), p. 55.

[127] *Ibid.*, p. 76.

[128] *Ibid.*, p. 77. Similar passages appear on pages 79–80.

[129] *Ibid.*, p. 88.

[130] *Maclaine Watson & Co. Ltd.* v. *Department of Trade and Industry*, judgement of 29 July 1987, *International Law Reports*, vol. 80 (1989), p. 47.

[131] *Ibid.* and *J. H. Rayner (Mincing Lane) Ltd.* v. *Department of Trade and Industry and Others, and Related Appeals*, judgement of 27 April 1988, *ibid.*, p. 57.

[132] *Ibid.*, p. 108.

[133] *Ibid.*, p. 109.

However, Lord Kerr's conclusion did not entirely rest on municipal law. He also stated the opinion that:

> In sum, I cannot find any basis for concluding that it has been shown that there is any rule of international law, binding upon the member states of the I.T.C., whereby they can be held liable—let alone jointly and severally—in any national court to the creditors of the I.T.C. for the debts of the I.T.C. resulting from contracts concluded by the I.T.C. in its own name.[134]

81. Lord Ralph Gibson concurred. He observed that:

> Where the contract has been made by the organisation as a separate legal personality, then, in my view, international law would not impose such liability upon the members, simply by reason of their membership, unless upon a proper construction of the constituent document, by reference to terms express or implied, that direct secondary liability has been assumed by the members.[135]

He also noted that:

> Nothing is shown of any practice of states as to the acknowledgement or acceptance of direct liability by any states by reason of the absence of an exclusion clause.[136]

Also the dissenting judge, Lord Nourse, gave decisive importance to the attitude taken by the member States, although he adopted the opposite presumption. He said that:

> [I]t is inherent in the views of the jurists and the Westland tribunal that the founding states of an international organisation can, by the terms of its constitution, provide for the exclusion or limitation, alternatively no doubt for the inclusion, of their liability for its obligations; and, moreover, that such provision will be determinative of that question for the purposes of international law. Thus the intention of the founding states is paramount ... And we must heed the importance which Shihata, like the Westland tribunal, would attach to the extent to which the states' intention was made known to third parties dealing with the I.T.C.[137]

Lord Nourse found that "the intention of the states who were parties to I.T.A.6 [the Sixth International Tin Agreement] was that the members of I.T.C. should be liable for its obligations"[138] and said that:

> [T]he ITC has separate personality in international law, but that its members are nevertheless jointly and severally, directly and without limitation liable for debts on its tin and loan contracts in England, if and to the extent that they are not discharged by the I.T.C. itself.[139]

82. The conclusion that the majority opinions had reached in the Court of Appeal was unanimously upheld by the House of Lords. Lord Templeman rejected the idea that liability of member States would "flow from a general principle of law", noting that: "No authority was cited which supported the alleged general principle."[140] With regard to the alleged rule of international law imposing on "states members of an international organisation, joint and several liability for the default of the organisation in the payment of its debts unless the treaty which establishes the international organisation clearly disclaims any liability on the part of the members", Lord Templeman found that: "No plausible evidence was produced of the existence of such a rule of international law before or at the time of I.T.A.6 in 1982 or thereafter."[141] As an additional argument the same judge held that:

> [I]f there existed a rule of international law which implied in a treaty or imposed on sovereign states which enter into a treaty an obligation (in default of a clear disclaimer in the treaty) to discharge the debts of an international organisation established by that treaty, the rule of international law could only be enforced under international law.[142]

Neither was Lord Oliver of Aylmerton persuaded of the existence in international law of a rule providing for liability, whether "primary or secondary", of members of an international organization. He said:

> A rule of international law becomes a rule—whether accepted into domestic law or not—only when it is certain and is accepted generally by the body of civilised nations; and it is for those who assert the rule to demonstrate it, if necessary before the International Court of Justice. It is certainly not for a domestic tribunal in effect to legislate a rule into existence for the purposes of domestic law and on the basis of material that is wholly indeterminate.[143]

83. The question of liability of member States was incidentally touched upon by the Government of Canada in relation to a claim for injuries caused by a crash of a Canadian helicopter in 1989, while it was operating in the Sinai for an organization established by Egypt and Israel, the Multilateral Force and Observers (MFO). An exchange of letters dated 4 and 9 November 1999 between Canada and MFO contained the following passage:

> The Government of Canada agrees that the payment of U.S. $3,650,000 shall constitute full and final satisfaction of, and the Government of Canada shall thereupon be deemed to unconditionally release and discharge the MFO and through it the State of Israel and the Arab Republic of Egypt from, any and all liability or obligation that the MFO may have in respect of the claims.[144]

One could find in this passage some support for the view that a claim could have been preferred against the two member States.

84. Some opinions on the question of the responsibility of member States were expressed by States in connection with the current study of the Commission. In this context, Germany recalled in its written comments that it had

> advocated the principle of separate responsibility before the European Commission of Human Rights (*M. & Co.*), the European Court of Human Rights (*Senator Lines*) and ICJ (*Legality of Use of Force*) and has rejected responsibility by reason of membership for measures taken by the European Community, NATO and the United Nations.[145]

---

[134] *Ibid.*

[135] *Ibid.*, p. 172.

[136] *Ibid.*, p. 174.

[137] *Ibid.*, p. 141.

[138] *Ibid.*, p. 145.

[139] *Ibid.*, p. 147.

[140] *Australia & New Zealand Banking Group Ltd.* et al. v. *Australia* et al., judgement of 26 October 1989, ILM, vol. XXIX, No. 3 (May 1990), p. 674.

[141] *Ibid.*, p. 675.

[142] *Ibid.*

[143] *Ibid.*, p. 706. A few months later, the view that member States could not be held responsible because of their part in the "internal decision-making process" of the organization was maintained by Mr. Advocate General Darmon in his opinion in the case *Maclaine Watson & Company Ltd* v. *Council and Commission of the European Communities*, case C–241/87, before the Court of Justice of the European Communities, *Reports of Cases before the Court of Justice and the Court of First Instance* (1990–5), p. I–1822, para. 144. A settlement was reached before the Court could give its judgement on this case.

[144] Similar wording had been used in an exchange of letters dated 3 May 1990 between the MFO Director-General and the Ambassador of the United States to Italy, relating to a claim arising from the crash of an aircraft. For further information, see *Yearbook ... 2004*, vol. II (Part One), document A/CN.4/545, sect. I.3, pp. 34–36 and annex thereto, p. 41.

[145] *Yearbook ... 2005*, vol. II (Part One), document A/CN.4/556, sect. O.3, p. 61.

85. In its report concerning its fifty-seventh session, the Commission had requested comments with regard to the question whether "a State could be held responsible for the internationally wrongful act of an international organization of which it is a member".[146] Only a few comments were expressed in the Sixth Committee on this point. While two statements suggested that the current draft articles should not deal with this question,[147] other statements expressed a different opinion[148] and proposed a variety of solutions. The delegation of China observed that, since the decisions and actions of an international organization were, as a rule, under the control, or reliant on the support, of member States, those member States that voted in favour of the decision in question or implemented the relevant decision, recommendation or authorization should incur a corresponding international responsibility.[149] Other delegations took the view that in principle member States were not responsible, but held that they could incur responsibility in "certain exceptional cases",[150] in case of "negligent supervision of organizations",[151] or "particularly with regard to international organizations with limited resources and a small membership, where each member State had a high level of control over the organization's activities".[152] Another delegation pointed out the possible relevance of "various factors".[153]

86. According to INTERPOL, one of "the *lex specialis* cases where the rules of an international organization specifically provide for the responsibility of a State for internationally wrongful acts of an international organization of which it is a member" would occur when "either the constituent instrument or another rule of the organization prescribes the derivative or secondary liability of the members of the organization for the acts or debts of the organization".[154] However, responsibility of States members under the rules of the organization does not imply that those States incur responsibility towards a third State unless their responsibility was made relevant with regard to that State under international law. Thus, contrary to the opinion expressed by INTERPOL it cannot be assumed, on the basis of the constituent instrument, that States members of the European Community would incur responsibility when the Community breaches a treaty obligation. Article 300, paragraph 7, of the Treaty establishing the European Community does not intend to create obligations for member States towards non-member States.[155] As was noted in a written comment by Germany, "the article only forms a basis for obligations under community law *vis-à-vis* the European Community and does not permit third parties to assert direct claims against the States members of the European Community".[156] For similar reasons, provisions that may be contained in status-of-forces agreements concerning distribution of liability between a State providing forces to an international organization and that organization cannot be regarded under international law as *per se* relevant in the relations with third States.[157]

87. When a treaty provides for the responsibility of member States,[158] or limits that responsibility or rules it out,[159] a special rule of international law may be established, on the assumption that the treaty provision becomes relevant in relation to a potentially claimant State.[160] Given the variety of this type of clause, it would be difficult to build an argument on the basis of this treaty practice and suggest a conclusion, one way or the other, for resolving the question of responsibility of member States.

88. Legal literature is divided on the question of whether States incur responsibility when an organization of which they are members commits an internationally wrongful act. Some authors hold member States to be responsible because they do not accept that the organization has its own legal personality or they consider that the legal personality of the organization can have legal effects only with regard to non-member States that recognize it.[161] These views conflict with the assumption, made in article 2 of the current draft, that the organization has "its own international legal personality".[162] Other authors maintain, on different premises, that member States are responsible if the organization fails to comply with its obligation to

---

[146] *Ibid.*, vol. II (Part Two), p. 13, para. 26 (*b*).

[147] Statements of Morocco (*Official Records of the General Assembly, Sixtieth Session, Sixth Committee*, 11th meeting, para. 43) and Argentina (12th meeting, para. 80).

[148] The statement of Sierra Leone (*ibid.*, 17th meeting, para. 11) stressed the "exceptional importance" of the issue.

[149] *Ibid.*, 11th meeting, para. 53.

[150] Statement of Italy, *ibid.*, 12th meeting, para. 3.

[151] Statement of Austria, *ibid.*, 11th meeting, para. 65.

[152] Statement of Belarus, *ibid.*, 12th meeting, para. 52.

[153] Statement of Spain, *ibid.*, 13th meeting, para. 53.

[154] Letter of 31 January 2006 (see footnote 51 above).

[155] Article 300, paragraph 7, reads as follows: "Agreements concluded under the conditions set out in this Article shall be binding on the institutions of the Community and on Member States." The European Court of Justice pointed out that this provision does not imply that member States are bound towards non-member States and thus may incur responsibility under international law. See *France* v. *Commission*, case C–327/91, judgment of 9 August 1994, *Reports of Cases before the Court of Justice* (1994–8), p. I–3674, para. 25.

[156] *Yearbook ... 2005*, vol. II (Part One), document A/CN.4/556, sect. O.1 (*a*) (iii), pp. 53–54.

[157] For an analysis of the agreements concerning the status of forces of NATO and the European Union, see Schmalenbach, *op. cit.*, pp. 556–564 and 573–575. See also *Yearbook ... 2005* (footnote 156 above), sect. O.2 (*c*) (ii), pp. 59–60. The model status-of-forces agreement between the United Nations and host countries (A/45/594, annex) does not contain provisions on liability.

[158] For instance, according to article XXII, para. 3 (*b*) of the Convention on the international liability for damage caused by space objects: "Only where the organization has not paid, within a period of six months, any sum agreed or determined to be due as compensation for such damage, may the claimant State invoke the liability of the members which are States Parties to this Convention for the payment of that sum." The fact that liability of members of an organization was only provided for the benefit of States parties to the Convention was criticized by Galicki, "Liability of international organizations for space activities", p. 207.

[159] As an example, article 24 of the International Cocoa Agreement, 2001 may be quoted: "A Member's liability to the Council and to other Members is limited to the extent of its obligations regarding contributions specifically provided for in this Agreement. Third parties dealing with the Council shall be deemed to have notice of the provisions of this Agreement regarding the powers of the Council and the obligations of the Members ..."

[160] This would require the acceptance or at least acquiescence of third States.

[161] For this view, see Münch, *op. cit.*, pp. 267–268; Seidl-Hohenveldern, "Die völkerrechtliche Haftung für Handlungen internationaler Organisationen im Verhältnis zu Nichtmitgliedstaaten", pp. 502–505; and Stein, "Kosovo and the international community—the attribution of possible internationally wrongful acts: responsibility of NATO or of its member States", p. 192.

[162] *Yearbook ... 2005*, vol. II (Part Two), p. 40, para. 205.

make reparation for an internationally wrongful act.[163] Their opinion has been opposed by several other authors who hold that, given the separate legal personality of the organization, member States do not incur any subsidiary responsibility.[164] However, among these authors, some accept that responsibility can nevertheless occur for member States in exceptional cases.[165]

89. The latter opinion also found an expression in the resolution that the Institute of International Law adopted in 1995 in Lisbon on the legal consequences for member States of the non-fulfilment by international organizations of their obligations towards third parties. According to article 6 (*a*) of that resolution:

> Save as specified in article 5, there is no general rule of international law whereby States members are, due solely to their membership, liable concurrently or subsidiarily, for the obligations of an international organization of which they are members.[166]

Article 5 reads as follows:

> (*a*) The question of the liability of the members of an international organization for its obligations is determined by reference to the Rules of the organization.
>
> (*b*) In particular circumstances, members of an international organization may be liable for its obligations in accordance with a relevant general principle of international law, such as acquiescence or the abuse of rights.
>
> (*c*) In addition, a member State may incur liability to a third party
>
> (i) through undertakings by the State, or
>
> (ii) if the international organization has acted as the agent of the State, in law or in fact.[167]

90. The general approach that was taken in the resolution of the Institute of International Law seems in line with the elements that are offered by the above analysis of practice. Apart from the interim arbitral award in the case concerning *Westland Helicopters* (see paragraph 76 above) and the minority opinion by Lord Nourse in the Court of Appeal in the International Tin Council case (see paragraph 81 above), the decisions considered above followed the view that there exists no presumption to the effect that member States incur responsibility (see paragraphs 77–82 above). The same view was shared by the great majority of States: all those (over 25) that were sued in the two affairs considered in paragraphs 76–82 above and most of those that commented on this question in connection with the present study (see paragraphs 84–85 above).

91. One case in which States are often held to be exceptionally responsible for an internationally wrongful act committed by an organization of which they are members is when States accept to be responsible. Acceptance generally implies only a subsidiary responsibility in the event that the organization fails to comply with its obligations towards a non-member State. For instance, in his opinion in the International Tin Council case, Lord Ralph Gibson referred to acceptance of responsibility in the "constituent document".[168] Acceptance can also be expressed in an instrument other than the constituent act. However, as was pointed out when considering article 300, paragraph 7, of the Treaty establishing the European Community (see paragraph 86 above), member States would incur responsibility in international law only if their acceptance of responsibility produced legal effects in their relations with the injured non-member State. This would be most likely to occur on the basis of a treaty provision that conferred rights on third States.[169] The injured State could not sustain its claim simply on the basis of the constituent instrument, which does not bind member States in their relations with non-member States.

92. While the case of acceptance of responsibility seems straightforward, there is another case that calls for a similar solution. This is when member States, by their conduct, cause a non-member State to rely, in its

[163] See Adam, *Les organismes internationaux spécialisés: contribution à la théorie générale des établissements publics internationaux*, p. 130; Ginther, *Die völkerrechtliche Verantwortlichkeit internationaler Organisationen gegenüber Drittstaaten*, pp. 177–179 and 184; Hoffmann, "Der Durchgriff auf die Mitgliedstaaten internationaler Organisationen für deren Schulden", p. 586; Pitschas, *Die völkerrechtliche Verantwortlichkeit der Europäischen Gemeinschaft und ihrer Mitgliedstaaten*, pp. 92–96; Sadurska and Chinkin, "The collapse of the International Tin Council: a case of State responsibility?", pp. 887–890; Schermers, "Liability of international organizations", p. 9; and Wenckstern, "Die Haftung der Mitgliedstaaten für internationale Organisationen", pp. 108–109. Brownlie, in *Principles of Public International Law*, p. 655, held that "in the case of more specialized organizations with a small number of members, it may be necessary to fall back on the collective responsibility of the member states".

[164] See Hartwig, *Die Haftung der Mitgliedstaaten für Internationale Organisationen* , pp. 290–296; Klein, *op. cit.*, pp. 509–510; Pellet, "L'imputabilité d'éventuels actes illicites: responsabilité de l'OTAN ou des États membres", pp. 198 and 201; Pernice, "Die Haftung internationaler Organisationen und ihrer Mitglieder", pp. 419–420; and Ritter, "La protection diplomatique à l'égard d'une organisation internationale", pp. 444–445. Also the authors referred to in footnote 160 above consider that member States are not responsible when the legal personality of the organization may be opposed to non-member States.

[165] Several authors held the view that an exception should be admitted when member States accept that they could be held responsible for an internationally wrongful act of the organization. In a seminal paper, "Role of law in economic development: the legal problems of international public ventures", p. 125, Shihata held, with regard to international companies, that "[a]ll relevant provisions and circumstances must be studied to ascertain what was intended by the parties in this respect and the extent to which their intention was made known to third parties dealing with the enterprise". With regard to members of an international organization, Seidl-Hohenveldern, "Liability of member States for acts or omissions of an international organization", p. 739, agreed that one should likewise take "all relevant provisions and circumstances into account". Klein, *op. cit.*, pp. 509–510, considered that the conduct of member States might imply that they provide a guarantee for the obligations arising for the organization. According to Herdegen, "The insolvency of international organizations and the legal position of creditors: some observations in the light of the International Tin Council crisis", p. 141: "Membership alone cannot serve as an appropriate basis for an extension of claims and liabilities, unless the member States clearly intended to share the organization's rights and obligations." Amerasinghe, "Liability to third parties of member States of international organizations: practice, principle and judicial precedent", p. 280, held that, on the basis of "policy reasons", "the presumption of nonliability could be displaced by evidence that members (some or all of them) or the organization with the approval of members gave creditors reason to assume that members (some or all of them) would accept concurrent or secondary liability even without an express or implied intention to that effect in the constituent instrument". According to Hartwig, *op. cit.*, pp. 299–300, and Hirsch, *op. cit.*, p. 165, an injured party would have the right to claim that members fulfil their obligations to provide funds to the organization concerned.

[166] Institute of International Law, *Yearbook*, vol. 66, part II (Session of Lisbon, 1996), p. 449.

[167] *Ibid.*

[168] See paragraph 81 above. In the same paragraph there is a quotation from Lord Nourse's opinion, which also refers to the "constitution" of the international organization concerned.

[169] The conditions set by article 36 of the Vienna Convention on the Law of Treaties would then apply.

dealings with the organization, on the subsidiary responsibility of the member States of that organization. Certain instances that have been envisaged in practice[170] could be covered by an exception that referred to reliance on the subsidiary responsibility of member States. One statement directly to the point was made in the arbitral award on the merits in the *Westland Helicopters* case. The tribunal referred to the "trust of third parties contracting with the Organization as to its ability to cope with its commitments because of the constant support of the member states".[171] Various factors could be relevant when it comes to establishing whether a non-member State had reason to rely on the member States' responsibility. Among those factors one could include, as was suggested in the comment made by Belarus, "small membership".[172] However, it cannot be assumed that the presence of one or more of those factors *per se* implies that member States incur responsibility.

93. The two exceptions mentioned in the preceding paragraphs do not necessarily concern all the States that are members of an international organization. For instance, should acceptance of subsidiary responsibility have been made only by certain member States, responsibility could be held to exist only for those States. On the other hand, should responsibility arise for the organization as a consequence of a decision taken by one of its organs, the fact that the decision in question was taken with the votes of some member States only does not imply that only those States would incur responsibility.[173] A distinction between States which vote in favour and the other States would not always be warranted. This would reflect also a policy reason, because giving weight to that distinction could negatively affect the decision-making process in many organizations, because the risk of incurring responsibility would hamper the reaching of consensus.

94. The solution suggested here finds some support in further policy reasons. First of all, should member States be regarded as generally responsible, albeit subsidiarily, the relations of international organizations with non-member States would be negatively affected, because they would find difficulties in acting autonomously. Moreover, as has been noted, "if members know that they are potentially liable for contractual damages or tortious harm caused by the acts of an international organization, they will necessarily intervene in virtually all decision-making by international organizations".[174] The two suggested exceptions also rest on policy reasons, because they link responsibility of member States to their conduct. Once member States have accepted responsibility or led a non-member State to rely on their responsibility, it seems fair that member States should face the consequences of their own conduct.

95. For the reasons explained in paragraph 57 above, the suggested draft article will only consider States as members of an international organization. However, as was observed by IAEA:

> *Prima facie*, any potential responsibility of a State member of an international organization and of an international organization that is a member of another international organization should be treated similarly.[175]

96. The foregoing remarks lead to the conclusion that only in exceptional cases could a State that is a member of an international organization incur responsibility for the internationally wrongful act of that organization. This could be expressed in a text like the one which follows:

"*Article 29. Responsibility of a State that is a member of an international organization for the internationally wrongful act of that organization*

"Except as provided in the preceding articles of this chapter, a State that is a member of an international organization is not responsible for an internationally wrongful act of that organization unless:

"(*a*) it has accepted with regard to the injured third party that it could be held responsible; or

"(*b*) it has led the injured third party to rely on its responsibility."

---

[170] See paragraphs 76, 83 and 85 above. Some of the exceptions referred to in the resolution of the Institute of International Law, quoted in paragraph 82 above, concern the same type of circumstance, while the case where "the international organization has acted as the agent of the State, in law or in fact" (art. 5 (*c*) (ii)) appears to raise a question of attribution of conduct.

[171] This passage was quoted in paragraph 78 above.

[172] *Official Records of the General Assembly, Sixtieth Session, Sixth Committee*, 12th meeting, para. 52.

[173] The importance of the circumstance of a vote in favour of the relevant decision was emphasized in the statements by China (*ibid.*, 11th meeting, para. 53) and Belarus (*ibid.*, 12th meeting, para. 51).

[174] Higgins, *loc. cit.*, p. 419.

[175] *Yearbook ... 2004*, vol. II (Part One), document A/CN.4/545, sect. B.1 (*b*), p. 23.

DOCUMENT A/CN.4/568 and Add.1

Comments and observations received from international organizations

[*Original: English*]
[*17 March and 12 May 2006*]

CONTENTS

Multilateral instruments cited in the present report

	Source
Treaty of Peace between the Allied and Associated Powers and Germany (Treaty of Versailles) (Versailles, 28 June 1919)	*British and Foreign State Papers, 1919,* vol. CXII (London, HM Stationery Office, 1922), p. 1.
Constitution of the United Nations Educational, Scientific and Cultural Organization (London, 16 November 1945)	United Nations, *Treaty Series*, vol. 4, No. 52, p. 275.
Articles of Agreement of the International Monetary Fund and Articles of Agreement of the International Bank for Reconstruction and Development (Washington, D.C., 27 December 1945)	*Ibid.*, vol. 2, No. 20, p. 39.
Treaty on principles governing the activities of States in the exploration and use of outer space, including the moon and other celestial bodies (Moscow, London and Washington, D.C., 27 January 1967)	*Ibid.*, vol. 610, No. 8843, p. 205.
Convention on international liability for damage caused by space objects (London, Moscow, Washington, D.C., 29 March 1972)	*Ibid.*, vol. 961, No. 13810, p. 187.
Vienna Convention on the Law of Treaties between States and International Organizations or between International Organizations (Vienna, 21 March 1986)	A/CONF. 129/15.
Treaty establishing the European Community, as incorporating the amendments made by the Treaty of Nice of 26 February 2001	Consolidated version of the Treaty on European Union, *Official Journal of the European Communities*, No. C 325, vol. 45 (24 December 2002), p. 33.

Works cited in the present report

CRAWFORD, James

The International Law Commission's Articles on State Responsibility: Introduction, Text and Commentaries. Cambridge, Cambridge University Press, 2002.

KLEIN, Pierre

La responsabilité des organisations internationales dans les ordres juridiques internes et en droit des gens. Brussels, Bruylant, 1998.

Introduction

1. At its fifty-fifth session in 2003, the International Law Commission asked the Secretariat to circulate, on an annual basis, the portions of its report relevant to the topic "Responsibility of international organizations" to international organizations for their comments.[1] Pursuant to that request, selected international organizations were invited to submit their comments on the relevant portions of the Commission's 2003, 2004 and 2005 reports.[2] Most recently, the Commission sought comments on chapter VI of its 2005 report[3] and on the issues of particular interest to it noted in paragraph 26 of the 2005 report.[4]

[1] *Yearbook ... 2003*, vol. II (Part Two), p. 18, para. 52.

[2] The written comments of international organizations received prior to 9 May 2005 are contained in *Yearbook ... 2004*, vol. II (Part One), document A/CN.4/545, and *Yearbook ... 2005*, vol. II (Part One), documents A/CN.4/547, p. 19 and A/CN.4/556, p. 27.

[3] *Yearbook ... 2005*, vol. II (Part Two), p. 38.

[4] Paragraph 26 of *Yearbook ... 2005*, vol. II (Part Two) (p. 13), reads as follows:

"The next report of the Special Rapporteur will address questions relating to (1) circumstances precluding wrongfulness, and (2) responsibility of States for the internationally wrongful acts of international

2. As at 12 May 2006, written comments had been received from the following seven international organizations (dates of submission in parentheses): INTERPOL (31 January 2006), OPCW (30 January 2006), World Bank (31 January 2006), WHO (21 February 2006), European Commission (3 February 2006), ILO (5 April 2006) and UNESCO (28 April 2006). These comments are reproduced below, in a topic-by-topic manner.

organizations. The Commission would welcome comments and observations relating to these questions, especially on the following points:

"(*a*) Article 16 of the articles on Responsibility of States for Internationally Wrongful Acts only considers the case that a State aids or assists another State in the commission of an internationally wrongful act. Should the Commission include in the draft articles on responsibility of international organizations also a provision concerning aid or assistance given by a State to an international organization in the commission of an internally wrongful act? Should the answer given to the question above also apply to the case of direction and control or coercion exercised by a State over the commission of an act of an international organization that would be wrongful but for the coercion?

"(*b*) Apart from the cases considered under (*a*), are there cases in which a State could be held responsible for the internationally wrongful act of an international organization of which it is a member?"

Comments and observations received from international organizations

A. General remarks

European Commission

The general view of the European Commission on the work of the International Law Commission in 2005 was expressed in the statement of the European Union and of the European Community to the Sixth Committee of the General Assembly on 25 October 2005 (see *Official Records of the General Assembly, Sixtieth Session, Sixth Committee*, 12th meeting).

The European Commission welcomes the progress made by the International Law Commission and congratulates the Special Rapporteur, Mr. Giorgio Gaja, for his third report.[5] The European Commission attaches great importance to the work of the International Law Commission, but necessarily looks at it from the perspective of a rather specific international organization. It is therefore restricting its remarks to a few aspects of the draft articles.

Articles 8, paragraph 1, 9, 10 and 11 of the present draft are identical to articles 12, paragraph 1, 13, 14 and 15 on responsibility of States for internationally wrongful acts.[6] There is indeed no need to deviate from the rules for States in this respect and hence the European Commission has no remarks.

Draft articles 12–14 on inter-temporal law reflect the precedents of articles 16–18 on responsibility of States for internationally wrongful acts.[7] They again do not require any comment from the European Commission.

International Labour Organization

This is the first time that ILO is contributing to this exercise. Some remarks will therefore inevitably be devoted to issues dealt with by the Commission prior to its fifty-seventh session, held in 2005. It is hoped that these remarks can still be taken into consideration by the Special Rapporteur and the Commission.

In general, it may be said that there is no significant practice as regards the international responsibility of ILO. There is, of course, abundant practice concerning the responsibility of the organization *vis-à-vis* its officials, including a rich case law elaborated by the ILO Administrative Tribunal. ILO does not, however, consider this practice to be relevant in the context of this exercise as it reflects a specific legal system, as explained below in more detail.

In general terms, ILO considers that the comments made on the relevant parts of the 2003 and 2004 Commission reports by some organizations, namely INTERPOL and IMF, regarding the differences between the law of State responsibility and the law of responsibility of international organizations, are sensible. In this connection two points seem particularly important to ILO. The first is the fact that issues implicating the organic principles or internal governance of international organizations are governed by international law, while, as regards States, municipal laws, including the national constitutions, are, from the standpoint of international law and of international tribunals, merely facts which express the will and constitute the activities of States.[8] On the other hand, for international organizations, unlike what happens for States, international responsibility must be examined in the light of the organizations' purposes and functions as specified or implied in their constituent documents and developed in practice, because they are not endowed with general competence.[9]

Organization for the Prohibition of Chemical Weapons

Regarding chapter VI, OPCW finds that it is quite comprehensive, thorough and balanced in its treatment of the wide range of issues that arise in the context of the international responsibility of international organizations. It goes a long way in clarifying and developing the state of international law on this topic.

United Nations Educational, Scientific and Cultural Organization

First, UNESCO would like to point out that it supports the choice of the Commission to rely in principle on the approach taken in the articles on responsibility of States

[5] *Yearbook ... 2005*, vol. II (Part One), document A/CN.4/553, pp. 7 *et seq.*

[6] *Yearbook ... 2001*, vol. II (Part Two), pp. 26–27.

[7] *Ibid.*, p. 27.

[8] *Yearbook ... 2005*, vol. II (Part One), document A/CN.4/556, comments by INTERPOL, sect. L.2, pp. 43–47.

[9] *Ibid.*, comments by IMF, sect. L.3, pp. 47–48.

for internationally wrongful acts.[10] However, as will be clarified below, UNESCO is of the opinion that, even in the absence of any relevant practice, the Commission should be careful not to adhere too strictly to those articles, when objective characteristics of international organizations appear to suggest that a different solution should be developed. Some of the articles provisionally adopted are based on elements of practice pertaining, in many cases, to a single type of activity (military actions conducted by peacekeeping forces). However, most of the international organizations do not perform such an activity. The different typology of acts and activities performed by international organizations and the ways in which they may entail the responsibility of an organization should be further investigated.

Concerning the Commission's request for information with respect to claims of violations of international law made against UNESCO, it appears that since its establishment no such claim has been made against the organization.

Nonetheless, reference may be made to civil lawsuits in which UNESCO was involved as a respondent that may be of relevance to the present study as they develop arguments (for instance, as regards the issue of attribution of conduct) that could be applicable by analogy to the field of responsibility for internationally wrongful acts.

World Health Organization

As far as chapter VI is concerned, WHO notes that the Commission is proceeding consistent with its decision to base itself on the articles on responsibility of States for internationally wrongful acts,[11] adapted as appropriate. WHO agrees in principle with the decision by the Commission to proceed in that manner in the absence of specific issues affecting the application to international organizations of the principles expressed in the aforementioned articles. At the same time, however, WHO shares the concern expressed by a number of international organizations in their comments on the draft articles, when they underscore the fundamental differences between States and international organizations *qua* subjects of international law, and between international organizations. Such differences would warrant a careful assessment on the part of the Special Rapporteur and the Commission as to solutions which might turn out to be counterproductive for the interests of international organizations. The scarcity of available practice, and the evidently less settled status of international law in this area as compared to that of responsibility of States, make the overall situation complex and delicate. This is particularly evident for provisions such as draft articles 12–14, which touch on issues of particular political sensitivity in the relations between an international organization and its member States.

In view of the foregoing considerations, WHO would recommend regular consultations between the Commission and the Special Rapporteur, on the one hand, and interested international organizations, on the other hand, in the course of the process leading to the adoption of further draft articles. WHO welcomes, in this connection, the fact that the responsibility of international organizations will be one of the items on the agenda of the forthcoming meeting of legal advisers of the United Nations system and that the Special Rapporteur has accepted to participate in that meeting.

As WHO has noted in a previous communication, it does not have any practice concerning claims of breaches by it of its international obligations; its replies to the queries raised by the Commission, therefore, can only be of a speculative nature, or based once again on analogies with the articles on responsibility of States for internationally wrongful acts. While the secretariat of WHO is keen to contribute to the further work of the Commission on this topic, it may not always be possible for it to take a formal position on legal questions of a general nature on which it has no practice and which may have policy implications. Consequently, the fact that WHO may not reply to some or all of the queries raised by the Commission should not be seen as either indifference on its part or acquiescence to the approach being followed by it.

B. Draft article 1—Scope of the draft articles

3. Draft article 1, as provisionally adopted by the Commission at its fifty-fifth session, in 2003, reads as follows:

Article 1. Scope of the present draft articles

1. The present draft articles apply to the international responsibility of an international organization for an act that is wrongful under international law.

2. The present draft articles also apply to the international responsibility of a State for the internationally wrongful act of an international organization. *

* *Yearbook ... 2003*, vol. II (Part Two), p. 18, para. 53.

International Labour Organization

With regard to draft article 1, paragraph 2, it would appear that joint responsibility[12] of a State in connection with the act of an international organization might be more specific to the European Community, as an international organization *sui generis*, rather than for any other international organization. In fact, as indicated in draft article 2, the legal personality of the organization should be the organization's "own" and therefore "distinct from that of its member-States".[13]

As regards the limited practice of ILO in this respect, ILO refers to its comments below on the specific questions asked by the Commission concerning the responsibility of a State in the cases of aid or assistance, direction and control or coercion exercised by a State over the commission of an act of an international organization.

C. Draft article 2—Use of terms

4. Draft article 2, as provisionally adopted by the Commission at its fifty-fifth session, in 2003, reads as follows:

[10] *Yearbook ... 2001*, vol. II (Part Two), p. 26, para. 76.

[11] *Ibid.*

[12] See *Yearbook ... 2004*, vol. II (Part One), document A/CN.4/541, p. 5, para. 8, and *Yearbook ... 2002*, vol. II (Part Two), p. 95, para. 479.

[13] See *Yearbook ... 2003*, vol. II (Part Two), p. 21, commentary to draft article 2, para. (10).

Article 2. Use of terms

For the purposes of the present draft articles, the term "international organization" refers to an organization established by a treaty or other instrument governed by international law and possessing its own international legal personality. International organizations may include as members, in addition to States, other entities.*

* *Yearbook ... 2003*, vol. II (Part Two), p. 18, para. 53.

UNITED NATIONS EDUCATIONAL, SCIENTIFIC AND CULTURAL ORGANIZATION

Under this provision, the term international organization is defined as referring to "an organization established by a treaty or other instrument governed by international law and possessing its own international legal personality. International organizations may include as members, in addition to States, other entities".[14]

The reference to organizations established "by another instrument governed by international law" finds confirmation in the UNESCO practice concerning the creation of intergovernmental organizations through a simplified procedure whereby UNESCO governing bodies (the General Conference or the Executive Board) adopt their statutes and those member States interested in their activities may notify the Director-General of their acceptance of the statutes. This was the case for the International Centre for the Study of the Preservation and Restoration of Cultural Property (ICCROM), established in Rome in 1959. At the time of the adoption by the UNESCO General Conference, no doubt was raised concerning the nature of the statutes of ICCROM, which appear to have been implicitly considered as being an international legally binding instrument creating an intergovernmental organization.[15] In an unpublished letter dated 22 May 1959 addressed to Francis Wolf, legal adviser to ILO, Claude Lussier, UNESCO deputy legal adviser, explained that the procedure followed for the establishment of ICCROM was one of the legal tools used within the organization to create bodies that complement and complete the activities of UNESCO. Among these tools, he indicated: (*a*) a multilateral intergovernmental agreement negotiated under the auspices of UNESCO (as in the case of CERN); and (*b*) a national act creating institutions operating under the legal system of a member State. The case of ICCROM is described as being "halfway" between these two solutions. In another legal opinion, the UNESCO legal adviser, Hanna Saba, stated that the Centre had been created by the General Conference and that it derived its international legal personality from the decision of that body.[16] Subsequently, the statutes of ICCROM were registered with the Secretariat of the United Nations, thereby confirming that they were considered as being an implied international agreement.

A more recent case concerns the International Centre for Synchrotron Light for Experimental Sciences and Applications in the Middle East (SESAME), which was established in 2002 with the structure of an intergovernmental organization. Its statutes were approved by the UNESCO Executive Board (which is a body with a restricted composition: 58 members elected by the General Conference) on delegated authority by the General Conference and entered into force after the Director-General had received a certain number (six) of instruments of acceptance from member States from the region concerned.[17]

D. Draft article 3—General principles

5. Draft article 3, as provisionally adopted by the Commission at its fifty-fifth session, in 2003, reads as follows:

Article 3. General principles

1. Every internationally wrongful act of an international organization entails the international responsibility of the international organization.

2. There is an internationally wrongful act of an international organization when conduct consisting of an action or omission:

(*a*) Is attributable to the international organization under international law; and

(*b*) Constitutes a breach of an international obligation of that international organization.*

* *Yearbook ... 2003*, vol. II (Part Two), p. 18, para. 53.

UNITED NATIONS EDUCATIONAL, SCIENTIFIC AND CULTURAL ORGANIZATION

Paragraph 2

With reference to the possibility that the responsibility of international organizations be entailed by a failure to act, UNESCO shares the view expressed by IMF (see *Yearbook ... 2004*, vol. II (Part One), document A/CN.4/545, sect. D.2, para. 4) as to the necessity to take into account the fact that omissions may simply result from the application of the decision-making process provided under the constitutive act of the international organization concerned. For instance, when unanimity is required for a decision of a governing body of the organization, it could be asked whether the fact that a member State has lawfully exercised its right of veto, thereby preventing the organization from taking action, would be of any relevance in order to exclude or limit the responsibility of that organization for an omission linked to a situation of political impasse.

The Special Rapporteur tried to reply to the argument raised by IMF by observing that difficulties with compliance due to the political decision-making process may also arise within States and with respect to obligations to take positive actions. In this connection, the Special Rapporteur mentioned the failure by the United Nations to prevent genocide in Rwanda (see *Yearbook ... 2005*, vol. II (Part One), document A/CN.4/553, paras. 8–10). However, it could be asked whether a situation in which the Security Council failed to find an agreement between its members for taking any necessary action in order to

[14] *Yearbook ... 2003*, vol. II (Part Two), p. 18, para. 53.

[15] See UNESCO, *Records of the General Conference, Ninth Session, New Delhi, 1956, Resolutions*, 9C/Resolution 4.53, available at http://unesdoc.unesco.org.

[16] Memorandum of 12 November 1959 from H. Saba to J. K. van der Haagen, Chief, Museums and Monuments Division, UNESCO (unpublished document).

[17] See 164 EX/Decision 3.33 of the Executive Board, Decisions adopted by the Executive Board at its 164th Session, Paris, 21–30 May 2002, available at http://unesdoc.unesco.org.

prevent a genocide could be comparable to the situation where a decision not to intervene was taken by the Secretary-General as the highest authority in the chain of command during a military operation of United Nations peacekeeping forces when massive genocidal acts were taking place: would the United Nations be considered responsible for omission in both cases to the same extent?

UNESCO is of the opinion that the consequences of the application of the principle set forth in draft article 3, paragraph 2, to international organizations should be further explored especially with respect to the type of organ (be it collective or individual, with a political or an administrative nature) responsible for the decision not to act. The fact that the social basis of an international organization is constituted by States, i.e. other subjects of international law, should be taken into account.

E. Draft article 4—General rule on attribution of conduct to an international organization

6. Draft article 4, as provisionally adopted by the Commission at its fifty-sixth session, in 2004, reads as follows:

Article 4. General rule on attribution of conduct to an international organization

1. The conduct of an organ or agent of an international organization in the performance of functions of that organ or agent shall be considered as an act of that organization under international law whatever position the organ or agent holds in respect of the organization.

2. For the purposes of paragraph 1, the term "agent" includes officials and other persons or entities through whom the organization acts.

3. Rules of the organization shall apply to the determination of the functions of its organs and agents.

4. For the purpose of the present draft article, "rules of the organization" means, in particular: the constituent instruments; decisions, resolutions and other acts taken by the organization in accordance with those instruments; and established practice of the organization.*

* *Yearbook ... 2004*, vol. II (Part Two), *p. 46*, para. 71.

International Labour Organization

Paragraph 2

The definition of the term "agent" in draft article 4, paragraph 2, "includes officials and other persons or entities through whom the organization acts". Given the general importance of the definition and its implications for the following provisions,[18] ILO has concerns over its wide scope.[19] The commentary to the provision explains, in particular, that the legal nature of the "agent" is "not decisive for the purpose of attribution of conduct".[20] The term could apparently also include entities "external" to an organization, such as private companies.[21] With reference to the comments received from other international organizations (see *Yearbook ... 2004*, vol. II (Part One), document A/CN.4/545, sects. A.2 and H.3) it seems similarly difficult for ILO to foresee a situation where the acts of such an entity could be attributable to ILO. It would therefore be welcome if the Commission provided such examples.

Paragraph 3

The question of the definition of the term "agent" seems all the more important in the light of draft article 4, paragraph 3, according to which "[r]ules of the organization shall apply to the determination of the functions of its organs and agents". While ILO welcomes the reference to the rules of the organization, the commentary explains that the wording "is intended to leave the possibility open that, in exceptional circumstances, functions may be considered as given to an organ or agent even if this could not be said to be based on the rules of the organization".[22] It remains unclear what such "exceptional circumstances" could be and what would be the bases of entrusting functions in such situations. In the view of ILO, if not based on the rules of the organizations, the conduct of a person or entity could be attributable to an organization only if acting on its instructions, or under its direction or control.[23]

United Nations Educational, Scientific and Cultural Organization

Paragraphs 2–3

The definition of the term "agent" in draft article 4, paragraph 2, raises particular concerns for UNESCO, as it would be applicable not only to UNESCO officials and experts on mission, but more in general to "other persons or entities through whom the organization acts".

Apparently, the existence of a functional link between the organization and its agent as a necessary condition in order to attribute his/her conduct to the organization is implied in the reference, in draft article 4, paragraph 1, to the fact that the organ or agent acts "in the performance of functions of that organ or agent".[24] Under draft article 4, paragraph 3, the rules of the organization are indicated as being in principle the parameter to determine these functions. However, the reference to the functional link is not sufficiently developed to clearly delimit the category of "agents".

[18] See *Yearbook ... 2004*, vol. II (Part Two), p. 50, para. 72, commentary to draft article 4, para. (14).

[19] Article 4 of the articles on responsibility of States for internationally wrongful acts, containing the basic rule of attribution of acts of State organs to the State, is limited to "any person or entity which has that status [of an organ] in accordance with the internal law of the State" (*Yearbook ... 2001*, vol. II (Part Two), p. 26, para. 76), i.e. any natural or legal person, such as an official, commission, department or other body exercising public authority (ibid., p. 40, commentary to draft article 4, para. (2)). The question of attribution of acts of "external" entities is covered in articles 5 (Conduct of persons or entities exercising elements of governmental authority) and 8 (Conduct directed or controlled by a State) (*ibid.*, p. 26), which, in the draft articles on the responsibility of international organizations, have been "merged" in the basic provision on attribution rendering it very large in scope.

[20] *Yearbook ... 2004*, vol. II (Part Two), p. 49, para. 72, commentary to draft article 4, para. (6).

[21] *Ibid.*, paras. (12)–(13).

[22] *Ibid.*, para. (9).

[23] See article 8 of the articles on responsibility of States for internationally wrongful acts (Conduct directed or controlled by a State) which contains the basic principle of attribution in international law, i.e. that acts are attributable only "if the person or group of persons is in fact acting on the instructions of, or under the direction or control of, that State" (*Yearbook ... 2001*, vol. II (Part Two), p. 26, para. 76).

[24] See *Yearbook ... 2004*, vol. II (Part Two), p. 49, para. 72, commentary to draft article 4, para. (7).

In this connection, UNESCO would like to mention the existence of a clause included in the contracts between the organization and its private contractors, which reads as follows:

> Neither the contractor, nor anyone whom the contractor employs to carry out the work is to be considered as an agent or member of the staff of UNESCO and, except as otherwise provided herein, they shall not be entitled to any privileges, immunities, compensation or reimbursements, nor are they authorized to commit UNESCO to any expenditure or other obligations.

UNESCO contractors may perform very different types of operational activities (including technical assistance) under fee contracts[25] and consultant contracts.[26] Although the same types of activity could be carried out by UNESCO officials, in the case of contractors UNESCO is of the view that acts performed by the latter may not be considered as acts of the organization, since the rules of the organization clearly exclude this possibility. Furthermore, the contracts in question only impose on contractors an obligation of result (for instance, the execution of a project in the field), while the organization has no direction or control over their actions nor may it exercise disciplinary powers on them.

However, in its commentary to draft article 4, paragraph 3, the Commission refers to the possibility that "in exceptional circumstances, functions may be considered as given to an organ or agent, even if this could not be said to be based on the rules of the organization".[27] When these exceptional circumstances would arise is not clearly explained. The commentary to article 4 appears to suggest that such a circumstance would occur with respect to the so-called *de facto* organs, i.e. persons or groups of persons acting in fact on the instructions, or under the direction or control of an organization,[28] but beyond the latter case UNESCO cannot imagine other cases in which the attribution of a conduct to an organization would not be based on its internal rules and regulations. In this regard, UNESCO invites the Commission to shed further light on the type of situations that would be practically envisaged. In the opinion of UNESCO, besides acts of officials or experts on mission performed in their official capacity, only the acts of persons or entities operating in fact on the instructions, or under the direction or control of an organization, could be attributed to the latter.

The conduct of contractors may give rise to legal problems when the terms of their contract are not clear as to the real nature of the link existing between them and the organization, which may be misleading for third parties. For example, the organization once concluded a contract in which the contractor was authorized to use the name and logo of UNESCO for the organization of cultural and sports events that were supposed to be financed by the contractor himself through a fund-raising campaign not directly involving UNESCO. Although the contract clearly indicated that the activity of the contractor would by no means entail the legal or financial responsibility of the organization and contained the clause quoted in paragraph 3 of the present set of comments, UNESCO was held partially liable, in an arbitral award, towards the contractor, who had to face relevant financial liabilities towards his creditors, for not fulfilling its obligation to cooperate with him, but also for having created an evident risk of ambiguity for third parties by authorizing the contractor to use its name and emblem. In this case, the contractor was not considered a UNESCO agent, but the organization was considered as bearing part of the responsibility, *inter alia*, for having created an ambiguity about his real status.[29]

Except for the case just mentioned, the clause mentioned above seems to protect UNESCO in an effective manner from claims that might arise from the conduct of its contractors. UNESCO is not aware of any specific cases in which the organization has been held directly or indirectly liable for actions performed by its contractors.

Draft article 4, paragraph 2, in connection with draft article 5

With reference to the "entities" through which an organization may act, UNESCO notes that the content of this notion is not sufficiently clarified in the commentaries to draft articles 4–5. UNESCO wonders whether the wide definition of "agents" included in draft article 4, paragraph 2, without any further qualifications, might leave the door open for the attribution to an organization of acts performed by State entities or private entities (such as universities, research institutes, etc.) that happen to be its "contractors". UNESCO agrees with the view expressed in the commentary to article 4, according to which the reference to the "conduct of persons or entities exercising elements of governmental authority" used in article 5 of the draft articles on responsibility of States for internationally wrongful acts would not be appropriate for international organizations;[30] however, in the view of UNESCO, further elaboration is needed on this point so as to better define the link that must exist between these entities and the organization concerned.

Within the UNESCO legal framework, reference may be made in this connection to National Commissions, which are not part of UNESCO, but are referred to in the

---

[25] A fee contract is concluded by UNESCO with an individual or legal entity having a specialized skill in order to obtain special goods or services such as the preparation or assignment of an unpublished manuscript or original work, the development of a new or improved product or process, or the provision of other services specially suited to the organization, in return for a lump sum (which includes the contractor's remuneration) and by a specified deadline (see *UNESCO Administrative Manual*, vol. I, chap. 7, item 700).

[26] A consultant is a high-level specialist employed by UNESCO for a specific short period of time, for instance, to carry out a priority task in its programme of activities, undertaking on-site analysis of complex problems and the search for innovative solutions in a field where the specialists required are not available in the secretariat; to attend a conference or meeting organized by the unit concerned as a technical adviser; to provide specialized tuition in a seminar or training course organized by the unit concerned; or to carry out a short mission in a member State, thereafter drawing up a report to advise the Government or a national institution on a matter related to the programme of activities of the unit concerned (*ibid.*, vol. II, chap. 24, item 2435).

[27] *Yearbook ... 2004*, vol. II (Part Two), p. 49, para. 72, commentary to draft article 4, para. (9).

[28] *Ibid.*, para. (13).

[29] A copy of the arbitral award was attached to the UNESCO submission.

[30] See *Yearbook ... 2004*, vol. II (Part Two), p. 49, para. 72, commentary to draft article 4, para. (12).

UNESCO Constitution.[31] They may be either governmental agencies, i.e. State organs (usually a department or unit within the competent ministry of a member State), but also non-governmental organizations. Under specific arrangements made in accordance with the Charter of National Commissions for UNESCO, these entities may be entrusted with specific tasks by organs of the organization.[32] The activities that can be subcontracted to these entities are very different in nature, however, unless a specific arrangement is made to this end, UNESCO never retains effective control over their conduct, since they are entities clearly separate from the organization. Since draft article 5 only refers to organs or agents "placed at the disposal of an international organization by a State or another international organization", the provision would appear not to be suitable for the case of National Commissions for UNESCO, especially when the agent placed at the disposal of UNESCO comes from non-governmental organizations. Nevertheless, National Commissions could fall within the wide definition of "agents" provided under draft article 4, paragraph 2, in which the requisite of effective control is not expressly set forth.

A clearer definition of the link between organizations and external entities which could possibly be considered as acting on behalf of the organization would be welcome, as UNESCO is particularly exposed to the risk of facing liability claims for the acts of legally separate entities which, also for historical reasons, have developed close relations with the organization. For instance, there exist a number of institutes and centres, referred to as "category 2 institutes and centres", which are nationally based institutions or intergovernmental organizations placed "under the auspices" of UNESCO. They are entities which are not legally part of the organization, but which are associated with it through formal arrangements approved by the General Conference and may contribute to the execution of the UNESCO programme.[33] Reference may also be made to the UNESCO clubs and associations, which were created all over the world at the end of the Second World War to publicize the work of the organization. They are private associations established under the domestic legislation of member States and UNESCO has no direct control over them. However, both category 2 institutes and centres and UNESCO clubs are authorized to use the name and logo of the organization in their promotional activities.

UNESCO is of the opinion that only acts of officials or experts on mission performed in their official capacity and acts of entities which are considered as being an integral part of the organization could be attributable to the organization. In all cases concerning contractors, be they private individuals, public or private legal entities or National Commissions, their actions cannot be attributed to UNESCO and may not entail its responsibility, unless specific arrangements have been made to place them under the control of the organization or unless the organization has subsequently ratified their actions.

Paragraph 4

UNESCO supports the inclusion of a reference to the rules of the organization in draft article 4, paragraph 4, concerning the general rule on the attribution of conduct. UNESCO considers the definition included in draft article 4, paragraph 4, as being adequate and approves the decision to enlarge the definition set forth in the Vienna Convention on the Law of Treaties between States and International Organizations or between International Organizations (art. 2, para. 1 (*j*)) to cover, together with "decisions" and "resolutions", "other acts taken by the organization". Within UNESCO there exists a body of detailed administrative regulations which govern the functioning of the organization and contain indications on the scope of the competences and functions of its organs.

F. Draft article 5—Conduct of organs or agents placed at the disposal of an international organization by a State or another international organization

7. Draft article 5, as provisionally adopted by the Commission at its fifty-sixth session, in 2004, reads as follows:

Article 5. Conduct of organs or agents placed at the disposal of an international organization by a State or another international organization

The conduct of an organ of a State or an organ or agent of an international organization that is placed at the disposal of another international organization shall be considered under international law an act of the latter organization if the organization exercises effective control over that conduct.*

* *Yearbook ... 2004*, vol. II (Part Two), *p. 46,* para. 71.

International Labour Organization

As the Special Rapporteur affirmed in his second report, "[m]ost of the practice concerning attribution of conduct in case of a State organ placed at an organization's disposal relates to peacekeeping forces" (*Yearbook ... 2004*, vol. II (Part One), document A/CN.4/541, para. 34). ILO notes that there is, however, a widespread practice whereby member States or other international organizations put their own officials at the disposal of

[31] Article VII, paragraph 2, of the Constitution states: "National Commissions or National Cooperating Bodies, where they exist, shall act in an advisory capacity to their respective delegations to the General Conference, to the representatives and alternates of their countries on the Executive Board and to their Governments in matters relating to the Organization and shall function as agencies of liaison in all matters of interest to it." (See UNESCO, *Basic Texts*, (Paris, 2004), or the UNESCO website at http://unesdoc.unesco.org.)

[32] Under article II, paragraph 2, of the Charter of National Commissions for UNESCO adopted by the UNESCO General Conference: "Depending on the arrangements made by each Member State, National Commissions may also be expected, *inter alia*: (a) To assume, alone or in collaboration with other bodies, responsibility for the operation of UNESCO projects in the country and for national participation in subregional, regional, or international UNESCO activities." Article III, paragraph 4, of the aforesaid Charter provides that National Commissions "must be able to contribute effectively to the implementation of UNESCO's programme: … (*b*) By assuming operational responsibility for some of UNESCO's programme activities". According to article V, paragraph 3, "UNESCO can extend and develop its action through National Commissions by: (*a*) Entering into contracts with them, wherever necessary, for the execution of activities included in its programme" (*ibid.*, pp. 148–150).

[33] See UNESCO, "Principles and guidelines for the establishment and functioning of UNESCO institutes and centres (category 1) and institutes and centres under the auspices of UNESCO (category 2)" (33 C/19 of 4 August 2005), in printed form or on the UNESCO website at http://unesdoc.unesco.org.

an international organization such as ILO. This practice has already been mentioned in the comments provided by INTERPOL (see *Yearbook ... 2005*, vol. II (Part One), document A/CN.4/556, sect. F.1).

The legal framework within which officials are put at the disposal of ILO may result in two different situations. The first is that the national official or the official of another international organization becomes an official of ILO. In such a case, ILO becomes responsible for the conduct of the official, as he or she becomes its agent.

The second situation arises when the official concerned is kept under employment contract with the releasing State or international organization. This form of secondment (also known as "loan" in the terminology of the United Nations common system) is based on an agreement between the State concerned and the international organization or between two organizations. The issue of effective control over the official's conduct is not so obvious. The statutory position of the official is determined by his or her terms of appointment with the releasing organization or State and that releasing organization or State remains responsible for all expenditures in connection with the assignment of the official, such as remuneration, leave, allowances, health care, pension, occupational accident or sickness. The releasing State or international organization typically retains its competence regarding disciplinary measures.

The official is, however, under the administrative supervision of an ILO official and benefits from the same facilities as the regular ILO staff regarding office space, computers and other facilities necessary to carry out his or her assignment in ILO. The official has a duty to respect standards of conduct and other rules applicable to ILO officials only to the extent specified in the agreement between the releasing organization or State and ILO.

In the light of the above, ILO would welcome further clarification of the expression "effective control" in the context of draft article 5.

G. Draft article 6—Excess of authority or contravention of instructions

8. Draft article 6, as provisionally adopted by the Commission at its fifty-sixth session, in 2004, reads as follows:

Article 6. Excess of authority or contravention of instructions

The conduct of an organ or an agent of an international organization shall be considered an act of that organization under international law if the organ or agent acts in that capacity, even though the conduct exceeds the authority of that organ or agent or contravenes instructions.*

* *Yearbook ... 2004*, vol. II (Part Two), *p. 46*, para. 71.

International Labour Organization

ILO agrees with the principle that an international organization may be held responsible for *ultra vires* conduct of its organs or officials, when such conduct exceeds the powers of a specific organ or official under the rules of the organization or, *a fortiori*, when the conduct goes beyond the powers conferred on the organization by its constituent instrument. However, there is a distinction to be made between those two situations. Where the conduct exceeds the power of an organ or official but remains within the powers of the organization, the situation is the same as for *ultra vires* conduct of organs of a State: third parties need protection as they cannot be expected to have knowledge of the internal legal rules of the State or organi-zation, which define the powers of the organ or official concerned. The situation is different where the conduct is *ultra vires* for the international organization, a case that is not conceivable for States due to their general competence. As in such cases third parties appear to require less protection, the introduction into the article of exceptions from the responsibility of the organization such as those suggested by INTERPOL and IMF (see *Yearbook ... 2005*, vol. II (Part One), document A/CN.4/556, sect. G) would seem appropriate.

Concerning the condition under which an *ultra vires* act of the organization requires that the concerned organ or official act in its official capacity, the Special Rapporteur noted that the wording "'in that capacity' is rather cryptic and vague" (see *Yearbook ... 2004*, vol. II (Part One), document A/CN.4/541, para. 57). While there certainly is a need in practice to establish more detailed criteria, it may be noted that in another context, that of applying privileges and immunities, international organizations already have a long and abundant practice in determining whether or not officials have acted in their official capacity, given that jurisdictional immunity is normally granted to officials only in respect of acts performed in that capacity.

H. Draft article 8—Existence of a breach of an international obligation

9. Draft article 8, as provisionally adopted by the Commission at its fifty-seventh session, in 2005, reads as follows:

Article 8. Existence of a breach of an international obligation

1. There is a breach of an international obligation by an international organization when an act of that international organization is not in conformity with what is required of it by that obligation, regardless of its origin and character.

2. Paragraph 1 also applies to the breach of an obligation under international law established by a rule of the international organization.*

* *Yearbook ... 2005*, vol. II (Part Two), p. 41, para. 205.

European Commission

Article 8, paragraph 1, and articles 9, 10 and 11 of the present draft are identical to article 12, paragraph 1, and articles 13, 14 and 15 on responsibility of States for internationally wrongful acts.[34] There is indeed no need to deviate from the rules for States in this respect and hence the European Commission has no remarks.

Article 8, paragraph 2, on non-compliance with an "obligation under international law established by a rule of the international organization", however, raises some questions. The rule does not give any guidance as to which sorts of rules of the international organization qualify as "obligations under international law". Certainly, in the

[34] *Yearbook ... 2001*, vol. II (Part Two), pp. 26–27.

case of the European Community, the important question would arise whether a violation of secondary Community law by a Community institution triggers the international responsibility of the European Community. Given that the European Court of Justice has characterized the European Community ever since the 1960s as a legal order of its own, the prevailing view inside the Community would be that it does not. (And the same would be true, in the view of the European Commission, of the breach of secondary Community law by a member State.) The commentary may be of some help in this respect, because it states that the article does not intend to take a position in the debate between those who regard the "internal" law of international organizations as partly or wholly autonomous in relation to international law and those who regard it as an integral part of international law. Nevertheless, it remains an open question whether article 8, paragraph 2, is an essential part of the draft articles.

International Labour Organization

Draft article 8, paragraph 2, provides that "paragraph 1 also applies to the breach of an obligation under international law established by a rule of the international organization". By leaving open the controversial question of the legal nature of the rules of international organizations, this provision does not seem to afford the necessary legal security to international organizations. On the other hand, the legal nature of those rules may not be determining, provided that organizations are able to rely on two provisos that would significantly limit the scope of a possible international responsibility for non-compliance with a rule of the international organization.

The first proviso would be a full application of the principle of *lex specialis derogat legi generali*. In its commentary to draft article 8, the Commission points to the fact that "[r]ules of an organization may devise specific treatment of breaches of obligations, also with regard to the question of the existence of a breach".[35] While the Commission puts forward two examples where the special rules would not necessarily prevail over principles set out in the draft articles, ILO considers that the vast majority of possible breaches of its internal rules, including in particular of its various administrative regulations and rules, would not entail an international responsibility of the organization under the draft articles, since the relevant obligations are created, fulfilled and sometimes enforced exclusively within the special internal legal order of the organization, of which they form part. In this regard, the ILO staff regulations constitute the most undisputable example. Because those regulations are adopted by the Governing Body of ILO to govern the relationship between the organization and its officials and that responsibility under those rules can be enforced through the Administrative Tribunal of ILO, there would remain no room for international responsibility under the *lex generalis* codified in the draft articles.

The second proviso would be that the distinct legal personality of an international organization is fully taken into account when determining whether a State is entitled to invoke the responsibility of that organization in case of a breach of the rules of the organization. For example, if the secretariat of an international organization were to cause a financial loss to the organization owing to non-compliance with the organization's financial regulations (e.g. regarding investment of funds or procurement), it should be recognized that the obligations breached are owed to the organization itself and not to the member States that contribute to the organization's budget. The legal personality of international organizations constitutes an effective "veil" in two directions: not only does it shield member States from being held responsible by third parties for their conduct within the international organization (on this point, see comments in section L below on the specific questions asked by the Commission), it also, conversely, prevents member States from invoking obligations that are in reality owed to the organization as a distinct subject of international law. In ILO practice, cases such as the above example would presumably be reported by the external auditor to the Governing Body and the Director-General would assume the political responsibility for the loss while, in turn, applying internal sanctions against the officials directly responsible.

Provided that the Commission will take into account the above two provisos when examining the question concerning *lex specialis* and the invocation of the responsibility of an international organization,[36] the uncertainties created by the wording of draft article 8, paragraph 2, would seem to be acceptable.

United Nations Educational, Scientific and Cultural Organization

Concerning the controversial legal nature of the rules of the organization in relation to international law, UNESCO notes that in the formulation of article 8, paragraph 2, on the existence of a breach of an international obligation, the Commission has chosen to leave the door open to the possibility of applying the principles established under the present draft articles to breaches of obligations arising from the rules of the organization. On this point, UNESCO shares the opinion expressed by other organizations that breaches of such obligations should be considered as a special regime and therefore excluded from the scope of the study.

As far as the employment relationship between an organization and its staff is concerned, the responsibility of the organization for breaches of internal rules is established within its internal legal order, under which appropriate legal remedies are in principle provided. This should be considered a "self-contained regime". In the case of UNESCO, the ILO Administrative Tribunal, which is competent to examine complaints concerning violations of UNESCO staff regulations and rules by the organization, is in a position to ensure the protection of UNESCO employees' fundamental rights, should the organization have violated them either by disregarding the staff regulations or by adopting staff regulations that are inconsistent with the general principles of international civil service law (concerning, for example, staff associations' collective rights).

[35] *Yearbook ... 2005*, vol. II (Part Two), p. 43, para. 206, commentary to article 8, para (7).

[36] The corresponding provisions of the articles on responsibility of States for internationally wrongful acts are articles 55 and 42, respectively (*Yearbook ... 2001*, vol. II (Part Two), pp. 29–30).

As regards the breach of obligations of an international organization towards its member States arising from its internal rules, the internal legal order of the organization generally provides a system of checks and balances between organs that should sufficiently protect the rights of member States established under the constituent treaty. In case a member State were of the opinion that the organization had violated those rights, it could have recourse to the dispute settlement remedies provided under the constituent treaty.[37]

In the light of the above, UNESCO considers draft article 8, paragraph 2, to be a mere tautology, as it simply affirms that the principles established under the draft articles would also apply to breaches of internal rules of the organization to the extent that they set out obligations under international law. The fact of admitting this possibility gives no clear indication about the scope of the present study and international organizations cannot accept such a degree of uncertainty on this fundamental issue.

World Health Organization

With reference to some of the articles provisionally adopted by the Commission, WHO concurs with the formulation of article 8, paragraph 2, concerning the relevance of the rules of an organization in the determination of the existence of a breach of its international obligations. As noted in the commentary to article 8 and as expressed in the comments of some organizations, the question of the legal nature of the rules of an organization (as defined in draft article 4) and their relation to international law is complex and does not lend itself to wholesale solutions. WHO would generally support the view that whether or not obligations arising for an organization under its rules may be considered international obligations depends on the source and subject matter of the rules concerned. Whereas there is no doubt that obligations arising directly under the constituent instrument of an organization *vis-à-vis* its member States are of an international nature, the same cannot be said in the view of WHO with regard to obligations arising between an organization and its officials under the staff regulations and rules. The solution adopted in article 8, paragraph 2, seems therefore an acceptable compromise on this point.

I. Draft article 15—Decisions, recommendations and authorizations addressed to Member States and international organizations

10. Draft article 15, as provisionally adopted by the Commission at its fifty-seventh session, in 2005, reads as follows:

Article 15. Decisions, recommendations and authorizations addressed to member States and international organizations

1. An international organization incurs international responsibility if it adopts a decision binding a member State or international organization to commit an act that would be internationally wrongful if committed by the former organization and would circumvent an international obligation of the former organization.

2. An international organization incurs international responsibility if:

(*a*) It authorizes a member State or international organization to commit an act that would be internationally wrongful if committed by the former organization and would circumvent an international obligation of the former organization, or recommends that a member State or international organization commit such an act; and

(*b*) That State or international organization commits the act in question in reliance on that authorization or recommendation.

3. Paragraphs 1 and 2 apply whether or not the act in question is internationally wrongful for the member State or international organization to which the decision, authorization or recommendation is directed.*

* *Yearbook ... 2005*, vol. II (Part Two), pp. 41–42, para. 205.

European Commission

The European Commission notes with interest how the International Law Commission approached the issue of "normative control" of decisions, recommendations and authorizations of international organizations in draft article 15. It agrees with the Chairman of the Drafting Committee that there are no clear practical examples to assist in formulating this particular provision. The European Commission would therefore suggest that the International Law Commission employ great care in its future discussion.

The European Commission welcomes the fact that article 15 distinguishes between binding decisions of an international organization (para. 1) and mere authorizations or recommendations (para. 2). The underlying idea is that an international organization should not be liable for acts of its member States, if the latter was not required by the organization to take a certain action, but decided to do so of their own volition, independently of the authorization or recommendation from the international organization.

Nevertheless, the distinction may not be refined enough. To give a Community law example, under article 249 of the Treaty establishing the European Community, secondary Community law may be binding in its entirety and directly applicable in all member States (regulations), or only binding as to the result to be achieved (directives), or binding only upon those to whom it is addressed (decisions). It is suggested that an obligation of result (as in a Community directive) comes very close to a binding decision, but nevertheless may leave a certain amount of discretion to the member States of an organization. Therefore, paragraphs 1–2 of draft article 15 may well be in need of some refinement on this point.

Coming back to article 15, paragraph 1, here the mandatory requirements for member States to commit an internationally wrongful act imposed by an international organization must also "circumvent" an international obligation of the international organization. However, the European Commission wonders whether the notion of circumvention is indispensable in the light of the International Law Commission's own commentary on article 15. If—as the commentary puts it—compliance by members with a binding decision is to be expected,[38] the

[37] See article XIV, paragraph 2, of the UNESCO Constitution, under which "[a]ny question or dispute concerning the interpretation of this Constitution shall be referred for determination to the International Court of Justice or to an arbitral tribunal, as the General Conference may determine under its Rules of Procedure".

[38] *Yearbook ... 2005*, vol. II (Part Two), p. 47, para. 206, commentary to article 15, para (5).

whole notion of circumvention may become superfluous. In the final part of paragraph 1 of article 15, "circumvent" could then better be read as "breach". On the other hand, if one takes the view that the idea of mandatory "law on the books" constituting a breach of international law is restricted to the limited domain of WTO law only and has not taken hold in general international law, or depends in any case on what the law actually states, then the notion of circumvention does not have a function in paragraph 1. It would seem commendable that the International Law Commission revisit this article and the comments pertaining to it at a later stage in order to create greater clarity on this issue.

International Criminal Police Organization

The INTERPOL General Secretariat wishes to reiterate its concerns and reservations with regard to the rule reflected in draft article 15, particularly as far as it concerns the responsibility of international organizations for acts of their members committed in reliance on a recommendation of an organization. The General Secretariat is not aware of precedent or practice involving an international organization consciously ordering or recommending its members to commit an internationally wrongful act, on which the rule proposed by the Commission could be founded. The conceptual underpinning of the proposed rule is also unclear, especially with regard to acts committed in reliance on mere recommendations of international organizations. In the case of INTERPOL, this is further complicated by the fact that article 9 of the Constitution expressly states that "Members shall do all within their power, in so far as compatible with their own obligations, to carry out the decisions of the General Assembly".

Moreover, the formulation of draft article 15 suggests that the proposed rule would apply even if a recommendation concerns a matter which the international organization is not competent to deal with. It would be difficult for INTERPOL to accept such effect, given that article 8 (*f*) of the INTERPOL Constitution expressly restricts the recommendatory powers of the General Assembly to matters with which the organization is competent to deal.

International Labour Organization

It is noteworthy that, under draft article 15, paragraph 1, an international organization incurs international responsibility by the mere fact of adopting a decision binding on a member State or international organization to commit an act of the wrongful nature described, without the act actually being taken on the part of the member State. Under this formulation, the very fact of creating an inconsistent international obligation, without more, would seem insufficient, especially if the member State were to invoke the wrongfulness in defence of its failure to comply. One of the two conditions for an internationally wrongful act of an international organization to arise is that the relevant conduct "constitutes a breach of an international obligation of that organization". ILO wonders whether the mere fact of adopting the binding decision referred to above, without the act being actually committed by the State, could constitute a breach of an international obligation of the organization concerned. In contrast, the commission of an act in reliance upon an authorization or recommendation to do so in draft article 15, paragraph 2, while appearing reasonable, would seem to contradict the premise under which the single prong for wrongfulness is established in paragraph 1.

United Nations Educational, Scientific and Cultural Organization

From a general point of view, UNESCO is in agreement with the structure and formulation chosen for this draft article. However, further elaboration on the possible cases that would fall under this clause would be welcome.

In particular, UNESCO is of the opinion that the scope of draft article 15, paragraph 2, should be further elucidated possibly in the commentary to the same provision, namely with reference to the expression "an act that would be internationally wrongful if committed by the former organization and would circumvent an international obligation of the former organization": should the committed internationally wrongful act and the circumvention necessarily refer to the same international obligation?

World Health Organization

Draft article 15 deals with an issue of potential political sensitivity for international organizations, in particular for a technical agency such as WHO whose normative functions mainly consist of recommendations addressed either by the governing bodies of the organization or by the secretariat to member States. WHO appreciates the point, expressed in paragraph (1) of the commentary to the article concerned,[39] that an international organization should not be allowed to "outsource" actions that would be unlawful if taken directly by that organization. At the same time, WHO finds it hard to envisage in practice a situation that would fall under draft article 15, paragraph 2, in particular in cases in which the conduct of the State or international organization to which an authorization or recommendation is addressed is not wrongful, as provided in paragraph 3 of the same article. Moreover, WHO notes the statements reproduced in the report of the Special Rapporteur and the position taken by some international organizations in their comments to the effect that an international organization should not be considered responsible for acts undertaken by its members on the basis of an authorization or recommendation issued by the organization. In this connection, therefore, it would be helpful if the commentary to draft article 15 could be revised in due course to offer practical examples of the situations that the Commission seems to have in mind.

J. Circumstances precluding wrongfulness—general considerations

International Criminal Police Organization

The issue of circumstances precluding the wrongfulness of the acts of international organizations has been addressed by international administrative tribunals. The case law of those tribunals confirms that circumstances precluding wrongfulness are inherent in the law of responsibility for the breach of international obligations.

[39] *Yearbook ... 2005*, vol. II (Part Two), p. 47, para. 206.

Therefore, the topic is rightfully considered for inclusion in the draft articles on responsibility of international organizations for internationally wrongful acts.

Nevertheless, it might be necessary to clarify the use of terms and reflect on the question whether the distinctions as made in the corresponding provisions of the Commission's articles on responsibility of States for internationally wrongful acts, i.e. consent, countermeasures, *force majeure*, distress, necessity and compliance with peremptory norms, are fully transferable to the responsibility of international organizations. In this context, the INTERPOL General Secretariat wishes to mention three cases decided by international administrative tribunals.

1. *Organization of American States Administrative Tribunal, Judgment No. 24*[40]

This case concerned a decision of OAS to relieve the complainant of the post of Director of the Office of the General Secretariat and terminate his contract with the organization, allegedly for reasons of *force majeure* said to be known to the complainant but beyond the control of the organization. In rejecting the argument, the Tribunal adhered to a restrictive notion of *force majeure*, and at the same time suggested that impossibility can also be a circumstance precluding wrongfulness:

> The Tribunal considers that in the present case there is no *force majeure* that would have made it impossible for the General Secretariat to fulfill the fixed-term contract, since it is much-explored law that by *force majeure* is meant an irresistible happening of nature. Nor is there any impossibility of fulfilling the contract for reasons outside the General Secretariat.

2. *International Labour Organization Administrative Tribunal, Judgment No. 339*[41]

In this case, the ILO Administrative Tribunal answered, *obiter dicta*, the question whether financial distress caused by reasons other than failure of countries to honour their membership dues to an organization can serve as a circumstance that precludes wrongfulness. The complainant was offered and accepted a "consultancy" contract with the organization in question. The project for which the complainant was to work was a UNDP project. UNDP ran into financial difficulties and had to suspend or cancel credits. The credits for the complainant's consultancy were cut off. The organization therefore told him that it had cancelled the offer of appointment. The Administrative Tribunal sided with the complainant:

> It is possible that an event such as the withdrawal of the UNDP finance might be shown as having such a crippling effect on the Organization's ability to continue with the contract as to constitute reasonable grounds for its termination. But there is no material in the dossier which would enable the Tribunal to reach any conclusion about the effect of the withdrawal. There is no reference to UNDP in the contract. Presumably it was to pay the complainant's salary in whole or in part, but there is no adequate statement anywhere in the dossier of what the financial arrangements were with FAO or of how they affected the Organization's ability to finance its contracts. The only communications disclosed from the UNDP are two cables. The first dated 22 January 1976 states that the UNDP is "unable to authorize" three months of the proposed consultancy and suggests another source. The second dated 29 January approves one proposed consultancy but is "unable to approve" the remaining three months of the complainant's consultancy. There is nothing in this to connect the disapprovals with any financial situation. The FAO's decision to cancel its arrangements with the complainant was not taken until 17 February; the delay suggests that there may have been other factors to consider. Finally, there is a great difference between stopping recruitments and terminating prematurely contracts which have already been concluded. Presumably on the information given to it by the Organization the UNDP believed that in the complainant's case all it was doing was to stop additional recruitment; it does not follow that it would have acted in the same way in the case of a concluded contract.

3. *International Labour Organization Administrative Tribunal, Judgment No. 2183*

In this case, the complainant was on sick leave for a long time and nobody could consult her e-mails. Her immediate supervisor asked for access to her computer account, consulted her e-mails and reported that he had separated the professional messages from the private messages, which had been stored in a new file. Having heard about what she described as an "e-mail violation", the complainant complained to the Director of Administration. The complainant was not satisfied with the reply received and she disputed its content. The organization countered with the plea of necessity. The Administrative Tribunal rejected the claim by applying the following principles to the facts of the case:

> Firstly, the CERN rules which applied at the relevant time ... indicate ... that:
>
> ... "The computing facilities, including networks, must not be used other than for their intended purpose in connection with the CERN official programme of work, unless subject to a special agreement."
>
> However, CERN acknowledges that, like other organisations, it tolerates the use of e-mail addresses for private purposes within appropriate limits, and "provided that this does not adversely affect the operation of the Organization".
>
> Secondly, the principle of the confidentiality of private messages stored in a professional e-mail account must be observed.
>
> Thirdly, in the event that access to an e-mail account becomes necessary for reasons of urgency or because of the prolonged absence of the account holder, it must be possible for organisations to open the account using appropriate technical safeguards. That state of necessity, justifying access to data which may be confidential, must be assessed with the utmost care.[42]

It must be noted that although the Tribunal utilized the term "state of necessity", it could be argued that the test set forth in article 16 (*a*) of the Commission's articles on responsibility of States for internationally wrongful acts[43] was not met.

International Labour Organization

Without prejudice to possible comments by ILO on the forthcoming work of the Commission concerning circumstances precluding wrongfulness, ILO considers that international organizations may invoke such circumstances, as recognized under general international law. ILO notes that the particular nature of international organizations should be adequately taken into consideration in the codification of those rules.

---

[40] Available at http://www.oas.org/tribadm/catalog_test/english/hist_76/24.doc. The judgements of the OAS Administrative Tribunal in general can be accessed at www.oas.org/tribadm/search_busqueda/query_en.asp.

[41] The judgements of the ILO Administrative Tribunal can be accessed at www.ilo.org/dyn/triblex/triblexmain.advancedSearch?p_lang=en.

[42] See footnote 41 above.

[43] *Yearbook ... 2001*, vol. II (Part Two), p. 27.

In response to the question whether the plea of necessity could be invoked by an international organization under a set of circumstances similar to those enumerated in article 25 of the articles on responsibility of States for internationally wrongful acts,[44] ILO is not aware of any relevant practice in that regard. ILO agrees that the plea of necessity is limited to exceptionable situations and admitted only under strict conditions, in particular that of safeguarding "an essential interest threatened by a grave and imminent peril".[45] In the light of the diverse mandates and functions of international organizations as well as the wide range of "essential interests"[46] invoked in State practice to justify the plea, ILO considers that international organizations should not be excluded from invoking the plea. ILO would welcome the Commission studying whether the "essential interests" of international organizations enshrined in their constitutive instruments could be invoked in this context.[47]

United Nations Educational, Scientific and Cultural Organization

As concerns the applicability to international organizations of the draft articles on responsibility of States for internationally wrongful acts, concerning the circumstances precluding wrongfulness, those provisions may in principle be transposed to the present study.

While draft articles on consent, self-defence, distress and *force majeure* do not seem to raise particular problems, the applicability *mutatis mutandis* of the provisions on countermeasures and necessity looks more problematic.

With reference to countermeasures, UNESCO is of the opinion that, should the issue of countermeasures be addressed in the draft, it should be clearly distinguished from that of sanctions, which may be adopted by an organization against its own member States.

With regard to necessity, UNESCO shares the position taken by the Special Rapporteur in his fourth report (A/CN.4/564 and Add.1–2, paras. 35–46),[48] according to which a reference to the constituent instrument would be too restrictive in order to define the "essential interest" that an organization may need to safeguard against a grave and imminent peril. UNESCO believes that the reference to the "functions" of the organization, included in the proposed draft article 22, would more appropriately delimit the scope of the provision.

K. Circumstances precluding wrongfulness—necessity

11. In its 2004 report the Commission posed the following question regarding necessity:

(*b*) Among the circumstances precluding wrongfulness, article 25 of the draft articles on responsibility of States for internationally wrongful acts refers to "necessity", which may be invoked by a State under certain conditions: first of all, that the "act not in conformity with an international obligation of that State … is the only way for the State to safeguard an essential interest against a grave and imminent peril". Could necessity be invoked by an international organization under a similar set of circumstances?[*]

[*] *Yearbook ... 2004*, vol. II (Part Two), p. 15, para. 25.

World Bank

In the Commission's draft articles on responsibility of States for internationally wrongful acts, necessity is acknowledged as a circumstance precluding wrongfulness, but only in exceptional cases and within stringent limits: pursuant to draft article 25,[49] a State may not invoke necessity unless (*a*) it is the only way to safeguard an essential interest against a grave and imminent peril, and (*b*) it does not seriously impair an essential interest of the State or States towards which the obligation that is breached exists, or of the international community as a whole. Moreover, necessity may not be invoked by a State that has contributed to the situation of necessity, or in breach of an obligation excluding the possibility of invoking necessity.

Within these strict limits, it is difficult to see why an international organization may not also invoke necessity. One of the fundamental prerequisites for invoking necessity is the safeguard of an "essential interest". As international organizations have a separate legal personality from that of their member States, and are therefore separate legal subjects, it cannot be denied, *a priori*, that they too have essential interests to safeguard in accordance with their constituent instruments.

The relevance of exceptional circumstances in World Bank operations is confirmed by certain clauses in the General Conditions, which are incorporated in World Bank financial agreements and to which reference can be made here by way of analogy. Section 6.02 (*e*) of the General Conditions Applicable to Loan and Guarantee Agreements for Single Currency Loans (dated 30 May 1995, as amended through 1 May 2004) provides for the possibility that the right of a borrower to make withdrawals from the Loan Account be suspended in whole or in part if:

> As a result of events which have occurred after the date of the Loan Agreement, an extraordinary situation shall have arisen which shall make it improbable that the Project can be carried out or that the Borrower or the Guarantor will be able to perform its obligations under the Loan Agreement or the Guarantee Agreement.

Likewise, section 6.02 (*k*) of the General Conditions Applicable to Loan and Guarantee Agreements for Fixed-Spread Loans (dated 1 September 1999, as amended through 1 May 2004) provides for the possibility of suspension if:

> An extraordinary situation shall have arisen under which any further withdrawals under the Loan would be inconsistent with the provisions of Article III, Section 3 of the Bank's Articles of Agreement.[50]

[44] *Yearbook ... 2001*, vol. II (Part Two), p. 28.

[45] *Gabčíkovo-Nagymaros Project (Hungary/Slovakia), Judgment, I.C.J. Reports 1997*, p. 40, para. 50.

[46] Crawford, *The International Law Commission's Articles on State Responsibility: Introduction, Text and Commentaries*, p. 183.

[47] See the response of the European Commission in *Yearbook ... 2005*, vol. II (Part One), document A/CN.4/556, sect. M.1.

[48] Reproduced in the present volume.

[49] *Yearbook ... 2001*, vol. II (Part Two), p. 28.

[50] Article III, section 3, of the Articles of Agreement reads as follows: "The total amount outstanding of guarantees, participations in loans and direct loans made by the Bank shall not be increased at any time, if by such increase the total would exceed one hundred percent of the unimpaired subscribed capital, reserves and surplus of the Bank."

Finally, regarding the peril that justifies the invocation of necessity, ICJ, in the *Gabčíkovo-Nagymaros Project* case, observed that peril has to be objectively established, and not merely apprehended as possible, and that a "peril" appearing in the long term might be held to be "imminent" as soon as it is established.[51] This latter clarification is of the utmost importance to World Bank practice, in which imminent perils may arise within the context of long-term financial commitments. Therefore, in the view of the World Bank, this clarification provided by ICJ should be reflected either in the text of the relevant article that will be adopted by the Commission or, at least, in the commentary accompanying it.

In consideration of the foregoing, the view of the World Bank is that the Commission's project:

(*a*) Should indicate that necessity, as one of the circumstances precluding wrongfulness, may be invoked by an international organization under similar circumstances to those in which a State may invoke necessity to safeguard an essential interest against a grave and imminent peril; and

(*b*) Should expressly state, preferably in the text of the relevant article, or at least in the commentary accompanying it, that a peril appearing in the long term might be held to be imminent as soon as it is established.

L. Responsibility of States for the internationally wrongful acts of international organizations

European Commission

With reference to the questions raised in paragraph 26 of the International Law Commission's 2005 report (see paragraph 1 of the Introduction above), the European Commission does not see a compelling reason why these questions should be treated. The draft deals with the international responsibility of an international organization. As draft article 16 already indicates, it is without prejudice to the international responsibility of States, including the member States of the international organization in question. The existing rules on State responsibility may well be applied by analogy when a State does not aid or assist another State but an international organization to commit an internationally wrongful act.

On the other hand, in its practice the European Commission has faced claims, according to which the European Community was said to be liable for aiding or assisting third States in the commission of internationally wrongful acts, thereby allegedly triggering the international responsibility of the Community itself. A pertinent example is a case that was brought in a court of a third State against the Community for allegedly having financed illegal activities of a public body, the employees of which allegedly caused the death of members of the applicant's family. In such a situation, it would be important to apply a similarly high threshold for triggering international liability as is laid down for assistance or aid by States under article 16[52] of the rules on State responsibility. Accordingly, assistance or aid for an internationally wrongful act could only trigger the international responsibility of an international organization if:

(*a*) The international organization does so with knowledge of the circumstances of the internationally wrongful act; and

(*b*) The act would be internationally wrongful if committed by the international organization.

International Criminal Police Organization

Regarding the issue of responsibility of States for the wrongful acts of international organizations, it would appear that—unless the Commission intends at some point to integrate the various areas of responsibility for internationally wrongful acts into one comprehensive framework—one would be venturing into the area of State responsibility rather than the responsibility of international organizations. The questions posed by the Commission reveal one consequence of the fact that international responsibility is commonly considered in relation to States as normal subjects of international law. The move to also study the responsibility of international organizations reflects the concomitant recognition of international organizations as subjects of international law. However, international responsibility is in essence a broader question inseparable from the question of who is the party that owes the international legal obligation that was breached. In other words, internationally wrongful acts of any subject (whether a State, an international organization, a natural person or a national legal person) pertain to the law of international responsibility. Thus, both theory and experience indicate that the question is broader than only the responsibility of States for the wrongful acts of international organizations. Consequently, singling out the responsibility of States for the wrongful acts of international organizations could prove to be unjustifiably selective.

The above becomes more clear when dealing with the two specific questions posed, namely (*a*) whether the draft articles should contain a provision on aid and assistance given by a State to an international organization in the commission of an internationally wrongful act; and (*b*) whether there are cases in which a State could be held responsible for the internationally wrongful act of an international organization of which it is a member. As will be explained below, those questions should be dealt with in the articles on responsibility of States for internationally wrongful acts.

[51] *Gabčíkovo-Nagymaros Project (Hungary/Slovakia), Judgment, I.C.J. Reports 1997*, p. 42, para. 54:

"The word 'peril' certainly evokes the idea of 'risk'; that is precisely what distinguishes 'peril' from material damage. But a state of necessity could not exist without a 'peril' duly established at the relevant point in time; the mere apprehension of a possible 'peril' could not suffice in that respect. It could moreover hardly be otherwise, when the 'peril' constituting the state of necessity has at the same time to be 'grave' and 'imminent'. 'Imminence' is synonymous with 'immediacy' or 'proximity' and goes far beyond the concept of 'possibility'. As the International Law Commission emphasized in its commentary, the 'extremely grave and imminent' peril must 'have been a threat to the interest at the actual time' ... That does not exclude, in the view of the Court, that a 'peril' appearing in the long term might be held to be 'imminent' as soon as it is established, at the relevant point in time, that the realization of that peril, however far off it might be, is not thereby any less certain and inevitable."

[52] *Yearbook ... 2001*, vol. II (Part Two), p. 27.

1. *Aiding, assisting, directing and controlling*

It is submitted that articles 16–17 of the articles on responsibility of States for internationally wrongful acts[53] are unduly restrictive in their scope. They only deal with cases of aiding and assisting another State, and directing and controlling another State in the commission of an internationally wrongful act, but not with cases of aiding and assisting in the commission of internationally wrongful acts by other subjects of international law, such as an international organization. Had articles 16–17 not been that restrictive, there would not have been a need to raise the question of whether the articles on the responsibility of international organizations should contain a provision on aid and assistance given by a State to an international organization in the commission of an internationally wrongful act, or directing and controlling an international organization in the commission of an internationally wrongful act. Given the restrictive formulations in articles 16–17, it would seem that the question posed by the Commission is one of the questions concerning State responsibility, which, by virtue of article 56 of the articles on responsibility of States for internationally wrongful acts,[54] continues to be governed by the applicable rules of international law. In this regard, it is recalled that the general formulation used by PCIJ in the *Factory at Chorzów* case,[55] is wide enough to cover cases of aiding and assisting or directing and controlling another subject of international law in the commission of an internationally wrongful act.

Hence, only if there exists no rule of general international law which holds that a State is responsible in cases of aiding and assisting or directing and controlling an international organization in the commission of an internationally wrongful act—which is not obvious —would there be a gap that needs to be filled through progressive development. But even then, it is not believed that the articles on the responsibility of international organizations would be the right place to do so. One could argue against limiting the responsibility of international organizations to aiding/controlling/coercing a State or another international organization in their breach of international law (see articles 12–14 of the draft).

2. *Member's responsibility*

To a certain extent, the foregoing discussion partly answers the question whether there are cases in which a State could be held responsible for the internationally wrongful act of an international organization of which it is a member. It is not clear what cases could be contemplated that are not already covered. One of the functions of article 57 of the articles on responsibility of States for internationally wrongful acts[56] is to exclude the question of the responsibility of any State for the conduct of an international organization from the scope of the articles. However, that provision does not exclude from the scope of the articles any question of responsibility of a State for its own conduct, that is, for conduct attributable to a State under part one, chapter II, of the articles on responsibility of States. The declared intention of the Commission under article 57 is to exclude these issues—although they formally fall within the scope of the articles on responsibility of States—since they concern questions of State responsibility akin to those dealt with in part one, chapter IV. Therefore, the scope of article 57 is narrow and covers only what is sometimes referred to as derivative or secondary liability of member States for acts or debts of an international organization.[57]

As previously observed by the INTERPOL General Secretariat (*Yearbook ... 2005*, vol. II (Part One), document A/CN.4/556, sect. M.2), the situation that might arise in case of the financial abandonment of an organization by its members calls for reflection in this context. It is recalled that in the *Effect of Awards* case,[58] ICJ clarified that the function of approving the budget does not mean that the plenary organ of an international organization has an absolute power to approve or disapprove the expenditure proposed to it, for some part of that expenditure arises out of obligations already incurred by the organization, and to this extent the plenary organ has no alternative but to honour those engagements. However, is the refusal of members to enable the organization to honour its engagements not covered by the provision regarding coercion? The case of the International Tin Council constitutes a singular case where members simply abandoned the organization, leading to defaults and its eventual demise. Conceivably, a case of such financial abandonment could be a case that would trigger the responsibilities of members under a rule akin to article 18 of the articles on responsibility of States for internationally wrongful acts.[59] Beyond this example, it remains unclear what should be covered under the heading of "responsibility of a State for internationally wrongful acts of an international organization".

(a) Lex specialis

It would seem that article 55 of the articles on responsibility of States for internationally wrongful acts[60] and article 74, paragraph 3, of the Vienna Convention on the Law of Treaties between States and International Organizations or between International Organizations already cover the *lex specialis* cases where the rules of an international organization specifically provide for the responsibility of a State for internationally wrongful acts of an international organization of which it is a member. That would be the case if either the constituent instrument or another rule of the organization prescribes the derivative or secondary liability of the members of the organization for the acts or debts of the organization. That is, for instance, the case with article 300, paragraph 7, of the Treaty establishing the European Community, which provides that agreements concluded by the European Community under the conditions set out in that article shall be binding on the institutions of the Community and on member States.

---

[53] *Yearbook ... 2001*, vol. II (Part Two), p. 27.

[54] *Ibid.*, p. 30.

[55] *Factory at Chorzów, Merits, Judgment No. 13, 1928, P.C.I.J., Series A, No. 17.*

[56] *Yearbook ... 2001*, vol. II (Part Two), p. 30.

[57] See Crawford, *op. cit.*, commentary on article 57, p. 311, para. (5).

[58] *Effect of Awards of Compensation Made by the United Nations Administrative Tribunal, Advisory Opinion, I.C.J. Reports 1954*, p. 59.

[59] *Yearbook ... 2001*, vol. II (Part Two), p. 27.

[60] *Ibid.*, p. 30.

(b) Pactum tertiis

Similarly, where an internationally wrongful act of an international organization results from the breach of an obligation imposed by an international agreement between the organization and a State or another international organization, it would follow from articles 34–35 of the Vienna Convention on the Law of Treaties between States and International Organizations or between International Organizations that only if the member countries of the wrongdoing organization have accepted to guarantee the discharge of the obligations under the agreement would they accrue responsibility for the breach of obligation by the organization.

(c) *Lack of funding*

One of the situations invoked in the doctrine justifying the responsibility of States for the wrongful acts of international organizations concerns the cases where an organization fails to meet its obligations because of lack of funding. Leaving aside the cases of financial obligations not governed by international law, there is some authority in the case law of the international courts and tribunals that implies that those cases are covered by the circumstances precluding wrongfulness.

Two judgements of international administrative tribunals illustrate this point. One concerns the situation that can arise when an organization faces financial difficulties resulting from extraneous factors, while the other concerns a situation caused by members' failure to meet their financial obligations to the organization.

As already mentioned above, in its Judgment No. 339, the ILO Administrative Tribunal answered positively the question whether financial distress caused by reasons other than failure of countries to honour their membership dues to an organization can serve as a circumstance that precludes wrongfulness. However, according to the OAS Administrative Tribunal, Judgment No. 124, when the cause is not extraneous but relates to the failure of members to meet their financial obligations, financial distress only leads to temporary impossibility of performance:

> The Tribunal holds that the Organization has an obligation to pay but recognizes, at the same time, that *exceptional circumstances* or *force majeure* may temporarily prevent it from meeting its legal obligation.
>
> Bearing that reality in mind, the legal tenet being applied here is that obligations are extinguished only in the manner provided for by the internal legal system of the Organization and by general principles of law such as waiver, payment, expiration, and indemnification, and not in any other way such as the nonpayment of quotas by the member states.
>
> Putting together both aspects—the nonpayment of quotas by the member states and the legally binding nature of the obligation—the Organization must open a special account on behalf of the General Secretariat staff, managed by and under the responsibility of the Treasurer, to set up a reserve for the employees, which shall be used solely and exclusively for paying any benefits owed by the Organization to its staff. The reserve shall be carried on the books and shall be paid out as the member states *become current in meeting* their financial obligations to the Organization by paying their quotas. (See articles 6 and 54 of the Charter and resolution AG/RES. 900 (XVII–O/87), in which the General Assembly stated that "payment of quotas and contributions is a legal commitment of the member states to the Organization of American States"; *see also* "The Mandatory Nature of the General Assembly Resolutions Setting the Quotas that the Member States are to Contribute to Fund the OAS", document OEA/Ser.G/CP/doc.1907/88 of July 7, 1988, pp. 1–2, prepared by the General Secretariat of the OAS and placed before the Permanent Council of the Organization. See also the Advisory Opinion "Certain Expenses of the United Nations (Article 17, paragraph 2 of the Charter)" dated July 20, 1962 (*I.C.J. Reports*, 1962) of the International Court of Justice, cited also by the General Secretariat of the OAS in the aforesaid document, in which the Court upheld the binding nature of quota determinations made by the UN General Assembly, and a memorandum from the United Nations Legal Counsel dated August 7, 1978, in which he maintained that Article 17 of the UN Charter "imposes on members the legal obligation to pay the quotas set for them by the General Assembly" (*Digest of United States Practice in International Law*, pp. 225–226).[61]

The latter judgement seems to suggest that, since under international law States that are members of an international organization are bound to pay the contributions assessed by the competent body of the organization, it is incumbent upon the organization to take measures to deal with situations where members are not current with their dues. However, the legal obligation inherent in membership in an international organization to pay the quotas set by the plenary organ remains *res inter alios acta*, and does not seem to amount to what is referred to as derivative or secondary liability of member States for acts or debts of an international organization.

(d) *Abandoning the general principles?*

As stated above, it remains unclear what should be covered under the heading of responsibility of a State for internationally wrongful acts of an international organization. Two other possibilities can be contemplated.

First, that as a matter of positive general international law the responsibility of a State for internationally wrongful acts of an international organization derogates from the general principles set forth in chapters I and III of the articles on responsibility of States for internationally wrongful acts.[62] Article 1 states that every internationally wrongful act of a State entails the responsibility of that State. Moreover, article 13 states that an act of a State does not constitute a breach of an international obligation unless the State is bound by the obligation in question at the time the act occurs. However, there exists no international practice that would support a finding that a derogating customary rule of international law has evolved, entailing that a State is also responsible for internationally wrongful acts of an international organization of which it is a member. Even a most favourable reading of the *Westland Helicopters Ltd/Arab Organization for Industrialization* (AOI) arbitration award[63] would still lead to the conclusion that the tribunal essentially deemed that the acts of AOI were attributable to the member States because AOI was substantially indistinguishable from them. Thus, apart from the fact that subsequently the Swiss judiciary rightfully annulled the award,[64] the *Westland Helicopters Ltd*/AOI arbitration award in fact constitutes an application of the general principles set forth in chapter I of the articles on responsibility of States for internationally wrongful acts.

---

[61] *Jairo Torres et al.* v. *Secretary General of the Organization of American States* (www.oas.org), p. 31.

[62] *Yearbook ... 2001*, vol. II (Part Two), pp. 26–27.

[63] *International Law Reports*, vol. 80 (1989), p. 595.

[64] *Ibid.*, p. 622.

Secondly, it might be that as a matter of *lege ferenda*, there should be a rule derogating from the general principles set forth in chapters I and III of the articles on responsibility of States for internationally wrongful acts. However, unlike domestic law systems, the international community has neither legal and administrative process of incorporation nor any common standards for international organizations. Thus, embarking on such an exercise will require dealing with the plethora of questions emanating from the diversity of international organizations. To mention just a few: should multilateral banking institutions be treated in the same way as non-banking international organizations? Should it matter that some organizations are integrationist and others not? Should a distinction be made between the types of obligations? Do the internal control mechanisms of all international organizations conform with the conditions that would allow such a rule to operate?

International Labour Organization

Question (a)

The basic position of ILO on question (*a*) is that articles 16–18 of the articles on responsibility of States for internationally wrongful acts[65] cannot be transposed into the draft articles on the responsibility of international organizations, unless their scope is clarified to the effect that they apply only to the responsibility of member States incurred when acting outside the constitutional framework of the organization.

If transposed to the responsibility of international organizations, articles 16–18 would require collaboration or other interaction between a State and the international organization in the commission of an internationally wrongful act of the organization. In this regard, there is a fundamental distinction to be made between the two different levels on which an international organization can interact with a member State. On the one hand, a member State can act within the constitutional framework and procedures of the organization. As a member of the organs of the organization, it contributes to the taking of collective decisions, including on the adoption (or non-adoption) of legal instruments of the organization. It also fulfils its basic obligations as a member under the constituent treaty, such as the payment of its assessed contributions. On the other hand, a member State may interact with an international organization beyond the scope of its constitutional obligations as a member of the organization; in such cases, the State and the organization relate to each other as two independent subjects of international law whose relationship would be governed by, *inter alia*, any relevant rules of international law applicable to their relations. This is the case, for example, when a State provides funds to the organization for its extrabudgetary technical cooperation activities or accepts such activities as a beneficiary, or when it offers to host its headquarters, offices or meetings and grants privileges and immunities to the organization.

It has been suggested in the Commission's commentary on article 57 of the articles on responsibility of States for internationally wrongful acts[66] that a State may incur international responsibility by virtue of its membership in an international organization. This would seem to imply that member States acting within the constitutional framework of an organization could be held responsible for the consequences of internationally wrongful acts committed by that organization. If articles 16–18 of the articles on responsibility of States were to be reproduced *mutatis mutandis* in the draft articles on the responsibility of international organizations, this would indeed be a possible consequence. In the view of ILO, such consequence would, however, not reflect applicable custom and practice.

As was properly stated in a 1995 resolution of the Institute of International Law, "there is no general rule of international law whereby States members are, due solely to their membership, liable concurrently or subsidiarily for the obligations of an international organization of which they are members".[67] In the absence of provisions to the contrary in constituent instruments of the organization concerned or otherwise failing the consent of the member States concerned, the latter are shielded by the organization's own and distinct legal personality. While constituent instruments of certain international organizations do make provision for the shared responsibility between an international organization and its member States,[68] this is not the case of the majority of them, including the Constitution of ILO,[69] and there is no practice to show the existence of such concurrent or subsidiary responsibility. While there is an opinion in academic writing contending that in certain cases member States could be held responsible for internationally wrongful acts of an international organization, it would seem that those are mainly based on the *International Tin Council* and the *Westland Helicopter* cases, whose scope and relevance seem to have been overestimated.[70] Without further entering into the general debate on this issue, ILO wishes to state that it does not consider those cases as precedents that would apply to the international responsibility of organizations such as ILO, whose mandate does not entail major economic operations under national laws.

A hypothetical transposition of articles 16–18 of the articles on responsibility of States for internationally wrongful acts[71] into the responsibility of international organizations would, in particular, seem to cover situations where member States have contributed to an internationally wrongful act of an international organization through their participation in the organization's decision that is at the origin of the wrongful act (which may be an action or omission) by voting for or against it, by abstaining, or

[65] *Yearbook ... 2001*, vol. II (Part Two), pp. 27.

[66] *Ibid.*, pp. 141–142.

[67] Resolution II, art. 6, adopted by the Institute of International Law at its Lisbon session in 1995, available on www.idi-iil.org.

[68] See, for example, the Convention on the international liability for damage caused by space objects, providing a system for sharing of liability between the organization and member States for damage caused by activities under the Treaty on principles governing the activities of States in the exploration and use of outer space, including the moon and other celestial bodies.

[69] Part XIII of the Treaty of Peace between the Allied and Associated Powers and Germany (Treaty of Versailles).

[70] See, for example, Klein, *La responsabilité internationale des organisations internationales dans les ordres juridiques internes et en droit des gens*, pp. 430–438.

[71] See footnote 65 above.

permitting or impeding consensus in the competent collective decision-making body. In this regard, in addition to the more general considerations raised in the preceding paragraph, there is a specific reason why ILO needs to rely on the "veil" of its international legal personality. All governing organs of ILO have a tripartite membership, which means that, in addition to government representatives, non-governmental members, i.e. employers' and workers' representatives, participate in the work and the decisions of those organs on an equal footing with Governments. In particular, the Governing Body of the International Labour Office, which is the pivotal organ of ILO, entrusted with important decision-making powers, is one-half composed of employer and worker members, who participate in the decisions of the Governing Body with an equal voting power. As they are elected by the International Labour Conference in their personal capacity, they cannot be considered to be the agents of any member Government, nor even of their respective employers' or workers' organizations.[72]

If member Governments could be held concurrently responsible for internationally wrongful acts of ILO resulting from Governing Body decisions, whereas employer and worker members of the Governing Body could arguably not, this would create a distortion incompatible with the structural principles inherent to the Constitution of ILO. The suggestion made by INTERPOL that draft article 1, paragraph 2, could also cover the responsibility of non-State entities (see *Yearbook ... 2005*, vol. II (Part One), document A/CN.4/556, sect. B) would help only to the extent that it also covered individual members of the organs of the organization, which are not themselves members of the organization. However, ILO would in any event not be favourable to any such extension of the scope of the draft articles, as there seems to be no practice in this regard.

In view of the above, ILO would suggest that the scope of articles 16–18, if transposed into the draft articles on responsibility of international organizations, be limited so as to exclude the concurrent or subsidiary responsibility of a member State acting exclusively within the constitutional framework and procedures of an organization except as the organization and its member States may expressly agree otherwise. This would, however, be without prejudice to that State's own responsibility under the articles on responsibility of States for internationally wrongful acts in case of breach of the organization's constituent instrument.

Provided that their scope were limited as described above, ILO would be favourable to transposing at least article 16 into these draft articles and would not object to the same as regards articles 17–18, although it is not aware of any practice regarding the latter two. As a general comment, it may be noted that the responsibility under those adapted articles would not need to be limited to States that are members of the international organization concerned, since some of the acts that would qualify as aid, assistance, direction, control or coercion under those articles could as well be committed by non-member States.

[72] See the Constitution of ILO, art. 7 (footnote 78 above).

As regards article 16, its application *mutatis mutandis* to the case of a State which aids or assists an international organization in the commission of an internationally wrongful act by the latter would seem to be justified. Such aid or assistance takes, for example, the form of providing funds to the organization for its extrabudgetary technical cooperation activities or hosting its headquarters, offices or meetings. The existence of concurrent responsibility of a State in those cases is confirmed in practice by the fact that States sometimes exclude that responsibility by way of agreement. For example, donor Governments of ILO sometimes exclude their responsibility for possible damages caused by activities of ILO under the financed projects.[73] ILO, in turn, regularly passes the primary responsibility for third-party claims in connection with those activities on to the Government of the beneficiary country.[74] Similarly, the headquarters agreement between ILO and Switzerland provides that "Switzerland shall not incur by reason of the activity of the International Labour Organisation on its territory any international responsibility for acts or omissions of the Organisation or of its agents acting or abstaining from acting within the limits of their functions".[75]

Concerning article 17 of the articles on responsibility of States for internationally wrongful acts, it is noted that the examples mentioned in the Commission's commentary to that article for direction of or control over a State by another State do not fit for international organizations.[76] In fact, it is not clear how a State could assume the direction or control of an international organization from outside its constitutional framework. In any event, any attempt to do so would constitute a breach of the principle of independence of the international organization and of the provisions of its constituent instrument that safeguard the independence of its executive head and other staff, which would entail the responsibility of the State itself. Assuming, however, that a State could establish a *de facto* direction or control over the organization, the provisions of article 17 would seem to provide an appropriate answer to the question of concurrent responsibility of the State.

Similarly, as regards article 18, ILO is not aware of any practice of a State coercing an international organization, but would consider that those provisions would be transferable to such hypothetical situations.

[73] For example, grant agreements with one donor Government agency contain the following clause: "[Donor] does not assume liability for any third-party claims for damages arising out of this grant."

[74] The ILO standard agreement with beneficiary Governments includes a clause similar to that usually contained in the UNDP Standard Basic Assistance Agreements (DP/107, annex I), reading as follows:

> "The Designated Institution shall handle and be responsible for any third-party claim or dispute arising from operations under this Agreement against the ILO, its officials or other persons performing services on its behalf, and shall hold them harmless in respect of such claims or disputes. Where a claim or dispute arises from the gross negligence or wilful misconduct of the above-mentioned individuals, the Parties shall consult with a view to finding a satisfactory solution."

[75] Agreement between the Swiss Federal Council and the International Labour Organisation concerning the legal status of the International Labour Organisation in Switzerland, art. 24 (United Nations, *Treaty Series*, vol. 15, No. 103, p. 383).

[76] *Yearbook ... 2001*, vol. II (Part Two), pp.68–69.

Question (b)

Apart from the cases considered above, ILO on the basis of its practice does not consider that there may be other cases in which a State could be held responsible for the internationally wrongful act of an international organization of which it is a member.

Organization for the Prohibition of Chemical Weapons

In chapter III.C of its 2005 report,[77] the Commission has invited comments and observation on three issues.

1. *Aiding or assisting, directing and controlling or coercing*

The first question (para. 26 (*a*)) is whether the Commission should include in the draft articles on responsibility of international organizations a provision concerning aid or assistance given by a State to an international organization in the commission of an internally wrongful act. The second is whether the answer to the first question should also apply to the case of direction and control or coercion exercised by a State over the commission of an act of an international organization that would be wrongful but for the coercion. In the view of OPCW, both issues are of great relevance in contemporary international affairs, and OPCW believes that the Commission should indeed examine them. In so doing, the Commission may wish to consider the practical consequences of the possible finding that a State is responsible in both scenarios. In addition, it would be desirable to clarify whether the wrongful act referred to in the second question is an internally wrongful act or an internationally wrongful act, as this is not specified in paragraph 26 (*a*).

2. *Responsibility of member States of an international organization*

The final question (para. 26 (*b*)) is whether there are cases in which a State could be held responsible for the internationally wrongful act of an international organization of which it is a member. In the view of OPCW, recent events, as can be observed in international and domestic litigation as well as in the academic literature, indicate that this is an issue of considerable practical significance, as the potential liability of member States has arisen for consideration on a number of occasions. The consensus in the academic literature, however, is that the legal situation is not entirely clear. Accordingly, consideration of the issue by the Commission could help to clarify the status of international law on the matter, regardless of the outcome of such consideration.

United Nations Educational, Scientific and Cultural Organization

In considering the issue referred to in question (*a*), the Commission should keep in mind that the international organizations to which the present draft principles would apply do have an international legal personality and, therefore, they are subjects which are in principle autonomous from their member States. Given this premise, it must be made clear that all actions taken by member States within the context of the constitutional framework of the organization (in terms of their contribution to their organization's decisions to act or not to act) would not entail their responsibility, unless a specific provision to this end is provided under its constitutive treaty. The responsibility of member States could be affirmed only when those States could be said to retain full control over the actions of the organization so that its legal personality would be considered a mere fiction.

In the light of the above, the aforesaid provision referring to the case of a State aiding or assisting an international organization in the commission of an internationally wrongful act should be limited, on the one hand, to the relations between the organization and non-member States and, on the other hand, as far as relations with member States are concerned, to those cases in which the organization and the member State concerned interact as independent subjects of international law. This would be the case when military forces of a member State collaborate with forces under the command of an organization in order to illegally overthrow a foreign Government or when a member State receives technical assistance from an organization and State agents collaborate with the organization's staff in carrying out internationally wrongful acts such as an illicit traffic of cultural objects.

In this regard, it is worth mentioning that in case of technical assistance activities, specific arrangements are made between the organization and the beneficiary State so as to exclude the responsibility of the former for claims or liabilities resulting from the activities performed by the organization's personnel in the country. The standard agreements on technical assistance between UNESCO and beneficiary countries include the following standard clause, which reflects an established practice followed for this type of agreement by the specialized agencies of the United Nations system:

> The Government shall be responsible for dealing with any claims which may be brought by third parties against UNESCO, its property and its personnel or other persons performing services on behalf of UNESCO and shall hold harmless UNESCO, its property, personnel and such persons in case of any claims or liabilities resulting from activities under this Plan of Operations, except where it is agreed by UNESCO and the Government that such claims or liabilities arise from the gross negligence or wilful misconduct of such personnel or persons.

Also, in those cases where a member State is willing to donate funds to the organization for technical assistance activities to be carried out in the territory of another member State, the donor Government often asks for the inclusion in the agreement with UNESCO of the following non-liability clause:

> [Member State X] does not assume liability for any third-party claims for damages arising out of this grant.

As for the situations in which a State would direct and control an international organization in the commission of an internationally wrongful act or exercise coercion on the latter, the case appears to be rather unlikely. In a very hypothetical case, coercion could be exercised by a State, for instance, over the organization's secretariat following a military occupation of the territory of the State hosting the coerced organization. However, within the constitutional

[77] *Yearbook ... 2005*, vol. II (Part Two), p.13.

framework of an organization, the exercise of direction or control by a member State over the organization's action does not appear to be possible given the legal guarantees usually provided for under constituent treaties.

World Health Organization

Coming to chapter III.C of the report,[78] WHO notes that the Commission is not requesting comments on any specific circumstance precluding wrongfulness and that the applicability of a claim of necessity to international organizations was the subject of a previous request for comments by the Commission. By way of general comment at this stage, WHO would recommend that the Special Rapporteur and the Commission bear in mind the fundamental differences between States and international organizations, and the differences of functions and purposes existing between international organizations, to assess which of the circumstances precluding wrongfulness listed in part one, chapter V, of the articles on responsibility of States for internationally wrongful acts[79] could be considered applicable to international organizations, especially taking into account the probable absence of practice in this area. For example, while it is evident that a circumstance such as self-defence is by its very nature only applicable to the actions of a State, it could be questioned whether the international obligations usually attributable to international organizations may be such that could plausibly lead to a breach of a peremptory norm of general international law under article 26 of the articles on State responsibility.[80]

The Commission is also asking whether it should include in the draft articles the case of a State aiding or assisting an international organization in the commission of an internationally wrongful act, as well as the cases of a State directing and controlling, or coercing, an international organization in the commission of an internationally wrongful act. These are the situations envisaged in articles 16–18 of the articles on responsibility of States for internationally wrongful acts,[81] as noted in the report. The general reply of WHO to this question is that, to the extent that either of the three cases in question would involve the international responsibility of an international organization, it would seem logical to include that situation in the draft articles. On the basis of the structure and content of the articles on State responsibility, that would generally seem to be the case for aid or assistance, or direction and control, by a State to an international organization in the commission of an internationally wrongful act. A different reply, however, would seem to apply to the case of an international organization being coerced by a State in the commission of an act that would be wrongful but for the coercion, since that particular situation would exclude the responsibility of the coerced organization.

[78] *Yearbook ... 2005*, vol. II (Part Two), p.13.

[79] *Yearbook ... 2001*, vol. II (Part Two), pp. 27–28.

[80] *Ibid.*, p. 28.

[81] *Ibid.*, p. 27.

UNILATERAL ACTS OF STATES

[Agenda item 6]

DOCUMENT A/CN.4/569 and Add.1

Ninth report on unilateral acts of States, by Mr. Víctor Rodríguez Cedeño, Special Rapporteur

[Original: Spanish]
[6 April 2006]

CONTENTS

Multilateral instruments cited in the present report

	Source
Convention respecting the Free Navigation of the Suez Maritime Canal (Constantinople, 29 October 1888)	N. Singh, ed., *International Maritime Law Conventions*, vol. 4 (London, Stevens, 1983), p. 2834.
Treaty of Peace between the Allied and Associated Powers and Germany (Treaty of Versailles) (Versailles, 28 June 1919)	*British and Foreign State Papers, 1919*, vol. CXII (London, HM Stationery Office, 1922), p. 1.
Convention on the Prevention and Punishment of the Crime of Genocide (New York, 9 December 1948)	United Nations, *Treaty Series*, vol. 78, No. 1021, p. 277.
Vienna Convention on the Law of Treaties (Vienna, 23 May 1969)	*Ibid.*, vol. 1155, No. 18232, p. 331.
Vienna Convention on Succession of States in respect of Treaties (Vienna, 23 August 1978)	*Ibid.*, vol. 1946, No. 33356, p. 3.
Convention on the rights of the child (New York, 20 November 1989)	*Ibid.*, vol. 1577, No. 27531, p. 3.
Inter-American Convention against Corruption (Caracas, 29 March 1996)	ILM, vol. 35, No. 5 (September 1996), p. 724.
Criminal Law Convention on Corruption (Strasbourg, 27 January 1999)	United Nations, *Treaty Series*, vol. 2216, No. 39391, p. 225.
Additional Protocol to the Criminal Law Convention on Corruption (Strasbourg, 15 May 2003)	*Ibid.*, vol. 2466, No. 39391, p. 168.

Works cited in the present report

Akehurst, Michael

"The hierarchy of the sources of international law", BYBIL 1974–1975 (Oxford), vol. 47, 1977, pp. 273–285.

Alexidze, Levan

"Legal nature of *jus cogens* in contemporary international law", *Collected Courses of The Hague Academy of International Law, 1981–III*. The Hague, Martinus Nijhoff, 1982. vol. 172, pp. 219–270.

Aspremont Lynden, Jean d'

"Les travaux de la Commission du droit international relatifs aux actes unilatéraux des États", RGDIP, vol. CIX, 2005, pp. 163–189.

Barberis, Julio A.

"Los actos jurídicos unilaterales como fuente del derecho internacional público", *in* Manuel Pérez González and others, eds., *Hacia un nuevo orden internacional y europeo: estudios en homenaje al Profesor Don Manuel Díez de Velasco*. Madrid, Tecnos, 1993, pp. 101–116.

Bondía García, David

Régimen jurídico de los actos unilaterales de los Estados. Barcelona, Bosch, 2004. 221 p.

Brownlie, Ian

Principles of Public International Law. 6th ed. Oxford, Oxford University Press, 2003. 742 p.

Capotorti, Francesco

"L'extinction et la suspension des traités", *Collected Courses of The Hague Academy of International Law, 1971–III*. Leiden, Sijthoff, 1972. vol. 134, pp. 417–587.

Carrillo Salcedo, Juan Antonio

"Reflections on the existence of a hierarchy of norms in international law, *European Journal of International Law* (Florence), vol. 8, 1997, pp. 583–595.

Casado Raigón, Rafael

Notas sobre el jus cogens *internacional*. Córdoba, Spain, 1991. 43 p.

Casado Raigón, Rafael and Eva María Vázquez Gómez

"La impronta del *ius cogens* en el proyecto de artículos de la Comisión de Derecho Internacional sobre la responsabilidad del Estado por hechos internacionalmente ilícitos", *in* Ana Salinas de Frías and Marina Vargas Gómez-Urrutia, eds., *Soberanía del Estado y derecho internacional: homenaje al profesor Juan Antonio Carrillo Salcedo*. Seville, University of Seville, 2005. vol. I, pp. 343–360.

Casanovas la Rosa, Oriol

"La modificación de los acuerdos internacionales por la práctica posterior", *Revista Española de Derecho Internacional*, vol. XXI, No. 1, January–March 1968, pp. 328–345.

Cassese, Antonio

International Law. Oxford, Oxford University Press, 2001. 469 p.

Charpentier, Jean

"Engagements unilatéraux et engagements conventionnels: différences et convergences", *in* Jerzy Makarczyk, ed., *Theory of International Law at the Threshold of the 21st Century*. The Hague, Kluwer, 1996, pp. 367–380.

Coussirat-Coustère, Vincent and Pierre Michel Eisemann, eds.

Repertory of international arbitral jurisprudence. vol. I, 1794–1918. Dordrecht, Martinus Nijhoff, 1989. 546 p.

Danilenko, Gennady M.

"International *jus cogens*: issues of law-making", *European Journal of International Law* (Florence), issue 1, 1991, pp. 42–65.

Degan, Vladimir-Djuro

"Unilateral act as a source of particular international law", *Finnish Yearbook of International Law* (Helsinki), vol. V, 1994, pp. 149–266.

Dehaussy, J.

"La déclaration égyptienne de 1957 sur le canal de Suez", *Annuaire français de droit international* (Paris), vol. VI, 1960, pp. 169–184.

Elias, T. O.

"Problems concerning the validity of treaties", *Collected Courses of The Hague Academy of International Law, 1971–III*. Leiden, Sijthoff, 1972. vol. 134, pp. 333–416.

Fernández Tomás, Antonio

"El *ius cogens* y las obligaciones derivadas de normas imperativas: entre el mito y la realidad", *in* Ana Salinas de Frías and Marina Vargas Gómez-Urrutia, eds., *Soberanía del Estado y derecho internacional: homenaje al profesor Juan Antonio Carrillo Salcedo*. Seville, University of Seville, 2005. Vol. I, pp. 619–638.

Gaja, Giorgio

"*Jus cogens* beyond the Vienna Convention", *Collected Courses of The Hague Academy of International Law, 1981–III*. The Hague, Martinus Nijhoff, 1982. vol. 172, pp. 271–316.

Gómez Robledo, Antonio

"Le *ius cogens* international: sa genèse, sa nature, ses fonctions", *Collected Courses of The Hague Academy of International Law, 1981–III*. The Hague, Martinus Nijhoff, 1982. Vol. 172, pp. 9–217.

El ius cogens *internacional: Estudio histórico-crítico*. Mexico, Universidad Nacional Autónoma de México, 2003. 195 p.

González Vega, Javier A.

"El reconocimiento de Belice ante la Corte de Constitucionalidad de Guatemala: la sentencia de 3 de noviembre de 1992", *Revista Española de Derecho Internacional*, vol. XLV, No. 2, July–December 1993, pp. 580–585.

Guggenheim, Paul

"The validity and the nullity of international legal acts", *Recueil des cours de l'Académie de droit international de La Haye, 1949–I*. Paris, Sirey, 1949. vol. 74, pp. 191–268.

Gutiérrez Espada, Cesáreo

Derecho Internacional Público. Madrid, Trotta, 1995. 699 p.

"Sobre las normas imperativas del derecho internacional", *Pacis Artes: Obra Homenaje al profesor Julio D. González Campos*, vol. I, *Derecho Internacional Público y Derecho Comunitario y de la Unión Europea*. Madrid, Editer, 2005, pp. 273–288.

Hannikainen, Lauri

Peremptory Norms (Jus Cogens) in International Law: Historical Development, Criteria, Present Status. Helsinki, Finnish Lawyers' Publishing Company, 1988. 781 p.

Haraszti, György

"Treaties and the fundamental change of circumstances", *Collected Courses of The Hague Academy of International Law, 1975–III*. Leiden, Sijthoff, 1977. vol. 146, pp. 1–93.

Higgins, Rosalyn

Problems and Process: International Law and How We Use It. Oxford, Clarendon Press, 1994. 274 p.

Jacqué, Jean-Paul

Éléments pour une théorie de l'acte juridique en droit international public. Paris, Librairie Générale de Droit et de Jurisprudence, 1972. 511 p.

"À propos de la promesse unilatéral", *Mélanges offerts à Paul Reuter—le droit international: unité et diversité*. Paris, Pedone, 1981, pp. 327–345.

Kiss, Alexandre-Charles

Répertoire de la pratique française en matière de droit international public. vol. I. Paris, Centre National de la Recherche Scientifique, 1962.

Koskenniemi, Martti

"Report of the Director of Studies of the English-speaking Section of the Centre", *in* Pierre Michel Eisemann and Martti Koskenniemi, eds., *State Succession: Codification Tested against the Facts*. The Hague, Martinus Nijhoff, 2000, pp. 65–132.

Lauterpacht, H., ed.

Annual Digest and Reports of Public International Law Cases: Years 1935–1937. London, Butterworth, 1941.

Annual Digest and Reports of Public International Law Cases: Years 1919–1942. London, Butterworth, 1947.

Annual Digest and Reports of Public International Law Cases: Years 1943–1945. London, Butterworth, 1949.

Marston, Geoffrey, ed.

"United Kingdom materials on international law 1981", BYBIL 1981, vol. 52, 1982, pp. 361–534.

"United Kingdom materials on international law 1982", BYBIL 1982, vol. 53, pp. 337–570.

"United Kingdom materials on international law 1987", BYBIL 1987, vol. 58 (1988), pp. 497–650.

Meron, Theodor

"Article 46 of the Vienna Convention on the Law of Treaties (*ultra vires* treaties): some recent cases", BYBIL 1978, vol. 49, 1979, pp. 175–199.

Moore, John Bassett

History and Digest of the International Arbitrations to which the United States has been a Party. Washington, D.C., Government Printing Office, 1898.

Nahlik, S. E.

"The grounds of invalidity and termination of treaties", *American Journal of International Law*, vol. 65, 1971, pp. 736–756.

Navarro Batista, Nicolás

"La práctica comunitaria sobre reconocimiento de Estados: nuevas tendencias", *Revista de Instituciones Europeas* (Madrid), vol. 22, No. 1, 1995, pp. 475–507.

Nicoloudis, E. P.

La nullité de jus cogens *et le développement contemporain du droit international public*. Athens, Papazissi, 1974.

Oraison, André

"Le dol dans la conclusion des traités", RGDIP, vol. 75, No. 3, July–September 1971, pp. 617–673.

L'erreur dans les traités. Paris, Librairie Générale de Droit et de Jurisprudence, 1972. 281 p.

Ortega Terol, Juan Miguel

Textos y documentos sobre los desmembramientos de la Unión Soviética y de Yugoslavia. Cuenca, Universidad de Castilla-La Mancha, 1996. 100 p.

"Aspectos teóricos y prácticos de la continuidad en la identidad del Estado", *Anuario de Derecho Internacional* (Pamplona), vol. XV, 1999, pp. 273–323.

Pecourt García, Enrique

"El principio del 'estoppel' en derecho internacional público", *Revista Española de Derecho Internacional*, vol. XV (1962), Nos. 1–2, págs. 97–139.

Poch de Caviedes, Antonio

"From the *clausula rebus sic stantibus* to the revision clause in international conventions", *Recueil des cours de l'Académie de droit international de La Haye, 1966–II*. Leiden, Sijthoff, 1968. vol. 118, pp. 105–208.

Remiro Brotóns, Antonio

Derecho Internacional Público. vol. II: Derecho de los Tratados, Madrid, Tecnos, 1987. 551 p.

Rodríguez Carrión, Alejandro J.

Lecciones de derecho internacional público. 5th ed. Madrid, Tecnos, 2002. 659 p.

ROUSSEAU, Charles

"Chronique des faits internationaux", RGDIP, vol. LXXXV, 1981.

"Chronique des faits internationaux", RGDIP, vol. LXXXVI, 1982.

"Chronique des faits internationaux", RGDIP, vol. LXXXVIII, 1984.

"Chronique des faits internationaux", RGDIP, vol. LXXXIX, 1985.

"Chronique des faits internationaux", RGDIP, vol. XCI, 1987.

"Chronique des faits internationaux", RGDIP, vol. XCII, 1988.

ROZAKIS, Christos L.

The concept of jus cogens *in the law of treaties*. Amsterdam, Elsevier, 1976. 206 p.

RUBIN, Alfred P.

"The international legal effects of unilateral declarations", *American Journal of International Law*, vol. 71, 1977, pp. 1–30.

RUDA, José M.

"Terminación y suspensión de los tratados", *in* Emmanuel G. Bello and Bola A. Ajibola, eds., *Essays in honour of Judge Taslim Olawale Elias*. vol. I: *Contemporary International Law and Human Rights*. Dordrecht, Martinus Nijhoff, 1992, pp. 93–116.

RUILOBA GARCÍA, Eloy

Circunstancias especiales y equidad en la delimitación de los espacios marítimos. Saragossa, Real Instituto de Estudios Europeos, 2001. 559 p.

SEVE DE GASTÓN, Alberto

"Los actos jurídicos internacionales unilaterales con especial atinencia a los intereses marítimos argentinos", *Anuario Argentino de Derecho Internacional* (Córdoba, Argentina), vol. I, 1983, pp. 251–357.

SICAULT, Jean-Didier

"Du caractère obligatoire des engagements unilatéraux en droit international public", RGDIP, vol. LXXXIII, 1979, pp. 633–688.

SINCLAIR, Sir Ian

The Vienna Convention on the Law of Treaties. 2th ed. Manchester, Manchester University Press, 1984. 270 p.

SKUBISZEWSKI, Krzysztof

"Unilateral acts of States", *in* Mohammed Bedjaoui, ed., *International Law: Achievements and Prospects*. Paris, UNESCO, 1991, pp. 221–240.

SZTUCKI, Jerzy

Jus cogens *and the Vienna Convention on the Law of Treaties: A Critical Appraisal*. Vienna, Springer-Verlag, 1974. 204 p.

TORRES CAZORLA, María Isabel

"Rights of private persons on State succession: an approach to the most recent cases", *in* Pierre Michel Eisemann and Martti Koskenniemi, eds., *State Succession: Codification Tested against the Facts*. The Hague, Martinus Nijhoff, 2000, pp. 663–717.

Los actos unilaterales de los Estados en el derecho internacional contemporáneo. Málaga, October 2001. 182 p. Mimeographed.

"El derecho del menor a una nacionalidad: análisis de los recientes casos de sucesión de Estados", *Los Derechos del Niño: Estudios con motivo del X Aniversario de la Convención de los Derechos del Niño*. Madrid, Ministry of Labour and Social Affairs, 2002, pp. 193–212.

"El último cambio de Yugoslavia: de la República Federativa de Yugoslavia (Serbia y Montenegro) a la Unión de Serbia y Montenegro", *Revista Española de Derecho Internacional* (Madrid), vol. LV, No. 1, January-June 2003, pp. 487–492.

URIOS MOLINER, Santiago

Actos unilaterales y derecho internacional público: delimitación de una figura susceptible de un régimen jurídico común. Castellón, Universitat Jaume I, April 2001. Mimeographed. (Thesis, University Jaume I, Spain)

VAN BOGAERT, E.

"Le sens de la clause '*rebus sic stantibus*' dans le droit des gens actuel", RGDIP, vol. LXX, 1966, pp. 49–74.

VENTURINI, Gian Carlo

"The scope and legal effects of the behaviour and unilateral acts of States", *Recueil des cours de l'Académie de droit international de La Haye*, 1964–II. Leiden, Sijthoff, 1964. Vol. 12, pp. 363–467.

VERDROSS, Alfred

"*Jus dispositivum* and *jus cogens* in international law", *American Journal of International Law* (Washington, D.C.), vol. 60, 1966, pp. 55–63.

VERHOEVEN, Joe

La reconnaissance internationale dans la pratique contemporaine: les relations publiques internationales. Paris, Pedone, 1975.

"La reconnaissance internationale: déclin ou renouveau?", *Annuaire français de droit international* (Paris), vol. XXXIX, 1993, pp. 7–40.

VERZIJL, J. H. W.

"La validité et la nullité des actes juridiques internationaux", *Revue de droit international* (París), vol. XV, No. 2, April-May-June 1935, pp. 284–339.

International Law in Historical Perspective. Part VI: Juridical facts as sources of international rights and obligations. Leiden, Sijthoff, 1973.

VIRALLY, Michel

"Réflexions sur le '*jus cogens*'", *Revue de droit international* (Paris), vol. XII, 1966, pp. 5–29.

VISSCHER, Paul DE

"Remarques sur l'évolution de la jurisprudence de la Cour Internationale de Justice relative au fondement obligatoire de certains actes unilatéraux", *in* Jerzy Makarczyk, ed., *Essays in International Law in honour of Judge Manfred Lachs*. The Hague, Martinus Nijhoff, 1984, pp. 459–465.

WEIL, Prosper

"Le droit international en quête de son identité: cours général de droit international public", *Collected Courses of The Hague Academy of International Law*, 1992–VI. The Hague, Martinus Nijhoff, 1996. vol. 237, pp. 9–370.

WEILER, J. H. H. and Andreas L. PAULUS

"The structure of change in international law or is there a hierarchy of norms in international law?", *European Journal of International Law* (Florence), vol. 8, 1997, pp. 545–565.

ZAFRA ESPINOSA DE LOS MONTEROS, Rafael

Aproximación a una teoría de los actos unilaterales de los Estados. University of Seville, 2001. Mimeographed.

Introduction

1. The International Law Commission considered the eighth report on unilateral acts of States[1] at its 2852nd to 2855th meetings, held on 15 and 19–21 July 2005. In accordance with the views expressed by the Working Group on unilateral acts of States and the members of the Commission, as well as the Governments represented in the Sixth Committee of the General Assembly, that report presented a number of examples of unilateral acts of States. While not all of these examples represented unilateral acts in the sense with which the Commission is concerned, they served to facilitate progress in the deliberations on the subject.

2. In the course of the Commission's discussions, it was once again pointed out that "the diversity of effects and the importance of the setting in which acts occurred made it very difficult to arrive at a 'theory' or 'regime' of unilateral acts".[2] Other members, however, thought that it was possible to establish such a regime,[3] albeit with the qualifications described below.

3. It was also pointed out, during the Commission's discussions on the topic, that "the practice studied so far, supplemented perhaps by further study of other acts ... might provide the basis for a formal definition that nevertheless retained some flexibility".[4] After establishing such a definition, "the Commission should study the capacity and authority of the author of a unilateral act".[5] It was also suggested that a "summary of the Commission's work on the subject, in the form of a declaration accompanied by general or preliminary conclusions and covering all the points which had been accepted by consensus", should be prepared.[6] It was further noted that it was "important not to overlook the need to ensure that States were still free to make political statements at any time without feeling constrained by the possibility of having to accept legal commitments".[7]

4. Another view, which had been put forward in the Commission a number of times before, was that "unilateral acts were so diverse, and so various and complex in nature, that they could not be codified in the form of draft articles";[8] an "'expository' study of the topic would thus be the best way to proceed, since the setting in which acts were performed was crucial to their identification".[9] Given the difficulties that the Commission had encountered in attempting to agree on general rules, it would be better, in the view of some members, to "aim in the direction of guidelines or principles which could help and guide States while providing for greater certainty in the matter".[10]

5. Another issue that was considered in the course of the Commission's discussions at its fifty-seventh session and at the meetings of the Working Group on unilateral acts[11] was that of the "revocability of a unilateral act",[12] which, it was said, must be taken up if the topic was to be thoroughly studied;[13] it is therefore addressed in detail in the present report.

6. The report and the Commission's deliberations thereon were considered by Member States in the Sixth Committee during the sixtieth session of the General Assembly in 2005. At the meetings held between 24 October and 3 November 2005, government representatives highlighted the difficulty of the topic[14] and expressed some concern about the slow progress of the Commission's work,[15] as well as their agreement with the approach taken in the eighth report of the Special Rapporteur;[16] they also raised more specific issues in relation to the topic. It was mentioned that the scope of the topic should be restricted to the obligation a State could assume through a unilateral declaration, the conditions governing its validity[17] and its effects on third States, including the corresponding rights of those States. That would obviate the need to examine the enormously complex issue of conduct.[18]

7. As to how the work on this topic should proceed, some delegations stressed the need to conclude the study in 2006[19] through the formulation of general conclusions based on the Commission's previous work,[20] albeit without losing sight of the specific nature of unilateral acts;

---

[1] *Yearbook ... 2005*, vol. II (Part One), document A/CN.4/557, p. 119.

[2] *Ibid.* (Part Two), para. 303, view expressed by Ms. Escarameia and Mr. Candioti.

[3] *Ibid.*, views of Messrs. Kamto, Pellet, Candioti and Ms. Xue, among others.

[4] *Ibid.*, view of Mr. Fomba.

[5] *Ibid.*, para. 305, in particular the views of Ms. Escarameia, Mr. Pellet and Mr. Daoudi.

[6] *Ibid.*, para. 307, views of Mr. Candioti and Ms. Xue.

[7] *Ibid.*, para. 309, view of Mr. Pellet.

[8] *Ibid.*, para. 310, views of Mr. Koskenniemi and Mr. Brownlie.

[9] *Ibid.*, view of Mr. Brownlie.

[10] *Ibid.*, para. 314, views of Mr. Candioti and Mr. Pellet, among others.

[11] Under the chairmanship of Mr. Pellet, the open-ended Working Group held four meetings (11 and 18 May, 1 June and 25 July 2005) (*ibid.*, paras. 327–332).

[12] *Ibid.*, para. 315.

[13] At the request of the members of the Commission, its Chairman at its fifty-seventh session, Mr. Momtaz, told government representatives in the Sixth Committee that the Commission would welcome comments from Governments on practice regarding the revocation or revision of unilateral acts, their particular circumstances and conditions, the effects of revocation or revision of a unilateral act, and the range of possible reactions from third parties (*Official Records of the General Assembly, Sixtieth Session, Sixth Committee*, 13th meeting, para. 80).

[14] *Ibid.*, 11th meeting, para. 59, statement by Spain; 16th meeting, para. 12, statement by the Russian Federation; 19th meeting, para. 14, statement by the Libyan Arab Jamahiriya; 20th meeting, para. 38, statement by the Bolivarian Republic of Venezuela.

[15] *Ibid.*, 11th meeting, para. 46, statement by Morocco; 14th meeting, para. 52, statement by Japan; 15th meeting, para. 10, statement by the Republic of Korea; 16th meeting, para. 52, statement by Guatemala; *ibid.*, para. 72, statement by Kenya.

[16] *Ibid.*, 14th meeting, para. 10, statement by Austria; para. 44, statement by New Zealand; para. 52, statement by Japan; *ibid.*, 16th meeting, para. 12, statement by the Russian Federation; para. 21, statement by Poland; para. 46, statement by Chile.

[17] *Ibid.*, 11th meeting, para. 59, statement by Spain; para. 74, statement by France.

[18] *Ibid.*, para. 59, statement by Spain; para. 74, statement by France; 16th meeting, para. 22, statement by Poland; along the same lines, Chile took the view that it would be better to consolidate the progress achieved with respect to unilateral acts *sensu stricto* before embarking on a detailed study of conduct (*ibid.*, para. 48).

[19] *Ibid.*, 12th meeting , para. 42, statement by Denmark on behalf of the Nordic countries; 16th meeting, para. 35, statement by Portugal.

[20] *Ibid.*, 12th meeting, para. 42, statement by Denmark on behalf of the Nordic countries; 13th meeting, para. 106, statement by Argentina; 15th meeting, para. 18, statement by China.

that is, without modelling the conclusions too closely on the provisions of the Vienna Convention on the Law of Treaties (hereinafter the 1969 Vienna Convention).[21] Other delegations, however, felt that provisions on the law of treaties could be useful as a point of departure and could even be used as a framework, *mutatis mutandis*.[22] One delegation said that the view it had expressed at previous sessions, to the effect that the topic should be set aside, had not changed;[23] another said that the difficulty of defining the nature of such acts suggested that they were unamenable to codification or progressive development.[24] Other delegations felt that the Commission's consideration of the topic made a positive contribution by identifying and clarifying the concept of unilateral acts[25] so that ideas or guiding principles could be formulated on the topic;[26] that might provide a good foundation to serve as a first step towards possible codification.

8. In response to the concerns expressed by the members of the Commission, and with a view to facilitating the consideration of the topic, the Special Rapporteur is submitting his ninth report this year. The report is divided into two chapters, the first of which refers to the grounds for invalidity of unilateral acts and the modification and suspension of such acts, together with other related concepts. While these issues have arisen in the course of previous years' deliberations, they have not been formally presented in the Special Rapporteur's reports. Chapter II of the present report deals with topics that have been considered before, from a structural standpoint, in the Commission and in the Working Group on unilateral acts of States established in 2004 and 2005 and chaired by Mr. Alain Pellet: the definition of unilateral acts in a way that distinguishes them from other acts which, although apparently unilateral, actually constitute a treaty relationship and are therefore subject to the regime established by the 1969 Vienna Convention. In turn, such acts, as manifestations of will in the strict sense, are distinguished from unilateral conduct that may produce similar legal effects. On this same subject, reference is made to the addressee or addressees of a unilateral act, although this does not affect the fact that the topic is limited to unilateral acts formulated by States. In this regard, the report presents two proposals that could form part of the definition of such acts and could determine the scope of the draft guiding principles; secondly, the report presents proposed language related to the formulation of the act: capacity of the State, persons authorized to act and to enter into legal commitments on the State's behalf in its international relations, and the subsequent confirmation of an act formulated without authorization; thirdly, proposed language is suggested in relation to the basis for the binding nature of unilateral acts; and lastly, a draft guiding principle is presented in relation to the interpretation of unilateral acts. A list of all the guiding principles being proposed, including those concerning the invalidity, termination and suspension of unilateral acts, which are discussed in chapter I, is annexed to the present document.

9. The Special Rapporteur proposes that chapter I of this report be considered in plenary session and that chapter II be referred to the Working Group on unilateral acts of States for further consideration, in line with the Working Group's mandate and in order to expedite the work on the topic at the current session.

[21] *Ibid.*, 14th meeting, para. 44, statement by New Zealand.

[22] *Ibid.*, 15th meeting, para. 10, statement by the Republic of Korea; 16th meeting, para. 54, statement by Guatemala.

[23] *Ibid.*, 14th meeting, para. 7, statement by the United Kingdom of Great Britain and Northern Ireland.

[24] *Ibid.*, 15th meeting, para. 2, statement by the United States of America.

[25] *Ibid.*, 16th meeting, para. 46, statement by Chile; para. 54, statement by Guatemala; 17th meeting, paras. 6 and 10, statement by Cuba; 18th meeting, para. 74, statement by Belarus.

[26] *Ibid.*, para. 93, statement by Malaysia.

Chapter I

Unilateral acts of States

A. Validity and duration of unilateral acts

10. In this section, the question of the validity and duration of unilateral acts of States is addressed, a topic which, though discussed by the Commission at previous sessions, must be examined in more detail in order to provide the basis for the guiding principles being proposed. Both the Commission and the Sixth Committee have expressed the need to address this topic as thoroughly as possible. With this objective in mind, an attempt will be made to describe the status of the issue, in the literature and in practice, notwithstanding the paucity of precedents.

1. Grounds for invalidity

11. The question of the validity of unilateral acts of States has been considered only rarely and tangentially in the legal literature.[27] While in the realm of the law of treaties the possible grounds for their invalidity, termination and suspension have been the subject of a huge number of studies and opinions in the literature,[28] this has not been the case in the area that is of concern here.[29] This is not to say that the topic has not sparked any interest;

[27] The analysis of this issue draws to a large extent on the conclusions put forward by Torres Cazorla, *Los actos unilaterales de los Estados en el derecho internacional contemporáneo*, pp. 115–172.

[28] It should be borne in mind that the 1969 Vienna Convention devotes 31 articles (42–72) and an annex to the invalidity, termination and suspension of the operation of treaties (part V). The Convention's goal was a laudable one: to lend stability and legal security to treaty relations by limiting the invalidity, termination and suspension of the operation of treaties to a few exceptional circumstances.

[29] The view expressed by Pecourt García, "El principio del *estoppel* en derecho internacional público", p. 125, may therefore continue to be valid, even though it was expressed before the 1969 Vienna Convention came into being. That view, which could also be applied to unilateral acts of States, is that: "The absence of an organic doctrine and a set of uniform principles governing the validity and invalidity of international legal acts makes it almost impossible to study those concepts in relation to a specific type of act, within a framework of general validity. This means that the question of the validity and invalidity of different types of international acts has to be considered within relatively autonomous conceptual and regulatory frameworks."

quite the contrary. In fact, almost as soon the Commission began to discuss this topic, government representatives in the Sixth Committee expressed the view that, in the future, the Commission should focus on aspects concerning the elaboration and conditions of validity of unilateral acts.[30] The Commission itself referred to a working group questions relating to the causes of invalidity; this was "a delicate matter which ... warranted more extensive study, along with the consideration of the question of the conditions of validity of a unilateral act".[31]

12. Views have been expressed in the literature to the effect that the principle of good faith creates a need to ensure compliance with unilateral commitments. This principle, in turn, reflects the moral obligation to honour one's promises or, alternatively, the social requirement of ensuring the stability of international relations, and is achieved through the sincerity of the declaring State or the expectation created among third parties that the unilateral act will be observed.[32] The same body of opinion holds that "thus, with regard to the fundamental requirement of stability in international relations, unilateral commitments offer guarantees of solidity comparable to those of treaty commitments".[33] This assessment also highlights the affinity between these two concepts—unilateral acts and international treaties—and illustrates one of the reasons why, in the view of the Special Rapporteur, the study of this topic should consider the provisions of the 1969 Vienna Convention that concern the possible invalidity, termination or suspension of treaties, even though these provisions cannot be transposed wholesale to the realm of unilateral acts, owing to the peculiar characteristics of such acts.[34]

13. The second major issue that the study will have to address is the near absence of discussion about the contingencies that may affect unilateral acts; there is a similar dearth of examples in international practice. Furthermore, attempts to extrapolate certain concepts emanating from internal law have given rise to some doubts in the literature, which not even case law, in the few instances in which it has dealt with this subject, has been able to dispel. As Guggenheim correctly pointed out:

> [B]y introducing into international law the private law theory relating to defects of consent, one is transposing into the sphere of inter-State relations a doctrine that was originally applied in the sphere of internal law, forgetting that a coherent theory on defects of consent can only be developed through a lengthy accumulation of precedents, which are lacking in international law.[35]

14. Perhaps as a consequence of this attempt to extrapolate rules of internal law to the international plane, the literature distinguishes between defects that directly affect the expression of will *per se*, thereby depriving it of its very essence, and defects that affect the will of the subject, rendering it irregular, but not necessarily eliminating it. Following this line of reasoning, the consequences initially arising from these two situations could also be different. Thus, as Venturini points out, "in the first case, the legal act, deprived of one of its constituent parts, must be considered null and void, while in the second case, mere irregularity, which is not manifest, simply means that the subject concerned has the right to challenge the act".[36] Taking a more pragmatic view, Verzijl believed that such distinctions, extrapolated from different legal systems,[37] might also be of interest for the purposes of public international law and might be applicable in particular to unilateral acts.[38]

15. This, then, is practically virgin territory, in which references in the literature are scarce—or tend to refer to the law of treaties—and practice is almost non-existent. These are all aspects which, of course, curtail and restrict the scope of the study of the topic, but an attempt will nonetheless be made, to the extent possible, to provide examples to illustrate the concepts discussed.

16. To what extent could the grounds for invalidity provided in the 1969 Vienna Convention be applicable to unilateral acts? It has been said that "when they operate as sources of legal rights and obligations, the common requirements for validity of unilateral acts are essentially the same as for validity of treaties".[39] According to this view, the requirements for validity would therefore be as follows: the unilateral act must have been issued by a person with the capacity to formulate it; its content must be materially possible and not prohibited by a peremptory norm of general international law (*jus cogens*); and the intention expressed by the author of the unilateral act must correspond to the author's true intention and must

[30] The statements made by Austria (*Official Records of the General Assembly, Sixtieth Session, Sixth Committee*, 13th meeting, para. 10), and Romania (18th meeting, para. 3) illustrate this point particularly well.

[31] *Yearbook ... 2001*, vol. II (Part One), document A/CN.4/519, p. 117, para. 4. See also paragraphs 5–6 and 19.

[32] Charpentier, "Engagements unilateraux et engagements conventionnels: différences et convergences", p. 378.

[33] *Ibid.*, p. 380.

[34] Both ideas are highlighted by Akehurst, "The hierarchy of the sources of international law", pp. 280–281, where he states that "these acts are so heterogeneous that it is very difficult to generalize about them … in other circumstances unilateral acts are sources of law, or at least of legal rights and obligations … Such acts are similar in their effects to treaties, and probably have the same hierarchical value as treaties; that is to say, a State can, by promise or waiver, lose liberties or rights which it enjoyed under treaties or customary rules, although a subsequent treaty or custom can extinguish the obligations assumed in the promise or revive the rights lost by the waiver".

[35] Guggenheim, "The validity and the nullity of international legal acts", p. 197.

[36] Venturini, "The scope and legal effects of the behaviour and unilateral acts of States", p. 420, although this author acknowledges that the distinction between invalidity and voidableness has not been fully accepted in the literature. In fact, in the end the 1969 Vienna Convention made no such distinction.

[37] Verzijl, "La validité et la nullité des actes juridiques internationaux", p. 298, who cites as examples the absolute non-existence of an act, as opposed to invalidity as such; invalidity and voidableness; absolute invalidity and relative invalidity; invalidity that can be declared by the courts *proprio motu* versus invalidity that must be recognized because the parties so decide; total invalidity and partial invalidity; invalidity that can be remedied versus invalidity that cannot; and invalidity with *ex nunc* and *ex tunc* effects.

[38] *Ibid.*, p. 306.

[39] Degan, "Unilateral act as a source of particular international law", p. 187. Practically the same view was upheld by Skubiszewski, "Unilateral acts of States", p. 230, where the author states the following: "Any unilateral act must express the true intention of its author. Hence unilateral acts obtained by error, fraud or corruption of a State representative are voidable, and those which result from coercion (whether of the State representative or the State itself) are null and void. In this respect there exists much analogy between invalidity of treaties and unilateral acts."

not be affected by defects or invalidating factors. As to the form that unilateral acts should take, it is assumed that there is considerable freedom here; however, as the same body of opinion points out, there are some unilateral acts for which formal notification is required in order to publicize them in a timely fashion and give them legal security[40] (as is the case, for example, in the law of the sea with respect to the delineation of baselines and the delimitation of the respective zones).[41] As stated in previous reports and again at the beginning of the present report, unilateral acts of this kind are linked to a treaty regime and are therefore governed by the specific treaty regime in which they are subsumed.

17. The grounds for invalidity that will be discussed here will be divided into the following three categories: (*a*) invalidity of a unilateral act on the ground that the representative lacks competence; (*b*) grounds for invalidity related to the expression of consent; and (*c*) invalidity of a unilateral act on the ground that it is contrary to a norm of *jus cogens*.

(a) *Invalidity of a unilateral act on the ground that the representative lacks competence*

18. As will be discussed in detail in chapter II, from international practice it can be inferred that, in addition to persons representing the State at the highest level, there are others who, by virtue of their functions and in a specific context, can act and enter into commitments on the State's behalf in its international relations, by formulating legally binding unilateral acts.

19. In accordance with the majority of legal experts and international practice, it may be assumed that those persons that represent the State at the highest level and therefore have the capacity to express the consent of the State in a treaty context also have the capacity to bind their State by means of unilateral acts. This is an extrapolation—with all the risks that analogies entail—of article 7, paragraph 2 (*a*), of the 1969 Vienna Convention. However, the international plane presents many complexities in this regard, of which one in particular will be mentioned: the possibility that other persons, some of whom are referred to in the article in question (diplomatic agents or representatives to an international conference) and some of whom are not (persons who produce appropriate full powers), may have some capacity to bind the State they represent. This question was discussed previously with regard to persons qualified to act and to enter into commitments on behalf of the State.

20. What would happen if a State representative were to overstep his or her authority? This question is more directly related to the approach widely taken in internal law. The respective constitutional texts tend to provide a fairly exhaustive list of which national bodies can participate—and how—in expressing the consent of the State to be bound where international treaties are concerned, but not where unilateral acts are concerned.[42]

21. The 1969 Vienna Convention's provisions on the possible factors affecting the competence of the State representative to bind the State by means of treaties reflect a cautious approach based on the premise that such provisions are in the nature of exceptions and, therefore, on the principle of preserving and maintaining the treaty relationship. The Special Rapporteur believes that the same principle must be given primacy where unilateral acts are concerned; failure to do so would generate distrust in international relations and, as a consequence, jeopardize the use of unilateral acts as a way for States to act and commit themselves at that level. Furthermore, the situation of uncertainty and failure to honour promises which invocation of one of the grounds for invalidity currently being discussed could create would tip the scales in favour of validating, where possible, a unilateral act that has this defect. In order to clarify this issue, the Special Rapporteur believes it would be very useful to discuss again, at least briefly, two of the provisions of part V of the Convention, in order to verify whether or not these provisions could be applicable to the subject that is of concern.

(i) *Article 46 of the 1969 Vienna Convention*

22. As is well known, article 46, paragraph 1, entitled "Provisions of internal law regarding competence to conclude treaties", states the following: "A State may not invoke the fact that its consent to be bound by a treaty has been expressed in violation of a provision of its internal law regarding competence to conclude treaties as invalidating its consent unless that violation was manifest

[40] ICJ took a very strict approach in this respect in its recent decision in the dispute between the Democratic Republic of the Congo and Rwanda (*Armed Activities on the Territory of the Congo (New Application: 2002) (Democratic Republic of the Congo* v. *Rwanda), Jurisdiction and Admissibility, Judgment, I.C.J. Reports 2006*, p. 25, para. 41), in which, referring specifically to the withdrawal of reservations, it stated the following: "Thus a clear distinction has to be drawn between a decision to withdraw a reservation to a treaty taken within a State's domestic legal order and the implementation of that decision by the competent national authorities within the international legal order, which can be effected only by notification of withdrawal of the reservation to the other States parties to the treaty in question."

[41] This is because of the unique nature of such acts, which are governed by treaties regarding the law of the sea. In this respect, as stated by Ruiloba García, *Circunstancias especiales y equidad en la delimitación de los espacios marítimos*, p. 34: "Maritime delimitation is heterogeneous in nature, insofar as each case of delimitation has its own specific characteristics that make it unique and unrepeatable, like a snowflake."

[42] In this sense, the Special Rapporteur fully shares the view expressed by Remiro Brotóns to the effect that:

> "[T]he constitutional enshrinement of parliamentary participation in treaties reflects a *static* vision of the ways in which international rules and obligations are produced. Treaties are by no means the only way. Autonomous unilateral acts of international relevance (recognition, promise, protest, reprisal) come to mind ... This is an area in which the Chambers—and sometimes even the Government, as a collegiate body—does not participate, even though it is illogical that something may be *promised* without the Chambers, but may be *undertaken* only with them by means of a treaty. In order to clarify this *grey area* a *new vision* is needed that offers solutions *other than* participation by the Chambers, in line with the fluidity of these commitments and the way they are incorporated into positive law. At the moment, only a few State systems have dared to venture into this territory, and the Spanish system is not one of them. The Constitutions of Denmark (art. 19.3) and Sweden (chap. X, arts. 2, 6–8; XIII, art. 2) can be cited as examples of an innovative model for full participation—but not strict control—by the Chambers in the most significant foreign policy decisions, whatever form they may take. These Constitutions provide for the establishment of smaller representative bodies, ready to meet at a moment's notice, which gather confidential information on developments in international relations and are consulted by the Government *before* important decisions are adopted."

(Remiro Brotóns, *Derecho Internacional Público*, p. 116)

and concerned a rule of its internal law of fundamental importance."[43]

23. The negative wording of this provision reflects the fact that it concerns an exception; in principle, no State may invoke a provision of its internal law regarding competence to conclude treaties with a view to declaring an agreement null and void. If this is true for treaties, the question arises as to whether this solution can be extrapolated to unilateral acts. With regard to the view expressed by PCIJ in 1932 in the case of the Treatment of Polish Nationals and Other Persons of Polish Origin in the Danzig Territory,[44] it should be pointed out that the 1969 Vienna Convention adopted a more nuanced position in this respect. This may be because the Commission, in view of historical precedents, took the realistic view[45] that some room should be left for certain particularly drastic cases,[46] such as those described in the articles to which reference is being made in this section. In principle, this is based on a concern for preserving the validity of treaties and considering the situations referred to below as exceptions.

24. It is necessary to discuss whether it is possible to invoke, as a ground for invalidating a unilateral act, the fact that the act was formulated in manifest violation of a provision of internal law that is of fundamental importance and concerns competence to conclude treaties. As pointed out above, the main problem here is that constitutional texts tend to specify the mechanisms and bodies that can participate in expressing the consent of the State where international treaties are concerned, but not where unilateral acts are concerned.

25. Article 46 of the 1969 Vienna Convention lays down three conditions for invoking the invalidity of a treaty: (*a*) the violation invoked must concern a rule of internal law of fundamental importance, meaning the Constitution and laws that have constitutional force and are in effect at the time (for this requirement to apply to unilateral acts, these laws would have to be in force both when the unilateral act in question was formulated and when the alleged invalidity is claimed); (*b*) the rule in question must concern competence to conclude treaties, a phrase which, if interpreted in its strictest sense, could, in the view of the Special Rapporteur, be extrapolated to unilateral acts, with the qualifications discussed below; and (*c*) the violation of internal law must be manifest, meaning that it must be objectively evident to any State dealing with the matter normally and in good faith.[47]

26. In his second report on unilateral acts of States, the Special Rapporteur proposed an article which, following fairly closely the provisions of the 1969 Vienna Convention, set out in seven paragraphs the possible grounds for invalidating a unilateral act. The draft article read as follows:

Article 7. Invalidity of unilateral acts

A State may invoke the invalidity of a unilateral act:

...

(*g*) If the expression of a State's consent to be bound by a unilateral act has been in clear violation of a norm of fundamental importance to its domestic law.[48]

27. This draft article was less restrictive than article 46 of the 1969 Vienna Convention, since it referred to a clear violation of a norm of fundamental importance, but did not specifically indicate that the norm should concern the competence to express consent (in this instance with respect to unilateral acts).[49]

---

[43] The explanation of what is understood by manifest violation is found in paragraph 2 of the same article, which states that a "violation is manifest if it would be objectively evident to any State conducting itself in the matter in accordance with normal practice and in good faith". In this respect, see Meron, "Article 46 of the Vienna Convention on the Law of Treaties (*ultra vires* treaties): some recent cases".

[44] *Treatment of Polish Nationals and Other Persons of Polish Origin in the Danzig Territory, Advisory Opinion, 1932, P.C.I.J., Series A/B, No. 44*, p. 24, which reads as follows:

> "It should however be observed that, while on the one hand, according to generally accepted principles, a State cannot rely, as against another State, on the provisions of the latter's Constitution, but only on international law and international obligations duly accepted, on the other hand and conversely, a State cannot adduce as against another State its own Constitution with a view to evading obligations incumbent upon it under international law or treaties in force. Applying these principles to the present case, it results that the question of the treatment of Polish nationals or other persons of Polish origin or speech must be settled exclusively on the bases of the rules of international law and the treaty provisions in force between Poland and Danzig."

[45] However, see *Yearbook ... 1966*, vol. II, document A/6309/Rev.1, p. 241, para. (7), which refers to this question, pointing out that:

> "State practice furnishes examples of claims that treaties were invalid on constitutional grounds, but in none of them was that claim admitted by the other party to the dispute. Moreover, in three instances—the admission of Luxembourg to the League, the Politis incident and the membership of Argentina—the League of Nations seems to have acted upon the principle that a consent given on the international plane by an ostensibly competent State agent is not invalidated by the subsequent disclosure that the agent lacked constitutional authority to commit his State."

[46] A historic example of a unilateral act that was contrary to important constitutional rules, making its performance impossible, was the case of *George Croft* (Portugal *v.* United Kingdom), which was resolved on 7 February 1856:

> "If at any time the Portuguese Government, or its legal representative, had given to the British Government, in its usual forms of international intercourse, a promise that Mr. Croft should be assisted in obtaining the satisfaction of his claims, or that he was to be held harmless in regard thereto, that there could be no doubt that a perfectly valid title to satisfaction or indemnification from the Portuguese state would arise therefrom, since those are constitutional forms recognized by the law of nations, in which the international obligations of one country toward another are contracted. But the same can not be asserted of a case where nothing else is apparent but an order which the government issued to its own authorities in favour of a foreign subject, without any promise having been previously made to that subject's government. If in such a case the order meets with constitutional obstacles, which render its execution impossible, no claim founded on international law can be made upon the government for damages on account of its order not having been carried into execution."

(Moore, *History and Digest of the International Arbitrations to which the United States has been a Party*, pp. 4982–4983). See also Coussirat-Coustère and Eisemann, *Repertory of International Arbitral Jurisprudence*, p. 46.

[47] See Elias, "Problems concerning the validity of treaties", pp. 357–358; see also *Yearbook ... 1966* (footnote 45 above), p. 242, para. (11). The Commission concluded that it would be impracticable and inadvisable to try to specify in advance the cases in which a violation of internal law may be held to be "manifest", since the question must depend to a large extent on the particular circumstances of each case.

[48] *Yearbook ... 1999*, vol. II (Part One), document A/CN.4/500 and Add.1, p. 207, para. 109.

[49] During discussions at the fifty-first session of the Commission in 1999, members expressed divergent views with respect to this article; some members maintained that this norm should follow article 46 of the 1969 Vienna Convention more closely, while others believed that the provision should reflect the flexibility inherent in unilateral acts (*ibid.*, vol. II (Part Two)), p. 136, para. 559.

28. The corresponding draft article presented in the third report on unilateral acts of States the following year (art. 5 (*h*)), was even more laconic, and established the following as grounds for invalidity: "If the unilateral act as formulated conflicts with a norm of fundamental importance to the domestic law of the State formulating it."[50] This wording elicited various reactions from the members of the Commission, as set out in the report on the work of its fifty-second session in 2000:

> In the view of some members, the subparagraph, as drafted, might be interpreted as giving priority to domestic law over commitments under international law, and this would be unacceptable. Some members also wondered whether the subparagraph might not lend itself to a situation whereby a State would utilize the provisions of its own national law to evade international obligations which it had assumed by a valid unilateral act.[51]

Furthermore, one of the suggestions made in the course of these discussions was that this subparagraph should bring out the fact that, at the time the act was formulated, there had been a breach of an internal norm of fundamental importance to domestic or constitutional law "concerning the capacity to assume international obligations or to formulate legal acts at the international level".[52] If that proposal was not accepted, the very general nature of the draft article might suggest that any violation of a norm of domestic law, albeit one of substantial importance, could cause the unilateral act to be declared invalid, with the risks that that entailed.

29. The inclination of the Special Rapporteur, which closely mirrors the arguments raised in Vienna and reflected in the 1969 Vienna Convention, is to take a restrictive approach to the grounds for invalidity in general and the one mentioned in the preceding paragraph in particular. In the interest of legal security, State representatives must be cautious in undertaking international commitments and, by extension, unilateral acts. Similarly, there is always the possibility of subsequently confirming the act in question. This solution not only avoids the drastic step of declaring an act invalid, but also puts the State in a much better position with respect to the undertaking of commitments and the honouring of promises.[53]

30. In accordance with the foregoing, the following draft guiding principle on compliance of the unilateral act with the domestic legal order could be formulated:

"*Invalidity of a unilateral act that conflicts with a norm of fundamental importance to the domestic law of the State formulating it*

"A State that has formulated a unilateral act may not invoke as grounds for invalidity the fact that the act conflicts with its domestic law, unless it conflicts with a norm of fundamental importance to its domestic law and the contradiction is manifest."

(ii) *Specific restrictions on authority to express the consent of a State*

31. Article 47 of the 1969 Vienna Convention, entitled "Specific restrictions on authority to express the consent of a State", is directly related to the topic of this discussion. According to that article:

> If the authority of a representative to express the consent of a State to be bound by a particular treaty has been made subject to a specific restriction, his omission to observe that restriction may not be invoked as invalidating the consent expressed by him unless the restriction was notified to the other negotiating States prior to his expressing such consent.

32. This rule is even more restrictive than article 46, discussed above. Nahlik's firm opinion in relation to both rules is that "practical cases in which either of the two articles concerned could be invoked will be extremely rare".[54] However, the application of the concept contained in article 47 cannot be extrapolated *in toto* to unilateral acts, given the aforementioned special features of these acts, which stem, principally, from the very means by which they are formulated. In contrast with international treaties, wherein State representatives would be able to inform the representatives of other States of any restrictions on the expression of consent, the very essence of a unilateral act, in respect of which there are no other negotiating parties, renders the aforementioned provision meaningless. In fact, this was not among the grounds for invalidity mentioned in the second and

---

[50] *Yearbook ... 2000*, vol. II (Part One), document A/CN.4/505, p. 264, para. 167.

[51] *Ibid.*, vol. II (Part Two), p. 98, para. 602.

[52] *Ibid.*, para. 603.

[53] An interesting case in this regard was resolved by the Constitutional Court of Guatemala in its ruling of 3 November 1992, which affirmed the validity of a series of actions undertaken by the President of the Republic, Jorge Serrano Elías, by virtue of which he had recognized Belize and established diplomatic relations with it. The historic confrontation between Belize and Guatemala gave rise to article 19, paragraph 1, of the transitory provisions of the 1985 Constitution of Guatemala, which states:

> "The Executive is empowered to take steps aimed at resolving the status of Guatemala's rights with respect to Belize, in line with its national interests. Any final agreement must be submitted by the Congress of the Republic to the popular consultation procedure established under article 173 of the Constitution."

The issue at stake was whether the recognition of Belize by Guatemala should be considered a "final agreement" and, if so, whether the manifestations and consequences of the President's actions should be considered invalid. The majority opinion of the judges who participated in the issuing of this ruling of the Constitutional Court was that the act of recognition was a result of the changes this dispute had undergone as a result of the independence of this territory from the United Kingdom, without it being regarded as a final step, in the sense and with the effects implied by the Constitution. Nevertheless, a different position was taken in the "reasoned dissent" of the President of the Court and two judges; following González Vega ("El reconocimiento de Belice ante la Corte de Constitucionalidad de Guatemala: la sentencia de 3 de noviembre de 1992", p. 580), who presented the same solution maintained by this minority, in the absence of participation by the Congress of the Republic and the people, the act of recognizing Belize did not represent the decision of the State, and therefore could produce no legal effect or be executed. That author therefore concluded the following:

> "Here is the clear consequence upheld by the minority in the Constitutional Court: the invalidity of the act of recognition, and implicitly its revocability, since it was issued by an organ without competence under the Guatemalan Constitution."

(*Ibid.*, p. 584)

There are perhaps many factors that led the Court to adopt its decision, such as the changes on the international scene, and the desire to avoid casting doubt on the Guatemalan position because of an act carried out by its highest representative. In this regard, see González Vega, *loc. cit.* Another case similar to the previous one was considered in the eighth report on unilateral acts of States (*Yearbook ... 2005* (footnote 1 above), pp. 123–125, paras. 13–35) and concerned a 1952 note from the Minister for Foreign Affairs of Colombia on the Los Monjes group of islands.

[54] Nahlik, "The grounds of invalidity and termination of treaties", p. 741.

third reports on unilateral acts of States,[55] although those reports did refer to one of the initial provisions of the draft articles: the one concerning the possibility of subsequent confirmation of a unilateral act, which was discussed earlier.

33. Two aspects were added to the similar provision in the 1969 Vienna Convention: the reference to the act of committing the State on the international plane (an essential aspect of unilateral acts, even though it could also be considered applicable to treaty law), and the provision on compulsory confirmation.

34. On this basis, the following draft guiding principle is presented, on the understanding that it might not be necessary, as another guiding principle on the confirmation or validation of a unilateral act has already been formulated and has been submitted for the consideration of the Working Group on unilateral acts of States:

"*Invalidity of an act formulated by a person not qualified to do so*

"A unilateral act formulated by a person not authorized or qualified to do so may be declared invalid, without prejudice to the possibility that the State from which the act was issued may confirm it in accordance with guiding principle 4."

(b) *Grounds for invalidity related to the expression of consent*

35. All the possible grounds for invalidity studied in this section share the common denominator of flawed consent to be bound by a unilateral act. The 1969 Vienna Convention again serves as a reference point. Three of these grounds (error, fraud and coercion) are rooted in the Roman-law tradition and were introduced into the Convention for basically two reasons: because they served as a type of safety valve in case any of these circumstances arose, although this rarely happens, and because their inclusion would obviate any argument that the Convention's provisions on grounds for invalidity were not exhaustive, thereby preventing States from seeking other possible grounds for invalidity. Each of them will now be looked at.

(i) *Error*

36. In its report to the General Assembly at its eighteenth session in 1966, which contained the draft articles on the law of treaties and commentaries thereon, the Commission stressed that "the instances in which errors of substance have been invoked as affecting the essential validity of a treaty have not been frequent. Almost all the recorded instances concern geographical errors, and most of them concern errors in maps".[56] If this is true with respect to treaties, it should also be true with respect to unilateral acts.

[55] *Yearbook ... 1999* and *Yearbook ... 2000* (see footnotes 48 and 50 above).

[56] *Yearbook ... 1966* (see footnote 45 above), p. 243, para. (1) of the commentary to article 45.

37. There have been very few cases, in either international practice or existing case law, in which error has been cited as a ground justifying a declaration of invalidity. There are, however, some illustrative cases. For example, in the *Legal Status of Eastern Greenland* case, Judge Anzilotti, in his dissenting opinion, stated that:

> A question of a totally different kind is whether the declaration of the Norwegian Minister for Foreign Affairs was vitiated, owing to a mistake on a material point, i.e. because it was made in ignorance of the fact that the extension of Danish sovereignty would involve a corresponding extension of the monopoly and of the régime of exclusion.
>
> ...
>
> My own opinion is that there was no mistake at all, and that the Danish Government's silence on the so-called monopoly question, and the absence of any observation or reservation in regard to it in M. Ihlen's reply, are easily accounted for by the character of this overture, which was made with a future settlement in view. But even accepting, for a moment, the supposition that M. Ihlen was mistaken as to the results which might ensue from an extension of Danish sovereignty, it must be admitted that this mistake was not such as to entail the nullity of the agreement. *If a mistake is pleaded it must be of an excusable character; and one can scarcely believe that a government could be ignorant of the legitimate consequences following upon an extension of sovereignty**; I would add that, of all the governments in the world, that of Norway was the least likely to be ignorant of the Danish methods of administration in Greenland, or of the part played therein by the monopoly system and the régime of exclusion.[57]

38. It is generally recognized that, in order to vitiate the consent of a State in a treaty, an error must relate to an issue that forms an essential basis of the State's consent to be bound by the treaty; the Special Rapporteur believes that this same solution should be applied, *mutatis mutandis*, to unilateral acts of States.[58]

39. In his second report on unilateral acts of States, the Special Rapporteur proposed a provision that was almost identical to the provision of the 1969 Vienna Convention concerning error (art. 48), although it condensed into one paragraph the basic features that such an error must have, as follows:

> A State may invoke the invalidity of a unilateral act:
>
> (*a*) If the expression of the State's consent to formulate the act was based on an error of fact or a situation which was assumed by that State to exist at the time when the act was formulated and formed an essential basis of its consent to be bound by the act. The foregoing shall not apply if the State contributed by its own conduct to the error or if the circumstances were such as to put that State on notice of a possible error.[59]

40. Various opinions were expressed on the matter within the Commission. For example, it was said that the wording should be further disassociated from the 1969 Vienna Convention, taking into account the difference between unilateral acts and international treaties;[60] it was also suggested that the word "consent" should not be used "because of its treaty connotations".[61] This suggestion

[57] *Legal Status of Eastern Greenland, Judgment, 1933, P.C.I.J., Series A/B, No. 53*, p. 92.

[58] As highlighted by Oraison, *L'erreur dans les traités*, p. 41.

[59] *Yearbook ... 1999* (see footnote 48 above), p. 207, para. 109, art. 7.

[60] The view was expressed that an error of fact committed by a State when formulating a declaration should be easier to correct than an error related to an international treaty, given the flexibility and speed with which unilateral acts are usually formulated, as opposed to treaties (*ibid.*, vol. II (Part Two), p. 135, para. 555).

[61] *Yearbook ... 2000*, vol. II (Part Two), p. 97, para. 593.

was retained in the third report on unilateral acts of States, which kept the entire draft article unchanged except the opening phrase, which read, "If the act was formulated on the basis",[62] instead of the phrasing previously used ("If the expression of the State's consent to formulate the act was based").

41. In reality, the Special Rapporteur believes that error, as a circumstance that can lead to the invalidity of a unilateral act, must have been an essential determinant of the State's conduct. Moreover, the requirement of good faith—directly linked to the fact that the State claiming invalidity must not have contributed to the error by its own conduct—serves to prevent possible conduct whose ultimate aim is to release the State in question from commitments undertaken in the international sphere.

42. Error must be claimed by the State that formulated the unilateral act and committed the error, although a hypothetical situation could arise in which a third State that is the beneficiary of the unilateral act discovers, in view of the circumstances of the case, that there has been an error and so informs the author State. In an even more unusual case, it could also transpire that the error was caused by the fraudulent conduct of a third party, which would give rise to two possible causes of invalidity and would invalidate the unilateral act in question, unless the circumstances of the case and the will of the State having formulated the act make it advisable that the act should remain in effect, through its confirmation.

43. Draft guiding principle 7, paragraph 1, which is reproduced below, addresses this potential cause of invalidity; the remaining paragraphs on grounds for invalidity will be cited further on, after the commentary relating to each of them:

"*Invalidity of unilateral acts*

"1. (*a*) A State that is the author of a unilateral act may not invoke error as grounds for declaring the act invalid, unless the act was formulated on the basis of an error of fact or a situation that was assumed by the State to exist at the time when the act was formulated and that fact or that situation formed an essential basis of its consent to be bound by the unilateral act;

"(*b*) The foregoing shall not apply if the author State contributed by its own conduct to the error or if the circumstances were such as to put that State on notice of the possibility of such an error."[63]

(ii) *Fraud*

44. In accordance with article 49 of the 1969 Vienna Convention: "If a State has been induced to conclude a treaty by the fraudulent conduct of another negotiating State, the State may invoke the fraud as invalidating its consent to be bound by the treaty." Whether this cause of invalidity of an international treaty could be applied, *mutatis mutandis*, to a unilateral act should therefore be considered. In Sicault's view, both fraud[64] and error are causes of invalidity that are fully applicable to unilateral acts. The reference to both causes is probably due to the fine line between them, which has been illustrated on several occasions in the legal literature.[65]

45. If this cause of invalidity is accepted in the case of unilateral acts, it should be subject to the same conditions required in order for fraud to be taken into consideration in a treaty context. Remiro Brotóns highlights three elements of the conduct of a third party that must be present in order for the conduct to be qualified as fraudulent and for the act whose formulation was induced to be declared invalid: (*a*) a material element, referred to as fraudulent conduct, which, in the Commission's view, encompasses "any false statements, misrepresentations or other deceitful proceedings";[66] (*b*) a psychological element, meaning the will or intention to mislead (in the context of unilateral acts, the will to induce the State formulating the act to implement the provisions thereof, regardless of their nature); and (*c*) a result, achieved by fraudulent means. In this connection, it is said that the fraud must be of an essential nature.[67]

46. With regard to unilateral acts, the proposal submitted to the Commission in the second report of the Special Rapporteur appears in what was then draft article 7 (*b*), according to which, "If a State has been induced to formulate an act by the fraudulent conduct of another State", it may invoke the invalidity of the act.[68] The report went on to state that: "Fraud can even occur through omission, as when a State which has knowledge of certain realities does not convey it, thus inducing another State to formulate a legal act."[69] However, this last point elicited various criticisms from several members of the Commission, who took the view that that interpretation "might encroach on certain accepted ways whereby States led their foreign policy and convinced other States to join in that policy".[70] Interpretation will have to be relied on to draw a distinction between situations in which fraud is present and those in which it is not.

47. The same draft guiding principle on grounds for invalidity contains a second paragraph, which reads as follows:

"2. Fraud may be invoked as grounds for declaring a unilateral act invalid if the author State was induced to

---

[62] *Ibid*., vol. II (Part One) (see footnote 50 above), p. 263, para. 167.

[63] To allow for the invocation of error by States other than the State that formulated the unilateral act, the following wording is submitted to the Commission for its consideration:

"Error may be invoked as grounds for declaring a unilateral act invalid if the act was formulated on the basis of an error of fact or a situation that was assumed by the State to exist at the time when the act was formulated and that fact or that situation formed an essential basis of its consent to be bound by the unilateral act."

[64] Sicault, "Du caractère obligatoire des engagements unilatéraux en droit international public", p. 667: "It must be admitted that if the author of a unilateral undertaking has been induced to enter into that undertaking by the fraudulent conduct of another subject of public international law, it may invoke the fraud as invalidating its consent to be bound by the undertaking."

[65] See Oraison, "Le dol dans la conclusion des traités", p. 622.

[66] *Yearbook ... 1966* (see footnote 45 above), p. 245, para. (3) of the commentary to article 46.

[67] Remiro Brotóns, *op. cit*., p. 435.

[68] *Yearbook ... 1999* (see footnote 48 above), p. 207, para. 109, and draft article 5 (*b*), of the third report, *Yearbook ... 2000* (see footnote 50 above), p. 264, para. 167, which is identical.

[69] *Yearbook ... 1999* (see footnote 48 above), p. 209, para. 136.

[70] *Ibid*., vol. II (Part Two), p. 135, para. 555.

formulate the act by the fraudulent conduct of another State."

(iii) *Corruption of a representative*

48. Although this cause of invalidity was a late addition to the draft articles that became the 1969 Vienna Convention, because it was originally thought to be subsumed under the concept of fraud, a decision was taken to include it in the text as article 50, which reads as follows: "If the expression of a State's consent to be bound by a treaty has been procured through the corruption of its representative directly or indirectly by another negotiating State, the State may invoke such corruption as invalidating its consent to be bound by the treaty." Of course, the strength of the term "corruption" makes it necessary to define the concept precisely. The customary decorations and hospitality which are a normal part of diplomatic practice would not be regarded as corruption; something extra would be required.[71] The lack of precedents may be due to the fact that States are reluctant to admit that their representatives are responsible for giving this defective form of consent.[72]

49. The role played by this potential cause of invalidity in the context of unilateral acts could be almost identical to the role it plays in the treaty context; an analysis of the way in which that cause was described in the second report on unilateral acts of States revealed certain limitations, which were subsequently removed in the third report. The original draft text (art. 7 (*c*)) read as follows:

> A State may invoke the invalidity of a unilateral act:
>
> ...
>
> (*c*) If the expression of a State's consent to be bound by a unilateral act has been procured through the corruption of its representative directly or indirectly by another State.[73]

50. The phrase "If the expression of a State's consent to be bound" limits the scope of application of the draft article, which was further refined in the third report on unilateral acts of States to read as follows: "If the act has been formulated as a result of corruption of the person formulating it, through direct or indirect action by another State."[74] The first part of the provision contains the amendment; it now reads "If the act has been formulated", and the term "representative" has been replaced with the phrase "person formulating it", which, while more general, introduces a greater degree of uncertainty.

51. A cause of this nature is certainly necessary and useful, given that the realities of international relations may give rise to such acts. Some members of the Commission expressed their support for its inclusion because of the need to combat that situation universally, as underlined by the Inter-American Convention against Corruption, and the Criminal Law Convention on Corruption, adopted by the Council of Europe, and its Additional Protocol. Another interesting development, described in the Commission's report to the General Assembly on the work of its fifty-second session in 2000, was the question raised as to "whether it was necessary to narrow down the possibility of corruption to 'direct or indirect action by another State'". This point highlighted something that has become an undeniable fact of international life today, given the enormous power that certain entities can acquire; namely, that: "The possibility could not be ruled out that the person formulating the unilateral act might be corrupted by another person or by an enterprise."[75]

52. In line with the foregoing, paragraph 3 of the draft guiding principle would read as follows:

> "3. Corruption of the representative of the State may be invoked as grounds for declaring a unilateral act invalid if the act was formulated owing to the corruption of the person formulating it."

(iv) *Coercion*

53. Together with error and fraud, and bearing in mind the nuances discussed below, coercion is the third cause of invalidity provided for in the 1969 Vienna Convention, and one which finds its origin in the strong tradition of Roman law. The Convention covers coercion of two types: coercion of a representative of a State (art. 51) and coercion of the State itself by the threat or use of force (art. 52). Both types seem to be fully applicable to unilateral acts of States.

a. *Coercion of a representative of a State*

54. In practice, there have been a number of cases in which coercion of a State representative, sometimes to the point where the latter fears for his or her life, has led to the conclusion of agreements and even to the formulation of acts which, without that coercion, would not have existed.[76] The notion of coercion, which must be used against a representative (as an individual, not as an organ of the State), encompasses a wide variety of situations, including, as pointed out by the Commission in its commentary on the draft articles, "any form of constraint or threat"[77] affecting the representative's physical integrity, freedom, career, property or social or family situation.

---

[71] For a definition of the term "corruption" see *Yearbook ... 1966* (footnote 45 above), p. 245, para. (4) of the commentary to article 47, which specifies that "only acts calculated to exercise a substantial influence on the disposition of the representative to conclude the treaty may be invoked as invalidating the expression of consent which he has purported to give on behalf of his State", not "a small courtesy or favour" that may be shown to him in connection with the conclusion of the treaty.

[72] As Sinclair states in *The Vienna Convention on the Law of Treaties*, p. 175: "There is no doubt a practical safeguard in that States will be reluctant to admit that their own representatives have been corrupted."

[73] *Yearbook ... 1999* (see footnote 48 above), p. 207, para. 109.

[74] *Yearbook ... 2000* (see footnote 50 above), p. 264, para. 167.

[75] *Ibid.*, vol. II (Part Two), p. 97, para. 594.

[76] An interesting example can be found in Remiro Brotóns, *op. cit.*, p. 438: "Once there, having been taken prisoner on 20 April, he [Ferdinand VII] was threatened with the death penalty for having committed high treason against his father, Charles IV, unless he abdicated, which he did on 6 May. One day earlier, in exchange for monetary compensation, Charles IV had ceded his rights to Napoleon, who, in turn, ceded them to his brother Joseph. Those acts were considered invalid on grounds of *fraud* and *violence* by the Cádiz Cortes, which subsequently, in 1811, issued a Decree proclaiming the invalidity of any undertaking made by Ferdinand VII while he was imprisoned at Valencey."

[77] *Yearbook ... 1963*, vol. II, document A/5509, p. 197, para. (2) of the commentary to article 35.

55. In the treaty context, one of the principal characteristics distinguishing coercion from corruption is the fact that the former can be employed by anyone, while the latter is only recognized when it is employed by another negotiating State. With regard to unilateral acts, there is value in incorporating both these elements into the definition of the two aforementioned concepts, since there is nothing to preclude the possibility that corruption may be imputable to individuals or entities which are not States as such, but whose ability to exert pressure may corrupt a representative by inducing him or her to undertake a commitment which, in the absence of such corruption, would not have been made.

56. It might be unwise to impose excessive restrictions on this cause of invalidity, such as those that were apparent in draft article 7 of the second report on unilateral acts of States, which provided that the invalidity of a unilateral act could be invoked "[i]f the expression of a State's consent to be bound by a unilateral act has been procured by the coercion of its representative through acts or threats directed against him".[78] The expression "directed against him" could be interpreted to mean that such coercion—in Spanish, "coacción" is a more appropriate term than "coerción", since the latter implies an element of physical force that is not necessarily present—could also be directed against the representative's immediate personal interests (such as his or her property or family) and thereby produce the desired result.

57. The following year's proposal included a number of amendments similar to those discussed in relation to corruption, but the rest of the aforementioned elements were generally retained; the proposal read as follows: "If the act has been formulated as a result of coercion of the person formulating it, through acts or threats directed against him."[79] The particular conclusiveness of this cause of invalidity was noted by the Commission, which took the view that

> the use of coercion on the person formulating the act was a special case, since, in those circumstances, the person involved was not expressing the will of the State he was supposed to represent, but that of the State using coercion. Without a will, there was no legal act and, if there was no act, there was nothing to be invalidated. Whereas other subparagraphs were cases of *negotium nullum*, the subparagraph in question was a case of *non negotium*.[80]

Accordingly, this situation gives rise to initial invalidity, since the act in question never existed, having been invalid from the outset.

58. The relevant paragraph of the draft guiding principle on grounds for invalidity could read as follows:

"4. Coercion of the person who formulated a unilateral act may be invoked as grounds for declaring its invalidity if that person formulated it as a result of acts or threats directed against him or her."

b. *Coercion of a State by the threat or use of force*

59. This is the most important and most modern cause of invalidity of treaties, and its genesis and development are linked to the prohibition of the threat or use of force in international relations and the scope of that prohibition, which has put an end to one of the traditional methods of acquiring territory (annexation), a practice that was usually sanctioned by means of an international treaty. However, a number of issues directly related to this cause of invalidity must be addressed. The first relates to the type of force referred to in article 52 of the 1969 Vienna Convention; the Declaration on the prohibition of military, political or economic coercion in the conclusion of treaties, that was annexed to the Final Act of the United Nations Conference on the Law of Treaties, which reflects the position taken by a large group of States (particularly those belonging to the group of developing countries), demonstrates the gulf between these countries (which favoured a broad interpretation of the concept of force) and the restrictive position that ultimately triumphed.[81] However, a question inevitably arises as to whether the same concept of force used in 1969 should be retained in the current international context or whether, with a view also to extrapolating the concept to future unilateral acts, a broader interpretation should be considered.

60. First, the second report on unilateral acts of States more or less reproduced—in almost identical terms, except for the heading—the provisions of the 1969 Vienna Convention; it therefore identified as a cause of invalidity the situation produced "[i]f the formulation of the unilateral act has been procured by the threat or use of force in violation of the principles of international law embodied in the Charter of the United Nations".[82]

61. In the course of the Commission's deliberations, a suggestion was made to the effect that an additional cause of invalidity should be included, namely unilateral acts formulated in violation of a Security Council resolution adopted under Chapter VII of the Charter of the United Nations, for example an act of recognition adopted in violation of a Council resolution which called on members of the Organization not to recognize a particular entity as a State.[83] Echoing this suggestion, the third report on unilateral acts of States proposed that a unilateral act could be regarded as invalid "[i]f, at the time of its formulation, the unilateral act conflicts with a decision of the Security Council",[84] with no further qualification.

---

[78] *Yearbook ... 1999* (see footnote 48 above), p. 207, para. 109, art. 7 (*d*).

[79] *Yearbook ... 2000* (see footnote 50 above), p. 264, para. 167, art. 5 (*d*).

[80] *Ibid.*, vol. II (Part Two), p. 97, para. 595.

[81] *Official Records of the United Nations Conference on the Law of Treaties, First and Second Sessions, Vienna, 26 March–24 May 1968 and 9 April–22 May 1969, Documents of the Conference* (United Nations publication, Sales No. E.70.V.5), document A/CONF.39/26. As Nahlik points out, *loc. cit.*, p. 744, the Declaration was the result of a compromise reached between the two positions, which limited article 52 of the Convention to such cases as would fall under the prohibition already found in the principles contained in the Charter of the United Nations.

[82] *Yearbook ... 1999* (see footnote 48 above), p. 207, para. 109, art. 7 (*e*).

[83] *Ibid.*, vol. II (Part Two), p. 136, para. 560. This suggestion was made by Mr. Dugard (*ibid.*, vol. I, 2595th meeting, para. 24) and also by Poland in the Sixth Committee (*Official Records of the General Assembly, Fifty-fourth Session, Sixth Committee*, 25th meeting, para. 122).

[84] *Yearbook ...2000* (see footnote 50 above), p. 264, para. 167, art. 5 (*g*).

62. The debates that have taken place within the Commission itself as to whether or not to include this subparagraph have been difficult: while some members have expressed support for the proposal, others have proposed that the scope of the subparagraph should be more limited, and still others have called for its deletion. There is no doubt that cases may arise in which a unilateral act might conflict with a Security Council decision adopted after the act was formulated; this would not necessarily lead to invalidation of the unilateral act, but instead may simply lead to its suspension until such time as, to cite an example, a Council sanction is lifted.[85] It might be appropriate to ask whether such a situation—relating to Council decisions—is covered by the provisions on peremptory norms, which are binding for all States. The basis for this could be an interpretation of Article 2, paragraph 6, and Articles 25 and 103 of the Charter of the United Nations;[86] accordingly, unilateral acts formulated in violation of such a norm would not be valid, and the operation of those formulated prior to the adoption of that norm would be suspended until such time as the decision was no longer in effect. The Commission should carefully consider and decide whether such a ground for invalidity should be included.

63. A further issue relating directly to the use of force and to the current normative framework concerns recognition and the role that it plays. Here the Special Rapporteur comes into conflict with those who subscribe to the doctrine of "limits on freedom of recognition". One of the most relevant of those limits, potentially falling within the scope of the subject that is of concern here, is that relating to the non-recognition of States founded through intervention or the use of force.[87]

64. Various cases are cited in registries of practice, which refer to numerous circumstances relating to recognition, such as the *Fritz Jellinek and others* v. *Victor G. Lévy* case resolved by the Commercial Court of the Seine in its decision of 18 January 1940, in which the Court refused to consider valid the expropriation of assets and other acts leading to the use of force by Germany against Czechoslovakia;[88] the Court of Paris, in its decision of 21 July 1953 concerning the case of *Administration des Domaines* v. *Dame Sorkin*, affirmed that no legal effects would follow from annexation or forced occupation,[89] as previously ruled by the Criminal Division of the Court of Cassation in its decision of 24 July 1946 (case of Wagner and others).[90] Similar rulings are found in many other case-law decisions.[91] More recent cases include non-recognition of the annexation by Israel of the Golan Heights and the ensuing protests,[92] direct opposition to the creation of a Turkish Cypriot state[93] and the occupation of Kuwait by Iraq.[94]

65. However, that position has not always been consistent; situations can be somewhat ambiguous as regards recognition, as in the case of Manchukuo: many States Members of the League of Nations maintained trade relations with that entity and gave a certain level of recognition to acts formulated by it, despite the condemnation issued by the League.[95] However, there have been a number of cases in which courts (usually national courts) have ruled against the recognition of certain territorial annexations, considering them invalid and therefore lacking legal

[85] *Ibid.*, p. 98, para. 601.

[86] Assuming, of course, that interpretation of those articles is not strictly literal; for example, Article 103 of the Charter should provide for obligations undertaken not only through treaties but also through unilateral acts if it is to apply in such cases. The Article states that: "In the event of a conflict between the obligations of the Members of the United Nations under the present Charter and their obligations under any other international agreement, their obligations under the present Charter shall prevail." From this it could logically be inferred that any unilateral act conflicting with such a provision would have no effect. In that respect, Article 25 of the Charter, which establishes that "[t]he Members of the United Nations agree to accept and carry out the decisions of the Security Council in accordance with the present Charter", clearly defines the nature of those decisions. Moreover, if the Special Rapporteur limits his consideration to decisions relating to the maintenance of international peace and security, the Charter even provides for application with respect to non-Member States of the Organization—whose number today is negligible—under Article 2, paragraph 6, which states that: "The Organization shall ensure that states which are not Members of the United Nations act in accordance with these Principles so far as may be necessary for the maintenance of international peace and security."

[87] On this subject, see Rodríguez Carrión, *Lecciones de Derecho Internacional Público*, p. 92, for a discussion of those limits and various examples.

[88] The Court ruled that "the French courts cannot allow acts of violent dispossession carried out by the German Reich against so-called 'non-Aryan' citizens, on that ground alone and without appropriate indemnification, to produce any effect within the territory of the Republic" (Kiss, *Répertoire de la pratique française en matière de droit international public*, p. 17, para. 29).

[89] Kiss, *op. cit.*, p. 28, para. 51: "Given the fact that Auschwitz, or more precisely, Osweicim, lies on Polish territory; it follows that the local law was Polish law, which *de facto* annexation or occupation by force could not invalidate."

[90] *Ibid.*, p. 29, No. 52: "Whereas the alleged declaration of annexation of Alsace by Germany, invoked as an argument, was nothing more than a unilateral act that could not modify legally the provisions of the treaty signed at Versailles on 28 June 1919 by the representatives of the German State".

[91] *Ibid.*, pp. 30–34, recounts various similar decisions by French courts.

[92] That non-recognition was expressed in numerous spheres: by the United States, the Ministries for Foreign Affairs of States members of the European Community, the Governments of Arab States, the Security Council, the General Assembly and the annual World Health Assembly of WHO, among others (see Rousseau, "Chronique des faits internationaux" (1982), pp. 596–598, and Marston, "United Kingdom materials on international law 1981", pp. 516–518).

[93] When, on 15 November 1983, a Turkish Cypriot state in northern Cyprus was proclaimed, the Turkish Cypriot Assembly declared that "the two peoples, Greek and Turkish, are destined to coexist side by side on the island. The new Republic will not unite with any other State. It will be non-aligned. ... The proclamation of independence will not hinder, but on the contrary facilitate the establishment of a real federation" (Rousseau, *loc. cit.* (1984), p. 431). The declaration was recognized by Turkey, but categorically rejected by Greece, the United Kingdom, France, the Federal Republic of Germany, Italy, the United States, Canada, Australia, India, Japan, the Union of Soviet Socialist Republics and the States of the socialist bloc. The proclamation was condemned by the Security Council and by the Council of Europe; the former considered it as legally invalid and called for its withdrawal under Security Council resolution 541 (1983) (*ibid.*, pp. 431–432).

[94] On 8 August 1990, the Spanish Office of Diplomatic Information issued the following communiqué: "The Government of Spain, in accordance with the Charter of the United Nations, considers unacceptable the acquisition of territories by force and, therefore, rejects and does not recognize the annexation of the State of Kuwait by the Republic of Iraq, proclaimed on this day by Baghdad" (*Actividades, Textos y Documentos de la Política Exterior Española* (Madrid, Ministry for Foreign Affairs and Cooperation, 1991), p. 53, and *Revista Española de Derecho Internacional*, vol. XLIII, No. 1 (1991), p. 144).

[95] See Guggenheim, *loc. cit.*, p. 229.

effect,[96] particularly since the Second World War. To some extent this issue is related directly to section (*c*) below, which concerns the presumed invalidity of a unilateral act that is contrary to a peremptory norm.

66. The following guiding principle could be formulated under principle 7 (Invalidity of unilateral acts):

"5. Any unilateral act formulated as a result of the threat or use of force in violation of the principles of international law embodied in the Charter of the United Nations is invalid."

(c) *Invalidity of a unilateral act on the ground that it is contrary to a norm of* jus cogens

67. The capacity to formulate unilateral acts is fundamentally limited by *jus cogens* norms,[97] since any unilateral act that conflicts with such norms is invalid, if it is assumed that the provisions of article 53 of the 1969 Vienna Convention apply[98] in general, and again *mutatis mutandis*, to unilateral acts.

68. Leaving aside the various opinions as to what norms might have the status of *jus cogens*,[99] and the difficult debates that led ultimately to the inclusion of that concept in the 1969 Vienna Convention,[100] the relationship between the unilateral act and the fact that it may conflict with a *jus cogens* norm will now be examined. In considering that question it should be borne in mind that, as pointed out by Brownlie: "The particular corollaries of the concept of *jus cogens* are still being explored."[101]

69. Peremptory norms "are a constraint on the capacity to formulate unilateral legal acts; this would include some norms deriving from the Charter of the United Nations and others contained in basic conventions, such as those relating to slavery and genocide, among many others".[102] Any unilateral act conflicting with such a norm would be considered invalid *ab initio*; it could therefore be expected to cause protests from the time of its formulation. However, practice in this regard is virtually non-existent.[103]

70. Following the same line of argument, it is relevant to highlight opinion No. 10 of 4 July 1992 rendered by the Arbitration Commission of the International Conference on the Former Yugoslavia (Badinter Commission) with reference to recognition of the Federal Republic of Yugoslavia (Serbia and Montenegro). Paragraph 4 of that text states that:

> [W]hile recognition is not a prerequisite for the foundation of a State and has only declarative value, it is none the less a discretionary act which other States may perform when they choose and in a manner of their own choosing, subject only to respect for the guiding norms of general international law, particularly those which prohibit the use of force in relations with other States or those which guarantee the rights of ethnic, religious or linguistic minorities.[104]

It is interesting to note that the paragraph presents "guiding" or peremptory norms as limiting freedom of recognition, from which it is logical to infer that such norms apply to all unilateral acts, of which recognition is but one example, and perhaps the most controversial of all.[105] In that regard, it is appropriate to recall the position that was adopted by virtually the entire international community with respect to the non-recognition of the South African Bantustans[106] or the presence of South Africa in

---

[96] Many of these cases are cited by Guggenheim, *loc. cit.*, p. 232, and are also recounted in Lauterpacht, *Annual Digest and Reports of Public International Law Cases, Years 1919–1942*, case No. 123, decision of the Cantonal Court of Utrecht, the Netherlands, of 8 September 1941; *ibid., Years 1943–1945*, case No. 9, p. 226, non-recognition by the United States of the annexation of Estonia, and cases Nos. 8 and 54, pp. 23 and 188, contained in the same volume, relating to recognition of the annexation by Germany of Austria; and *ibid., Years 1935–1937*, case No. 38, p. 119, resolved on 11 May 1937 by the British Supreme Court.

[97] However, some authors are highly critical of the application to unilateral acts of tenets of treaty law relating to *jus cogens*. For example, Weil, "Le droit international en quête de son identité: cours général de droit international public", p. 282, writes that: "In short, one must cease referring to *jus cogens* in relation to unilateral acts or actions by States, and leave that theory to treaty law, where it should have remained."

[98] Article 53 (Treaties conflicting with a peremptory norm of general international law ("*jus cogens*")) stipulates:

"A treaty is void if, at the time of its conclusion, it conflicts with a peremptory norm of general international law. For the purposes of the present Convention, a peremptory norm of general international law is a norm accepted and recognized by the international community of States as a whole as a norm from which no derogation is permitted and which can be modified only by a subsequent norm of general international law having the same character."

[99] Examples of these opinions can be found in Alexidze, "Legal nature of *jus cogens* in contemporary international law"; Carrillo Salcedo, "Reflections on the existence of a hierarchy of norms in international law"; Casado Raigón, *Notas sobre el "jus cogens" internacional*; Casado Raigón and Vázquez Gómez, "La impronta del *ius cogens* en el proyecto de artículos de la Comisión de Derecho Internacional sobre la responsabilidad del Estado por hechos internacionalmente ilícitos"; Danilenko, "International *jus cogens*: issues of law-making"; Fernández Tomás, "El *ius cogens* y las obligaciones derivadas de normas imperativas: entre el mito y la realidad"; Gaja, "*Jus cogens* beyond the Vienna Convention"; Gómez Robledo, "Le *ius cogens* international: sa genèse, sa nature, ses fonctions"; and *El* ius cogens *internacional: estudio histórico-crítico*; Gutiérrez Espada, "Sobre las normas imperativas del derecho internacional"; Hannikainen, *Peremptory Norms (Jus Cogens) and International Law: Historical Development, Criteria, Present Status*; Nicoloudis, *La nullité de* jus cogens *et le développement contemporain du droit international public*; Rozakis, *The Concept of* jus cogens *in the Law of Treaties*; Sztucki, Jus cogens *and the Vienna Convention on the Law of Treaties*; Verdross, "*Jus dispositivum* and *jus cogens* in international law"; Virally, "Réflexions sur le *jus cogens*"; and Weiler and Paulus, "The structure of change in international law or is there a hierarchy of norms in international law?".

[100] See *Yearbook ... 1999* (footnote 48 above), pp. 209–210, para. 139.

[101] Brownlie, *Principles of Public International Law*, p. 490.

[102] *Yearbook ... 1999* (see footnote 48 above), p. 210, para. 140.

[103] As pointed out by Verzijl, *International Law in Historical Perspective*, pp. 76–77: "As concerns unilateral acts, I only cite here the cases of occupation of a part of the high seas, for example contiguous to the territorial sea; the annexation of foreign territory in the course of a war prior to the conclusion of a peace treaty ...; a declaration of contraband relative to objects and materials which are insusceptible of such a declaration; adherence or accession to an open convention contrary to the conditions upon which the admissibility of such an adherence or accession depends; the establishment of a so-called pacific blockade pretending to produce legal effects to the detriment of a third State, etc."

[104] A/48/874-S/1994/189, annex. As highlighted by Navarro Batista, "La práctica comunitaria sobre reconocimiento de Estados: nuevas tendencias", p. 484, attention should be drawn to the "conditionality" to which the acts of recognition in question are subject in such cases. Hence the author affirms that "[i]n reality, the efforts undertaken in the literature to underline the unconditional nature of acts of recognition seem to be less a reflection of State practice than a (laudable) attempt to restrict a reality that is considered rather unfortunate and too susceptible to political fickleness".

[105] See Verhoeven, "La reconnaissance internationale: déclin ou renouveau?", in particular pp. 32–39.

[106] The Minister of State, Foreign and Commonwealth Office of the United Kingdom responded as follows:

Namibia;[107] the policy of apartheid pursued in those territories and the obstacles to Namibia's independence were cited, respectively, as the grounds for non-recognition of situations conflicting with true peremptory norms.[108] States are increasingly voicing opposition to the adoption by other States of internal norms that conflict with certain non-derogable norms.[109]

71. In view of the above, a possible guiding principle, following on from the above-mentioned paragraphs, could be as follows:

"6. Any unilateral act which at the time of its formulation is contrary to (or conflicts with) a peremptory norm of general international law (*jus cogens*) is invalid."

72. Having analysed the various possible grounds for invalidity that might be invoked with respect to a unilateral act, one must ask oneself who would have the authority to declare the presumed invalidity of that act, and what possible channels might be established under international law—bearing in mind that one is in the territory of legal speculation—to give effect to such a declaration. This is a highly abstract area in which, if a third party (usually an international court of law or arbitration) could declare, *ex officio* or otherwise, the invalidity of a unilateral act, most of those ambiguities would disappear. However, it is clear that what would presumably be gained in terms of legal certainty would be lost in terms of the very essence of unilateral acts, which would be subject to a regime that was not accepted for inclusion even in the 1969 Vienna Convention.

73. What does appear to be logical is that a State that formulates a unilateral act should normally be able to invoke its invalidity, with the caveat that special attention must be paid to good faith in this context; otherwise, any State wishing to eliminate commitments that it had undertaken previously through unilateral acts would declare those acts invalid *ipso facto*, thus creating a situation of considerable uncertainty and raising numerous doubts as to the seriousness with which that State conducts its foreign policy, and conflicting with the very spirit in which such acts are examined, which seeks to ensure confidence and legal certainty in international relations. In that context, good faith assumes a role of particular importance when such commitments are undertaken.

74. However, are all grounds for invalidity equal, or should key distinctions be made between them with respect both to their effects and to who is authorized to declare such invalidity? In principle, if the same criteria that emerged from the United Nations Conference on the Law of Treaties—which gave rise to the 1969 Vienna Convention—are applied, a dual regime may emerge. Thus, one could speak of relative or partial invalidity (with reference to articles 46–50 of the Convention) in cases where the invocation of invalidity is regarded essentially as the exclusive right of the party affected and the effects of such invalidity are limited, except where the ground invoked is the illicit conduct of another party. So-called "absolute" invalidity would apply in the event of invocation of one of the other grounds for invalidity cited above (coercion—of a representative of a State or of a State—or incompatibility between the act and a *jus cogens* norm), in which case invalidity may be invoked not only by the State that formulated the treaty (or, for present purposes, the unilateral act), but also by any other State, bearing in mind the much more serious nature of these circumstances.

75. As in other areas of international law, the problem lies in the impossibility of identifying a body that has the competence to ensure that unilateral acts comply with this regime or the authority to declare an act invalid, either *ex officio* or by submission of the State that formulated the act or of a third State aware of the existence of that ground for invalidity. Given that problems in addressing this issue have already arisen in relation to international treaties, an area in which normative channels appear to be much more clearly defined, the Special Rapporteur believes that with respect to unilateral acts it is all but impossible, given the current international situation, to propose and adopt a mechanism to settle any disputes that may arise in connection with unilateral acts and their possible invalidity. The very term "unilateral" suggests that perhaps the only viable and genuine alternative could be for the State that has formulated the unilateral act to function as the entity that has the authority—and the obligation, if the gravity of the case so requires—to draw attention to any defects in the act, thereby making the situation known and preventing the act from continuing to produce effects.

76. Of course, the consideration of this topic is fundamentally speculative, since applicable law is still somewhat uncertain, despite the effort to draw up guiding principles on the subject. In any event, as in the context of the law of treaties, the topic is important, if controversial. It should be studied in a possible subsequent phase of the work in this area.

77. Another question which is related to the invalidity of unilateral acts and to which there is no generally accepted answer is whether or not a presumably invalid

---

"The United Kingdom, like all other countries except South Africa, do not recognise Transkei, Bophuthatswana, Venda and Ciskei as independent, sovereign States. British officials therefore do not have any dealings with anyone who purports to represent their so-called 'Governments'."

(Marston, *loc. cit.*, *1982*, p. 358)

[107] The Minister of State, Foreign and Commonwealth Office of the United Kingdom stated that:

"The question of recognition does not arise. As a matter of fact, a system of courts exists in Namibia as part of South Africa's administration of that territory. We do not recognise that South Africa has any right to continue to administer Namibia ... We do not intervene during the course of judicial proceedings in Namibia or elsewhere and that has been the policy of successive governments."

(*Ibid.*, *1987*, p. 528).

[108] On this issue, Cassese, *International Law*, p. 144, states that: "It would follow among other things that whenever an entity with all the hallmarks of statehood emerges as a result of aggression, or is grounded on systematic denial of the rights of minorities or of human rights, other States are legally bound to withhold recognition."

[109] See, *inter alia*, the example cited by Cassese, *ibid.*, p. 430, endnote No. 94, concerning the message relating to the International Convention on the Prevention and Punishment of the Crime of Genocide and the corresponding revision of criminal law sent to the Parliament by the Federal Council of the Swiss Government on 31 March 1999, which stated that: "Given that the prohibition of genocide is a peremptory norm of *jus gentium* (*jus cogens*), States cannot agree to reject it. Therefore, a peace treaty that sanctions amnesty for acts of genocide should not be considered as legally valid. Consequently, from the perspective of international law, a national law that authorizes or itself prescribes an act of genocide against a certain group may in no case serve to legitimize the conduct of the perpetrators of such an act or their accomplices."

unilateral act can be validated. The answer to this question, whether affirmative or negative, must be qualified to reflect the particular circumstances of each case, as no definitive "yes" or "no" answers can be given in relation to unilateral acts. It could, in any case, be argued that, with respect to especially serious grounds for invalidity—coercion or the fact that the unilateral act in question conflicts with a norm of *jus cogens*—the possibility of validation is quite remote.[110] The situation is likely to be different, or at least the validation is unlikely to be so problematic, with respect to other circumstances that can give rise to invalidity. Cases of error, fraud or a representative's overstepping his or her authority, among others, probably could be validated if the subsequent conduct of the State having formulated the unilateral act clearly warranted that consequence.

78. Even ICJ, in some of its judgments, points to this possibility of validation, although the judgments in question refer to international treaties. This was clearly apparent, for example, in the ruling handed down in the case concerning the *Arbitral Award Made by the King of Spain on 23 December 1906*.[111] Similarly, the judgment in the case concerning the Temple of Preah Vihear is also very illustrative, although it actually addresses the question of whether the subsequent conduct of one of the parties to a dispute can be deemed to validate a purportedly erroneous initial act.[112]

B. Termination and suspension of unilateral acts and other related concepts

79. Having considered possible grounds for the invalidity of unilateral acts, the application of such acts will now be examined, especially with regard to the duration of their effects over time. This includes the termination, suspension, modification and revocation of an act.

80. In relation to unilateral acts, the principle of good faith is a kind of substantive paradigm that implies that such acts should be maintained over time. Logically, as Barberis notes, "the author of a unilateral legal act does not have the power to establish arbitrarily, by means of another unilateral legal act, a rule that derogates from the one established by means of the earlier act".[113] Virtually the same opinion has been expressed by Venturini, who notes that, with respect to unilateral acts, "revocation is admissible only in the case envisaged by the general norms of the international legal system, because otherwise, the compulsory value of those same acts would be abandoned to the arbitrary power of their authors".[114]

81. The Commission is faced with the arduous task of trying to identify the rules of general international law under which a unilateral act may be revoked.[115] The Special Rapporteur wonders whether there is any certainty to be derived from international practice in this area—of which there has been very little—or from the literature—which also offers few examples—as to what circumstances would make it permissible to terminate, modify or suspend the application of a unilateral act.

82. Before venturing into this uncharted territory, the various concepts to which reference will be made must be defined, at least at a basic level: the possibility of terminating a unilateral act (although in many cases the literature uses the term "revocation" to refer to this situation, since it concerns unilateral acts) and the possibility of suspending a unilateral act or modifying its content; this last situation often entails the formulation of a new unilateral act (or even the conclusion of a treaty containing the modified version of the original unilateral act). The cases that can arise in this connection are as varied as international circumstances themselves. An attempt will therefore be made to cover as many hypothetical situations as possible, bearing in mind, however, that neither practice nor the literature offers much information in this regard. Accordingly, relevant treaties must be investigated, by identifying possibilities that can be extrapolated to unilateral acts as a category, and an attempt must be made to determine the consequences that might ensue for such acts.

83. In relation to unilateral acts, two terms are used interchangeably in the literature to refer to the cessation of the effects of an act of this kind: "revocation", which is used very frequently, and "termination", which is of course implied by the other term. In the view of the Special Rapporteur, there is a nuance of meaning that differentiates between the two concepts, even though they are used interchangeably. Termination may be due to external factors (such as a situation in which the subject matter of the unilateral act has ceased to exist or a fundamental change has taken place in the circumstances that gave rise to the act) or even intrinsic ones (the inclusion of a

[110] Except in situations that are almost purely hypothetical; for example, if a new norm of *jus cogens* were to emerge with which the unilateral act previously considered invalid is consistent, or even if a fundamental change in circumstances were to prompt a State to formulate a unilateral act that is identical in substance to an act formulated under coercion, even though the element of coercion is absent in the case of the latter act. If the intention of the State that formulates the new unilateral act is to apply it retroactively to the time when the presumably invalid act was formulated, should that right be denied or, conversely, should the previous unilateral act be validated without qualification? The Special Rapporteur believes that the latter option is valid if it accurately reflects the State's intention.

[111] *Arbitral Award Made by the King of Spain on 23 December 1906, Judgment, I.C.J. Reports 1960*, especially pp. 213–214), in which it is stated that:

> "In the judgment of the Court, Nicaragua, by express declaration and by conduct, recognized the Award as valid and it is no longer open to Nicaragua to go back upon that recognition and to challenge the validity of the Award. Nicaragua's failure to raise any question with regard to the validity of the Award for several years after the full terms of the Award had become known to it further confirms the conclusion at which the Court has arrived. The attitude of the Nicaraguan authorities during that period was in conformity with Article VII of the Gámez-Bonilla Treaty which provided that the arbitral decision whatever it might be—and this, in the view of the Court, includes the decision of the King of Spain as arbitrator—'shall be held as a perfect, binding and perpetual Treaty between the High Contracting Parties, and shall not be subject to appeal'."

[112] *Temple of Preah Vihear, Merits, Judgment, I.C.J. Reports 1962*, pp. 22–24 (among others).

[113] Barberis, "Los actos jurídicos unilaterales como fuente del derecho internacional público", p. 113.

[114] Venturini, *loc. cit.*, p. 421.

[115] As early as 1998, when the Special Rapporteur submitted his first report on unilateral acts of States, some members of the Commission mentioned the need to study these issues; see the views of Mr. Hafner and Mr. Yamada, *Yearbook ... 1998*, vol. I, 2526th meeting, pp. 56–57, paras. 71–72, and of Mr. Pambou-Tchivounda and Mr. Herdocia Sacasa, *ibid.*, p. 57, paras. 76–78.

time limit or even a resolutive condition in the unilateral act, provided that its purpose is legitimate and it does not impose obligations on third parties without their consent). The term "revoke" implies that something (in this case, a unilateral act) is considered to have been terminated or to have no further effect because the State having formulated it so intends.[116] The Special Rapporteur believes that the word "termination" is broader, as it also covers other situations in which a unilateral act ceases to have effect as a result of circumstances unrelated to the will of the State having formulated the act.

84. Suspension—unlike termination, which is definitive—means the provisional and temporary cessation of the observance of the unilateral act in question. Contrary to what might, in principle, be assumed, these two concepts have many features in common; this may be one of the main reasons they are dealt with together in the 1969 Vienna Convention, in part V, section 3.

85. Circumstances may arise in which unilateral acts must be adapted to reflect contemporary realities; nothing is immutable, and unilateral acts need not necessarily be an exception. The question, then, is why the modification of their content should not be allowed, as it is in the case of international treaties. The crucial point is that, in the case of unilateral acts, it is the will of the party formulating them that determines whether the act should continue to have the same content or whether it can be modified in some way; otherwise, one would be dealing with something else (a bilateral agreement, in most cases), not a unilateral act. The possibility of modifying a unilateral act is therefore the prerogative of the party having formulated it, although the changes made should not affect the essence of the original unilateral act, since, if they did, they would in fact amount to a new unilateral act that would invalidate the earlier one.

86. The absence, in the literature, of discussion of the (possible) modification of unilateral acts directly mirrors the situation with respect to the modification of treaties. This is a logical consequence of the very nature of the international system.[117]

87. To ensure that the discussion of these concepts is based on a precise understanding of them, their content must, at the outset, be analysed.

> [I]t may happen that a State formulates a promise for a term of 10 years or subjects it to certain resolutive conditions. In such cases, if the term expires or the condition is met, the promise ceases without the need for any act of revocation. Another case may occur in which the author of the promise or the waiver expressly provides for the possibility of revoking it under certain circumstances. However, if the possibility of revocation derives neither from the context of the unilateral legal act nor from its nature, a unilateral promise and a unilateral waiver are, in principle, irrevocable.[118]

There have also, as international case law has affirmed from time to time, been acts that can be revoked, but with certain limitations, as ICJ highlighted in the case concerning *Military and Paramilitary Activities in and against Nicaragua*, in its judgment of 26 November 1984 on the jurisdiction of the Court and the admissibility of the application. According to the Court:

> [T]he right of immediate termination of declarations with indefinite duration is far from established. It appears from the requirements of good faith that they should be treated, by analogy, according to the law of treaties, which requires a reasonable time for withdrawal from or termination of treaties that contain no provision regarding the duration of their validity.[119]

88. Also relevant in this regard is the view expressed by Gutiérrez Espada, who states:

> It seems reasonable to assume that, in principle, any unilateral act may be revoked by its author, unless the circumstances unequivocally and categorically indicate otherwise. While we may invoke the "denunciation" of treaties by way of analogy, we must also bear in mind that denunciation is possible only in certain conditions ... the revocability of unilateral acts is likewise subject to certain limitations.[120]

Virtually the same position is expressed in the separate opinion of Judge Mosler in the above-mentioned case concerning *Military and Paramilitary Activities in and against Nicaragua*.[121]

89. There are some situations in which unilateral acts may be modified or terminated even though these outcomes are not genuinely intended by their author. Inability to comply, the fact that the subject matter has ceased to exist or a fundamental change in circumstances are valid reasons to terminate or modify a unilateral act, while the emergence of a new peremptory norm of general international law will terminate any unilateral act that conflicts with it.

90. When the law of treaties was being codified, Sir Gerald Fitzmaurice, who at the time was the Special Rapporteur on the subject, submitted a draft article 22, paragraph 2 of which provided as follows (expressly referring to the possibility that a unilateral act may be revocable):

---

[116] According to the definition given in the dictionary published by the Real Academia Española (Spanish Royal Academy), the Spanish term "*revocar*" means to render ineffective a concession, mandate or decision. According to the *Concise Oxford English Dictionary*, the English term "revoke" means to "end the validity or operation of (a decree, decision or promise)". In the 1969 Vienna Convention the term "revocation" is used in article 37; that provision was cited in the Commission by Mr. Galicki as a possible source of guidance in this regard (*Yearbook ... 1998*, vol. I, 2527th meeting, p. 59, para. 10).

[117] Casanovas la Rosa, "La modificación de los acuerdos internacionales por la práctica posterior", p. 330, indicates that:

> "Whereas in domestic legal systems most contracts are implemented on a one-time basis and ongoing contracts are less common, in the international system there are many treaties and agreements whose purpose is to regulate the relations between the parties on a more or less permanent basis. If we add the observation that the international system does not impose the formal requirements which, in the field of private law, are necessary for the validity of many contracts, nor does it have any authorities with compulsory jurisdiction that can determine, at any given time, the exact nature of the rights and obligations of the parties in case of dispute, it may easily be supposed that the modification of agreements through subsequent practice may apply much more broadly in the international sphere than in the domestic sphere. However, the discussion of situations of this type in international case law has been infrequent and, in some respects ... ambiguous."

[118] Barberis, *op. cit.*, p. 113.

[119] *Military and Paramilitary Activities in and against Nicaragua (Nicaragua* v. *United States of America), Jurisdiction and Admissibility, Judgment, I.C.J. Reports 1984*, p. 420, para. 63.

[120] Gutiérrez Espada, *Derecho Internacional Público*, p. 597.

[121] *I.C.J. Reports 1984* (see footnote 119 above), p. 466.

Unless the declaration specifies its own irrevocability, the State or States in whose favour it was made cannot object to its withdrawal or modification at the will of the declarant State; provided that, if this has consequences analogous to those indicated in paragraph 4 (c) of article 20 of the present text,[122] the declarant State shall be liable to pay compensation, or make other appropriate reparation, in respect of the loss or damage caused.[123]

91. The content of article 37, paragraph 2, of the 1969 Vienna Convention is similar to this proposal.[124] Thus, if the intention referred to in that article is absent, the right in question may be revocable;[125] however, no reference is made to the possibility of reparation for potential harm caused. This issue is related to international responsibility, which the codifiers did not address.

92. Interpreting this provision and relating it directly to the issue of interest here—that is, to unilateral acts—Urios Moliner affirms, rightly in the view of the Special Rapporteur, that:

[D]eclarations of this kind are in principle irrevocable and not subject to modification, unless this possibility is implied by the terms of the declaration and the circumstances and conditions necessary for this purpose, as laid down in the declaration, are met, or the party or parties having suffered the harm give their consent, or there is a fundamental change in the circumstances that gave rise to the declaration.[126]

In short, the aim is to ensure the maintenance of unilateral acts, which may be terminated or have their provisions modified or suspended only in exceptional and non-arbitrary situations.

93. It is clear that this subject area has given rise to many differences of opinion, which are directly reflected in the debates of the Sixth Committee; the idea that unilateral acts are irrevocable unless their addressees consent to their revocation[127] has been challenged by other views. These include the position that a unilateral act may be revoked if it is made subject to a time limit or to the fulfilment of a condition, or to general principles such as *rebus sic stantibus*,[128] the exception for *force majeure* or other principles. It might even be said that certain acts should be considered revocable under all but the most limited circumstances.[129]

94. The Special Rapporteur believes that Germany was correct when, in its reply to the questionnaire on unilateral acts, it pointed out that the question of whether or not a unilateral act could be revoked could not be assessed in the abstract without regard to the concrete circumstances of the act in question; any attempt to subject the issue to an abstract, across-the-board principle would be meaningless.[130] Other State representatives supported the idea that unilateral acts could be revoked.[131] The views expressed are indicative of a wide variety of approaches. An attempt will therefore be made to draw a distinction between situations that were provided for at the time a unilateral act was formulated or that stem directly from the will of the party having formulated it, on the one hand, and circumstances in which an external factor gives rise to the change in question, on the other.

1. Situations arising from the will of the party formulating the unilateral act

95. A State that formulates a unilateral act, as a manifestation of its will, may suspend or modify the act or limit its duration, if the intent to do so was clearly expressed, like the unilateral act in question, at the time or times when the act was formulated.

96. Logically, it should be possible to impose a time limit on a unilateral act[132] by clearly stating this condition at the time the act is formulated. The Special Rapporteur believes that the same logic would apply in the case of a suspension of operation, if some sort of moratorium—or period during which the act shall not apply—is provided

[122] This refers to a situation in which a third State, by acting in such a way as to exercise the rights conferred by the treaty, incurs damage over and above what it would have incurred if it had not so acted or had not exercised any such rights.

[123] *Yearbook ... 1960*, vol. II, document A/CN.4/130, p. 81.

[124] When a right has arisen for a third State in conformity with article 36, the right may not be revoked or modified by the parties if it is established that the right was intended not to be revocable or subject to modification without the consent of the third State.

[125] Contrary to what might be assumed, and according to Capotorti, "L'extinction et la suspension des traités", p. 496, on this point the 1969 Vienna Convention took a significant step forward in relation to the traditional view—reflected, for example, in the draft Convention on the Law of Treaties, prepared by Harvard Law School—that rights conferred on third parties by an international treaty are in all cases revocable by the parties; at least the Vienna Convention limits this possibility to some extent, when the treaty in question so provides.

[126] Urios Moliner, *Actos unilaterales y derecho internacional público: delimitación de una figura susceptible de un régimen jurídico común*, p. 125.

[127] The representative of the Republic of Korea said that, in order to protect the rights of addressees and preserve international legal stability, it should not be permissible for States to revoke or modify unilateral acts without the consent of the other States concerned (*Official Records of the General Assembly, Sixtieth Session, Sixth Committee*, 15th meeting, para. 10). The representative of Belarus said that unilateral acts could be terminated by States only by agreement with subjects of international law that had taken note of them and modified their conduct accordingly (*ibid.*, 18th meeting, para. 75).

[128] The representative of the Republic of Korea said that the principle of *rebus sic stantibus* could also be considered as grounds for the revocability and modification of unilateral acts (*ibid.*, 15th meeting, para. 10).

[129] See also the summary of the discussion held in the Sixth Committee after the introduction of the Special Rapporteur's second report on unilateral acts of States (Topical summary of the discussion in the Sixth Committee on the report of the Commission during the fifty-fourth session of the General Assembly (A/CN.4/504 and Add.1), para. 156).

[130] *Yearbook ... 2000*, vol. II (Part One), document A/CN.4/511, pp. 266–267. As far back as 1973, Verzijl, *op. cit.*, expressed the same view, p. 106, stating: "Their susceptibility of unilateral withdrawal depends on their specific character and cannot, therefore, be discussed as a problem capable of a solution which applies to all cases." The same idea was expressed in the Sixth Committee, at its sixtieth session, by the representative of Japan (*Official Records of the General Assembly, Sixtieth Session, Sixth Committee*, 14th meeting, para. 54), who noted that his Government considered that the revocability and modification of unilateral acts depended on the form, content, authors and addressees of the act, and must be determined by examining each category or type of unilateral act.

[131] These included the representatives of El Salvador and Georgia, although Finland, Israel and Italy took a more nuanced approach by referring to that possibility, but with certain limitations (see *Yearbook ... 2000* (footnote 130 above), p. 281).

[132] Such a time limit may, as in the case of international treaties, take various forms: a fixed date, the passage of a period of time or the fulfilment of a given event which acts as a resolutive condition are perhaps the most common forms. The time limit may even be determined by the cessation of a given activity, which implies the acceptance of an obligation from that moment onward.

for at the time of its formulation. The act would regain its legal effects at a later date (once the period provided for had expired or the established condition had been fulfilled).

97. The termination, suspension or modification of a unilateral act becomes more complex when the possibility of doing so is not—as is more often the case—provided for at the time the act is formulated. In this case the question arises as to whether it is possible to do so, taking into account that it would be the State which formulated the act that also seeks to terminate it. The question becomes even more complex in the case of unilateral acts which have generated, or which may generate, expectations among third parties. The little information to be gleaned from practice and from the literature is discussed below.

98. It has been asserted that, in general terms, the author of a unilateral promise may revoke it or modify its content, provided that the addressees of the promise have expressly given their consent, or that there is no opposition from the persons affected by it. This idea, which may appear very reasonable in theory, is less so in the case of a promise which has *erga omnes* effects,[133] or whose addressees are undetermined, or where there are doubts as to their identity. Rubin makes an interesting point in this context, asserting that

> it is certainly possible in some cases for a single party legally to terminate its apparent treaty obligations without violating the principle of good faith. There is no apparent reason why obligations assumed by unilateral declaration should be harder to terminate than obligations assumed by treaty.[134]

99. In the Security Council, the representative of France expressed a similar sentiment with respect to Egypt's declaration on the Suez Canal.[135] He then proceeded to question the declaration's irrevocability, which he did not believe to have the same value as the promise itself, stating: "[A] unilateral declaration, even if registered, obviously cannot be anything more than a unilateral act, and we must draw the conclusion from these findings that just as the Declaration was issued unilaterally, it can be amended or annulled in the same manner."[136] The Secretary-General adopted an almost identical position at a press conference held on 25 April 1957 concerning the same declaration.[137] Because this was a period when even the very definition of a unilateral act was unclear, the intent of the formulating State affected the possibility of revoking such an act.

100. The main problem lies in the fact that a promise generates—or may generate—expectations on the part of third parties, which appear to have a certain right to assume that such a promise will be honoured, within limits. In this regard, Jacqué states:

> A unilateral promise creates, for the benefit of its addressee(s), as soon as they are informed of its existence, a right to expect that the author of the promise will honour its commitment. However, just as treaty law authorizes the parties, under certain circumstances, to terminate a treaty before it expires, the Court does not guarantee the irrevocability and absolute immutability of a unilateral promise.[138]

However, in 1974 ICJ, in it own words, suggested that such a possibility of revocation is not, and is very far from being, absolute: "The Court finds that the unilateral undertaking resulting from these statements cannot be interpreted as having been made in implicit reliance on an *arbitrary power** of reconsideration."[139]

101. The question of whether or not a promise can be revoked raises difficult issues which can be resolved only by referring to the concrete circumstances of the case. While the principle of good faith plays a vitally important role here, since the promise generates certain expectations which could be disappointed if the promise is revoked, this undertaking need not be regarded as a perpetual obligation from which the State can never free itself. A relative, flexible position should therefore be adopted, as noted by de Visscher, "whose relativity, *ratione personae, ratione temporis* and *ratione materiae*, should be seen in the light of the political and legal context of each case".[140] Such relativism may lead to problems, but the

---

[133] See Sicault, *loc. cit.*, p. 650.

[134] Rubin, "The international legal effects of unilateral declarations", p. 10.

[135] Declaration (with letter of transmittal to the Secretary-General of the United Nations) on the Suez Canal and the arrangements for its operation (Cairo, 24 April 1957), by which the Government of Egypt undertook to abide by its obligations under the 1888 Convention respecting the Free Navigation of the Suez Maritime Canal (United Nations, *Treaty Series*, vol. 265, No. 3821, p. 299).

[136] *Official Records of the Security Council, Twelfth Year*, 776th meeting, para. 59. See also Kiss, *op. cit.*, p. 618. A virtually identical position regarding the possibility of revoking a unilateral act was also taken by the Minister for Foreign Affairs of France during a meeting of the Ministers for Foreign Affairs of France, the Soviet Union, the United Kingdom and the United States, held in Geneva on 8 November 1955: "It is quite true that the guarantees currently enjoyed by the USSR because of the existence of the measures taken by Western defence organizations are unilateral in nature, and therefore revocable" (*ibid.*, p. 618).

[137] In which he stated: "The registration as such does not make the document irrevocable, because it is ... binding upon the party submitting it, with the character they have given to the document itself. That is to say ... it can be superseded ... by another declaration" (cited by Dehaussy, "La déclaration egyptienne de 1957 sur le Canal de Suez", p. 180, footnote (32)).

[138] Jacqué, "A propos de la promesse unilatérale", p. 342.

[139] *Nuclear Tests (Australia* v. *France), Judgment, I.C.J. Reports 1974*, p. 270, para. 51. The Court would express a similar opinion in the case concerning *Military and Paramilitary Activities in and against Nicaragua* (*I.C.J. Reports 1984* (see footnote 119 above), p. 418, para. 59), stating that "the unilateral nature of declarations does not signify that the State making the declaration is free to amend their scope and contents of its solemn commitments as it pleases" (The "unilateral nature of declarations" refers to declarations of acceptance of the jurisdiction of the Court, although the Special Rapporteur believes that this idea can be extrapolated in a generalized way to all unilateral declarations that may be formulated by States.)

[140] De Visscher, "Remarques sur l'évolution de la jurisprudence de la Cour Internationale de Justice relative au fondement obligatoire de certains actes unilatéraux", p. 464. Let us consider a real case in which the socio-political circumstances of the State which made the promise prevented the performance thereof. In a statement, Japanese Prime Minister Zeuko Suzuki indicated that Japan, after holding the appropriate consultations with the United States, would authorize the transit of ships carrying nuclear weapons (Rousseau, *loc. cit.* (1981), p. 905). He was thus publicly expressing a derogation from one of the three basic principles underlying Japan's nuclear policy: non-possession, non-production and non-introduction of this type of weapon in Japan. The furore caused by these remarks forced the Minister to reverse course, and he subsequently announced to the press that Japan would deny such authorization. This position was reiterated on 9 August 1984 by Japanese Prime Minister M. Y. Nakasone, who, during a ceremony commemorating the nuclear attack on Nagasaki, stated that Japan would not permit United States warships carrying nuclear missiles to use its ports (*ibid.* (1985), p. 166).

law must be applied in a manner that takes into account its capacity to adapt to circumstances. Thus, in considering whether a promise may be changed (through termination, suspension or modification), special attention should be paid to the circumstances that make such a change necessary, as well as to the good faith of the State that formulated the unilateral act and wishes to change it. In fact, it could even be argued, moving further into the realm of alternatives characterized as *de lege ferenda*, that when expectations generated among third parties are seriously disappointed, it should be possible to request reparation if it can be proved that the State seeking to terminate or radically alter the content of the obligation that it assumed unilaterally is acting arbitrarily or in bad faith.

102. Turning to the concept of recognition, the Special Rapporteur finds that ideas on this subject have gone through a number of different phases, with the result that the views expressed in the literature as to whether or not an act of recognition is revocable have changed considerably. Practice in this area is almost non-existent, and opinions have been divided between the assertion of the irrevocable nature of recognition[141] (or, at least, of what has been called *de jure* recognition) and *de facto* recognition (which is considered to be provisional and therefore revocable). Since the extent of the difference of opinion is matched by the lack of any significant practice that might offer a certain degree of clarity, it is best to adopt a cautious approach.

103. Such caution is demonstrated, for example, by certain authors who, while starting from the assumption that recognition is revocable, assert that "recognition may be revoked and there exists no right to its maintenance. However, as long as the recognition is not withdrawn, the beneficiary or beneficiaries have the right to demand that its author respect the obligations deriving from the act by which it has recognized a certain situation".[142] The same position has been taken by other authors, who distinguish between purely unilateral recognition, which they believe is revocable, and situations where an act of recognition is included in an international treaty, in which case the opposite effect is produced. At the present time, it seems that this position not only gives rise to many uncertainties, but also asserts a distinction whereby treaty provisions are assumed to offer more security and certainty than unilateral acts. The Special Rapporteur believes that this distinction is simply not realistic, given the current state of affairs.

104. The consequences deriving from recognition are so significant that care must be taken in making categorical assertions about its potential revocability. One complex case involved the former Yugoslav republics, which at a certain point recognized (through treaty provisions) the continuity of what was then called[143] the Federal Republic of Yugoslavia (Serbia and Montenegro);[144] this situation led to an obvious contradiction with respect to the Convention on the rights of the child. The events occurred as follows: on 3 January 1991 the Socialist Federal Republic of Yugoslavia ratified the Convention, making a reservation to article 9, paragraph 1,[145] which it then withdrew (this time as the Federal Republic of Yugoslavia) on 28 January 1997.[146] This action led to subsequent communications from Slovenia (28 May 1997), Croatia (3 June 1997), Bosnia and Herzegovina (4 June 1997)[147] and the former Yugoslav Republic of Macedonia (10 October 1997).[148] Bosnia and Herzegovina, Croatia and Slovenia asserted that "[t]he State which in 1991 notified its ratification of the [said Convention] and made the reservation was the former Socialist Federal Republic of Yugoslavia (SFRY), but the State which on 28 January 1997 notified the withdrawal of its reservation was the Federal Republic of Yugoslavia".[149] Moreover, they drew attention to Security Council resolutions 757 (1992) and 777 (1992) and to General Assembly resolution 47/1, which indicated that the Socialist Federal Republic of Yugoslavia had ceased to exist and that the Federal Republic of Yugoslavia could not be considered its sole successor. In view of the ambiguity involved (a reserving State that has ceased to exist and a presumed successor that withdraws a reservation that it did not make), the Secretary-General was requested to clarify the situation. The former Yugoslav Republic of Macedonia stated "that the Federal Republic of Yugoslavia has neither notified its succession to the Convention, nor has it adhered to the Convention in any other appropriate manner consistent with the International Treaty Law. Accordingly, the Federal Republic of Yugoslavia is not, and can not be considered as a Party to the Convention".[150] Thus,

[141] Very illuminating in this respect are the proposals noted by Verhoeven, *La reconnaissance internationale dans la pratique contemporaine: les relations publiques internationales*, p. 650, footnote (69).

[142] Jacqué, *Éléments pour une théorie de l'acte juridique en droit international*, p. 337.

[143] In this regard, see a discussion of the situation concerning the name of the Federal Republic of Yugoslavia *in* Torres Cazorla, "El último cambio de Yugoslavia: de la República Federativa de Yugoslavia (Serbia y Montenegro) a la Unión de Serbia y Montenegro".

[144] See paragraph 17 of the ICJ judgment of 11 July 1996, *Application of the Convention on the Prevention and Punishment of the Crime of Genocide, Preliminary Objections, Judgment, I.C.J. Reports 1996*, p. 610. In this case it is clear that Bosnia and Herzegovina wanted the Federal Republic of Yugoslavia to be considered as a successor State, with that position being accepted, at least with respect to the Convention, by the Court. The respective accords signed bilaterally between the Federal Republic of Yugoslavia and the other former Yugoslav republics, aimed at normalizing their relations, appeared to accept the idea of the continuity of the personality of the Socialist Federal Republic of Yugoslavia in the Federal Republic of Yugoslavia (Serbia and Montenegro). Examples in this regard include article 4 of the Agreement on the Regulation of Relations and Promotion of Cooperation between the Republic of Macedonia and the Federal Republic of Yugoslavia of 8 April 1996 (S/1996/291, appendix). See also ILM, vol. XXXV, No. 5 (September 1996), p. 1248; article 5 of the Agreement on Normalization of Relations between the Federal Republic of Yugoslavia and the Republic of Croatia, of 23 August 1996 (*ibid.*, p. 1221; and A/51/318-S/1996/706, annex); and paragraph IV of the joint declaration of the President of the Republic of Serbia and the President of Bosnia and Herzegovina, of 3 October 1996 (A/51/461-S/1996/830, annex). See also *Review of International Affairs*, No. 1049–1050, p. 15. For an analysis of these and other related questions, see Torres Cazorla, "Rights of private persons on State succession: an approach to the most recent cases", pp. 674–677.

[145] United Nations, *Multilateral Treaties Deposited with the Secretary-General: Status as at 31 December 2005*, vol. I (United Nations publication, Sales No. E.06.V.2), p. 335, note 3.

[146] *Ibid.*, p. 340, note 38.

[147] *Ibid.*

[148] United Nations, *Treaty Series*, vol. 1993, No. 27531, p. 316.

[149] *Ibid.*, *Multilateral Treaties* ... (see footnote 145 above), p. 340, note 38.

[150] See footnote 148 above.

although initially the former Yugoslav republics had appeared to recognize the continuity of the Federal Republic of Yugoslavia, they expressed the opposite view a year later.[151] The complex situation in which the Federal Republic found itself for almost a decade thus illustrates how such problematic circumstances can arise.[152]

105. The Special Rapporteur believes that the circumstances of the case, good faith and the possibility that a unilateral act may have generated expectations in third parties must be the essential elements to be taken into account in determining whether a State can put forward a further expression of unilateral will which modifies the initial unilateral act.[153] However, any attempt to establish fixed rules on this subject is inevitably frustrated by the very nature of the unilateral act, which is infinitely flexible. The absence (albeit deliberate and desired by States) of a body responsible for considering and resolving potentially problematic situations which might arise in this respect is another important obstacle to be considered, and is at this point insuperable. The Special Rapporteur believes that only Article 33 of the Charter of the United Nations, with the freedom it allows regarding the choice of the means for the pacific settlement of disputes, can serve as a guide in this respect.

106. A situation which combines elements of the two situations mentioned above and which generally implies the possibility of terminating a unilateral act normally arises when the unilateral act in question has been performed in its entirety. Such cases may involve a wide variety of circumstances: for example, the unilateral act may be completed through a single action (as with a promise to cancel a debt) or the obligation constituting the unilateral act may have a specific content which, once exhausted, renders the continued validity of the act futile. In a treaty context, performance serves as a reason for the expiry of so-called contractual treaties, which are defined as treaties that give rise to legal relationships of a specific nature. Once the obligation arising from such a treaty is fulfilled, the treaty ceases to operate.[154]

107. Various guiding principles relating to the possible grounds for termination mentioned above might be formulated as a single draft principle, which would initially include the following grounds, submitted for the consideration of the Commission:

"*Termination of unilateral acts (part one)*

"A unilateral act may be terminated or revoked by the formulating State:

"(*a*) If a specific time limit for termination of the act was set at the time of its formulation (or if termination was implicit following the performance of one or more acts);

"(*b*) If the act was subject to a resolutive condition at the time of its formulation."

108. Termination of a unilateral act because its subject matter has ceased to exist is to a certain degree related to another cause, which shall be considered in the next section: the potential termination, modification or suspension of operation due to supervening impossibility of performance. This cause, unlike those which are currently of concern, was included in the 1969 Vienna Convention.

2. Situations arising from circumstances unrelated to the will of the party formulating the unilateral act

109. The grounds for termination, modification or suspension of an international treaty have long been a central focus of study and have given rise to considerable misgivings, particularly in cases where such changes have been brought about or intended by only one of the parties to the treaty. Although these misgivings are well founded, questions also arise with respect to other grounds where a situation unrelated to the will of the formulating State—of a unilateral act, in this case—leads to the termination, modification or suspension of the act.[155] In the analysis of the different situations which could lead to such changes, the Special Rapporteur will first examine several possibilities that are expressly provided for in the 1969 Vienna Convention[156] and that could apply to unilateral acts, and then, in the next section, other circumstances will be considered.[157]

(a) *Situations provided for in the 1969 Vienna Convention*

110. Article 61 of the 1969 Vienna Convention concerns a ground for terminating or suspending the operation of an international treaty which, in the opinion of the Special Rapporteur, is fully applicable to unilateral acts. This ground, supervening impossibility of performance, could also justify the termination of a unilateral act if, as stated in article 61, paragraph 1, "the impossibility results from the permanent disappearance or destruction of an object indispensable for the execution of the treaty", or the suspension of the act's operation if the impossibility is merely temporary. The rule of *ad impossibilia nemo tenetur* is fully applicable in this case, since the State would

[151] An exhaustive account of this situation is contained in Torres Cazorla, "El derecho del menor a una nacionalidad: análisis de los recientes casos de sucesión de Estados", pp. 200–201.

[152] An excellent discussion of all these issues can be found in Ortega Terol, "Aspectos teóricos y prácticos de la continuidad en la identidad del Estado", pp. 287–300.

[153] This further manifestation of will which seeks to terminate the unilateral act could even consist of the signing of an international treaty whose content is contrary to that of the previous unilateral act. This could give rise to a number of possible situations: the State or States for which the previous unilateral act generated certain expectations might also be parties to the treaty, in which case no problems would occur; or they might not be parties, in which case obligations of various and sometimes contradictory kinds would arise, thereby leading to a problem of non-compliance, with either the unilateral act or the treaty. The issue of international responsibility would be a matter of considerable interest in this particular connection.

[154] See Capotorti, *loc. cit.*, pp. 525–526.

[155] This is in line with Capotorti, *loc. cit.*, p. 514.

[156] The first part of the analysis will deal with supervening impossibility of performance, fundamental change of circumstances, emergence of a new peremptory norm of general international law (*jus cogens*) and, to a degree, severance of diplomatic or consular relations (arts. 61–64 of the Convention).

[157] These circumstances include the subsequent emergence of a new international custom, a war or State succession, all of which could result in the modification of the unilateral act in question, as will be shown.

otherwise be obliged to do the impossible. The loss or disappearance of an object indispensable for the execution of the unilateral act is the basic feature of this ground for termination (for example, the loss of a territory or a strip of coastline with respect to which the unilateral act produced effects).[158]

111. The impossibility referred to in article 61, which is applicable by analogy to unilateral acts, must have the following characteristics: (*a*) the impossibility must be supervening; (*b*) the impossibility must be definitive or irreversible, since it would otherwise lead to suspension rather than termination; and (*c*) it must affect an object which is indispensable for the execution of the act, since the impossibility must be instrumental, although not necessarily physical or material.

112. An interesting question arises if the State that formulated the unilateral act contributed by its own conduct to the emergence of the material impossibility and is ultimately responsible for the loss. However, it is important to distinguish between two factors which are not differentiated in the 1969 Vienna Convention: the situation of loss, which could—and logically should—lead to the termination or possible suspension of the unilateral act, and the possible international responsibility incurred by the State which, through its conduct, caused the material impossibility. This does not mean that the party concerned cannot invoke impossibility, which is a fact, but rather that it cannot be absolved of its international responsibility *vis-à-vis* third parties. This issue is likely to cause controversy in the majority of cases, which can be settled by the means provided under international law.

113. The invocation of a fundamental change of circumstances as a ground for terminating an international treaty is one of the most extensively studied issues in the legal literature.[159] The contrast between this ground and the rule of *pacta sunt servanda* is one of the most complex debates in treaty law.[160] The necessary flexibility of the international order, where the will of the State and the external reality that determines it play a fundamental role, demonstrates the significance of this clause; this is only logical since the strict application of the *pacta sunt servanda* principle, without exception, "will violate the *pacta* principle itself by giving it a sacred, almost mystical, character and elevating it to a *noli me tangere*".[161] The importance of this ground for termination may be the primary and ultimate reason for the degree of detail and the negative wording of article 62 of the 1969 Vienna Convention, which limit the possibility of invoking that circumstance. This reflects the restrictive position taken in the literature on the possible invocation of this ground, as a logical consequence of the need to prevent arbitrary actions which otherwise might be taken. Regarding the fundamental character that the changed circumstance must have, it has been logically affirmed in the literature that

> [t]he changed circumstance must be fundamental; it must affect, as has been said, the *fundamentum* or very basis of the treaty, and must be extraordinary in that it transcends or exceeds the ordinary changes that are rightly and typically anticipated in the drawing up of private contracts or international treaties.[162]

114. The definition of a fundamental change of circumstances is subject to a wide variety of interpretations and may even be applied to a situation of war between the parties. In the *Rann of Kutch* case between India and Pakistan, India compared the Ihlen declaration, which was taken into account by PCIJ in the dispute between Denmark and Norway,[163] to the circumstances of the current case, declaring before the Tribunal that

> the Ihlen declaration was made at a time when there was no dispute between Denmark and Norway; the attitude changed when the dispute arose subsequently. The declaration cannot be put on a par with one sentence in one letter after an acute dispute had arisen and when "parties are fighting each other, as it were, in correspondence over a particular attitude".[164]

115. It has been maintained that articles 61 (Supervening impossibility of performance) and 62 (Fundamental change of circumstances) of the 1969 Vienna Convention[165] could be applied *mutatis mutandis* to certain unilateral acts (particularly those which give rise to obligations), given that the conditions for modification and termination are very close to those provided for in treaty law with respect to the suspension or termination of obligations arising from an international treaty.[166] However,

---

[158] As noted in the literature, this circumstance is somewhat similar to a fundamental change of circumstances, which will be analysed further on. In "Terminación y suspensión de los tratados", p. 103, Ruda writes:

> "It is undeniable that the disappearance or destruction of the object of the treaty constitutes a fundamental change in the circumstances that existed at the time the treaty was concluded, but the International Law Commission interprets these situations as two legally distinct grounds. The difference, in our understanding, is that supervening impossibility of performance is an objective criterion, whereas a fundamental change of circumstances is determined subjectively; this distinction is worthy of separate study."

[159] See Haraszti, "Treaties and the fundamental change of circumstances", pp. 46–64.

[160] The bibliography on this subject is extensive. The Special Rapporteur will simply mention the statement made by Van Bogaert prior to the conclusion of the studies which led to the 1969 Vienna Convention, "Le sens de la clause '*rebus sic stantibus*' dans le droit des gens actuel", p. 50, to the effect that "[i]t is useful to note that *pacta sunt servanda* and *rebus sic stantibus* are the two elements which ensure that the law is efficient and, at the same time, equitable".

[161] Poch de Caviedes, "From the *clausula rebus sic stantibus* to the revision clause in international conventions", p. 168.

[162] *Ibid.*, p. 170.

[163] *Legal Status of Eastern Greenland* (see footnote 57 above), p. 70.

[164] *International Law Reports* (London), vol. 50, 1976, p. 379. See also the case concerning the Indo-Pakistan Western boundary (*Rann of Kutch*) between India and Pakistan, UNRIAA, vol. XVII, p. 410.

[165] According to Sicault, *loc. cit.*, pp. 654–655, a fundamental change of circumstances may be invoked by a State that formulates a unilateral promise as a ground for revoking the promise, if the following three conditions are met: (*a*) the existence of those circumstances must have constituted an essential basis of the consent to be bound by the promise; (*b*) the change of circumstances must radically transform obligations still to be performed under the unilateral act; and (*c*) the change of circumstances must not have resulted from a breach by the author of the promise of an international obligation (either of an obligation under the promise or of any other obligation).

[166] There is one particularly sensitive area in which States often show great suspicion or formulate protests when other parties adopt controversial conduct: issues related to disarmament or to moratoriums on nuclear testing. What is more, States often make commitments that are not strictly unilateral, but are directly related to the conduct of another State. One example of this was the announcement by the Soviet Union on 18 December 1986 that it would resume nuclear testing whenever the United States did so, thereby ending the moratorium which had been in place since 6 August 1985. After the United States conducted an underground nuclear test on 3 February 1987 at the Nevada nuclear testing ground (followed by further tests on 11 February and 18 March),

in the context of unilateral acts such situations entail an additional circumstance which normally does not occur in treaty law, namely the unilateral modification of the content of the unilateral act. This explains the cautious attitude of ICJ in its consideration of the invocation of a fundamental change of circumstances, as shown by the *Gabčíkovo-Nagymaros Project* case:

> A fundamental change of circumstances must have been unforeseen; the existence of the circumstances at the time of the Treaty's conclusion must have constituted an essential basis of the consent of the parties to be bound by the Treaty. The negative and conditional wording of Article 62 of the Vienna Convention on the Law of Treaties is a clear indication moreover that the stability of treaty relations requires that the plea of fundamental change of circumstances be applied only in exceptional cases.[167]

116. Sometimes the psychological element or the belief by the formulating State that there has been a fundamental change in the circumstances that prompted it to adopt its initial position take on special importance. An interesting example is the position adopted by Poland, which initially notified ILO of its withdrawal from that organization and subsequently invalidated the withdrawal through another notification the day before the initial notice was to have taken effect.[168]

117. Could the severance of diplomatic or consular relations result in such a change as to bring about the termination or suspension—or perhaps modification—of a unilateral act? In principle, if one were to follow the approach that was taken in codifying international treaties, such a severance of relations need not bring about significant changes, except as could otherwise be inferred from the contents of the unilateral act itself (for example, if diplomatic or consular relations are a condition without which the unilateral act would not have been formulated or if it would be very difficult to carry out in the absence of this circumstance). Accordingly, article 63 of the 1969 Vienna Convention provides that:

> "The severance of diplomatic or consular relations between parties to a treaty does not affect the legal relations established between them by the treaty except insofar as the existence of diplomatic or consular relations is indispensable for the application of the treaty."

The Convention uses the word "indispensable"; thus it may be inferred that the same requirement should apply to unilateral acts. However, the Special Rapporteur is reluctant to subscribe to that view; indeed, it is his understanding that typically, where diplomatic or consular relations have been severed, it is highly unlikely that the State which formulated the act will be prepared to continue to carry it out, at least in the same manner.

118. The emergence of a new peremptory norm of general international law (*jus cogens*), as provided in article 64 of the 1969 Vienna Convention, more or less stands in logical correlation to article 53 of the Convention, to which reference has already been made. Article 64 provides that: "If a new peremptory norm of general international law emerges, any existing treaty which is in conflict with that norm becomes void and terminates." However, despite the words at the end of that article ("becomes void and terminates"), one is dealing here with a case of extinction upon the emergence of a norm of *jus cogens* and not properly of invalidity, as discussed earlier. The consequences of this are substantial: the effects which the treaty produced up until the new norm's emergence will remain unaffected wherever possible, as opposed to what would occur in a case of invalidity as such. That is the major distinction between the two provisions mentioned above.

119. In view of the foregoing, the following paragraphs may be formulated with regard to other possible causes of termination under the above-mentioned guiding principle:

"*Termination of unilateral acts (continued)*

"A unilateral act may be terminated or revoked by the formulating State:

"...

"(*c*) If the subject matter of the unilateral act has ceased to exist;

"(*d*) If there has been a fundamental change in the circumstances that prompted the formulation of the act (*rebus sic stantibus*) which renders its fulfilment impossible;

"(*e*) If a peremptory norm of international law has emerged following its formulation which conflicts with the act."

(b) *Situations not expressly provided for in the 1969 Vienna Convention*

120. An issue of relevance that arises with respect to unilateral acts is whether a customary rule that emerges subsequent to the formulation of a unilateral act may result in the termination, modification or suspension of the act as being in conflict with that rule. This issue, the answer to which is uncertain, was raised by the Commission when the law of treaties was being codified. However, the Commission decided, given the numerous difficulties involved in the controversial issue of the possible conflict between treaty and customary rules, that the issue was too complex to be covered in all its aspects without jeopardizing the work of codification and progressive development.[169] Possibly, a normative basis on which to tackle this issue may be found in the area of universal or general custom;

---

the Soviet Government officially announced on 4 February that the United States action had ended the moratorium. The Soviet Union resumed nuclear testing on 26 February in Kazakhstan (Rousseau, *loc. cit.* (1987), p. 945).

[167] *Gabčíkovo-Nagymaros Project (Hungary/Slovakia), Judgment, I.C.J. Reports 1997*, p. 65, para. 104.

[168] On 17 November 1984, Poland, through its representative in Geneva, gave notice to the ILO Governing Body of its withdrawal from that organization. Its letter reiterated the charges it had been levelling for three years against ILO, including interference in Poland's internal affairs, a continuing anti-Polish campaign and a hostile attitude towards Poland (Rousseau, *loc. cit.* (1985), p. 467). That notice would be rendered invalid when, on the morning of 16 November 1987, the Government of Poland informed the ILO Director-General that it was withdrawing its previous notice, being satisfied that the problems caused by actions taken against Poland within ILO, which had made it impossible for Poland to participate in the organization's work, would be settled once and for all. Poland's withdrawal from the organization was to have become effective on 16 November 1987 at midnight (*ibid.* (1988), p. 407).

[169] See Capotorti, *loc. cit.*, p. 518.

on the other hand, the Special Rapporteur finds regional custom more problematic, given that the existence of a unilateral act contrary to what is claimed to be regional or even local custom could act as a serious impediment to such custom gaining currency or even being opposable to the State which formulated the unilateral act. Practice shows that the opposite situation is more frequent; that is to say, the existence of many unilateral acts on a particular matter tends to bring about a change in the legal regime in effect until that time. Such a new approach may even be set forth in a treaty.[170]

121. A second case not addressed in the 1969 Vienna Convention is the issue as to what happens to unilateral acts when their author undergoes a substantial transformation. In other words, what happens in case of State succession? Should the previous undertakings entered into under unilateral acts remain in force or do such undertakings become ineffective when such a circumstance occurs, especially in cases where the predecessor State disappears? This issue, which is not easy where international treaties are concerned,[171] is even less so in the case of unilateral acts, where the conflict between two competing needs that arise at the international level becomes even more evident: the need to ensure a certain stability in international relations, with adherence to international undertakings deriving from unilateral acts being a key reflection of this. In each case, the solution will depend on the particular circumstances, as well as whether it is still possible for the State or States emerging from the succession to comply with the unilateral act. In the view of the Special Rapporteur, there are no criteria that point *a priori* to a restrictive approach one way or another. Clearly, however, where a State has undergone a very significant transformation as a result of a succession, the unilateral act may as a result be modified.

122. On the other hand, there also arises the issue as to whether the outbreak of an armed conflict can cause the termination or suspension of a unilateral act in effect between the two belligerent States. As with the issue discussed above, the 1969 Vienna Convention merely states that it does not cover this situation. Article 73 of the Convention expressly states that: "The provisions of the present Convention shall not prejudge any question that may arise in regard to a treaty from a succession of States or from the international responsibility of a State or from the outbreak of hostilities between States." Given its controversial nature, this issue was set aside. The Commission has now reverted to it and appointed Mr. Brownlie as Special Rapporteur for the topic; he submitted his first report in 2005.[172]

123. On this point, it is the view of the Special Rapporteur that, more clearly than in any other circumstance, the unilateral act at issue must be looked at to determine whether war affects the performance of a particular unilateral act. Perhaps, where the act constitutes a promise or waiver which operates to the advantage of the State with which the author State is at war, the author State may elect to terminate it or, at a minimum, to suspend it. In addition, a fundamental change of circumstances may even be invoked. A highly politicized institution such as recognition is usually subject to change in cases of armed conflict and may even give rise to other situations, such as recognition of the state of armed conflict, with the consequences that this entails.[173]

124. The above discussion on the validity, grounds for invalidity and application of unilateral acts, which is heavily influenced by the Vienna regime, is intended to complement earlier reports, to clarify these issues to the extent possible and, indeed, to provide the Commission with a set of guiding principles in this specific area. All these comments, with the exception of those relating to suspension, have already been set out in the relevant section, but the Special Rapporteur elected to reiterate them as a whole at this juncture in order not to lose sight of the overall picture.

"*Suspension of unilateral acts*

"A unilateral act may be suspended by the formulating State:

"(*a*) If a circumstance that would allow for its suspension was specified at the time of its formulation;

"(*b*) If the act was subject to a suspensive condition at the time of its formulation;

"(*c*) If its subject matter has temporarily ceased to exist;

"(*d*) If there has been a fundamental change in the circumstances that prompted the formulation of the act which temporarily renders its fulfilment impossible."

[170] This is what occurred, for example, in the law of the sea with respect to the extension of the territorial sea to 12 nautical miles and the establishment of the exclusive economic zone, the origin of which is directly tied to the concept of a "patrimonial sea" (Seve de Gastón, "Los actos jurídicos internacionales unilaterales con especial atinencia a los intereses marítimos argentinos", p. 260, who provides an overview of all these issues and an illustrative listing of unilateral acts of States (sorted by continent), *ibid.*, pp. 260–261 and 295–357.

[171] The lack of an international consensus in favour of the principle of continuity with respect to international treaties to which the predecessor was a party, as opposed to the *tabula rasa* approach, is becoming evident. This is demonstrated by two factors. The first is the limited acceptance of the Vienna Convention on Succession of States in respect of Treaties (hereinafter the 1978 Vienna Convention), which resulted in it not securing the number of ratifications required for its entry into force until 1996. The second factor is reflected in the many divergences observed in international practice over the last decade, with continuity, notification of succession, accession to or termination of the effects of the international treaties of the predecessor all being frequently observed. As Koskenniemi has highlighted in "Report of the Director of Studies of the English-speaking section of the Centre", p. 89: "The only relatively undoubted normative conclusion one can draw remains procedural: that States should negotiate in good faith. That obligation is not, however, dependent on the 1978 Vienna Convention but on a structural requirement of the diplomatic system."

[172] In 2005, the first report on the effects of armed conflicts on treaties (*Yearbook ... 2005*, vol. II (Part One), document A/CN.4/552, p. 209) was submitted together with a memorandum by the Secretariat entitled "The effect of armed conflict on treaties: an examination of practice and doctrine" (A/CN.4/550 and Corr.1–2), reproduced on the website of the Commission.

[173] For an exhaustive discussion of this issue, see Verhoeven, *op. cit.*, pp. 100–167.

Chapter II

Draft guiding principles for consideration by the Working Group

125. As mentioned at the beginning of this report, the Commission is being provided with draft guiding principles on the various issues discussed earlier in the Commission and in the Sixth Committee. These draft guiding principles could be considered by the Working Group on unilateral acts of States to be reconvened this year. This set of guiding principles covers the validity and termination of unilateral acts, a topic discussed in chapter I of the present report.

A. Definition of a unilateral act

126. One of the most extensively debated issues in the Commission since it began considering this topic in 1997 has been the definition of a unilateral act, which is crucial for developing rules or guiding principles governing the operation of such acts. The first issue in this regard is the distinction between unilateral legal acts and unilateral acts of States not aimed at establishing or confirming a legal relationship; that is, unilateral political acts. From the outset, special emphasis has been placed on the need to make a distinction between the two types, which is a difficult proposition for the purposes of which it is crucial to determine the intention of the author State. Unilateral legal acts would, of course, be subject to international law and failure to comply therewith would cause the author State to incur international responsibility. Unilateral political acts would commit the State only in the political context, and the State would incur only political consequences for non-compliance.

127. Without revisiting the topic, it should be recalled that the Commission has held detailed discussions, in the plenary and in the Working Group on unilateral acts of States, on some acts that are within the framework of international political relations and, as such, fall outside the scope of international law, including the unilateral declarations of nuclear-weapon States referred to as negative security assurances, formulated at various levels and in various international bodies and contexts. In the view of the majority of members, such declarations are political in nature and as such are not legally binding on the declaring States. A detailed review of the texts of such declarations and of the circumstances or contexts in which they were formulated shows that the declaring States had no intention of entering into legal obligations in connection with such negative security assurances. These were therefore unilateral political declarations not subject to international law.

128. From the outset the members also generally agreed to single out those unilateral legal acts of States that are clearly part of a treaty relationship and as such fall under the 1969 Vienna Convention. These are acts which are unilateral in form, that is, formulated by a single State—but are part of a treaty relationship. Examples include signature, ratification, formulation and withdrawal of reservations, notification and deposit of relevant treaty instruments, among others. A unilateral act, *sensu stricto*, establishes a relationship between the author State and the addressee or addressees, but this relationship is distinct from a treaty relationship.

129. Another category to be identified is unilateral acts connected with a particular regime authorized by a specific set of rules. Declarations establishing exclusive economic zones or, in general, the delimitation of maritime zones are examples of such acts.

130. Also excluded are declarations of acceptance of the compulsory jurisdiction of ICJ, which, although they are also unilateral as to their form, fall under the Vienna regime on the law of treaties. While such declarations are formally unilateral, most international scholarship and case law consider them as being part of a treaty relationship and as such falling within the Vienna regime. However, these are *sui generis* optional declarations to which certain rules, such as the rules of interpretation, should be applied more flexibly. It should be recalled, in this regard, that in the case concerning *Military and Paramilitary Activities in and against Nicaragua*, the United States contended that such declarations

> are *sui generis*, are not treaties, and are not governed by the law of treaties, and States have the sovereign right to qualify an acceptance of the Court's compulsory jurisdiction, which is an inherent feature of the Optional-Clause system as reflected in, and developed by, State practice.[174]

131. While mindful of their *sui generis* nature, as it had been in previous cases, such as the *Anglo-Iranian Oil Co.* case, ICJ took the view that such declarations were indeed part of a treaty relationship. Declarations accepting the Court's jurisdiction, it noted, were not a treaty text resulting from negotiations between two or more States but "the result of unilateral drafting".[175] The fact that such declarations are registered and deposited with the Secretary-General supports this view. From a reading of the Court's 1984 judgment, it may be concluded that, even though such declarations fall under a treaty regime, the fact that they were unilaterally drafted should be taken into account when interpreting them.

132. The unilateral acts that have been under consideration by the Commission since 1997, namely unilateral declarations made by one or more States with a view to producing certain legal effects, should be distinguished, at least as far as their formulation or realization are concerned, from equally unilateral conduct which, without being an act in the strict sense of the term, is capable of producing similar legal effects. Considering both unilateral acts and unilateral conduct in the same study was not deemed acceptable by the majority, although some members and some Governments were of the view that their consideration should be related, since, even though they could be "formulated" or "realized" under different circumstances, they could have similar effects. Although, in the view of the Special Rapporteur, there are clear differences between acts and conduct, at least with regard to their formulation, it was felt that conduct should not be excluded from the study and from adequate consideration

[174] *I.C.J. Reports 1984* (see footnote 119 above), p. 415, para. 53.

[175] *Anglo-Iranian Oil Co., Preliminary Objection, Judgment, I.C.J. Reports 1952*, p. 105.

by the Commission. The guiding principles with regard to unilateral acts in the strict sense could be applicable *mutatis mutandis* to unilateral conduct by States.

133. Based on the reports of the Special Rapporteur, the Commission very thoroughly reviewed a series of classic unilateral acts which are considered as such by most legal scholars (recognition, promise, waiver, protest), and concluded that, while it was a useful intellectual exercise that in some ways enriched the international doctrine on the subject, the Commission was aware that the characterization of the act does not alter its legal effects. A unilateral act, as the Commission concluded at the time, may be characterized in various ways, without influencing the legal effects that the author of the act is seeking to produce. Independently of its characterization, what was important was to determine whether the author State, at the time it formulated the act, intended to commit itself legally in relation to the addressee or addressees.

134. The unilateral act of interest to the Commission is a declaration, made by one or more States, whose form—it should be made clear—is not important and which contains an expression of unilateral will formulated with the intention of assuming certain obligations or of confirming certain rights. It is an act whose process of elaboration differs from the process of elaboration of a treaty in which two or more States participate; this makes it difficult to determine the intention of the author to be legally bound.

135. The author of the act seeks through such a declaration "to produce certain legal effects", a more generic expression that encompasses both the obligations that the declaring State may assume and the rights that it may reaffirm through such an act. This question has been extensively debated in the literature and in the Commission. A State, it was affirmed, may assume unilateral obligations in the exercise of its sovereignty, but cannot impose obligations on another State without the latter's consent, as was established in the regime on the law of treaties. However, some members expressed the view that to refer exclusively to the assumption of obligations would limit the scope of the draft articles and that reference should be made to the production of legal effects that cover both the possibility of assuming obligations and that of reaffirming rights.

136. A unilateral act should be formulated "under international law", since it is itself derived from international law and thus becomes a source of obligations[176] (and even of the reaffirmation of rights), like treaty or customary norms or acts of international organizations.

137. As a reflection of what has been stated above and in accordance with the results of the Commission's deliberations and the conclusions of the Working Group on unilateral acts of States established to consider the question, the following draft guiding principle is presented. The draft text covers in general terms the constituent elements of the draft definition which the Special Rapporteur presented in his first report[177] and which served at the time as an initial basis of discussion to develop the study of the subject.

"*Principle 1. Definition of a unilateral act*

"A unilateral act of a State means a unilateral declaration formulated by a State with the intent of producing certain legal effects under international law."

138. In the context of the definition and its scope, reference should now be made to the addressee (or addressees) of the act. While the subject under consideration and the draft guiding principles concern unilateral acts formulated by a State, it is important to note that such acts may be addressed to another State, to a group of States, to the international community as a whole, to an international organization or to any other entity subject to international law.

139. It is therefore necessary to include a reference to this characteristic in the definition (para. 2). The Commission is presented with two options for this paragraph, the first of which enumerates the possible addressees of unilateral acts, thereby giving the paragraph a more restrictive character, while the second and broader option specifies that a unilateral act must be formulated in accordance with international law, but does not specify to whom it must be addressed.[178]

"*Principle 1*

"2. *Addressees of unilateral acts of States*

"Option A

"A unilateral act may be addressed to one or more States, the international community as a whole, one or more international organizations or any other entity subject to international law.

"Option B

"A unilateral act formulated in accordance with international law will produce legal effects, regardless of to whom it was addressed."

B. Formulation of a unilateral act

1. Capacity of a State to formulate a unilateral act

140. As is the case under the law of treaties, the State has capacity to formulate unilateral acts. Indeed, the State may, in the exercise of its sovereignty, formulate declarations with the intent to produce certain legal effects, assuming unilateral obligations that, given their nature, do not require acceptance or any reaction on the part of the addressee. The term used is "formulate", which is similar to the terms

[176] In this connection, reference must be made to the terms used by ICJ in its judgment of 3 February 2006 on admissibility in the case concerning *Armed Activities on the Territory of the Congo, I.C.J. Reports 2006* (see footnote 40 above), p. 26, para. 45 (in which it uses the expression "unilateral commitment having legal effects"), and p. 27, para. 46 (in which it refers to "performance, on behalf of the said State, of unilateral acts having the force of international commitments").

[177] *Yearbook ... 1998*, vol. II (Part One), p. 319, document A/CN.4/486.

[178] It suffices to recall in this regard some of the examples mentioned in the eighth report on unilateral acts of States, which include among the addressees of a unilateral act even the officers of an international organization or entities that are not States as such (*Yearbook ... 2005* (see footnote 1 above), p. 126, paras. 44–54 and pp. 133–135, paras. 138–156).

"elaboration" or "conclusion" used in treaty law. Indeed, it has been noted that "formulation" reflects the unilateral form of the act, while the "elaboration" or "conclusion" of a treaty presumes agreement or a common intent, which is unnecessary in the context of unilateral acts.

141. In this way, closely following the language of the 1969 Vienna Convention (art. 6), every State has capacity to formulate a unilateral act, provided, in this case, that it is done "in accordance with international law". The guiding principle would therefore be drafted as follows:

"*Principle 2. Capacity of States to formulate unilateral acts*

"Every State possesses capacity to formulate unilateral acts in accordance with international law."

2. Persons having competence to formulate unilateral acts on behalf of a State

142. A somewhat more complex question concerning the formulation of unilateral acts is that of the competence of the persons who can formulate an act of this nature on behalf of the State and commit the State in its international relations. The question has been considered by the Commission on various occasions, particularly during the debates that followed the presentation of the second and third reports on unilateral acts of States. As will be recalled, the Special Rapporteur presented some general and preliminary ideas on the subject, which were consistent with the opinions expressed both by the members of the Commission and by some of the States that responded to the questionnaire sent out by the Secretariat.[179]

143. Like the formula which must be taken as the point of departure, in accordance with the Vienna regime on the law of treaties, certain persons may without authorization act and bind the State in its international relations (Heads of State, Heads of Government and ministers for foreign affairs), on the assumption that these individuals have full powers to do so. As ICJ recently observed in accordance with its consistent jurisprudence:

> [I]t is a well-established rule of international law that the Head of State, the Head of Government and the Minister for Foreign Affairs are deemed to represent the State merely by virtue of exercising their functions, including for the performance, on behalf of the said State, of unilateral acts having the force of international commitments.[180]

144. Paragraph 1 of the draft guiding principle, which contains this general rule, would read as follows:

"*Principle 3. Competence to formulate unilateral acts on behalf of the State*[181]

"1. By virtue of their office, Heads of State, Heads of Government and ministers for foreign affairs are considered to represent their State and to have the capacity to formulate unilateral acts on its behalf."[182]

145. In addition to the persons referred to in draft principle 3, paragraph 1, there might be other persons who could act on behalf of the State and bind it by formulating a unilateral declaration. Within the Sixth Committee, various opinions have been expressed indicating a reluctance to broaden the circle of persons qualified to formulate unilateral acts.[183] Moreover, within the Commission itself, a number of members cited examples to show that, although in many cases representatives to international conferences had made declarations that appeared to be binding in some way on the States they were representing, ultimately that did not prove to be the case.[184]

146. It is true that this provision raises many problems, as indicated above; nonetheless, it is a common practice, especially in the context of certain international bodies or organizations, for representatives of the State other than those mentioned above to perform acts by which they may and in fact do bind the State that they represent.[185]

147. In the Commission's deliberations, the possibility has been put forward that persons other than the Head of State or Government or the minister for foreign affairs may also be authorized under international law to act on behalf of and bind the State in this sphere. During these debates the view has been expressed that a person other than those mentioned might act and bind the State in this sphere if that person can be considered authorized to do so. This narrow innovation would reflect the evolving nature of international relations and the possibility that some persons may be empowered to act and do in fact act on behalf of the State. The special nature of unilateral acts, in this view, makes it necessary to devise a more flexible rule than the rule for treaties, while framing it in such a way that only in specific cases and circumstances may the State be bound by persons other than those traditionally contemplated under the Vienna regime.

148. In its judgment of 3 February 2006 on the jurisdiction of the Court and the admissibility of the application

---

[179] See, for example, the opinions of Argentina and Israel, *Yearbook ... 2000* (see footnote 130 above), pp. 271–272.

[180] *I.C.J. Reports 2006* (see footnote 40 above), p. 27, para. 46.

[181] This heading reflects the wording suggested by Mr. Pambou-Tchivounda (*Yearbook ... 2000*, vol. I, 2628th meeting, p. 128, para. 31).

[182] The need to have a restrictive criterion for determining who has the capacity to bind the State through the formulation of unilateral acts was stressed by many of the States that answered the questionnaire sent out by the Secretariat (see *Yearbook ... 2000* (footnote 130 above), p. 265). In that regard, in a meeting of the Commission, Mr. Momtaz expressed the view that the capacity to formulate a unilateral act should be restricted to those persons mentioned in article 7, paragraph 2 (*a*), of the 1969 Vienna Convention (see *Yearbook ... 2002*, vol. I, 2723rd meeting, p. 82, para. 30).

[183] The representative of Chile, for instance, in discussing the possibility of adopting a flexible criterion for determining which persons should have the capacity to formulate unilateral acts, said that his delegation was opposed to adopting rules more flexible than those contained in the 1969 Vienna Convention. See *Official Records of the General Assembly, Sixtieth Session, Sixth Committee*, 16th meeting, para. 47, in which he stated that such flexibility was dangerous and could lead to abuses, since it was left to the addressee State to determine whether the person who had formulated a given declaration, without being formally empowered to do so, was actually authorized to bind the State that person claimed to represent. Under article 7, paragraph 1 (*b*), of the Convention, flexibility in the matter of representing the State was limited to the practice of the States concerned, so that the decision was not left to one State alone. The representative of Kenya agreed and expressed the view that the category of persons with capacity to bind the State should be restricted to that defined in article 7 of the Convention (*ibid.*, para. 73).

[184] See the examples cited by Mr. Hafner in *Yearbook ... 1999*, vol. I, 2595th meeting, p. 205, para. 34.

[185] Consider, for example, what occurs when State representatives, who are of ministerial rank but are not necessarily ministers for foreign affairs, meet in the Council of the European Union.

filed by the Democratic Republic of the Congo against Rwanda, ICJ noted that

with increasing frequency in modern international relations other persons representing a State in specific fields may be authorized by that State to bind it by their statements in respect of matters falling within their purview. This may be true, for example, of holders of technical ministerial portfolios exercising powers in their field of competence in the area of foreign relations, and even of certain officials.[186]

This citation supports the notion that persons other than those authorized to act on behalf of the State in the treaty sphere may bind the State through the formulation of a unilateral statement or declaration, as can be inferred from the text of the ICJ judgment in the cited case, with reference to the actions of the Minister of Justice of Rwanda.

149. The Special Rapporteur should add that, in addition to the possibility of inferring from practice that a person may act on behalf of and bind the State that he/she represents in a given sphere, the circumstances in which a particular unilateral act has been formulated are also relevant, as will be seen below. The manner in which it was formulated, the terms of the declaration (and, as ICJ indicated, the clarity and precision of those terms) and the context, which together provide all the relevant information surrounding the unilateral act, will be critical factors.

150. On the understanding that the above question will be considered in greater detail further on in relation to the interpretation of unilateral acts, the Special Rapporteur will now present guiding principle 3, paragraph 2, which is worded as follows:

"In addition to the persons mentioned in the previous paragraph, other persons may be considered able to formulate unilateral acts on behalf of the State if that may be inferred from the practice followed in that regard by the formulating State and from the circumstances in which the act was formulated."

3. Subsequent confirmation of a unilateral act formulated without authorization

151. As is the case in treaty law, a unilateral act may be confirmed by the State when it has been formulated by a person not authorized or qualified to do so. In previous reports the Special Rapporteur suggested that, given the nature of unilateral acts, such confirmation must be explicit; however, that view did not meet with broad support from the members of the Commission.

152. In addition to the consideration given to the question in chapter I of the present report in relation to the grounds for invalidity of a unilateral act, the Special Rapporteur will now present the following draft guiding principle concerning confirmation:

"*Principle 4. Subsequent confirmation of an act formulated by a person without authorization (or not qualified to do so)*

"A unilateral act formulated by a person not authorized (or qualified) to act on behalf of the State, in accordance with the previous guiding principles, may be confirmed subsequently by the State either expressly or through conclusive acts from which such confirmation can be clearly inferred."

C. Basis for the binding nature of unilateral acts

153. Since the first report on the topic was submitted to the Commission,[187] the question of the basis of unilateral acts, that is, what makes them binding, has come up for discussion on a number of occasions, but there has been no unanimity of opinion on the matter. Without going into great detail and reverting to previous reports and debates in the Commission, the Special Rapporteur merely notes that neither the legal literature[188] nor the members of the Commission have taken a unified position that would allow him to determine clearly what constitutes the basis for the binding nature of unilateral acts.[189]

154. One basic principle that must be taken into account is good faith, if the view expressed by ICJ in 1974 is followed:

One of the basic principles governing the creation and performance of legal obligations, whatever their source, is the principle of good faith. Trust and confidence are inherent in international co-operation, in particular in an age when this co-operation in many fields is becoming increasingly essential. Just as the very rule of *pacta sunt servanda* in the law of treaties is based on good faith, so also is the binding character of an international obligation assumed by unilateral declaration. Thus interested States may take cognizance of unilateral declarations and place confidence in them, and are entitled to require that the obligation thus created be respected.[190]

155. Realistically, the intention of the State that formulated the unilateral act also constitutes an element that must be given considerable weight in determining the basis of the binding nature of unilateral acts. This opinion, expressed within the Commission,[191] finds support in the legal literature[192] and ICJ decisions.[193] In the judgment of 3 February 2006 cited above, the Court reaffirmed the necessity of taking into account the "actual content [of a

---

[186] *I.C.J. Reports 2006* (see footnote 40 above), p. 27, para. 47.

[187] See *Yearbook ... 1998* (footnote 177 above), pp. 336–337, paras. 152–162.

[188] On this point, Bondía García, *Régimen jurídico de los actos unilaterales de los Estados*, notably on page 76, chooses to offer a dual basis: a subjective criterion, consisting in the intent of the State to give binding effect to the unilateral act, and an objective criterion, which is based on the protection of legitimate confidence (good faith); in another example from Spanish legal literature, Zafra Espinosa de los Monteros, *Aproximación a una teoría de los actos unilaterales de los Estados*, pp. 54–56, opts to follow closely the view expressed by ICJ in the *Nuclear Tests* cases and makes good faith and mutual trust the basis of the binding character.

[189] An attempt was made to base the binding nature of unilateral acts on a rule such as *acta sunt servanda* or *declaratio est servanda*, but that solution met with many criticisms. Some members of the Commission went so far as to say that "there was no need to invent any special rule such as *declaratio est servanda* ... The principle of good faith was enough" (view of Mr. Lukashuk, *Yearbook ... 1998*, vol. I, 2524th meeting, p. 37, para. 47).

[190] *I.C.J. Reports 1974* (see footnote 139 above), p. 268, para. 46.

[191] *Yearbook ... 2000* (see footnote 50 above), p. 252, paras. 35–36.

[192] In this regard, see Higgins, *Problems and Process: International Law and How We Use It*, p. 35; see also Bondía García, *op. cit.*, pp. 76–77.

[193] Turning once again to *Nuclear Tests (Australia* v. *France)*, for example, the following is found: "[I]n whatever form these statements were expressed, they must be held to constitute an engagement of the State, having regard to their intention and to the circumstances in which they were made" (*I.C.J. Reports 1974* (see footnote 139 above), p. 269, para. 49).

statement] as well as the circumstances in which it was made" (in other words, its context); the Court goes on to say that "a statement of this kind can create legal obligations only if it is made in clear and specific terms".[194]

156. In the light of the foregoing, a guiding principle could be framed concerning the basis for the binding nature of unilateral acts, worded as follows:[195]

"*Principle 10. Basis for the binding nature of unilateral acts*

"The binding nature of the unilateral acts of States is based on the principle of good faith and the intent to be bound of the State that formulated the act."

D. Interpretation of unilateral acts

157. Given the nature of unilateral acts, to formulate rules of interpretation for them similar to those already existing for treaties proves practically impossible. In both the fourth and the fifth reports[196] presented to the Commission, a few preliminary criteria were formulated to offer some guidelines for the interpretation of unilateral acts. The diverse views expressed by Commission members illustrated clearly the many difficulties involved in arriving at generally acceptable criteria for interpreting unilateral acts.[197] Some of the suggestions of the Special Rapporteur in the above-mentioned reports, such as a reference to recourse to the preparatory work, preambles or annexes, which are useful in connection with international treaties, had to be abandoned, because they did not find favour with the majority of the Commission members[198] or of the authors of the legal literature.[199]

158. The Special Rapporteur should point out that the unilateral statements considered by ICJ, whether or not they were formulated in the context of a treaty relationship, were subject to interpretation, so that it is appropriate to mention them at this point. The Court concluded that a restrictive interpretation was called for when States made statements by which their freedom of action was to be limited, and it stressed the need to consider the circumstances in which such a unilateral act was formulated, as well as the clarity and precision of its terms, as mentioned earlier.[200]

159. All the above elements may be used to interpret a unilateral act; in this sphere context plays a key role and must be given considerable weight when assessing a unilateral act and deducing the possible legal consequences deriving from it.

160. Following that line of thought, the Special Rapporteur arrives at the following draft guiding principle:

"*Principle 11. Interpretation of unilateral acts*

"The context in which a unilateral act was formulated by a State, together with the clarity and precision of its terms, shall be given weight in interpreting it."

161. The Special Rapporteur believes that he has fulfilled the task entrusted to him by the Commission by presenting the draft guiding principles, duly supported by reasoning, applicable to unilateral acts of States. If the Commission thinks it is appropriate, the draft principles could be referred to the Working Group on unilateral acts of States and at a later stage to the Drafting Committee for consideration. The Special Rapporteur feels that the guiding principles could be useful to States in assessing in practice the effects that might be produced by unilateral acts of States, a topic that the Commission has been considering since 1997.

---

[194] *I.C.J. Reports 2006* (see footnote 40 above), p. 28, paras. 49–50.

[195] The numerical placement of this draft guiding principle was changed because the Special Rapporteur feels that the proposed principles outlined in chapter I of this report, on the grounds for invalidity and termination of unilateral acts, should be presented first, before this guiding principle, as can be seen in the annex, where all the principles are laid out in consecutive order.

[196] In this regard, see *Yearbook ... 2001* (footnote 31 above), pp. 128–136, paras. 101–154, and *Yearbook ... 2002*, vol. II (Part One), document A/CN.4/525 and Add.1–2, paras. 120–135, where a general rule of interpretation and some supplementary means of interpretation were put forward.

[197] See *Yearbook ... 2001*, vol. II (Part Two), in particular pp. 204–205, paras. 239–244. At that time it was felt to be premature to deal with the issue of interpretation; some members felt that the provisions of the 1969 Vienna Convention could be helpful, while others expressed just the opposite view, given the unique nature of unilateral acts. The notions of object and purpose and of the context of a unilateral act were stressed during that session of the Commission.

[198] See *Yearbook ... 2002*, vol. II (Part Two), p. 86, paras. 405–406.

[199] See d'Aspremont Lynden, "Les travaux de la Commission du droit international relatifs aux actes unilatéraux des États", pp. 180–181, devoted in particular to the interpretation of unilateral acts.

[200] See *I.C.J. Reports 1974* (footnote 139 above), p. 267, para. 44, and *I.C.J. Reports 2006* (footnote 40 above), p. 28, paras. 49–50.

Annex

DRAFT GUIDING PRINCIPLES

In order to provide the Commission with an overview of the various draft guiding principles submitted for its consideration during this session, they are all presented below in order in a systematic fashion.

Principle 1.[*] *Definition of a unilateral act*

A unilateral act of a State means a unilateral declaration formulated by a State with the intent of producing certain legal effects under international law.

Addressees of unilateral acts of States

Option A

A unilateral act may be addressed to one or more States, the international community as a whole, one or more international organizations or any other entity subject to international law.

Option B

A unilateral act formulated in accordance with international law will produce legal effects, regardless of to whom it was addressed.

Principle 2. Capacity of States to formulate unilateral acts

Every State possesses capacity to formulate unilateral acts in accordance with international law.

Principle 3. Competence to formulate unilateral acts on behalf of the State

1. By virtue of their office, Heads of State, Heads of Government and ministers for foreign affairs are considered to represent their State and to have the capacity to formulate unilateral acts on its behalf.

2. In addition to the persons mentioned in the previous paragraph, other persons may be considered able to formulate unilateral acts on behalf of the State if that may be inferred from the practice followed in that regard by the formulating State and from the circumstances in which the act was formulated.

Principle 4. Subsequent confirmation of an act formulated by a person without authorization (or not qualified to do so)

A unilateral act formulated by a person not authorized (or qualified) to act on behalf of the State, in accordance with the previous guiding principles, may be confirmed subsequently by the State either expressly or through conclusive acts from which such confirmation can be clearly inferred.

Principle 5. Invalidity of an act formulated by a person not qualified to do so

A unilateral act formulated by a person not authorized or qualified to do so may be declared invalid, without prejudice to the possibility that the State from which the act was issued may confirm it in accordance with guiding principle 4.

Principle 6. Invalidity of a unilateral act that conflicts with a norm of fundamental importance to the domestic law of the State formulating it

A State that has formulated a unilateral act may not invoke as grounds for invalidity the fact that the act conflicts with its domestic law, unless it conflicts with a norm of fundamental importance to its domestic law and the contradiction is manifest.

Principle 7. Invalidity of unilateral acts

1. (*a*) A State that is the author of a unilateral act may not invoke error as grounds for declaring the act invalid, unless the act was formulated on the basis of an error of fact or a situation that was assumed by the State to exist at the time when the act was formulated and that fact or that situation formed an essential basis of its consent to be bound by the unilateral act;

(*b*) The foregoing shall not apply if the author State contributed by its own conduct to the error or if the circumstances were such as to put that State on notice of the possibility of such an error.

2. Fraud may be invoked as grounds for declaring a unilateral act invalid if the author State was induced to formulate the act by the fraudulent conduct of another State.

3. Corruption of the representative of the State may be invoked as grounds for declaring a unilateral act invalid if the act was formulated owing to the corruption of the person formulating it.

4. Coercion of the person who formulated a unilateral act may be invoked as grounds for declaring its invalidity if that person formulated it as a result of acts or threats directed against him or her.

5. Any unilateral act formulated as a result of the threat or use of force in violation of the principles of international law embodied in the Charter of the United Nations is invalid.

6. Any unilateral act which at the time of its formulation is contrary to (or conflicts with) a peremptory norm of general international law (*jus cogens*) is invalid.

Principle 8. Termination of unilateral acts

A unilateral act may be terminated or revoked by the formulating State:

(*a*) If a specific time limit for termination of the act was set at the time of its formulation (or if termination was implicit following the performance of one or more acts);

[*] Contains two potential paragraphs: one relating to the definition itself and another concerning the addressees of the unilateral act.

(*b*) If the act was subject to a resolutive condition at the time of its formulation;

(*c*) If the subject matter of the unilateral act has ceased to exist;

(*d*) If there has been a fundamental change in the circumstances that prompted the formulation of the act (*rebus sic stantibus*) which renders its fulfilment impossible;

(*e*) If a peremptory norm of international law has emerged following its formulation which conflicts with the act.

Principle 9. Suspension of unilateral acts

A unilateral act may be suspended by the formulating State:

(*a*) If a circumstance that would allow for its suspension was specified at the time of its formulation;

(*b*) If the act was subject to a suspensive condition at the time of its formulation;

(*c*) If its subject matter has temporarily ceased to exist;

(*d*) If there has been a fundamental change in the circumstances that prompted the formulation of the act which temporarily renders its fulfilment impossible.

Principle 10. Basis for the binding nature of unilateral acts

The binding nature of the unilateral acts of States is based on the principle of good faith and the intent to be bound of the State that formulated the act.

Principle 11. Interpretation of unilateral acts

The context in which a unilateral act was formulated by a State, together with the clarity and precision of its terms, shall be given weight in interpreting it.

RESERVATIONS TO TREATIES

[Agenda item 7]

DOCUMENT A/CN.4/572*

Note on draft guideline 3.1.5 (Definition of the object and purpose of the treaty), by Mr. Alain Pellet, Special Rapporteur

[*Original: French*]
[*21 June 2006*]

1. At the Commission's fifty-seventh session, in 2005, the Special Rapporteur proposed, in his tenth report on reservations to treaties,[1] draft guideline 3.1.5 concerning the definition of the object and purpose of the treaty, which plays a key role in determining the validity of a reservation. This draft text was worded:

3.1.5 *Definition of the object and purpose of the treaty*

For the purpose of assessing the validity of reservations, the object and purpose of the treaty means the essential provisions of the treaty, which constitute its *raison d'être*.[2]

2. The Commission's consideration of this draft guideline was very brief, owing to a lack of time, and several members were unable to express their views on it during the fifty-seventh session. Although most of the members who took the floor did not voice any radical objections to the Special Rapporteur's proposal, several speakers rightly contended that the proposed definition was rather unworkable and of no obvious usefulness.[3]

3. In the Sixth Committee of the General Assembly, the draft text proposed by the Special Rapporteur was, on the whole, well received by Member States, and some intimated that the Commission should pursue its consideration thereof.[4] The comment was also made, however, that the definition was of scant use because it was couched in vague terms providing little clarification.[5]

4. Although some Commission members[6] and a few delegations in the Sixth Committee[7] may have demurred, the Special Rapporteur still believes[8] that the Guide to Practice must of necessity contain a definition of the object and purpose of the treaty. Apparent difficulty with its formulation should not be a reason for foregoing definition of a notion central to the law of reservations and, what is more, to the law of treaties as a whole. Moreover, it must be borne in mind that the purpose of the Guide to Practice is to elucidate and clarify the rules governing reservations to treaties established by the two Vienna Conventions on the law of treaties.[9] In the opinion of the Special Rapporteur, not to define a notion that is so enigmatic yet, at the same time, so central to the assessment of a reservation's validity would leave a major gap in the Guide, which would defeat its purpose of assisting States in their practice with regard to reservations.

5. It is, however, indisputable that the object and purpose of a given treaty can be determined only by reference to the text and particular nature of each treaty. Yet while there is no such thing as a "one-size-fits-all" definition and it is inevitable that some degree of subjectivity will persist in each individual case, it is possible to limit the latter's effect. As the Special Rapporteur emphasized in his tenth report on reservations to treaties, guidelines on

---

* Incorporating A/CN.4/572/Corr.1.

[1] *Yearbook ... 2005*, vol. II (Part One), document A/CN.4/558 and Add.1–2, p. 141.

[2] *Ibid.*, p. 164, para. 89.

[3] Mr. Gaja (*ibid.*, vol. I, 2857th meeting, p. 192, para. 43), Ms. Escarameia (*ibid.*, 2858th meeting, p. 193, para. 3), Mr. Koskienniemi (*ibid.*, p. 197, para. 31), Mr. Fomba (*ibid.*, para. 34), Mr. Economides (*ibid.*, p. 200, para. 72), Ms. Xue (*ibid.*, pp. 201–202, para. 86) and Mr. Rodríguez Cedeño (*ibid.*, p. 203, para. 101).

[4] Russian Federation (*Official Records of the General Assembly, Sixtieth Session, Sixth Committee*, 16th meeting, para. 18), Mexico (*ibid.*, 15th meeting, para. 5) and Argentina (*ibid.*, 13th meeting, para. 103).

[5] Sweden, on behalf of the Nordic countries (*ibid.*, 14th meeting, para. 21) and China (*ibid.*, 15th meeting, para. 19).

[6] Mr. Gaja (*Yearbook ... 2005*, vol. I, 2857th meeting, p. 192, para. 43) and Mr. Koskienniemi (*ibid.*, 2858th meeting, p. 197, para. 31).

[7] United Kingdom (*Official Records of the General Assembly, Sixtieth Session, Sixth Committee*, 14th meeting, para. 5), New Zealand (*ibid.*, para. 45) and Guatemala (*ibid.*, para. 65).

[8] See also the conclusions of the Special Rapporteur during the deliberations of the fifty-seventh session, *Yearbook ... 2005*, vol. I, 2859th meeting, p. 207, para. 16: "[I]t was essential to try to define the concept of object and purpose, since it was fundamental to the law of reservations and to the law of treaties in general."

[9] Vienna Convention on the Law of Treaties (Vienna, 23 May 1969), United Nations, *Treaty Series*, vol. 1155, No. 18232, p. 331, and the Vienna Convention on the Law of Treaties between States and International Organizations or between International Organizations (Vienna, 21 March 1986), A/CONF.129/15. See also the comments of the Russian delegation to the Sixth Committee, *Official Records of the General Assembly, Sixtieth Session, Sixth Committee*, 16th meeting, para. 18: "It might be difficult to define a treaty's object and purposes in an accurate or objective manner, but such a definition might be a useful guideline for the purpose of interpreting a specific international treaty in conjunction with the reservations made thereto."

the definition of the object and purpose of the treaty "will, to be sure, not resolve all problems", but

> they can certainly contribute to a solution if they are applied in good faith and with a little common sense, and it would appear to be legitimate to transpose the principles in articles 31–32 of the 1969 and 1986 Vienna Conventions … to the determination of the object and purpose of a treaty.[10]

6. Having carefully listened to the Commission members who expressed an opinion on this point and having studied the comments of delegations in the Sixth Committee, the Special Rapporteur has come to the conclusion that the definition currently proposed in draft guideline 3.1.5 falls somewhat short of the clarification which he deems essential, and that the bald reference to the *raison d'être* of the treaty is likely to replace one enigma[11] with another.

7. Following up a suggestion made at the fifty-seventh session,[12] the Special Rapporteur considers that it might be advisable to take as a model the wording found in the second part of draft guideline 3.1.12 (Reservations to general human rights treaties)[13] and to link the reservation to the impact it will have (or is intended to have) on the general architecture of the treaty. With this in mind, the following definition could be adopted as a basis for the work of the Drafting Committee:

"3.1.5 *Definition of the object and purpose of the treaty*

"For the purpose of assessing the validity of reservations, the object and purpose of the treaty means the essential rules, rights and obligations indispensable to the general architecture of the treaty, which constitute the *raison d'être* thereof and whose modification or exclusion could seriously disturb the balance of the treaty."

8. Alternatively, along the same line of thought, the following definition could be adopted. It differs from the previous one in that it places greater emphasis on the procedural angle:

"3.1.5 *Incompatibility of a reservation with the object and purpose of the treaty*

"A reservation shall be incompatible with the object and purpose of the treaty if it has a serious impact on the essential rules, rights or obligations indispensable to the general architecture of the treaty, thereby depriving it of its *raison d'être*."

9. These alternative texts[14] might seem more workable than the wording proposed in 2005, since they preserve a vital degree of flexibility while ultimately leaving something to the subjective assessment of the interpreter. Furthermore, they make it clear that, although the notion of the object and purpose of the treaty is, in the Special Rapporteur's view, identical in the various provisions of the 1969 and 1986 Vienna Conventions that contain a reference to it,[15] the two texts plainly indicate that they are supposed to apply only to the issue of the validity of reservations.

---

[10] *Yearbook ... 2005* (see footnote 1 above), p. 164, para. 91.

[11] See Isabelle Buffard and Karl Zemanek, "The 'object and purpose' of a treaty: an enigma?", *Austrian Review of International and European Law*, vol. 3 (1998), pp. 311–343.

[12] Mr. Gaja (*Yearbook ... 2005*, vol. I, 2857th meeting, p. 192, para. 46).

[13] "To assess the compatibility of a reservation with the object and purpose of a general treaty for the protection of human rights, account should be taken of the indivisibility of the rights set out therein, the importance that the right which is the subject of the reservation has within the general architecture of the treaty, and the seriousness of the impact the reservation has upon it." (*Yearbook ... 2005* (see footnote 1 above), p. 167, para. 102.)

[14] The Special Rapporteur has a definite preference for the first set, which he thinks is more consonant with the general spirit of the definitions adopted thus far in the Guide to Practice.

[15] See the tenth report on reservations to treaties, *Yearbook ... 2005* (see footnote 1 above), p. 161, paras. 77–78.

DOCUMENT A/CN.4/574

Eleventh report on reservations to treaties, by Mr. Alain Pellet, Special Rapporteur

[*Original: French*]
[*10 August 2006*]

CONTENTS

Multilateral instruments cited in the present report

	Source
Convention on the Prevention and Punishment of the Crime of Genocide (New York, 9 December 1948)	United Nations, *Treaty Series*, vol. 78, No. 1021, p. 277.
Convention for the Protection of Human Rights and Fundamental Freedoms (European Convention on Human Rights) (Rome, 4 November 1950)	*Ibid.*, vol. 213, No. 2889, p. 221.
Vienna Convention on Diplomatic Relations (Vienna, 18 April 1961)	*Ibid.*, vol. 500, No. 7310, p. 95.
Vienna Convention on Consular Relations (Vienna, 24 April 1963)	*Ibid.*, vol. 596, No. 8638, p. 261.
International Convention on the Elimination of All Forms of Racial Discrimination (New York, 21 December 1965)	*Ibid.*, vol. 660, No. 9464, p. 195.
International Covenant on Civil and Political Rights (New York, 16 December 1966)	*Ibid.*, vol. 999, No. 14668, p. 171.
Optional Protocol to the International Covenant on Civil and Political Rights (New York, 16 December 1966)	*Ibid.*
Vienna Convention on the Law of Treaties (Vienna, 23 May 1969)	*Ibid.*, vol. 1155, No. 18232, p. 331.
Agreement on the International Carriage of Perishable Foodstuffs and on the Special Equipment to be used for such Carriage (ATP) (Geneva, 1 September 1970)	*Ibid.*, vol. 1028, No. 15121, p. 121.
Convention on the prevention and punishment of crimes against internationally protected persons, including diplomatic agents (New York, 14 December 1973)	*Ibid.*, vol. 1035, No. 15410, p. 167.
Customs Convention on the International Transport of Goods under Cover of TIR Carnets (TIR Convention) (Geneva, 14 November 1975)	*Ibid.*, vol. 1079, No. 16510, p. 89.
International Tropical Timber Agreement (Geneva, 18 November 1983)	*Ibid.*, vol. 1393, No. 23317, p. 67.
Wheat Trade Convention (London, 14 March 1986)	*Ibid.*, vol. 1429, No. 24237, p. 71.
Vienna Convention on the Law of Treaties between States and International Organizations or between International Organizations (Vienna, 21 March 1986)	*Official Records of the United Nations Conference on the Law of Treaties between States and International Organizations or between International Organizations*, vol. II (United Nations publication, Sales No. E.94.V.5).
United Nations Convention against Illicit Traffic in Narcotic Drugs and Psychotropic Substances (Vienna, 20 December 1988)	United Nations, *Treaty Series*, vol. 1582, No. 27627, p. 95.
Convention on the rights of the child (New York, 20 November 1989)	*Ibid.*, vol. 1577, No. 27531, p. 3.
Convention on the Safety of United Nations and Associated Personnel (New York, 9 December 1994)	*Ibid.*, vol. 2051, No. 35457, p. 363.
International Convention for the Suppression of Terrorist Bombings (New York, 15 December 1997)	*Ibid.*, vol. 2149, No. 37517, p. 256
Rome Statute of the International Criminal Court (Rome, 17 July 1998)	*Ibid.*, vol. 2187, No. 38544, p. 3.
International Convention for the Suppression of the Financing of Terrorism (New York, 9 December 1999)	*Ibid.* , vol. 2178, No. 38349, p. 197.

Works cited in the present report

ABI-SAAB, Georges

"Concluding remarks", *in* Vera Gowlland-Debbas, ed., *Multilateral Treaty-Making: The Current Status of Challenges to and Reforms Needed in the International Legislative Process.* The Hague, Martinus Nijhoff, 2000, pp. 137–142. (Nijhoff Law Specials, vol. 47)

BARATTA, Roberto

Gli effetti delle riserve ai trattati. Milan, Giuffrè, 1999. 437 p.

BOWETT, D. W.

"Reservations to non-restricted multilateral treaties", BYBIL, *1976–1977*, vol. 48, 1978, pp. 67–92.

CLARK, Belinda

"The Vienna Convention reservations regime and the Convention on Discrimination against Women", *American Journal of International Law*, vol. 85, No. 2, April 1991, pp. 281–321.

COCCIA, Massimo

"Reservations to multilateral treaties on human rights", *California Western International Law Journal*, vol. 15, No. 1, winter 1985, pp. 1–51.

EDWARDS JR., Richard W.

"Reservations to treaties", *Michigan Journal of International Law*, vol. 10, No. 2, spring 1989, pp. 362–405.

GAMBLE JR., John King

"The 1982 U.N. Convention on the Law of the Sea: a 'midstream' assessment of the effectiveness of article 309", *San Diego Law Review*, vol. 24, No. 3, 1987, pp. 627–644.

GREIG, D. W.

"Reservations: equity as a balancing factor?", *Australian Year Book of International Law 1995*, vol. 16, pp. 21–172.

HORN, Frank

Reservations and Interpretative Declarations to Multilateral Treaties. The Hague, T.M.C. Asser Instituut, 1988. 514 p. (Thesis, University of Uppsala, Sweden)

IMBERT, Pierre-Henri

Les réserves aux traités multilatéraux: évolution du droit et de la pratique depuis l'avis consultatif donné par la Cour internationale de Justice le 28 mai 1951. Paris, Pedone, 1978. 503 p.

JOVANOVIĆ, Stevan

Restriction des compétences discrétionnaires des États en droit international. Paris, Pedone, 1988. 240 p.

KOHONA, Palitha T. B.

"Some notable developments in the practice of the UN Secretary-General as depositary of multilateral treaties: reservations and declarations", *American Journal of International Law*, vol. 99, No. 2, April 2005, pp. 433–450.

"Reservations: discussion of recent developments in the practice of the Secretary-General of the United Nations as depositary of multilateral treaties", *Georgia Journal of International and Comparative Law*, vol. 33, No. 2, 2005, pp. 415–450.

LIJNZAAD, Liesbeth

Reservations to UN-Human Rights Treaties: Ratify and Ruin? Dordrecht, Martinus Nijhoff, 1995.

MIGLIORINO, Luigi

"La revoca di riserve e di obiezioni a riserve", *Rivista di diritto internazionale*, vol. LXXV, No. 2, 1992, pp. 315–334.

MÜLLER, Daniel

"Article 20", *in* Olivier Corten and Pierre Klein, eds., *Les Conventions de Vienne sur le droit des traités: commentaire article par article.* vol. I. Brussels, Bruylant, 2006, pp. 797–882.

"Article 21", *in* Olivier Corten and Pierre Klein, eds., *Les Conventions de Vienne sur le droit des traités: commentaire article par article.* vol. I. Brussels, Bruylant, 2006, pp. 883–934.

PELLET, Alain

"Conclusions générales", *La codification du droit international.* Société Française pour le Droit International, Colloque d'Aix-en-Provence. Paris, Pedone, 1999, pp. 329–341.

"Responding to new needs through codification and progressive development", *in* Vera Gowlland-Debbas, ed., *Multilateral Treaty-Making: The Current Status of Challenges to and Reforms Needed in the International Legislative Process.* The Hague, Martinus Nijhoff, 2000, pp. 13–23. (Nijhoff Law Specials, vol. 47)

"Article 22", *in* Olivier Corten and Pierre Klein, eds., *Les Conventions de Vienne sur le droit des traités: commentaire article par article.* vol. I. Brussels, Bruylant, 2006, pp. 935–970.

PELLET, Alain and William SCHABAS

"Article 23", *in* Olivier Corten and Pierre Klein, eds., *Les Conventions de Vienne sur le droit des traités: commentaire article par article.* vol. I. Brussels, Bruylant, 2006, pp. 971–1022.

REDGWELL, Catherine

"Universality or integrity? Some reflections on reservations to general multilateral treaties", BYBIL, *1993*, vol. 64, 1994, pp. 245–282.

REUTER, Paul

Introduction to the Law of Treaties. 2nd ed. London, Kegan Paul International, 1995. 294 p. Translated by José and Peter Haggenmacher.

RIQUELME CORTADO, Rosa

Las reservas a los tratados: lagunas y ambigüedades del régimen de Viena. Murcia, University of Murcia, 2004. 434 p.

SZAFARZ, Renata

"Reservations to multilateral treaties", *Polish Yearbook of International Law*, vol. III, 1970, pp. 293–316.

TOMUSCHAT, Christian

"Admissibility and legal effects of reservations to multilateral treaties: comments on arts. 16 and 17 of the ILC's 1966 draft articles on the law of treaties", *Heidelberg Journal of International Law*, vol. 27, 1967, pp. 463–482.

ZEMANEK, Karl

"Some unresolved questions concerning reservations in the Vienna Convention on the Law of Treaties", *in* Jerzy Makarczyk, ed., *Essays in International Law in honour of Judge Manfred Lachs.* The Hague, Martinus Nijhoff, 1984, pp. 323–336.

Introduction[1]

1. The seventh report on reservations to treaties presented a brief summary of the Commission's earlier work on the subject.[2] This seemed appropriate since the Commission was entering a new quinquennium. The main conclusions drawn from the consideration of the seventh report by the Commission and by the Sixth Committee of the General Assembly were presented in the eighth report on reservations to treaties.[3] Reverting to that practice, this year's report summarizes briefly the lessons that can be drawn from consideration of the eighth, ninth and tenth reports by the Commission and by the Sixth Committee before proceeding to give a brief account of the main developments in the area of reservations that have occurred during recent years and have come to the attention of the Special Rapporteur.

A. Eighth report on reservations to treaties and the outcome

1. CONSIDERATION OF THE EIGHTH REPORT BY THE COMMISSION

2. At its fifty-fifth session in 2003, the Commission adopted 11 draft guidelines presented by the Special

[1] The Special Rapporteur would like to express his special thanks to Daniel Müller, doctoral candidate at the University of Paris X-Nanterre and researcher at the Nanterre International Law Centre for his especially useful assistance in the drafting of this report. It is based, in particular, on his commentary to articles 20–21 of the Vienna Convention on the Law of Treaties (hereinafter the 1969 Vienna Convention) and the Vienna Convention on the Law of Treaties between States and international organizations or between international organizations (hereinafter the 1986 Vienna Convention), "Article 20" and "Article 21". Some developments in the present report are also based on the commentary to articles 22 ("Article 22" prepared by the Special Rapporteur) and 23 (Pellet and Schabas, "Article 23").

[2] *Yearbook ... 2002*, vol. II (Part One), document A/CN.4/526 and Add.1–3, pp. 7–14, paras. 2–47.

[3] *Yearbook ... 2003*, vol. II (Part One), document A/CN.4/535 and Add.1, pp. 33–35, paras. 2–16.

Rapporteur in his seventh report relating to withdrawal and modification of reservations,[4] which had already been referred to the Drafting Committee during the Commission's fifty-fourth session but which, owing to lack of time, the Committee had been unable to consider during that session,[5] together with the corresponding commentary.[6] The Commission thus continued to fill in the gaps in part III of the Guide to Practice having to do with the formulation and withdrawal of reservations, acceptance and objections.[7] The Commission also referred to the Drafting Committee the draft guidelines presented in the Special Rapporteur's eighth report relating to withdrawal and modification of interpretative declarations.[8]

3. Regarding the issue of the enlargement or widening of the scope of a reservation, most members of the Commission were in favour of the draft guideline proposed by the Special Rapporteur,[9] bringing the solution to this problem into line with that of late formulation of a reservation. Nevertheless, some members of the Commission disagreed with the proposal, arguing that it could jeopardize legal certainty and would be contrary to the definition of reservations contained in the 1969 Vienna Convention.[10] Finally, following a vote, the draft guideline was also sent to the Drafting Committee and the Commission decided to request the comments of States on the issue.[11]

4. The draft guidelines on the definition of objections to reservations presented in the eighth report on reservations to treaties[12] elicited a critical[13] and fruitful exchange of views, particularly on the issue of the intention of the objecting State and the effects they purported to produce. The Special Rapporteur took note of these debates and proposed a more neutral formulation of the definition of objections. Nevertheless, the corresponding draft guidelines were not referred to the Drafting Committee and the Special Rapporteur proposed to give the matter further thought in the following report.[14]

5. Owing to lack of time, the Drafting Committee was unable to consider the draft guidelines referred to it by the plenary Commission during its fifty-fifth session in 2003.

2. Consideration of chapter VIII of the 2003 report of the Commission in the Sixth Committee

6. Chapter VIII of the Commission's report on the work of its fifty-fifth session in 2003 was devoted to reservations to treaties.[15] As usual, a very brief summary of the topic was provided in chapter II[16] and the "specific issues on which comments would be of particular interest to the Commission"[17] were set out in chapter III. As regards reservations to treaties, the Commission solicited the observations and comments of States on two points: first, the Commission asked States for their views on objections to reservations and for specific examples of their usual practice, in order to supplement its information in relation to the definition of and reasons for objections;[18] secondly, the Commission requested the comments of States on draft guideline 2.3.5 (Enlargement of the scope of a reservation), which had elicited divergent views within the Commission.[19]

7. Concerning enlargement of the scope of a reservation, some delegations were of the view that there were differences between enlargement of the scope of a reservation and late formulation of a reservation and that the Commission should exclude the possibility of States enlarging the scope of a reservation so as not to jeopardize legal certainty.[20] However, most delegations stated a preference for bringing the rules for enlargement of the scope of a reservation into line with those already elaborated by the Commission for late formulation of a reservation.[21] It was underlined that such enlargements did not necessarily constitute an abuse of rights by the reserving State, but could be made in good faith and might even be necessary in order to take into account new constraints resulting, for example, from changes in the internal law of the State concerned.[22]

8. Regarding objections to reservations and the definition of objections, different delegations had very divergent views on almost all the elements of the proposed definition.

9. According to an extreme view, it was not necessary to include a definition of objections in the Guide to Practice, since article 20, paragraphs 4 (*b*) and 5, and article 21 of the 1969 Vienna Convention were sufficient in that regard.[23]

[4] *Yearbook ... 2002* (see footnote 2 above), annex, p. 43.

[5] *Yearbook ... 2003* (see footnote 3 above), p. 34, para. 6.

[6] *Ibid.*, vol. II (Part Two), pp. 70–92, para. 368.

[7] See the provisional plan of the study presented by the Special Rapporteur in his second report (*Yearbook ... 1996*, vol. II (Part One), document A/CN.4/477 and Add.1, pp. 48–49, para. 37); this plan was also mentioned in the seventh report (*Yearbook ... 2002* (see footnote 2 above), p. 9, para. 18).

[8] Draft guidelines 2.4.9 (Modification of interpretative declarations), 2.4.10 (Modification of a conditional interpretative declaration), 2.5.12 (Withdrawal of an interpretative declaration) and 2.5.13 (Withdrawal of a conditional interpretative declaration), *Yearbook ... 2003* (see footnote 3 above), pp. 40–42, paras. 49–68.

[9] Draft guideline 2.3.5 (Enlargement of the scope of a reservation), *ibid.*, p. 39, para. 46.

[10] *Yearbook ... 2003*, vol. II (Part Two), p. 63, paras. 353–354.

[11] See paragraphs 6–7 below.

[12] *Yearbook ... 2003* (see footnote 3 above), pp. 48–49, paras. 98–105.

[13] See also the ninth report on reservations to treaties, *Yearbook ... 2004*, vol. II (Part One), document A/CN.4/544, pp. 254–255, paras. 6–11.

[14] See paragraph 17 below.

[15] *Yearbook ... 2003*, vol. II (Part Two), pp. 59–92.

[16] *Ibid.*, p. 13, para. 18. The Special Rapporteur continues to have grave doubts about the usefulness of these "summaries", which provide little information and risk giving readers in too much of a hurry a pretext for not referring to the pertinent chapters.

[17] *Ibid.*, p. 14.

[18] *Ibid.*, p. 15, paras. 34–38.

[19] *Ibid.*, para. 39.

[20] Austria (*Official Records of the General Assembly, Fifty-eighth Session, Sixth Committee*, 19th meeting, para. 97); Greece (*ibid.*, 20th meeting, para. 53).

[21] Israel (*ibid.*, 17th meeting, para. 47); Slovenia (19th meeting, para. 4); the Netherlands (*ibid.*, para. 23); Argentina (*ibid.*, para. 89); Romania (*ibid.*, para. 62); Sweden, on behalf of the Nordic countries (*ibid.*, para. 29); Italy (*ibid.*, para. 33); China (*ibid.*, para. 44); Chile (*ibid.*, para. 78); Kenya (*ibid.*, 21st meeting, para. 36).

[22] France (*ibid.*, 19th meeting, para. 37); Chile (*ibid.*, para. 79).

[23] Portugal (*ibid.*, para. 14); Pakistan (*ibid.*, 20th meeting, para. 67); United States of America (*ibid.*, para. 9). The Special Rapporteur considers this idea rather surprising, since these articles do not in any way define an objection.

10. However, the choice made by the Special Rapporteur and endorsed by the Commission to try to define what constituted an objection was accepted by most delegations, who considered that any definition of an objection should necessarily take into account the author's intention and the legal effects the latter intended to produce.[24]

11. The proposed definition did, however, attract some criticism. According to some delegations, the intentional element limited to the legal effects intended by the author of the objection to the reservation was too restrictive: States made objections for a variety of reasons, often of a purely political nature, but also because they considered a reservation to be contrary to the object and purpose of a treaty.[25] According to those delegations, the definition proposed by the Special Rapporteur[26] would deny States the flexibility that they currently enjoyed.[27]

12. Some delegations maintained that the legal effects envisaged were too broad and diverged too far from the regime of the 1969 Vienna Convention.[28] In the view of these States, only the effects contemplated by the Convention should be retained for the purposes of the definition, on the understanding, however, that room should be left for a "reservations dialogue" with the aim of persuading the reserving State to modify the reservation.[29] It was also maintained, however, that the definition of objections should include all negative reactions to the reservation,[30] and it was argued that it was advisable not to limit it to the legal effects established by the 1969 and 1986 Vienna Conventions, since the legal effects of an objection depended above all on the intention of the objecting State.[31] Nonetheless, some States emphasized that objections with "super-maximum effects"[32] destroyed a basic element of the consent of the State to become a party to the treaty.[33]

13. Lastly, some delegations proposed that the definition should evoke the strictly relative scope of the effects of an objection between the State author of the reservation in question and the State author of the objection.[34]

14. On a more general note, the delegations welcomed the guidelines adopted by the Commission;[35] some modifications were proposed,[36] and the Special Rapporteur will bear them in mind during the second reading of the Guide to Practice. It was also suggested that the commentary should indicate more systematically which of the guidelines were interpretative guidelines intended to clarify the provisions of the 1969 and 1986 Vienna Conventions and which of them were merely recommendations to States.[37] The Special Rapporteur is not convinced that this is any more feasible than to distinguish between rules that constitute codification *sensu stricto* and those that represent progressive development.[38]

15. It was also indicated that the modalities of the "reservations dialogue", which seemed to have aroused considerable interest among States, should not be predetermined, as there were many ways in which States could explain their intentions with respect to a reservation or objection.[39]

B. Ninth report on reservations to treaties and the outcome

1. Consideration of the ninth report by the Commission

16. At its fifty-sixth session in 2004, the Commission provisionally adopted the draft guidelines referred to the Drafting Committee during its preceding session (see paragraphs 2–3 above) with the commentaries thereto.[40]

17. In his ninth report on reservations to treaties,[41] which was really in the nature of an adjustment to chapter II of his eighth report,[42] the Special Rapporteur had re-examined the issue of the definition of objections taking into account the criticisms levelled against his proposal during the Commission's preceding session (see paragraph 4 above) and within the Sixth Committee (see paragraphs 8–13 above). The new definition, more neutral as regards the difficult (and premature) question of the validity of an objection, and draft guideline 2.6.2 defining an objection to the late formulation or widening of the scope

---

[24] See, particularly, Argentina (*ibid.*, 19th meeting, para. 89); Romania (*ibid.*, para. 63); Japan (*ibid.*, para. 48); Australia (*ibid.*, 20th meeting, para. 16); Malaysia (*ibid.*, para. 20).

[25] Netherlands (*ibid.*, 19th meeting, para. 21; Sweden, on behalf of the Nordic countries (*ibid.*, para. 28); United States (*ibid.*, 20th meeting, para. 9); Israel (*ibid.*, 17th meeting, para. 45).

[26] The definition of objection proposed by the Special Rapporteur reads as follows:

> "'Objection' means a unilateral statement, however phrased or named, made by a State or an international organization in response to a reservation to a treaty formulated by another State or international organization, whereby the State or organization purports to prevent the reservation having any or some of its effects."

(*Yearbook ... 2003*, vol. II (Part Two), p. 64, para. 363)

[27] United States (*Official Records of the General Assembly, Fifty-eighth Session, Sixth Committee*, 20th meeting, para. 9).

[28] See, however, Slovenia (*ibid.*, 19th meeting, para. 4); Malaysia (*ibid.*, 20th meeting, para. 20).

[29] France (*ibid.*, 19th meeting, para. 38); Malaysia (*ibid.*, 20th meeting, para. 20).

[30] Italy (*ibid.*, 19th meeting, para. 31).

[31] The Netherlands (*ibid.*, para. 21); Cyprus (*ibid.*, para. 70); Greece (*ibid.*, 20th meeting, para. 51); Bulgaria (*ibid.*, para. 63); Argentina (*ibid.*, 19th meeting, para. 89); Romania (*ibid.*, para. 63); Japan (*ibid.*, para. 48); Australia (*ibid.*, 20th meeting, para. 16); Malaysia (*ibid.*, para. 20).

[32] *Yearbook ... 2003*, vol. II (Part Two), p. 64, para. 363.

[33] Islamic Republic of Iran (*Official Records of the General Assembly, Fifty-eighth Session, Sixth Committee*, 20th meeting, para. 70).

[34] Viet Nam (*ibid.*, para. 23).

[35] India (*ibid.*, 21st meeting, para. 41); Hungary (*ibid.*, para. 7); Slovenia (*ibid.*, 19th meeting, para. 3); Cyprus (*ibid.*, para. 70); Romania (*ibid.*, para. 62); Sweden, on behalf of the Nordic countries (*ibid.*, para. 24); Bulgaria (*ibid.*, 20th meeting, para. 63).

[36] Austria (*ibid.*, 19th meeting, para. 92); Viet Nam (*ibid.*, 20th meeting, para. 22).

[37] Poland (*ibid.*, 19th meeting, para. 103); Austria (*ibid.*, para. 93); Guatemala (*ibid.*, para. 9).

[38] See Pellet, "Conclusions générales", p. 330, and "Responding to new needs through codification and progressive development (keynote address)", especially pp. 15–16; and Abi-Saab, "Concluding remarks", particularly p. 138.

[39] Japan (*Official Records of the General Assembly, Fifty-eighth Session, Sixth Committee,* 19th meeting, para. 47).

[40] *Yearbook ... 2004*, vol. II (Part Two), pp. 106 *et seq.*, para. 295.

[41] *Yearbook ... 2004* (see footnote 13 above).

[42] *Yearbook ... 2003* (see footnote 3 above), p. 42.

of a reservation were finally referred, with some changes, to the Drafting Committee; however, it was unable to consider them during the fifty-sixth session.

2. Consideration of chapter IX of the 2004 report of the Commission in the Sixth Committee

18. Chapter IX of the Commission's report on the work of its fifty-sixth session[43] deals with the topic of reservations to treaties. In accordance with established practice, a brief summary is given in chapter II[44] and chapter III concerns specific issues on which comments would be of particular interest to the Commission. With regard to reservations to treaties, the Commission asked States for their comments and observations on the terminology to be used in future to describe reservations that did not satisfy the requirements of article 19 of the 1969 Vienna Convention ("lawfulness", "permissibility", "admissibility" or "validity").[45]

19. A number of comments were made on the terminology question posed by the Commission, but no clear trend emerged. While the English terms "unlawful" and "wrongful" were categorically rejected, the French words "*licéité*", "*recevabilité*" and "*validité*" had both defenders and detractors. Some delegations maintained that the English terms "permissible/impermissible" (as a rendering of "*licite/illicite*" in French) seemed to enjoy broad acceptance and had the required neutrality.[46] However, the view was expressed that the term "permissibility" implied the existence of an organ empowered to rule on the compatibility of a reservation with the treaty.[47] It was also said that the term "validity" might prejudge the legal effects of a reservation.[48] Furthermore, the expression "invalid reservation" was viewed as potentially confusing because it implied that the reservation was formulated by an unauthorized representative of the State in question.[49]

20. Another view was that a distinction should be drawn between reservations that did not fulfil the conditions of article 19 (*a*)–(*b*) of the 1969 Vienna Convention and reservations that did not meet the condition set out in article 19 (*c*). While the former must be regarded as "impermissible", the latter should be characterized as "invalid".[50]

21. The term "admissibility" was favoured by various delegations as most accurately reflecting the situation between equal sovereign States.[51]

22. However, other delegations preferred the word "validity" because it appeared in a number of articles of the 1969 Vienna Convention other than article 19 and was therefore the most appropriate term.[52] Some delegations also stressed that the provisions of articles 2, paragraph 1 (*d*), and 23, paragraph 1, of the Convention on the timing and form of a reservation were also conditions of "validity".[53] Support was also expressed for the term "validity", on condition that a clear distinction was drawn between "opposability" and "validity". "Non-opposability" was considered the most appropriate penalty of "invalidity";[54] *prima facie*, the Special Rapporteur shares this view, but this issue will be considered in greater detail in a future report.

23. Some delegations took advantage of the terminology question posed by the Commission to restate their position on determining the validity of a reservation and its effects.[55]

24. With regard to the definition of objections to reservations, States also expressed a fairly wide range of views, which were very similar to those put forward the previous year (see paragraphs 8–13 above). While some delegations regarded the definition of objections as too narrow, particularly as regards the effects intended by the author of the objection,[56] other delegations expressed concern about the excessive flexibility of the definition in relation to the 1969 Vienna Convention.[57] It was also proposed, by way of a compromise between too broad and too narrow a definition, to define the objection as a reaction purporting to make the effects of the reservation non-opposable in relations between the State author of the objection and the State author of the reservation.[58] However, yet another group of delegations expressed satisfaction with the proposed definition, while observing that the central question, namely the effects of reservations in relation to objections, remained unresolved.[59] Nevertheless, a number of delegations maintained that the definition of objections should not leave room for an objection to have "super-maximum" effect, which clearly contravened the fundamental legal principles of treaties.[60] On the other hand, it was pointed out that the proposed definition might not adequately cover "minimum effect" objections, which, under certain conditions, actually produced the same effects as the reservation in question; an alternative definition was therefore proposed.[61]

---

[43] *Yearbook ... 2004*, vol. II (Part Two), pp. 97–110, paras. 248–295.

[44] *Ibid.*, p. 13, para. 17. See also footnote 16 above.

[45] *Ibid.*, p. 16, paras. 33–37.

[46] Greece (*Official Records of the General Assembly, Fifty-ninth Session, Sixth Committee*, 24th meeting, para. 10); Japan (*ibid.*, 25th meeting, para. 6); Malaysia (*ibid.*, para. 40).

[47] Republic of Korea (*ibid.*, para. 31).

[48] Germany (*ibid.*, 23rd meeting, para. 68); Portugal (*ibid.*, 24th meeting, para. 2).

[49] Singapore (*ibid.*, 25th meeting, para. 21).

[50] Sweden, on behalf of the Nordic countries (*ibid.*, 24th meeting, para. 14); Singapore (*ibid.*, 25th meeting, para. 20).

[51] Republic of Korea (*ibid.*, para. 31).

[52] United States (*ibid.*, 24th meeting, para. 7); Spain (*ibid.*, para. 21).

[53] Belgium (*ibid.*, 25th meeting, paras. 13–15).

[54] Poland (*ibid.*, 24th meeting, para. 24); Japan (*ibid.*, 25th meeting, para. 6); Belgium (*ibid.*, para. 12); Malaysia (*ibid.*, para. 40).

[55] See, for example, Belgium (*ibid.*, paras. 12–15); Singapore (*ibid.*, paras. 20–22).

[56] Italy (*ibid.*, 24th meeting, para. 34); Russian Federation (*ibid.*, 25th meeting, para. 23).

[57] France (*ibid.*, 24th meeting, para. 16).

[58] *Ibid.*, para. 18).

[59] Spain (*ibid.*, para. 20).

[60] France (*ibid.*, paras. 16–17); Australia (*ibid.*, 25th meeting, para. 44); Islamic Republic of Iran (*ibid.*, 24th meeting, para. 36); Chile (*ibid.*, 22nd meeting, para. 89). See, however, the far-reaching view expressed by Sweden (on behalf of the Nordic countries) on objections with "super-maximum" effect (*ibid.*, 24th meeting, para. 13).

[61] See Poland (*ibid.*, para. 23): "'Objection' means a unilateral statement, however phrased or named, made by a State or an international organization, whereby the State or organization purports to express an act of non-acceptance (or rejection) of the reservation, certain legal effects being attributable to this act."

25. Several delegations reverted to the issue of the widening of the scope of reservations, maintaining that the draft guidelines adopted by the Commission did not do enough to discourage the practice.[62] However, it was again pointed out (see paragraph 7 above) that widening or enlarging the scope of a reservation might be justified in certain circumstances, although only in exceptional cases.[63]

26. Other comments were made on matters relating essentially to form.[64] The Special Rapporteur will bear them in mind during the second reading of the Guide to Practice.

C. Tenth report on reservations to treaties and the outcome

1. Consideration of the tenth report by the Commission

27. At its fifty-seventh session, in 2005, the Commission adopted the draft guidelines dealing with the definition of objections, which had been referred to the Drafting Committee at the preceding session, together with commentaries.[65]

28. In his tenth report on reservations to treaties, the Special Rapporteur had introduced the issue of the validity of reservations while reserving for later the discussion of the outstanding questions concerning the formulation of reservations, acceptances and objections. Owing to time constraints, the Commission was not able to consider the tenth report in its entirety. Consideration of the draft guidelines dealing with the compatibility of a reservation with the object and purpose of the treaty,[66] which had already given rise to a brief discussion,[67] as well as the question of the determination of the validity of reservations,[68] were reserved for the fifty-eighth session in 2006.

29. In general, the Commission looked favourably upon the other draft guidelines proposed by the Special Rapporteur in his tenth report on reservations to treaties. Only a few drafting changes were suggested. Those draft guidelines were therefore referred to the Drafting Committee[69] together with draft guidelines 1.6 (Scope of definitions)[70] and 2.1.8 (Procedure in case of manifestly [impermissible] reservations),[71] which had already been provisionally adopted, but that had to be reviewed in the light of the terminology change approved by the Commission, which, in accordance with the Special Rapporteur's proposal,[72] finally decided to use the more neutral term "validity" instead of "permissibility" (*licéité*), since the latter implicitly referred to the law of responsibility.[73]

30. However, the Drafting Committee was unable to consider the draft guidelines referred to it and deferred that task to the Commission's fifty-eighth session in 2006.

31. The Commission also welcomed the Special Rapporteur's proposal to organize, during its fifty-eighth or fifty-ninth session, a meeting with the human rights treaty bodies to discuss, *inter alia*, the issues of the validity of reservations, particularly in relation to the object and purpose of a treaty. However, that project has come up against a number of obstacles, which should perhaps be discussed by the Planning Group at the current session.

2. Consideration of chapter X of the 2005 report of the Commission in the Sixth Committee

32. Chapter X of the Commission's report on the work of its fifty-seventh session[74] in 2005 deals with the topic of reservations to treaties. In accordance with established practice, a brief summary is given in chapter II[75] and chapter III deals with specific issues on which comments would be of particular interest to the Commission. With regard to reservations to treaties, the Commission put a single question to States.[76]

33. That question read as follows:

> States often object to a reservation that they consider incompatible with the object and purpose of the treaty, but without opposing the entry into force of the treaty between themselves and the author of the reservation. The Commission would be particularly interested in Governments' comments on this practice. It would like to know, in particular, what effects the authors expect such objections to have, and how, in Governments' view, this practice accords with article 19 (*c*) of the 1969 Vienna Convention on the Law of Treaties.

34. A number of delegations submitted comments in response to the Commission's question, which, according to some, touched on a crucial and difficult aspect of the law governing reservations, even though, in practice, the issue of incompatibility with the object and purpose of a treaty arose in a relatively small number of rather extreme cases.[77] However, it must be admitted that the views expressed on that occasion were highly divergent.

35. Regardless of the concrete effects of an objection to a reservation regarded as incompatible with the object

---

[62] United Kingdom of Great Britain and Northern Ireland (*ibid.*, 22nd meeting, para. 36); Austria (*ibid.*, 23rd meeting, para. 79).

[63] Russian Federation (*ibid.*, 25th meeting, para. 23).

[64] Malaysia (*ibid.*, para. 41); Australia (*ibid.*, para. 45); Russian Federation (*ibid.*, para. 23).

[65] *Yearbook ... 2005*, vol. II (Part Two), pp. 76 *et seq.*, para. 438.

[66] *Yearbook ... 2005*, vol. II (Part One), document A/CN.4/558 and Add.1–2, p. 141.

[67] *Yearbook ... 2005*, vol. I, 2856th–2858th meetings.

[68] *Yearbook ... 2005* (see footnote 66 above), pp. 176–189, paras. 147–208. See the Special Rapporteur's explanations, *ibid.*, vol. I, 2854th meeting.

[69] Draft guidelines 3.1 (Freedom to formulate reservations), 3.1.1 (Reservations expressly prohibited by the treaty), 3.1.2 (Definition of specified reservations), 3.1.3 (Reservations implicitly permitted by the treaty) and 3.1.4 (Non-specified reservations authorized by the treaty).

[70] For the text of this draft guideline and the commentary thereto, see *Yearbook ... 1999*, vol. II (Part Two), p. 126.

[71] *Yearbook ... 2002*, vol. II (Part Two), pp. 45–46.

[72] *Yearbook ... 2005* (see footnote 66 above), pp. 147–148, paras. 2–8, and *ibid.*, vol. I, 2854th meeting.

[73] *Ibid.*, vol. I, 2859th meeting; *ibid.*, vol. II (Part Two), p. 64, para. 358.

[74] *Ibid.*, vol. II (Part Two), pp. 63–82, paras. 333–438.

[75] *Ibid.*, p. 11, para. 18. See also footnote 16 above.

[76] *Yearbook ... 2005*, vol. II (Part Two), p. 14, para. 29.

[77] United Kingdom (*Official Records of the General Assembly, Sixtieth Session, Sixth Committee*, 14th meeting, para. 3).

and purpose of the treaty pursuant to article 19 (*c*), of the 1969 and 1986 Vienna Conventions, overall the comments reflected the notion that, in formulating such objections, States were expressing their disagreement with the reservation by judging it invalid. A number of delegations therefore took the view that such an objection, and especially an accumulation of similar objections, constituted an important element in determining the object and purpose of the treaty.[78]

36. Some delegations maintained that a simple objection to a reservation incompatible with the object and purpose of the treaty could result only in the application of the whole treaty without taking account of the reservation,[79] which amounts to what has been called the "super-maximum" effect of the objection. Other delegations, however, rejected the possibility of such an effect as contrary to the basic principle of consent underlying the law of treaties.[80] In the view of those States, applying the treaty without taking account of the reservation could be envisaged only in exceptional circumstances, where the reserving State could be considered as having accepted or acquiesced in such an effect.[81]

37. Most of the delegations that responded to the Commission's question explained a decision not to oppose the entry into force of a treaty by the desire to enter into treaty relations with the reserving State despite a reservation considered incompatible with the object and purpose of the treaty. That attitude was not justified solely by political or extralegal reasons.[82] Some delegations clearly maintained that, by employing such a "paradoxical" method of formulating a simple objection to a reservation incompatible with the object and purpose of the treaty, the objecting State could attempt to initiate a "reservations dialogue" in order to convince the reserving State to reconsider its reservation or withdraw it altogether.[83]

38. More generally, several delegations took the view that States found it difficult to consider the plethora of reservations formulated by other States. They also stressed that political considerations often led States to refrain from reacting to such reservations. In the light of the practical and political problems, those delegations took the view that the effect to be attached to silence on the part of States in such circumstances was far from clear; however, under no circumstances should that silence be interpreted as an implicit validation of the reservation.[84]

39. Referring more specifically to the Special Rapporteur's tenth report and the draft guidelines proposed or already adopted, the feedback from those delegations that made comments was generally positive.

40. It was maintained that the term "freedom" ("*faculté*") in the title of draft guideline 3.1 (Freedom to formulate reservations) did not fit the content of the Vienna regime and should be changed to "right" ("*droit*").[85] Some delegations had doubts about the presumption of validity of reservations implicit in the draft guideline (although it should be recalled that the draft guideline merely reproduces the provisions of article 19 of the 1969 and 1986 Vienna Conventions). According to those States, there must be a balance between, on the one hand, the broadest possible participation in the treaty and, on the other, the integrity of that treaty.[86] It was also suggested that implicit prohibitions applicable to reservations should be incorporated into the draft guideline.[87]

41. The draft guidelines dealing with the object and purpose of the treaty and the definition of that concept, which the Commission had been unable to discuss in depth, were well received by those States that participated in the debate, some of which indicated that the Commission should continue to consider them.[88] Other delegations, however, wondered whether it was necessary or useful to seek to define the "object and purpose" of a treaty, taking the view that it would be more helpful to determine how that concept had been approached in individual cases.[89] It was also pointed out that the suggested definition was not really serviceable owing to the vague and elusive terms employed.[90]

42. With regard to draft guideline 3.1.7 (Vague, general reservations), it was maintained that automatically qualifying a general or vague reservation as incompatible with the object and purpose of the treaty was too severe, although the practice of formulating such reservations should certainly be discouraged.[91] There was also a suggestion to delete draft guideline 3.1.12 (Reservations to general human rights treaties), which risked introducing different standards for human rights treaties.[92] In addition, some delegations cautioned against combining the issues of reservations and dispute settlement. They took the view that draft guideline 3.1.13 (Reservations to treaty clauses concerning dispute settlement or the monitoring of the implementation of the treaty) might discourage States from participating in the treaty in question;[93] furthermore, it was pointed out that reservations to such clauses had

---

[78] Japan (*ibid.*, para. 57); Belgium (*ibid.*, 16th meeting, paras. 67 and 69); Greece (*ibid.*, 19th meeting, para. 39).

[79] Sweden (on behalf of the Nordic countries) (*ibid.*, 14th meeting, paras. 22–23); Spain (*ibid.*, 17th meeting, para. 24); Malaysia (*ibid.*, 18th meeting, para. 86); Greece (*ibid.*, 19th meeting, para. 39).

[80] United Kingdom (*ibid.*, 14th meeting, para. 3); Australia (*ibid.*, para. 40); France (*ibid.*, para. 72); Italy (*ibid.*, 16th meeting, para. 20); Portugal (*ibid.*, para. 44); Spain (*ibid.*, 17th meeting, para. 25).

[81] United Kingdom (*ibid.*, 14th meeting, para. 4).

[82] Portugal (*ibid.*, 16th meeting, para. 43).

[83] France (*ibid.*, 14th meeting, para. 72); Italy (*ibid.*, 16th meeting, para. 20); Portugal (*ibid.*, para. 44); Spain (*ibid.*, 17th meeting, para. 25). In the same vein, see Japan (*ibid.*, 14th meeting, para. 57); Belgium (*ibid.*, 16th meeting, para. 69); Romania (*ibid.*, para. 77).

[84] United Kingdom (*ibid.*, 14th meeting, paras. 2 and 5); Austria (*ibid.*, para. 13); Portugal (*ibid.*, 16th meeting, para. 38). In this connection, see also *Yearbook ... 2005* (footnote 66 above), paras. 204–205.

[85] United Kingdom (*Official Records of the General Assembly, Sixtieth Session, Sixth Committee*, 14th meeting, para. 6).

[86] Malaysia (*ibid.*, 18th meeting, para. 87).

[87] Spain (*ibid.*, 17th meeting, para. 19); Bolivarian Republic of Venezuela (*ibid.*, 20th meeting, para. 37).

[88] Russian Federation (*ibid.*, 16th meeting, para. 18); Mexico (*ibid.*, 15th meeting, para. 5); Argentina (*ibid.*, 13th meeting, para. 103).

[89] United Kingdom (*ibid.*, 14th meeting, para. 5); New Zealand (*ibid*, para. 45); Guatemala (*ibid.*, para. 65).

[90] Sweden, on behalf of the Nordic countries (*ibid.*, para. 21); China (*ibid.*, 15th meeting, para. 19).

[91] Austria (*ibid.*, 14th meeting, paras. 15–16).

[92] Malaysia (*ibid.*, 18th meeting, para. 89).

[93] Malaysia (*ibid.*, para. 90); Portugal (*ibid.*, 16th meeting, para. 40).

never been found to be contrary to the object and purpose of the treaty in the case law of ICJ.[94] Other delegations, however, took the view that the draft guideline struck a good balance between preservation of the object and purpose of the treaty and the freedom to choose mechanisms for settling disputes or monitoring the implementation of the treaty.[95]

43. These questions, however, were to be discussed in more detail by the Commission at its fifty-eighth session in 2006. The many comments relating specifically to the concrete effects of an objection,[96] which went above and beyond the issue of definition, will be taken into consideration by the Special Rapporteur in his next report, which will address the effects of accepting and objecting to reservations.

D. Recent developments with regard to reservations to treaties

44. In its judgment on jurisdiction and admissibility in the case of *Armed Activities on the Territory of the Congo (New Application: 2002) (Democratic Republic of the Congo* v. *Rwanda)*[97] ICJ ruled on some noteworthy and important questions concerning the right to make reservations to treaties.

45. First, ICJ addressed the purely procedural problem of the withdrawal of a reservation. The Democratic Republic of the Congo argued before the Court that Rwanda had withdrawn its reservation to article IX of the Convention on the Prevention and Punishment of the Crime of Genocide by simply adopting a *décret-loi*, by means of which the Government of Rwanda withdrew reservations made by Rwanda upon accession to or approval and ratification of international human rights instruments. The Court did not, however, endorse that argument:

> It is a rule of international law, deriving from the principle of legal security and well established in practice, that, subject to agreement to the contrary, the withdrawal by a contracting State of a reservation to a multilateral treaty takes effect in relation to the other contracting States only when they have received notification thereof. This rule is expressed in Article 22, paragraph 3 (*a*), of the Vienna Convention on the Law of Treaties, which provides as follows: "3. Unless the Treaty otherwise provides, or it is otherwise agreed: (*a*) the withdrawal of a reservation becomes operative in relation to another Contracting State only when notice of it has been received by that State." Article 23, paragraph 4, of that same Convention further provides that "[t]he withdrawal of a reservation or of an objection to a reservation must be formulated in writing".
>
> ... In the Court's view, the adoption of that *décret-loi* and its publication in the Official Journal of the Rwandese Republic cannot in themselves amount to such notification. In order to have effect in international law, the withdrawal would have had to be the subject of a notice received at the international level.[98]

46. ICJ thereby confirmed the rules contained in draft guidelines 2.5.2 (Form of withdrawal)[99] and 2.5.8 (Effective date of withdrawal of a reservation),[100] already adopted, which merely restate the rules resulting from the 1969 Vienna Convention.

47. Secondly, the Democratic Republic of the Congo contended before ICJ that the Rwandan reservation to article IX of the Convention on the Prevention and Punishment of the Crime of Genocide was invalid. Having reaffirmed the position it had taken in its advisory opinion of 28 May 1951 on the question concerning reservations to the Convention,[101] according to which a reservation to that Convention would be permitted provided it was not incompatible with the object and purpose of the Convention, the Court concluded:

> Rwanda's reservation to Article IX of the Genocide Convention bears on the jurisdiction of the Court, and does not affect substantive obligations relating to acts of genocide themselves under that Convention. In the circumstances of the present case, the Court cannot conclude that the reservation of Rwanda in question, which is meant to exclude a particular method of settling a dispute relating to the interpretation, application or fulfilment of the Convention, is to be regarded as being incompatible with the object and purpose of the Convention.[102]

The Court accordingly gave effect to Rwanda's reservation to article IX of the Convention, as it had already had occasion to do when considering comparable reservations in its orders on requests for the indication of provisional measures in the *Legality of Use of Force* cases.[103]

48. In substance, this solution is reflected in draft guideline 3.1.13 (Reservations to treaty clauses concerning dispute settlement or the monitoring of the implementation of the treaty), proposed by the Special Rapporteur in his tenth report on reservations to treaties.[104]

49. In their joint separate opinion, however, several judges stated the view that the principle applied by ICJ in its judgment might not be absolute in scope. They stressed that there might be situations where reservations to clauses concerning dispute settlement could be contrary to the treaty's object and purpose: it depended on the particular case.[105] Such is the thrust of the last part of draft guideline 3.1.13 as proposed by the Special Rapporteur

---

[94] Malaysia (*ibid.*, 18th meeting, para. 90); see also paragraphs 49–50 above.

[95] Spain (*Official Records of the General Assembly, Sixtieth Session, Sixth Committee*, 17th meeting, para. 18).

[96] See, for example, the comments of the Netherlands (*ibid.*, 14th meeting, para. 30), Guatemala (*ibid.*, para. 61) and Poland (*ibid.*, 16th meeting, para. 31).

[97] *Armed Activities on the Territory of the Congo (New Application: 2002) (Democratic Republic of the Congo* v. *Rwanda), Jurisdiction and Admissibility, Judgment, I.C.J. Reports 2006*, p. 6.

[98] *Ibid.*, pp. 25–26, paras. 41–42.

[99] "The withdrawal of a reservation must be formulated in writing." (*Yearbook ... 2003*, vol. II (Part Two), p. 74). For the commentary to this draft guideline, see pages 74–76.

[100] "Unless the treaty otherwise provides, or it is otherwise agreed, the withdrawal of a reservation becomes operative in relation to a contracting State or a contracting organization only when notice of it has been received by that State or that organization." (*ibid.*, p. 83.) For the commentary to this draft guideline, see pages 83–86.

[101] *Reservations to the Convention on the Prevention and Punishment of the Crime of Genocide, Advisory Opinion, I.C.J. Reports 1951*, p. 15.

[102] *I.C.J. Reports 2006* (see footnote 97 above), p. 32, para. 67.

[103] *Legality of Use of Force (Yugoslavia* v. *Spain)* and *(Yugoslavia* v. *United States of America), Provisional Measures, Orders of 2 June 1999, I.C.J. Reports 1999*, p. 772, paras. 32–33, and p. 924, paras. 24–25, respectively.

[104] See footnote 106 below.

[105] Joint separate opinion of Judges Higgins, Kooijmans, Elaraby, Owada and Simma, *I.C.J. Reports 2006* (see footnote 97 above), pp. 70–71, para. 21.

in his tenth report, which provides for two exceptions in which the principle would not apply.[106]

50. More generally, the authors of the joint separate opinion proposed a more nuanced reading of the 1951 advisory opinion. In particular, their opinion reflected the view that States did not have the sole competence to assess the compatibility of a reservation with the object and purpose of a treaty, and that the positions that several judicial and treaty monitoring bodies had taken were not contrary to the advisory opinion but simply constituted legal developments of questions not put before ICJ in 1951.[107]

51. Thirdly, however, with regard to the Rwandan reservation to article 22 of the International Convention on the Elimination of All Forms of Racial Discrimination, ICJ took a substantially different approach, bearing in mind the mechanism for assessing the validity of reservations which the Convention itself provides for:

> The Court notes that the Convention on Racial Discrimination prohibits reservations incompatible with its object and purpose. The Court observes in this connection that, under Article 20, paragraph 2, of the Convention, "[a] reservation shall be considered incompatible ... if at least two-thirds of the States Parties to [the] Convention object to it". The Court notes, however, that such has not been the case as regards Rwanda's reservation in respect of the Court's jurisdiction. Without prejudice to the applicability *mutatis mutandis* to Rwanda's reservation to Article 22 of the Convention on Racial Discrimination of the Court's reasoning and conclusions in respect of Rwanda's reservation to Article IX of the Genocide Convention (see paragraphs 66–68 above),[108] the Court is of the view that Rwanda's reservation to Article 22 cannot therefore be regarded as incompatible with that Convention's object and purpose. The Court observes, moreover, that the DRC itself raised no objection to the reservation when it acceded to the Convention.[109]

52. In relation to the argument of the Democratic Republic of the Congo that the reservation in question was without legal effect because, on the one hand, the prohibition on racial discrimination was a peremptory norm of general international law and, on the other, such a reservation was in conflict with a peremptory norm, ICJ referred:

> to its reasoning when dismissing the DRC's similar argument in regard to Rwanda's reservation to Article IX of the Genocide Convention (see paragraphs 64–69 above)[110]: the fact that a dispute concerns non-compliance with a peremptory norm of general international law cannot suffice to found the Court's jurisdiction to entertain such a dispute, and there exists no peremptory norm requiring States to consent to such jurisdiction in order to settle disputes relating to the Convention on Racial Discrimination.[111]

53. For their part, the bodies created within the United Nations or by international human rights conventions have continued to develop and harmonize their approaches to this issue. For example, in 2004, Ms. Françoise Hampson presented her final working paper on reservations to human rights treaties (E/CN.4/Sub.2/2004/42), a study of the formulation of reservations, State responses and the reactions of monitoring bodies and mechanisms. Highly interesting and well-balanced findings emerged from this far-reaching study. Notably, the author came to the following conclusions:

(*a*) "Nothing ... suggests that a special regime applies to human rights treaties or to a particular type of treaty which type includes human rights treaties" (para. 6);

(*b*) "A judicial or quasi-judicial body has an inherent jurisdiction to determine ... (*a*) whether a statement is a reservation or not; and (*b*) if so, whether it is a valid reservation; and (*c*) to give effect to a conclusion with regard to validity"(para. 37);

(*c*) "General comments and concluding observations of a treaty body are not binding on a State party. Neither are the conclusions of the Human Rights Committee acting under the Optional Protocol to the International Covenant on Civil and Political Rights. It is submitted, nevertheless, that the conclusion of the treaty body, whilst not binding, will have considerable persuasive force, not least because it is likely to reach similar conclusions with regard to similar reservations by other parties" (para. 18).

It is worth drawing attention in particular to paragraph 38 of the study:

> It has been suggested that monitoring mechanisms do not have the authority to "determine" anything, since their findings are not legally binding. It is submitted that this is to confuse two separate issues. The first question is the scope of its authority to reach conclusions with regard to the substance. The second question is the binding character of the conclusions with regard to the substance. The fact that the conclusions of a monitoring body with regard to the substance are not legally binding does not mean that findings with regard to jurisdiction are not binding. It would, for example, be *ultra vires* the power of a monitoring body to exercise an authority which it does not have, even with the consent of the State in question.

These conclusions largely parallel those reached by the Special Rapporteur in his tenth report on reservations to treaties and are reflected, in particular, in draft guidelines 3.2–3.2.4.[112]

54. Pursuant to decision 2004/110 of the Sub-Commission on the Promotion and Protection of Human Rights (E/CN.4/2005/2, p. 74), this working paper was communicated to all treaty bodies and to the Commission. Ms. Hampson

---

[106] The text of the draft guideline 3.1.13 states:

"A reservation to a treaty clause concerning dispute settlement or the monitoring of the implementation of the treaty is not, in itself, incompatible with the object and purpose of the treaty, unless:

"(*a*) The provision to which the reservation relates constitutes the *raison d'être* of the treaty; or

"(*b*) The reservation has the effect of excluding its author from a dispute settlement or treaty implementation monitoring mechanism with respect to a treaty provision that the author has previously accepted, if the very purpose of the treaty is to put such a mechanism into effect."

(*Yearbook ... 2005* (see footnote 66 above), p. 166, para. 99).

[107] *I.C.J. Reports 2006* (see footnote 97 above), paras. 4–23. In their joint separate opinion (p. 68, para. 14), the five signatories had this to say about the Commission's work on reservations to treaties:

"The study of reservations to treaties, in all its complexity, is under preparation in the International Law Commission. (On the issues under consideration in this opinion, see, in particular, Second Report on Reservations to Treaties, by Mr. Alain Pellet, Special Rapporteur, Report of the International Law Commission to the General Assembly on the work of its Forty-ninth Session [...] [*Yearbook ... 1997*, vol. II (Part Two), pp. 44–57]; Tenth Report on Reservations to Treaties, by Mr. Alain Pellet, Special Rapporteur [...] [*Yearbook ... 2005*, vol. II (Part One), document A/CN.4/558 and Add.1–2].)

[108] See paragraph 47 above of the present report.

[109] *I.C.J. Reports 2006* (see footnote 97 above), p. 35, para. 77.

[110] See paragraph 47 above of the present report.

[111] *I.C.J. Reports 2006* (see footnote 97 above), p. 35, para. 78.

[112] *Yearbook ... 2005* (see footnote 66 above), pp. 177–183, paras. 151–180.

recommended that any further consideration of the question of reservations to human rights treaties should be suspended pending the upcoming work of the Commission on the topic (E/CN.4/Sub.2/2004/42, para. 72).

55. The third inter-committee meeting[113] and the sixteenth meeting of chairpersons of the human rights treaty bodies, held in Geneva on 21–22 June and from 23 to 25 June 2004, respectively, also considered the question of reservations to human rights treaties and found that "although not all treaty bodies were confronted with this issue, it would be useful to adopt a common approach".[114] A working group on reservations was established, as recommended at the fourth inter-committee meeting[115] to consider the report on the practice of human rights treaty bodies with respect to reservations to international human rights treaties (HRI/MC/2005/5 and Add.1), which is prepared and regularly updated by the Secretariat; the group is made up of one representative of each committee. At its meeting held on 8–9 June 2006,[116] the working group adopted the following recommendations for the attention of the fifth inter-committee meeting:[117]

1. The working group welcomes the report on the practice of human rights treaty bodies with respect to reservations to international human rights treaties (HRI/MC/2005/5) and its updated version (HRI/MC/2005/5/Add.1) which the secretariat had compiled for the fourth inter-committee meeting.

2. The working group recommends that while any declaration made at the time of ratification may be considered as a reservation, however it was termed, care must be exercised before concluding that the declaration should be considered as a reservation, even if the State had not used that term.

3. The working group recognizes that, despite the specific nature of the human rights treaties, which do not constitute a simple exchange of obligations between States but are the legal expression of the essential rights that each individual must be able to exercise as a human being, general treaty law is applicable to the human rights instruments and must be applied taking fully into account their specific nature, including their content and control mechanisms.

4. The working group considers that when reservations are authorized, whether explicitly or implicitly, they can contribute to the attainment of the objective of universal ratification. Unauthorized reservations, including those that are incompatible with the object and purpose of the treaty, do not contribute to attainment of the objective of universal ratification.

5. The working group considers that treaty bodies are competent to assess the validity of reservations, with a view to performing their functions, and possibly the implications of a finding of invalidity of a reservation, particularly in the examination of individual communications or in exercising other investigative functions in the case of treaty bodies that have such competence.

6. The working group considers that the identification of criteria for determining the validity of reservations in the light of the object and purpose of a treaty may be useful not only for States when they are considering making reservations, but also for treaty bodies in the performance of their functions. In this regard, the criteria contained in the draft methodological guidelines set out in the tenth report of the Special Rapporteur of the International Law Commission on reservations to treaties (A/CN.4/558/Add.1) constitute a step forward. The working group was pleased with its dialogue with the International Law Commission and welcomes the idea of further dialogue.

7. The working group considers that the only foreseeable consequences of invalidity are that the State could be considered as not being a party to the treaty, or as a party to the treaty but the provision to which the reservation has been made would not apply, or as a party to the treaty without the benefit of the reservation. The consequence that applies in a particular situation depends on the intention of the State at the time it enters its reservation. This intention must be identified during a serious examination of the available information, with the presumption, which may be refuted, that the State would prefer to remain a party to the treaty without the benefit of the reservation, rather than being excluded.

8. The working group welcomes the inclusion of a provision on reservations in the draft harmonized guidelines on reporting under the international human rights treaties, including the common core document and treaty-specific reports (HRI/MC/2006/3). It emphasizes the importance of dialogue between the treaty bodies and States making reservations; such dialogue would aim to distinguish more precisely the scope and consequences of reservations and possibly encourage the State party to reformulate or withdraw its reservations.

9. The working group recommends that another meeting be convened in the light of the latest discussions in the International Law Commission on reservations to treaties.[118]

56. At the regional level, the European Observatory of Reservations to International Treaties, set up at the end of the 1990s by the Council of Europe's *Ad Hoc* Committee of Legal Advisers on Public International Law (CAHDI),[119] has continued to promote and foster a common approach and response by States members of the Council to reservations formulated to conventions concluded both within and outside the framework of the Council. Pursuant to a decision taken in 2002,[120] the Council of Europe committed itself to a genuine joint action based on a list of problematic reservations to treaties relating to the fight against terrorism drawn up by the Observatory. The Committee of Ministers, at the deputy level, called on member States to consider withdrawing their possibly problematic reservations and invited the Secretary General of the Council to notify non-member States of the conclusions of CAHDI with regard to their reservations. The Committee of Ministers also encouraged member States "to volunteer to approach the non-member states concerned with regard to their respective reservations".[121] Interestingly, since these notifications were issued, a genuine dialogue has been taking place between the reserving States and the authorities of the Council. For example, the Russian Federation responded to the Secretary General's notification

[113] These meetings were attended by members of the following human rights treaty bodies: Human Rights Committee, Committee on Economic, Social and Cultural Rights, Committee on the Rights of the Child, Committee on the Elimination of Discrimination against Women, Committee on the Elimination of Racial Discrimination, Committee against Torture and Committee on Migrant Workers.

[114] Report of the third inter-committee meeting of human rights treaty bodies (A/59/254, annex, para. 18). See also the report of the fourth inter-committee meeting of human rights treaty bodies (A/60/278, annex, para. 14).

[115] A/60/278, annex, paras. 14 and 35 (VI).

[116] At the meeting of 8 June, Mr. George Korontzis, Senior Assistant Secretary to the Commission, gave the working group information on the recent work of the Commission on the topic of reservations.

[117] When the present report was being finalized, the report of this meeting (A/61/385, annex), held from 19 to 21 June 2006, was not yet available.

[118] Report of the meeting of the working group on reservations (HRI/MC/2006/5), para. 16.

[119] See the third report on reservations to treaties, *Yearbook ... 1998*, vol II (Part One), document A/CN.4/491 and Add.1–6, p. 233, paras. 28–29, and the report of the Group of Specialists on Reservations to International Treaties (DI-S-RIT (98) 10).

[120] *Yearbook ... 2003* (see footnote 3 above), p. 36, para. 23.

[121] Council of Europe, Committee of Ministers, 904th meeting of the Ministers' Deputies (CM(2004)174), para. 4; see also the decision of 2 November 2005, *ibid.*, 944th meeting (CM(2005)148), para. 3.

in 2005, explaining its reservation to the International Convention for the Suppression of the Financing of Terrorism; CAHDI consequently withdrew this reservation from its list of problematic reservations.[122] Showing that they too are responsive to the steps taken by the Council authorities, States not members of the Council have been providing explanations and clarifications of their reservations to instruments relating to the fight against terrorism that have been judged problematic.[123]

E. General presentation of the eleventh report

57. With the exception of a possible annex to reconsider the definition of the object and purpose of the treaty in the light of the discussion of the tenth report at the Commission's fifty-seventh session in 2005 (see paragraph 28 above), the present report is entirely devoted to procedural questions, in order to complete the examination of part III of the provisional plan of the study presented by the Special Rapporteur in his second report[124] and endorsed by the Commission in 1996.[125] It begins with an examination of questions relating to the formulation of objections, which had already been dealt with to some extent in the eighth and ninth reports on reservations to treaties.[126] The formulation of acceptances[127] and reactions to interpretative declarations are then examined.

[122] See CAHDI, 29th meeting, Strasbourg, 17–18 March 2005, meeting report (CAHDI (2005) 8), paras. 84–85.

[123] Such is the case of Malaysia, which provided information and clarifications concerning its declaration to the Convention on the prevention and punishment of crimes against internationally protected persons, including diplomatic agents (CAHDI, 30th meeting, Strasbourg, 19–20 September 2005, meeting report (CAHDI (2005) 19), paras. 42–43).

[124] *Yearbook ... 1996* (see footnote 7 above).

[125] See *Yearbook ... 1997*, vol. II (Part Two), pp. 52–53, paras. 116–123. See also the seventh report on the law of reservations, *Yearbook ... 2002* (footnote 2 above), p. 9, para. 18.

[126] *Yearbook ... 2003* (see footnote 3 above), p. 42, and *Yearbook ... 2004* (see footnote 13 above), paras. 1–29.

[127] After giving the question much thought, the Special Rapporteur believes that the "reservations dialogue" cannot be discussed until the question of the effects of reservations and of acceptances of, and objections to, reservations has been considered.

Formulation and withdrawal of acceptances and objections

A. Formulation and withdrawal of objections to reservations

58. At its fifty-seventh session, in 2005, the Commission adopted draft guideline 2.6.1 on the definition of objections. It reads:

> 2.6.1 *Definition of objections to reservations*
>
> "Objection" means a unilateral statement, however phrased or named, made by a State or an international organization in response to a reservation to a treaty formulated by another State or international organization, whereby the former State or organization purports to exclude or to modify the legal effects of the reservation, or to exclude the application of the treaty as a whole, in relations with the reserving State or organization.[128]

59. This definition—which it might be preferable to include in the first section of the Guide to Practice on second reading—is deliberately incomplete[129] in that, unlike the definition of reservations,[130] it does not specify the instances when an objection may be formulated and does not specify which categories of States or international organizations can formulate an objection. These are important elements for assessing the extent of the freedom to make objections (sect. 1 below). This study will also have to be supplemented by specific provisions on the procedure to be followed for formulating objections (sect. 2 below) and of the conditions and effects of their withdrawal or modification (sect. 3 below).

1. Freedom to make objections

60. It is now well established that a State or an international organization may make an objection to a reservation formulated by another State or another international organization, irrespective of the question of the validity of the reservation.[131] Nevertheless, although that power is quite extensive (see paragraphs 63 and 66 below), it is not unlimited, and it therefore seems preferable to speak of a "freedom" rather than a "right".[132] On the other hand, although reservations are only "formulated" by their authors, since they do not take effect until the other States or international organizations concerned have consented to them in one form or another,[133] the same is not true of objections, which are "made" solely by being unilaterally formulated by their authors, at least when they are parties to the treaty.[134]

[128] *Yearbook ... 2005*, vol. II (Part Two), p. 77, para. 438.

[129] See the commentary to this draft guideline 2.6.1, *ibid.*, pp. 77–78, paras. (4), (6) and (7).

[130] See draft guideline 1.1, *Yearbook ... 2003*, vol. II (Part Two), p. 65, para. 367.

[131] Throughout the present report, the Special Rapporteur sets aside the possible impact of the non-validity of the reservation on the effects of its acceptance or any objection to it. It is proposed that this matter will be studied when the effects of acceptances and objections come to be addressed.

[132] Similarly with regard to reservations, see the presentation of draft guideline 3.1 in the tenth report on reservations to treaties (*Yearbook ... 2005* (footnote 66 above), pp. 148–149, para. 12). In his first report on the law of treaties, however, Sir Humphrey Waldock mentioned "the right [of any State] to object" (*Yearbook ... 1962*, vol. II, document A/CN.4/144 and Add.1, p. 62). After a lengthy discussion in the Commission on the question of the connection between objections and the compatibility of a reservation with the object and purpose of the treaty (*ibid.*, vol. I, 651st–654th and 656th meetings, pp. 139–168 and 172–175; see also paragraph 62 below), this requirement, which was included in draft article 19, paragraph 1 (*a*), as proposed by the Special Rapporteur, completely disappeared in the text of draft article 18 proposed by the Drafting Committee, which combined draft articles 18 and 19. In this respect, the Special Rapporteur noted that his two drafts "had been considerably reduced in length without, however, leaving out anything of substance" (*ibid.*, 663rd meeting, p. 223, para. 36). Neither during the debates nor in the later texts submitted to or adopted by the Commission, was the issue of the "right" to make objections revisited.

[133] See *Yearbook ... 2005* (footnote 66 above), p. 149, para. 14.

[134] The situation may be different in two cases: the first being where the treaty itself has yet to enter into force, which goes without saying, and the second—considered below (para. 83)—where the objecting State or international organization intends to become a party, but has not yet expressed its definitive consent to be bound.

61. The *travaux préparatoires* of the 1969 Vienna Convention leave no doubt as to the discretionary nature of the formulation of objections, but are not very enlightening on the question of who may formulate them.

62. Adopted after heated debate in the Commission,[135] draft article 20, paragraph 2 (*b*), adopted on first reading by the Commission in 1962, established a link between objections and the incompatibility of reservations with the object and purpose of the treaty, which seemed to be the *sine qua non* for validity in both cases.[136] In response to the comments made by the Australian, Danish and United States Governments,[137] however, the Special Rapporteur reverted to the position taken by the Commission on first reading, omitting the reference to the criterion of compatibility from his proposed draft article 19, paragraph 3 (*b*).[138] The opposing opinion was nonetheless supported once more by Sir Humphrey Waldock in the Commission's debates,[139] but that did not prevent the Drafting Committee from once again leaving out any reference to the compatibility criterion—without, however, providing any explanation.[140] In accordance with that position, draft article 19, paragraph 4 (*b*), adopted on second reading in 1965, merely provided that "[a]n objection by another contracting State to a reservation precludes the entry into force of the treaty as between the objecting and reserving States unless a contrary intention is expressed by the objecting State".[141] Despite the doubts voiced by a number of delegations,[142] the United Nations Conference on the Law of Treaties of 1968–1969 made no further reference to the lack of a connection between objections and the criteria of a reservation's validity. In response to a question by Canada, however, the Expert Consultant, Sir Humphrey Waldock, was particularly clear in his support for the position adopted by the Commission:

> The second question was, where a reservation had not been expressly authorized, and at the same time was not one prohibited under article 16, paragraph (*c*), could a contracting State lodge an objection other than that of incompatibility with the object and purpose of the treaty? The answer was surely Yes. Each contracting State remained *completely free** to decide for itself, in accordance with its own interests, whether or not it would accept the reservation.[143]

63. On this point, the Vienna regime deviates from the solution adopted by ICJ in its 1951 advisory opinion,[144] which, in this regard, is certainly outdated and no longer corresponds to current positive law.[145] A State or an international organization has the right to formulate an objection both to a reservation that does not meet the criteria for validity and to a reservation that it deems to be unacceptable "in accordance with its own interests" (para. 62 above), even if it is valid. In other words, States and international organizations are free to object for any reason whatsoever and that reason may or may not have to do with the non-validity of the reservation.[146]

64. This solution is based on the principle of consent, which underlies the reservations regime and indeed all treaty law, as ICJ recalled in its 1951 advisory opinion:

> It is well established that in its treaty relations a State cannot be bound without its consent, and that consequently no reservation can be effective against any State without its agreement thereto.[147]

---

[135] The criterion of compatibility with the object and purpose of the treaty played a large part in the early debates on reservations (*Yearbook ... 1962*, vol. I, 651st–654th and 656th meetings, pp. 139–168 and 172–175). One of the leading advocates of the link between this criterion and reactions to a reservation was Mr. Rosenne, who based his arguments on the ICJ advisory opinion (see footnote 144 below) (*ibid.*, 651st meeting, p. 144, para. 79).

[136] According to that provision: "An objection to a reservation by a State which considers it to be incompatible with the object and purpose of the treaty precludes the entry into force of the treaty as between the objecting and the reserving State, unless a contrary intention shall have been expressed by the objecting State" (*Yearbook ... 1962*, vol. II, document A/5209, p. 176).

[137] See the fourth report on the law of treaties, *Yearbook ... 1965*, vol. II, document A/CN.4/177 and Add.1 and 2, pp. 45–47.

[138] *Ibid.*, p. 52, para. 10.

[139] *Ibid.*, vol. I, 799th meeting, p. 169, para. 65. See also Mr. Tsuruoka, *ibid.*, para. 69. For an opposing view, see Mr. Tunkin, *ibid.*, p. 167, para. 37.

[140] *Ibid.*, 813th meeting, pp. 265–268, paras. 30–71 and, in particular, paras. 57–66.

[141] *Ibid.*, vol. II, document A/6009, p. 162.

[142] See, in particular, the United States amendment (*Official Records of the United Nations Conference on the Law of Treaties, First and Second Sessions, Vienna, 26 March–24 May 1968 and 9 April–22 May 1969, Documents of the Conference* (United Nations publication, Sales No. E.70.V.5) (A/CONF.39/14), p. 136, para. 179 (v) (*d*), and the comments of the United States representative (*ibid., First Session, Vienna, 26 March–24 May 1968, Summary records of the plenary meetings and of the meetings of the Committee of the Whole* (United Nations publication, Sales No. E.68.V.7), 21st meeting, p. 108, para. 11). See also the critical comments made by Australia (*ibid.*, 22nd meeting, para. 49), Japan (*ibid.*, 21st meeting, para. 29), the Philippines (*ibid.*, para. 58), United Kingdom (*ibid.*, para. 74), Switzerland (*ibid.*, para. 41) and Sweden (*ibid.*, 22nd meeting, para. 32).

[143] *Ibid.*, 25th meeting, para. 3.

[144] The Court considered that "it is the compatibility of a reservation with the object and purpose of the Convention that must furnish the criterion for the attitude of a State in making the reservation on accession as well as for the appraisal by a State in objecting to the reservation. Such is the rule of conduct which must guide every State in the appraisal which it must make, individually and from its own standpoint, of the admissibility of any reservation" (*I.C.J. Reports 1951* (see footnote 101 above, p. 24.) See also Coccia, "Reservations to multilateral treaties on human rights", pp. 8–9; Edwards Jr., "Reservations to treaties", p. 397; Lijnzaad, *Reservations to U.N. Human Rights Treaties. Ratify and Ruin?*, p. 51; and Zemanek, "Some unresolved questions concerning reservations in the Vienna Convention on the Law of Treaties", p. 333.

[145] It is also unlikely that it reflected the state of positive law in 1951. No one seems to have ever claimed that the freedom to formulate objections in the context of the system of unanimity was subject to the reservation being contrary to the object and purpose of the treaty.

[146] Subject, of course, to the general principles of law which may limit the exercise of the discretionary power of States at the international level and the principle prohibiting abuse of rights.

[147] *I.C.J. Reports 1951* (see footnote 101 above), p. 21. The dissenting judges also stressed this principle in their joint opinion:

> "The consent of the parties is the basis of treaty obligations. The law governing reservations is only a particular application of this fundamental principle, whether the consent of the parties to a reservation is given in advance of the proposal of the reservation or at the same time or later."

(*Ibid.*, pp. 31–32). See also the famous PCIJ dictum in the *"Lotus"* case :

> "The rules of law binding upon States therefore emanate from their own free will as expressed in conventions or by usages generally accepted as expressing principles of law and established in order to regulate the relations between these co-existing independent communities or with a view to the achievement of common aims. Restrictions upon the independence of States cannot therefore be presumed."

(*"Lotus", Judgment No. 9, 1927, P.C.I.J., Series A, No. 10*, p. 18). See also *Yearbook ... 1996* (footnote 7 above), p. 57, paras. 97 and 99.

65. A State (or an international organization) is, therefore, never bound by treaty obligations[148] that are not in its interests. A State that formulates a reservation is simply proposing a modification of the treaty relations envisaged by the treaty.[149] No State, however, is obliged to accept those modifications—except for those resulting from reservations expressly authorized by the treaty, provided, of course, that they are not contrary to the object and purpose of the treaty.[150] Limiting the right to raise objections to reservations that are contrary to one of the criteria for validity established in article 19 would not only violate the sovereign right to accept or refuse treaty obligations,[151] but would also have the effect of establishing an actual right to make reservations. Such a right, which definitely does not exist, would contravene the very principle of the sovereign equality of States, since it would allow the reserving State (or international organization) to unilaterally impose its will on the other Contracting Parties.[152] In practice, this would render the mechanism of acceptances and objections null and void.[153]

66. It therefore seems to be indisputable that States and international organizations have the discretionary right to make objections to reservations. This should be reflected in a draft guideline that emphasizes that a State or international organization not only has the right to raise an objection to a reservation, but may exercise that right in a discretionary manner; in other words, it may raise an objection for any reason, even merely for political reasons or reasons of expediency, without having to explain its reasons (on this point, see, however, paragraphs 105–111 below).

67. However, "discretionary" does not mean "arbitrary"[154] and, even though this right undoubtedly stems from the power of a State to exercise its own judgement, it is not absolute. Above all, it must be exercised within the limits arising from the procedural and form-related constraints that are developed in greater detail later in the present report. Thus, for example, it should be emphasized at the outset that a State or international organization that has accepted a reservation loses its right to formulate an objection later to the same reservation. This can be derived implicitly from the presumption of acceptance of reservations established in article 20, paragraph 5, of the 1969 and 1986 Vienna Conventions, which presumption will be discussed in more detail later, during the discussion of the acceptance procedure (see paragraph 57 above).

"2.6.3 *Freedom to make objections*

"A State or an international organization may formulate an objection to a reservation for any reason whatsoever, in accordance with the provisions of the present Guide to Practice."

68. This freedom to make objections for any reason whatsoever also encompasses the freedom to oppose the entry into force of the treaty as between the reserving State or international organization, on the one hand, and the author of the objection, on the other. This is made possible by articles 20, paragraph 4 (*b*), and 21, paragraph 3, of the 1969 and 1986 Vienna Conventions, which specify the effects of an objection.

69. Arriving at those provisions, in particular article 20, paragraph 4 (*b*), of the 1969 Vienna Convention, proved difficult. This was because the Commission's early special rapporteurs, staunch supporters of the system of unanimity, were barely interested in objections, the effects of which were, in their view, purely mechanical (see paragraph 88 below): it seemed self-evident to them that an objection prevents the reserving State from becoming a party to the treaty.[155] Even though he came to support a more flexible system, Sir Humphrey Waldock still adhered to that view in 1962, as is demonstrated by draft article 19, paragraph 4 (*c*), presented in his first report on the law of treaties: "the objections shall preclude the entry into force of the treaty as between the objecting and the reserving States."[156]

70. The members of the Commission,[157] including the Special Rapporteur,[158] were, however, inclined to abandon that categorical approach in favour of a simple presumption in order to bring the wording of this provision more into line with the ICJ 1951 advisory opinion, which stated:

> As no State can be bound by a reservation to which it has not consented, it necessarily follows that each State objecting to it will or will not, on the basis of its individual appraisal within the limits of the criterion of the object and purpose stated above, consider the reserving State to be a party to the Convention.[159]

71. By strictly aligning themselves with this position, the members of the Commission introduced a simple presumption in favour of the non-entry into force of the treaty as between the reserving State and the objecting State and, at the same time, limited the possibility of opposing the treaty's entry into force in cases where the reservation was contrary to its object and purpose.[160] Draft article 20, paragraph 2 (*b*), adopted at its first reading, therefore provided the following:

---

[148] This clearly does not mean that States are not bound by legal obligations emanating from other sources.

[149] See *Yearbook ... 2005* (footnote 66 above), para. 14.

[150] See Horn, *Reservations and Interpretative Declarations to Multilateral Treaties*, p. 121; Tomuschat, "Admissibility and legal effects of reservations to multilateral treaties: comments on arts. 16 and 17 of the ILC's 1966 draft articles on the law of treaties", p. 466.

[151] See Tomuschat, *loc. cit.*

[152] See, in this regard, the ninth of the guiding principles applicable to unilateral declarations of States capable of creating legal obligations, adopted by the Commission at its fifty-eighth session, *Yearbook ... 2006*, vol. II (Two), para. 176.

[153] See Müller, "Article 20", p. 837, para. 74. See also the statement made by Mr. Pal in the Commission (*Yearbook ... 1962*, vol. I, 653rd meeting p. 153, para. 5).

[154] See, in particular, Jovanović, *Restriction des compétences discrétionnaires des États en droit international.*

[155] See Reuter, *Introduction to the Law of Treaties*, p. 83, para. 134.

[156] *Yearbook ... 1962* (see footnote 132 above), p. 62.

[157] See, in particular, Mr. Tunkin (*Yearbook ... 1962*, vol. I, 653rd meeting, p. 156, para. 26, and 654th meeting, p. 162, para. 11), Mr. Rosenne (*ibid.*, 653rd meeting, p. 157, para. 30), Mr. Jiménez de Aréchaga (*ibid.*, p. 158, para. 48), Mr. de Luna (*ibid.*, p. 160, para. 66) and Mr. Yasseen (*ibid.*, 654th meeting, p. 161, para. 6).

[158] *Ibid.*, p. 162, paras. 17 and 20.

[159] *I.C.J. Reports 1951* (see footnote 101 above), p. 26.

[160] See paragraph 62 and footnote 135 above.

An objection to a reservation by a State which considers it to be incompatible with the object and purpose of the treaty precludes the entry into force of the treaty as between the objecting and the reserving State, unless a contrary intention shall have been expressed by the objecting State.[161]

72. If the possibility of making an objection is no longer linked to the criterion of compatibility with the object and purpose of the treaty,[162] the freedom of the objecting State to oppose the treaty's entry into force in its relations with the reserving State becomes unconditional. The objecting State may, therefore, exclude all treaty relations between itself and the reserving State for any reason. The wording ultimately retained by the Commission went so far as to make this effect automatic: an objection (whatever the reason) precluded the entry into force of the treaty, unless the State concerned expressed its contrary intention.[163] During the United Nations Conference on the Law of Treaties at Vienna, the thrust of that presumption was reversed, not without heated debate, in favour of the entry into force of the treaty as between the objecting State and the reserving State.[164]

73. As open to criticism as this new approach may seem, the fact remains that the objecting State is still free to oppose the entry into force of the treaty in its relations with the reserving State. The reversal of the presumption simply requires the objecting State to make an express declaration to that effect, even though it remains completely free regarding its reasons for making such a declaration.

74. In practice, States have been curiously eager to state specifically that their objections do not prevent the treaty from entering into force *vis-à-vis* the reserving State, even though, by virtue of the presumption contained in article 20, paragraph 4 (*b*), of the 1969 and 1986 Vienna Conventions, that would automatically be the case. Nor is this practice due to a desire to justify the objection, since States raise minimum-effect objections (specifically stating that the treaty will enter into force in their relations with the reserving State) even to reservations that they deem incompatible with the purpose and object of the treaty.[165] It is possible, however, to find examples of objections where States specifically state that their objection does prevent the treaty from entering into force in their relations with the reserving State.[166] Such cases, though rare,[167] show that States can and do raise such objections when they see fit.

75. It follows that the power to make an objection for any reason whatsoever also means that the objecting State or international organization may freely oppose the entry into force of the treaty in their relations with the reserving State or organization. The author of the objection therefore remains completely free to modify the effects of the objection as it pleases and without having to justify its

---

[161] *Yearbook ... 1962* (see footnote 136 above), p. 176. See also page 181, paragraph (23) of the commentary to article 20.

[162] On this point, see the explanations given in paragraph 62 above.

[163] Draft article 17, paragraph 4 (*b*), adopted on second reading, provided as follows:

> "An objection by another contracting State to a reservation precludes the entry into force of the treaty as between the objecting and reserving States unless a contrary intention is expressed by the objecting State."

(*Yearbook ... 1966*, vol. II, document A/6309/Rev.1, p. 202)

[164] The question had already been raised during the discussion of the draft articles adopted on first reading by the members of the Commission and by the Czechoslovak and Romanian delegations in the Sixth Committee (Sir Humphrey Waldock, fourth report (*Yearbook ... 1965* (footnote 132 above), pp. 48–49). The idea of reversing the presumption had been advocated by a number of Commission members (Mr. Tunkin (*ibid.*, vol. I, 799th meeting, p. 167, para. 39) and Mr. Lachs (*ibid.*, 813th meeting, p. 268, para. 62)). Nonetheless, the proposals made in this regard by Czechoslovakia (A/CONF.39/C.1/L.85, *United Nations Conference on the Law of Treaties* (footnote 142 above), p. 135), Syria (A/CONF.39/C.1/L.94, *ibid.*) and the Union of Soviet Socialist Republics (A/CONF.39/C.1/L.115, *ibid.*, p. 133) were rejected by the Conference in 1968 (*ibid.*, p. 137, para. 182 (*j*), and *ibid.*, *First Session*, 25th meeting, p. 135, paras. 35 *et seq.*). It was only in 1969 that a new Soviet amendment in this regard (A/CONF.39/L.3, *ibid.*, *First and Second Sessions*, pp. 265–266) was finally adopted by 49 votes to 21, with 30 abstentions (*ibid.*, *Second Session, Vienna, 9 April–22 May 1969, Summary records of the plenary meetings and of the meetings of the Committee of the Whole* (United Nations publication, Sales No. E.70.V.6), tenth plenary meeting, p. 35, para. 79).

[165] See Belgium's objections to the Egyptian and Cambodian reservations to the Vienna Convention on Diplomatic Relations (United Nations, *Multilateral Treaties Deposited with the Secretary-General: Status as at 31 December 2005*, vol. I (United Nations publication, Sales No. E.06.V.2), chap. III.3) and the objections of Germany to several reservations concerning the same Convention (*ibid.*). It is, however, interesting to note that, even though Germany considers all the reservations in question as "incompatible with the letter and spirit of the Convention", Germany stated for only some objections that they did not prevent the entry into force of the treaty as between Germany and the reserving States; it did not take a position on the other cases. Many examples can be found in the objections to the reservations formulated to the International Covenant on Civil and Political Rights, in particular the objections that were raised to the United States reservation to article 6 of the Covenant by Belgium, Denmark, Finland, France, Italy, the Netherlands, Norway, Portugal, Spain and Sweden (*ibid.*, chap. IV.4). All these States considered the reservation to be incompatible with the object and purpose of the Covenant, but nonetheless did not oppose its entry into force in their relations with the United States. Only Germany remained silent regarding the entry into force of the Covenant, despite its objection to the reservation (*ibid.*). The phenomenon is not, however, limited to human rights treaties. See, for example, the objections made by Austria, France, Germany and Italy to Viet Nam's reservation to the United Nations Convention against Illicit Traffic in Narcotic Drugs and Psychotropic Substances (*ibid.*, chap. VI.19) and the objections made by the States members of the Council of Europe to the reservations to the International Convention for the Suppression of Terrorist Bombings (*ibid.*, vol. II, chap. XVIII.9) and to the International Convention for the Suppression of the Financing of Terrorism (*ibid.*, chap. XVIII.11).

[166] See, for example, the objections of China and the Netherlands to the reservations made by a number of socialist States to the Convention on the Prevention and Punishment of the Crime of Genocide (United Nations, *Multilateral Treaties ...* (footnote 165 above), vol. I, chap. IV.1), the objections of Israel, Italy and the United Kingdom to the reservations formulated by Burundi to the Convention on the prevention and punishment of crimes against internationally protected persons, including diplomatic agents (*ibid.*, vol. II, chap. XVIII.7), the objections of France and Italy to the United States reservation to the Agreement on the International Carriage of Perishable Foodstuffs and on the Special Equipment to be used for such Carriage (*ibid.*, vol. I, chap. XI.B.22) and the objections of the United Kingdom to the Syrian and Vietnamese reservations and the objections of New Zealand to the Syrian reservation formulated to the 1969 Vienna Convention (*ibid*, vol. II, chap. XXIII.1).

[167] This is not to imply that maximum-effect objections accompanied by the declaration provided for in article 20, paragraph 4 (*b*), are a type of objection that is disappearing, as suggested by Riquelme Cortado (*Las reservas a los tratados: lagunas y ambigüedades del Régimen de Viena*, p. 283). It has been argued that the thrust of the presumption retained at the United Nations Conference on the Law of Treaties (in favour of the entry into force of the treaty) and political considerations may explain the reluctance of States to resort to maximum-effect objections (see Redgwell, "Universality or integrity? Some reflections on reservations to general multilateral treaties", p. 267). See, however, the explanations provided by States to the question raised by the Commission on this subject, paras. 33–38 above, in particular para. 37.

decision. It might be useful to state this clearly in a draft guideline 2.6.4, entitled as follows:

"2.6.4 *Freedom to oppose the entry into force of the treaty* vis-à-vis *the author of the reservation*

"A State or international organization that formulates an objection to a reservation may oppose the entry into force of the treaty as between itself and the reserving State or international organization for any reason whatsoever, in accordance with the provisions of the present Guide to Practice."

76. Draft guideline 2.6.1 on the definition of objections to reservations does not, in fact, resolve the question of which States or international organizations have the freedom to make objections to a reservation formulated by another State or another international organization, a question which the Commission explicitly set aside when it adopted the draft guideline (see paragraph 59 above).

77. The 1969 and 1986 Vienna Conventions provide some guidance on this matter. Article 20, paragraph 4 (*b*), of the 1986 Convention refers to "an objection by a contracting State or by a contracting organization". However, it should not necessarily be inferred from this phrase that only contracting States or organizations within the meaning of article 2, paragraph 1 (*f*), are authorized to formulate objections.[168] Article 20, paragraph 4 (*b*), simply determines the possible effects of an objection raised by a contracting State or by a contracting organization; however, the fact that paragraph 4 does not specify the effects of objections formulated by States other than contracting States or by organizations other than contracting organizations does not necessarily mean that such other States or organizations may not formulate objections.[169] In reality, it may be wise for States or international organizations that intend to become parties, but have not yet expressed their definitive consent to be bound, to express their opposition to a reservation. These "pre-emptive" objections will have the effects envisaged in articles 20–21 only when their author becomes a contracting State or a contracting organization.[170]

78. The limitation on the possible authors of an objection that article 20, paragraph 4 (*b*), of the 1969 and 1986 Vienna Conventions might seem to imply is not found in article 21, paragraph 3, on the effects of the objection on the application of the treaty in cases where the author of the objection has not opposed the entry into force of the treaty between itself and the reserving State. Above all, as article 23, paragraph 1, of the 1969 Convention clearly states, reservations, express acceptances and objections must be communicated not only to the contracting States but also to "other States entitled to become parties to the treaty". Such a notification has meaning only if these other States can, in fact, react to the reservation by way of an express acceptance or an objection. The specific effects of these reactions is a separate issue.

79. The draft article 19 proposed by Sir Humphrey Waldock in his first report on the law of treaties, an article devoted entirely to objections and their effects, provided, moreover, that "any State which is *or is entitled to become a party** to a treaty shall have the right to object".[171]

80. The practice of the Secretary-General as depositary of multilateral treaties with regard to objections formulated by non-contracting or non-signatory States is ambiguous in this regard. Such objections are termed "communications" and, since they are deemed to have no legal effect, they are not registered under Article 102 of the Charter of the United Nations, nor are they published in the Treaty Series.[172] The reason for this is that, except in a few specific cases,[173] an objection formulated by a signatory State has no effect as long as the State that formulated the objection does not become a party to the treaty in question. The practice of the Secretary-General does not therefore shed much light on the freedom to formulate objections, because simply saying that an objection has no effect does not mean that it cannot be formulated.

81. The freedom to make objections is not, therefore, limited to contracting States or international organizations. However, this does not mean that just any State or international organization can raise an objection. There is clearly no reason why a State or an international organization that has no intention of becoming a party to a treaty should be able to express an opinion about reservations to it; such an objection would, in this specific case, have no effect, not even a potential effect.

82. These considerations, taken together, suggest that only States and organizations that are Contracting Parties or are "entitled to become parties to the treaty" may object to reservations that have been formulated. Such a limitation, though it may seem superfluous for "open" treaties containing the words "any State", is needed to cover the specific situation of treaties with limited participation, regardless of whether or not they are subject to the unanimity requirement imposed by article 20, paragraph 2, of the 1969 and 1986 Vienna Conventions.

83. However, it should be noted that, while objections formulated by parties to the treaty are "made" from the very moment that they are formulated, in the sense that they produce their effects immediately (see paragraph 60 above), it could be asked whether those emanating from States or international organizations that are not parties to the treaty could be deemed to be "made" when the objections will not have concrete effects until the treaty enters into force with regard to them. In the view of the Special Rapporteur, this nuance should be reflected by using the

[168] This position seems to be defended by Clark, "The Vienna Convention reservations regime and the Convention on Discrimination against Women", p. 297.

[169] In this regard, see Imbert, *Les réserves aux traités multilatéraux*, p. 150.

[170] In its 1951 advisory opinion, ICJ considered that "an objection to a reservation made by a State which is entitled to sign or accede but which has not yet done so, is without legal effect" (*I.C.J. Reports 1951* (see footnote 101 above, p. 30). However, this in no way implies that these States may not formulate objections.

[171] *Yearbook ... 1962* (see footnote 132 above), p. 62.

[172] *Summary of Practice of the Secretary-General as Depositary of Multilateral Treaties* (United Nations publication, Sales No. E.94.V.15), document ST/LEG/7/Rev.1, para. 214.

[173] See article 20, paragraph 2, of the 1969 and 1986 Vienna Conventions: an objection prevents the requirement of unanimous acceptance provided for in this article from being met.

word "formulated" rather than "made" in draft guideline 2.6.5, which might be adopted in order to clarify draft guidelines 2.6.1–2.6.2 on these points. The effect of this change should not, however, be exaggerated: in this case, contrary to what happens in the case of reservations, the effects of the objection are not subject to a specific reaction by the reserving State or by another party to the treaty.

84. Consequently, draft guideline 2.6.5 might be worded as follows:

"2.6.5 *Author of an objection*

"An objection to a reservation may be formulated by:

"(*a*) Any contracting State and any contracting international organization; and

"(*b*) Any State and any international organization that is entitled to become a party to the treaty."

85. Even though, according to the definition contained in draft guideline 2.6.1, an objection is a unilateral statement,[174] it is perfectly possible for a number of States and/or a number of international organizations to formulate an objection jointly. Practice in this area is not highly developed; it is not, however, non-existent.[175] A particularly striking example is to be found in the objections formulated in identical terms by Belgium, Denmark, France, Germany, Ireland, Italy, Luxembourg, the Netherlands, the United Kingdom and the European Community with respect to the similar declarations made by Bulgaria and the German Democratic Republic to the Customs Convention on the International Transport of Goods under Cover of TIR Carnets.[176] The European Community has also formulated a number of objections "[o]n behalf of the European Economic Community and of its member States".[177]

86. Technically, moreover, there is nothing to prevent the joint formulation of an objection, just as there is nothing to prevent the joint formulation of reservations.[178] However, this in no way affects the unilateral nature of the objection. For these reasons, the Commission will undoubtedly wish to adopt a draft guideline modelled on the equivalent draft guideline relating to the joint formulation of reservations.[179]

"2.6.6 *Joint formulation of an objection*

"The joint formulation of an objection by a number of States or international organizations does not affect the unilateral nature of that objection."

2. Procedure for the formulation of objections

87. The procedural rules concerning the formulation of objections are not notably different from those that apply to the formulation of reservations. This is, perhaps, the reason why the Commission apparently did not pay very much attention to these issues during the preparatory work for the 1969 Vienna Convention.

88. That lack of interest can easily be explained in the case of the special rapporteurs who advocated the traditional system of unanimity, namely Messrs J. L. Brierly, H. Lauterpacht and G. G. Fitzmaurice.[180] While it was only logical, in their view, that an acceptance, which is at the heart of the traditional system of unanimity, should be provided with a legal framework, particularly where its temporal aspect was concerned, an objection, which they saw simply as a refusal of acceptance that prevented unanimity from taking place and, consequently, the reserving State from becoming a party to the instrument, did not seem to warrant specific consideration.

89. It was only logical that Sir Humphrey Waldock's first report on the law of treaties, which introduced the "flexible" system in which objections play if not a more important then at least a more ambiguous role, contained an entire draft article on procedural issues relating to the formulation of objections.[181] Despite the very detailed

[174] See also the commentary to draft guideline 2.6.1 (Definition of objections to reservations), *Yearbook ... 2005*, vol. II (Part Two), para. 438, para. (6) of the commentary.

[175] In the context of regional organizations, in particular the Council of Europe, States strive to coordinate and harmonize their reactions and objections to reservations. Even though member States continue to formulate objections individually, they coordinate not only on the timing, but also on the wording, of objections, especially in the case of objections to reservations relating to counter-terrorism conventions (see also paragraph 56 above); see, for example, the objections of certain States members of the Council of Europe to the International Convention for the Suppression of Terrorist Bombings (United Nations, *Multilateral Treaties* ... (footnote 165 above), vol. II, chap. XVIII.9) and to the International Convention for the Suppression of the Financing of Terrorism (*ibid*., chap. XVIII.11).

[176] *Ibid*., vol. I, chap. XI.A.16.

[177] United Nations, *Treaty Series*, vol. 1404, No. 23317, p. 426, objection to a declaration made by the Union of Soviet Socialist Republics with respect to the International Tropical Timber Agreement. See also the identical objection to the declaration made by the Union of Soviet Socialist Republics with respect to the Wheat Trade Convention (*ibid*., vol. 1455, No. 24237, p. 286). In the same vein, see the practice followed at the Council of Europe since 2002 with respect to reservations to conventions relating to the fight against terrorism (para. 56 above).

[178] *Yearbook ... 1998* (see footnote 119 above), pp. 246–247, paras. 130–133.

[179] Draft guideline 1.1.7 (Reservations formulated jointly): "The joint formulation of a reservation by a number of States or international organizations does not affect the unilateral nature of that reservation." (*Ibid*., vol. II (Part Two), p. 106). For the commentary to this draft guideline, see pages 106–107. See also draft guideline 1.2.2 (Interpretative declarations formulated jointly) and the commentary thereto (*Yearbook ... 1999*, vol. II (Part Two), pp. 106–107).

[180] Even though Mr. Lauterpacht's proposals *de lege ferenda* envisaged objections, the Special Rapporteur did not consider it necessary to set out the procedure that should be followed when formulating them. See the alternative drafts for article 9, *Yearbook ... 1953*, vol. II, document A/CN.4/63, pp. 91–92.

[181] This draft article 19 read as follows:

"2. (*a*) An objection to a reservation shall be formulated in writing by the competent authority of the objecting State or by a representative of the State duly authorized for that purpose.

"(*b*) The objection shall be communicated to the reserving State and to all other States which are or are entitled to become parties to the treaty, in accordance with the procedure, if any, prescribed in the treaty for such communications.

"(*c*) If no procedure has been prescribed in the treaty but the treaty designates a depositary of the instruments relating to the treaty, then the lodging of the objection shall be communicated to the depositary whose duty it shall be:

(*Continued on next page*.)

nature of this provision, the report limits itself to a very brief commentary by indicating that "[t]he provisions of this article are for the most part a reflex of provisions contained in [the articles on the power to formulate and withdraw reservations (art. 17) and on consent to reservations and its effects (art. 18)] and do not therefore need further explanation".[182]

90. After major reworking of the draft articles on acceptance and objection initially proposed by the Special Rapporteur,[183] only draft article 18, paragraph 5, presented by the Drafting Committee in 1962 deals with the formulation and the notification of an objection,[184] a provision which, in the view of the Commission, "do[es] not appear to require comment".[185] That lack of interest continued into 1965, when the draft received its second reading. And even though objections found a place in the new draft article 20 devoted entirely to questions of procedure, the Special Rapporteur still did not consider it appropriate to comment further on those provisions.[186]

91. The desirability of parallel procedural rules for the formulation, notification and communication of reservations, on the one hand, and of objections, on the other, was stressed throughout the debate in the Commission and was finally reflected in article 23, paragraph 1, of the 1969 Vienna Convention, which sets forth the procedure for formulating an express acceptance of or an objection to a reservation. In 1965, Mr. Castrén rightly observed:

> Paragraph 5 [of draft article 20, which, considerably shortened and simplified, was the source for article 23, paragraph 1] laid down word for word precisely the same procedural rules for objections to a reservation as those applicable under paragraph 1 to the proposal and notification of reservations. Preferably, therefore, the two paragraphs should be amalgamated or else paragraph 5 should say simply that the provisions of paragraph 1 applied also to objections to a reservation.[187]

92. Therefore, it may be wise to simply take note, within the framework of the Guide to Practice, of this procedural parallelism between the formulation of reservations and the formulation of objections. It is particularly important to note that the requirement of a marked formalism that is a consequence of these similarities between the procedure for the formulation of objections and the procedure for the formulation of reservations is justified by the highly significant effects that an objection may have on the reservation and its application as well as on the entry into force and the application of the treaty itself.[188]

93. The parallel cannot be complete, however. It is clear that some rules of procedure applicable to the formulation of reservations cannot be transposed to the formulation of objections. This is clearly the case with respect to the time at which an objection may be formulated; the question of the confirmation of an objection formulated before the author is a party must obviously be posed in different terms.[189] Moreover, while the requirement of written form applies to the formulation of an objection as well as that of a reservation, it is no doubt helpful to say so specifically. These three questions at least merit separate draft guidelines.

94. In contrast, the rules regarding the authorities competent to formulate reservations at the international level and the consequences (or the absence of consequences) of the violation of internal rules regarding the formulation of reservations, the rules regarding the notification and communication of reservations and the rules regarding the functions of the depositary in this area would seem to be transposable *mutatis mutandis* to the formulation of objections. Rather than reproducing draft guidelines 2.1.3 (Formulation of a reservation at the international level),[190] 2.1.4 (Absence of consequences at the international level of the violation of internal rules regarding the

(Footnote 181 continued.)

"(i) To transmit the text of the objection to the reserving State and to all other States which are or are entitled to become parties to the treaty; and

"(ii) To draw the attention of the reserving State and the other States concerned to any provisions in the treaty relating to objections to reservations.

"3. (*a*) In the case of a plurilateral or multilateral treaty, an objection to a reservation shall not be effective unless it has been lodged before the expiry of twelve calendar months from the date when the reservation was formally communicated to the objecting State; provided that, in the case of a multilateral treaty, an objection by a State which at the time of such communication was not a party to the treaty shall nevertheless be effective if subsequently lodged when the State executes the act or acts necessary to enable it to become a party to the treaty.

(*b*) In the case of a plurilateral treaty, an objection by a State which has not yet become a party to the treaty, either actual or presumptive, shall:

(i) Cease to have effect, if the objecting State shall not itself have executed a definitive act of participation in the treaty within a period of twelve months from the date when the objection was lodged;

(ii) Be of no effect, if the treaty is in force and four years have already elapsed since the adoption of its text.

(*Yearbook ... 1962* (see footnote 132 above), p. 62)

[182] *Ibid.*, p. 68, para. (22) of the commentary on article 19.

[183] The only explanation that can be found in the work of the Commission for merging the draft articles initially proposed by Sir Humphrey Waldock is found in his presentation of the report of the Drafting Committee at the 663rd meeting of the Commission (see footnote 132 above). On that occasion, the Special Rapporteur stated that "the new article 18 covered both acceptance of and objection to reservations; the contents of the two former articles 18 and 19 had been considerably reduced in length without, however, leaving out anything of substance" (*Yearbook ... 1962*, vol. I, 663rd meeting, p. 223, para. 36).

[184] *Ibid.*, 668th meeting, p. 258, para. 30. See also draft article 19, paragraph 5, adopted on first reading, *ibid.*, vol. II (see footnote 136 above), p. 176.

[185] *Ibid.*, vol. II, p. 180, para. (18) of the commentary to article 19.

[186] See *Yearbook ... 1965* (footnote 137 above), pp. 53–54, para. 14, 15 and 19.

[187] *Ibid.*, vol. I, 799th meeting, p. 168, para. 53.

[188] See articles 20, paragraph 4 (*b*), and 23, paragraph 3, of the 1969 and 1986 Vienna Conventions.

[189] See article 23, paragraph 3, of the 1969 and 1986 Vienna Conventions.

[190] "2.1.3 *Formulation of a reservation at the international level*

"1. Subject to the customary practices in international organizations which are depositaries of treaties, a person is considered as representing a State or an international organization for the purpose of formulating a reservation if:

"(*a*) That person produces appropriate full powers for the purposes of adopting or authenticating the text of the treaty with regard to which the reservation is formulated or expressing the consent of the State or organization to be bound by the treaty; or

"(*b*) It appears from practice or other circumstances that it was the intention of the States and international organizations concerned to consider that person as competent for such purposes without the person's having to produce full powers.

"2. By virtue of their functions and without having to produce full powers, the following are considered as representing a State for the purpose of formulating a reservation at the international level:

"(*a*) Heads of State, Heads of Government and ministers for foreign affairs;

formulation of reservations),[191] 2.1.5 (Communication of reservations),[192] 2.1.6 (Procedure for communication of reservations)[193] and 2.1.7 (Functions of depositaries),[194] simply replacing "reservation" with "objection" in the text of the drafts, it is the opinion of the Special Rapporteur that referring to these draft guidelines is sufficient.[195]

"2.6.9 *Procedure for the formulation of objections*

"Draft guidelines 2.1.3, 2.1.4, 2.1.5, 2.1.6 and 2.1.7 are applicable *mutatis mutandis* to objections."

(a) *Form of an objection*

(i) *Written form*

95. Pursuant to article 23, paragraph 1, of the 1986 Vienna Convention, an objection to a reservation "must be formulated in writing and communicated to the contracting States and contracting organizations and other States entitled to become parties to the treaty".

96. As is the case for reservations,[196] the requirement that an objection to a reservation must be formulated in writing was never called into question, but was presented as self-evident in the debates in the Commission and at the United Nations Conferences on the Law of Treaties. In his first report, Sir Humphrey Waldock, the first special rapporteur to draft provisions on objections (see also paragraphs 87–89 above), already provided in draft article 19, paragraph 2 (*a*), which dealt entirely with objections to reservations, that "[a]n objection to a reservation shall be formulated in writing",[197] without making this formal requirement the subject of commentary.[198] While the procedural guidelines were comprehensively revised by the Special Rapporteur in the light of the comments of two Governments suggesting that "some simplification of the procedural provisions"[199] was desirable, the requirement of a written formulation for an objection to a reservation was always explicitly stipulated:

(*a*) In article 19, paragraph 5, adopted on first reading (1962): "An objection to a reservation shall be formulated in writing and shall be notified";[200]

(*b*) In article 20, paragraph 5, proposed by the Special Rapporteur in his fourth report (1965): "An objection to a reservation must be in writing";[201]

(*c*) In article 20, paragraph 1, adopted on second reading (1965): "A reservation, an express acceptance of a reservation and an objection to a reservation must be

---

"(*b*) Representatives accredited by States to an international conference for the purpose of formulating a reservation to a treaty adopted at that conference;

"(*c*) Representatives accredited by States to an international organization or one of its organs, for the purpose of formulating a reservation to a treaty adopted by that organization or body;

"(*d*) Heads of permanent missions to an international organization, for the purpose of formulating a reservation to a treaty between the accrediting States and that organization."

(*Yearbook ... 2002*, vol. II (Part Two), p. 30, para. 103. See also the commentary, pp. 30–32)

[191] "2.1.4 *Absence of consequences at the international level of the violation of internal rules regarding the formulation of reservations*

"1. The determination of the competent authority and the procedure to be followed at the internal level for formulating a reservation is a matter for the internal law of each State or the relevant rules of each international organization.

"2. A State or an international organization may not invoke the fact that a reservation has been formulated in violation of a provision of the internal law of that State or the rules of that organization regarding competence and the procedure for formulating reservations as invalidating the reservation."

(*Ibid.*, p. 32)

[192] "2.1.5 *Communication of reservations*

"1. A reservation must be communicated in writing to the contracting States and contracting organizations and other States and international organizations entitled to become parties to the treaty.

"2. A reservation to a treaty in force which is the constituent instrument of an international organization or to a treaty which creates an organ that has the capacity to accept a reservation must also be communicated to such organization or organ."

(*Ibid.*, p. 34)

[193] "2.1.6 *Procedure for communication of reservations*

"1. Unless otherwise provided in the treaty or agreed by the contracting States and contracting organizations, a communication relating to a reservation to a treaty shall be transmitted:

"(*a*) If there is no depositary, directly by the author of the reservation to the contracting States and contracting organizations and other States and international organizations entitled to become parties to the treaty; or

"(*b*) If there is a depositary, to the latter, which shall notify the States and organizations for which it is intended as soon as possible.

"2. A communication related to a reservation shall be considered as having been made by the author of the reservation only upon receipt by the State or by the organization to which it was transmitted, or as the case may be, upon its receipt by the depositary.

"3. The period during which an objection to a reservation may be raised starts at the date on which a State or an international organization received notification of the reservation.

"4. Where a communication relating to a reservation to a treaty is made by electronic mail or by facsimile, it must be confirmed by diplomatic note or depositary notification. In this case, the communication is considered as having been made on the date of the electronic mail or facsimile."

(*Ibid.*, p. 38)

Paragraph 3 of this guideline raises problems in that it makes a rule regarding the period during which an objection to a reservation may be raised; this problem is discussed at length in paragraphs 126–129 below.

[194] "2.1.7 *Functions of depositaries*

"1. The depositary shall examine whether a reservation to a treaty formulated by a State or an international organization is in due and proper form and, where appropriate, bring the matter to the attention of the State or international organization concerned.

"2. In the event of any difference appearing between a State or an international organization and the depositary as to the performance of the latter's functions, the depositary shall bring the question to the attention of:

"(*a*) The signatory States and organizations and the contracting States and contracting organizations; or

"(*b*) Where appropriate, the competent organ of the international organization concerned.

(*Ibid.*, p. 42.)

[195] The Commission proceeded in the same manner in draft guidelines 1.5.2 (referred to draft guidelines 1.2 and 1.2.1), 2.4.3 (referred to draft guidelines 1.2.1, 2.4.6 and 2.4.7) and, even more obviously, in 2.5.6 (referred to draft guidelines 2.1.5, 2.1.6 and 2.1.7) (*Yearbook ... 2003*, vol. II (Part Two), pp. 66, 68 and 69).

[196] See draft guideline 2.1.1 (Written form) and commentary, *Yearbook ... 2002*, vol. II (Part Two), pp. 28–29, para 103.

[197] See footnote 181 above.

[198] *Yearbook ... 1962* (see footnote 132 above), p. 68, para. (22) of the commentary on article 19, which refers the reader to the commentary on article 17 (*ibid.*, p. 66, para. (11)).

[199] *Yearbook ... 1965* (see footnote 137 above), p. 53, para. 13. The Governments were those of Denmark and Sweden (*ibid.*, pp. 46–47).

[200] *Yearbook ... 1962* (see footnote 136 above), p. 176.

[201] *Yearbook ... 1965* (see footnote 137 above), p. 53.

formulated in writing and communicated to the other contracting States."[202]

The written form was not called into question at the Vienna Conference in 1968 and 1969 either. On the contrary, all proposed amendments to the procedure in question retained the requirement that an objection to a reservation must be formulated in writing.[203]

97. That objections must be in written form is well established. Notification, another procedural requirement applicable to objections (by virtue of article 23, paragraph 1, of the 1969 and 1986 Vienna Conventions), requires a written document; oral communication alone cannot be filed or registered with the depositary of the treaty or communicated to other interested States. Furthermore, considerations of legal security justify and call for the written form. One must not forget that an objection has significant legal effects on the opposability of a reservation, the applicability of the provisions of a treaty as between the reserving State and the objecting State (art. 21, para. 3, of the Vienna Conventions) and the entry into force of the treaty (art. 20, para. 4). In addition, an objection reverses the presumption of acceptance arising from article 20, paragraph 5, of the Conventions, and written form is an important means of proving whether a State did indeed express an objection to a reservation during the period of time prescribed by this provision or whether, by default, it must be considered as having accepted the reservation.

98. It seems, therefore, necessary to carry over the first part of article 23, paragraph 1, of the 1969 and 1986 Vienna Conventions in a draft guideline 2.6.7, which would parallel draft guideline 2.1.1.

"2.6.7 *Written form*

"An objection must be formulated in writing."

(ii) *Expression of intention to oppose the entry into force of a treaty*

99. As already noted (see paragraphs 68–75 above), a State objecting to a reservation may oppose the entry into force of a treaty as between itself and the reserving State. In order for this to be so, according to article 20, paragraph 4 (*b*), of the 1986 Vienna Convention that intent must still be "definitely expressed by the objecting State or organization".

100. Following the reversal of the presumption regarding the effects of the objection on the entry into force of the treaty as between the reserving State and the objecting State (see paragraphs 69–72 above), a clear and unequivocal statement is needed in order for the treaty not to enter into force.[204] This is certainly true of the objection of the Netherlands to reservations to article IX of the Convention on the Prevention and Punishment of the Crime of Genocide, which states that "[t]he Government of the Kingdom of the Netherlands ... does not deem any State which has made or will make such reservation a party to the Convention".[205] France also very clearly expressed such an intention regarding the reservation of the United States to the Agreement on the International Carriage of Perishable Foodstuffs and on the Special Equipment to be used for such Carriage (ATP), by declaring that it would "not be bound by the ATP Agreement in its relations with the United States of America".[206] Similarly, the United Kingdom stated in its objection to the reservation of the Syrian Arab Republic to the 1969 Vienna Convention that it did "not accept the entry into force of the Convention as between the United Kingdom and Syria".[207]

101. On the other hand, the mere fact that the reason for the objection is that the reservation is considered incompatible with the object and purpose of the treaty is not sufficient.[208] Practice is indisputable in this regard, since States quite frequently base their objections on such incompatibility, all the while clarifying that the finding does not prevent the treaty from entering into force as between them and the author of the reservation.[209] The objections of Israel, Italy and the United Kingdom regarding the reservation of Burundi to the Convention on the prevention and punishment of crimes against internationally protected persons, including diplomatic agents termed the reservation incompatible with the object and purpose of the Convention. Notwithstanding, the authors of the objections state, somewhat ambiguously, that they would not "consider Burundi as having validly acceded to the Convention until such time as the reservation is withdrawn".[210] This declaration could lead to debate as to the clarity of the intention expressed.

[202] *Ibid.* (see footnote 141 above), p. 162. Draft article 20 of 1965 became draft article 18 with modification, in the text adopted by the Commission in 1966 (*Yearbook ... 1966* (see footnote 163 above), p. 208).

[203] See the Spanish amendment (A/CONF.39/C.1/L.149): "A reservation, an acceptance of a reservation, and an objection to a reservation must be formulated in writing and duly communicated by the reserving, accepting or objecting State to the other States which are parties, or are entitled to become parties, to the treaty." (*United Nations Conference on the Law of Treaties* (footnote 142 above), p. 138, para. 192 (i)).

[204] See Baratta, *Gli effetti delle riserve ai trattati*, p. 352. The author states: "There is no doubt that in order for the expected consequence of the rule regarding a qualified objection to be produced, the author must state its intention to that effect."

[205] United Nations, *Multilateral Treaties* ... (see footnote 165 above), chap. IV.1. See also the objection of China (*ibid.*).

[206] *Ibid.*, chap. XI.B.22. See also the objection of Italy (*ibid.*).

[207] *Ibid.*, vol. II, chap. XXIII.1. See also the objection of the United Kingdom to the reservation of Viet Nam (*ibid.*).

[208] This remark, which concerns only the contents of declarations made pursuant to article 20, paragraph 4 (*b*), of the 1969 and 1986 Vienna Conventions, does not pre-empt the different question of determining whether a reservation incompatible with the object and purpose of a treaty is or is not automatically null and void; that question was examined in the tenth report on reservations (*Yearbook ... 2005* (see footnote 66 above), paras. 195–200) and will be discussed again in the next report.

[209] Among many examples, see the objections of several States members of the Council of Europe to the reservation of the Syrian Arab Republic to the International Convention for the Suppression of the Financing of Terrorism on the basis of the incompatibility of the reservation with the object and purpose of the Convention (Austria, Belgium, Canada, Denmark, Estonia, Finland, France, Germany, Latvia, Norway, the Netherlands, Portugal, Sweden) (United Nations, *Multilateral Treaties* ... (see footnote 165 above), chap. XVIII.11). In every case it is stated that the objection does not preclude the entry into force of the Convention between the objecting State and the Syrian Arab Republic. See also the examples cited in footnote 165 above.

[210] *Ibid.*, vol. II, chap. XVIII.7.

102. Neither the 1969 and 1986 Vienna Conventions nor the *travaux préparatoires* give any useful indication regarding the time at which the objecting State or international organization must clearly express its intention to oppose the entry into force of the treaty as between itself and the reserving State. One can, however, proceed by deduction. According to the presumption of article 20, paragraph 4 (*b*), of the Vienna Conventions, whereby an objection does not preclude the entry into force of a treaty in treaty relations between an objecting State or international organization and the reserving State or international organization unless the contrary is expressly stated, an objection that is not accompanied by such a declaration results in the treaty entering into force, subject to article 21, paragraph 3, of the Conventions concerning the effect of a reservation on relations between the two parties. If the objecting State or international organization expressed a different intention in a subsequent declaration, it would not only undermine legal security but would also enlarge its objection: a minimum-effect objection would become a maximum-effect objection (see paragraph 177 below), which, as shall be seen, is certainly not possible (see paragraphs 176–180 below and draft guideline 2.7.9).

103. Therefore, in order effectively to oppose the entry into force of a treaty as between itself and the reserving State, the objecting State must necessarily formulate the declaration provided for in article 20, paragraph 4 (*b*), of the 1969 and 1986 Vienna Conventions at the same time that it formulates the objection. The declaration on the non-entry into force of the treaty in bilateral relations then becomes a specific element of the very content of the maximum-effect objection, of which it must be an integral part.

104. These two conditions—a clear declaration, expressed in the objection itself—limit, then, the freedom of a State or international organization to oppose the entry into force of a treaty (see paragraphs 68–75 above and draft guideline 2.6.4). They are reflected in draft guideline 2.6.8, which might be worded as follows:

"2.6.8 *Expression of intention to oppose the entry into force of the treaty*

"When a State or international organization making an objection to a reservation intends to oppose the entry into force of the treaty as between itself and the reserving State or international organization, it must clearly express its intention when it formulates the objection."

(iii) *Statement of reasons*

105. Despite the link initially established between an objection, on the one hand, and the compatibility of the reservation with the object and purpose of the treaty, on the other hand (see paragraph 62 above), Sir Humphrey Waldock never at any point envisaged requiring a statement of the reasons for an objection. Neither of the Vienna Conventions contains such a provision. This is highly regrettable.

106. Of course, as explained above (see paragraphs 60–83), a State or international organization may object to a reservation for any reason whatsoever, irrespective of the validity of the reservation. "No State can be bound by contractual obligations it does not consider suitable."[211] Furthermore, during discussions in the Sixth Committee, several States indicated that quite often the reasons a State has for formulating an objection are purely political.[212] Since this is the case, stating a reason risks uselessly embarrassing an objecting State or international organization, without any gain to the objecting State or international organization or to the other States or international organizations concerned.

107. But the question is different where a State or international organization objects to a reservation because it considers it invalid (for whatever reason). Leaving aside the possibility that States may have a legal obligation[213] to object to reservations that are incompatible with the object and purpose of a treaty, nevertheless, in a "flexible" treaty regime the objection clearly plays a vital role in the determination of the validity of a reservation. In the absence of a mechanism for reservation control, the onus is on States and international organizations to express, through objections, their view, necessarily subjective, on the validity of a given reservation.[214] Such a function can only be fulfilled, however, by objections motivated by considerations regarding the non-validity of the reservation in question. It is difficult to see why an objection formulated for purely political reasons should be taken into account in evaluating the conformity of a reservation with the requirements of article 19 of the 1969 and 1986 Vienna Conventions. Even if only

---

[211] Tomuschat, *loc. cit.*, p. 466.

[212] See the statement of the United States representative in the Sixth Committee during the fifty-eighth session of the General Assembly: "Practice demonstrated that States and international organizations objected to reservations for a variety of reasons, often political rather than legal in nature, and with different intentions" (*Official Records of the General Assembly, Fifty-eighth Session, Sixth Committee*, 20th meeting, para. 9). During the sixtieth session, the representative of the Netherlands stated that "[i]n the current system, the political aspect of an objection, namely, the view expressed by the objecting State on the desirability of a reservation, played a central role, and the legal effects of such an objection were becoming increasingly peripheral" (*ibid., Sixtieth Session, Sixth Committee*, 14th meeting, para. 31); on the political aspect of an objection, see Portugal (*ibid.*, 16th meeting, para. 44). See also Inter-American Court of Human Rights, *Caesar* v. *Trinidad and Tobago*, judgment of 11 March 2005, Merits, Reparations and Costs, Series C, No. 123, separate opinion of Judge A. A. Cançado Trindade, para. 24.

[213] The Netherlands observed that "States parties, as guardians of a particular treaty, appeared to have a moral, if not legal, obligation to object to a reservation that was contrary to the object and purpose of that treaty" (*Official Records of the General Assembly, Sixtieth Session, Sixth Committee*, 16th meeting, para. 29). According to this line of reasoning, "a party is required to give effect to its undertakings in good faith and that would preclude it from accepting a reservation inconsistent with the object and purpose of the treaty" (Final working paper submitted by Françoise Hampson (E/CN.4/Sub.2/2004/42) on reservations to human rights treaties (see paragraph 53 above), para. 24); Ms. Hampson observed, however, that there appeared to be no general obligation to object to incompatible reservations (*ibid.*, para. 30); this is also the *prima facie* position of the Special Rapporteur.

[214] Some treaty regimes go so far as to rely on the number of objections in order to determine the admissibility of a reservation. See, for example, article 20, paragraph 2, of the International Convention on the Elimination of All Forms of Racial Discrimination, which states: "A reservation incompatible with the object and purpose of this Convention shall not be permitted, nor shall a reservation the effect of which would inhibit the operation of any of the bodies established by this Convention be allowed. *A reservation shall be considered incompatible or inhibitive if at least two-thirds of the States Parties to this Convention object to it**."

for this reason, it would seem reasonable, even necessary, to indicate to the extent possible the reasons for an objection.

108. In addition, statement of the reasons for an objection not only allows a reserving State or international organization to understand the views of the other States and international organizations concerned regarding the validity of the reservation; it also provides important evidence to the monitoring bodies called on to decide on the conformity of a reservation with the treaty. Thus, in the *Loizidou* case, the European Court of Human Rights found confirmation of its conclusions regarding the reservation of Turkey in the declarations and objections made by other States parties to the European Convention on Human Rights.[215] Similarly, in the working paper she submitted to the Sub-Commission on the Promotion and Protection of Human Rights in 2004, Ms. Hampson stated that "[i]n order for a treaty body to discharge its role, it will need to examine, amongst other materials, the practice of the parties to the treaty in question with regard to reservations and objections".[216] The Human Rights Committee itself, in its general comment No. 24, which, while demonstrating deep mistrust with regard to the practice of States concerning objections and with regard to the conclusions that one may draw from it in assessing the validity of a reservation, nevertheless states that "an objection to a reservation made by States may provide some guidance to the Committee in its interpretation as to its compatibility with the object and purpose of the Covenant".[217]

109. State practice shows that States often indicate in their objections not only that they consider the reservation in question contrary to the object and purpose of the treaty but also, in more or less detail, how and why they reached that conclusion. At the sixtieth session of the General Assembly, the representative of Italy to the Sixth Committee expressed the view that the Commission should encourage States to make use of the formulas set forth in article 19 of the 1969 Vienna Convention, with a view to clarifying their objections.[218]

110. In view of these considerations and the absence of an obligation in the Vienna regime to state the reasons for objections, it would seem useful to include in the Guide to Practice a draft guideline encouraging States (and international organizations) to expand and develop the practice of stating reasons.[219] However, it must be clearly understood that such a provision would be only a recommendation, a guideline for State practice and would not codify an established rule of international law.[220]

111. The Special Rapporteur is thus proposing draft guideline 2.6.10, which might read as follows:

"2.6.10 *Statement of reasons*

"Whenever possible, an objection should indicate the reasons why it is being made."

(b) *Confirmation of objections*

112. Contrary to what is provided in article 23, paragraph 2, of the 1969 Vienna Convention for reservations,[221] an objection does not require formal confirmation by its author if it was made prior to the formal confirmation of the reservation, in accordance with article 23, paragraph 3 of the Convention, which states:

> An express acceptance of, or an objection to, a reservation made previously to confirmation of the reservation does not itself require confirmation.

113. That provision was only included at a very late stage of the preparatory work for the 1969 Vienna Convention. The early draft articles relating to the procedure applicable to the formulation of objections did not refer to cases where an objection might be made to a reservation that had yet to be formally confirmed. It was only in 1966 that the non-requirement of confirmation of an objection was expressed in draft article 18, paragraph 3, adopted on second reading,[222] without explanation or illustration; however, it was presented at that time as *lex ferenda*.[223]

114. This is doubtless a common sense rule: the formulation of the reservation concerns all States and international organizations that are Contracting Parties or entitled to become parties; acceptances and objections affect primarily the bilateral relations between the author of a reservation and each of the accepting or objecting States or organizations. The reservation is an "offer" addressed to all Contracting Parties, which may accept or reject it; it is the reserving State or organization that endangers the integrity of the treaty and risks reducing it to a series of bilateral relations. On the other hand, it is not important whether the acceptance or objection is made before or after the confirmation of the reservation: what is important is that the reserving State or organization is aware of

---

[215] *Loizidou* v. *Turkey*, European Court of Human Rights, *Series A: Judgments and Decisions*, vol. 310 (Preliminary Objections), Judgment of 23 March 1995, pp. 28–29, para. 81. See also the statement of Sweden on behalf of the Nordic countries, in the Sixth Committee (*Official Records of the General Assembly, Sixtieth Session, Sixth Committee*, 14th meeting, para. 22).

[216] E/CN.4/Sub.2/2004/42 (see footnote 213 above), para. 28. See more generally, paragraphs 21–35 of this important study.

[217] Report of the Human Rights Committee, *Official Records of the General Assembly, Fiftieth Session, Supplement No. 40* (A/50/40), vol. I, annex V, para. 17.

[218] *Official Records of the General Assembly, Sixtieth Session, Sixth Committee*, 16th meeting, para. 20.

[219] This idea had already been received favourably by the Commission (*Yearbook ... 2003*, vol. II (Part Two), p. 63, para. 352).

[220] This is not the first guideline constituting a recommendation to appear in the Guide to Practice. See draft guideline 2.5.3 on the periodic review of the usefulness of reservations (*ibid.*, p. 76, para. 368).

[221] See also draft guideline 2.2.1 (Formal confirmation of reservations formulated when signing a treaty): "If formulated when signing a treaty subject to ratification, act of formal confirmation, acceptance or approval, a reservation must be formally confirmed by the reserving State or international organization when expressing its consent to be bound by the treaty. In such a case the reservation shall be considered as having been made on the date of its confirmation." (*Yearbook ... 2001*, vol. II (Part Two), p. 180, para. 157.) For the commentary to this draft guideline, see pages 180–183 (*ibid.*).

[222] See *Yearbook ... 1966* (footnote 163 above), p. 208.

[223] "[T]he Commission did not consider that an objection to a reservation made previously to the latter's confirmation would need to be reiterated after that event" (*ibid.*, para. (5) of the commentary).

its partners' intentions,[224] which is the case if the communication procedure established in article 23, paragraph 1, has been followed.

115. State practice regarding the confirmation of objections is sparse and inconsistent: sometimes States confirm their previous objections once the reserving State has itself confirmed its reservation, but at other times they refrain from doing so.[225] Although the latter approach seems to be more usual, the fact that these confirmations exist does not invalidate the positive quality of the rule laid down in article 23, paragraph 3; they are precautionary measures by no means dictated by a feeling of legal obligation (*opinio juris*).

116. In view of these considerations, it will be sufficient, in the Guide to Practice, to repeat the rule expounded in article 23, paragraph 3, of the 1969 and 1986 Vienna Conventions:

"2.6.11 *Non-requirement of confirmation of an objection made prior to formal confirmation of a reservation*

"An objection to a reservation made by a State or an international organization prior to confirmation of the reservation in accordance with draft guideline 2.2.1 does not itself require confirmation."

117. Article 23, paragraph 3, of the 1969 and 1986 Vienna Conventions does not, however, answer the question of whether an objection made by a State or an international organization that, when making it, has yet to express its consent to being bound by the treaty must subsequently be confirmed if it is to produce the effects envisaged. Although Sir Humphrey Waldock did not overlook the possibility that an objection might be formulated by signatory States or by States only entitled to become parties to the treaty,[226] the question of the subsequent confirmation of such a reservation was never raised.[227] A proposal in that regard made by Poland at the United Nations Conference on the Law of Treaties[228] was not considered. Accordingly the Conventions have a gap that the Commission should endeavour to fill.

118. State practice in this regard is all but non-existent. One of the rare examples is provided by the objections formulated by the United States to a number of reservations to the 1969 Vienna Convention itself.[229] In its objection to the reservation by the Syrian Arab Republic, the United States—which has yet to express its consent to be bound by the Convention—specified that it

> intends, at such time as it may become a party to the Vienna Convention on the Law of Treaties, *to reaffirm its objection** to the foregoing reservation and to reject treaty relations with the Syrian Arab Republic under all provisions in Part V of the Convention with regard to which the Syrian Arab Republic has rejected the obligatory conciliation procedures set forth in the Annex to the Convention.[230]

Curiously, the second United States objection, formulated against the reservation by Tunisia, does not contain the same statement.

119. In its 1951 advisory opinion, ICJ also seemed to take the view that objections made by non-States parties do not require confirmation. It considered that:

> Pending ratification, the provisional status created by signature confers upon the signatory a right to formulate as a precautionary measure objections which have themselves a provisional character. These would disappear if the signature were not followed by ratification, *or they would become effective on ratification**.
>
> ...
>
> The reserving State would be given notice that as soon as the constitutional or other processes, which cause the lapse of time before ratification, have been completed, it would be confronted with a valid objection which carries full legal effect.[231]

The Court thereby seemed to accept that an objection automatically takes effect as a result of ratification alone, without the need for confirmation.[232] Nonetheless, it has yet to take a formal stand on this question and the debate has been left open.

120. It is possible, however, to deduce, from the omission from the text of the 1969 and 1986 Vienna Conventions of any requirement that an objection made by a State or an organization prior to ratification or approval being confirmed, that neither the members of the Commission nor the delegates at the United Nations Conference on the

---

[224] In its advisory opinion of 28 May 1951, *Reservations to the Convention on the Prevention and Punishment of the Crime of Genocide*, ICJ described the objection made by a signatory as a "warning" addressed to the author of the reservation (*I.C.J. Reports 1951* (see footnote 101 above), p. 29). See also paragraphs 119 and 122 below.

[225] For example, Australia and Ecuador did not confirm their objections to the reservations formulated at the time of the signing of the Convention on the Prevention and Punishment of the Crime of Genocide by the Byelorussian SSR, Czechoslovakia, Ukraine and the Union of Soviet Socialist Republics, when those States ratified that Convention while confirming their reservations (United Nations, *Multilateral Treaties* ...(see footnote 165 above), chap. IV.1). Similarly, Ireland and Portugal did not confirm the objections they made to the reservation formulated by Turkey at the time of the signing of the Convention on the rights of the child when Turkey confirmed its reservation in its instrument of ratification (*ibid.*, chap. IV.11). On the other hand, Finland, which had objected to a reservation Qatar had made to the same Convention, confirmed its objection when Qatar confirmed its reservation at the time of ratification (*ibid.*, p. 331).

[226] See in particular draft article 19, paragraph 3 (*b*), proposed by Sir Humphrey Waldock in his first report on the law of treaties (*Yearbook ... 1962* (footnote 132 above), p. 62) and draft article 20, paragraph 6, proposed in his fourth report on the law of treaties (*Yearbook ... 1965* (footnote 137 above), p. 53).

[227] Except, perhaps, in a comment made incidentally by Mr. Tunkin, *Yearbook ... 1965*, vol. I, 799th meeting, p. 167, para. 38: "It was clearly the modern practice that a reservation was valid only if made or confirmed at the moment when final consent to be bound was given, and that was the presumption reflected in the 1962 draft. The same applied to objections to reservations. The point was partially covered in paragraph 6 of the Special Rapporteur's new text for article 20."

[228] A/CONF.39/6/Add.1, p. 18. The Polish Government proposed that article 18, paragraph 2 (which became article 23), should be worded as follows: "If formulated on the occasion of the adoption of the text or upon signing the treaty subject to ratification, acceptance or approval, a reservation as well as an eventual objection to it must be formally confirmed by the reserving and objecting States when expressing their consent to be bound by the treaty. In such a case the reservation and the objection shall be considered as having been made on the date of their confirmation."

[229] The reservations in question are those formulated by the Syrian Arab Republic and Tunisia (United Nations, *Multilateral Treaties* ... (see footnote 165 above), vol. II, chap. XXIII.1).

[230] *Ibid.*

[231] *I.C.J. Reports 1951* (see footnote 101 above), pp. 28–29.

[232] See in this sense Horn, *op. cit.*, p. 137.

Law of Treaties[233] considered that such a confirmation was necessary. The fact that the Polish amendment,[234] which aimed to bring objections in line with reservations in that respect, was not adopted further confirms this argument. These considerations are further strengthened if one bears in mind that, when the requirement of formal confirmation of reservations formulated when signing the treaty, an obligation now firmly enshrined in article 23, paragraph 2, of the Conventions, was adopted by the Commission, it was more in the nature of progressive development than codification *sensu stricto*.[235] Therefore, the disparity on this score between the procedural rules laid down for the formulation of reservations, on the one hand, and the formulation of objections, on the other, could not have been due to a simple oversight but could reasonably be considered deliberate.

121. There are other grounds for the non-requirement of formal confirmation of an objection made by a State or an international organization prior to the expression of its consent to be bound by the treaty. Whereas reservations are often considered as "a necessary evil, but still an evil",[236] in that they endanger the integrity of a treaty, objections are merely a reaction open to the other States or international organizations concerned and are aimed at monitoring or restricting, in the absence of a centralized monitoring mechanism, the freedom to formulate reservations. An objection may, of course, produce effects on a treaty that are far from negligible and may possibly even prevent it from entering into force. Yet reservations are undoubtedly the true "evil";[237] it is they that must be restricted not only in substance but also in form, so that the reserving State or international organization can assess the scope of its unilateral declaration. Objections are by no means anodyne, of course: they alone enable the other Contracting Parties to give their point of view as to the validity or appropriateness of a reservation. From this perspective, formal requirements, provided they are not excessive, may serve to discourage the practice of reservations, insofar as that may be done.

122. A reservation formulated before the reserving State or international organization becomes a Contracting Party to the treaty should produce no legal effect and will remain a "dead letter" until such a time as the State's consent to be bound by the treaty is effectively given. Requiring formal confirmation of the reservation is justified in this case in particular by the fact that the reservation, once accepted, modifies that consent. The same is not true of objections. Although objections, too, only produce the effects provided for in articles 20, paragraph 4, and 21, paragraph 3, of the 1969 and 1986 Vienna Conventions once the objecting State or international organization has become a Contracting Party, they are not without significance even before then. They express their author's opinion of a reservation's validity or admissibility and, as such, may be taken into consideration by the bodies having competence to assess the validity of reservations (see paragraph 108 above). Moreover, and on this point the ICJ advisory opinion remains valid, objections give notice to reserving States with regard to the attitude of the objecting State *vis-à-vis* their reservation. As the Court observed:

> The legal interest of a signatory State in objecting to a reservation would thus be amply safeguarded. The reserving State would be given notice that as soon as the constitutional or other processes, which cause the lapse of time before ratification, have been completed, it would be confronted with a valid objection which carries full legal effect and consequently, it would have to decide, when the objection is stated, whether it wishes to maintain or withdraw its reservation.[238]

Such an objection, formulated prior to the expression of consent to be bound by the treaty, therefore encourages the reserving State to reconsider, modify or withdraw its reservation in the same way as an objection raised by a contracting State. This notification would, however, become a mere possibility if the objecting State were required to confirm its objection at the time it expressed its consent to be bound by the treaty. The requirement for an additional formal confirmation would thus, in the view of the Special Rapporteur, largely undermine the significance attaching to the freedom of States and international organizations that are not yet Contracting Parties to the treaty to raise objections.

123. Moreover, non-confirmation of the objection in such a situation poses no problem of legal security. The objections formulated by a signatory State or by a State entitled to become a party to the treaty must, like any notification or communication relating to the treaty,[239] be made in writing and communicated and notified, in the same way as an objection emanating from a party. Furthermore, unlike a reservation, an objection modifies traditional relations only with respect to the bilateral relations between the reserving State—which has been duly notified—and the objecting State. The rights and obligations assumed by the objecting State *vis-à-vis* other States parties to the treaty are not affected in any way.

124. In conclusion, it may reasonably be considered that the formal confirmation of an objection formulated by a State or an international organization that has not yet expressed its consent to be bound by the treaty is by no means essential. The silence of the 1969 and 1986 Vienna Conventions on this point should, however, be rectified in order to remove any doubts concerning this point. This could be achieved through a draft guideline 2.6.12 worded as follows:

"2.6.12 *Non-requirement of confirmation of an objection made prior to the expression of consent to be bound by a treaty*[240]

"If an objection is made prior to the expression of consent to be bound by the treaty, it does not need to be formally

[233] *Ibid.*

[234] See footnote 228 above.

[235] See Sir Humphrey Waldock's first report (*Yearbook ... 1962* (footnote 132 above), p. 66, para. (11) of the commentary on article 17; Greig, "Reservations: equity as a balancing factor?", p. 28; and Horn, *op. cit.*, p. 41. See also the commentary to draft guideline 2.2.1 (Formal confirmation of reservations formulated when signing a treaty), *Yearbook ... 2001*, vol. II (Part Two), p. 181, para. 157, para. (8).

[236] *Yearbook ... 1965*, vol. I, 797th meeting, p. 151, para. 38 (Mr. Ago); see also Gamble Jr., "The 1982 U.N. Convention on the Law of the Sea: a 'midstream' assessment of the effectiveness of article 309", p. 628.

[237] The Special Rapporteur does not think that reservations are necessarily an evil in all cases and regardless of circumstances.

[238] *I.C.J. Reports 1951* (see footnote 101 above), p. 29.

[239] See article 78 of the 1969 Vienna Convention and article 79 of the 1986 Vienna Convention.

[240] The title of this draft guideline is modelled on that of draft guideline 2.4.4 (Non-requirement of confirmation of interpretative declarations made when signing a treaty), *Yearbook ... 2001*, vol. II (Part Two), p. 193.

confirmed by the objecting State or international organization at the time it expresses its consent to be bound."

(c) *Time at which an objection may be raised*

125. The question of the time at which and until which a State or an international organization may raise an objection is partially and indirectly addressed by article 20, paragraph 5, of the 1969 and 1986 Vienna Conventions. In its 1986 form, this provision states:

> For the purposes of paragraphs 2 and 4,[241] and unless the treaty otherwise provides, a reservation is considered to have been accepted by a State or an international organization if it shall have raised no objection to the reservation by the end of a period of twelve months after it was notified of the reservation or by the date on which it expressed its consent to be bound by the treaty, whichever is later.

126. It should be noted that draft guideline 2.1.6 (Procedure for communication of reservations), paragraph 3, adopted by the Commission in 2002, draws an express conclusion from this provision with respect to the period of time during which an objection may be raised. According to that paragraph:

> The period during which an objection to a reservation may be raised starts at the date on which a State or an international organization received notification of the reservation.[242]

127. This stipulation, which appeared neither in the proposals of the Special Rapporteur[243] nor in the report of the Drafting Committee,[244] was added to draft guideline 2.1.6 in plenary meeting, on the basis of a proposal by Mr. Gaja[245] which at the time was well received by the Special Rapporteur.[246] On reflection, however, this reference to the period of time during which an objection may be formulated presents two difficulties:

(*a*) First, the logic might be questioned of including in a draft guideline on the procedure for communicating reservations a rule that concerns not reservations, but objections;[247]

(*b*) Secondly, and this is a matter of greater concern, the third paragraph of the draft guideline, although not inaccurate, is incomplete and could cause confusion: it addresses only (and, moreover, incompletely[248]) the question of the date from which an objection may be formulated (*dies a quo*) but leaves entirely unanswered the question of the *dies ad quem*; clearly, the latter cannot be dealt with on the basis of omission, and it is difficult to deal with it in isolation and to determine the date on which the period of time expires without reference to the date on which it commences.[249]

128. That being the case, it appears essential to include in that section of the Guide to Practice a comprehensive draft guideline on the time period for formulating objections; this is the purpose of draft guideline 2.6.13, which might be worded by adhering quite closely to the relevant part of the text of article 20, paragraph 5, of the 1986 Vienna Convention:

"2.6.13 *Time period for formulating an objection*

"Unless the treaty otherwise provides, a State or an international organization may formulate an objection to a reservation by the end of a period of 12 months after it is notified of the reservation or by the date on which such State or international organization expresses its consent to be bound by the treaty, whichever is later."

129. It is clear that this draft guideline to a certain degree duplicates draft guideline 2.1.6, paragraph 3, while completing it and removing its ambiguities. There are thus two avenues open to the Commission. On the one hand, it might decide to delete draft guideline 2.1.6, paragraph 3 (and paragraph (24) of the commentary to this provision), which would be consistent but would present the difficulty of reopening a provision already adopted. On the other hand, it might decide to retain both provisions (which are not incompatible but might be confusing if they were both retained) and keep open the option of introducing the necessary consistency by deleting draft guideline 2.1.6, paragraph 3, on second reading of the draft Guide to Practice. The Special Rapporteur will defer to the wisdom of the Commission on this point.

130. Draft guideline 2.6.13, however, provides only a partial response with respect to the date from which an objection to a reservation may be formulated. It does state that the time period during which the objection may

---

[241] Paragraph 2 refers to reservations to treaties with limited participation; paragraph 4 establishes the effects of the acceptance of reservations and objections in all cases other than those of reservations expressly authorized by the treaty, with reference to treaties with limited participation and the constituent acts of international organizations.

[242] *Yearbook ... 2002*, vol. II (Part Two), p. 26.

[243] See *Yearbook ... 2001*, vol. II (Part One), document A/CN.4/518 and Add.1–3, pp. 160–161, paras. 153 and 155, containing draft guidelines 2.1.6 and 2.1.8 as proposed by the Special Rapporteur, which provided the basis for the draft guideline 2.1.6 ultimately adopted by the Commission.

[244] See the presentation of the report of the Drafting Committee by Mr. Yamada, *Yearbook ... 2002*, vol. I, 2733rd meeting, p. 150, paras. 21–24.

[245] *Ibid.*, p. 152, para. 43.

[246] *Ibid.*, para. 45.

[247] It should be noted that the very brief commentary which accompanies this provision gives no indication of the reasons that led the Commission to take this decision:

"Paragraph 3 of draft guideline 2.1.6 deals with the specific case of the time period for the formulation of an objection to a reservation by a State or an international organization. It is based on the principle embodied in article 20, paragraph 5, of the 1986 Vienna Convention (itself based on the corresponding provision of the 1969 Vienna Convention), which reads:

'... unless the treaty otherwise provides, a reservation is considered to have been accepted by a State or an international organization if it shall have raised no objection to the reservation by the end of a period of twelve months after it was notified of the reservation or by the date on which it expressed its consent to be bound by the treaty, whichever is later.'

"It should be noted that, in such cases, the date of effect of the notification may differ from one State or organization to another, depending on the date of reception."

(*Ibid.*, vol. II (Part Two), p. 42, para. (24) of the commentary to draft guideline 2.1.6). The positions of Mr. Gaja and the Special Rapporteur (footnotes 245 and 246 above), are scarcely more illuminating in this regard: they both limit themselves to a reference to article 20, paragraph 5, of the 1969 and 1986 Vienna Conventions.

[248] See paragraphs 130–135 and draft guideline 2.6.14 below.

[249] In any case, the commentary to draft guideline 2.1.6, paragraph 3 (footnote 247 above) refers expressly to article 20, paragraph 5, of the 1969 and 1986 Vienna Conventions, which makes the same point.

be formulated commences when the reservation is notified to the State or international organization that intends to raise an objection, which implies that the objection may be formulated as from that date. But this does not necessarily mean that it may not be made earlier. Similarly, the definition of objections adopted by the Commission in 2005 (see paragraph 58 above) provides in this regard that a State or an international organization may make an objection "*in response to a reservation to a treaty formulated** by another State or international organization", which seems to suggest that an objection may be made by a State or an international organization only after a reservation has been *formulated. A priori*, this seems quite logical, but this conclusion is probably hasty.

131. State practice demonstrates, in fact, that States also raise objections for "pre-emptive" purposes. Chile, for example, formulated the following objection to the 1969 Vienna Convention:

> The Republic of Chile formulates an objection to the reservations which have been made or may be made in the future relating to article 62, paragraph 2, of the Convention.[250]

In the same vein, Japan raised the following objection:

> The Government of Japan objects to any reservation intended to exclude the application, wholly or in part, of the provisions of article 66 and the Annex concerning the obligatory procedures for settlement of disputes and does not consider Japan to be in treaty relations with any State which has formulated or will formulate such reservation, in respect of those provisions of Part V of the Convention regarding which the application of the obligatory procedures mentioned above are to be excluded as a result of the said reservation.[251]

However, in the second part of this objection, Japan noted that the effects of this objection (an intermediate effect[252]) should apply *vis-à-vis* the Syrian Arab Republic and Tunisia. It went on to reiterate its declaration to make it clear that the same effects should be produced *vis-à-vis* the German Democratic Republic and the Union of Soviet Socialist Republics, which had formulated reservations similar to those of the Syrian Arab Republic and Tunisia.[253] Other States, for their part, have raised new objections in reaction to every reservation to the same provisions newly formulated by another State party.[254]

132. The objection of Japan to the reservations formulated by Bahrain[255] and Qatar to the Vienna Convention on Diplomatic Relations also states that not only are the two reservations specifically concerned not regarded as valid, but that this [Japan's] "position is applicable to any reservations to the same effect to be made in the future by other countries".[256]

133. The objection of Greece regarding the Convention on the Prevention and Punishment of the Crime of Genocide also belongs in the category of advance objections. It states:

> We further declare that we have not accepted and do not accept any reservation which has already been made or which may hereafter be made by the countries signatory to this instrument or by countries which have acceded or may hereafter accede thereto.[257]

A general objection was also raised by the Netherlands concerning the reservations to article IX of the same convention. Although this objection lists the States that had already made such a reservation, it concludes: "The Government of the Kingdom of the Netherlands therefore does not deem any State which has made or which will make such reservation a party to the Convention."[258] That objection was, however, withdrawn in 1996 with respect to the reservations made by Malaysia and Singapore and, on the same occasion, withdrawn in relation to Bulgaria, Hungary and Mongolia which had, for their part, withdrawn their reservations.

134. State practice is therefore far from uniform in this regard. However, the Special Rapporteur believes that there is nothing to prevent a State or international organization from formulating pre-emptive or precautionary objections, before a reservation has been formulated or, in the case of reservations already formulated, from declaring its opposition, in advance, to any similar or identical reservation. Such objections do not, of course, produce the effects envisaged in articles 20, paragraph 4, and 21, paragraph 3, of the 1969 and 1986 Vienna Conventions,[259] until a corresponding reservation is formulated by another contracting State or contracting organization. This situation is rather similar to that of a reservation formulated by a State or international organization that is a signatory but not yet a party, against which another State or organization raises an objection, for objections of this kind do not require formal confirmation once the reservation is confirmed at the time when the reserving State expresses its consent to be bound by the treaty (see paragraphs 117–124 and draft guideline 2.6.11 above). A pre-emptive objection nonetheless constitutes notice that its author will not accept certain reservations. As ICJ noted, such notice safeguards the rights of the objecting State and warns other States intending to formulate a corresponding reservation that such a reservation will be met with an objection (see the passages from the Court's 1951 advisory opinion cited in paragraph 122 above).

---

[250] United Nations, *Multilateral Treaties* ... (see footnote 165 above), vol. II, chap. XXIII.1.

[251] *Ibid.*

[252] On the "intermediate" effect of an objection, see *Yearbook ... 2003* (footnote 3 above), p. 47, para. 95.

[253] United Nations, *Multilateral Treaties* ... (see footnote 165 above), vol. II, chap. XXIII.1.

[254] See, for example, the declarations and objections of Germany, the Netherlands, New Zealand, the United Kingdom and the United States to the comparable reservations of several States to the 1969 Vienna Convention (*ibid.*).

[255] *Ibid.*, vol. I, chap. III.3. With regard to the reservation formulated by Bahrain on 2 November 1971, the objection of Japan, dated 27 January 1987, must be regarded as late. It is certainly because of the fact that the objection by Japan also concerns the reservation formulated by Qatar on 6 June 1986 that the Secretary-General published it as an "objection" and not as a simple "communication", as is normally the case. This does not, however, prejudge the concrete effects that this late objection might produce.

[256] *Ibid.*

[257] *Ibid.*, chap. IV.1. Despite this general objection, Greece raised two further objections with regard to the reservation of the United States (*ibid.*).

[258] *Ibid.*

[259] Nor any other effects, assuming other effects to be legally possible.

135. The question now is whether a separate guideline on this point should be included in the Guide to Practice or whether it is enough to state in the commentary to guideline 2.6.13 on the time period for formulating an objection that the date of notification of the reservation constitutes the *dies a quo* for the calculation of that period, but does not necessarily constitute the date from which an objection may be made. The benefits of pre-emptive objections seem sufficient to warrant the adoption of a separate draft guideline enshrining this practice, which might be worded as follows:

"2.6.14 *Pre-emptive objections*

"A State or international organization may formulate an objection to a specific potential or future reservation, or to a specific category of such reservations, or exclude the application of the treaty as a whole in its relations with the author of such a potential or future reservation. Such a pre-emptive objection shall not produce the legal effects of an objection until the reservation has actually been formulated and notified."

136. Just as it is possible to formulate an objection in advance, there is nothing to prevent States or international organizations from formulating objections late, in other words after the end of the 12-month period (or any other time period specified by the treaty), or after the expression of consent to be bound in the case of States and international organizations that accede to the treaty after the end of the 12-month period.

137. This practice is far from uncommon. In a study published in 1988, Horn found that of 721 objections surveyed, 118 had been formulated late,[260] and this figure has since increased.[261] Many examples can be found[262] relating to human rights treaties,[263] but also to treaties covering subjects as diverse as the law of treaties,[264] the fight against terrorism,[265] the Convention on the Safety of United Nations and Associated Personnel[266] and the Rome Statute of the International Criminal Court.[267]

138. This practice should certainly not be condemned. On the contrary, it allows States and international organizations to express—in the form of objections—their views as to the validity of a reservation, even when the reservation was formulated more than 12 months earlier, and this practice has its advantages, even if these late objections do not produce any immediate legal effects. As it happens, the position of the States and international organizations concerned regarding the validity of a reservation is an important element for the interpreting body, whether a monitoring body or international court, to take into consideration when determining the validity of the reservation (see also paragraph 108 above). Furthermore, an objection, even a late objection, is important in that it may lead to a reservations dialogue.[268]

139. However, it follows from article 20, paragraph 5, of the 1969 and 1986 Vienna Conventions that if a State or international organization has not raised an objection by the end of a period of 12 months following the formulation of the reservation, or by the date on which it expressed its consent to be bound by the treaty, it is considered to have accepted the reservation, with all the consequences that this entails. Without going into details of the effects of tacit acceptance of this kind, which will be developed further in the next report by the Special Rapporteur, suffice it to say that the effect of such acceptance is, in principle, that the treaty enters into force between the reserving State (or international organization) and the State (or organization) considered to have accepted the reservation. This result cannot be called into question by an objection formulated several years after the cut-off date without seriously affecting legal security. The practice of the Secretary-General as the depositary of multilateral treaties confirms this view. The Secretary-General receives late objections and communicates them to the

[260] Horn, *op. cit.*, p. 206. See also Riquelme Cortado, *op. cit.*, pp. 264–265.

[261] Riquelme Cortado, *op. cit.*, p. 265.

[262] The examples cited hereafter are solely cases identified by the Secretary-General and, consequently, notified as "communications". The study is complicated by the fact that, in the collection of multilateral treaties deposited with the Secretary-General, the date indicated is not that of notification but of deposit of the instrument containing the reservation.

[263] See the very comprehensive list drawn up by Riquelme Cortado, *op. cit.*, p. 265, footnote 316.

[264] *Ibid.*, footnote 317.

[265] See the late objections to the declaration made by Pakistan (13 August 2002) upon accession to the International Convention for the Suppression of Terrorist Bombings: Republic of Moldova (6 October 2003), Russian Federation (22 September 2003) and Poland (3 February 2004) (United Nations, *Multilateral Treaties ...* (footnote 165 above), vol. II, chap. XVIII.9, note 5); and the late objections to the reservations formulated by the following States in regard to the International Convention for the Suppression of the Financing of Terrorism: reservation by Belgium (17 May 2004): Russian Federation (7 June 2005) and Argentina (22 August 2005); reservation by Jordan (28 August 2003): Belgium (24 September 2004), Russian Federation (1 March 2005), Japan (14 July 2005), Argentina (22 August 2005); reservation by the Democratic People's Republic of Korea (12 November 2001, at the time of signature; as the State did not ratify the Convention, the reservation was not confirmed): Republic of Moldova (6 October 2003), Germany (17 June 2004), Argentina (22 August 2005) (*ibid.*, chap. XVIII.11, notes 4, 5 and 8).

[266] See the late objections by Portugal (15 December 2005) in regard to the declaration by Turkey (9 August 2004) (*ibid.*, chap. XVIII.8, note 4).

[267] See the late objections by Ireland (28 July 2003), the United Kingdom (31 July 2003), Denmark (21 August 2003) and Norway (29 August 2003) to the interpretative declaration (considered by objecting States to constitute a prohibited reservation) by Uruguay (28 June 2002) (*ibid.*, chap. XVIII.10, note 7).

[268] Following the late objection by Sweden, Thailand withdrew its reservation in respect of the Convention on the rights of the child (*ibid.*, vol. I, chap. IV.11, note 13). With regard to the interpretative declaration of Uruguay in respect of the Rome Statute of the International Criminal Court (see footnote 267 above), Uruguay justified its declaration, in a communication dated 21 July 2003, providing assurance that its interpretative declaration did not constitute a reservation of any kind. Baratta considered that:

> "Objections are a tool used not only and not chiefly to express disapproval of the reservation of another and sometimes to point out its incompatibility with further obligations under international law, but also and mainly to induce the author of the reservation to reconsider and possibly to withdraw it."

(*Op. cit.*, pp. 319–320)

other States and organizations concerned, not as objections but as a "communication".[269]

140. States seem to be aware that a late objection cannot produce the normal effects of an objection made in good time. The United Kingdom, in its objection (made within the required 12-month period) to the reservation of Rwanda to article IX of the Convention on the Prevention and Punishment of the Crime of Genocide, said that it wished "to place on record that they take the same view [in other words, that they were unable to accept the reservation] of the similar reservation [to that of Rwanda] made by the German Democratic Republic as notified by the circular letter ... of 25 April 1973".[270] It is clear that the British objection to the reservation of the German Democratic Republic was late. The careful wording of the objection shows that the United Kingdom did not expect it to produce the legal effects of an objection formulated within the period specified by article 20, paragraph 5 of the 1969 Vienna Convention.

141. The communication of 21 January 2002 by Peru in relation to a late objection by Austria[271]—only a few days late—concerning its reservation to the 1969 Vienna Convention is particularly interesting:

> [The Government of Peru refers to the communication made by the Government of Austria relating to the reservation made by Peru upon ratification]. In this document, Member States are informed of a communication from the Government of Austria stating its objection to the reservation entered in respect of the Vienna Convention on the Law of Treaties by the Government of Peru on 14 September 2000 when depositing the corresponding instrument of ratification.
>
> As the [Secretariat] is aware, article 20, paragraph 5, of the Vienna Convention states that "a reservation is considered to have been accepted by a State if it shall have raised no objection to the reservation by the end of a period of twelve months after it was notified of the reservation (...)". The ratification and reservation by Peru in respect of the Vienna Convention were communicated to Member States on 9 November 2000.
>
> Since the communication from the Austrian Government was received by the Secretariat on 14 November 2001 and circulated to Member States on 28 November 2001, the Peruvian Mission is of the view that there is tacit acceptance on the part of the Austrian Government of the reservation entered by Peru, the 12-month period referred to in article 20, paragraph 5, of the Vienna Convention having elapsed without any objection being raised. The Peruvian Government considers the communication from the Austrian Government as being without legal effect, since it was not submitted in a timely manner.[272]

Although it would appear excessive to consider the communication from Austria as being completely without legal effect, the communication from Peru shows very clearly that a late objection does not preclude the presumption of acceptance under article 20, paragraph 5, of the 1969 and 1986 Vienna Conventions.

142. It follows from the above that while a late objection may constitute an important element in determining the validity of a reservation, it cannot produce the "normal" effects of an objection envisaged by articles 20, paragraph 4 (*b*), and 21, paragraph 3, of the 1969 and 1986 Vienna Conventions.[273]

143. States should certainly not be discouraged from formulating late objections: quite the opposite. However, it must be stressed that such late objections cannot produce the effects envisaged by the 1969 and 1986 Vienna Conventions. This is how article 20, paragraph 5, of the Conventions should be understood.

"2.6.15 *Late objections*

"An objection to a reservation formulated after the end of the time period specified in guideline 2.6.13 does not produce all the legal effects of an objection that has been made within that time period."

144. The wording of this draft guideline remains sufficiently flexible to allow for the well-established State practice of late objections. It does not prohibit a State or international organization from raising an objection after the end of the specified time period—either 12 months (or any other period provided for by the treaty) after it received notice of the reservation, or after the date on which it expressed its consent to be bound by the treaty, if this is later. However, the word "formulate" is preferable to "make" (see paragraph 60 above), since a late objection cannot produce the "normal" effects of an objection made within the period specified in article 20, paragraph 5, of the 1969 and 1986 Vienna Conventions, reproduced in guideline 2.6.13 (Time period for formulating an objection). The fact that a late objection cannot produce the "normal" effects of an objection does not mean that it has no effect at all (see paragraph 138 above).

3. Withdrawal and modification of objections to reservations

145. The question of the withdrawal of objections to reservations, like that of the withdrawal of reservations, is addressed only very cursorily in the 1969 and 1986 Vienna Conventions,[274] which merely provide indications on how objections may be withdrawn and when such withdrawals become operative. The modification of objections is not addressed at all.

---

[269] *Summary of Practice* ... (see footnote 172 above), para. 213. In *Multilateral Treaties* ... (see footnote 165 above), however, several examples of late objections are given in the "Objections" section. This is the case, for example, for the objection raised by Japan (27 January 1987) to the reservations formulated by Bahrain (2 November 1971) and Qatar (6 June 1986) to the Vienna Convention on Diplomatic Relations. While the objection was very late concerning the reservation made by Bahrain, it was received in good time concerning the reservation made by Qatar; it was no doubt for that reason that the objection was communicated as such, and not simply as a "communication" (*ibid.*, chap. III.3). This is also the case for the objection by the United Kingdom (21 November 1975) to the reservation of Rwanda (16 April 1975), which also applies to the reservation of the German Democratic Republic (25 April 1975) (see paragraph 140 below).

[270] *Multilateral Treaties* ... (see footnote 165 above), chap. IV.1.

[271] This late objection was notified as a "communication" (*ibid.*, vol. II, chap. XXIII.1, note 18).

[272] *Ibid.*

[273] However, this does not prejudge the question of whether, and how, the reservation presumed to be accepted produces the "normal" effect provided for under article 21, paragraph 1, of the Conventions. The consent of the other States is not in itself enough to produce this effect; the reservation must also meet the conditions for validity set out in articles 19 and 23 of the Conventions.

[274] Especially concerning the effects of the withdrawal of reservations (see Szafarz, "Reservations to multilateral treaties", p. 314).

146. Article 22 provides as follows:

2. Unless the treaty otherwise provides, an objection to a reservation may be withdrawn at any time.

3. Unless the treaty otherwise provides, or it is otherwise agreed:

(*b*) the withdrawal of an objection to a reservation becomes operative only when notice of it has been received by the State which formulated the reservation.

Article 23, paragraph 4, stipulates how objections may be withdrawn:

The withdrawal of a reservation or of an objection to a reservation must be formulated in writing.

147. The Commission has done very little work on the withdrawal of objections. The question is not dealt with at all in the work of the early special rapporteurs; this is hardly surprising, given their advocacy of the traditional theory of unanimity (see paragraph 88 above), which logically precluded the possibility of an objection being withdrawn. Just as logically, it was the first report by Sir Humphrey Waldock, who favoured the flexible system, which contained the first proposal for a provision concerning the withdrawal of objections to reservations. He proposed the following draft article 19, paragraph 5:

A State which has lodged an objection to a reservation shall be free to withdraw it unilaterally, either in whole or in part, at any time. Withdrawal of the objection shall be effected by written notification to the depositary of the instruments relating to the treaty, and failing any such depositary, to every State which is or is entitled to become a party to the treaty.[275]

After major reworking of the provisions on the form and procedure relating to reservations and objections,[276] this draft article—which simply reiterated *mutatis mutandis* the similar provision on the withdrawal of a reservation[277]—was abandoned, without the reasons for this being clear from the Commission's work. The draft article is found neither in the text adopted on first reading, nor in the Commission's final draft.

148. It was only during the United Nations Conference on the Law of Treaties that the issue of the withdrawal of objections was reintroduced into the text of articles 22–23, based on a Hungarian amendment[278] which realigned the procedure for the withdrawal of objections with that of withdrawal of reservations. As Ms. Bokor-Szegó explained, on behalf of the Hungarian delegation:

[I]f a provision on the withdrawal of reservations was included, it was essential that there should also be a reference to the possibility of withdrawing objections to reservations, particularly since that possibility already existed in practice.[279]

The representative of Italy at the Conference also argued in favour of aligning the procedure for the withdrawal of an objection to a reservation with that for the withdrawal of a reservation:

The relations between a reservation and an objection to a reservation was the same as that between a claim and a counter-claim. The extinction of a claim, or the withdrawal of a reservation, was counterbalanced by the extinction of a counter-claim or the withdrawal of an objection to a reservation, which was equally a diplomatic and legal procedural stage in treaty-making.[280]

149. However, there is virtually no State practice in this area. Horn could only identify one example of a clear, definite withdrawal of an objection.[281] In 1982, Cuba notified the Secretary-General of the withdrawal of objections it had made when ratifying the Convention on the Prevention and Punishment of the Crime of Genocide with respect to the reservations to articles IX and XII formulated by several socialist States.[282]

150. Although the provisions of the 1969 Vienna Convention do not go into detail on the issue of withdrawal of objections, it is clear from the *travaux préparatoires* that, in principle, the withdrawal of objections follows the same rules as the withdrawal of reservations, just as the formulation of objections follows the same rules as the formulation of reservations (see paragraphs 89–92 above). To make the relevant provisions clear and specific, therefore, the draft guidelines already adopted by the Commission on the question of the withdrawal (and modification) of reservations,[283] can be taken as a basis, with the necessary changes to take account of the specific nature of objections. However, this should not be seen in any way as an attempt to revive the theory of parallelism of forms;[284] it is not a matter of aligning the procedure for the withdrawal of objections with the procedure for their formulation, but of applying the same rules to the withdrawal of an objection as those applicable to the withdrawal of a reservation. The two acts, of course, have different effects on the life of the treaty and differ in their nature and their addressees. Nevertheless, they are similar enough to be governed by comparable formal systems and procedures, as was suggested during the preparatory work for the Convention.

151. Following the example of the draft guidelines on the withdrawal and modification of reservations, five issues should be addressed concerning, respectively: the

[275] *Yearbook ... 1962* (see footnote 132 above), p. 62.

[276] See footnote 132 above.

[277] Draft article 17, paragraph 6, provided as follows: "A State which has formulated a reservation is free to withdraw it unilaterally, either in whole or in part, at any time, whether the reservation has been accepted or rejected by the other States concerned. Withdrawal of the reservation shall be effected by written notification to the depositary of instruments relating to the treaty and, failing any such depositary, to every State which is or is entitled to become a party to the treaty." (*Yearbook ... 1962* (see footnote 132 above), p. 61). The similarity between the two texts was highlighted by Sir Humphrey Waldock, who considered in the commentary on draft article 19, paragraph 5, that the latter provision reflected draft article 17, paragraph 6, and "[did] not therefore need further explanation" (*ibid.*, p. 68, para. (22)).

[278] A/CONF.39/L.18, *Official Records of the United Nations Conference on the Law of Treaties, First and Second Sessions* (footnote 142 above), p. 267. The Hungarian amendment was adopted, with a slight modification, by 98 votes to none, *ibid., Second Session* (see footnote 164 above), eleventh plenary meeting, p. 38, para. 41.

[279] *Ibid., Second Session* (see footnote 164 above), p. 37, para. 14.

[280] *Ibid.*, pp. 37–38, para. 27.

[281] Horn, *op. cit.*, p. 227.

[282] United Nations, *Multilateral Treaties* ... (see footnote 165 above), chap. IV.1, p. 134, note 30.

[283] Draft guidelines 2.5.1–2.5.11. For the relevant texts and commentaries, see *Yearbook ... 2003*, vol. II (Part Two), pp. 70–92, para. 368.

[284] See *Yearbook ... 2002* (footnote 2 above), pp. 24–25, para. 119.

form and procedure for withdrawal; the effects of withdrawal; the time at which withdrawal of the objection produces those effects; partial withdrawal; and the possible widening of the scope of the objection.

(a) *Form and procedure for withdrawing objections*

152. The question of the form for withdrawing an objection is answered in the 1969 and 1986 Vienna Conventions, in particular in articles 22, paragraph 2, and 23, paragraph 4 (see paragraph 146 above). Neither the possibility of withdrawing an objection at any time nor the requirement that it should be done in written form requires further elaboration—the provisions of the Conventions themselves are sufficient, especially considering that there is virtually no State practice in this regard. The applicable rules should logically be modelled on those relating to the withdrawal of reservations, regarding both the possibility of withdrawing an objection at any time and the written form.

153. On the first point, it will be noted, however, that paragraph 1 (relating to the withdrawal of reservations) and paragraph 2 (relating to the withdrawal of objections) of article 22 of the 1969 and 1986 Vienna Conventions are worded differently: whereas paragraph 1 is careful to state, with regard to a reservation, that "the consent of a State which has accepted the reservation is not required for its withdrawal",[285] paragraph 2 does not make the same specification as far as objections are concerned. But this difference should not be interpreted *a contrario*: the reason for the absence of the clause is that, in the latter case, the purely unilateral character of the withdrawal is self-evident. Proof of this, moreover, is that the part of the Hungarian amendment[286] which would have brought the wording of paragraph 2 into line with that of paragraph 1 was set aside at the request of the British delegation,

> in view of the differing nature of reservations and objections to reservations; the consent of the reserving State was self-evidently not required for the withdrawal of the objection, and an express provision to that effect might suggest that there was some doubt on the point.[287]

This is a convincing rationale for the different wording of the two provisions, which does not need to be revisited.

154. On the other hand, with regard to form, reservations and objections are treated the same way in article 23, paragraph 1, of the 1969 and 1986 Vienna Conventions.

155. In the light of these observations, it therefore seems reasonable in draft guidelines 2.7.1 and 2.7.2 simply to reproduce the rules contained respectively in articles 22, paragraph 2, and 23, paragraph 4, of the 1969 and 1986 Vienna Conventions, without modifying them:

"2.7 *Withdrawal and modification of objections to reservations*

"2.7.1 *Withdrawal of objections to reservations*

"Unless the treaty otherwise provides, an objection to a reservation may be withdrawn at any time.

"2.7.2 *Form of withdrawal of objections to reservations*

"The withdrawal of an objection to a reservation must be formulated in writing."

156. As for questions relating to the formulation and communication of a withdrawal, none of the provisions contained in either the 1969 or the 1986 Vienna Convention is useful or specific. The *travaux préparatoires* (see paragraphs 147–148 above), however, reveal that the procedure for the withdrawal of an objection is identical to that of a reservation. Accordingly, in the Guide to Practice it is sufficient to refer back to the relevant provisions[288] relating to the procedure to be followed for withdrawing a reservation, which apply *mutatis mutandis* to the withdrawal of an objection.[289]

"2.7.3 *Formulation and communication of the withdrawal of objections to reservations*

"Guidelines 2.5.4, 2.5.5 and 2.5.6 are applicable *mutatis mutandis* to the withdrawal of objections to reservations."

---

[285] On this point, see draft guideline 2.5.1 and commentary, *ibid.*, pp. 20–21, paras. 85–90.

[286] A/CONF.39/L.18 (see footnote 278 above). This amendment resulted in the inclusion of paragraph 2 in article 23 (see paragraph 148 above).

[287] *Official Records of the United Nations Conference on the Law of Treaties, Second Session* (see footnote 164 above), p. 38, para. 31.

[288] In other words, the following draft guidelines:

"2.5.4 [2.5.5] *Formulation of the withdrawal of a reservation at the international level*

"1. Subject to the usual practices in international organizations which are depositaries of treaties, a person is competent to withdraw a reservation made on behalf of a State or an international organization if:

"(*a*) That person produces appropriate full powers for the purposes of that withdrawal; or

"(*b*) It appears from practice or other circumstances that it was the intention of the States and international organizations concerned to consider that person as competent for such purposes without having to produce full powers.

"2. By virtue of their functions and without having to produce full powers, the following are competent to withdraw a reservation at the international level on behalf of a State:

"(*a*) Heads of State, Heads of Government and Ministers for Foreign Affairs;

"(*b*) Representatives accredited by States to an international organization or one of its organs, for the purpose of withdrawing a reservation to a treaty adopted by that organization or body;

"(*c*) Heads of permanent missions to an international organization, for the purpose of withdrawing a reservation to a treaty between the accrediting States and that organization.

"2.5.5 [2.5.5 *bis*, 2.5.5 *ter*] *Absence of consequences at the international level of the violation of internal rules regarding the withdrawal of reservations*

"1. The determination of the competent body and the procedure to be followed for withdrawing a reservation at the internal level is a matter for the internal law of each State or the relevant rules of each international organization.

"2. A State or an international organization may not invoke the fact that a reservation has been withdrawn in violation of a provision of the internal law of that State or the rules of that organization regarding competence and the procedure for the withdrawal of reservations as invalidating the withdrawal.

"2.5.6 *Communication of withdrawal of a reservation*

"The procedure for communicating the withdrawal of a reservation follows the rules applicable to the communication of reservations contained in guidelines 2.1.5, 2.1.6 [2.1.6, 2.1.8] and 2.1.7."

(*Yearbook ... 2003*, vol. II (Part Two), p. 69, para. 367). For the commentaries to these draft guidelines, see pages 76–81, paragraph 368 (*ibid.*).

[289] See footnote 195 above.

(b) *Effects of the withdrawal of an objection*

157. At the suggestion of the Special Rapporteur,[290] the Commission considered the effects of the withdrawal of a reservation at the same time that it examined the procedure for withdrawal.[291] Yet, whereas withdrawing a reservation simply restores the integrity of the treaty in its relations between the author of the reservation and the other parties, the effects of withdrawing an objection are likely to be manifold.

158. Without doubt, a State or an international organization which withdraws its objection to a reservation must be considered to have accepted the reservation. This follows implicitly from the presumption of article 20, paragraph 5, of the 1969 Vienna Convention, which considers the lack of an objection by a State or an international organization to be an acceptance. Bowett also asserts that "the withdrawal of an objection to a reservation ... becomes equivalent to acceptance of the reservation".[292] It has also been argued that "the withdrawal of an objection is a specific form of the acceptance of the reservation".[293]

159. It is questionable, however, and in any case premature,[294] to maintain that the consequence of withdrawing an objection is that "the reservation has full effect".[295] As it happens, the effects of the withdrawal of an objection, or the resulting "deferred" acceptance, can be manifold and complex, depending on factors relating to the nature not only of the reservation[296] but also of the objection itself:[297]

(*a*) If the objection was not accompanied by the definitive declaration provided for in article 20, paragraph 4 (*b*), of the 1969 Vienna Convention, the reservation produces its "normal" effects as provided for in article 21, paragraph 1;

(*b*) If the objection was a "maximum-effect" objection, the treaty enters into effect between the two parties and the reservation produces its full effects in accordance with the provisions of article 21;

(*c*) If the objection was a cause precluding the treaty from entering into force between all parties pursuant to article 20, paragraph 2, or with regard to the reserving State in application of article 20, paragraph 4, the treaty enters into force (and the reservation produces its effects).[298]

160. Not only would it therefore seem difficult to adopt a provision covering all the effects of the withdrawal of an objection, owing to the complexity of the question, but it might also pre-empt the future work of the Commission on the effects of a reservation and the acceptance of a reservation. At this stage in the proceedings, then, it seems wiser, and in any case sufficient, to note that the withdrawal of an objection to a reservation is equivalent to its acceptance and that a State which has withdrawn its objection must be considered to have accepted the reservation. Such a provision implicitly refers to acceptances and their effects.

"2.7.4 *Effect of withdrawal of an objection*

"A State that withdraws an objection formulated earlier against a reservation is considered to have accepted that reservation."

(c) *Effective date of withdrawal of an objection*

161. The 1969 Vienna Convention contain a very clear provision concerning the time at which the withdrawal of an objection becomes operative. Article 22, paragraph 3, states:

Unless the treaty otherwise provides, or it is otherwise agreed:

(*a*) ...

(*b*) the withdrawal of an objection to a reservation becomes operative only when notice of it has been received by the State which formulated the reservation.

162. This provision differs from the corresponding rule on the effective date of withdrawal of a reservation in that, in the latter case, the withdrawal "becomes operative in relation to another contracting State only when notice of it has been received by that State" (art. 22, para. 3 (*a*)). The reasons for this difference in wording can easily be understood. Whereas withdrawing a reservation hypothetically modifies the content of treaty obligations between the reserving State or international organization and all the other contracting States or organizations, in general withdrawing an objection to a reservation modifies only the bilateral treaty relationship between the reserving State or organization and the objecting State or organization. Ms. Bokor-Szegó, representative of Hungary at the 1969 United Nations Conference on the Law of Treaties, explained the difference in the wording between subparagraph (*a*) and the subparagraph (*b*) proposed by her delegation as follows (see paragraph 148 above):

[W]ithdrawal of an objection directly concerned only the objecting State and reserving State.[299]

163. However, as indicated earlier in paragraph 159, the effects of withdrawing an objection to a reservation may go beyond this strictly bilateral relationship between the reserving party and the objecting party. All depends on the content and scale of the objection: the result of its withdrawal may even be that a treaty enters into force between all the States and international organizations that ratified it. This occurs in particular when an objection has prevented

[290] *Yearbook ... 2002* (see footnote 2 above), p. 31, para. 152.

[291] See draft guideline 2.5.7 (Effect of withdrawal of a reservation) and the commentary, *Yearbook ... 2003*, vol. II (Part Two), pp. 81–83.

[292] "Reservations to non-restricted multilateral treaties", pp. 87–88. See also Migliorino, "La revoca di riserve e di obiezioni a riserve", p. 329.

[293] Szafarz, *loc. cit.*, p. 314.

[294] The question of the effects of reservations, acceptances and objections will be the subject of a later report, as was indicated in the provisional outline of the study (see footnote 7 above).

[295] Bowett, *loc. cit.*, p. 88.

[296] And its validity or non-validity—but that is a totally different problem.

[297] In this vein, see Szafarz, *loc. cit.*, p. 314, and Migliorino, *loc. cit.*, p. 329.

[298] Numerous other situations are possible, in particular if one accepts the validity of objections with "intermediate" or "super-maximum" effect. For definitions of these notions, see footnotes 307–310 below.

[299] *Official Records of the United Nations Conference on the Law of Treaties, Second Session* (see footnote 164 above), p. 37, para. 14.

a treaty from entering into force between the parties to a treaty with limited participation (art. 20, para. 2) or, a less likely scenario, when the withdrawal of an objection allows the reserving State or international organization to be a party to the treaty in question and thus brings the number of parties up to that required for the treaty's entry into force. Accordingly, it could be questioned whether it is legitimate that the effective date of withdrawal of an objection to a reservation should depend solely on when notice of that withdrawal is given to the reserving State, which is certainly the chief interested party but not necessarily the only one. In the above-mentioned situations, limiting the requirement to give notice in this way means that the other contracting States or organizations are not in a position to determine the exact date when the treaty enters into force.

164. This disadvantage appears to be more theoretical than real, however, since the withdrawal of an objection must be communicated not only to the reserving State but also to all the States and organizations concerned or to the depositary of the treaty, who will transmit the communication.[300]

165. The other disadvantages of the rule setting the effective date at notification of the withdrawal were discussed by the Commission, with regard to reservations, when it adopted draft guideline 2.5.8 (Effective date of withdrawal of a reservation).[301] They concern the immediacy of that effect, on the one hand, and, on the other, the uncertainty facing the author of the withdrawal as to the date notification is received by the State or international organization concerned. The same considerations apply to the withdrawal of an objection, but there they are less problematic.[302] As far as the immediacy of the effect of the withdrawal is concerned, it should be borne in mind that the chief interested party is the author of the reservation, who would like the reservation to produce all its effects on another Contracting Party: the quicker the objection is withdrawn, the better it is from the author's perspective.

166. In view of these considerations, it does not seem necessary to modify the rule set forth in article 22, paragraph 3 (*b*), of the 1969 Vienna Convention. Taking into account the recent practice of the principal depositaries of multilateral treaties and, in particular, that of the Secretary-General,[303] who use modern, rapid means of communication to transmit notifications, States and international organizations other than the reserving State or organization should normally receive the notification at the same time as the directly interested party. Consequently, it might be both useful and justifiable simply to reproduce the provision of the Convention in a draft guideline, while pointing out the problem in the commentary, as was done for the similar rule concerning the withdrawal of a reservation.[304]

167. In accordance with the Commission's practice, a draft guideline should be adopted that reproduces article 22, paragraph 3 (*b*), of the 1986 Vienna Convention, which is more comprehensive than the corresponding 1969 provision in that it takes into account international organizations, without altering the meaning in any way.

"2.7.5 *Effective date of withdrawal of an objection*

"Unless the treaty otherwise provides, or it is otherwise agreed, the withdrawal of an objection to a reservation becomes operative only when notice of it has been received by the State or international organization which formulated the reservation."

168. For the reasons given in the commentary to draft guideline 2.5.9 (Cases in which a reserving State or international organization may unilaterally set the effective date of withdrawal of a reservation),[305] another partially analogous draft guideline should be adopted to allow for the situation where the objecting State or international organization unilaterally sets the effective date of withdrawal of its objection. With regard, however, to the case where the objecting State decides to set as the effective date of withdrawal of its objection an earlier date than that on which the reserving State received notification of the withdrawal, a situation corresponding to draft guideline 2.5.9 (*b*),[306] such an approach places the reserving State in a particularly awkward position. The State that has withdrawn its objection is considered as having accepted the reservation, and therefore, in accordance with the provisions of article 21, paragraph 1, it may invoke the effect of the reservation on a reciprocal basis. The reserving State would then have incurred international obligations without being aware of it, and this could seriously undermine legal security in treaty relations. This hypothesis should therefore be omitted from draft guideline 2.7.9, with the consequence that only a date later than the date of notification may be set by an objecting State when withdrawing an objection.

"2.7.6 *Cases in which an objecting State or international organization may unilaterally set the effective date of withdrawal of an objection to a reservation*

"The withdrawal of an objection takes effect on the date set by its author where that date is later than the date on which the reserving State received notification of it."

(d) *Partial withdrawal of objections and its effects*

169. As with the withdrawal of reservations, it is quite conceivable that a State (or international organization)

[300] This follows from draft guideline 2.7.3 and of draft guidelines 2.5.6 (Communication of withdrawal of a reservation) and 2.1.6 (Procedure for communication of reservations), to which it refers. Consequently, the withdrawal of the objection must be communicated "to the contracting States and contracting organizations and other States and international organizations entitled to become parties to the treaty" (*Yearbook ... 2003*, vol. II (Part Two), p. 67).

[301] See the commentary to draft guideline 2.5.8 (Effective date of withdrawal of a reservation), *ibid.*, p. 83–86, para. 368.

[302] *Ibid.*, p. 85, para. (12) of the commentary.

[303] See paragraphs. (14)–(18) of the commentary to draft guideline 2.1.6 (Procedure for communication of reservations), *Yearbook ... 2002*, vol. II (Part Two), pp. 40–41, para. 103. See also Kohona, "Some notable developments in the practice of the UN Secretary-General as depositary of multilateral treaties: reservations and declarations", and "Reservations: discussion of recent developments in the practice of the Secretary-General of the United Nations as depositary of multilateral treaties".

[304] See draft guideline 2.5.8 and the commentary, *Yearbook ... 2003*, vol. II (Part Two), pp. 83–86, para. 368.

[305] *Ibid.*, p. 86.

[306] *Ibid.*, p. 87, paras. (4)–(5) of the commentary to draft guideline 2.5.9.

might modify an objection to a reservation by partially withdrawing it:

(*a*) In the first place, a State might change an objection with "maximum"[307] (or even "super-maximum"[308]) or intermediate[309] effect into a "normal" or "simple" objection;[310] in such cases, the modified objection will produce the effects foreseen in article 23, paragraph 3. Moving from an objection with maximum effect to a simple objection or one with intermediate effect also brings about the entry into force of the treaty as between the author of the reservation and the author of the objection.[311]

(*b*) In the second place, it would appear that there is nothing to prevent a State from "limiting" the actual content of its objection (by accepting certain aspects of reservations that lend themselves to being separated out in such a way)[312] while maintaining its principle; in this case, the relations between the two States are governed by the new formulation of the objection.

170. To the Special Rapporteur's knowledge, no case of such a partial withdrawal of an objection has occurred in State practice. This does not, however, appear to be sufficient grounds for ruling out such a hypothesis. In his first report on the law of treaties, Sir Humphrey Waldock expressly provided for the possibility of a partial withdrawal of this kind. Draft article 19, paragraph 5, which was devoted entirely to objections but subsequently disappeared in the light of changes made to the structure of the draft articles (see paragraph 89 above), states:

> A State which has lodged an objection to a reservation shall be free to withdraw it unilaterally, either in whole or *in part**, at any time.[313]

The commentaries to this provision[314] presented by the Special Rapporteur offer no explanation of the reasons why he proposed it. Nonetheless, it is noteworthy that this draft article 19, paragraph 5, should again be identical to the corresponding proposal concerning the withdrawal of reservations,[315] as was made explicit in Sir Humphrey's commentary.[316]

171. Although there is no relevant practice, there is certainly no reason to rule out the possibility of an objection being partially withdrawn. Accordingly, the arguments which led the Commission to allow for the possibility of partial withdrawal of reservations[317] may be transposed *mutatis mutandis* to partial withdrawal of objections, even though in this case the result is not to ensure a more complete application of the provision of the treaty but, on the contrary, to give full effect (or greater effect) to a reservation. Consequently, just as partial withdrawal of a reservation follows the rules applicable to full withdrawal,[318] it would seem that the procedure for the partial withdrawal of an objection should be modelled on that of its total withdrawal.

172. Nevertheless it would be difficult to model a concise definition of what is meant by "the partial withdrawal of an objection" on the provision adopted by the Commission to define the partial withdrawal of a reservation, which, in the terms of draft guideline 2.5.10 "limits the legal effect of the reservation and achieves a more complete application of the provisions of the treaty, or of the treaty as a whole, to the withdrawing State or international organization".[319] As far as the partial withdrawal of an objection is concerned, the difficulty of determining the effects of total withdrawal (see paragraphs 157–160 above), reveals the scale of the problems: in this case the reservation is not simply accepted; rather, the objecting State or international organization merely wishes to alter slightly the effects of an objection which, in the main, is maintained. Although it is neither possible nor useful to take a position at this stage on the effects of an objection, there is no doubt that they are quite diverse and are (chiefly) felt in the relations between the author of the objection and the author of the reservation—as provided in article 21, paragraph 3, of the 1969 and 1986 Vienna Conventions—but may also have an impact on the treaty itself if, for example, the withdrawal of an objection with "maximum" effect, replaced by a simple objection, enables the treaty to enter into force.

173. In view of this complexity, it is probably wise, and sufficient, to adopt a draft guideline 2.7.7 worded in general terms:

---

[307] An objection with "maximum" effect is an objection in which its author expresses the intention of preventing the treaty from entering into force as between itself and the author of the reservation in accordance with the provisions of article 20, paragraph 4 (*b*), of the 1969 and 1986 Vienna Conventions. See *Yearbook ... 2003* (footnote 3 above), p. 47, para. 95; see also paragraph 103 above.

[308] An objection with "super-maximum" effect states not only that the reservation to which the objection is made is not valid, but also that, consequently, the treaty applies *ipso facto* as a whole in the relations between the two States. See *Yearbook ... 2003* (footnote 3 above), p. 48, para. 96.

[309] By making an objection with "intermediate" effect, a State expresses the intention to be associated with the author of the reservation but considers that the exclusion of treaty relations should go beyond what is provided for in article 21, paragraph 3, of the 1969 and 1986 Vienna Conventions (*ibid.*, p. 47, para. 95).

[310] "Normal" or "simple" objections are those with "minimum" effect, as provided for in article 21, paragraph 3, of the 1969 and 1986 Vienna Conventions (*ibid.*).

[311] If, on the contrary, an objection with "super-maximum" effect were abandoned and replaced by an objection with maximum effect, the treaty would no longer be in force between the States or international organizations concerned; even if an objection with super-maximum effect were held to be valid, that would enlarge the scope of the objection, which is not possible (see paragraphs 176–180 and draft guideline 2.7.9 below).

[312] In some cases, the question of whether, in the latter hypothesis, it is really possible to speak of a "limitation" of this kind is debatable—but neither more nor less than the question of whether modifying a reservation is tantamount to its partial withdrawal.

[313] *Yearbook ... 1962* (see footnote 132 above), p. 62—see paragraph 147 above.

[314] *Ibid.*, p. 68.

[315] See draft article 17, paragraph 6, *ibid.*, p. 61.

[316] *Ibid.*, p. 68.

[317] See the commentary to draft guideline 2.5.10 (Partial withdrawal of a reservation), *Yearbook ... 2003*, vol. II (Part Two), pp. 89–90, paras. (11)–(12) of the commentary.

[318] See draft guideline 2.5.10 (Partial withdrawal of a reservation), paragraph 2: "The partial withdrawal of a reservation is subject to the same formal and procedural rules as a total withdrawal and takes effect on the same conditions." (*Ibid.*, p. 87.)

[319] *Ibid.*, para. 1.

"2.7.7 *Partial withdrawal of an objection*

"1. Unless the treaty provides otherwise, a State or an international organization may partially withdraw an objection to a reservation. The partial withdrawal limits the legal effects of the objection on the treaty relations between the author of the objection and that the author of the reservation or on the treaty as a whole.

"2. The partial withdrawal of an objection is subject to the same formal and procedural rules as a total withdrawal and takes effect on the same conditions."

174. As for the effects of a partial withdrawal, the difficulty of determining them *in abstracto* calls for a guideline sufficiently broad and flexible to cover every possible case that might arise. The wording currently adopted with regard to the effects of the partial withdrawal of a reservation[320] would seem to meet these requirements. The partial withdrawal modifies the initial objection to the extent of the new formulation. The objection therefore continues to produce its effects as specified by the new text.

175. Even less than in the case of the partial withdrawal of reservations should it be possible for other States or international organizations or the reserving State or organization to react to the partial withdrawal of an objection. The objection itself produces its effects regardless of any reaction in accordance with the principle of the freedom of States or international organizations to make objections.[321] If they may make them as they wish, they may also withdraw them or limit their legal effects.

"2.7.8 *Effect of a partial withdrawal of an objection*

"The partial withdrawal of an objection modifies the legal effect of the objection to the extent of the new formulation of the objection."

(e) *Widening of the scope of an objection to a reservation*

176. Neither the Commission's *travaux préparatoires* nor the 1969 and 1986 Vienna Conventions contain provisions or indications on the question of the widening of the scope of an objection previously made by a State or international organization, and there is no State practice in this area.

177. In theory, it is conceivable that a State or international organization that has already raised an objection to a reservation may wish to widen the scope of its objection, for example by adding the declaration provided for in article 20, paragraph 4 (*b*) of the 1969 and 1986 Vienna Conventions, thereby transforming it from a simple objection, which does not preclude the entry into force of the treaty as between the objecting and reserving parties, into a qualified objection, which precludes any treaty-based relations between the objecting and reserving parties. This example alone demonstrates the problems of legal security that would result from such an approach. Any hint of an intention to widen or enlarge the scope of an objection to a reservation could seriously undermine the status of the treaty in the bilateral relations between the reserving party and the author of the new objection. Moreover, since in principle the reserving party does not have the right to respond to an objection, to allow the widening of the scope of an objection would amount to exposing the reserving State to the will of the author of the objection, who could change the treaty relations between the two parties at will, at any time.

178. It is therefore easy to understand the lack of State practice, which suggests that States and international organizations consider that the widening of the scope of an objection to a reservation is simply not possible.

179. Other considerations support this conclusion. In its work on reservations, the Commission has already examined the similar issues of the widening of the scope of a reservation[322] and the widening of the scope of a conditional interpretative declaration.[323] In both cases the widening is understood as the late formulation of a new reservation or a new conditional interpretative declaration.[324] However, a State or international organization that withdraws its objection to a reservation is considered to have accepted the reservation (see paragraphs 157–160 above), which precludes it from subsequently raising another objection against it. Furthermore, because of the presumption contained in article 20, paragraph 5, of the 1969 and 1986 Vienna Conventions, the late formulation of an objection can have no legal effect. Any declaration formulated after the end of the 12-month period, or any other period specified by the treaty in question, is no longer considered as an objection properly speaking, but as the renunciation of a prior acceptance, without regard for the commitment entered into with the reserving State,[325] and the practice of the Secretary-General as depositary of multilateral treaties confirms this conclusion.[326]

180. Therefore, it seems necessary to specify firmly in a draft guideline 2.7.9 that it is not possible to widen the scope of an objection to a reservation.

"2.7.9 *Prohibition against the widening of the scope of an objection to a reservation*

"A State or international organization which has made an objection to a reservation cannot subsequently widen the scope of that objection."

---

[320] See draft guideline 2.5.11 (Effect of a partial withdrawal of a reservation):

"1. The partial withdrawal of a reservation modifies the legal effect of the reservation to the extent of the new formulation of the reservation. Any objection made to the reservation continues to have effect as long as the author does not withdraw it, to the extent that the objection does not apply exclusively to that part of the reservation which has been withdrawn.

"2. No objection may be made to the reservation resulting from a partial withdrawal, unless that partial withdrawal has a discriminatory effect."

(*Ibid.*, p. 91)

[321] See paragraphs 60–67 and draft guideline 2.6.3 (Freedom to make objections) above.

[322] See draft guideline 2.3.5 (Widening of the scope of a reservation) and commentary, *Yearbook ... 2004*, vol. II (Part Two), p. 106, para. 295.

[323] See draft guideline 2.4.10 (Limitation and widening of the scope of a conditional interpretative declaration) and commentary, *ibid.*

[324] See the commentary to draft guideline 2.3.5, *ibid.*, para. (1), and the commentary to draft guideline 2.4.10, *ibid.*, p. 109, para. (1).

[325] See also paragraphs 136–144 above.

[326] See paragraph 139 and footnote 269 above.

EXPULSION OF ALIENS

[Agenda item 8]

DOCUMENT A/CN.4/573*

Second report on the expulsion of aliens, by Mr. Maurice Kamto, Special Rapporteur

[*Original: French*]
[*20 July 2006*]

CONTENTS

* Incorporating A/CN.4/573/Corr.1.

Multilateral instruments cited in the present report

	Source
Treaty of Peace between the Allied and Associated Powers and Germany (Treaty of Versailles) (Versailles, 28 June 1919)	*British and Foreign State Papers, 1919*, vol. CXII (London, HM Stationery Office, 1922), p. 1.
Treaty of Peace between the Principal Allied and Associated Powers and Poland (Versailles, 28 June 1919)	*Ibid.*, p. 225.
Convention fixing the Rules to be observed for the Granting of Asylum, adopted by the VIth International Conference of American States (Havana, 20 February 1928)	League of Nations, *Treaty Series*, vol. CXXXII, No. 3046, p. 323.
Convention on Political Asylum (Montevideo, 26 December 1933)	*Final Act of the Seventh International Conference of American States*, Montevideo, Uruguay, 3–26 December 1933, p. 168.
Agreement concerning prosecution and punishment of the major war criminals of the European Axis (London, 8 August 1945)	United Nations, *Treaty Series*, vol. 82, No. 251, p. 279.
Constitution of the International Refugee Organization and Agreement on interim measures to be taken in respect of refugees and displaced persons (New York, 15 December 1946)	*Ibid.*, vol. 18, No. 283, p.3.
International Labour Organisation Convention (No. 97) concerning migration for employment (Geneva, 1 July 1949)	*Ibid.*, vol. 120, No. 1616, p. 71.
Geneva Conventions for the protection of war victims (Geneva, 12 August 1949)	*Ibid.*, vol. 75, Nos. 970–973, pp. 31 *et seq.*
Geneva Convention for the Amelioration of the Condition of the Wounded and Sick in Armed Forces in the Field	*Ibid.*, No. 970, p. 31.
Geneva Convention for the Amelioration of the Condition of Wounded, Sick and Shipwrecked Members of Armed Forces at Sea	*Ibid.*, No. 971, p. 85.
Geneva Convention relative to the Treatment of Prisoners of War	*Ibid.*, No. 972, p. 135.
Geneva Convention relative to the Protection of Civilian Persons in Time of War	*Ibid.*, No. 973, p. 287.
Convention for the Protection of Human Rights and Fundamental Freedoms (European Convention on Human Rights) (Rome, 4 November 1950)	*Ibid.*, vol. 213, No. 2889, p. 221.
Convention relating to the Status of Refugees (Geneva, 28 July 1951)	*Ibid.*, vol. 189, No. 2545, p. 137.
Protocol relating to the Status of Refugees (New York, 31 January 1967)	*Ibid.*, vol. 606, No. 8791, p. 267.
Convention on diplomatic asylum (Caracas, 28 March 1954)	*Ibid.*, vol. 1438, No. 24377, p. 101.
Convention on territorial asylum (Caracas, 28 March 1954)	*Ibid.*, No. 24378, p. 127.
Convention relating to the Status of Stateless Persons (New York, 28 September 1954)	*Ibid.*, vol. 360, No. 5158, p. 117.
European Convention on Establishment (Paris, 13 December 1955)	*Ibid.*, vol. 529, No. 7660, p.141.

	Source
Treaty establishing the European Community (Rome, 25 March 1957), incorporating the amendments made by the Treaty of Nice of 26 February 2001	Consolidated version of the Treaty on European Union, *Official Journal of the European Union*, vol. 45, No. C 325 (24 December 2002) p. 1.
European Convention on Extradition (Paris, 13 December 1957)	United Nations, *Treaty Series*, vol. 359, No 5146, p. 273.
Convention on the reduction of statelessness (New York, 30 August 1961)	*Ibid.*, vol. 989, No. 14458, p. 175.
Vienna Convention on Consular Relations (Vienna, 24 April 1963)	*Ibid.*, vol. 596, No. 8638, p. 261.
Optional Protocol to the Vienna Convention on Consular Relations concerning the Compulsory Settlement of Disputes (Vienna, 24 April 1963)	*Ibid.*, No. 8640, p. 487.
International Covenant on Civil and Political Rights (New York, 16 December 1966)	*Ibid.*, vol. 999, No. 14668, p. 171.
Optional Protocol to the International Covenant on Civil and Political Rights (New York, 16 December 1966)	*Ibid.*
OAU Convention governing the specific aspects of refugee problems in Africa (Addis Ababa, 10 September 1969)	*Ibid.*, vol. 1001, No. 14691, p. 45.
American Convention on Human Rights: "Pact of San José, Costa Rica" (San José, 22 November 1969)	*Ibid.*, vol. 1144, No. 17955, p. 123.
Convention (No. 143) concerning migrations in abusive conditions and the promotion of equality of opportunity and treatment of migrant workers (Geneva, 24 June 1975)	*Ibid.*, vol. 1120, No. 17426, p. 323.
Convention against torture and other cruel, inhuman or degrading treatment or punishment (New York, 10 December 1984)	*Ibid.*, vol. 1465, No. 24841, p. 85.
The Schengen acquis—Agreement between the Governments of the States of the Benelux Economic Union, the Federal Republic of Germany and the French Republic on the gradual abolition of checks at their common borders (Schengen, 14 June 1985)	*Official Journal of the European Communities*, No. L 239 (22 September 2000), pp. 13–18.
The Schengen acquis—Convention implementing the Schengen Agreement of 14 June 1985 between the Governments of the States of the Benelux Economic Union, the Federal Republic of Germany and the French Republic on the gradual abolition of checks at their common borders (Schengen, 19 June 1990)	*Ibid.*, pp. 19–62.
International Convention on the Protection of the Rights of All Migrant Workers and Members of their Families (New York, 18 December 1990)	United Nations, *Treaty Series*, vol. 2220, No. 39481, p. 3.
Treaty of Amsterdam Amending the Treaty on European Union, the Treaties Establishing the European Communities and Certain Related Acts (Amsterdam, 2 October 1997)	*Official Journal of the European Communities*, No. C 340 (10 November 1997), p. 1.
European Convention on Nationality (Strasbourg, 6 November 1997)	United Nations, *Treaty Series*, vol. 2135, No. 37248, p. 213.
Rome Statute of the International Criminal Court (Rome, 17 July 1998)	*Ibid.*, vol. 2187, No. 38544, p. 3.
Partnership agreement between the members of the African, Caribbean and Pacific Group of States of the one part, and the European Community and its Member States, of the other part (Cotonou, 23 June 2000)	*Official Journal of the European Communities*, No. L 317, vol. 43 (13 December 2000), p. 3.

Works cited in the present report

Abraham, Ronny

"La reconduite à la frontière des demandeurs d'asile", *Revue française de droit administratif* (Paris), vol. 8, No. 1, January–February 1992, pp. 90–103.

Basdevant, Jules

Dictionnaire de la terminologie du droit international. Paris, Sirey, 1960.

Benoît-Rohmer, Florence

"Reconduite à la frontière: développements récents", *Revue du droit public et de la science politique en France et à l'étranger*, vol. 110, 1994, pp. 429–478.

Boeck, Charles de

"L'expulsion et les difficultés internationales qu'en soulève la pratique", *Collected Courses of The Hague Academy of International Law, 1927–III.* Paris, Hachette, 1928. Vol. 18, pp. 447–647.

Borchard, Edwin M.

The Diplomatic Protection of Citizens Abroad or the Law of International Claims. New York, Banks Law Publishing Co., 1919.

Brownlie, Ian

Principles of Public International Law. 6th ed. Oxford, Oxford University Press, 2003.

Chaltiel, Florence

"Le juge administratif, juge de l'immigration", *Revue du droit public*, vol. 116, No. 1, 2000, pp. 153–193.

Cholewinski, Ryszard

Migrant Workers in International Human Rights Law: Their Protection in Countries of Employment. Oxford, Clarendon Press, 1997. 405 p.

Daillier, Patrick and Alain Pellet

Droit international public. 7th ed. Paris, LGDJ, 2002. 1510 p.

Dent, John A.

Research Paper on the Social and Economic Rights of Non-Nationals in Europe. London, European Council on Refugees and Exiles, November 1998. 130 p.

D'Haëm, Rudolph

La reconduite à la frontière des étrangers en situation irrégulière. Paris, Presses Universitaires de France, 1997. 128 p. (Que sais-je?)

DOEHRING, Karl

"Aliens, expulsion and deportation", *in* Rudolf Bernhardt, ed., *Encyclopedia of Public International Law.* Amsterdam, Elsevier, 1985. vol. 8, pp. 14–16.

DRAPER, Gerald

The Red Cross Conventions. New York, Praeger, 1958.

ECONOMIDÈS, Constantin P.

"Les effets de la succession d'États sur la nationalité des personnes physiques", RGDIP, vol. 103/1999/3, pp. 577–599.

ELLES, Baroness

International Provisions Protecting the Human Rights of Non-Citizens. United Nations publication, Sales No. E.80.XIV.2 (E/CN.4/Sub.2/392/Rev.1).

FABRE-ALIBERT, Véronique

"Réflexions sur le nouveau régime juridique des étrangers en France", *Revue du droit public et de la science politique en France et à l'étranger* (Paris), vol. 110, 1994, pp. 1165–1195.

FAVOREU, Louis and Loïc Philip

Les grandes décisions du Conseil constitutionnel. 5th ed. Paris, Sirey, 1989. 808 p.

FLECK, Dieter, ed.

The Handbook of Humanitarian Law in Armed Conflicts. Oxford, Oxford University Press, 1995. 589 p.

FRANCK, Claude

"L'évolution des méthodes de protection des droits et libertés par le Conseil constitutionnel sous la septième législature", *Semaine Juridique*, vol. 60, No. 38, 17 September 1986, doctrine 3256.

GAJA, Giorgio

"Expulsion of aliens: some old and new issues in international law", *Bancaja Euromediterranean Courses of International Law.* Elcano, Aranzadi, 1999. vol. III, pp. 283–314.

GARNER, Bryan A.

A Dictionary of Modern Legal Usage. 2nd ed. Oxford, Oxford University Press, 1995.

GARNER, Bryan A., ed.

Black's Law Dictionary. 8th ed. St. Paul, Minn., West, 2004.

GAY, Jean-Christophe

Les discontinuités spatiales. Paris, Economica, 1995. 112 p. (Collection "Géopoche")

GENEVOIS, Bruno

"Un statut constitutionnel pour les étrangers", *Revue française de droit administratif,* vol. 9, No. 5, September–October 1993, pp. 871–900.

GRAHL-MADSEN, Atle

The Status of Refugees in International Law, vol. II, *Asylum, Entry and Sojourn.* Leiden, Sijthoff, 1972. 482 p.

GRIFFIN, W. Martin

"Colonial expulsion of aliens", *American Law Review* (St. Louis), vol. XXXIII, 1899, pp. 90–96.

GUIMEZANES, N.

"La loi du 9 septembre 1986 sur les conditions d'entrée et de séjour des étrangers en France", *Semaine juridique*, Édition générale, No. 3, 1987, part I (doctrine), 3270.

HATHAWAY, James C.

The Rights of Refugees under International Law. Cambridge, Cambridge University Press, 2005.

INSTITUTE OF INTERNATIONAL LAW

Annuaire de l'Institut de droit international. vol. 11, 1891–1892. Hamburg Session, September 1892. Brussels, Weissenbruch, 1892. 441 p.

"Règles internationales sur l'admission et l'expulsion des étrangers proposées par l'Institut de droit international et adoptées par lui à Genève, le 9 septembre 1892", *Annuaire de l'Institut de droit international.* vol. 12, 1892–1894. Geneva Session, September 1892. Paris, Pedone-Lauriel.

"Régime de la neutralité", *Annuaire de l'Institut de droit international.* vol. 21. Ghent Session, September 1906. Paris, Pedone, 1907.

"Statut juridique des apatrides et des réfugiés", *Annuaire de l'Institut de droit international.* vol. 39–II, Brussels Session, April 1936. Brussels, Falk, 1936.

"Asylum in public international law (excluding neutral asylum)", *Annuaire de l'Institut de droit international.* vol. 43–II. Bath Session, September 1950. Basel, Editions juridiques et sociologiques, 1950.

INTERNATIONAL LAW ASSOCIATION

Report of the Fifty-Fifth Conference held at New York, 21–26 August 1972. London, ILA, 1974.

JAHN, Eberhard

"Refugees", *in* Rudolf Bernhardt, ed., *Encyclopedia of Public International Law*. vol. 4. Amsterdam, Elsevier, 2000, pp. 72–76.

JENNINGS, Sir Robert and Sir Arthur WATTS, eds.

Oppenheim's International Law, vol. I, *Peace*, parts 2 to 4. 9th ed. Harlow, Longman, 1992.

JULIEN-LAFERRIÈRE, François

"Le mythe de 'l'immigration zéro'", *L'actualité juridique: droit administratif,* No. 2, 20 February 1994, pp. 83–95.

KISS, Alexandre-Charles

Répertoire de la pratique française en matière de droit international public. Vols. II and VI. Paris, Centre national de la recherche scientifique, 1966 and 1969.

LADHARI, Mohamed

"La reconduite à la frontière des étrangers en situation irrégulière", *Les Petites Affiches*, No. 96, 10 August 1990, pp. 13–26.

LOCHAK, Danièle

"L'entrée et le séjour des étrangers en France: une législation sous influence", *L'actualité juridique: droit administratif,* No. 10, 20 October 1989, pp. 586–597.

MANGOLDT, Hans VON

"Stateless persons", *in* Rudolf Bernhardt, ed., *Encyclopedia of Public International Law.* Amsterdam, Elsevier, 2000. Vol. 4, pp. 656–660.

MILLER, Hunter, ed.

Treaties and Other International Acts of the United States of America. vol. 2, documents 1–40: 1776–1818. Washington, D.C., Government Printing Office, 1931.

Treaties and Other International Acts of the United States of America. vol. 4, documents 80–121: 1836–46. Washington, D.C., Government Printing Office, 1934.

NOREK, Claude

"Le droit d'asile en France dans la perspective communautaire", *Revue française de droit administratif* (Paris), vol. 5, No. 2, March–April 1989, pp. 200–206.

PARRY, Clive, ed.

The Consolidated Treaty Series. vol. 88, 1838–1839. Dobbs Ferry, New York, Oceana, 1969.

PELLONPÄÄ, Matti

Expulsion in International Law: A Study in International Aliens Law and Human Rights with Special Reference to Finland. Helsinki, Suomalainen Tiedeakatemia, 1984, pp. 292. (Academic dissertation, University of Helsinki)

PILLET, A. and J.-P. NIBOYET

Manuel de droit international privé. Paris, Sirey, 1924.

REWALD, Roman

"Judicial control of administrative discretion in the expulsion and extradition of aliens", *American Journal of Comparative Law*, vol. 34 (Supplement), 1986, pp. 451–465.

RIVIER, Alphonse

Principes du droit des gens. vol. 1. Paris, Arthur Rousseau, 1896. 596 p.

ROUSSEAU, Charles

Droit international public. vol. II: *Les sujets de droit.* Paris, Sirey, 1974. 797 p.

SALMON, Jean, ed.

Dictionnaire de droit international public. Brussels, Bruylant, 2001.

SANDOZ, Yves, Christophe SWINARSKI and Bruno ZIMMERMANN, eds.

Commentary on the Additional Protocols of 8 June 1977 to the Geneva Conventions of 12 August 1949. Geneva, ICRC/Martinus Nijhoff, 1987.

SOHN, Louis B. and Thomas BUERGENTHAL, eds.

The Movement of Persons across Borders. Washington, D.C., American Society of International Law, October 1992. (Studies in Transnational Legal Policy, No. 23)

TEITGEN-COLLY, Catherine and François JULIEN-LAFERRIÈRE

"Chronique de législation: étrangers", *L'actualité juridique: droit administratif* (Paris), No. 11, 20 November 1998, pp. 922–930.

TREBILCOCK, Anne M.

"Sex discrimination", *in* Rudolf Bernhardt, ed., *Encyclopedia of Public International Law.* vol. 4. Amsterdam, Elsevier, 2000, pp. 390–394.

TURPIN, Dominique

"La réforme de l'ordonnance du 2 novembre 1945 sur la condition des étrangers par la loi du 10 janvier 1980", *Revue critique de droit international privé* , 1980, pp. 41–57.

"Les nouvelles conditions de l'expulsion des réfugiés", *Revue française de droit administratif*, vol. 2 (2), March–April 1986, pp. 137–154.

VINCENT, J.-Y.

"Le nouveau régime de l'entrée et du séjour des étrangers en France", *La Revue Administrative*, No. 196, July–August 1980, pp. 363–382.

"La réforme de l'expulsion des étrangers par la loi du 29 octobre 1981", *Semaine juridique*, Édition générale, 1982, part I (doctrine), 3054.

VISSCHER, Charles DE

Theory and Reality in Public International Law. Rev. ed. English translation by P. E. Corbett. Princeton, N.J., Princeton University Press, 1968. 527 p.

WARZAZI, Halima Embarek

"Exploitation of labour through illicit and clandestine trafficking" (E/CN.4/Sub.2/L.640 of 20 November 1975). United Nations, Economic and Social Council, Commission on Human Rights, Sub-Commission on Prevention of Discrimination and Protection of Minorities, Twenty-ninth Session.

WHITEMAN, Marjorie M.

Digest of International Law. vol. 10. Washington, D.C., Department of State, 1968.

Introduction

1. It is appropriate to begin this second report with a brief review of the history of the topic, as the Special Rapporteur did not honour that tradition in his preliminary report on the expulsion of aliens.[1] A concise overview of the main ideas put forward in the preliminary report and an update on recent developments relating to the topic will follow, before the general presentation of this report.

A. Review of the history of the topic

2. At its fiftieth session, in 1998, the International Law Commission took note of the report of the Planning Group, which identified, *inter alia*, the topic of the expulsion of aliens for inclusion in the long-term programme of work of the Commission.[2]

3. At its fifty-second session, in 2000, the Commission included the topic entitled "Expulsion of aliens" in its long-term programme of work,[3] and a preliminary general scheme or syllabus on the topic was annexed to the report of the Commission.[4] The General Assembly took note of the topic's inclusion in paragraph 8 of its resolution 55/152 of 12 December 2000.

4. During its fifty-sixth session, in 2004, the Commission decided to include the topic "Expulsion of aliens" in its current programme of work and appointed Mr. Maurice Kamto as Special Rapporteur for the topic.[5] The General Assembly, in paragraph 5 of its resolution 59/41 of 2 December 2004, endorsed that decision of the Commission.

5. At the fifty-seventh session of the Commission, in 2005, the Special Rapporteur introduced his preliminary report,[6] which the Commission considered at its 2849th to 2852nd meetings from 11 to 15 July 2005.[7]

B. Consideration of the preliminary report on the expulsion of aliens

6. In his preliminary report, the Special Rapporteur outlined his understanding of the subject and sought the

[1] *Yearbook ... 2005*, vol. II (Part One), document A/CN.4/554, pp. 193 *et seq*.

[2] See *Yearbook ... 1998*, vol. II (Part Two), pp. 110–111, para. 554.

[3] *Yearbook ... 2000*, vol. II (Part Two), p. 131, para. 729.

[4] *Ibid.*, annex, pp. 142–143.

[5] See *Yearbook ... 2004*, vol. I, 2830th meeting, para. 4. See also volume II (Part Two), p. 120, para. 364.

[6] See footnote 1 above.

[7] See *Yearbook ... 2005*, vol. I, pp. 125–153.

opinion of the Commission on a few methodological issues to guide his future work.

1. Consideration by the Commission

7. The Commission endorsed most of the Special Rapporteur's choices and his draft workplan annexed to the preliminary report on the expulsion of aliens. However, it was suggested that the workplan should include a specific examination of the principles applicable to the expulsion of aliens. It was proposed, in particular, that the study should take into account the provisions of international human rights law requiring decisions on expulsion to be taken in accordance with law, with regard both to rules of procedure and to the conditions for expulsion; the application of the principle of non-discrimination; balancing a State's interest in expelling with the individual's right to privacy and family life; and the question of the risk that an individual's rights might be infringed in the State of destination.

8. As the Special Rapporteur explained, these principles, which are at the heart of the problem of the expulsion of aliens in international law, had, of course, not been overlooked; but it had not seemed appropriate to him to examine them within the framework of a preliminary report. However, part one, chapter II, of his draft workplan, devoted to general principles, very clearly showed that all of the relevant principles in this area would be reviewed in detail in subsequent reports.

9. Some members of the Commission were of the view that there was no need to include in the topic the questions of refusal of admission and immigration, movements of population, situations of decolonization and self-determination or the position of the occupied territories in the Middle East. Nevertheless, the Commission agreed with the Special Rapporteur that the draft articles to be developed on the topic must present as exhaustive a legal regime as possible, founded on fundamental principles forming the legal basis for the expulsion of aliens under international law.

2. Consideration by the Sixth Committee

10. The representatives of several States made statements during the consideration of chapter VIII (Expulsion of aliens) of the report of the Commission[8] by the Sixth Committee during the sixtieth session of the General Assembly. Speakers generally emphasized the importance, interest and urgency of the topic, but also its complexity and difficulty.[9] On the whole, like the Commission itself, they clearly supported the general approach to the topic proposed by the Special Rapporteur.[10]

11. During the debate a number of suggestions were made. With respect to approach, it was considered that codification of the topic required, as the Special Rapporteur himself had stated, a thorough comparative study of national laws, particularly if the question of the grounds for expulsion were to be considered,[11] the relevant rules of international law and international and regional jurisprudence.[12] In that regard, it was suggested that the work done over the past four years under the Berne Initiative and by IOM and the Global Commission on International Migration, which had presented its report to the Secretary-General of the United Nations on 5 October 2005,[13] should be taken into consideration.

12. With respect to content, the suggestions were more varied and at times contradictory, especially concerning the scope of the topic. While some representatives maintained on principle that all issues relating to immigration or border control policy (non-admission and refoulement) should be excluded from the scope of the topic,[14] others considered on the contrary that refusal of entry to an immigrant on board a ship or aircraft under the control of the expelling State should be considered to fall within the framework of expulsion.[15] It was also suggested that questions relating to international humanitarian law[16] should not be included in the topic, such as the expulsion of nationals of enemy States in the event of armed conflict or the large-scale expulsion of a population as a result of a territorial dispute.[17] Moreover, attention was drawn to the need to consider the question of the return of the expelled person to the State of origin, including the return of stateless persons who had been deprived of their nationality before obtaining a new nationality.[18] In that connection, it was suggested that the decision of a Government to expel aliens should not give rise to any obligation on the part of other States to receive them. Similarly, the question of States transited by the expelled person was raised, and it was suggested that these States should also not have the obligation to readmit expelled aliens into their territory.

13. One delegation expressed strong doubts that the topic deserved autonomous treatment in terms of existing conventional and customary international law, or that expulsion could be qualified as a "unilateral act of a State". The same delegation considered that the reference to diplomatic protection was out of place in the context of the topic, since diplomatic protection was exercised only where there was a breach of international law by a State and only after the exhaustion of local remedies.[19]

---

[8] *Ibid.*, vol. II (Part Two), p. 54.

[9] See the topical summary of the discussion in the Sixth Committee on the report of the Commission during the sixtieth session of the General Assembly (A/CN.4/560), paras. 128–152.

[10] See especially the statements by Canada (*Official Records of the General Assembly, Sixtieth Session, Sixth Committee*, 12th meeting, paras. 111–112); China (*ibid.*, 11th meeting, para. 54); and Poland (*ibid.*, 13th meeting, paras. 62–64).

[11] See the statements by Austria (*ibid.*, 11th meeting, para. 66) and Japan (*ibid.*, 12th meeting, paras. 8–9).

[12] See the above-cited statement by China (*ibid.*, 11th meeting, para. 54) and the statements by Romania (*ibid.*, para. 78) and by New Zealand (*ibid.*, paras. 109–110).

[13] See the above-cited statement by Canada (*ibid.*, 12th meeting, paras. 111–112).

[14] See, in particular, the above-cited statement by Romania (*ibid.*, 11th meeting, para. 78); the statement by Sweden on behalf of the Nordic countries (*ibid.*, 13th meeting, paras. 21–23) and the statement by the Republic of Korea (*ibid.*, 11th meeting, paras. 88–91).

[15] See the above-cited statement by China (*ibid.*, para. 54) and the statement by the Republic of Korea (*ibid.*, paras. 88–91); for an opposing view, see the above-cited statement by the representative of the Nordic countries (*ibid.*, 13th meeting, paras. 21–23).

[16] See the statement by Morocco (*ibid.*, 11th meeting, para. 45).

[17] See the above-cited statement by China (*ibid.*, para. 54).

[18] See the above-cited statement by Canada (*ibid.*, 12th meeting, paras. 111–112).

[19] See the statement by Portugal (*ibid.*, paras. 38–39).

14. The questions and doubts raised in those statements will be answered or resolved in this report and subsequent reports of the Special Rapporteur. Suffice it to say at this stage that, in the first place, if, as was recognized in the statement just cited, there exist rules of customary law on the matter, then the topic lends itself to codification without there being any need to demonstrate its autonomy with respect to related matters already governed by international agreements; in the second place, the reference to diplomatic protection is not intended to reopen that topic, the consideration of which has been virtually completed by the Commission, which has adopted a set of draft articles on it. But to rule out diplomatic protection on principle would be to presume that expulsion could never be carried out in violation of international law, which seems unlikely. The Special Rapporteur remains convinced that a State's responsibility may be engaged owing to the conditions of expulsion of an alien from its territory. Arbitral decisions in the late nineteenth and early twentieth centuries[20] sufficiently demonstrate this point; the *Diallo* case[21] pending before ICJ also provides guidance along the same lines, subject to what the Court ultimately decides in this case. Nevertheless, the Special Rapporteur does not intend to develop a special responsibility regime for the matter; he intends to refer to the relevant rules governing the responsibility of States for internationally wrongful acts.

C. Recent developments relating to the topic

15. Under this heading, the Special Rapporteur does not intend to cover all the developments in recent years, or even since his preliminary report, on the question of the expulsion of aliens. He proposes, more modestly, to present the main trends in State practice in the matter since the publication of the preliminary report as well as the current thinking on the subject within the United Nations and in other international forums. The latest jurisprudence and legal writings will be referred to in due course in relation to the particular question under discussion in order to avoid the risk of repetition which would result from introducing them both at this stage and then again later to shed light on one aspect of the topic or another.

1. Recent practice of some States

16. The question of expulsion of aliens is complicated further by the dramatic and complex problem of combating terrorism and the no less alarming problem of rampant irregular immigration.

(a) *Combating terrorism and expulsion*

17. The phenomenon of expulsion of aliens, even considered *sensu stricto* as excluding the question of non-admission and refoulement, has continued to grow, as the requirements of combating terrorism have increased distrust towards aliens on the part of many States. In this respect, some countries have begun to amend their legislation to place greater restrictions on the conditions for entry and stay in their territory. In articles in *The Guardian* of 12 August 2005, the British Lord Chancellor, Lord Falconer, was reported as saying that things had changed after the London attacks of 7 and 21 July 2005 and that there was a need for a text laying out for judges the "correct interpretation of the European Convention [for the Protection of Human Rights and Fundamental Freedoms]". He added: "I want a law which says that the Home Secretary, supervised by the courts, has got to balance the rights of the individual deportee against the risk to national security."[22] That was the rationale that led the British authorities to expel nine Algerian nationals suspected of being involved in terrorist activities. The British Home Secretary, Charles Clarke, said in that connection: "In accordance with my powers to deport individuals whose presence in the United Kingdom is not conducive to the public good for reasons of national security, the Immigration Service has today detained 10 foreign nationals who I believe pose a threat to national security."[23]

18. Acting on the same rationale, France established regional centres to combat Islamic fundamentalism, which resulted in the expulsion, for their radical preaching, of former Algerian imams, including Chellali Benchellali, Abdelkader Bouziane and Abdel Aissaoui. The Prime Minister of France said that he was "convinced that the denunciation of the Islamist preachers calling for violence, the dismantling of fundamentalist networks and the expulsion of foreign nationals who do not respect our values and our laws constitute the starting point for effective counter-terrorism efforts".[24] The French Minister of the Interior on 29 July 2005 announced the expulsion, by the end of August, of some 10 Islamists to their country of origin as an action against "radical preachers who may influence the very young or very susceptible".[25] That the persons concerned were deprived of their French nationality, acquired through naturalization, to make it possible to expel them is legally significant, because it is unusual in French practice. The Minister of the Interior said in this connection: "For those who have French nationality, I would like to revive the procedures for deprivation of citizenship. It is not actually something new; it is a provision that exists in our Penal Code and has simply not been used."[26] Besides article 25 of the Civil Code, article 26 of Ordinance No. 45–2658 of 2 November 1945, as amended by the French Parliament in June and July 2004,[27] and Act No. 2003–1119 of 26 November 2003 on immigration control, stay of aliens in France and nationality allow for expulsion on the grounds of incitement to discrimination, hatred or violence directed against a person or group, against women, for example.

---

[20] A number of these arbitral decisions are cited by Boeck, "L'expulsion et les difficultés internationales qu'en soulève la pratique", especially pp. 486–494.

[21] *Ahmadou Sadio Diallo (Republic of Guinea* v. *Democratic Republic of the Congo), Order of 7 November 2002, I.C.J. Reports 2002*, p. 607.

[22] *The Guardian*, Friday 12 August 2005 (http://www.guardian.co.uk).

[23] *The Independent*, 11 August 2005. See also *El Watan* (Algerian daily), 13 August 2005 (http://www.elwatan.com).

[24] Statement by Prime Minister Dominique de Villepin cited by Colette Thomas in her article "Paris et Londres coopèrent dans la lutte contre le terrorisme", published on 25 July 2005 on Radio France International (http://www.rfi.fr).

[25] Interview with the Minister of the Interior, Nicolas Sarkozy, in the French daily, *Le Parisien*, Friday 29 July 2005.

[26] *Ibid.*

[27] On 15 July 2004, the French Senate adopted without amendments on first reading the bill adopted by the National Assembly on first reading during the twelfth legislative term (Assemblée nationale (12e législ.): 1654, 1670 et T.A. 309; Sénat: 360 et 403 (2003–2004) (http://ameli.senat.fr).

19. France is not the only European country to have a legal arsenal aimed at facilitating the expulsion of radical imams. In the United Kingdom of Great Britain and Northern Ireland, since April 2003, the Government has had the option of depriving any person of citizenship constituting a threat to the country, as it did with the Muslim cleric Abu Hamza al-Masri after he called for a jihad. Austria has also tightened its legislation; among the new measures in effect since 1 January 2006 is a provision for the expulsion of preachers whose speech is a danger to public safety. In Germany, a law that entered into force at the beginning of 2005 is also intended to facilitate the expulsion of "spiritual instigators of disorder".[28]

(b) *Irregular immigration and expulsion*

20. Faced with an influx of poor immigrants, the developed countries are transforming themselves into impenetrable fortresses. Increasingly, they are closing their gates to certain categories of aliens by tightening control over immigration and making the conditions for entry or stay in their territories more stringent.[29] Addressing a meeting of prefects on 9 September 2005, the Minister of the Interior of France defined his policy in terms of quantitative goals and demanded results from the members of his audience:

> When we last met, I gave you numerical goals, asking you to remove a minimum of 23,000 aliens with irregular status this year. I note that by the end of August, 12,849 aliens had been effectively removed: in other words, 56 per cent of our goal was achieved in eight months. Therefore you have five months in which to step up your efforts. I also see that there are disparities in the results between some prefectures and others.
>
> Now, I expect everyone to mobilize their efforts, and I invite those prefects whose results are below average to apply to the National Centre for Leadership and Resources for operational support.[30]

As he saw it, nothing should stop the prefects in the fulfilment of their mission:

> And you must not hesitate to use all the room for manoeuvre authorized by the law. It is there for a purpose. You should therefore use the powers vested in you by the Code of Entry and Residence of Aliens, whatever petitions are made locally. I would ask you to show that you can resist pressure from this or that "group" or "association"; they represent no one but themselves.[31]

Nothing was to stand in the way of action; neither the concerns of these officials about the reception of asylum-seekers, nor any other considerations based on the case law of the European Court of Human Rights concerning the universal right to lead a family life in the place of one's choice. He explained.

> To facilitate removal, I have also decided to accelerate the programme of administrative custody …
>
> At the same time, at my request, the Minister for Foreign Affairs has instituted a procedure whereby we can sanction countries that are not cooperative in the matter of issuing travel documents by limiting the number of short-term visas France allows to their nationals. This concerns about a dozen countries, which you have identified, including Serbia and Montenegro, Guinea, Sudan, Cameroon, Pakistan, Georgia, Belarus and Egypt.[32]

21. One might question the legality of such diplomatic reprisals against what then became known as the "countries of illegal emigration", as contrasted with "safe countries".[33] It really does look, however, as though here the end was being used to justify the means. The Minister of the Interior was not at any pains to hide his determination to achieve his ultimate goal. He concluded his speech in unambiguous terms, mingling exaltation with threats:

> You need to become involved personally, resolutely and consistently, if you are to achieve results. This is what you are here for, and this is what justifies your existence, because it is on this that you will be judged in the end. Our joint success and the standard of living of the French are at stake.[34]

However, the effectiveness of such policies is doubtful. There has been a move forward from the myth of "zero immigration"[35] to the illusion of "selective immigration",[36] while the root causes of undeclared immigration are ignored, namely, the economic imbalance in the world and the extreme poverty of the countries of origin of the illegal immigrants. Certainly, in Mr. Sarkozy's explanatory statement given to the National Assembly on 30 April 2003 on the bill finally passed by both chambers of the French parliament in 2006, he criticizes "the zero immigration dogma" which would, he said, "be harmful" to France. His bill, which proposes thorough and far-reaching amendments to the law regarding expulsion and the related penalty of being barred from French territory, which could be imposed on aliens for a certain number of offences, "maintains the possibility of issuing an expulsion order or imposing the penalty of being barred from French territory against aliens who do not have personal

[28] Myriam Berber, "Expulsions et déchéance de nationalité pour les imams radicaux", published on 29 July 2005, on Radio France International (http://www.rfi.fr). Italy and Spain, for their part, while clearly threatened by radical groups, do not have any specific regulations. Other European States, in particular the Nordic countries, have chosen for the moment, for the sake of freedom of expression, not to take special measures, preferring to resolve problems on a case-by-case basis.

[29] While recognizing that "Europe also needs immigration" and that it "is not a luxury because immigration contributes decisively to economic growth in Europe" (Romano Prodi, then President of the European Commission, on 15 October 2003, at a pre-European Council press conference in Brussels), European leaders are unanimous in their "commitment to the fight against illegal immigration" in a more effective way. Among the measures envisaged or already implemented are the setting of quotas, visa policy, biometric means of identification, the establishment of an agency for the management of operational cooperation at the external borders (proposed by the European Commission on 20 November 2003 (COM(2003) 687 final/2)), the establishment of a European border police force or a European corps of border guards (see Communication from the Commission on the topic (COM (2002) 233 final)). On all these points, see *Justice & Security* (www.euroactiv.com, 13 December 2005).

[30] The text of this speech is annexed by Alain Gresh to his article entitled "M. Sarkozy contre l'anti-France", *Le Monde diplomatique*, 26 September 2005 (www.monde-diplomatique.fr). See also www.interieur.gouv.fr.

[31] *Ibid.*

[32] *Ibid.*

[33] Alain Morice, "Europe blocks right to asylum", *Le Monde diplomatique*, 17 March 2004, English language edition translated by Paul Jones (www.monde-diplomatique.fr).

[34] Speech by Mr. Sarkozy, cited above (see footnote 30).

[35] This was the goal announced by Mr. Charles Pasqua, Minister of State and Minister of the Interior and Regional Development of France, back on 2 June 1993 (see his interview, *Le Monde*, 2 June 1993), which gave birth to the so-called "Pasqua Law" adopted by the French parliament on 15 December 1993 and promulgated on 30 December 1993; on this topic see also Julien-Laferrière, "Le mythe de 'l'immigration zéro'".

[36] This is the conceptual shorthand of Mr. Nicolas Sarkozy, then Minister of the Interior of France (*BBC News*, 18 May 2006 (http://news.bbc.co.uk)).

or family ties with France" and provides for what he calls a mechanism "for deferred expulsion", the equivalent of a solemn warning procedure.[37]

22. In Belgium, under the law of 15 December 1980 on entry into the territory, residence, settlement and removal of aliens, amended several times in pursuit of the goal of "halting all new immigration", a policy adopted by the Government in 1974 and still in force, 14,110 people were expelled or repatriated in 2003, of whom 7,742 were expelled by air after having spent in some cases only a few weeks, but in many cases several years in Belgium. During that same year, 3,339 others were "turned back (*refoulés*)" without having crossed the Belgian frontier.[38] On 17 February 2005, the Netherlands parliament approved by a large majority the decision to expel 26,000 foreigners whose status was irregular, the so-called aliens "without papers".[39] With regard to the Spanish enclave of Ceuta, in Morocco, whose streets swarm with hundreds of asylum-seekers, the president of the Spanish Refugee Aid Commission expressed his dismay: "It is painful to say so, but Spain is hostile to refugees because of government policy ... The democratic Spain of 2003 has forgotten the Spain of 1939, when hundreds of thousands of its children fled Franco's repressive regime and settled around the globe."[40]

23. On the topic of expulsion, the developing harmonization of European migration policy laid down in the Treaty of Amsterdam was embodied on 9 March 2004 in the first specific step taken to establish a common policy for compulsory return, initially raised during the Informal Justice and Home Affairs Council meeting on 22–23 January 2004 in Dublin: the first Community charter flight was organized jointly by Belgium, Luxembourg and the Netherlands, to fly to Priština and Tirana.[41] This policy was extended progressively in spite of opposition from the European Parliament as expressed in a motion dated 1 April 2004. In fact, during a meeting of ministers of the interior of five European countries (G5) held on 5 July 2005 in Evian, France, they announced the organization of "joint expulsions" of illegal immigrants by France, Germany, Italy, Spain and the United Kingdom—to their countries of origin. The individuals concerned were sent on a "pooled flight". An operation of this kind, which had been done in the past, for instance by Germany and Italy, was repeated at the end of July 2005 with a "Franco-British pooled flight", to remove "some 40" immigrants who had entered France and the United Kingdom illegally.[42] This type of operation entails the risk of acting hastily or making an unfortunate error, since the expelling States might be sending illegal immigrants back to their country of origin without making sure that their lives are not threatened or that they are not going to be subjected to torture or inhuman, cruel and degrading treatment. Apart from these considerations, in such case the issue arises of whether or not these are collective expulsions. Moreover, the practice seems to be leading to an increasingly worrisome situation in which refugees may be treated like any other migrants, a situation which is a real threat to the very institution of asylum.

24. The European countries' desire to stem migration in general and to combat clandestine immigration by every possible means has in effect given rise to two new legal phenomena: "readmission agreements" and "transit agreements".

25. A readmission agreement is a bilateral agreement establishing the legal framework and the conditions for "removal" of illegal immigrants from the country where they are staying. It is a treaty concluded between the State "receiving" the illegal immigrants and the State of origin, or presumed State of origin, of such immigrants, under which the latter State agrees to accept the immigrants concerned, who have been identified and transferred under the responsibility and at the expense of the expelling State. This practice is becoming increasingly common; a country like Spain has signed such agreements with several States and is in the process of concluding as many more as possible. Some readmission agreements concluded by Spain contain provisions under which a sum of money is paid to those who are repatriated, in order to facilitate their reintegration into the country of destination.[43]

26. The "transit agreement" has a different purpose, and is far more questionable from a substantive standpoint, as can be seen from the one concluded on 8 January 2003 between Senegal and Switzerland. Under the terms of this "transit agreement", Senegal undertakes to receive and redirect all Africans that Switzerland may expel or ban from its territory, and as the receiving country, to identify their State of origin. In this respect, article 15 of the protocol refers laconically to "special services", for which the cost will be "settled by agreement between the parties".[44] This legal peculiarity dubbed a "transit agreement" would thus open the door to sordid financial dealings between Governments over the persons of illegal immigrants in disregard of basic respect for human dignity and the plight of the individuals concerned. The conclusion of the agreement collapsed in the face of public outcry in Senegal and the efforts of Swiss human rights activists.

2. International migration: report of the Global Commission on International Migration

27. The phenomenon of migration has assumed unprecedented proportions, to which globalization has undoubtedly contributed. The complexity of the problem, together with its economic impact and political sensitivity, have made it a subject of concern for the international community. Accordingly the General Assembly decided, in its resolution 58/208 of 23 December 2003, to devote a high-level dialogue to international migration at its sixty-first session in 2006. The Assembly also requested the

[37] See the bill adopted by the National Assembly and considered by the Senate under reference No. 362 dated 17 May 2006 (www.senat.fr).

[38] See Francisco Padilla, "La politique belge en matière d'expulsion des étrangers" (www.universal-embassy.be).

[39] Morice, *loc. cit.* (see footnote 33 above).

[40] *Ibid.*

[41] In order to implement this policy, the European Commission decided to offer financial support of 30 million euros.

[42] See Karine G. Barzegar, "Paris et Londres expulsent 'cette semaine' une 'quarantaine' de clandestins afghans par 'vol groupé'", *Associated Press*, 26 July 2005.

[43] Diplomatic source.

[44] Morice, *loc. cit.* (see footnote 33 above).

Secretary-General to report to it at its sixtieth session on the organizational details of the high-level dialogue, and recalled the request in its resolution 59/241 of 22 December 2004. In his report on international migration and development to the sixtieth session of the Assembly, the Secretary-General suggested the organizational arrangements for the high-level dialogue and the dates, 14–15 September 2006.[45]

28. By December 2003, a core group of States, encouraged by the Secretary-General, had set up the Global Commission on International Migration (GCIM), an independent body[46] whose aim is to create a framework for formulating a coherent and comprehensive response to international migration. In October 2005, GCIM produced an in-depth study in the form of a report entitled "Migration in an interconnected world: new directions for action".[47] Although GCIM is mainly concerned with studying the link between migration and economic development, in particular the impact of migration on development in migrants' countries of origin and destination alike, the International Law Commission, when it considers the agenda item "Expulsion of aliens", should not overlook the work done by this group of high-level experts. Apparently GCIM has also given thought to the challenge of irregular migration[48] and the human rights rules applicable to these so-called illegal migrants.[49]

29. According to the GCIM report, there is a broad consensus that both the number of migrants and the proportion of irregular migrants have increased. OECD estimates that migrants with irregular status account for from 10 to 15 per cent of the 56 million migrants in Europe, where about 500,000 new undocumented migrants arrive every year. In the United States of America, the number of irregular migrants (of whom half are of Mexican origin) is more than 10 million, and is growing by about 500,000 per year. Irregular migration is by no means confined to developed countries. Asia is the continent with the largest number of migrants with irregular status. It is estimated that there are 20 million in India alone, for example. They also make up the majority of migrants in Africa and Latin America,[50] where the close similarities of population groups living on either side of frontiers and the extremely porous nature of those frontiers make migratory movements easier. In Africa in particular, immigration is regarded as irregular only by State authorities, whereas the populations concerned see it as a natural movement among members of the same community and largely ignore international boundaries, which they regard as abstract and artificial in any case.

30. Irregular migration is one of the telling signs of the socio-economic imbalances aggravated by economic globalization and the rapid impoverishment of underdeveloped countries. But it also reflects the misery of populations in countries where extreme poverty is compounded by the consequences of repeated conflict and political intolerance. In such circumstances, migrants are willing to sacrifice anything to escape from their conditions and environments, as was dramatically demonstrated by the sight of throngs of young Africans storming the barbed wire fences around the Spanish enclaves of Ceuta and Melilla. The number of clandestine immigrants who die every year in their attempt to cross barriers—natural ones, like the Mediterranean, or erected by States, like those on the frontiers of Spain—in order to reach Europe is estimated at 2,000. Similarly, about 400 Mexicans die every year trying to cross the border into the United States.[51]

3. Euro-African Ministerial Conference on Migration and Development (Rabat, 10–11 July 2006)

31. The Euro-African Ministerial Conference on Migration and Development was attended by the representatives of 30 European countries, the Russian Federation, Turkey and Ukraine, 27 African countries, Mexico and 21 international organizations.

32. The Action Plan adopted at the Conference set out to tackle irregular migratory flows by cooperating in the fight against illegal immigration and by reinforcing the national border control capacity of countries of transit and departure. Under the heading of cooperation in the fight against illegal immigration, the Conference called for, *inter alia*, cooperating logistically and financially for the voluntary return of migrants in transit countries; setting up, while ensuring respect for human dignity and the fundamental rights of individuals, efficient readmission systems among all countries concerned, in particular through the effective implementation of the relevant provisions of article 13 of the Cotonou Agreement[52] and the conclusion of readmission agreements between the North, West and Central African countries concerned and also between the European Community or one of its member States and North, West and Central African countries; providing technical and logistical support for identifying the nationality of illegal migrants; facilitating the reintegration of irregular migrants who have returned to their home country; informing and sensitizing potential migrants on the risks of illegal immigration; and making available financial resources to assist countries facing emergency situations concerning illegal migration. As can be seen, the underlying but dominant concern of the

[45] A/60/205 of 8 August 2005.

[46] In August 2005, GCIM, an informal consultative body with its secretariat in Geneva, comprised over 30 States from every region of the world, including Algeria, Australia, Bangladesh, Belgium, Brazil, Canada, Egypt, Finland, France, Germany, the Holy See, Hungary, India, Indonesia, Iran (Islamic Republic of), Japan, Mexico, Morocco, the Netherlands, Nigeria, Norway, Pakistan, Peru, the Philippines, South Africa, Spain, Sri Lanka, Sweden, Switzerland, Turkey and the United Kingdom, as well as the European Union.

[47] Report of the Global Commission on International Migration, available at the following website: www.gcim.org.

[48] *Ibid.*, pp. 32–41.

[49] *Ibid.*, pp. 53–64.

[50] *Ibid.*, pp. 32–33.

[51] *Ibid.*, p. 34. See also the figures put forward by several associations that keep updated lists of victims; they have estimated at over 4,000 the number of deaths documented between mid-May 1992 and December 2003 in connection with clandestine migration towards Europe. Sources: Association des familles victimes de l'immigration clandestine (AFVIC); Gay, *Les discontinuités spatiales*; Olivier Clochard and Philippe Rekacewicz, "En dix ans plus de 4 000 morts aux frontières de l'Union Européenne", *Le Monde diplomatique*, www.monde-diplomatique.fr, March 2004.

[52] Partnership agreement between the members of the African, Caribbean and Pacific Group of States of the one part, and the European Community and its Member States, of the other part, signed in Cotonou on 23 June 2000.

Conference participants was the systematic expulsion of illegal migrants to their countries of origin. This is not made explicit, but the principle seems to be accepted, as the remaining text refers solely to setting the conditions for returning and reintegrating the persons to be expelled and getting their States of nationality to facilitate both the identification of their nationality and their readmission to their national territory.

33. In addition, the Euro-African Ministerial Conference on Migration and Development called for the national border control capacity of these countries and transit countries to be strengthened through improved training of staff employed in the relevant services and equipment used in transborder operational cooperation; it also urged cooperation aimed at providing the countries concerned with a computerized database for effectively combating irregular migration and cooperation in putting in place an early warning system, based on the European model, to allow for the immediate transmission of precursory signals warning of potential clandestine immigration and the activities of criminal smuggling organizations.

34. However, in the Rabat Declaration, entitled "Euro-African Partnership for Migration and Development",[53] while the ministers for foreign affairs of the participating States reaffirmed their commitment to "fighting against illegal migration, including readmission of illegal migrants", they also recommended "implementing an active policy of integration for legal migrants and combating exclusion, xenophobia and racism", while committing themselves to working in close partnership "following a comprehensive, balanced, pragmatic and operational approach, and respecting the rights and dignity of migrants and refugees". These are empty words, however, since for the European countries the main aim of the Euro-African Ministerial Conference on Migration and Development was to lay the foundations for the mass expulsion, with international legitimacy, of illegal migrants originating in African countries. There remains very little opposition, if any, to these expulsions of aliens with irregular status since these States are exercising their unquestionable sovereign right. Being aware of the need to respect the fundamental rights and dignity of the persons concerned is really all that is required of them under international law, something the Special Rapporteur intends to pay particular attention to under this topic.

35. The contributions of the members of the Commission, and later the States, to the debate on the preliminary report on the expulsion of aliens[54] and the varied and, at times, contradictory suggestions they made, together with the above-mentioned developments in recent State practice with regard to the expulsion of aliens and the reflections of GCIM and the Euro-African Ministerial Conference on Migration and Development, which underline the extent of the phenomenon of irregular migration in the world and put forward ways of addressing it, all demonstrate the need to define the topic by determining its exact scope.

[53] Rabat Declaration available at www.maec.gov.ma.

[54] See footnote 1 above.

D. Scope of the topic

36. One of the aims of the preliminary report on the expulsion of aliens was to provoke discussion in the Commission and in the Sixth Committee on the methodological issues and the scope of the topic. The debate in both bodies revealed agreement that certain questions should be included when addressing the topic under examination, although there were differences of opinion on other questions. However, no one held the view that the subject should not be addressed by the Commission.[55]

37. There appeared to be a consensus that the topic should include persons residing in the territory of a State of which they did not have nationality, with a distinction being made between persons in a regular situation and those in an irregular situation, including those who had been residing for a long time in the expelling State. Refugees, asylum-seekers, stateless persons and migrant workers should also be included.[56]

38. On the other hand, some members of the Commission and some representatives of States members of the Sixth Committee were of the view that it would be difficult to include denial of admission with regard to new illegal immigrants or those who had not yet become established in the receiving country. Others felt that the scope of the topic should exclude persons who had changed nationality following a change in the status of the territory where they were resident in the context of decolonization.

39. In the opinion of the Special Rapporteur, such cases cannot be excluded in principle. A distinction must be drawn between cases where a change of nationality leads to a (collective) transfer of populations who benefit from a new nationality because of a change in territorial status, and those in which persons accorded the said nationality are expelled. An expulsion of the latter kind should be subject to an ordinary law regime, and there is no reason to exclude it from the scope of the topic.

40. As far as the question of non-admission (or "expulsion" of illegal immigrants) is concerned, the practice of certain States and the identification as an alien of anyone who has crossed the frontier and entered the territory of the State in which he or she is present suggest *prima facie* that this question cannot be excluded from the scope of the topic without severely limiting it. Indeed, according to the Republic of Korea to do so "would not only unduly limit the scope of the Commission's work; it would also leave unaddressed the interests and concerns of many illegal

[55] The representative of Hungary to the Sixth Committee had expressed the view at the fifty-ninth session of the General Assembly that the topic "should have been taken up by other institutions and bodies within the United Nations system, such as the Office of the United Nations High Commissioner for Refugees or the Commission on Human Rights" (*Official Records of the General Assembly, Sixtieth Session, Sixth Committee*, 13th meeting, para. 9). Taking note of the preliminary report of the Special Rapporteur on the subject at the sixtieth session of the General Assembly, he stated that in the view of his country it was incumbent upon the Special Rapporteur and the Commission "to take great care in determining the exact scope and content of the future study" (*ibid.*).

[56] See *Yearbook ... 2005*, vol. II (Part Two), p. 58, para. 273.

residents around the world".[57] The traditional notion of expulsion, however, concerns aliens whose entry or stay are lawful, whereas non-admission concerns those whose entry into or stay on its territory a State seeks to prevent; removal of an illegal immigrant who is at the border or has just crossed it is strictly speaking non-admission, not expulsion. It is by virtue of this judicious distinction that non-admission does not, in the opinion of the Special Rapporteur, fall within the scope of this topic.

41. As for the expulsion of aliens in situations of armed conflict, the Special Rapporteur found no valid reason for excluding it from the scope of the topic. In view of the methodological option chosen by the Commission, namely to make full use of the existing treaty rules for the purpose of codifying this topic, the existence of specific rules on the matter under international humanitarian law should not be an obstacle to including this issue in the scope of the topic, quite the contrary. Moreover, owing to the contribution made by the award rendered on 17 December 2004 in the *Eritrea* v. *Ethiopia* case,[58] in which the issue of expulsion through deprivation of nationality is complicated by that of expulsion in a context of armed conflict, the traditional rules on the matter can be revisited.

[57] *Official Records of the General Assembly, Sixtieth Session, Sixth Committee*, 11th meeting, para. 89.

[58] Eritrea–Ethiopia Claims Commission, *Partial Award, Civilians Claims, Ethiopia's Claim 5, between the Federal Democratic Republic of Ethiopia and the State of Eritrea* (The Hague, 17 December 2004).

E. General presentation of this report

42. The aim of this report is to examine the general rules applicable to the expulsion of aliens as they derive from customary law, treaty law, case law and State practice, and in the light of the way the question is dealt with in the legal literature. As a result of that examination, it will be possible to address some of the questions and suggestions formulated when the preliminary report on the expulsion of aliens[59] was considered.

43. In this regard, the Special Rapporteur will generally follow, in greater detail, the approach outlined in the draft workplan annexed to his preliminary report on the expulsion of aliens, which was approved by the Commission[60] and most of the States that expressed their views on the topic in the Sixth Committee during the sixtieth session of the General Assembly, as indicated in paragraph 10 of the present report. He did, however, reverse the order of "Scope" and "Definitions", placing the latter after the former, and reorganized the content of "Scope", moving much of it into the "Definitions" chapter, so that "Scope" now covers the standard categories of aliens to which expulsion applies. For the sake of precision, in the present report, which examines some of the general rules on the expulsion of aliens, the questions that will lead to the formulation of draft articles on the topic's scope and the definitions of its key terms will be examined in greater depth.

[59] See footnote 1 above.

[60] See *Yearbook ... 2005*, vol. II (Part Two), p. 57–58, paras. 269–272.

GENERAL RULES

44. The consideration of the preliminary report on the expulsion of aliens showed that the main point of debate and controversy, within both the Commission and the Sixth Committee, was the scope of the topic. Hence, this report will focus first on determining the scope. Once the topic has been delimited, the next step will be to define, more precisely than in the preliminary report, the concepts relating to the topic, before undertaking an examination of the general principles of international law governing the matter.

CHAPTER I

Scope

45. The introduction to the present report describes the scope of the topic in broad outline. The task now is to delimit it more precisely, by indicating the various categories of persons concerned. In keeping with the observations made in paragraphs 37–41 of the report and consistent with the preference expressed by both the Commission and the Sixth Committee for the elaboration of a legal regime as comprehensive as possible on the topic, the Special Rapporteur will proceed to address each of the following situations one by one: aliens residing lawfully in the territory of a State, aliens with irregular status, refugees, displaced persons, asylum-seekers and asylum recipients, stateless persons, former nationals of a State, persons who have become aliens through loss of nationality following the emergence of a new State, nationals of a State engaged in armed conflict with the receiving State and migrant workers.

46. Falling outside the scope of the topic are several categories of aliens for whom the conditions and procedures for expulsion are governed by special rules. This is the case in particular with aliens who are entitled to certain privileges and immunities, notably diplomats, consular authorities, members of special missions serving in a foreign country, international civil servants, members of the armed forces on official mission or members of a multinational armed force[61] who are subject to special rules (*leges speciales*) rather than the general rules applicable to the expulsion of aliens under international law.

47. Although it has been asserted that international law does not prohibit the expulsion of nationals,[62] the Special Rapporteur does not believe that international law

[61] See the memorandum by the Secretariat on the expulsion of aliens (A/CN.4/565), paras. 28–35, available on the website of the Commission (www.un.org/law/ilc/index.htm).

[62] *Ibid.*, para. 36 and footnotes 53–61.

authorizes it. On the contrary, the general principles point in the opposite direction. In the draft regulations for the expulsion of aliens submitted to the Institute of International Law during its session held in Hamburg, Germany, in September 1892, Mr. Féraud-Giraud proposed the following rule on the subject:

> A State may not, through administrative or judicial channels, expel its own nationals, regardless of their differences of religion, race or national origin.
>
> Such an act constitutes a serious violation of international law when it has the intentional result of removing to other territories individuals who have been convicted of a crime or who are simply the subject of legal proceedings.[63]

48. Generally speaking, this is a logical rule arising from the personal jurisdiction of the State, which imposes on it the responsibility of ensuring the protection of its own nationals, both within and outside its national territory.[64] The rule of non-expulsion of nationals can be considered "undisputed" and, thus, even if it is not expressed, it is implied.[65] It is for that reason that the domestic laws of some countries expressly prohibit the expulsion of nationals.[66] Such a rule, implicit in which is the right of a national to reside or remain in his or her own country,[67] or to enter that country,[68] does not allow for the expulsion by a State of its nationals. Furthermore, as a consequence of the preceding rule, the State is bound to admit its nationals who have been expelled from another country, but not the nationals of other States expelled by them or by third States; a State can only be required to admit nationals of other States if it has expressly agreed to do so, generally under an international agreement.[69] More specifically, it should be noted that some human rights treaties expressly prohibit the expulsion of a person from the territory of a State of which he or she is a national.[70]

49. In addition to the fact that practice provides very few examples of the expulsion of a person by the State of which he or she is a national, these arguments show that such cases of expulsion constitute real exceptions, which, moreover, are only possible with the express agreement of the receiving State. In any case, as a national is not and cannot simultaneously be an alien, the legal regime governing expulsion of nationals falls outside the scope of the topic of expulsion of aliens.

[63] *Annuaire de l'Institut de droit international* (1891–1892), pp. 278–279.

[64] See Daillier and Pellet, *Droit international public*, pp. 493–501, paras. 322–327.

[65] Boeck, *loc. cit.*, p. 447.

[66] See A/CN.4/565 (footnote 61 above), para. 36, footnote 60.

[67] *Ibid.*, footnote 56.

[68] The International Rules on the Admission and Expulsion of Aliens, proposed by the Institute of International Law and adopted by the Institute on 9 September 1892 in Geneva, contain an article which stipulates that, in principle, a State may not prohibit either its nationals or persons who are no longer nationals of that State, but have not acquired the nationality of any other State from entering or remaining in its territory (*Annuaire de l'Institut de droit international* (1892–1894), p. 219).

[69] See Jennings and Watts, *Oppenheim's International Law*, pp. 944–945.

[70] See A/CN.4/565 (footnote 61 above), para. 36, footnote 55.

A. Aliens residing lawfully in the territory of the expelling State

50. An alien residing lawfully in a foreign State can be understood to mean a person who has entered a country lawfully or who has been formally admitted and resides there in conformity with the laws and/or regulations of that country governing the conditions under which aliens may be present or reside. The question of whether a distinction should be made between aliens in transit, aliens admitted on a temporary or short-term basis, long-term residents, and so forth, will not be addressed at this point. The only issue of concern for the moment is the legality of their presence in the territory of the receiving State, although the length of their stay might possibly have some implications with respect to the consequences of expulsion.

51. Lawful entry into the territory of the receiving State implies crossing the frontier of that State with travel documents that are recognized as valid by the State's authorities. Lawful stay means that the alien, having crossed the border legally, meets the conditions of stay, that is, the conditions for continued presence in the country concerned in accordance with its national law.

52. However, it is not always necessary for an alien to have entered the territory of the receiving State lawfully in order for his or her presence there to be lawful. In some countries, a person who has entered the territory of the receiving State illegally can subsequently have his or her situation regularized and obtain legal resident status.[71] This practice is becoming increasingly common in the main countries that receive clandestine immigrants, particularly in Europe and in the Americas, where regularization occurs either collectively or individually on a case-by-case basis, depending on the country.[72]

53. The expulsion of an alien residing lawfully in the territory of the expelling State has often been the only situation envisaged by most treaties. Several international conventions containing provisions on expulsion thus cover only that possibility.[73]

B. Aliens with irregular status

54. Some treaties distinguish between aliens who are lawfully present and those whose status is irregular, but they do not provide a definition of the term "illegal alien". Some national legislation provides elements of a definition of this category of aliens, although the terms used to refer to them vary from country to country.[74]

[71] See Grahl-Madsen, *The Status of Refugees in International Law.* vol. II. *Asylum, Entry and Sojourn*, p. 348; see also A/CN.4/565 (footnote 61 above), para. 44.

[72] This is the case, in particular, in Italy and Spain, where groups of illegal aliens have collectively had their status regularized in recent years; in France, where, after a wave of mass regularizations, there has been a hardening of attitudes towards aliens with irregular status, with a shift towards, at best, regularization on a case-by-case basis; and in the United States, where the federal Administration recently proposed mass regularization of Mexican immigrants, but still faces some opposition in Congress.

[73] See, in particular, the International Covenant on Civil and Political Rights (art. 13); the Convention relating to the Status of Refugees (art. 32); the Convention relating to the Status of Stateless Persons (art. 31); and the European Convention on Establishment. See also A/CN.4/565 (footnote 61 above), para. 755, footnotes 1760–1763.

[74] See A/CN.4/565 (footnote 61 above), para 129, footnotes 249–258.

55. An alien with irregular status can be understood to mean a person whose presence in the territory of the receiving State is in violation of the legislation of that State concerning the admission, stay or residence of aliens. First of all, an alien's status may be illegal by virtue of the conditions under which he or she entered the State. This is the case with illegal or clandestine migrants. Hence, any alien who crosses the frontier of the expelling State in violation of its rules concerning the admission of aliens will be considered to have irregular status. Secondly, the illegal status may be the result not of the conditions of entry but of the conditions of stay in the territory of the expelling State. In such cases, although the alien has crossed the frontier of the State legally and has therefore been lawfully admitted, he or she subsequently fails to comply with the conditions of stay stipulated by the laws of the receiving State. This occurs, for example, when a lawfully admitted alien remains in the territory of the State beyond the period set by the competent authorities of that State. Thirdly, an alien's presence in the expelling State may also be illegal for both of the aforementioned reasons, as would be the case if an alien had entered the receiving State illegally and had not subsequently had his or her status regularized, thus failing to comply with both the conditions of admission and the conditions of stay.

56. The conditions of stay for aliens comprise two aspects: the residence permit that legalizes the alien's presence in the territory of the State for a specific period, which may or may not be renewable, and the rules that must be complied with during the alien's stay, for example, rules relating to the activities in which the alien may or may not engage during his or her stay. It is a basic principle that a person who voluntarily enters and resides in the territory of a foreign State must comply with the conditions of stay or residence in that State, including acceptance of its legal institutions and rules.[75] These are conditional rules, and failure to comply with them may result in revocation or cancellation of the residence permit and may change the alien's status from legal to illegal, making him or her subject to possible expulsion.

C. Refugees

57. The term "refugee" has different meanings depending on whether it is considered from a sociological or a legal viewpoint. Its sociological meaning is long-standing, broad and somewhat loose. In this context, the term "refugee" has long been used to refer to persons who, for whatever reason, have been forced to leave their homes to find refuge elsewhere.[76] "Elsewhere" was not defined in relation to State boundaries. This use of the term "refugee" has not completely disappeared today. Certain international forums—employing journalese, whether consciously or not—use the term to refer to persons displaced within their own country and living in physical conditions comparable to those of displaced persons who have taken refuge in a foreign country. Such persons are also referred to as "internal refugees" or "internally displaced persons". They nonetheless need international assistance, and the General Assembly has on several occasions requested UNHCR to extend them humanitarian assistance.[77]

58. The term "refugee" has a much more precise meaning in law, however. In this regard, it generally refers to persons forced to leave their country to find refuge in another country. As stated in the ICJ judgment in the *Asylum* case between Colombia and Peru, "the refugee is within the territory of the State of refuge";[78] in other words, he would not have the status of refugee if he were in the territory of his State of nationality. Under the various international conventions on refugees, refugees are persons who flee their State owing to persecution or well-founded fear of being persecuted for reasons of race, religion, nationality, membership of a social group or political opinion. According to some authors, persons who flee their country for reasons other than those mentioned above are "displaced persons"[79] and not refugees in the legal sense. The latter term also includes persons who are outside their State of nationality or residence but who are unable or, for valid reasons, unwilling to return to their country.[80]

59. Leaving aside the incidental and other circumstantial aspects of the definition of the term "refugee" contained in the Convention relating to the Status of Refugees, it is clear, under article 1, section A, paragraph (2), of the Convention, that the term "refugee" refers to any person who, as a result of particular events:

> and owing to well-founded fear of being persecuted for reasons of race, religion, nationality, membership of a particular social group or political opinion, is outside the country of his nationality and is unable or, owing to such fear, is unwilling to avail himself of the protection of that country; or who, not having a nationality and being outside the country of his former habitual residence as a result of such events, is unable or, owing to such fear, is unwilling to return to it.

60. The OAU Convention governing the specific aspects of refugee problems in Africa adopted a broader definition of the concept of "refugee". The OAU Convention provides that, in addition to the persons covered by the Convention relating to the Status of Refugees,[81] the term "refugee":

> shall also apply to every person who, owing to external aggression, occupation, foreign domination or events seriously disturbing public order in either part or the whole of his country of origin or nationality, is compelled to leave his place of habitual residence in order to seek refuge in another place outside his country of origin or nationality.[82]

61. This broad definition of the term "refugee" has had an impact beyond Africa and constitutes a significant contribution by Africa to determining the meaning of the concept. At the beginning of the 1980s, it became clear that the international community was open to

[75] See Borchard, *The Diplomatic Protection of Citizens Abroad or the Law of International Claims*, p. 179.

[76] See Jahn, "Refugees", p. 72.

[77] *Ibid.*, p. 73.

[78] *Asylum, Judgment, I.C.J. Reports 1950*, p. 274.

[79] Sohn and Buergenthal, *The Movement of Persons across Borders*, p. 99.

[80] See the Convention relating to the Status of Refugees, its Protocol, and the Constitution of the International Refugee Organization and Agreement on interim measures to be taken in respect of refugees and displaced persons; see also Jahn, *loc. cit.*, p. 72.

[81] Definition used in article I, paragraph 1, of the OAU Convention.

[82] Art. I, para. 2; the Convention has also been published in fascicle form by the Media Relations and Public Information Service of UNHCR (Geneva).

the OAU definition when the Executive Committee of the UNHCR Programme observed in 1981 that the increased number of large-scale refugee influx situations in different areas of the world, especially in developing countries, had changed the composition of groups of asylum-seekers, which included not only those who were refugees within the meaning of the Convention relating to the Status of Refugees and its Protocol, but also those referred to in article I, paragraph 2, of the OAU Convention governing the specific aspects of refugee problems in Africa.[83]

62. Following that statement by UNHCR in 1981, the States of Central America in 1984 adopted the Cartagena Declaration on Refugees, which recommended that the definition of "refugee" be extended to cover "persons who have fled their country because their lives, safety or freedom have been threatened by generalized violence, foreign aggression, internal conflicts, massive violation of human rights or other circumstances which have seriously disturbed public order".[84]

63. Although OAS had adopted a somewhat narrower definition in article 22, paragraph 7, of the American Convention on Human Rights: "Pact of San José, Costa Rica", the more extensive definition was subsequently endorsed both by the Inter-American Commission on Human Rights and by the OAS General Assembly.[85]

64. A number of differences can be found in the wording of the definition. The variations essentially relate to the question of whether all groups that flee the territory of their State of origin may be regarded as refugees, irrespective of the reasons for which they are forced to leave. It has been said that, in addition to the "core meaning" of the term "refugee", there are "grey areas"[86] covering persons who are not afforded any protection by the Government of their State of origin. These "grey areas" are vague and imprecise and could give rise to dispute between candidates for refugee status or the international organizations assisting them and the host States, since there is a tendency to include victims of certain types of social constraints, victims of economic changes—sometimes referred to as "economic refugees"—or persons who leave their country purely for personal convenience. It is therefore of both theoretical and practical interest to elaborate a precise definition of the concept of "refugee" in international law and for the purposes of this study.

65. In the light of the above observations and on the basis of State and international organization practice, it can be said that the definition of the term "refugee" in international law includes the following essential elements: (*a*) an individual who has crossed the frontier of his or her State of origin; (*b*) the individual must have crossed the frontier because of some constraint; (*c*) the reasons for that constraint must be clearly identifiable: well-founded fear of being persecuted for reasons of race, religion, nationality, membership of a particular social group or political opinion, internal or international armed conflict, political violence, external aggression or occupation or foreign domination. In other words, "refugee" can be understood to mean a person who is outside his or her country of nationality or, if he or she is stateless, the country of his or her habitual residence, or a person who is obliged to seek refuge outside his or her country of origin owing to well-founded fear of being persecuted for reasons of race, religion, nationality, membership of a particular social group or political opinion, or owing to external aggression, occupation, foreign domination, internal or international armed conflict or events seriously disturbing public order in either a part or the whole of his or her country of origin or nationality.

66. The term "refugee" thus defined refers both to a state and to a status. It is, first of all, a state, in that any person to whom the foregoing definition applies is considered to be a refugee, even if he or she has not been granted the legal status of refugee by the host country. Secondly, it is a status, in that the acquisition of said legal status, under circumstances and through procedures established by international conventions[87] and national legislation, allows the person in question to enjoy the legal protection afforded to refugees. On the basis of this concept of legal status, a distinction is drawn between humanitarian intervention to assist a person who is in the situation (state) of being a refugee and the legal protection and rights conferred by the legal status of refugee.

67. This distinction is important with regard to the expulsion of aliens. While a person with refugee status may be expelled from the host State only in exceptional cases and under certain specific circumstances, the expulsion of persons whose state is that of refugee and who may be seeking refugee status is subject, as will be seen, to less restrictive rules. An individual seeking refugee status may be treated in some cases as an illegal or clandestine migrant, and thus an alien with irregular status, whereas an individual granted refugee status is governed by a specific legal regime, particularly in relation to expulsion.

68. It is generally agreed that the rights accruing to refugees should be accorded to all those who, *prima facie*, appear to be refugees under the legal system of any State party to the relevant international conventions, irrespective of the legality of their status.[88] There is, however, dispute as to the meaning of the terms "lawful presence" and "lawful stay". Some commentators consider that a refugee's presence is not lawful until it has been recognized as such by a State party to the Convention relating to the

[83] See Sohn and Buergenthal, *op. cit.*, p. 103; and A/CN.4/565 (footnote 61 above), para. 153.

[84] Cartagena Declaration on Refugees (22 November 1984), *Annual Report of the Inter-American Commission on Human Rights* (OAS document OEA/Ser.L/V/II.66,doc.10, rev.1), pp. 190–193 (1984–1985), para. 3.

[85] See A/CN.4/565 (footnote 61 above), para. 156.

[86] *Ibid.*, para. 157.

[87] Under article 1, section A, of the Convention relating to the Status of Refugees, a refugee who has dual nationality must be able to prove that he or she fears persecution in, or no longer enjoys the protection of, either country of nationality. Moreover, a refugee who does not avail himself or herself of the protection of a country of which he or she has nationality or who, having lost his or her nationality, has reacquired it, may no longer enjoy the protection of UNHCR.

[88] See Grahl-Madsen, *op. cit.*, p. 94; see also Dent, *Research Paper on the Social and Economic Rights of Non-Nationals in Europe*, commissioned by the European Council on Refugees and Exiles (ECRE), p. 15.

Status of Refugees,[89] that is, until the person acquires refugee status.

69. The situation is somewhat confused in that refugees awaiting a decision on their legal status do not clearly belong either in the category of "lawfully present" or in the category of "unlawfully present", and it is better to regard them as lawfully present in the physical sense, but not in the sense that they could claim all the rights accorded to those with the legal status of refugee.[90]

70. Other authors argue, however, that refugees may be considered to be lawfully present once they have been admitted to the procedure for acquiring the legal status of refugee or for admission to the host State. Nonetheless, they take the view that, where the host State has not specified the mechanisms or the procedure for acquiring the legal status of refugee, the presence in that State's territory of refugees seeking such status should be considered tacitly lawful.[91]

71. Whatever the subtleties of one approach or another, it should nonetheless be noted that all of them draw a distinction between those applying for refugee status or waiting to be granted it and those who have been granted it. All also agree that the legal situation of each of the two groups is different. The controversial point is how to define the legal situation of an applicant for refugee status between the time of submission of the application and the time of receipt of a response. Some authors consider that one should speak of lawful stay subject to a time limit.[92] In fact, the answer depends on national law, and the question will be duly considered when the conditions for expulsion are analysed.

D. Displaced persons

72. A refugee is different from a displaced person. A displaced person who is by force of circumstances in a foreign territory, outside his or her State of origin or nationality, is in a situation comparable to that of a refugee. However, displaced persons cannot be assimilated to refugees, even though they generally have the same need for protection. The distinction between the two situations lies in the reasons for taking refuge in a foreign country. Displaced persons who are outside the territory of their country of origin or nationality are in that situation for reasons other than those set out in the definition of "refugee" in international law: they are outside their country because of natural or man-made disasters. The category of displaced persons essentially consists of victims of such disasters, who are commonly known as "ecological" or "environmental" refugees. It is these persons whom the General Assembly has had in mind since 1977 when referring to "refugees and displaced persons".

[89] See, for example, Pellonpää, *Expulsion in International Law: A Study in International Aliens Law and Human Rights with Special Reference to Finland*, p. 292.

[90] See Grahl-Madsen, *op. cit.*, p. 362.

[91] See Hathaway, *The Rights of Refugees under International Law*, cited by Dent, *op. cit.*, p. 17.

[92] Some commentators understand "lawful stay" (or "legal stay") to mean presence for three months or more: see Grahl-Madsen, *op. cit.*, p. 374.

E. Asylum-seekers and asylum recipients

1. Concept

73. The right of asylum is today established as a rule of customary international law, although it has its origins in national law.[93] Article 14, paragraph 1, of the Universal Declaration of Human Rights states:

> Everyone has the right to seek and to enjoy in other countries asylum from persecution.[94]

74. This rule is reinforced by the Declaration on Territorial Asylum, article 1, paragraph 1, of which states:

> Asylum granted by a State, in the exercise of its sovereignty, to persons entitled to invoke article 14 of the Universal Declaration of Human Rights, including persons struggling against colonialism, shall be respected by all other States.[95]

75. The exercise of this right is a matter of State sovereignty.

76. The institution of asylum has a longer history in international law than the concept of refugee, although the two concepts have features in common. In the resolutions of the Institute of International Law adopted at its Bath session in 1950, "the term 'asylum' means the protection which a State grants on its territory, or in some other place under the control of certain of its organs, to a person who comes to seek it".[96]

77. This definition renders the general meaning of asylum. However, the legal regime governing the right of asylum varies depending on the place where the right is exercised and on the rules applicable to the asylum recipient.

2. Types of asylum

78. There are three different types of asylum: territorial or internal asylum, extraterritorial or diplomatic asylum, and neutral asylum.

79. The first two types are linked to criteria of a geographical nature or relating to territorial competence. The third is linked to the nature of the recipients and the rules applicable to them.

80. The right of territorial asylum is understood to mean the right of a State of refuge to grant shelter or protection on its territory to a foreigner who requests it.[97] In addition to persons facing persecution, the Declaration on Territorial Asylum states that persons "struggling against

[93] For example, in France, paragraph 4 of the preamble to the Constitution of 27 October 1946, which is incorporated in the preamble to the Constitution of 4 October 1958, provides that "[a]ny man persecuted in virtue of his actions in favour of liberty may claim the right of asylum upon the territories of the Republic" (www.conseil-constitutionnnel.fr).

[94] General Assembly resolution 217 (III) A of 10 December 1948, art. 14, para. 1.

[95] General Assembly resolution 2312 (XXII) of 14 December 1967.

[96] Institute of International Law, resolution entitled "Asylum in public international law (excluding neutral asylum)", art. 1, *Annuaire de l'Institut de droit international* (1950), p. 389.

[97] See De Visscher, *Theory and Reality in Public International Law*; and Salmon, *Dictionnaire de droit international public*, p. 94.

colonialism"[98] are among those who may be granted territorial asylum. However, anyone who is the subject of "prosecutions genuinely arising from non-political crimes or from acts contrary to the purposes and principles of the United Nations" pursuant to article 14, paragraph 2, of the Universal Declaration of Human Rights.[99] 81. Treaty law has helped to define the concept of territorial asylum. The Convention on territorial asylum specifies the causes of persecution that may give victims a right to territorial asylum. Article II of the Convention stipulates:

> The respect which, according to international law, is due the jurisdictional right of each State over the inhabitants in its territory, is equally due, without any restriction whatsoever, to that which it has over persons who enter it proceeding from a State in which they are persecuted for their beliefs, opinions, or political affiliations, or for acts which may be considered as political offenses.
>
> Any violation of sovereignty that consists of acts committed by a government or its agents in another State against the life or security of an individual, carried out on the territory of another State, may not be considered attenuated because the persecution began outside its boundaries or is due to political considerations or reasons of state.

82. Similarly, article 22, paragraph 7, of the American Convention on Human Rights provides:

> Every person has the right to seek and be granted asylum in a foreign territory, in accordance with the legislation of the state and international conventions, in the event he is being pursued for political offenses or related common crimes.

83. The right of extraterritorial asylum is understood to mean the right of a State to grant individuals refuge in places that are outside its territory but are subject to its jurisdiction. Various places fall into this category. According to the Institute of International Law:

> Asylum may be granted on the premises of diplomatic missions, consulates, warships, government ships used for public services, military aircraft, and premises within the jurisdiction of another organ of a foreign State authorised to exercise authority over that territory.[100]

84. The granting of extraterritorial asylum is largely dependent on political considerations. This applies in particular when extraterritorial asylum takes the form of diplomatic asylum. It is a treaty right[101] of the head of mission of the sending State to refuse to hand over to the authorities of the receiving State political figures who are nationals of the receiving State who take refuge in the mission premises and to obtain safe-conducts for such persons allowing them to leave their country.[102]

85. In the *Asylum* case,[103] Víctor Raúl Haya de la Torre, head of the American People's Revolutionary Alliance party, who was being prosecuted along with other members of the party for the "crime of military rebellion",[104] had sought asylum at the Embassy of Colombia in Lima. The Ambassador of Colombia informed the Minister for Foreign Affairs of Peru in a letter dated 3 January 1949—in accordance with the second provision of article 2 of the Convention fixing the Rules to be observed for the Granting of Asylum, signed by the two countries at Havana in 1928—that Mr. Haya de la Torre had "been given asylum at the seat of [the] mission"[105] and stated in a further letter dated 14 January that, pursuant to instructions received from the Chancellery of his country, the Government of Colombia, in accordance with the right conferred upon it by article 2 of the Convention on Political Asylum, signed by the two countries at Montevideo on 26 December 1933, had "qualified Señor Víctor Raúl Haya de la Torre as a political refugee".[106]

86. The Government of Peru disputed the legality of the asylum granted and refused to issue the safe-conduct requested by Colombia. ICJ observed that, under article 2, paragraph 2, of the Convention fixing the Rules to be observed for the Granting of Asylum, the essential justification for asylum was in the imminence or persistence of a danger for the person of the refugee, and that it was incumbent upon Colombia to submit proof of facts to show that the above-mentioned condition was fulfilled. In the Court's opinion, the asylum cases cited by Colombia were not such as to allow the Court "to assess the value of such cases as precedents tending to establish the existence of a legal obligation upon a territorial State to recognize the validity of asylum which has been granted against proceedings instituted by local judicial authorities".[107] Moreover, it emerged from those cases that, in a general way, "considerations of convenience or simple political expediency seem to have led the territorial State to recognize asylum without that decision being dictated by any feeling of legal obligation".[108]

87. These remarks showed, in the opinion of ICJ,

> that asylum as practised in Latin America is an institution which, to a very great extent, owes its development to extra-legal factors. The good-neighbour relations between the republics, the different political interests of the governments, have favoured the mutual recognition of asylum apart from any clearly defined juridical system.[109]

88. However, ICJ also noted that the parties had not disputed that "asylum may be granted on humanitarian grounds in order to protect political offenders against the violent and disorderly action of irresponsible sections of the population".[110]

89. While some of the ICJ remarks suggest that general international law does not recognize the right to diplomatic asylum as a legal institution generating rights and obligations, it is apparent that such a right may be founded on custom, not only on regional or local custom, but also on general custom. That is doubtless the sense in

[98] Art. 1, para. 1. (see footnote 95 above).

[99] See footnote 94 above.

[100] Institute of International Law, "Asylum in public international law (excluding neutral asylum)", art. 3, p. 390.

[101] Diplomatic asylum is quite frequently granted by certain countries, particularly in Latin America, where it is a well-established institution of regional international law. See, by way of illustration, the Convention fixing the Rules to be observed for the Granting of Asylum, adopted by the VIth International Conference of American States; and the Convention on diplomatic asylum.

[102] Salmon, *op. cit.*, p. 94.

[103] *I.C.J. Reports 1950* (see footnote 78 above).

[104] *Ibid.*, p. 273.

[105] *Ibid.*

[106] *Ibid.*

[107] *Ibid.*, p. 286.

[108] *Ibid.*

[109] *Ibid.*

[110] *Ibid.*, pp. 282–283.

which the codification efforts undertaken by the Institute of International Law at its Bath session in 1950 should be understood.

> Asylum may be granted to any person whose life, liberty, or person is threatened by violence emanating from the local authorities or against which they are obviously powerless to protect him, or even which they tolerate or provoke. These provisions shall apply in the same conditions when such threat is the result of civil strife.
>
> In cases where the powers of government in the country are manifestly disorganized or under the control of any faction to such an extent that private individuals no longer have sufficient guarantees for their safety, diplomatic agents ... may grant or continue to afford asylum even against prosecutions instituted by bodies exercising authority on the spot.[111]

90. In the case of diplomatic asylum, in contrast to territorial asylum, the refugee is within the territory of the State in which the offence was committed, and the decision to grant asylum therefore involves a derogation from its sovereignty in that it depends essentially on the State granting diplomatic asylum, which is restricted only in that it cannot make a "unilateral and definitive qualification"[112] of the nature of the offence of which the asylum-seeker is accused binding on the State in which the offence was committed. Because a decision to grant asylum withdraws the offender from the jurisdiction of the territorial State and constitutes an intervention in matters which are exclusively within the competence of that State, ICJ takes the view that: "Such a derogation from territorial sovereignty cannot be recognized unless its legal basis is established in each particular case."[113]

91. Neutral asylum usually applies in situations of conflict. In its September 1906 resolution on neutrality, the Institute of International Law defined it as follows: "The right to neutral asylum is the right of a neutral State to grant, within its jurisdiction, shelter to those seeking refuge from the calamities of war" (art. 7).[114]

92. Refuge may consist of shelter and temporary leave to remain in the territory or on a government vessel of the neutral State; it may be granted to members of the armed forces of the belligerents, escaped prisoners of war, sick or wounded civilians or refugees fleeing armed conflict. Those granted neutral asylum may not continue to participate in the fighting or even retain the means to fight. Accordingly, active members of armed forces must be disarmed and interned, while escaped prisoners of war may be assigned to quarters if they wish to remain in the neutral State.[115]

93. Neutrality in this instance must be understood as a State's non-involvement in the conflict. In that connection, the law of armed conflict obliges the State not party to the conflict

> to care for the civilian wounded and sick ... and to treat them humanely, but unlike the provisions laid down with regard to the military wounded and sick, there is no obligation to keep them until hostilities have ended. The civilian wounded and sick may request repatriation, particularly through the diplomatic representation of their country. They may also seek asylum in the State in whose territory they have landed, or in another State.[116]

94. Neutral asylum does not give the recipient permanent status. It is intended to address—for a limited time and essentially for humanitarian reasons—a situation of serious crisis which places his life in danger. It therefore differs from the traditional form of asylum whose nature and significance have already been explored, particularly as the recipient of neutral asylum, as indicated above, can request asylum from the neutral State or another State.

95. Nonetheless, recipients of neutral asylum are also affected by the issue of expulsion of aliens, as the protection which they are provided and the neutral State's obligations to them show clearly that they cannot be removed from the territory of that State at just any time or in just any manner.

3. Asylum-seekers and refugees

96. The distinction between the institution of asylum and the concept of a refugee is not always clear to everyone. Laws in a number of countries use both interchangeably,[117] while laws in others use "asylum" in a broader sense than "refugee".[118] In that respect, the latter coincide with international law. The International Law Association has drawn a distinction between the two, attributing a broader meaning to "asylum" than to "refugee".[119] Its draft convention on territorial asylum defines the two terms as follows:

> Article 1 (*a*) All States shall have a right to grant asylum to all victims of or who have well-grounded fear of persecution and to political offenders ...
>
> (*b*) The High Contracting Parties undertake to grant refuge in their territories to all those who are seeking asylum from persecution on grounds of race, religion, nationality, membership of a particular social group, which shall be understood to include any regional or linguistic group, or adherence to a particular political opinion.[120]

97. There is no limit placed on the forms of persecution that can result in the granting of asylum, in contrast to the forms of persecution which open the way to refugee status. In recent years, for example, persecution on the basis of gender or gender-linked practices has been advanced as the basis for claims of asylum.[121]

98. Some authors, in examining their countries' domestic laws, have also underlined the need to distinguish between asylum and refugee status. Asylum is presented as a sovereign decision of a State which has the "effect of granting an alien's request to remain", while recognition of refugee status by the competent national authority "confers on the recipient particular rights going beyond

---

[111] See footnote 100 above.

[112] *I.C.J. Reports 1950* (see footnote 78 above), p. 275.

[113] *Ibid.*

[114] Institute of International Law, *Annuaire de l'Institut de droit international* (1906), p. 375.

[115] See Salmon, *op. cit.*, p. 95.

[116] Sandoz, Swinarski and Zimmerman, *Commentary on the Additional Protocols of 8 June 1977 to the Geneva Conventions of 12 August 1949*, p. 334.

[117] See examples in A/CN.4/565 (footnote 61 above), para. 171, footnote 344.

[118] *Ibid.*, footnote 345.

[119] International Law Association, *Report of the Fifty-Fifth Conference held at New York, 21–26 August 1972*, pp. 196–211.

[120] *Ibid.*, p. 207.

[121] See Trebilcock, "Sex discrimination", p. 395.

the right to remain".[122] With that distinction in mind, France's Constitutional Council, deeming the right of asylum to be a fundamental right, that is, a right which in French law is "one of the essential guarantees of adherence to other rights and freedoms",[123] has affirmed that aliens may invoke a right to which the French people have solemnly declared their commitment, the right "whereby any man persecuted in virtue of his actions in favour of liberty may claim the right of asylum upon the territories of the Republic".[124]

99. The situation of an asylum-seeker is similar to that of a refugee in that the return (refoulement) of both is subject to limits which do not apply to the expulsion of an alien without either refugee or asylum-seeker status. The Convention relating to the Status of Refugees says that the contracting States may not "expel or return ('*refouler*') a refugee in any manner whatsoever to the frontiers of territories where his life or freedom would be threatened" (art. 33, para. 1). Usually, an alien seeking asylum is permitted to remain provisionally in the territory until his or her application has been ruled on. French judicial precedent, for example, has recognized that an asylum-seeker claiming refugee status should be allowed to remain provisionally in French territory until the French Office for the Protection of Refugees and Stateless Persons or, where applicable, the Redress Commission, has ruled on his or her application.[125] While the French Constitutional Council considered that this principle was founded on the preamble to the French Constitution of 1946, the Council of State considered that it was founded on article 31, paragraph 2, of the Convention relating to the Status of Refugees and on the act of 25 July 1952 establishing the Office for the Protection of Refugees and Stateless Persons.[126]

F. Stateless persons

100. The term "stateless person" refers, put briefly, to a person who has no nationality. In more elaborate terms, it can be considered to refer to a person who does not have the nationality of any State, or who does not have nationality by virtue of the application of the relevant national law of the State concerned. Some consider that it may also be construed to include a person who has a nationality but does not enjoy the protection of his or her Government.[127] This broader view of the meaning of the term should be treated with caution, as it could make implementation difficult in practice. At what point does one consider that a State is not protecting one of its nationals? Does the obligation entail the obligation to take measures or to produce results? Who decides whether a State is inadequately fulfilling its obligation to protect? What about the many poor countries which often fail to give their nationals appropriate protection even in situations where such protection is essential?

101. On the other hand, from a legal standpoint it is easy to conceive that a person might become stateless by reason of not acquiring a nationality at birth, usually referred to as "original nationality", or subsequently by losing or being deprived of the nationality of a State without having acquired the nationality of another State.[128] These are the typical forms of statelessness.

102. The Convention relating to the Status of Stateless Persons provides a precise definition of statelessness inspired by the resolution adopted by the Institute of International Law at its 1936 session in Brussels. The latter definition reads: "The term *stateless person* refers to any person who is not considered by any State to hold its nationality."[129] Similarly, but with a choice of words and a precision which improve upon the Institute of International Law definition, article 1, paragraph 1, of the Convention states: "For the purpose of this Convention, the term 'stateless person' means a person who is not considered as a national by any State under the operation of its law."

103. Some countries' laws either use the definition of the Convention relating to the Status of Stateless Persons or define "stateless persons" in the commonly understood sense of a person who is without nationality or known nationality.[130]

104. Notwithstanding the Convention on the reduction of statelessness,[131] there are still stateless persons in a number of countries. This situation has a bearing on the topic under consideration in that the stateless person does not have the status of national of the host State, while not having the nationality of any other State either. In other words, a stateless person is an alien everywhere from the legal standpoint; for that reason, international law extends particular protection to stateless persons.

G. Former nationals

105. The term "former national" refers to a person who no longer has the nationality of the State of which he or she was previously a national. Such a situation may arise from loss of nationality or from deprivation of nationality.[132]

---

[122] Norek, "Le droit d'asile en France dans la perspective communautaire", p. 204.

[123] Franck, "L'évolution des méthodes de protection des droits et libertés par le Conseil constitutionnel sous la septième législature".

[124] Constitutional Council, decision 93–325 DC of 13 August 1993, *Journal Officiel*, 18 August 1993, p. 11722; see also Fabre-Alibert, "Réflexions sur le nouveau régime juridique des étrangers en France", p. 1183. Because the right to asylum is considered a fundamental right in French law, there is well-established judicial precedent that legislation cannot "regulate the conditions applying to that right except with the aim of making it more substantive or reconciling it with other rules or principles of constitutional rank" (Constitutional Council, decision 84–181 DC of 10–11 October 1984, quoted in Favoreu and Philip, *Les grandes décisions du Conseil constitutionnel*, p. 609).

[125] See Abraham, "La reconduite à la frontière des demandeurs d'asile: conclusions sur Conseil d'État, Assemblée, 13 décembre 1991" (2 espèces: 1) *M. Nkodia (Alfonso)*, 2) *Préfet de l'Hérault c. M. Dakoury*); and, in the same vein as this judicial precedent, decision 93–325 DC (footnote 124 above), para. 84.

[126] See Fabre-Alibert, *loc. cit.*, p. 1184.

[127] See Mangoldt, "Stateless persons", p. 656, and A/CN.565 (footnote 61 above), para. 173.

[128] See Jennings and Watts, *op. cit.*, pp. 886–890.

[129] Institute of International Law, "Statut juridique des apatrides et des réfugiés", p. 294.

[130] See A/CN.565 (footnote 61 above), para. 175, footnotes 350–355.

[131] Article 8, paragraph 1, of the Convention provides: "A Contracting State shall not deprive a person of its nationality if such deprivation would render him stateless."

[132] For example, pursuant to section 2 of Act No. 1968–LF–3 of 11 June 1968, setting up the Cameroon Nationality Code: "Cameroon nationality is acquired or lost after birth either by operation of law or by the decision of a public authority under the law." (*Journal officiel de la République fédérale du Cameroun*, 15 July 1968)

106. Loss of nationality results from a voluntary act undertaken by a national of a State which has the effect of ending his or her status as a national of that State. Usually, such a situation is a consequence of naturalization, whereby a person, of his or her own free will, acts to acquire voluntarily a new nationality, losing the former nationality if the laws of the State of which he or she was formerly a national or the State of which he or she has become a national prohibits dual or multiple nationality. Domestic legislation in a number of States, particularly new States, contains such clauses disallowing multiple nationality.[133]

107. Deprivation of nationality, unlike loss of nationality, is the effect of an act by the State which deprives a person of his or her nationality. Deprivation of nationality may be a penalty for failure on the part of a naturalized person to comply with the laws on nationality of the State of which he or she has become a national.[134] In such instances, deprivation is usually by administrative act. However, it can also be decreed by legislative act in particular situations, for example, when nationals become—*de jure* or *de facto*—nationals of another State following the separation of that State into two or more States.

108. Such a situation arose when Eritrea separated from Ethiopia following the April 1993 referendum on self-determination, in which the people of Eritrea opted for independence. Many people of Ethiopian nationality, but of Eritrean origin, lived in Ethiopia, had assets there and carried on habitual activities there. Eritrea alleged that Ethiopia had "wrongfully denationalized, expelled, mistreated and deprived of property tens of thousands of Ethiopian citizens of Eritrean origin in violation of multiple international legal obligations".[135]

109. Ethiopia challenged that allegation, and its opposition gave rise to the *Eritrea* v. *Ethiopia* case, submitted for arbitration to a Claims Commission, which rendered a partial award in that connection on 17 December 2004.[136] The case, which will be examined in greater detail several times in the context of this topic, raises the issue of loss or deprivation of nationality in connection with succession of States, as well as the deprivation of dual nationals of one of their nationalities followed by expulsion in the event of armed conflict on the grounds that they have become nationals of an enemy State.

H. Persons who have become aliens through loss of nationality following the emergence of a new State

110. A new State may emerge through decolonization, transfer or separation of part of the territory, unification, dissolution or break-up of an existing State. The sovereign prerogatives of the new State, whether it is considered a successor State or otherwise, include the power to grant or refuse its nationality according to the rules of its domestic law. However, as the Commission pointed out in the preamble to its draft articles on nationality of natural persons in relation to the succession of States, this must be "within the limits set by international law", and, when decisions are taken in that connection, "due account should be taken both of the legitimate interests of States and those of individuals".[137] The major concern of individuals is in fact to possess a nationality, and the right of every individual to a nationality is emerging as a fundamental principle of international law.[138] Article 1 of the above-mentioned Commission draft articles, adopted in 1999 on second reading, recalls that principle: "Every individual who, on the date of the succession of States, had the nationality of the predecessor State, irrespective of the mode of acquisition of that nationality, has the right to the nationality of at least one of the States concerned."[139]

111. One of the main aims of the draft articles on nationality of natural persons in relation to the succession of States, which have the effect of introducing a "presumption of nationality", is to prevent statelessness, and they could consequently be considered "to strike a satisfactory balance between the practical needs relating to the succession of States and concerns relating to human rights and could help to stabilize what is still inconsistent practice".[140] However, the draft articles do not completely eliminate the risk of statelessness. Moreover, they by no means prevent individuals with dual nationality arising from the emergence of a new State from losing one of those nationalities, thus becoming aliens in the State whose nationality they have lost and therefore liable to expulsion. As the distribution of population between the original State and the new State formed from it is usually based on ethnicity, the original—or old—State has only to decide to deprive of their nationality those members of the ethnic group making up the population of the new State who have opted for the nationality of the new State in order for many individuals to become suddenly aliens in a State in which they may have been established for a very long time. The *Eritrea* v. *Ethiopia* case[141] illustrates this theory quite well, except for the consideration that the decision to deprive Ethiopian nationals of Eritrean origin of their Ethiopian nationality was sparked by the outbreak of war between the two countries in 1998.

I. Nationals of a State engaged in armed conflict with the host State

112. It was long held, until the late nineteenth century at least, that States had the right to expel from their

[133] Section 31 of the Cameroon Nationality Code (see footnote 132 above) also provides:

"Cameroonian nationality is lost by:

"(*a*) Any Cameroon adult national who wilfully acquires or keeps a foreign nationality;

"(*b*) Renunciation under this law;

"(*c*) Any person who, occupying a post in a public service of an international or foreign body, retains that post notwithstanding an injunction by the Cameroonian Government to resign it."

[134] Eritrea–Ethiopia Claims Commission (see footnote 58 above), para. 10.

[135] *Ibid.*

[136] *Ibid.*

[137] *Yearbook ... 1999*, vol. II (Part Two), p. 20, para. 47.

[138] As set forth in article 15 of the Universal Declaration of Human Rights (see footnote 94 above) and recalled in articles 4 and 18 of the European Convention on Nationality.

[139] See footnote 137 above; see also, in connection with the draft articles, the reports of Mr. Václav Mikulka, Special Rapporteur on this topic (1995–1998) (*Yearbook ... 1995*, vol. II (Part One), p. 157, document A/CN.4/467; *Yearbook ... 1996*, vol. II (Part One), p. 119, document A/CN.4/474; *Yearbook ... 1997*, vol. II (Part One), p. 7, document A/CN.4/480 and Add.1; and *Yearbook ... 1998*, vol. II (Part One), p. 301, document A/CN.4/489); and Economides, "Les effets de la succession d'États sur la nationalité des personnes physiques".

[140] Daillier and Pellet, *op. cit.*, p. 543, para. 354.

[141] See footnote 58 above.

territories nationals of an enemy Power. This right was exercised on the basis of a distinction between friendly aliens and enemy aliens, without distinguishing among the latter between those who were participating in some way in the war effort of their country of origin or who had a hostile attitude towards the host State and those who were living there peacefully. British legal theorists took a clear-cut position on this matter, stating that:

> Nothing could be clearer than the right of the British executive in time of war to exclude the subjects of the unfriendly power. The same is true of the entry of foreign sovereigns or ambassadors at any time as they represent the sovereignty of a foreign State, and their forcible entry at any time would constitute a *casus belli*. In either case no injury resulting to them through their exclusion from British territory by British executive officers, would afford them a ground of action in an English court.[142]

113. Such a radical concept is no longer acceptable today, when the international community's sustained attention to the protection of human rights has led to the softening, even in some cases the abandonment, of certain traditional practices that are incompatible with those rights.

114. Nevertheless, it cannot be maintained that the principle or practice of expelling "enemy" aliens or nationals of a State engaged in armed conflict with the host State has disappeared. In the case of *Eritrea* v. *Ethiopia*, Eritrea accused Ethiopia of engaging in "ethnic cleansing"[143] by carrying out a mass expulsion of Ethiopians of Eritrean origin, that is, expelling its own nationals in violation of international law. The Eritrea–Ethiopia Claims Commission, concurring with Ethiopia's arguments in this regard, noted that international humanitarian law gives belligerents broad powers to expel nationals of the enemy State from their territory during a conflict. The Commission cited in this regard one of the authorities on international law, *Oppenheim's International Law*, which states:

> The right of states to expel aliens is generally recognised. It matters not whether the alien is on a temporary visit, or has settled down for professional business or other purposes on its territory, having established his domicile there.
>
> On the other hand, while a state has a broad discretion in exercising its right to expel aliens, its discretion is not absolute. Thus, by customary international law it must not abuse its right by acting arbitrarily in taking its decision to expel an alien, and it must act reasonably in the manner in which it effects an expulsion. Beyond this, however, customary international law provides no detailed rules regarding expulsion, and everything accordingly depends upon the merits of the individual case. Theory and practice correctly make a distinction between expulsion in time of hostilities and in time of peace. A belligerent may consider it convenient to expel all hostile nationals residing, or temporarily staying, within its territory: although such a measure may be very hard on individual aliens, it is generally accepted that such expulsion is justifiable.[144]

This opinion is shared by most writers on international humanitarian law.[145]

115. The Eritrea–Ethiopia Claims Commission also held, in this context, that Ethiopia had acted lawfully in depriving a substantial number of dual nationals (Ethiopians-Eritreans) of their Ethiopian nationality following identification through Ethiopia's security committee process. It added: "Ethiopia could lawfully expel these persons as nationals of an enemy belligerent, although it was bound to ensure them the protections required by Geneva Convention IV and other applicable international humanitarian law."[146]

J. Migrant workers

116. The problem of the migrant worker exists on every continent, as demonstrated by the regional seminars on the issue.[147] The phenomenon is growing continuously with the development of international transport. The resultant diversity of migrant workers means that each case requires individual attention. The lack of such attention often opens the way to the enactment in receiving countries of rules that discriminate against this category of worker.[148]

117. A "migrant worker" is a person who migrates from one country to another in order to obtain employment, rather than to work on his or her own account.[149] The term is defined along these lines in ILO Convention (No. 97) concerning migration for employment and Convention (No. 143) concerning migrations in abusive conditions and the promotion of equality of opportunity and treatment of migrant workers, as "a person who migrates from one country to another with a view to being employed otherwise than on his own account and includes any person regularly admitted as a migrant for employment".[150]

118. Similarly, article 2, paragraph 1, of the International Convention on the Protection of the Rights of All Migrant Workers and Members of their Families[151]—which entered

---

[142] Griffin, "Colonial expulsion of aliens", p. 91.

[143] Eritrea–Ethiopia Claims Commission (see footnote 58 above), p. 19, para. 80.

[144] Jennings and Watts, *op. cit.*, pp. 940–941, para. 413; see also Eritrea–Ethiopia Claims Commission (footnote 58 above), p. 19, para. 81.

[145] See, for example, Doehring, "Aliens, expulsion and deportation", p. 16: "[A] State may nonetheless be justified in expelling such a group without regard to the individual behaviour of its members, if the security and the existence of the expelling State would otherwise be seriously endangered, for example ... during a state of war"; Draper, *The Red Cross Conventions*, pp. 36–37, quoted in Whiteman, *Digest of International Law*, p. 274 (citing "the customary right of a State to expel all enemy aliens at the onset of a conflict"); and Fleck, *The Handbook of Humanitarian Law in Armed Conflicts*, p. 287, sect. 589, para. 5.

[146] Eritrea–Ethiopia Claims Commission (see footnote 58 above), p. 20, para. 82.

[147] See Elles, *International Provisions Protecting the Human Rights of Non-Citizens*, pp. 21–22. For a more detailed exposition on the protection of the rights of migrant workers provided in studies produced for the United Nations, see the study by Mrs. Halima Embarek Warzazi on the exploitation of labour through illicit and clandestine trafficking (E/CN.4/Sub.2/351); General Assembly resolution 2920 (XXVII) of 15 November 1972; the final report by Mrs. Warzazi (E/CN.4/Sub.2/L.629) of 4 July 1975, which, together with the report of the seminar on the human rights of migrant workers held in Tunis from 12 to 24 November 1975 (ST/TAO/HR/50), was submitted by the Commission on Human Rights to the General Assembly at its thirty-first session (see General Assembly resolution 31/127 of 16 December 1976).

[148] See Elles, *op. cit.*, p. 22.

[149] See Cholewinski, *Migrant Workers in International Human Rights Law: Their Protection in Countries of Employment*, p. 101; see also pages 102 and 150; see further Dent, *op. cit.*, pp. 24 and 27.

[150] Convention (No. 97), art. 11, para. 1. It will be noted that Convention (No. 143) includes in the definition a person "who has migrated" from one country to another.

[151] This Convention was inspired by the study on the condition of migrant workers undertaken by the Sub-Commission on Prevention of Discrimination and Protection of Minorities at the request of the Economic and Social Council (see Council resolution 1789 (LIV) of 18 May 1973).

into force on 1 July 2003—defines a migrant worker as "a person who is to be engaged, is engaged or has been engaged in a remunerated activity in a State of which he or she is not a national".

119. It should be noted that the expression "to be engaged" refers to the intending migrant worker who has a contract of employment. These definitions all exclude any person seeking work in a foreign country for the first time without having already concluded a contract of employment with an employer, as well as illegal migrant workers. They also exclude other categories of person, including frontier workers, members of the liberal professions and artistes who enter a country on a short-term basis, persons coming specifically for purposes of training or education and persons employed in a host country for a limited period of time to undertake a specific assignment.

120. On the other hand, the ILO conventions do not exclude persons with refugee status, in contrast to the International Convention on the Protection of the Rights of All Migrant Workers and Members of their Families, which excludes refugees and stateless persons from its scope.[152] The rationale is that these categories of person already enjoy a specific international status that affords them special protection. It has been noted, however, that their exclusion from the scope of the Convention gives rise to an anomalous situation whereby asylum-seekers are regarded as "migrant workers" if they have permission to work in the host country, but lose that status under the Convention once they are granted refugee or exile status.[153]

121. There are a variety of international legal instruments offering extensive protection to migrant workers.[154] With regard to the topic under consideration, the principle established is that migrant workers may not be expelled collectively, while individual expulsions are themselves subject to certain conditions, which will be examined subsequently, in the context of expulsion regimes.

122. Identification has just been made of various categories of person who, by virtue of their situation (the fact that they are present, either legally or illegally, in the territory of a State of which they are not nationals), their legal status (refugees, asylum-seekers, stateless persons, persons with dual or multiple nationality who have been deprived of the nationality of the territorial State) or their activities (migrant workers) are among the aliens whose expulsion falls within the framework of this topic. On this basis, the Special Rapporteur wishes to propose, for the purpose of delimiting the scope of the topic, the following draft article:

"*Article 1. Scope*

"1. The present draft articles shall apply to any person who is present in a State of which he or she is not a national (*ressortissant*).

"2. They shall apply, in particular, to aliens who are present in the host country, lawfully or with irregular status, to refugees, asylum-seekers, stateless persons, migrant workers, nationals (*ressortissants*) of an enemy State and nationals (*ressortissants*) of the expelling State who have lost their nationality or been deprived of it."

[152] See article 3 of the Convention, which lists the categories of person to whom the Convention does not apply.

[153] See Cholewinski, *op. cit.*, p. 153.

[154] These legal instruments, some of universal, some of regional or bilateral character, will be enumerated and analysed in due course in subsequent reports, particularly when the principles applicable to, grounds for and consequences of expulsion are examined.

Chapter II

Definitions

123. One of the chief difficulties of this topic lies in determining the exact meaning and content of such key concepts as "alien" and "expulsion". They should therefore be defined as clearly as possible by seeking their exact meaning in law or, at the very least, the sense in which they are to be used for the purposes of this study and the draft articles to result from it. As stated in the preliminary report on the expulsion of aliens,[155] the concept of expulsion can be understood only in relation to that of alien, and the latter will therefore be discussed first.

A. Alien

124. The term "alien" cannot be defined in itself but only in relation to what it is not, that is, a national or a person who holds the nationality of a given State or who is a *ressortissant* of that State. Accordingly, an alien is a person who is under the jurisdiction of another nation or State, a person who does not hold the nationality of the forum State.[156] It is in this sense that the term "alien" is used in the Declaration on the Human Rights of Individuals Who are not Nationals of the Country in which They Live, which applies it "to any individual who is not a national of the State in which he or she is present".[157]

125. "Alien" could thus be defined by starting from an opposition founded on a single criterion: the link of nationality with the territorial State. However, this criterion would not suffice to define *a contrario* all the persons covered by the category of "alien" as envisaged by this topic, particularly since the language of international law employs, in addition to the term "national", such

[155] See footnote 1 above.

[156] Salmon, *op. cit.*, pp. 468–469.

[157] General Assembly resolution 40/144 of 13 December 1985, annex, art. 1.

synonyms as "citizen", "subject" and "*ressortissant*",[158] which do not necessarily imply the same type of legal link between the individual and the territorial State. Accordingly, the concept of "alien" will be approached by proceeding from the aforementioned opposite concepts. The advantage of such an approach is that, if one determines which of these concepts is best able to capture all of the persons who come under a State's jurisdiction, one will thereby identify the appropriate term for designating the relationship that binds an alien to his or her State of origin or affiliation.

126. In very specific terms, it is a matter of answering the following question: is the term "alien" to be understood solely as the opposite of a person holding the nationality of the territorial State (a national) or can it also be understood in relation to citizens, subjects or *ressortissants* of a State of origin or affiliation? Each of these ideas will be examined in turn.

1. National

127. Used as a noun, the term "national" means a person who possesses the nationality of the State in which he or she is present, nationality being the legal link that binds a person—a natural person in this case—to a State, either from birth or, subsequent to birth, by naturalization, marriage or operation of law. As stated by ICJ in its judgment in the *Nottebohm* case:

> According to the practice of States, to arbitral and judicial decisions and to the opinions of writers, nationality is a legal bond having as its basis a social fact of attachment, a genuine connection of existence, interests and sentiments, together with the existence of reciprocal rights and duties. It may be said to constitute the juridical expression of the fact that the individual upon whom it is conferred, either directly by the law or as the result of an act of the authorities, is in fact more closely connected with the population of the State conferring nationality than with that of any other State. Conferred by a State, it only entitles that State to exercise protection *vis-à-vis* another State, if it constitutes a translation into juridical terms of the individual's connection with the State which has made him its national.[159]

128. An alien may be a national of a State of origin or affiliation or, on the contrary, a non-national of the territorial State or the forum State. However, this criterion of the bond of nationality is too restrictive where the concept of "alien" is concerned, since not every alien is necessarily a national of a given State.

129. In any case, one will refrain in the context of the present topic from defining "alien" by invoking the criterion of nationality. Not only are the conditions for acquiring nationality strictly a matter for the internal law of each State—the State being able to confer or deny its nationality as it sees fit—but the debate on the issue of nationality in international jurisprudence has also proved to be extremely complex.[160] With regard to international law, the Special Rapporteur, Mr. John R. Dugard, explained in his first report on diplomatic protection[161] that, while the *Nottebohm* case was seen as authority for the position that there should be an effective or genuine link between the individual and the State of nationality, the judgment in this case was "atypical",[162] first, because there was suspicion about the manner in which Liechtenstein had conferred nationality on Nottebohm and, secondly, because the latter had close ties to Guatemala. The ensuing debate revealed a doctrinal disagreement within the Commission itself concerning the criteria for the conferment of nationality: *jus soli*, *jus sanguinis*, nationality by adoption, legitimation, recognition, marriage or some other means, "involuntary naturalization", "voluntary naturalization", or "valid naturalization" to use the terminology applied in the *Flegenheimer* case,[163] the "bona fide" criterion? This controversy is best avoided, particularly since it is always national legislation that stipulates the criteria for the conferment of nationality, irrespective of the views expounded in the legal literature and case law.

2. Citizen

130. In international law, the word "citizen" means an individual enjoying political rights that enable him or her to participate in the life of the State.[164] This general definition does not enable the nature of the link between the citizen and the State in question to be determined. It may be a link of nationality for, in some sense, citizen is synonymous with national or *ressortissant*. This is confirmed by a legal opinion prepared by the Office of Legal Affairs of the United Nations, which in 1980 wrote that:

> "Nationality" and "citizenship" are largely within the competence of municipal law except where the discretion of the State is restricted by its international obligations. Both terms refer to the status of the individual in his relationship with the State. They are sometimes used synonymously but they do not necessarily describe the same relationship towards the State.[165]

131. Indeed, citizenship does not always coincide with nationality, at least as far as the legal basis of each and the nature of the respective connection with the State are concerned. European Union law provides an excellent illustration of this point. It affirms that citizenship is that of the Union, while nationality is that

[158] With regard to the term "subject", Rivier writes: "Subject, national, citizen, *régnicole*: so many synonyms the opposite of which is alien" (*Principes du droit des gens*, p. 137).

[159] *Nottebohm, Second Phase, Judgment, I.C.J. Reports 1955*, p. 23.

[160] See, for example, the debate on the issue in the PCIJ advisory opinion of 15 September 1923. Referring to the provisions of article 93 of the Treaty of Peace between the Principal Allied and Associated Powers and Poland, the Court stated that "[they] considerably extend the conceptions of minority and population, since they allude on the one hand to the *inhabitants* of the territory" (*Acquisition of Polish Nationality, Advisory Opinion, 1923, P.C.I.J., Series B, No. 7*, p. 14).

[161] *Yearbook ... 2000*, vol. II (Part One), p. 205, document A/CN.4/506 and Add.1.

[162] *Ibid.*, vol. II (Part Two), p. 79, para. 457.

[163] *Flegenheimer* case, decision No. 182 of 20 September 1958 (UNRIAA, vol. XIV (Sales No. 65.V.4), p. 377. See also *Yearbook ... 2000* (footnote 161 above), p. 228, para. 111, and *ibid.*, vol. II (Part Two), p. 80, paras. 464–465.

[164] Article 25 of the International Covenant on Civil and Political Rights (see General Assembly resolution 2200 (XXI) A, annex, of 16 December 1966) provides:

> "Every citizen shall have the right and the opportunity, without any of the distinctions mentioned in article 2 and without unreasonable restrictions:
>
> (*a*) To take part in the conduct of public affairs, directly or through freely chosen representatives;
>
> (*b*) To vote and to be elected ...;
>
> (*c*) To have access, on general terms of equality, to public service in his country."

[165] *United Nations Juridical Yearbook, 1980* (United Nations publication, Sales No. E.83.V.1), p. 190, para. 3.

of each member State. In this regard, article 17 (former art. 8) of the Treaty establishing the European Community provides:

1. Citizenship of the Union is hereby established. Every person holding the nationality of a Member State shall be a citizen of the Union ...

2. Citizens of the Union shall enjoy the rights conferred by this Treaty and shall be subject to the duties imposed thereby.[166]

132. Clearly, access to European citizenship is conditional on possession of the nationality of a State member of the European Union. At the same time, the enjoyment by a national of one State member of the Union of the rights associated with European citizenship in another State member of the Union of which that individual is not a national is not dependent on the latter legal link, that of nationality, but solely on the link of citizenship. In other words, a European cannot be an alien in any State member of the European Union, even though the individual only possesses the nationality of a single member State. In this respect, citizenship is broader than nationality and removes from the category of alien persons who would be included in it based solely on the criterion of nationality.

3. Subject

133. A subject is a person under the authority of a monarch or prince to whom he or she owes allegiance. A subject is to a monarchy what a citizen is to a republic. One speaks, for example, of citizens of the Republic of France, of the United States or of the Republic of Cameroon, but of Belgian, British or Spanish subjects. It is in this sense that the Convention relative to Successions between Belgium and Spain signed in Madrid on 1 March 1839, governing the right of the subjects of one State to acquire and inherit property in the other stipulated that "when goods acquired, by any means, by Belgian subjects in the States of His Majesty the King of Belgium, are exported, no taxes on emigration (*droit de détraction*) or immigration shall be levied on such goods".[167]

134. In the colonial era, the term "subjects" was used to refer to indigenous nationals living in the colonies as opposed to "citizens" coming from the parent State.[168] A note by the Legal Service of the Ministry for Foreign Affairs of France, dated 12 January 1935, stated:

In France, the term "*ressortissant*" is generally considered to include not only French persons in metropolitan France, but also colonial subjects and nationals of protectorate countries …

As regards the subjects, the matter is clear; as regards the protégés, who are sometimes mentioned as a separate category from *ressortissants*, the matter is less certain.[169]

135. In the *Dictionnaire de droit international public* it is said that the term "subject" is also a "synonym of national or citizen".[170] But based on the foregoing, it can be said that the term "*ressortissant*" can cover all three categories of persons.

4. Ressortissant

136. In current usage, the term "*ressortissant*" is synonymous with "*national*" [both usually translated as "national" in English]. The synonymity of the two terms is evident in several international legal instruments[171] and in international jurisprudence.

137. In the question submitted by the Council of the League of Nations to PCIJ in connection with the Court's advisory opinion No. 7, the Council seems to use "*ressortissant*" to mean "person possessing the nationality of". In its introduction to the question, the Council states:

The Polish Government has decided to treat certain persons, who were formerly German nationals [*ressortissants*], as not having acquired Polish nationality and as continuing to possess German nationality, which exposes them in Poland to the treatment laid down for persons of non-Polish nationality, and in particular of German nationality.[172]

138. In its judgment in the case concerning *Certain German Interests in Polish Upper Silesia*, PCIJ held that:

[T]he conception of a "national" [*ressortissant*] also covers, in the Court's opinion, communes such as the City of Ratibor. It is true that, as has been explained in connection with the case of the Königs-und Laurahütte Company, the term "national" [*ressortissant*] in the Geneva Convention generally contemplates physical persons. But a relation analogous to that which exists between physical persons and a State, and which is called nationality, also exists, although in a different form, in the case of corporations of municipal law.[173]

139. The question concerning the *Treatment of Polish Nationals and Other Persons of Polish Origin or Speech in the Danzig Territory* reveals a restrictive interpretation of the concept of "nationals", suggesting that other persons of the same origin and speaking the same language might not automatically be nationals, and that the latter term does not mean precisely the same thing as "*ressortissants*". PCIJ also noted in this case that "if only discrimination on account of Polish nationality, origin or speech is prohibited, it would be possible for Danzig to exclude all Poles from its territory, provided that the exclusion applied equally to other foreigners",[174] thus underlining the distinction between nationals of a State and persons whose country of origin is that State.

140. However, it appears from the same opinion that the term "*ressortissant*" might well cover all three categories of persons concerned in this case. Indeed, PCIJ points out that when the Conference of Ambassadors drafted the convention on the legal status of the Free City of Danzig,

[166] It is to be noted that, under the Treaty, European citizens have numerous rights, including the right to move and reside freely within the territory of the member States (art. 18); the right to vote and to stand as candidates at municipal elections and elections to the European Parliament in the member State in which they reside (art. 19); the right to diplomatic protection by any member State in third countries in which their member State is not represented (art. 20); the right to petition and to apply to the Ombudsman (art. 21).

[167] Parry, *The Consolidated Treaty Series*, art. 2, p. 330.

[168] See Salmon, *op. cit.*, p. 1061.

[169] Kiss, *Répertoire de la pratique française en matière de droit international public*, vol. II, p. 236, No. 438. See also Pillet and Niboyet, *Manuel de droit international privé*, p. 66, footnote (2).

[170] See footnote 168 above.

[171] For example, article 30, paragraph 1, of the European Convention on Establishment reads: "For the purpose of this Convention, 'nationals' [*ressortissants*] means physical persons possessing the nationality of one of the Contracting Parties."

[172] *Acquisition of Polish Nationality* (see footnote 160 above), p. 6.

[173] *Certain German Interests in Polish Upper Silesia, Merits, Judgment No. 7, 1926, P.C.I.J., Series A, No. 7*, p. 74.

[174] *Treatment of Polish Nationals and Other Persons of Polish Origin or Speech in the Danzig Territory, Advisory Opinion, 1932, P.C.I.J., Series A/B, No. 44*, p. 41.

it had before it three preliminary drafts, one of which was submitted by the City of Danzig and the other two by Poland: "The Danzig draft contained detailed provisions relating to the rights of the nationals [*ressortissants*] of the two contracting Parties. … The second Polish draft contained provisions for national treatment of Polish nationals [*ressortissants*] based on the principle of reciprocity." The Court adds that "[t]he question of national treatment of Polish nationals [*ressortissants*] … had been raised in both the Danzig and the Polish drafts… but instead of granting to Polish nationals [*ressortissants*] at Danzig national treatment … the Conference of Ambassadors dealt with the matter in Article 30", which accords "to Polish nationals [*nationaux*] and other persons of Polish origin or speech ... not national treatment, but the régime of minority protection".[175]

141. In its advisory opinion of 6 April 1935 concerning *Minority Schools in Albania*, PCIJ affirmed the inclusive nature of the term "*ressortissant*" *vis-à-vis* "national" when it wrote that in order to attain the idea underlying all treaties for the protection of minorities, it was necessary first to "ensure that nationals[176] belonging to racial, religious or linguistic minorities shall be placed in every respect on a footing of perfect equality with other nationals [*ressortissants*] of the State".[177] The Court also noted that "[a]ll Albanian nationals [*ressortissants*] enjoy the equality in law stipulated in Article 4"[178] of the Declaration of 2 October 1921, and established that article 5, paragraph 1, of the Declaration "confers on Albanian nationals [*ressortissants*] of racial, religious or linguistic minorities the right that is stipulated in the second sentence of that paragraph".[179]

142. In the case concerning *Rights of Nationals of the United States of America in Morocco*, as in all cases brought before ICJ and its predecessor in which nationals of one of the parties are concerned, the term "*ressortissant*" is translated as "nationals" in English. In this case, France asked the Court to adjudge and declare that "the privileges of the nationals of the United States of America in Morocco are only those which result from the text of Articles 20 and 21 of the Treaty of September 16th, 1836".[180] The United States held that "[t]he jurisdiction conferred upon the United States by the Treaties of 1787 and 1836 was jurisdiction, civil and criminal, in all cases arising between American citizens",[181] and that the United States had acquired in Morocco, through the effect of the most-favoured-nation clause and through custom, "jurisdiction in all cases in which an American citizen or protégé was defendant".[182] It is true that article 21 of the 1836 Treaty of Peace uses the term "citizen"[183] and not "national" (*ressortissant*), but it is clear that the term is being used to mean the same thing as "national". The Court itself used the two terms as equivalents. In stating the reasons for the judgment, the Court recalled that the most extensive privileges in the matter of consular jurisdiction granted by Morocco were granted in respect of "British nationals"[184] (*ressortissants*) on the basis of the General Treaty with Great Britain of 1856;[185] that jurisdiction in civil and criminal matters was established under the Treaty of Commerce between Morocco and Spain (Madrid, 20 November 1861)[186] "for cases in which Spanish nationals [*ressortissants*] were defendants";[187] and that, accordingly, the United States had "acquired by virtue of the most-favoured-nation clauses, civil and criminal consular jurisdiction in all cases in which United States nationals [*ressortissants*] were defendants".[188] In one section of the operative part of the judgment, the Court found, unanimously, that the United States was

> not entitled to claim that the application to citizens of the United States of all laws and regulations in the French Zone of Morocco requires the assent of the Government of the United States, but that the consular courts of the United States may refuse to apply to United States citizens laws or regulations which have not been assented to by the Government of the United States.[189]

The terms "nationals", "citizens" and "*ressortissants*" appear, at first glance, to be equivalent. However, is it not apparent in the reference made in this case by the United States, in its submission, to "all cases in which an American citizen or protégé was defendant",[190] that the term "*ressortissant*" might have a broader meaning in international law than "national" and "citizen"?

143. The tie of nationality being the foundation for a State's action with regard to diplomatic protection, the term "*ressortissant*" as used in various cases concerning diplomatic protection brought before ICJ is synonymous with "national" or "person having the nationality of".

144. In the case concerning *United States Diplomatic and Consular Staff in Tehran*,[191] the parties and ICJ itself used the terms "*ressortissant*" and "citizen" interchangeably and in a limited sense to mean "national" or

---

[175] *Ibid.*, pp. 33–34.

[176] "*Ressortissants*" in French.

[177] *Minority Schools in Albania, Advisory Opinion, 1935, P.C.I.J., Series A/B, No. 64*, p. 17.

[178] *Ibid.*, p. 19.

[179] *Ibid.*, p. 22.

[180] *Rights of Nationals of the United States of America in Morocco, Judgment, I.C.J. Reports 1952*, p. 179. In French: "[L]es privilèges des ressortissants des États-Unis d'Amérique au Maroc sont uniquement ceux qui résultent du texte des articles 20 et 21 du traité du 16 septembre." The Treaty of Peace (Meknès, 16 September 1836) is reproduced in Miller, Treaties and Other International Acts of the United States of America, vol. 4, p. 33.

[181] *I.C.J. Reports 1952* (see footnote 180 above), p. 186. The *Treaty of Peace and Friendship* between Morocco and the United States (28 June and 15 July 1786) is reproduced in Miller, *op. cit.*, vol. 2, p. 185.

[182] *I.C.J. Reports 1952* (see footnote 180 above), p. 186.

[183] That article stipulated: "If a citizen of the United States should kill or wound a Moor, or, on the contrary, if a Moor shall kill or wound a citizen of the United States, the law of the country shall take place, and equal justice shall be rendered, the Consul assisting at the trial." (*Ibid.*, p. 189)

[184] *Ibid.*, p. 190.

[185] See Exchange of notes constituting an agreement concerning the Convention of Commerce and Navigation between the United Kingdom and the Shereefian Empire signed on 9 December 1856 (Rabat, 1 March 1957), United Nations, *Treaty Series*, vol. 310, No. 4480, p. 3.

[186] *Tratados de España: Documentos internacionales del Reinado de Doña Isabel II desde 1842 a 1868* (Madrid, Ginesta, 1869), p. 245.

[187] *I.C.J. Reports 1952* (see footnote 180 above), p. 190.

[188] *Ibid.*

[189] *Ibid.*, p. 213.

[190] *Ibid.*, p. 189.

[191] *United States Diplomatic and Consular Staff in Tehran, Judgment, I.C.J. Reports 1980*, p. 3.

"individual of American nationality". Thus, in its submissions on the case, the United States Government maintained that it had carried out its mission in the Islamic Republic of Iran "with the aim of extricating American nationals [*ressortissants*]"[192] who had been victims of the Iranian armed attack on its embassy, and had demanded the immediate "release of all United States nationals [*ressortissants*]"[193] held in the embassy building and reparation "in its own right and in the exercise of its right of diplomatic protection of its nationals [*ressortissants*]".[194] Recalling the facts of the case in its judgment, the Court noted that after the Iranian "militants"[195] had seized the embassy, "other United States personnel and one United States private citizen [*ressortissant*] seized elsewhere in Tehran"[196] had been subsequently taken to the embassy and held hostage. The Court also referred, some paragraphs later, to the "total number of United States citizens [*citoyens*] seized"[197] and to "two other persons of United States nationality [*ressortissants*] not possessing either diplomatic or consular status".[198] Visas "issued to Iranian citizens [*citoyens*] for future entry into the United States were cancelled"[199] and the United States Government prohibited travel by its citizens [*ressortissants*] to Iran. The Court, in stating the reasons for its judgment, noted that "the United States Government may have had understandable preoccupations with respect to the well-being of its nationals [*ressortissants*] held hostage in its Embassy for over five months".[200] In paragraph 3 of its judgment, it decided that Iran "must immediately terminate the unlawful detention of ... diplomatic and consular staff and other United States nationals [*ressortissants*] now held hostage in Iran".[201]

145. Also using the term "*ressortissant*" in the sense of "national", Germany considered in its submissions in the *LaGrand* case[202] that by not informing Karl and Walter LaGrand without delay following their arrest of their rights under the Vienna Convention on Consular Relations, the United States had "violated its international legal obligations to Germany, in its own right and in its right of diplomatic protection of its nationals [*ressortissants*]";[203] and that pursuant to those international legal obligations, the United States should provide Germany with the guarantee that "in any future cases of detention of or criminal proceedings against German nationals [*ressortissants*]",[204] the law and practice of the United States would not hinder the application of international law.[205] ICJ, recalling the facts of the case, noted that "Walter LaGrand and Karl LaGrand were born in Germany in 1962 and 1963 respectively, and were German nationals [*ressortissants*]".[206] It did not accept the objections of the United States that Germany did not have "standing to assert those rights on behalf of its nationals [*ressortissants*]".[207] The Court's use of the term "*ressortissant*" as synonymous with "person possessing the nationality of" becomes very clear when "the Court concludes that Article 36, paragraph 1, creates individual rights, which, by virtue of Article I of the Optional Protocol, may be invoked in this Court by the national State of the detained person".[208] The Court also states, in paragraph (7) of its judgment, that "should nationals [*ressortissants*] of the Federal Republic of Germany nonetheless be sentenced to severe penalties, without their rights under"[209] the Vienna Convention having been respected, the United States, by means of its own choosing, should allow the review and reconsideration of the conviction.

146. In the case concerning *Avena and Other Mexican Nationals*, Mexico, in its final submissions, asked ICJ to adjudge and declare that the United States had "violated its international legal obligations to Mexico, in its own right and in the exercise of its right of consular protection of its nationals [*ressortissants*]".[210] It also asserted its own claims, basing them on the injury which it contended that "*it has itself suffered, directly and through its nationals* [*ressortissants*]".[211] The use of the term "*ressortissant*" as synonymous with "national" or "possessor of the nationality of a State", as noted in the *LaGrand* case,[212] is confirmed here. After recalling the text of paragraph 77 of the judgment issued in the *LaGrand* case, the Court examined "the question of the alleged dual nationality of certain of the Mexican nationals [*ressortissants*] the subject of Mexico's claims".[213] The United States objected to that claim, maintaining that it was

> an accepted principle that, when a person arrested or detained in the receiving State is a national [*ressortissant*] of that State, then even if he is also a national [*ressortissant*] of another State party to the Vienna Convention, Article 36 has no application ...; and Mexico has indicated that, for the purposes of the present case it does not contest that dual nationals have no right to be advised of their rights under Article 36.[214]

The Court pointed out "that Mexico, in addition to seeking to exercise diplomatic protection of its nationals [*ressortissants*]",[215] was making a claim in its own right, and that it could claim a breach of article 36 of the Vienna Convention on Consular Relations "in relation to any of its nationals [*ressortissants*]",[216] and the United States was "thereupon free to show that, because the person concerned was also a United States national [*ressortissant*], Article 36 had no application to that person".[217] Even more significantly, the Court noted that Mexico

---

[192] *Ibid.*, p. 18, para. 32.

[193] *Ibid.*, p. 6, para. 8.

[194] *Ibid.*, p. 7.

[195] *Ibid.*, p. 12, para. 17.

[196] *Ibid.*

[197] *Ibid.*, p. 13, para. 21.

[198] *Ibid.*, para. 22.

[199] *Ibid.*, p. 17, para. 31.

[200] *Ibid.*, p. 43, para. 93.

[201] *Ibid.*, p. 44, para. 95.

[202] *LaGrand (Germany* v. *United States of America), Judgment, I.C.J. Reports 2001*, p. 466; see also *Vienna Convention on Consular Relations (Paraguay* v. *United States of America), Provisional Measures, Order of 9 April 1998, I.C.J. Reports 1998*, p. 248).

[203] *I.C.J. Reports 2001* (see footnote 202 above), p. 471, para. 10.

[204] *Ibid.*, p. 473, para. 11.

[205] *Ibid.*, para. 12.

[206] *Ibid.*, pp. 474–475, para. 13.

[207] *Ibid.*, p. 483, para. 42.

[208] *Ibid.*, p. 494, para. 77.

[209] *Ibid.*, p. 516, para. 128.

[210] *Avena and Other Mexican Nationals (Mexico* v. *United States of America), Judgment, I.C.J. Reports 2004*, p. 35, para. 40.

[211] *Ibid.*, pp. 35–36. The term is used in this way in many other paragraphs of the French version of the judgment. In addition to those cited above, see also paragraphs 69 and 102.

[212] See footnote 202 above.

[213] *I.C.J. Reports 2004* (see footnote 210 above), p. 36, para. 41.

[214] *Ibid.*

[215] *Ibid.*, para. 42.

[216] *Ibid.*, p. 37.

[217] *Ibid.*

claimed to have met the burden of proof to show that the 52 persons involved in the case "were Mexican nationals [*ressortissants*] ... by providing to the Court the birth certificates of these nationals [*ressortissants*], and declarations from 42 of them that they have not acquired United States nationality".[218] If the burden of proof was to be shared in this instance, it was because, in the view of the United States, "persons of Mexican nationality may also have acquired United States citizenship by operation of law, depending on their parents' dates and places of birth, places of residency, marital status at time of their birth and so forth".[219] The Court found that it was "for Mexico to show that the 52 persons listed ... held Mexican nationality at the time of their arrest", and noted that to that end Mexico had "produced birth certificates and declarations of nationality, whose contents have not been challenged by the United States".[220] It is clear that, in the language of the parties and of the Court, no distinction is made between the notions of "*ressortissant*", "national" and even "citizen". The United States "told the Court that millions of aliens reside, either legally or illegally, on its territory, and moreover that its laws concerning citizenship are generous".[221] The Court pointed out that:

> [T]he language that a person speaks, or his appearance, does not necessarily indicate that he is a foreign national ..., and ... in view of the large numbers of foreign nationals living in the United States, these very circumstances suggest that it would be desirable for enquiry routinely to be made of the individual as to his nationality upon his detention.[222]

It noted that no evidence had been brought before it to suggest that there were, in the case of one of the persons concerned (Mr. Salcido, case No. 22), at the same time "indications of Mexican nationality, which should have caused rapid enquiry by the arresting authorities".[223] The Court also referred to "Mexican nationals [*ressortissants*]" in subparagraphs (6), (7), (9) and (11) of the judgment.[224]

147. Side by side with this limited meaning of "*ressortissant*" as "possessing the nationality of", the term also has an overly broad meaning in international law, especially when used in conjunction with the adjective "enemy". The term "*ressortissant enemi*" [enemy alien] denotes a natural or legal person believed by a belligerent to be subject by law to the authority of an enemy Power, depending on the criteria used to determine that connection, which may vary in domestic laws from one State to another.[225] The crux of the matter is the loyalty of a person to such a Power or, more precisely, and as ICJ indicated, citing the reply of Liechtenstein in the *Nottebohm* case, "nationality, residence ..., personal or business associations as evidence of loyalty ... or inclusion in the Black List".[226] Clearly, the range of persons to whom this applies is very broad, since it suffices that they should have shown evidence of their loyalty to the enemy Power in question without there being any need to establish their nationality[227] in order to consider them "*ressortissants*" of that Power.

148. The Special Rapporteur does not envisage the concept of "*ressortissant*" in such a broad sense in the context of the present topic. There exists an intermediate meaning that falls between the limitation of the term to the idea of nationality and its extension to all persons that a State at war may decide to consider enemy aliens on the basis of their culpable loyalty to an enemy State. Of course, States may decide, by agreement, to assign to the term whatever meaning they wish. However, the Special Rapporteur is striving for a definition that, while broad, remains precise, applying not only to nationals, but also to persons who are subject to the authority of a given State as the result of a particular legal connection, such as status of refugee or asylum-seeker, the legal relationship resulting from a situation of statelessness, or even a relationship of subordination, such as that created by a mandate or protectorate. For example, according to a note dated 12 January 1935 by the Legal Service of the Ministry for Foreign Affairs of France (see paragraph 134 above): "The following formula is suggested: 'All French *ressortissants*, including French protégés'."[228]

149. However, the precise sense in which the term is to be used in the context of the present topic is conveyed in the award rendered by the Franco-German Mixed Arbitral Tribunal on 30 December 1927 in the *Falla-Nataf and Brothers* v. *Germany* case:

> Whereas the defendant contends that the claimant, being of Tunisian nationality and as such a French protégé, may not be regarded as a *ressortissant* of an Allied or Associated Power ...
>
> Whereas the term "*ressortissant*" as used in article 297 of the Treaty of Versailles is not limited to *nationals* of a State, but comprises also all persons connected with a State by a juridical link other than nationality proper.[229]

150. "*Ressortissant*" is therefore understood to mean any person who, as the result of any legal relationship, including nationality, comes under the authority of a given State.

151. In view of the above considerations, it is reasonable to propose that the term "alien" denotes, in the context of this topic, a *ressortissant* of a State other than the receiving State or the territorial State, or, conversely, a "*non-ressortissant*"[230] of the latter.

152. Of course, a concept as broad as that of "*ressortissant*" presents the risk that individuals may claim falsely or purely opportunistically to be *ressortissants* of a State when in fact they neither possess its nationality nor have any solid connection with it, simply because they prefer, for various reasons, to be expelled to that State. It cannot be denied that such a risk exists, and in fact such situations are known to arise frequently in practice. However,

[218] *Ibid.*, p. 41, para. 55.

[219] *Ibid.*, para. 56.

[220] *Ibid.*, para. 57.

[221] *Ibid.*, p. 44, para. 64.

[222] *Ibid.*

[223] *Ibid.*, para. 66.

[224] *Ibid.*, p. 71–73, para. 153.

[225] See Salmon, *op. cit.*, p. 1001.

[226] *I.C.J Pleadings, Nottebohm*, vol. I (Liechtenstein *v.* Guatemala), p. 411.

[227] Note by the Legal Service of the Ministry for Foreign Affairs of France (18 February 1937) (Kiss, *op. cit.*, vol. VI, No. 883, p. 441).

[228] *Ibid.*, vol. II, No. 438, p. 236.

[229] *Recueil des décisions des tribunaux arbitraux mixtes institués par les Traités de paix* (Paris), vol. VII, 1928, p. 655.

[230] A Working Group of the Third Committee of the General Assembly set out a somewhat confused explanation of the concept of "non-citizen" in a document of 24 October 1980 (*United Nations Juridical Yearbook, 1980* (see footnote 165 above), pp. 189–191).

it is the responsibility of each State to preserve its nationality, its citizenship and the other legal connections that link its *ressortissants* to it, by ensuring that they acquire, or are issued by its authorities, official documents attesting to their status, particularly civil registry documents, national identity cards and passports. It is not the responsibility of the expelling State to verify the authenticity of those documents, but of course that of the State to which the person being expelled claims to belong.

B. Expulsion

153. The word "expulsion" is generally used in a broad and non-specific sense to denote a set of measures or actions carried out with the aim or having the effect of compelling an individual to leave the territory of a State. Expulsion is thus understood in relation to a given territorial space or, more broadly, to the territory or territories over which the expelling State exercises sovereignty. Its exact meaning will be derived, on the one hand, by distinguishing it from certain closely related concepts, and by determining the exact role played by the crossing of the territorial frontier of the expelling State in the process of expulsion.

1. Expulsion and related concepts

154. The term "expulsion" exists side by side with many related terms that have points in common, some of which may form part of the expulsion process as envisaged in the context of the present topic, while others are quite distinct. Particular attention will be paid to the terms "deportation", "extradition", "removal", "escort to the border", "refoulement", "non-admission" and "transfer".

(a) *Deportation*

155. The term "deportation" has a specific historical background in that it is closely linked to certain dramatic events during the Second World War. In that context, and more generally in the context of the laws of war, it is understood as the forced displacement or forced transfer of individuals or groups of the civilian population—who are protected persons under the provisions of the Geneva Conventions of 12 August 1949—from an occupied territory. In that regard, the Charter of the International Military Tribunal at Nuremberg, contained in the Agreement for the prosecution and punishment of the major war criminals of the European Axis signed in London on 8 August 1945, refers to "the deportation to slave labour or for any other purpose of civilian population of or in occupied territory"[231] as one of the crimes coming within the jurisdiction of the Tribunal for which there shall be individual responsibility.

156. The principle is that "[i]ndividual or mass forcible transfers, as well as deportations of protected persons from occupied territory to the territory of the Occupying Power or to that of any other country, occupied or not, are prohibited".[232] In 1992 the Security Council expressed its "grave alarm" at reports of "mass forcible expulsion and deportation of civilians" within the territory of the former Yugoslavia and especially in Bosnia and Herzegovina.[233]

157. Outside this historical context and that of the law of war, the term "deportation" is not used in a uniform sense in international law. The terms "deportation" and "expulsion" appear to be regarded as interchangeable in Anglo-American practice, despite the fact that, technically, there is a difference between the two procedures. In international law a distinction is made between deportation, meaning the power of a State to expel an alien forcibly to any country chosen by the deporting State, and expulsion, meaning that an alien may be expelled from the territory of the expelling State, which should seek the agreement of the person to be expelled in determining the destination, which should in all cases be the State of which that person is a national/*ressortissant*.[234]

158. It has been suggested that the term "deportation" should be understood as meaning measures undertaken by the competent national authority to bring about the expulsion of aliens,[235] the rationale being that authors in the Anglo-Saxon legal system, as has been seen, use the words "expulsion" and "deportation" interchangeably to mean the same thing.[236] While this may not raise any particular semantic problems in the English language, the word is heavily freighted with connotations as a result of the historical context outlined above and is not understood in the same way in all languages. In particular, it would be difficult to convey in French the idea that deportation could be a simple auxiliary measure or the actual execution of the expulsion. Therefore, the Special Rapporteur proposes that the term "deportation" should be understood, at least as far as French is concerned, in the same sense in which it is used in the law of war, as described above, and its usage limited to that context.

(b) *Extradition*

159. Extradition is an institution of judicial cooperation between States. It is a legal mechanism whereby State A (the "requested State") voluntarily surrenders an

[231] Art. 6 (*b*), p. 288.

[232] Geneva Convention relative to the Protection of Civilian Persons in Time of War, art. 49. It is conceded, however, that "the Occupying Power may undertake total or partial evacuation of a given area if the security of the population or imperative military reasons so demand. Such evacuations may not involve the displacement of protected persons outside the bounds of the occupied territory except when for material reasons it is impossible to avoid such displacement. Persons thus evacuated shall be transferred back to their homes as soon as hostilities in the area in question have ceased" (*ibid.*); see also articles 70 and 147 of the same Convention.

[233] Security Council resolution 771 (1992).

[234] See Sohn and Buergenthal, *op. cit.*, p. 90, para. 12.03. Garner, *Black's Law Dictionary*, p. 471, defines the word "deportation" as "[t]he act or an instance of removing a person to another country; esp., the expulsion or transfer of an alien from a country". See also Garner, *A Dictionary of Modern Legal Usage*, pp. 266–267. This variation in the use of the term "deportation" can also be seen in some national legislation where it is barely distinguished from expulsion; for example, see the legislations of Nigeria, the Republic of Korea and Spain in A/CN.4/565 (footnote 61 above), para. 183, footnote 371.

[235] A/CN.4/565 (see footnote 61 above), para. 184.

[236] For example, Rewald speaks of "[e]xpulsion of aliens (which involves deportation and extradition)" ("Judicial control of administrative discretion in the expulsion and extradition of aliens", p. 451); "Governing rule 12", published in *Studies in Transnational Legal Policy*, vol. 23 (1992), p. 89, is entitled "Expulsion or deportation of aliens"; in the editorial note, "Constitutional restraints on the expulsion and exclusion of aliens", *Minnesota Law Review*, vol. XXXVII (1952–1953), p. 440, it is stated that: "Recent Supreme Court decisions have helped to crystallize the always-competing policies underlying the question of the constitutional restraints on the handling of the expulsion and exclusion powers. The number of deportations is increasing, and the Attorney General announced that he would exclude a long-time resident from re-entry into the country where he has made his home."

individual (in this case, a defendant) present on its territory to State B (the "requesting State") at the latter's request,[237] where that request is made with a view to instituting criminal proceedings or enforcing a sentence.[238]

160. Unlike expulsion, therefore, extradition is not a unilateral decision taken by one State. It is the response of one State (the requested State) to the request of another (the requesting State). Whereas expulsion is legally based on the domestic law of the expelling State, the legal basis of extradition does not derive in its entirety from the domestic legal order of the extraditing State; usually it is based on a combination of the national legislation of the States involved in the extradition procedure, together with the provisions of bilateral and multilateral international legal instruments. The mechanism is also underpinned by the principle of reciprocity. Pursuant to article 1 of the European Convention on Extradition, the "Contracting Parties undertake to surrender to each other, subject to the provisions and conditions laid down in this Convention, all persons against whom the competent authorities of the requesting Party are proceeding for an offence or who are wanted by the said authorities for the carrying out of a sentence or detention order".

161. When the obligation to extradite is laid down neither by treaty nor by customary law—as was claimed, for example, by Peru in the *Haya de la Torre* case[239]—whether or not to proceed with extradition is the sovereign decision of the requested State. Such a decision, however, is invariably taken in response to a request by the requesting State; a State may not extradite *proprio motu*. On the other hand, it may deny such a request, in particular when its own nationals are concerned. In a joint declaration appended to the order issued by ICJ on 14 April 1992 in response to the request for the indication of provisional measures in the *Lockerbie* case, four members of the Court wrote:

> 1. Before the Security Council became involved in the case the legal situation was, in our view, clear. The United Kingdom and the United States were entitled to request Libya to extradite the two Libyan nationals charged by the American and British authorities with having contributed to the destruction of the aeroplane lost in the Lockerbie incident. For this purpose they could take any action consistent with international law. For its part, Libya was entitled to refuse such an extradition and to recall in that connection that, in common with the law of many other countries, its domestic law prohibits the extradition of nationals.
>
> 2. In so far as general international law is concerned, extradition is a sovereign decision of the requested State, which is never under an obligation to carry it out.[240]

(c) *Removal*

162. Removal is a generic term encompassing the different ways or procedures of excluding an alien from a given country. Strictly speaking, it is not a legal term although it is commonly used in French legal literature on the expulsion of aliens.[241] The term "*éloignement*" (removal) is understood to refer both to "expulsion" and to what is known under French law as "*la reconduite à la frontière*" (escort to the border).[242]

163. Nevertheless, in addition to this distinction, based mainly on the different rules of procedure applicable to the two measures, it is also noted that "whatever the motive, the removal of aliens derives ... from a single legal regime, that of expulsion".[243]

164. Account should therefore be taken of the proposal made by the Special Rapporteur in his preliminary report on the expulsion of aliens[244] to use the terms "expulsion" and "removal" in a broad sense, a proposal approved by the Commission.[245]

(d) *Escort to the border*

165. Under French law, in which this term appears in the legislation on the entry and stay of aliens, a distinction is made between expulsion and escort to the border. The term "expulsion" is applied to the removal of aliens, with regular or irregular status, whose presence on French territory poses a serious threat to public order,[246] whereas the expression "escort to the border" refers to measures to remove aliens with irregular status with regard to the alien police legislation.[247] Like expulsion in the restricted sense used in French legislation, escort to the border is subject to the issue of an order, the difference being that the order is issued, not by the Minister of the Interior, but by the Commissioner of the Republic. Unlike those subjected to expulsion *sensu stricto*, aliens who are escorted to the border do not have the right of appeal to the Refugee Appeals

---

[237] Brownlie writes: "Where this co-operation rests on a procedure of request and consent, regulated by certain general principles, the form of international judicial assistance is called extradition." (*Principles of Public International Law*, p. 313)

[238] See, for example, Jennings and Watts, *op. cit.*, pp. 948–950, para. 415. While Gaja believes that extradition "may be considered as a subcategory of expulsion to which particular rules apply", he also acknowledges that, owing to its specific regime, it "is generally considered as a separate legal measure and as such is outside the scope" of any study on expulsion ("Expulsion of aliens: some old and new issues in international law", p. 291).

[239] *Haya de la Torre, Judgment, I.C.J. Reports 1951*, p. 71.

[240] Joint declaration of Judges Evensen, Tarassov, Guillaume and Aguilar Mawdsley, *Questions of Interpretation and Application of the 1971 Montreal Convention arising from the Aerial Incident at Lockerbie (Libyan Arab Jamahiriya* v. *United Kingdom), Provisional Measures, Order of 14 April 1992, I.C.J. Reports 1992*, p. 24.

[241] See, for example, D'Haëm, *La reconduite à la frontière des étrangers en situation irrégulière*. He refers to the consensus in France since 1981 on a specific procedure allowing for "the removal from French territory of aliens who have entered it and resided there in irregular conditions" (p. 3); to "escort to the border" as a "type of removal" with only temporary effect, and to the "effective removal of the clandestine alien" (p. 4); or of "aliens in the process of removal" (p. 5); see also Teitgen-Colly and Julien-Laferrière, "Chronique de législation: étrangers", pp. 927–929; and Lochak, "L'entrée et le séjour des étrangers en France: une législation sous influence", p. 595.

[242] D'Haëm, *op. cit.*, p. 3: he considers that "escort to the border" is a "special removal measure" as distinct "from the other removal measure that is expulsion".

[243] *Ibid.*, p. 5.

[244] A/CN.4/554 (see footnote 1 above).

[245] *Ibid.*, para. 13.

[246] See article 23 of Ordinance No. 45–2658 of 2 November 1945 on the conditions of entry and residence of aliens in France (*Journal officiel*, 4 November 1945).

[247] For the legal regime governing this concept in France, see in particular Ladhari, "La reconduite à la frontière des étrangers en situation irrégulière"; Abraham, *loc. cit.*, p. 91; Benoît-Rohmer, "Reconduite à la frontière: développements récents", p. 429; and D'Haëm, *op. cit.*, p. 3.

Commission, but may return to France, whereas expelled aliens must await the repeal of the order in question.[248]

166. This distinction is not altogether clear, however, inasmuch as under Act No. 80–9 of 10 January 1980, for example, escort to the border is regarded simply as a means of enforcing expulsion measures; article 6 of that law provides that "an expelled alien may be escorted to the border".[249] Nonetheless, both cases involve measures of "*éloignement*" to remove the alien from the territory, the rest being a matter of the procedure and legal force pertaining to each measure. Consequently, at least for the purposes of the topic in question, it is preferable not to make a distinction between "expulsion" and "escort to the border", but to consider the latter as one of a number of expulsion measures, in the broad sense of the term "expulsion".

(e) *Refoulement*

167. At first glance, it would appear that the term "refoulement" refers to the exclusion from a State's territory of recently arrived clandestine immigrants, whereas expulsion would apply to persons with legal status, asylum-seekers or those requesting refugee status, and possibly also to individuals with irregular status who have lived for a long time in the territory of the expelling State. More simply, refoulement could be regarded as applying to aliens with irregular status, whereas expulsion applies to aliens with legal status. Arguments for the latter line of reasoning can be found in the note on international protection presented by UNHCR on 9 August 1984, according to which "[t]he observance of the principle of non-refoulement is closely related to the determination of refugee status".[250] This statement might appear to suggest that there might be refoulement of a person refused refugee status and non-refoulement in the opposite situation. As shown by the title of article 33, "Prohibition of expulsion or return (refoulement)", of the Convention relating to the Status of Refugees, it is clear that the Convention distinguishes between the two terms; yet neither the content of article 33 nor that of article 1, containing the definition of the term "refugee", enables one to differentiate between the two expressions.[251]

168. Another distinction made between expulsion and refoulement is that expulsion is a measure taken to protect public order, resorted to only when the presence of an alien on the territory poses a serious threat to that order, whereas refoulement is a measure taken to remove an alien with irregular status: "The prohibition against expelling an alien solely on the grounds of having violated the regulations regarding stay does not mean that he or she is immune from any measure to remove him or her from the territory. Now, as before 1980, expulsion is being replaced by refoulement."[252] Commenting on the amendment of the Ordinance of 2 November 1945 by the Act of 10 January 1980, another author writes: "Aliens with irregular status are no longer subjected to refoulement, they are expelled."[253]

169. In any event, legal writers are not unanimous on this score, and the terminology is by no means sufficiently clear. For example, one author has written that the French law of 9 January 1980 on the prevention of clandestine immigration reduced France's obligations under the relevant international conventions "merely to a prohibition against refoulement or expulsion towards a territory where the life or freedom of the persons concerned would be threatened".[254] The same author adds that the situation of candidates for refugee status is relatively uncertain and in no way prevents an expulsion order being issued;[255] that most requests for refugee status are rejected, after an appeal—with suspensive effect—before the Refugee Appeals Commission; and that it becomes difficult, after a long period of three years, reduced in 1985 to one year "to return [*refouler*] those concerned", many of whom disappear without trace.[256] With regard to the candidates for refugee status in a well-known case brought before the Administrative Court of Pau, this author writes that "the individuals concerned, who were neither returned *manu militari* nor escorted to the border, were better treated than many asylum-seekers".[257]

170. As can be seen, no real terminological distinction can be drawn among the three terms "expulsion", "escort to the border" and "refoulement"; they are used interchangeably, without any particular semantic rigour. The word "expulsion" will consequently be used in the context of the present topic as a generic term to mean all situations covered by all three terms and many others, such

[248] Guimezanes, "La loi du 9 septembre 1986 sur les conditions d'entrée et de séjour des étrangers en France", para. 15.

[249] *Journal officiel de la République française*, 11 January 1980, p. 71; see also Turpin, "La réforme de l'ordonnance du 2 novembre 1945 sur la condition des étrangers par la loi du 10 janvier 1980", p. 41; and Vincent, "Le nouveau régime de l'entrée et du séjour des étrangers en France", p. 363.

[250] *Official Records of the United Nations General Assembly, Thirty-fifth Session*, document A/AC.96/643, para. 17.

[251] See also the Convention against torture and other cruel, inhuman or degrading treatment or punishment, art. 3; the Declaration on Territorial Asylum (footnote 95 above), art. 3, para. 1; the OAU Convention governing the specific aspects of refugee problems in Africa, art. II, para. 3; and the American Convention on Human Rights: "Pact of San José, Costa Rica", art. 22, para. 8.

[252] Vincent, "La réforme de l'expulsion des étrangers par la loi du 29 octobre 1981".

[253] Turpin, "La réforme …", p. 42.

[254] *Ibid.*, "Les nouvelles conditions de l'expulsion des réfugiés", p. 140.

[255] *Ibid.*

[256] *Ibid.*, p. 141.

[257] *Ibid.* It should be pointed out that a person who is subjected to refoulement because he or she has been refused admission could run the risk of persecution in his or her country of origin. What can be done? Not yet having the status of refugee, that person ought not to be entitled to benefit from the provisions of article 33, paragraph 1, of the Convention relating to the Status of Refugees. It is this interpretation that seems to have inspired the United States Supreme Court in the case *Sale* v. *Haitian Centers Council* (opinion of 21 June 1993, ILM, vol. XXXII, No. 4 (July 1993), pp. 1052 *et. seq.*); see, however, the contrary opinion of Gaja, who bases his critique in particular on a report of the Inter-American Commission on Human Rights, according to which "the United States Government [had] breached its treaty obligations in respect of Article 33" of the Convention "because this provision has 'no geographical limitations'" (*loc. cit.*, p. 291). This interpretation is no doubt correct from the standpoint of the protection of human rights. But if it is considered that refoulement is a consequence of the non-admission, and since the non-admission concerns aliens who have not yet entered the territory of the State carrying out the refoulement—in other words aliens who have not yet crossed the frontier, as it is defined for the purposes of the present topic, then one cannot impose on the State refusing to admit an alien the same obligations that it would have in cases of expulsion; it must be agreed, therefore, that non-admission and expulsion are not the same thing. This, at least, is the conclusion reached by the Special Rapporteur with regard to the exact content of each of these two concepts.

as "return of an alien to a country"[258] or "exclusion of an alien",[259] this list not being exhaustive.

(f) *Non-admission*

171. A sovereign State is always free to refuse any alien access to its territory.[260] Accordingly, the preamble of the International Rules on the Admission and Expulsion of Aliens adopted by the Institute of International Law on 9 September 1892 proclaimed that "for each State, the right to admit or not admit aliens to its territory or to admit them only conditionally or to expel them is a logical consequence … of its independence".[261]

172. This sovereign right of a State to oppose entry to its territory by undesirable aliens, or those not meeting the conditions set by the laws on entry and stay, is valid even for aliens who have formally filed an application for refugee status[262] while they remain in the international zone and in centres where candidates for admission to the country's territory are detained. The criterion of crossing the frontier or entering the territory is important for distinguishing non-admission from expulsion in the broad sense since, in the view of the Special Rapporteur, aliens who have crossed the immigration control barriers and are in the territory of the receiving State, outside the special zones where candidates for admission are detained, may be subject only to expulsion and no longer to non-admission.

173. Refusal of admission may consist in an express decision by the competent authorities of the State to which the request for admission is made, or in the refusal to grant a visa, a necessary but not sufficient condition for access to the territory of most States. In general, diplomatic and consular authorities have the discretionary power to refuse or grant a visa to an alien who requests it.[263] The decision to refuse entry to the alien may be executed *ex officio* by the administration,[264] in other words without the need for a court decision. This lies outside the scope of expulsion even in the broad sense. Non-admission therefore does not fall within the scope of the definition of expulsion for the purposes of this topic.

(g) *Transfer, surrender, rendition*

174. Like expulsion, transfer describes the forced movement of individuals from one State to another, in other words, beyond its frontier. It differs, however, not only from exclusion, which is a sovereign decision made by the expelling State on the basis of domestic legal procedures, but also from extradition, which, as was seen earlier, is a special institution combining rules of domestic law with the rules of international treaty or customary law. Technically speaking, transfer consists in making an individual available to the jurisdiction of a foreign State or an international jurisdiction that requests it, so that the individual may appear in person or give evidence or assist in an investigation. In principle, such a procedure requires an international treaty that obliges all the States parties to carry out such a transfer. According to the Model Treaty on Mutual Assistance in Criminal Matters adopted by the General Assembly in 1990, a person in custody may be transferred to the requesting State, subject to his or her consent and if the requested State agrees and its law so permits.[265]

175. In recent years the practice of transfer has developed as a result of the setting up of international criminal courts. In accordance with the international legal instruments relating to these courts, a State may transfer an individual to the International Tribunal for the Former Yugoslavia, the International Tribunal for Rwanda and the International Criminal Court.[266] Pursuant to the Rules of Procedure and Evidence of the International Tribunal for the Former Yugoslavia,[267] the Tribunal may request the transfer of a suspect (rule 40 *bis*) or a witness (rule 90 *bis*).[268] The Rome Statute of the International Criminal Court uses the term "surrender" (*remise*) when referring to the transfer of an individual by a State to the Court.[269] It should be noted that in the draft statute for an international criminal court, adopted by the Commission in 1994, the term "transfer" (*transfert*) is used to cover all cases where suspects are made available to the court in order to be tried.[270]

176. There have been certain abuses in the practice of transfer. There have been cases of "extrajudicial transfer" of individuals arrested in a foreign country and then taken

[258] Term found, for example, in the pleading of the Government Commissioner (Abraham, *loc. cit.*, p. 93) alongside the expression "escort to the border" (*ibid.*, p. 90); see also D'Haëm, *op. cit.*, p. 111.

[259] Expression commonly used in the English-language legal literature; see, for example, "Constitutional restraints on the expulsion and exclusion of aliens" (footnote 236 above); see also the PCIJ advisory opinion, *Treatment of Polish Nationals* ... (footnote 174 above).

[260] See Boeck, *loc. cit.*, p. 456; see also Guimezanes, *loc. cit.*, para. 5.

[261] *Annuaire de l'Institut de droit international* (see footnote 68 above), p. 219. It went on: "Considering, however, that humanity and justice oblige States to exercise this right while respecting, to the extent compatible with their own security, the rights and freedom of aliens who wish to enter their territory or who are already there."

[262] Turpin, "Les nouvelle conditions …", p. 141.

[263] See, for example, Chaltiel, "Le juge administratif, juge de l'immigration", p. 168; and Lochak, *loc. cit.*, p. 592; see also the ruling of the Council of State of France handed down on 28 February 1986 in Ngako Jeuga, *Recueil des décisions du Conseil d'État statuant au Contentieux, et du Tribunal des Conflits, et des jugements des Tribunaux administratifs* (Paris, Sirey, 1986), p. 49.

[264] See Genevois, "Un statut constitutionnnel pour les étrangers", annex, Constitutional Council of France, decision No. 93–325 DC of 13 August 1993, p. 888, para. 5.

[265] General Assembly resolution 45/117 of 14 December 1990, annex, art. 13, para. 1.

[266] For example, the transfer by Serbia and Montenegro of Slobodan Milosevic, former President of the Federal Republic of Yugoslavia, to the International Tribunal for the Former Yugoslavia; the transfer by Cameroon of Théoneste Bagosora to the International Tribunal for Rwanda; the transfer by the Democratic Republic of the Congo of a Congolese warlord from the Ituri region to the International Criminal Court in 2006; the transfer by Nigeria in 2006 of Charles Taylor, former President of Liberia, to the Special Court for Sierra Leone in The Hague.

[267] See IT/32/Rev.38.

[268] A detained witness shall be transferred in accordance with the request of the Tribunal, conditional on his or her return within the period decided by the Tribunal (rule 90 *bis* (A)). In the case of a suspect, on the other hand, the total period of detention shall in no case exceed 90 days, at the end of which, in the event the indictment has not been confirmed and an arrest warrant signed, the suspect shall be released or be delivered to the authorities of the requested State (rule 40 *bis* (D)).

[269] Art. 59.

[270] *Yearbook ... 1994*, vol. II (Part Two), p. 63, art. 53.

to the United States to answer criminal charges.[271] Such abuses have increased with the struggle against international terrorism, and have taken the form of what has been called "extraordinary transfer" or "extraordinary rendition", a variant of—albeit different from—"extrajudicial transfer". In both cases, United States courts have tended to overlook the circumstances of arrest. Nevertheless, when they arrive in the United States, suspects in cases of "traditional"—so to speak—extrajudicial transfer benefit from normal due process for criminal cases, whereas in cases of "extraordinary transfer" no rules apply and the rule of law is totally absent: usually suspected of terrorism, the detained individual is held incommunicado and has no rights.[272] The United States Supreme Court recently called for a return to legality with regard to the individuals detained at Guantánamo Bay, Cuba.[273]

177. Whether it is consistent with or lies outside international law, the concept of transfer does not fall within the scope of expulsion in the meaning of the present topic: on the one hand, because its legal basis lies totally within the international legal order—unlike expulsion; on the other hand, because transfer concerns the nationals of the transferring State as well as aliens residing in its territory, whereas expulsion concerns only aliens, it being a well-established principle that no State may expel its own nationals.

2. Territory, frontier and expulsion

178. Expulsion entails the idea of the forced displacement of an individual outside the known limits of one place to another place. When considered with regard to States, it refers to the displacement of an individual under constraint beyond the territorial frontier of the expelling State to a State of destination. It now has to be determined what is meant by a State's territory and its frontier in the context of the present topic.

(a) *Territory*

179. The territory of a State may be described as being "the land surface and its vertical extensions, which are the subsoil, on the one hand, and the airspace over the subjacent surface, on the other".[274] This representation of territory combines, as can be seen, the notion of territory *sensu stricto*, derived from the word "terra", and that of space, referring to airspace. Although it is qualified as "comprehensive",[275] this definition does not cover all the spaces that may be included in the notion of territory. Territory also contains other maritime spaces under a State's sovereignty, such as its internal waters (including estuaries and small bays) and territorial sea, in addition to its superjacent airspace.[276]

180. According to a definition that is compatible with all aspects of a State's territorial sovereignty and which, in the view of the Special Rapporteur, is relevant to the present topic, territory is understood to be the space where "the State exercises all of the powers deriving from sovereignty";[277] it therefore excludes spaces where it exercises only sovereign rights or functional jurisdiction, such as the continental shelf and the contiguous zone, fishing zone and exclusive economic zone.

181. International law does not require that the territory of a State belong to one single holder, or even that its various land or island components be situated in the same geographic area in the vicinity of the main part of the State. Historically, enclaves and territorial corridors have been known to exist and even now, several former colonial and non-colonial Powers possess island or continental territorial dependencies in several regions of the world.

182. While the delimitation of State territory is not legally required in order for a State to exist, there is no doubt that defining a territory means defining its frontiers, as ICJ pointed out in the *Territorial Dispute* case.[278]

(b) *Frontier*

183. The term "frontier" has been defined empirically as "a line determining where the territories of two neighbouring States respectively begin and end".[279] But a frontier does not separate only neighbouring States; it also separates a State from all other States, neighbouring or distant. In this regard, the frontier is not only a physical line separating territorial areas. It is an international limit of State sovereignty and jurisdiction.[280] As the arbitral tribunal charged with determining the maritime boundary between Guinea-Bissau and Senegal indicated, an international boundary is the line formed by a series of points delineating the furthest limits within which the legal order of a State is applicable,[281] be it a land or maritime border.

---

[271] For example, the case of Manuel Noriega, the former Head of State of Panama, abducted in his country and transferred to the United States to answer primarily drug trafficking charges.

[272] On this distinction between "extrajudicial transfer" and "extraordinary transfer" or "extraordinary rendition", see the article, "Torture, American style", by Bob Herbert in *The New York Times*, 11 February 2005; and the initial findings of the report drafted at the request of the European Union on the complicity of some European countries in this type of transfer (or rendition) practised by the United States via Europe since the second war between the coalition and Iraq in 2003 (Council of Europe, Parliamentary Assembly, Committee on Legal Affairs and Human Rights, "Alleged secret detentions and unlawful inter-state transfers of detainees involving Council of Europe member states", available at http://assembly.coe.int). It should be highlighted that the same reasoning led the United States authorities to surrender to the Syrian authorities Maher Arar, a 34-year-old Canadian national of Syrian origin, arrested at J. F. Kennedy airport, New York, in September 2002.

[273] A decision of the United States Supreme Court of 29 June 2006 declared unconstitutional the military courts set up to try the Guantanamo prisoners and recommended that President George W. Bush work with Congress to find a solution to replace them. In a memorandum dated 7 July 2006, the Deputy Secretary of Defense, Mr. Gordon England, said that the Supreme Court had determined that article 3, common to all four Geneva Conventions of 12 August 1949, "applies as a matter of law to the conflict with Al Qaeda" (www.defense.gov) and by extension to the Guantanamo detainees (see also *Le Monde*, 13 July 2006).

[274] Rousseau, *Droit international public*, pp. 36–37.

[275] *Ibid.*, p. 37.

[276] See, on this point, the ICJ judgment of 27 June 1986 in *Military and Paramilitary Activities in and against Nicaragua (Nicaragua* v. *United States of America), Merits, Judgment, I.C.J. Reports 1986*, p. 111, para. 212.

[277] Daillier and Pellet, *op. cit.*, p. 414, para. 270.

[278] *Territorial Dispute (Libyan Arab Jamahiriya/Chad), Judgment, I.C.J. Reports 1994*, p. 20, para. 38.

[279] Basdevant, *Dictionnaire de la terminologie du droit international*, p. 293.

[280] *Black's Law Dictionary* defines boundary as "[a] line marking the limit of the territorial jurisdiction of a state or other entity having an international status" (Garner, p. 198).

[281] Decision of 31 July 1989, case concerning the delimitation of maritime boundary between Guinea-Bissau and Senegal, UNRIAA, vol. XX (Sales No. E/F.93.V.3), p. 119. Also published in RGDIP,

184. The legal regime of the frontier derives as much from the rules of international law as from those of the domestic law of each State regarding entry into and departure from the territory. However, this legal regime can also be established by mutual agreement of the States in a constructed legal space. Thus, the European Union member States parties to the Schengen acquis—Agreement between the Governments of the States of the Benelux Economic Union, the Federal Republic of Germany and the French Republic on the gradual abolition of checks at their common borders, and the Convention implementing it, decided gradually to abolish checks at their common borders;[282] however, its provisions were not, according to the Constitutional Council of France, "comparable to the abolition or modification of the frontiers that legally delimit the territorial jurisdiction of the State".[283]

185. After careful consideration, perhaps a combination of the frontier line and the concept of frontier zone, at times criticized,[284] to be sure, but reinterpreted and adapted in the context of this topic, corresponds better to the concept of frontier in relation to admission or non-admission and expulsion of aliens. The frontier understood as a territorial limit outside of which the expelling State wishes to place the alien is a multifunctional zone comprising a group of carefully delineated areas with varying legal status. The issue comes down to official points of entry and departure. Whereas illegal immigration is the clandestine breach by an alien of the frontier at any possible point, expulsion generally only happens through official points of entry and departure, including ports, airports and land frontier posts. These official points of entry and departure include checkpoints and, in international airports and certain ports, special areas for the detention of aliens denied entry or in the process of expulsion, and international areas where aliens are considered still outside the territory. The expelled alien held in a special area at an airport, port or land frontier post while waiting to be placed on board a plane, ship or vehicle is already expelled from the legal standpoint, which does not alter the obligation to respect the dignity and the fundamental rights attached to the alien as a human being.

186. In this regard, the frontier cannot be treated as a line, but as a zone with limits fixed by State regulations according to the areas that are established there. It is a zone of limits. The crossing of the line by the expelled person takes but a moment, though it is certainly critical to the process of expulsion. Therefore it could be said that, for the purposes of this topic, the frontier of a State comprises the zone at the limits of the territory of a State in which a national of another State no longer benefits from the status of resident alien and beyond which the national expulsion procedure is completed.

3. Constituent elements of expulsion

187. Expulsion is an act of the expelling State. Can it also be the conduct of that State? It is, in any case, coercive in nature.

(a) *Act or conduct*

188. In the domestic law of most States, expulsion is a unilateral act by the State, taking the form of a unilateral administrative act, since it is a decision of administrative authorities.[285] It is a formal act that may be contested before the courts of the expelling State, since expulsion is a procedural process, each stage of which can be contested.

189. Does expulsion therefore presuppose a formal measure in every case? As noted by Gaja, it seems that it should also be considered that expulsion occurs even in the absence of a formal legal act, as soon as a State creates the conditions making life impossible for the person in question. In practice, there seems to be little difference between a formal measure of expulsion and State conduct designed to force an individual from its territory, since in both cases the person in question must leave. "It seems reasonable to encompass both cases within the concept of expulsion."[286]

190. In this regard, the author draws support for his argument from two awards by the Iran–United States Claims Tribunal. In *International Technical Products Corporation* v. *The Government of the Islamic Republic of Iran*, the Tribunal accepted,

> in principle, the possibility that the constituent elements of expulsion ("removal, either 'voluntarily', under threat of forcible removal or forcibly") can be fulfilled in exceptional cases even where the alien leaves the country without being directly and immediately forced or officially ordered to do so. Such cases would seem to presuppose at least (1) that the circumstances in the country of residence are such that the alien cannot reasonably be regarded as having any real choice, and (2) that behind the events or acts leading to the departure there is an intention of having the alien ejected and these acts, moreover, are attributable to the State in accordance with principles of state responsibility.[287]

191. In the case of *Jack Rankin* v. *The Islamic Republic of Iran*, the Iran-United States Claims Tribunal noted that upon his return to Iran in February 1979, the Ayatollah Khomeini had called for the departure of all aliens and, consequently, his Government had implemented a policy that had forced numerous aliens to leave the Islamic Republic of Iran. The Tribunal added:

> However, it does not automatically follow that all U.S. nationals who departed from Iran ... after the implementation of this policy were wrongfully expelled. It is necessary to examine the circumstances of each departure and to identify the general and specific acts relied on

vol. XCIV (1990), p. 253. See further the arbitral award of 13 October 1995 in the *Laguna del Desierto* case concerning a boundary dispute between Argentina and Chile on the delimitation of the frontier line between boundary post 62 and Mount Fitzroy, UNRIAA, vol. XXII (Sales No. E/F.00.V.7), p. 153; and *Frontier Dispute (Benin/ Niger), Judgment, I.C.J. Reports 2005*, p. 142, para. 124.

[282] See Daillier and Pellet, *op. cit.*, p. 465, para. 298.

[283] Constitutional Council, decision No. 91–294 DC of 25 July 1991, *Journal Officiel*, No. 174 (27 July 1991).

[284] See the arbitral award of 16 November 1957 in the case concerning *Lake Lanoux*, UNRIAA, vol. XII (Sales No. 63.V.3), p. 307, and compare the arbitral award of 19 February 1968 in the case concerning the *Indo-Pakistan Western Boundary (Rann of Kutch)* between India and Pakistan, *ibid.*, vol. XVII (Sales No. E/F.80.V.2), pp. 1–576.

[285] In the *Diallo* case, pending before ICJ, expulsion was pronounced by a decision of the Prime Minister at the time (see footnote 21 above).

[286] Gaja, *loc. cit.*, p. 290.

[287] *International Technical Products Corporation* v. *The Government of the Islamic Republic of Iran*, award of 19 August 1985, *Iran-United States Claims Tribunal Reports*, vol. 9 (1987), p. 18.

and evidenced to determine how they affected or motivated at that time the individual who now is alleging expulsion and whether such acts are attributable to Iran.[288]

192. Therefore, when a formal act of expulsion has been taken by a State, it is necessary to establish, on the basis of the examination of facts or of the circumstances of the departure of the person in question from the host State, if the conduct having brought about this departure is attributable to the State.[289] Expulsion will therefore be understood within the context of this topic as an act or conduct of a State that compels an alien to leave its territory.

(b) *Constraint*

193. Expulsion is never an act or event requested by the expelled person, nor is it an act or event to which the expelled person consents. It is a formal measure or a situation of irresistible force that compels the person in question to leave the territory of the expelling State. This element of constraint is important in that it distinguishes expulsion from normal or ordinary departure of the alien from the territory. This is the element that arouses the attention or interest not only of the State of destination of the expelled person, but also of third States with respect to the situation thus created to the extent that the exercise of this incontestable right of a State places at issue the protection of fundamental human rights. Even before the violence perpetrated by some members of the security forces during the execution of expulsion orders, the formal measure ordering the expulsion is an injunction and hence a legal constraint, just as the conduct which forces the alien to depart is a constraint in that it is physically experienced as such.

194. An attempt has been made to differentiate the two concepts of "expulsion" and "alien". Now the challenge is to connect them in order to elicit their meaning and also the sense of some key concepts that will enable more efficient treatment of the topic. In the light of the above exposition, the following article devoted to definitions can be proposed:

"*Article 2. Definitions*

"For the purposes of the present draft articles:

"1. The expulsion of an alien means the act or conduct by which an expelling State compels a *ressortissant* of another State to leave its territory.

"2. It is understood that:

"(*a*) an alien means a *ressortissant* of a State other than the territorial or expelling State;

"(*b*) expulsion means an act or conduct by which the expelling State compels an alien to leave its territory;

"(*c*) frontier means the zone at the limits of the territory of an expelling State in which the alien no longer enjoys resident status and beyond which the national expulsion procedure is completed;

"(*d*) *ressortissant* means any person who, by any legal bond including nationality, comes under [the jurisdiction] [the personal jurisdiction] of a State;

"(*e*) territory means the domain in which the State exercises all the powers deriving from its sovereignty."

---

[288] *Jack Rankin* v. *The Islamic Republic of Iran*, award of 3 November 1987, *Iran-United States Claims Tribunal Reports*, vol. 17 (1988), pp. 147–148; see also *Alfred L. W. Short* v. *The Islamic Republic of Iran*, award of 14 July 1987, *ibid.*, vol. 16 (1988), pp. 85–86. The mechanism of attribution is explained by article 8 of the articles on responsibility of States for internationally wrongful acts of which the General Assembly took note in 2001 in its resolution 56/83 (see *Yearbook ... 2001*, vol. II (Part Two), p. 26, para. 76).

[289] See Gaja, *loc. cit.*, p. 290.

THE EFFECTS OF ARMED CONFLICTS ON TREATIES

[Agenda item 9]

DOCUMENT A/CN.4/570*

Second report on the effect of armed conflicts on treaties, by Mr. Ian Brownlie, Special Rapporteur

[*Original: English*]
[*16 June 2006*]

CONTENTS

Multilateral instruments cited in the present report

	Source
Geneva Conventions for the protection of war victims (Geneva, 12 August 1949)	United Nations, *Treaty Series*, vol. 75, Nos. 970–973, pp. 31 *et seq.*
Geneva Convention for the Amelioration of the Condition of the Wounded and Sick in Armed Forces in the Field	*Ibid.*, No. 970, p. 31.
Geneva Convention for the Amelioration of the Condition of Wounded, Sick and Shipwrecked Members of Armed Forces at Sea	*Ibid.*, No. 971, p. 85.
Geneva Convention relative to the Treatment of Prisoners of War	*Ibid.*, No. 972, p. 135.
Geneva Convention relative to the Protection of Civilian Persons in Time of War	*Ibid.*, No. 973, p. 287.
Vienna Convention on the Law of Treaties (Vienna, 23 May 1969)	*Ibid.*, vol. 1155, No. 18232, p. 331.
Vienna Convention on the Law of Treaties between States and International Organizations or between International Organizations (Vienna, 21 March 1986)	*Official Records of the United Nations Conference on the Law of Treaties between States and International Organizations or between International Organizations*, vol. II (United Nations publication, Sales No. E.94.V.5).

* Incorporating A/CN.4/570/Corr.1.

Introduction

1. The purpose of the present report is to present the first seven draft articles of the original draft, contained in the first report on the effects of armed conflicts on treaties,[1] submitted in 2005 at the fifty-seventh session of the International Law Commission, with reference to issues raised in the subsequent debates in the Commission and the Sixth Committee of the General Assembly. The presentation of the first seven draft articles would seem to be a practical way of moving forward. The Special Rapporteur had, during the debate at the fifty-seventh session of the Commission, emphasized that the first presentation was provisional in character and did not involve a rush to judgement.[2]

[1] *Yearbook ... 2005*, vol. II (Part One), document A/CN.4/552, p. 209.

[2] *Ibid.*, vol. II (Part Two), p. 28, para. 124.

CHAPTER I

Preliminary issues

2. The responses to the first report on the effects of conflicts on treaties have helped to clarify a number of issues.

3. Several delegations favoured the inclusion of treaties concluded by international organizations (China,[3] Indonesia,[4] Jordan,[5] Morocco,[6] Nigeria,[7] and Poland.[8] During the debate in the Commission, several members supported the inclusion of such treaties.[9] However, there was no general agreement that this was necessary and reference was made to article 74, paragraph 1, of the Vienna Convention on the Law of Treaties between States and International Organizations or between International Organizations.

4. General support was expressed for the view of the Special Rapporteur that the topic should form part of the law of treaties and not part of the law relating to the use of force. As the topical summary of the discussion held in the Sixth Committee during its sixtieth session (A/CN.4/560, para. 47) indicates, at the same time it was observed that the subject was closely related to other domains of international law, such as international humanitarian law, self-defence and State responsibility.

[3] *Official Records of the General Assembly, Sixtieth Session, Sixth Committee*, 18th meeting, para. 8.

[4] *Ibid.*, 20th meeting, para. 9.

[5] *Ibid.*, 19th meeting, para. 32.

[6] *Ibid.*, 11th meeting, para. 41.

[7] *Ibid.*, 20th meeting, para. 47.

[8] *Ibid.*, 19th meeting, para. 20.

[9] *Yearbook ... 2005*, vol. II (Part Two), p. 29, para. 129.

CHAPTER II

Draft articles

Draft article 1. Scope

The present draft articles apply to the effects of an armed conflict in respect of treaties between States.

5. In the Sixth Committee the view was expressed that, since article 25 of the Vienna Convention on the Law of Treaties (hereinafter the 1969 Vienna Convention) allowed for the provisional application of treaties, it seemed advisable that the draft articles should apply to treaties that were being provisionally applied.[10]

6. In the Commission it was suggested that a distinction be made between States which are Contracting Parties, under article 2, paragraph (1) (*f*), of the 1969 Vienna Convention, and those which are not. While some members preferred including treaties which had not yet entered into force, others considered that only treaties in force at the time of the conflict should be covered by the draft articles.[11]

[10] Comment by the Netherlands, *Official Records of the General Assembly, Sixtieth Session, Sixth Committee*, 18th meeting, para. 40.

Draft article 2. Use of terms

For the purposes of the present draft articles:

(*a*) "Treaty" means an international agreement concluded between States in written form and governed by international law, whether embodied in a single instrument or in two or more related instruments, and whatever its particular designation;

(*b*) "Armed conflict" means a state of war or a conflict which involves armed operations which by their nature or extent are likely to affect the operation of treaties between States parties to the armed conflict or between States parties to the armed conflict and third States, regardless of a formal declaration of war or other declaration by any or all of the parties to the armed conflict.

[11] *Yearbook ... 2005*, vol. II (Part Two), p. 29, para. 130.

A. Treaty

7. This formulation did not provoke any comment.

B. Armed conflict

8. This definition of armed conflict was examined in the first report.[12] The draft articles proposed by the Special Rapporteur include the effect on treaties of internal conflicts. At the same time, a proportion of the doctrine regards the distinction between international armed conflict and non-international armed conflict as basic in character, and would exclude the latter for present purposes.

9. This question provoked marked differences of opinion in the Sixth Committee. Five delegations were opposed to the inclusion of internal armed conflicts (Algeria,[13] Austria,[14] China,[15] Indonesia[16] and the Islamic Republic of Iran[17]). Six delegations were in favour of including non-international armed conflicts (Greece,[18] Morocco,[19] Nigeria,[20] the Netherlands,[21] Poland[22] and Slovakia[23]). The policy considerations which should apply point in different directions. If the principle of continuity were to be adopted, then the inclusion of non-international armed conflicts would militate in favour of stability. However, the principle of continuity is in many ways conditional, and widening the breadth of the definition of armed conflict would increase the scope of the problem.

10. A number of sources relating to the task of definition were invoked, as follows:

(*a*) The *Prosecutor* v. *Duško Tadić*: "[A]n armed conflict exists whenever there is a resort to armed force between States or protracted armed violence between governmental authorities and organized armed groups or between such groups within a State";[24]

(*b*) The 1969 Vienna Convention (art. 73), refers to "the outbreak of hostilities between States";

(*c*) There is the possible relevance of the report of the High-level Panel on Threats, Challenges and Change (A/59/565 and Corr.1, sect. IV).

11. Two other points should be borne in mind. The first was made by the Netherlands delegation:

> The final point to be raised in relation to the definition of armed conflict is that military occupations should indeed be included, even if not accompanied by protracted armed violence or armed operations. The fact that a State is under occupation can affect its ability to fulfil its treaty obligations. This is in keeping with the relevant provisions of international humanitarian law, notably article 2 of the four Geneva Conventions of 1949, which is *lex specialis* in this field. If such an occupation is sufficient to trigger the applicability of the specific norms related to armed conflicts, then it would also seem sufficient to trigger the applicability of the draft articles on the effect of armed conflicts on treaties. In this regard, the decision of the Special Rapporteur to include a reference in draft article 5, paragraph 1, of international humanitarian law as *lex specialis* is worthy of support.[25]

12. A concern was expressed during the debate at the fifty-seventh session of the Commission that the language proposed by the Special Rapporteur applied to situations that might fall outside the ordinary concept of armed conflict, such as violent acts by drug cartels, criminal gangs and domestic terrorists. However, the wording of draft article 2 (*a*), is intended to avoid such mischaracterizations. It is surely obvious that the application of the concept of "armed conflict" must be appropriately contextual. If this involves "circularity", as contended by some members of the Commission, then so be it.

13. The definition of armed conflict should be dealt with on a pragmatic basis. It would be helpful if a general indication on the inclusion or not of non-international armed conflicts could be obtained from the plenary. It must be clear that it would be inappropriate to seek to frame a definition of "armed conflict" for all departments of public international law.

Draft article 3. Ipso facto *termination or suspension*

The outbreak of an armed conflict does not *ipso facto* terminate or suspend the operation of treaties as:

(*a*) Between the parties to the armed conflict;

(*b*) Between one or more parties to the armed conflict and a third State.

14. The precise origin and significance of draft article 3 is explained in the first report on the effects of armed conflicts on treaties.[26] Draft article 3 is the most significant product of the resolution adopted by the Institute of International Law in 1985.[27] The majority of the delegations in the Sixth Committee did not find draft article 3 to be problematical. Austria expressed the view that the underlying concept of draft article 3 "constituted the point of departure of the whole set of draft articles".[28] There is considerable support for the view that the formulation "*ipso facto*" should be replaced with "necessarily".[29]

15. As the Special Rapporteur explained to the Commission, the purpose of draft article 3 is essentially constitutional, and the operative provisions are in draft articles 4–7. Thus, in the report of the Commission it is stated that:

> The Special Rapporteur characterized draft article 3 as being primarily expository in nature: in the light of the wording of subsequent

[12] *Yearbook ... 2005* (see footnote 1 above), P. 215, paras. 16–22.

[13] *Official Records of the General Assembly, Sixtieth Session, Sixth Committee*, 20th meeting, para. 64.

[14] *Ibid.*, 18th meeting, para. 26.

[15] *Ibid.*, para. 8.

[16] *Ibid.*, 20th meeting, para. 9.

[17] *Ibid.*, 18th meeting, para. 2.

[18] *Ibid.*, 19th meeting, para. 36.

[19] *Ibid.*, 11th meeting, para. 41.

[20] *Ibid.*, 20th meeting, para. 47.

[21] *Ibid.*, 18th meeting, paras. 43–44.

[22] *Ibid.*, 19th meeting, para. 18.

[23] *Ibid.*, para. 45.

[24] *The Prosecutor* v. *Duško Tadić a/k/a/ "DULE"*, case No. IT–94–1–AR72, International Tribunal for the Former Yugoslavia, Appeals Chamber, decision on the defence motion for interlocutory appeal on jurisdiction (2 October 1995), para. 70. See also ILM, vol. XXXV, No. 1 (January 1996), p. 32.

[25] Summarized in *Official Records of the General Assembly, Sixtieth Session, Sixth Committee*, 18th meeting, para. 44.

[26] *Yearbook ... 2005* (see footnote 1 above), paras. 25–28.

[27] Institute of International Law, *Yearbook*, vol. 61, part II, session of Helsinki 1985 (Paris, Pedone, 1986), pp. 278–283.

[28] *Official Records of the General Assembly, Sixtieth Session, Sixth Committee*, 18th meeting, para. 27.

[29] For the debate in the Commission see *Yearbook ... 2005*, vol. II (Part Two), pp. 30–31, paras. 142–148.

articles, particularly draft article 4, it was not strictly necessary. Its purpose was merely to emphasize that the earlier position, according to which armed conflict automatically abrogated treaty relations, had been replaced by a more contemporary view according to which the mere outbreak of armed conflict, whether declared war or not, did not *ipso facto* terminate or suspend treaties in force between parties to the conflict. He would, however, not oppose the deletion of the provision if the Commission so desired. Its formulation was based on article 2 of the resolution adopted by the Institute of International Law in 1985.[30]

16. And further:

While support was expressed for the Special Rapporteur's proposal, some members pointed out that there existed examples of instances of practice, referred to both in the Special Rapporteur's report and the Secretariat's memorandum, that appeared to suggest that armed conflicts cause the automatic suspension of various categories of treaty relations, in whole or in part. Indeed, it was suggested that the articles should not rule out the possibility of automatic suspension or termination in some cases. In terms of another suggestion, the provision could simply state that the outbreak of armed conflict did not necessarily terminate or suspend the operation of any treaty.[31]

17. In conclusion, and further by way of emphasis, draft article 3 is only a precursor to draft articles 4–7.

Draft article 4. The indicia of susceptibility to termination or suspension of treaties in case of an armed conflict

1. The susceptibility to termination or suspension of treaties in case of an armed conflict is determined in accordance with the intention of the parties at the time the treaty was concluded.

2. The intention of the parties to a treaty relating to its susceptibility to termination or suspension shall be determined in accordance:

(*a*) With the provisions of articles 31 and 32 of the Vienna Convention on the Law of Treaties; and

(*b*) The nature and extent of the armed conflict in question.

18. Draft article 4 represents the mode of practical implementation of the principle affirmed in draft article 3. The majority of responses to the draft accepted the principle lying behind draft article 4, but there were reservations about the problem of proving intention. The policy adopted by the Special Rapporteur is indicated clearly in the first report on the effects of armed conflicts on treaties.[32]

19. The reservations of members of the Commission (and some delegations) relating to the role of intention call for close examination. In the first place, given the character of the subject matter (as a part of the law of treaties), it is unrealistic to assert that the role of intention should be marginalized. At the same time, the Special Rapporteur recognizes that it is necessary to consider other factors, including the object and purpose of the treaty and the specific circumstances of the conflict. The existing content of draft article 4 is certainly not incompatible with reference to such other factors and no doubt the formulation can be improved.

[30] *Ibid.*, para. 142.

[31] *Ibid.*, para. 143.

[32] *Yearbook ... 2005* (see footnote 1 above), paras. 45–54.

20. During the debate in the Sixth Committee, a useful proposal was made for the reformulation of draft article 4:

1. Where a treaty indicates the intention of the parties relating to the termination or suspension of the treaty in case of an armed conflict, or where such intention may be deduced from the interpretation of the treaty, that intention shall stand.

2. In any other case, the intention of the parties to a treaty with regard to its termination or suspension in case of an armed conflict shall, in the event of disagreement between the parties in that regard, be determined by any reasonable means, which may include the *travaux préparatoires* of the treaty or the circumstances of its conclusion.

3. The foregoing shall be without prejudice to any decision that the parties may, by mutual agreement and without a breach of *jus cogens*, make at any time.[33]

21. There is, however, a need to avoid the assumption that draft article 4 should cover all possible issues in the same text. Draft article 4 was intended as a foundation provision which prefigures the following provisions and, in particular, draft article 7. The commentary to draft article 7 in the first report on the effects of armed conflicts on treaties[34] refers to a quantity of State practice on the various contextual bases on which intention may be discovered. Further materials are referred to in the memorandum prepared by the Secretariat (A/CN.4/550 and Corr.1–2).[35]

22. In addition, a proportion of the municipal case law indicates the significance of implications drawn from the object and purpose of a treaty. Relevant decisions include the following: *Établissements Cornet* v. *Vve Gaido*;[36] *In re Barrabini*;[37] *State* v. *Reardon*;[38] *Lanificio Branditex* v. *Societa Azais e Vidal*;[39] *Silverio* v. *Delli Zotti*;[40] *In re Utermöhlen*;[41] *The Society for the Propagation of the Gospel in Foreign Parts* v. *The Town of New Haven and William Wheeler*;[42] *Techt* v. *Hughes*;[43] *Goos* v. *Brocks*;[44] *Karnuth* v. *United States*;[45] *The Sophie Rickmers* v. *United States*;[46] *Clark* v. *Allen*;[47] *In re Meyer's Estate*;[48] *Brownell*

[33] Statement by Guatemala, *Official Records of the General Assembly, Sixtieth Session, Sixth Committee*, 19th meeting, para. 4.

[34] *Yearbook ... 2005* (see footnote 1 above), pp. 220–224, paras. 62–83.

[35] Available on the website of the Commission (www.un.org/law/ilc/).

[36] Case No. 155, France, Court of Appeal of Aix (7 May 1951), ILR (1951), p. 506.

[37] Case No. 156, France, Court of Appeal of Paris (28 July 1950), *ibid.*, p. 507.

[38] United States of America, Supreme Court of Kansas (15 May 1926), 120 Kan. 614; 245 p. 158.

[39] Italy, Court of Cassation (Joint Session) (8 November 1971), ILR, vol. 71, p. 595.

[40] Case No. 118, Luxembourg, High Court of Justice (30 January 1952), *ibid.* (1952), p. 558.

[41] Case No. 129, Netherlands, Court of Cassation (2 April 1948), *Annual Digest and Reports of Public International Law Cases, year 1949* (London, Butterworth, 1955), p. 380.

[42] United States, Supreme Court (1823), 21 U.S. 464.

[43] *Ibid.*, Court of Appeals of New York (8 June 1920), 229 N.Y. 222.

[44] *Ibid.*, Supreme Court of Nebraska (1929), 117 Neb. 750, 223 N.W. 13.

[45] *Ibid.*, Supreme Court (1929), 279 U.S. 231.

[46] *Ibid.*, Southern District Court of New York (1930), 45 F.2d 413.

[47] *Ibid.*, Supreme Court (1947), 331 U.S. 503.

[48] *Ibid.*, District Court of Appeal, California (1951), 107 Cal. App. 2d 799.

v. *City and County of San Francisco*;[49] *Argento* v. *Horn*;[50] *Gallina* v. *Fraser*.[51]

23. These decisions establish the general tendency of municipal courts in various jurisdictions to refer to the object and purpose of a treaty when deciding upon the effect of an armed conflict.

24. There is a particular question raised in several responses. Thus, the United States delegation observed:

> The Special Rapporteur considered that the intention of the parties at the time of the conclusion of the treaty should be determinative. This seems to my Government to be problematic, since generally when parties negotiate they do not consider how its provisions might apply during armed conflict.[52]

25. With respect, this is to introduce a false dilemma. It is a common experience in the interpretation of treaties (and legislation) that the intention of the parties (or other actors) must be "reconstructed" as a practical hypothesis. And in this context the Special Rapporteur would agree with the further observation of the United States delegation:

> In order to address the issue it is necessary to consider other factors, including the object and purpose of the treaty, the character of the specific provisions in question, and the circumstances relating to the conflict.[53]

Similar proposals emerged during the debate within the Commission.[54]

26. There remain certain structural problems. These include the relationship of draft article 4 and draft article 7. It is the intention of the Special Rapporteur that these provisions would be applicable on a basis of coordination. It could be argued that, if draft article 4 is redrafted to refer to other factors, including object and purpose, then draft article 7 would become redundant.

27. In that case, the present content of draft article 7 would be incorporated in the commentary. However, this way of proceeding would involve a loss of substance. In fact, much, if not all, of draft article 7 reflects State practice and fairly uniform judicial standards.

28. And there is an additional structural problem. The drafting of draft article 4 entails reference to articles 31–32 of the 1969 Vienna Convention. This incorporation is necessarily mechanical but there could be no question of fashioning "designer" principles of interpretation for exclusive use in the present context.

Draft article 5. Express provisions on the operation of treaties

1. Treaties applicable to situations of armed conflict in accordance with their express provisions are operative in case of an armed conflict, without prejudice to the conclusion of lawful agreements between the parties to the armed conflict involving suspension or waiver of the relevant treaties.

2. The outbreak of an armed conflict does not affect the competence of the parties to the armed conflict to conclude treaties in accordance with the Vienna Convention on the Law of Treaties.

29. The purpose of this provision is explained in the first report on the effects of armed conflicts on treaties.[55] General support was expressed in the Commission. It was accepted that the provision was necessary for the sake of clarity.

30. During the debate in the Commission reference was made to the principle enunciated in the ICJ advisory opinion concerning nuclear weapons[56] to the effect that, while certain human rights and environmental principles do not cease in time of armed conflict, their application is determined by "the applicable *lex specialis*, namely, the law applicable in armed conflict which is designed to regulate the conduct of hostilities".[57] The Special Rapporteur agrees that this principle be appropriately reflected in the draft articles.

31. In paragraph 2 of the draft article the term "competence" should be replaced by "capacity".

Draft article 6. Treaties relating to the occasion for resort to armed conflict

A treaty, the status or interpretation of which is the subject matter of the issue which was the occasion for resort to armed conflict, is presumed not to be terminated by operation of law, but the presumption will be rendered inoperable by evidence of a contrary intention of the Contracting Parties.

32. The basis of this draft article is examined in the first report on the effects of armed conflicts on treaties.[58] The thinking derives from the experience of the Special Rapporteur in the context of peaceful settlement of boundary disputes by judicial or other means. This draft attracted criticism in the Commission. The view was expressed that the draft article was, strictly speaking, not necessary in the light of draft article 3, which provision extended to a treaty whose interpretation might be the occasion for a conflict.[59] It was pointed out that the matter could be dealt with in the commentary to draft article 3.[60] A number of delegations expressed similar views during the debate in the General Assembly.[61]

---

[49] *Ibid.* (1954), 271 P.2d 974.

[50] *Ibid.*, Court of Appeals Sixth Circuit (1957), 241 F.2d 258.

[51] *Ibid.*, District Court, Connecticut (1959), 177 F.Supp. 856, ILR, vol. 31, p. 356.

[52] Summarized in *Official Records of the General Assembly, Sixtieth Session, Sixth Committee*, 20th meeting, para. 32. See also *Yearbook ... 2005*, vol. II (Part Two), p. 32, para. 152.

[53] Summarized in *Official Records of the General Assembly, Sixtieth Session, Sixth Committee*, 20th meeting, para. 32.

[54] See *Yearbook ... 2005*, vol. II (Part Two), p. 32, para. 153.

[55] *Yearbook ... 2005* (see footnote 1 above), pp. 219–220, paras. 55–58.

[56] *Legality of the Threat or Use of Nuclear Weapons, Advisory Opinion, I.C.J. Reports 1996*, p. 226.

[57] *Ibid.*, p. 240, para. 25. See also *Yearbook ... 2005, vol. II (Part Two)*, pp. 32–33, para. 159. See further the statement of the United States, *Official Records of the General Assembly, Sixtieth Session, Sixth Committee*, 20th meeting, para. 33.

[58] *Yearbook ... 2005* (see footnote 1 above), p. 220, paras. 59–61.

[59] *Ibid.*, vol. II (Part Two), p. 33, para. 164.

[60] *Ibid.*

[61] See, for example, Romania, *Official Records of the General Assembly, Sixtieth Session, Sixth Committee*, 19th meeting, para. 42.

33. The view of the Special Rapporteur is that the draft article should be deleted, and, if it is thought appropriate, the issue should be referred to in the commentary to draft article 3.

Draft article 7. The operation of treaties on the basis of necessary implication from their object and purpose

1. In the case of treaties the object and purpose of which involve the necessary implication that they continue in operation during an armed conflict, the incidence of an armed conflict will not as such inhibit their operation.

2. Treaties of this character include the following:

(*a*) Treaties expressly applicable in case of an armed conflict;

(*b*) Treaties declaring, creating, or regulating permanent rights or a permanent regime or status;

(*c*) Treaties of friendship, commerce and navigation and analogous agreements concerning private rights;

(*d*) Treaties for the protection of human rights;

(*e*) Treaties relating to the protection of the environment;

(*f*) Treaties relating to international watercourses and related installations and facilities;

(*g*) Multilateral law-making treaties;

(*h*) Treaties relating to the settlement of disputes between States by peaceful means, including resort to conciliation, mediation, arbitration and the International Court of Justice;

(*i*) Obligations arising under multilateral conventions relating to commercial arbitration and the enforcement of awards;

(*j*) Treaties relating to diplomatic relations;

(*k*) Treaties relating to consular relations.

34. The policy of this presentation was explained by the Special Rapporteur in his introduction to the debate as follows:

> The Special Rapporteur observed that draft article 7 dealt with the species of treaties the object and purpose of which involved the necessary implication that they would continue in operation during an armed conflict. Paragraph 1 established the basic principle that the incidence of armed conflict would not, as such, inhibit the operation of those treaties. Paragraph 2 contained an indicative list of some such categories of treaties. It was observed that the effect of such categorization was to create a set of weak rebuttable presumptions as to the object and purpose of those types of treaties, i.e. as evidence of the object and purpose of the treaty to the effect that it survives a war. He clarified that while he did not agree with all the categories of treaties in the list, he had nonetheless included them as potential candidates for consideration by the Commission. The list reflected the views of several generations of writers and was to a considerable extent reflected in available State practice, particularly United States practice dating back to the 1940s. While closely linked to draft articles 3 and 4, the draft article was primarily expository and could accordingly be excluded.[62]

35. The legal background to draft article 7 is examined extensively in the first report on the effects of armed conflicts on treaties.[63] Reference is made to the substantial memorandum prepared by the Secretariat (A/CN.4/550 and Corr.1–2).[64] The role of draft article 7 can be analysed as follows:

(*a*) It can be justified as a piece of expository drafting which gives effect to the application of the principle established in draft article 4 in the sphere of State practice and the experience of municipal courts;

(*b*) As a drafting matter, draft article 7 is strictly superfluous. It is merely indicative and it provides a vehicle for the substantial research materials which have been used by the Special Rapporteur;

(*c*) In any event there is the view, expressed by a number of Commission members, and by Governments, that the use of categories as a tool of analysis was inherently flawed. The statement of the United States in the Sixth Committee, at the sixtieth session of the General Assembly, expresses this viewpoint very clearly:

> Article 7 deals with the operation of treaties on the basis of implications drawn from their object and purpose. It is the most complex of the draft articles. It lists 12 categories of treaties that, owing to their object and purpose, imply that they should be continued in operation during an armed conflict. This is problematic because attempts at such broad categorization of treaties always seem to fail. Treaties do not automatically fall into one of several categories. Moreover, even with respect to classifying particular provisions, the language of the provisions and the intention of the parties may differ from similar provisions in treaties between other parties. It would be more productive if the Commission could enumerate factors that might lead to the conclusion that a treaty or some of its provisions should continue (or be suspended or terminated) in the event of armed conflict. The identification of such factors would, in many cases, provide useful information and guidance to States on how to proceed.[65]

36. There is a distinction to be drawn here. On the one hand, it may be accepted that the use of categories of the type set forth in draft article 7 is heavy-handed and inadequate for drafting purposes. On the other hand, as indicated in the first report on the effects of armed conflicts on treaties, most of the categories deployed are derived precisely from the policy and legal assessments of leading authorities, together with a significant amount of case law and practice. In other words, these materials indicate the very factors to which the United States refers in the statement quoted above.

37. At the end of the day, it may be that the solution lies within the realm of presentation. On this basis, draft article 7 would be deleted: as has been emphasized already, its purpose was indicative and expository. The question then is to find an appropriate container for the materials on which draft article 7 has been built. The obvious answer would be an annex containing an analysis of the State practice and case law which could be prepared by the Secretariat with assistance from the Special Rapporteur.

38. A number of specific points arose in the discussion both in the Commission and in the Sixth Committee,

[62] *Yearbook ... 2005*, vol. II (Part Two), pp. 33–34, para. 167.

[63] *Ibid.* (see footnote 1 above), pp. 220–228, paras. 62–118.

[64] See footnote 35 above.

[65] Summarized in *Official Records of the General Assembly, Sixtieth Session, Sixth Committee*, 20th meeting, para. 34.

apart from the general modalities of the categorization approach. In relation to subparagraph (*a*), the view was expressed that this category was unnecessary as it was already covered by draft article 5.[66] While this is analytically correct, the comment ignores the expository purpose of draft article 7. In fact, the category involved has generated some significant discussion of policy.

39. The United Kingdom of Great Britain and Northern Ireland regarded the inclusion of treaties relating to the protection of the environment as problematical.[67]

40. Within the Commission, the category of treaties concerning a permanent regime or status was subjected to criticism as being ambiguous and open-ended.[68] The Special Rapporteur would point out that the category has been accorded major support in the doctrine, and is recognized by other legal sources.

41. The "system" problem which emerges from the discussion overall is the operation of a *lex specialis* in time of armed conflict, which operation rules out any principle of general continuity. This outcome affects the sphere of human rights. Here, although there is a good basis for continuity, the protection of human rights must be related to the law of armed conflict. And the same analysis applies to the application of environmental principles in armed conflict.

42. In the light of such considerations, it is clear that the formulation of specific principles of continuity is problematical. The indicative list may reflect the policies adopted by municipal courts and some executive advice to courts. It is not possible to argue that the list is supported by State practice in a conventional mode.[69]

---

[66] *Yearbook ... 2005*, vol. II (Part Two), p. 34, para. 171.

[67] *Official Records of the General Assembly, Sixtieth Session, Sixth Committee*, 20th meeting, para. 1.

[68] See, *inter alia*, *Yearbook ... 2005*, vol. II (Part Two), p. 34, para. 171.

[69] See the view of India, summarized in *Official Records of the General Assembly, Sixtieth Session, Sixth Committee*, 18th meeting, para. 64.

THE OBLIGATION TO EXTRADITE OR PROSECUTE *(AUT DEDERE AUT JUDICARE)*

[Agenda item 10]

DOCUMENT A/CN.4/571

Preliminary report, by Mr. Zdzislaw Galicki, Special Rapporteur

[*Original: English*]
[*7 June 2006*]

CONTENTS

Multilateral instruments cited in the present report

	Source
International Convention for the Suppression of Counterfeiting Currency (Geneva, 20 April 1929)	League of Nations, *Treaty Series*, vol. CXII, No. 2623, p. 371.
Convention for the Prevention and Punishment of Terrorism (Geneva, 16 November 1937)	*Ibid.*, document C.546.M.383.1937.V.
Geneva Conventions for the protection of war victims (Geneva, 12 August 1949)	United Nations, *Treaty Series*, vol. 75, Nos. 970–973, pp. 31, 85, 135 and 287.
Protocol additional to the Geneva Conventions of 12 August 1949, and relating to the protection of victims of international armed conflicts (Protocol I) (Geneva, 8 June 1977)	*Ibid.*, vol. 1125, No. 17512, p. 3.
European Convention on Extradition (Paris, 13 December 1957)	*Ibid.*, vol. 359, No. 5146, p. 273.
Convention on the High Seas (Geneva, 29 April 1958)	*Ibid.*, vol. 450, No. 6465, p. 11.
Single Convention on Narcotic Drugs, 1961 (New York, 30 March 1961)	*Ibid.*, vol. 520, No. 7515, p. 151.
Protocol amending the Single Convention on Narcotic Drugs, 1961 (Geneva, 25 March 1972)	*Ibid.*, vol. 976, No. 14151, p. 3.
Convention for the suppression of unlawful seizure of aircraft (The Hague, 16 December 1970)	*Ibid.*, vol. 860, No. 12325, p. 105.

	Source
Convention on psychotropic substances (Vienna, 21 February 1971)	*Ibid.*, vol. 1019, No. 14956, p. 175.
Convention for the suppression of unlawful acts against the safety of civil aviation (Montreal, 23 September 1971)	*Ibid.*, vol. 974, No. 14118, p. 177.
International Convention on the Suppression and Punishment of the Crime of Apartheid (New York, 30 November 1973)	*Ibid.*, vol. 1015, No. 14861, p. 243.
Convention on the prevention and punishment of crimes against internationally protected persons, including diplomatic agents (New York, 14 December 1973)	*Ibid.*, vol. 1035, No. 15410, p. 167.
European Convention on the Suppression of Terrorism (Strasbourg, 27 January 1977)	*Ibid.*, vol. 1137, No. 17828, p. 93.
Convention on the physical protection of nuclear material (Vienna, 26 October 1979)	*Ibid.*, vol. 1456, No. 24631, p. 101.
International Convention against the taking of hostages (New York, 17 December 1979)	*Ibid.*, vol. 1316, No. 21931, p. 205.
United Nations Convention on the Law of the Sea (Montego Bay, 10 December 1982)	*Ibid.*, vol. 1833, No. 31363, p. 3.
Convention against torture and other cruel, inhuman or degrading treatment or punishment (New York, 10 December 1984)	*Ibid.*, vol. 1465, No. 24841, p. 85.
Convention for the suppression of unlawful acts against the safety of maritime navigation (Rome, 10 March 1988)	*Ibid.*, vol. 1678, No. 29004, p. 201.
United Nations Convention against Illicit Traffic in Narcotic Drugs and Psychotropic Substances (Vienna, 20 December 1988)	*Ibid.*, vol. 1582, No. 27627, p. 95.
International Convention Against the Recruitment, Use, Financing and Training of Mercenaries (New York, 4 December 1989)	*Ibid.*, vol. 2163, No. 37789, p. 75.
Convention on the Safety of United Nations and Associated Personnel (New York, 9 December 1994)	*Ibid.*, vol. 2051, No. 35457, p. 363.
International Convention for the Suppression of Terrorist Bombings (New York, 15 December 1997)	*Ibid.*, vol. 2149, No. 37517, p. 256.
Rome Statute of the International Criminal Court (Rome, 17 July 1998)	*Ibid.*, vol. 2187, No. 38544, p. 3.
International Convention for the Suppression of the Financing of Terrorism (New York, 9 December 1999)	*Ibid.*, vol. 2178, No. 38349, p. 197.
United Nations Convention against Transnational Organized Crime (New York, 15 November 2000)	*Ibid.*, vol. 2225, No. 39574, p. 209.
Protocol to Prevent, Suppress and Punish Trafficking in Persons, Especially Women and Children, supplementing the United Nations Convention against Transnational Organized Crime (New York, 15 November 2000)	*Ibid.*, vol. 2237, No. A–39574, p. 319.
Protocol against the Smuggling of Migrants by Land, Sea and Air, supplementing the United Nations Convention against Transnational Organized Crime (New York, 15 November 2000)	*Ibid.*, vol. 2241, No. A–39574, p. 480.
Protocol against the Illicit Manufacturing of and Trafficking in Firearms, Their Parts and Components and Ammunition, supplementing the United Nations Convention against Transnational Organized Crime (New York, 31 May 2001)	*Ibid.*, vol. 2326, No. A–39574, p. 211.
United Nations Convention against Corruption (New York, 31 October 2003)	*Ibid.*, vol. 2349, No. 42146, p. 41.
International Convention for the Suppression of Acts of Nuclear Terrorism (New York, 13 April 2005)	*Ibid.*, vol. 2445, No. 44004, p. 89.
Council of Europe Convention on the Prevention of Terrorism (Warsaw, 16 May 2005)	Council of Europe, *Treaty Series*, No. 196.

Works cited in the present report

AMNESTY INTERNATIONAL

Universal Jurisdiction: The Duty of States to Enact and Implement Legislation. London, International Secretariat, 2001.

BASSIOUNI, M. Cherif and Edward M. WISE

Aut Dedere Aut Judicare: The Duty to Extradite or Prosecute in International Law. Dordrecht, Martinus Nijhoff, 1995. 340 p.

BROOMHALL, Bruce

"Towards the development of an effective system of universal jurisdiction for crimes under international law", *New England Law Review* (Boston), vol. 35, No. 2, winter 2001, pp. 399–420.

DUGARD, John and Christine VAN DEN WYNGAERT

"Reconciling extradition with human rights", *American Journal of International Law* (Washington, D.C.), vol. 92, No. 2, April 1998, pp. 187–212.

ENACHE-BROWN, Colleen and Ari FRIED

"Universal crime, jurisdiction and duty: the obligation of *aut dedere aut judicare* in international law", McGill Law Journal (Montreal), vol. 43, 1997–1998, pp. 613–633.

FISHER, Keith R.

"*In rem* alternatives to extradition for money laundering", *Loyola of Los Angeles International and Comparative Law Review*, vol. 25, No. 3, summer 2003, pp. 409–456.

GROTIUS, Hugo

De Jure Belli ac Pacis (1646). Book II. English translation by Francis W. Kelsey, *in* James Brown Scott, ed., The Classics of International Law. Oxford, Clarendon Press, 1925. Vol. 2.

GUILLAUME, Gilbert

"Terrorisme et droit international", *Collected Courses of The Hague Academy of International Law*, 1989–III. Dordrecht, Martinus Nijhoff, 1990. vol. 215, pp. 287–416.

HARVARD LAW SCHOOL

"Research in international law, II: jurisdiction with respect to crime", Supplement to the *American Journal of International Law* (Washington, D.C.), vol. 29, 1935, pp. 435–651.

HENZELIN, Marc

Le principe de l'universalité en droit pénal international: droit et obligation pour les États de poursuivre et juger selon le principe de l'universalité. Basel, Helbing & Lichtenhahn, 2000.

HUDSON, Manley O., ed.

International Legislation: A Collection of the Texts of Multipartite International Instruments of General Interest. vol. VII (1935–1937), Nos. 402–505. Washington, D.C., Carnegie Endowment for International Peace, 1941.

INSTITUT DE DROIT INTERNATIONAL

Tableau des résolutions adoptées (1957–1991). Paris, Pedone, 1992. 165 p.

JENNINGS, Sir Robert and Sir Arthur WATTS, eds.

Oppenheim's International Law. vol. I: Peace, parts 2–4. 9th ed. Harlow, Longman, 1992.

LARSAEUS, Nina

"The relationship between safeguarding internal security and complying with international obligations of protection: the unresolved issue of excluded asylum seekers", *Nordic Journal of International Law*, vol. 73, No. 1, 2004, pp. 69–97.

PLACHTA, Michael

"*Aut dedere aut judicare*: an overview of modes of implementation and approaches", *Maastricht Journal of European and Comparative Law*, vol. 6, 1999, pp. 331–365.

"The *Lockerbie* case: the role of the Security Council in enforcing the principle *aut dedere aut judicare*", *European Journal of International Law*, vol. 12, No. 1, February 2001, pp. 125–140.

ROHT-ARRIAZA, Naomi

"State responsibility to investigate and prosecute grave human rights violations in international law", *California Law Review* (Berkeley), vol. 78, No. 2, March 1990, pp. 449–513.

Preface

1. At its fifty-sixth session, in 2004, the International Law Commission, on the basis of the recommendation of a Working Group on the long-term programme of work, identified the topic "Obligation to extradite or prosecute (*aut dedere aut judicare*)" for inclusion in its long-term programme of work.[1] The General Assembly, in resolution 59/41 of 2 December 2004, took note of the Commission's report concerning its long-term programme of work. At its 2865th meeting, held on 4 August 2005, the Commission considered the selection of a new topic for inclusion in the Commission's current programme of work and decided to include the topic "Obligation to extradite or prosecute (*aut dedere aut judicare*)" on its agenda, and appointed Mr. Zdzislaw Galicki as the Special Rapporteur for this topic.[2]

2. The topic in question had already appeared in the list of planned topics at the first session of the Commission in 1949,[3] but had been largely forgotten for more than half a century until it was briefly addressed in articles 8–9 of the 1996 draft Code of Crimes against the Peace and Security of Mankind.[4] These articles set out minimum contours of the principle of *aut dedere aut judicare* and the linked principle of universal jurisdiction. It is important to remember that the draft Code was largely a codification exercise of customary international law as it stood in 1996, as confirmed two years later with the adoption of the Rome Statute of the International Criminal Court, rather than a progressive development of international law.

3. The text presented below has been prepared by the Special Rapporteur as a very preliminary set of initial observations concerning the substance of the topic, marking the most important points for further considerations and including a very general road map for the future work of the Commission in this field.

[1] See *Yearbook ... 2004*, vol. II (Part Two), p. 120, para. 362; for the syllabus on the topic, see paragraphs 21–24 (*ibid.*).

[2] *Yearbook ... 2005*, vol. II (Part Two), p. 92, para. 500.

[3] *Yearbook ... 1949*, document A/925, p. 283, para. 16 (4).

[4] *Yearbook ... 1996*, vol. II (Part Two), pp. 27 and 30.

Introduction

4. The formula "extradite or prosecute" (in Latin: *aut dedere aut judicare*) is commonly used to designate the alternative obligation concerning the treatment of an alleged offender, "which is contained in a number of multilateral treaties aimed at securing international co-operation in the suppression of certain kinds of criminal conduct".[5]

5. As stressed in the doctrine, "[t]he expression *aut dedere aut judicare* is a modern adaptation of a phrase used by Grotius: *aut dedere aut punire* (either extradite or punish)".[6] It seems, however, that for applying it now, a more permissive formula of the alternative obligation

[5] Bassiouni and Wise, *Aut Dedere Aut Judicare*: *The Duty to Extradite or Prosecute in International Law*, p. 3. A rich collection of international criminal law conventions establishing a duty to extradite or prosecute has been gathered, classified into numerous categories and commented on by those two authors, *ibid.*, pp. 75–302. It may be a good starting point for the further work of the Commission.

[6] *Ibid.*, p. 4. See also Grotius, *De Jure Belli ac Pacis*, chap. XXI, paras. III–IV, pp. 526–529.

to extradition ("prosecute" (*judicare*) instead of "punish" (*punire*)) is suitable, having additionally in mind that Grotius contended that a general obligation to extradite or punish exists with respect to all offences by which another State is injured.

6. A modern approach does not seem to go so far as Grotius did, taking also into account that an alleged offender may be found not guilty. Furthermore, it leaves without any prejudice a question if the discussed obligation is deriving exclusively from relevant treaties or if it also reflects a general obligation under customary international law, at least with respect to specific international offences.

7. There are also some other formulas applied by the doctrine to describe the obligation in question, such as, for example, *judicare aut dedere* or *aut dedere aut prosequi*,[7] or even *aut dedere, aut judicare, aut tergiversari*.[8] At "the enforcement level, there is also the option of the enforcement of foreign criminal sentences under the principle of *aut dedere aut poenam persequi*".[9]

8. It was also noted by some authors that it is necessary to distinguish between the principle of universal jurisdiction and the *aut dedere aut judicare* principle. According to their opinion:

> The latter expression is essentially a modern adaptation of the phrase *aut dedere aut punire* used by Grotius in *De Jure Belli ac Pacis* to describe a natural right of an injured state to exact punishment, either by itself or by the state hosting the suspect. The modern expression, however, seems to suit the contemporary meaning better, as it does not, strictly speaking, imply an obligation to "punish" but rather to adjudicate or prosecute, or even just to "take steps towards prosecution".[10]

The question of the mutual relationship between the two said principles will meet its preliminary considerations in chapter II of the present report. A full analysis of the link between the principle of universal jurisdiction in criminal matters and the *aut dedere aut judicare* principle should have, without any doubt, an important place in the future work of the Commission on the present topic.

9. Although the obligation to extradite or prosecute may look, at first, like a very traditional one, one should not be misled, however, by its ancient, Latin formulation. The obligation to extradite or prosecute cannot be treated as a traditional topic only. Its evolution from the period of Grotius up to recent times and its significant development as an effective tool against growing threats arising for States and individuals from criminal offences can easily lead to one conclusion—that it reflects new developments in international law and pressing concerns of the international community.

10. The Commission, which incorporated the *aut dedere aut judicare* rule in the draft Code of Crimes against the Peace and Security of Mankind,[11] has simultaneously explained the principle and its rationale as follows:

> The obligation to prosecute or extradite is imposed on the custodial State in whose territory an alleged offender is present. The custodial State has an obligation to take action to ensure that such an individual is prosecuted either by the national authorities of that State or by another State which indicates that it is willing to prosecute the case by requesting extradition. The custodial State is in a unique position to ensure the implementation of the Code by virtue of the presence of the alleged offender in its territory. Therefore the custodial State has an obligation to take the necessary and reasonable steps to apprehend an alleged offender and to ensure the prosecution and trial of such an individual by a competent jurisdiction. The obligation to extradite or prosecute applies to a State which has custody of "an individual alleged to have committed a crime". This phrase is used to refer to a person who is singled out, not on the basis of unsubstantiated allegations, but on the basis of pertinent factual information.[12]

11. The Commission noted that the duty either to prosecute or extradite would depend on the sufficiency of the evidence, although it noticed simultaneously that:

> The national laws of various States differ concerning the sufficiency of evidence required to initiate a criminal prosecution or to grant a request for extradition.[13]

12. Recognizing the importance of the principle concerned for the effective operation of extradition, on 1 September 1983 the Institute of International Law at its Cambridge session in the United Kingdom, adopted a resolution on new problems of extradition, which contained a part VI entitled "*Aut judicare aut dedere*", stating in paragraph 1 that:

> The rule *aut judicare aut dedere* should be strengthened and amplified, and it should provide for detailed methods of legal assistance.[14]

13. It was underlined in the doctrine that to determine the effectiveness of the system based on the obligation to extradite or prosecute three problems have to be addressed:

> [F]irst, the status and scope of application of this principle under international law; second, the hierarchy among the options embodied in this rule, provided that the requested state has a choice; third, practical difficulties in exercising *judicare*.[15]

14. Such practical difficulties and obstacles exist, as it seems, equally in the field of *dedere* and *judicare*. The serious weaknesses in the current system of extradition and mutual legal assistance derive, to a great extent, from the outdated bilateral extradition and mutual legal assistance treaties. There are numerous grounds of refusal which are not appropriate when crimes under international law are concerned, but there are also important safeguards that often are missing regarding the extradition of persons to countries where they would face unfair

---

[7] See Guillaume, "Terrorisme et droit international" (p. 371), who said that "the true option which is open to States is necessarily *aut dedere aut prosequi*".

[8] Which freely translated means "to hand over, to prosecute, or to shuffle and find excuses" (Fisher, "*In rem* alternatives to extradition for money laundering", p. 412).

[9] Plachta, "The *Lockerbie* case: the role of the Security Council in enforcing the principle a*ut dedere aut judicare*", p. 131.

[10] Larsaeus, "The relationship between safeguarding internal security and complying with international obligations of protection: the unresolved issue of excluded asylum seekers", p. 79.

[11] See paragraph 24 below for the text of the appropriate article 9 of the draft Code.

[12] *Yearbook ... 1996*, vol. II (Part Two), p. 31, para. (3) of the commentary to article 9.

[13] *Ibid.*, para. (4).

[14] Institut de droit international, *Tableau des résolutions adoptées (1957–1991)*, p. 161.

[15] Plachta, "*Aut dedere aut judicare*: an overview of modes of implementation and approaches", p. 332.

trials, torture or the death penalty.[16] On the other hand, there are also numerous obstacles to the effectiveness of prosecution systems that are not appropriate to such crimes, including statutes of limitation, immunities and prohibitions of retrospective criminal prosecution over conduct that was criminal under international law at the time it occurred.

[16] Interesting observations on *aut dedere aut judicare* as a solution in confrontation between the tendency to suppress international crimes and the protection of basic human rights have been made by Dugard and Van den Wyngaert in "Reconciling extradition with human rights", pp. 209–210.

15. It also seems necessary to find out if there is any hierarchy of particular obligations which may derive from the obligation to extradite or prosecute, or whether it is just a matter of discretion of States concerned.

Chapter I

Universality of suppression and universality of jurisdiction

16. In particular, the obligation to extradite or prosecute during the last decades has been included in all so-called sectoral conventions against terrorism, starting with the Convention for the suppression of unlawful seizure of aircraft, which states in article 7:

> The Contracting State in the territory of which the alleged offender is found, shall, if it does not extradite him, be obliged, without exception whatsoever and whether or not the offence was committed in its territory, to submit the case to its competent authorities for the purpose of prosecution.

17. As noted in the doctrine, two variants of the above-mentioned Convention formula can be identified:

> (*a*) the alternative obligation to submit a case for prosecution is subject, where a foreigner is involved, to whether a state has elected to authorize the exercise of extraterritorial jurisdiction;
>
> (*b*) the obligation to submit a case for prosecution only arises when a request for extradition has been refused.[17]

Both of them are reflected in subsequently concluded universal and regional conventions against various kinds of international or transnational crimes.

18. Through such a formulation, as contained in the Convention for the suppression of unlawful seizure of aircraft, the obligation in question has been significantly strengthened by combining it with the principle of universality of suppression of appropriate terrorist acts. The principle of universality of suppression should not be identified, however, with the principle of universality of jurisdiction or universality of competence of judicial organs. The universality of suppression in this context means, as a result of application of the obligation to extradite or prosecute between States concerned, that there is no place where an offender could avoid criminal responsibility and find a so-called safe haven.

19. There are various descriptions of the concept of universal jurisdiction in criminal matters. One of them which seems practicable describes universal jurisdiction as:

> [T]he ability of the prosecutor or investigating judge of any state to investigate or prosecute persons for crimes committed outside the state's territory which are not linked to that state by the nationality of the suspect or of the victim or by harm to the state's own national interests.[18]

[17] Plachta, "*Aut dedere aut judicare* ...", p. 360. By way of example, the following conventions may be mentioned: with respect to variant (*a*): United Nations Convention against Illicit Traffic in Narcotic Drugs and Psychotropic Substances, art. 6, para. 9; and with respect to variant (*b*) European Convention on the Suppression of Terrorism, art. 7.

20. Consequently, crimes subject to universal jurisdiction—according to the authors of the definition quoted above—would fall into the following three categories:

> (*1*) Crimes under international law, such as war crimes, crimes against humanity and genocide, as well as torture, extrajudicial executions and "disappearances";
>
> (*2*) Crimes under national law of international concern, such as hijacking or damaging aircraft, hostage-taking and attacks on diplomats; and
>
> (*3*) Ordinary crimes under national law, such as murder, abduction, assault and rape.[19]

21. On the other hand, a concept of the principle of universal jurisdiction and competence, especially in later years, is often connected with the establishment of international criminal courts and their activities. In practice, however, the extent of such quasi-universal "jurisdiction and competence" depends on the number of States accepting the establishment of such courts and is not directly connected with the obligation to extradite or prosecute. It has to be stressed, however, in order to avoid misunderstandings, that although international criminal courts exercise international jurisdiction of varying geographic reach, including a universal one, it should not be treated as universal jurisdiction as defined above, which is a form of jurisdiction exercised only by States. The two types of jurisdiction are usually seen as complementary, but of an entirely different nature.

22. It seems inevitable, when analysing various aspects of the applicability of the obligation to extradite or prosecute, to trace the evolution of the principle of universality of jurisdiction from its traditional perception to the provisions of the Rome Statute of the International Criminal Court. Looking at this evolution, an interesting example of one of the earliest attempts to analyse the phenomenon of universal jurisdiction may be found in the draft Convention on jurisdiction with respect to crime, prepared in 1935 by the Research in International Law under the

[18] Amnesty International, *Universal Jurisdiction: The Duty of States to Enact and Implement Legislation*, introduction, p. 1.

[19] *Ibid.*

auspices of the Harvard Law School.[20] Two articles were included, dealing with the problem in question: article 9 entitled "Universality—piracy" and article 10, entitled "Universality—other crimes". The latter article provided that:

A State has jurisdiction with respect to any crime committed outside its territory by an alien, other than the crimes mentioned in Articles 6, 7, 8 and 9,[21] as follows:

(*a*) When committed in a place not subject to its authority but subject to the authority of another State, if the act or omission which constitutes the crime is also an offence by the law of the place where it was committed, if surrender of the alien for prosecution has been offered to such other State or States and the offer remains unaccepted, and if prosecution is not barred by lapse of time under the law of the place where the crime was committed. The penalty imposed shall in no case be more severe than the penalty prescribed for the same act or omission by the law of the place where the crime was committed.

(*b*) When committed in a place not subject to the authority of any State, if the act or omission which constitutes the crime is also an offence by the law of a State of which the alien is a national, if surrender of the alien for prosecution has been offered to the State or States of which he is a national and the offer remains unaccepted, and if prosecution is not barred by lapse of time under the law of a State of which the alien is a national. The penalty imposed shall in no case be more severe than the penalty prescribed for the same act or omission by the law of a State of which the alien is a national.[22]

23. The above-quoted formula combines elements of the universal jurisdiction of a State with the jurisdictional powers of a State based on principles of territoriality and nationality, as well as the additional element of the alternative possibility of extradition ("surrender"), which can be considered as a reflection of the principle of *aut dedere aut judicare*. However, the whole construction of these provisions seems to be aimed at the right of a State to extradite or prosecute rather than the obligation to do so.

24. In the realm of prior codification, the obligation in question may be found in article 9, entitled "Obligation to extradite or prosecute", contained in the draft Code of Crimes against the Peace and Security of Mankind, adopted by the Commission at its forty-eighth session, in 1996.[23] This article states as follows:

Without prejudice to the jurisdiction of an international criminal court, the State Party in the territory of which an individual alleged to have committed a crime set out in article 17, 18, 19 or 20 is found shall extradite or prosecute that individual.[24]

25. Simultaneously, article 8 of the draft Code of Crimes against the Peace and Security of Mankind, entitled "Establishment of jurisdiction", requires each "State Party" to

take such measures as may be necessary to establish its jurisdiction over the crimes set out in articles 17, 18, 19 and 20, irrespective of where or by whom those crimes were committed.[25]

In the commentary to this article, the Commission stated:

Jurisdiction over the crimes covered by the Code is determined in the first case by international law and in the second case by national law. As regards international law, any State party is entitled to exercise jurisdiction over an individual allegedly responsible for a crime under international law set out in articles 17 to 20 who is present in its territory under the principle of "universal jurisdiction" set forth in article 9. The phrase "irrespective of where or by whom those crimes were committed" is used in the first provision of the article to avoid any doubt as to the existence of universal jurisdiction for those crimes.[26]

26. Although the Commission did not use the term "universal jurisdiction" in draft article 9, the above-quoted commentary expresses the opinion of the Commission that, at least in terms of the list of "crimes under international law" (i.e. genocide, crimes against humanity, crimes against United Nations and associated personnel and war crimes) contained in articles 8–9, it considers them as being subject to "universal jurisdiction". Similarly, the Commission recognized that the same crimes are also subject to the obligation of *aut dedere aut judicare*.

27. It is interesting, however, that when the concept of the obligation to extradite or prosecute was introduced in the draft Code of Offences against the Peace and Security of Mankind, by the then Special Rapporteur, Mr. Doudou Thiam, for the first time in 1986, the draft article concerned was entitled "Universal offence" and provided for the duty of every State "to try or extradite any perpetrator of an offence against the peace and security of mankind arrested in its territory".[27]

28. The following year the title of the article concerned was changed by the Special Rapporteur to "*Aut dedere aut punire*".[28] Once again, the formulation of the obligation was modified to "obligation to try or extradite"[29] when adopted on first reading, before it reached its final form (extradite or prosecute) in the above-quoted draft Code of Crimes against the Peace and Security of Mankind finally adopted by the Commission in 1996.

29. An analogous formulation, although limited to specified "crimes against diplomatic agents and other internationally protected persons", was used in article 6 by the Commission, when elaborating the draft articles on the prevention and punishment of crimes against diplomatic agents and other internationally protected persons in 1972.[30] The *aut dedere aut judicare* principle is reproduced without change in article 7 of the Convention on

[20] "Research in international law, II: jurisdiction with respect to crime", p. 439.

[21] "Crimes mentioned" in the said articles included such crimes as those concerning "security of the State", "Counterfeiting", "Piracy", as well as crimes committed outside the territory of a State by an alien "in connection with the discharge of a public function which he was engaged to perform for that State" or "while engaged as one of the personnel of a ship or aircraft having the national character of that State".

[22] Harvard Law School, *loc. cit.*, pp. 440–441.

[23] *Yearbook ... 1996*, vol. II (Part Two), p. 17.

[24] *Ibid.*, p. 30. These are such crimes as "Crime of genocide", "Crimes against humanity", "Crimes against United Nations and associated personnel" and "War crimes".

[25] *Ibid.*, p. 27.

[26] *Ibid.*, p. 29, para. (7) of the commentary.

[27] *Yearbook ... 1986*, vol. II (Part One), document A/CN.4/398, fourth report on the draft Code of Offences against the Peace and Security of Mankind, by Mr. Doudou Thiam, Special Rapporteur, p. 82, art. 4, para. 1.

[28] *Yearbook ... 1987*, vol. II (Part One), document A/CN.4/404, p. 3.

[29] *Article 4 (Obligation to try or extradite)*:

"1. A State in whose territory an individual alleged to have committed a crime against the peace and security of mankind is present shall either try or extradite him."

(*Yearbook ... 1988*, vol. II (Part Two), p. 66); see also later *Yearbook ... 1994*, vol. II (Part One), document A/CN.4/460, p. 102.

[30] *Article 6*:

"The State Party in whose territory the alleged offender is present shall, if it does not extradite him, submit, without exception whatsoever and without undue delay, the case to its competent authorities for the purpose of prosecution, through proceedings in accordance with the laws of that State."

(*Yearbook ... 1972*, vol. II, document A/8710/Rev.1, p. 318)

the Prevention and Punishment of Crimes against Internationally Protected Persons, including Diplomatic Agents, adopted by the General Assembly on 14 December 1973.[31]

30. In the above-quoted practice of the Commission it is clearly visible that the *aut dedere aut judicare* principle went through a kind of evolution, as concerns both its form and content. This evolution may be helpful at present for a decision to be taken by the Commission as to the final formulation of the obligation to extradite or prosecute. It would seem especially important to establish whether the most common translation of *judicare* should be retained or perhaps be replaced by "try" or "adjudicate".

[31] General Assembly resolution 3166 (XXVIII), annex.

Chapter II

Universal jurisdiction and the obligation to extradite or prosecute

31. A close and mutual relationship between these two institutions has been noted and stressed in a well-known legal memorandum prepared by a non-governmental organization:

> There are two important related, but conceptually distinct, rules of international law.
>
> **Universal jurisdiction** is the *ability* of the court of any state to try persons for crimes committed outside its territory which are not linked to the state by the nationality of the suspect or the victims or by harm to the state's own national interests. Sometimes this rule is called permissive universal jurisdiction. This rule is now part of customary international law, although it is also reflected in treaties, national legislation and jurisprudence concerning crimes under international law, ordinary crimes of international concern and ordinary crimes under national law …
>
> Under the related ***aut dedere aut judicare*** (extradite or prosecute) rule, a state may not shield a person suspected of certain categories of crimes. Instead, it is *required* either to exercise jurisdiction (which would necessarily include universal jurisdiction in certain cases) over a person suspected of certain categories of crimes or to extradite the person to a state able and willing to do so or to surrender the person to an international criminal court with jurisdiction over the suspect and the crime. As a practical matter, when the *aut dedere aut judicare* rule applies, the state where the suspect is found must ensure that its courts can exercise all possible forms of geographic jurisdiction, including universal jurisdiction, in those cases where it will not be in a position to extradite the suspect to another state or to surrender that person to an international criminal court.[32]

32. During the discussion held in the Sixth Committee of the General Assembly at its sixtieth session, in 2005, some delegations, welcoming the inclusion of the topic, "The obligation to extradite or prosecute (*aut dedere aut judicare*)", expressed the view that:

> the analysis of this topic should take into account the principle of universal jurisdiction in criminal matters. The growing practice, especially in recent years, of including the obligation to extradite or prosecute in numerous international treaties and its application by States in their mutual relations raised the question of unification of different aspects of the operation of that obligation. Among the most important problems requiring urgent clarification was the possibility of recognizing the obligation in question not only as a treaty-based one but also as one having its roots, at least to some extent, in customary rules.[33]

33. A direct link existing between the institution of universal jurisdiction and the obligation to extradite or prosecute was also stressed by many scholars:

> Treaties setting out a regime of "universal jurisdiction" typically define a crime and then oblige all parties either to investigate and (if appropriate) prosecute it, or to extradite suspects to a party willing to do so. This is the obligation of *aut dedere, aut judicare* ("either extradite or prosecute").[34]

34. Not all of the authors are, however, in agreement as concerns the application of the principle (and obligation!) of *aut dedere aut judicare* to all crimes covered by the principle of universal jurisdiction. As summarized by one scholar:

> The suggestion … that the principle of *aut dedere aut judicare* would apply to all universally condemnable crimes as a matter of customary international law, or the theory … that the principle would, in some cases, even amount to an *erga omnes* obligation are, however, both extreme positions. While I have not found enough evidence to support such an obligation, I would not rule out that the principle may have reached customary status with regard to some conventions, or even groups of conventions.[35]

[32] Amnesty International, *op. cit.*, chap. 1, pp. 11–12.

[33] Topical summary of the discussion held in the Sixth Committee of the General Assembly during its sixtieth session (A/CN.4/560), para. 243.

[34] Broomhall, "Towards the development of an effective system of universal jurisdiction for crimes under international law", p. 401.

[35] Larsaeus, *loc. cit.*, p. 91.

Chapter III

Sources of the obligation to extradite or prosecute

A. International treaties

35. A preliminary task in future codification work on the topic in question would be to complete a comparative list of relevant treaties and formulations used by them to reflect this obligation. Some attempts have already been made in the doctrine, listing a large number of such treaties and conventions.[36] These are both substantive treaties, defining particular offences and requiring their criminalization and the prosecution or extradition of offenders, as well as procedural conventions, dealing with extradition and other matters of legal cooperation between States.

36. In examining those treaties it will be necessary to look closely at least at the provisions of international criminal law conventions establishing a duty to extradite or prosecute, dealing—as listed in the doctrine—with such matters as:

> (1) the prohibition against aggression, (2) war crimes, (3) unlawful use of weapons, (4) crimes against humanity, (5) the prohibition against

[36] See Bassiouni and Wise, *op. cit.*, pp. 75–302; see also Jennings and Watts, *Oppenheim's International Law*, pp. 953–954.

genocide, (6) racial discrimination and apartheid, (7) slavery and related crimes, (8) the prohibition against torture, (9) unlawful human experimentation, (10) piracy, (11) aircraft hijacking and related offenses, (12) crimes against the safety of international maritime navigation, (13) use of force against internationally protected persons, (14) taking of civilian hostages, (15) drug offenses, (16) international traffic in obscene publications, (17) protection of national and archaeological treasures, (18) environmental protection, (19) theft of nuclear materials, (20) unlawful use of the mails, (21) interference with submarine cables, (22) counterfeiting, (23) corrupt practices in international commercial transactions, and (24) mercenarism.[37]

This catalogue, though intended to cover all categories of treaties concerned, has become non-exhaustive, not including—for instance—the most recent counter-terrorism treaties, as well as conventions on the suppression of various international or transnational crimes.[38]

37. Another catalogue of selected international treaties with universal jurisdiction and *aut dedere aut judicare* obligations is contained in an above-quoted memorandum prepared by Amnesty International. It includes 21 conventions concluded during the period 1929–2000, which are considered by the authors of the said memorandum as the most representative for the question of universal jurisdiction and *aut dedere aut judicare* obligations. These are the following instruments:[39]

(1) International Convention for the Suppression of Counterfeiting Currency; (2) Geneva Conventions for the protection of war victims; (3) Convention on the High Seas; (4) Single Convention on Narcotic Drugs, 1961; (5) Convention for the suppression of unlawful seizure of aircraft; (6) Convention on psychotropic substances; (7) Convention for the suppression of unlawful acts against the safety of civil aviation; (8) Protocol amending the Single Convention on Narcotic Drugs, 1961; (9) International Convention on the Suppression and Punishment of the Crime of *Apartheid*; (10) Convention on the prevention and punishment of crimes against internationally protected persons, including diplomatic agents; (11) Protocol additional to the Geneva Conventions of 12 August 1949, and relating to the protection of victims of international armed conflicts (Protocol I); (12) International Convention against the taking of hostages; (13) Convention on the physical protection of nuclear material; (14) United Nations Convention on the Law of the Sea; (15) Convention against torture and other cruel, inhuman or degrading treatment or punishment; (16) Convention for the suppression of unlawful acts against the safety of maritime navigation; (17) International Convention Against the Recruitment, Use, Financing and Training of Mercenaries; (18) Convention on the Safety of United Nations and Associated Personnel; (19) International Convention for the Suppression of Terrorist Bombings; (20) International Convention for the Suppression of the Financing of Terrorism; and (21) United Nations Convention against Transnational Organized Crime.

38. It seems that the existing treaty practice, significantly enriched during the last decades, especially through various conventions against terrorism and other crimes threatening the international community, has already created a sufficient basis for considering the extent to which the obligation to extradite or prosecute, so important as a matter of international criminal policy, has become a matter of concrete legal obligation.

39. Moreover, several treaties (for example, the Convention against torture and other cruel, inhuman or degrading treatment or punishment) compel States parties to introduce rules to enforce the *aut dedere aut judicare* principle, according to which the State which does not order extradition is obliged to prosecute. Similarly, under international humanitarian law, States have the obligation to look for and prosecute those alleged to be responsible for grave breaches of the Geneva Conventions of 12 August 1949 and their Protocol I, or otherwise responsible for war crimes, and to prosecute such persons or extradite them for trial in another State. States will therefore have to set up appropriate mechanisms to ensure the effective enforcement of this principle, as well as to ensure more generally an effective framework for judicial cooperation with other States in these matters.

B. International custom and general principles of law

40. One of the crucial problems which has to be solved by the Commission during the elaboration of principles concerning the obligation to extradite or prosecute will be, without any doubt, to find a generally acceptable answer to the question of whether the legal source of the obligation to extradite or prosecute should be limited to the treaties which are binding the States concerned, or be extended to appropriate customary norms or general principles of law. There is no consensus among the doctrine concerning this question, although a large and growing number of scholars are in favour of supporting the concept of an international legal obligation *aut dedere aut judicare* as a general duty based not only on the provisions of particular international treaties, but also on generally binding customary norms, at least concerning certain categories of crimes.[40]

41. Some of the authors try to prove the existence of such customary norms through general practice deriving from treaties:

[I]t is reasonable to assert that if a state has signed and ratified a significant number of treaties containing the *aut dedere aut judicare* formula, then that state has demonstrated through this practice that *aut dedere aut judicare* is a customary norm. The state, through the act of signing related international agreements, articulates the belief that *aut dedere aut judicare* is an accepted norm and that it is the most effective way of preventing certain forms of conduct. This belief satisfies the requirement of *opinio juris* when establishing customary norms. If a state accedes to a large number of international treaties, all of which have a variation of the *aut dedere aut judicare* principle, there is strong evidence that it intends to be bound by this generalizable provision, and that such practice should lead to the entrenchment of this principle in customary law. By agreeing to the formula of *aut dedere aut judicare* in multiple treaties that are concerned with international offenses, a state has indicated that with respect to international offenses it believes that the best way to ensure compliance is to impose such an obligation.[41]

---

[37] Bassiouni and Wise, *op. cit.*, p. 73.

[38] See, for example, the United Nations Convention against Transnational Organized Crime, and the Protocols thereto, or the International Convention for the Suppression of Acts of Nuclear Terrorism. See also the Council of Europe Convention on the Prevention of Terrorism, which in article 18 provides for the obligation to "[e]xtradite or prosecute", although it does not deal directly with acts of terrorism but only with offences connected with terrorism.

[39] See Amnesty International, *op. cit.*, chap. 15, p. 18.

[40] See Bassiouni and Wise, *op. cit.*; and Roht-Arriaza, "State responsibility to investigate and prosecute grave human rights violations in international law", p. 466, noting that treaties imposing an *aut dedere aut judicare* obligation, "whether addressing international or national crimes, show an increasing tendency in international law to require states to investigate and prosecute serious offenses". See also Henzelin, *Le principe de l'universalité en droit pénal international: droit et obligation pour les États de poursuivre et juger selon le principe de l'universalité*, noting tendencies in the direction of a customary international law rule of *aut dedere aut judicare* with respect to certain crimes.

[41] Enache-Brown and Fried, "Universal crime, jurisdiction and duty: the obligation of *aut dedere aut judicare* in international law", p. 629.

42. A careful and thorough evaluation of possible customary grounds for the *aut dedere aut judicare* obligation is necessary for a final definition of the legal nature of this obligation. The extent to which such a definition will be based on either the codification of international law or the progressive development of this law depends mostly on the possibility of finding solid grounds in generally accepted customary norms.

C. National legislation and practice of States

43. When examining the question of sources from which the obligation to extradite or prosecute may derive, one should not limit oneself to traditional sources of international law, like international treaties and customary rules, but extend one's analysis to national legislation and the practice of States. This practice is very rich and worth considering in depth. Taking into account national legislation and practice in the sphere of universal jurisdiction, as well as the internal application by States of the *aut dedere aut judicare* principle, may be helpful for a better understanding of the way in which the traditional perception of this principle should be considered in the light of modern concepts of universal jurisdiction.

44. In this connection, as far as internal legislation is concerned, there are numerous examples where the power to exercise universal jurisdiction is not limited to crimes under international law, but is also extended to ordinary crimes found in the national law of most States. Almost two centuries ago, Austria became the first State, as far as is known, to have enacted legislation providing for universal jurisdiction over ordinary crimes under national law. It is worth recalling, for instance, that the Austrian Penal Code, following the 1803 legislation, includes provisions reflecting the *aut dedere aut judicare* principle in connection with universal jurisdiction. "First, article 64.1.6 provides that certain crimes under Austrian law committed abroad are punishable under Austrian criminal law, regardless of the criminal law of the place where they occurred, when Austria is under an obligation to punish them." Secondly,

> [A]rticle 65.1.2 of the Penal Code provides that courts may exercise universal jurisdiction over offences committed abroad, provided that (1) the acts are also punishable in the place where they are committed (double criminality requirement), (2) the suspect, if a non-national, is present in Austria and (3) he or she cannot be extradited to the other State for reasons other than the nature and characteristics of the offence. Crimes under international law are not political offences.[42]

45. Argentina was also among the States which had the earliest legislation providing for universal jurisdiction over all or most crimes in their penal codes and imposing an *aut dedere aut judicare* obligation with regard to foreigners found on its territory suspected of committing ordinary crimes abroad. Article 5 of the Argentine extradition law adopted in 1885 provided:

> In cases in which, under the provisions of this Act, the Government of the Republic is not bound to hand over the offenders requested, they shall be tried by the county's courts and sentenced to the penalties specified by law for crimes or offences committed within the territory of the Republic.[43]

46. Another interesting example of internal State practice—though applied many years later—may be found in the text of the reservation made by Belgium on 27 September 2001 (repeated on 17 May 2004) to the International Convention for the Suppression of the Financing of Terrorism, where it has been stated that:

> Belgium recalls that it is bound by the general legal principle *aut dedere aut judicare*, pursuant to the rules governing the competence of its courts.[44]

47. Summing up what has been said here in a preliminary way about the sources of the obligation to extradite or prosecute, it seems to be obvious that the main stream of considerations concerning the obligation to extradite or prosecute goes through the norms and practice of international law. It cannot be forgotten, however, that "efforts towards optimalization of the regulatory mechanism rooted in the principle *aut dedere aut judicare* may be undertaken either on the international level or on the domestic level".[45] Internal criminal, procedural and even constitutional regulations should be taken into consideration here on an equal level with international legal norms and practices.

48. Based on what has been said up to now, with regard to the preliminary plan of action, the Special Rapporteur is convinced that the sources of the obligation to extradite or prosecute should include general principles of law, national legislation and judicial decisions, and not just treaties and customary rules.

[42] Amnesty International, *op. cit.*, chap. 6, pp. 5–6.

[43] *Ibid.*, chap. 4, p. 11.

[44] United Nations, *Treaty Series*, vol. 2261, No. A–38349, p. 271.

[45] Plachta, "*Aut dedere aut judicare* ...", p. 332.

Chapter IV

Scope of the obligation to extradite or prosecute

49. The obligation to extradite or prosecute is constructed in the alternative giving a State the choice to decide which part of this obligation it is going to fulfil. It is presumed that after fulfilling one part of this composed obligation—either *dedere* or *judicare*—the State is free from fulfilling the other one. There is a possibility, however, that a State may wish to fulfil both parts of the obligation in question. For example, after establishing its jurisdiction, prosecuting, putting on trial and sentencing an offender, the State may decide to extradite (or surrender) such an offender to another State, also entitled to establish its jurisdiction, for the purpose of enforcing the judgement.

50. A detailed description of the obligation to extradite or prosecute differs significantly if various international conventions formulating the *aut dedere aut judicare* principle are compared. In the above-quoted Convention for the suppression of unlawful seizure of aircraft, the formulation applied was rather a simple one, providing that

the contracting State in the territory of which the alleged offender is found, shall "if it does not extradite him, be obliged, without exception whatsoever and whether or not the offence was committed in its territory, to submit the case to its competent authorities for the purpose of prosecution".[46] An analogous obligation, established for instance by the United Nations Convention against Corruption, is much more elaborated:

> A State Party in whose territory an alleged offender is found, if it does not extradite such person in respect of an offence to which this article applies solely on the ground that he or she is one of its nationals, shall, at the request of the State Party seeking extradition, be obliged to submit the case without undue delay to its competent authorities for the purpose of prosecution.[47]

The substantive scope of the obligation to extradite or prosecute is also extended, as the Convention provides in addition, in the same article, that:

> The States Parties concerned shall cooperate with each other, in particular on procedural and evidentiary aspects, to ensure the efficiency of such prosecution.[48]

51. Although the Commission in the quoted provision of the draft Code of Crimes against the Peace and Security of Mankind (para. 24 above) has recognized the existence of the obligation in question, it has done it, however, exclusively in relation to a strictly limited and defined group of offences, described generally as crimes against the peace and security of mankind (with the exclusion of the "Crime of aggression"). In any case, this recognition may be considered as a starting point for further considerations as to what extent this obligation may be extended to other kinds of offences.

52. Furthermore, it is worth noting that the Commission has introduced a concept of "triple alternative", considering a possibility of parallel jurisdictional competence to be exercised not only by interested States, but also by international criminal courts. It has been a significant step forward in the development of the traditional "alternative model" of the *aut dedere aut judicare* principle.

53. One of the earliest examples of such "third choice" may be found in the Convention for the Creation of an International Criminal Court, opened for signature at Geneva, on 16 November 1937.[49] The said court was intended to be established for the trial of persons accused of an offence dealt with in the Convention for the Prevention and Punishment of Terrorism of the same date.[50] In accordance with the provisions of article 2 of the first convention, the persons accused could be prosecuted either by a State before its own courts, or extradited to the State entitled to demand extradition, or committed for trial to the international criminal court. Unfortunately, the said Convention has never entered into force and the court in question could not be established.

54. Alternative competences of the International Criminal Court, established on the basis of the Rome Statute of the International Criminal Court, are generally known. The Rome Statute gives a choice between the State exercising jurisdiction over an offender or having him surrendered to the jurisdiction of the International Criminal Court.

55. In addition, there is already judicial practice, which deals with the said obligation and has confirmed its existence in contemporary international law. The *Lockerbie* case before ICJ brought a lot of interesting materials in this field, especially through dissenting opinions of five judges to the decisions of the Court "not to exercise its power to indicate provisional measures" as requested by the Libyan Arab Jamahiriya.[51] Although the Court itself was rather silent with regard to the obligation in question, the dissenting judges confirmed in their opinions the existence of "the rule of customary international law, *aut dedere aut judicare*"[52] and of "a right recognized in international law and even considered by some jurists as *jus cogens*".[53] These opinions, though not confirmed by the Court, should be taken into account when considering the trends of contemporary development of the said obligation.

56. As was correctly noted in the doctrine and which should be followed in future codification work to be continued by the Commission:

> [T]he principle *aut dedere aut judicare* can not be perceived as a panacea whose universal application will cure all the weaknesses and ailments that extradition has been suffering from for a long time ...
>
> In order to establish *aut dedere aut judicare* as a universal rule of extradition, the efforts should be made to gain the acceptance of the proposition that first, such a rule has become an indispensable element of the suppression of criminality and bringing offenders to justice in an international arena, and second, that it is untenable to continue limiting its scope to international crimes (and not even all of them) as defined in international conventions.[54]

57. In the light of what has been said above, it has been decided by the Commission that the topic "Obligation to extradite or prosecute (*aut dedere aut judicare*)" has achieved sufficient maturity for its codification, with a possibility of including some elements of progressive development. This developing nature of the obligation in question was also underlined by some scholars:

> The crystallization of an emerging rule of customary law that would oblige states to extradite or prosecute those reasonably suspected of international crimes should therefore be encouraged.[55]

---

[46] See paragraph 16 above.

[47] Art. 44, para. 11.

[48] *Ibid.* See also General Assembly resolution 58/4 of 31 October 2003, annex.

[49] League of Nations, document C.547(1).M.384(1).1937.V, reproduced in United Nations, *Historical Survey of the Question of International Criminal Jurisdiction (Memorandum by the Secretary-General)* (Sales No. 1949.V.8), p. 88, appendix 8. See also Hudson, *International Legislation: A Collection of the Texts of Multipartite International Instruments of General Interest*, p. 878.

[50] For the text of the convention see Hudson, *op. cit.*, p. 862.

[51] Two identical decisions were adopted by ICJ concerning *Questions of Interpretation and Application of the 1971 Montreal Convention arising from the Aerial Incident at Lockerbie (Libyan Arab Jamahiriya* v. *United Kingdom), Provisional Measures, Order of 14 April 1992*, and *ibid.* (*Libyan Arab Jamahiriya* v. *United States of America*), *Provisional Measures, Order of 14 April 1992, I.C.J. Reports 1992*, pp. 3 and 114 respectively.

[52] *Ibid.*, pp. 51 and 161 (Judge Weeramantry, dissenting opinion).

[53] *Ibid.*, pp. 82 and 187 (Judge Ajibola, dissenting opinion).

[54] Plachta, "*Aut dedere aut judicare* ...", p. 364.

[55] Broomhall, *loc. cit.*, p. 406.

Chapter V

Methodological questions

58. The identification of legal rules concerning the obligation to extradite or prosecute that the international community will be ready to approve and follow, either as binding norms or as a "soft-law" instrument, requires extensive and comprehensive work, including both international and national elements.

59. At this stage it seems premature to decide if the final product of the Commission's work should take the form of draft articles, guidelines or recommendations. The Special Rapporteur will try, however, to formulate in subsequent reports draft rules concerning the concept, structure and operation of the *aut dedere aut judicare* principle, without any prejudice concerning their final legal form. However, it would be of high importance for the Special Rapporteur to obtain opinions of other members of the Commission about the final form of the work undertaken now on the topic in question.

60. The Commission could address a written request for information to member States. It would welcome any information Governments may wish to provide concerning their practice with regard to this topic, particularly dealing with more contemporary practice. Any further information that Governments consider relevant to the topic would also be welcomed by the Commission and by the Special Rapporteur. In particular, such information should deal with:

(*a*) International treaties by which a given State is bound, containing the obligation to extradite or prosecute, and reservations made by the State to limit the application of the obligation to extradite or prosecute;

(*b*) Internal legal regulations, adopted and applied by a given State, including constitutional provisions and penal codes or codes of criminal procedures, concerning the obligation to extradite or to prosecute;

(*c*) Judicial practice of a given State reflecting the application and its extent, or non-application, of the principle of universal jurisdiction and obligation *aut dedere aut judicare*;

(*d*) To what crimes/offences the principle of universal jurisdiction and the *aut dedere aut judicare* obligation are applied in the legislation/practice of a given State;

(*e*) What obstacles a given State meets, both in international and internal forums, having a negative impact on the possible application of:

(i) Universal jurisdiction;

(ii) The *aut dedere aut judicare* principle.

Chapter VI

Preliminary plan of action

61. In the light of the preliminary observations made above, the 10 main points to be considered at the beginning by the Commission could be as follows:

1. First of all, there is a necessity for a comprehensive comparative analysis of appropriate provisions concerning the obligation to extradite or prosecute, contained in the relevant conventions and other international instruments, together with a systematic identification of existing similarities and differences. Although there were attempts to collect and systematize such international instruments, updating appropriate information may be of paramount importance for the subsequent effective work of the Commission.

2. The above-mentioned analysis should include the presentation of the evolution and development of the obligation to extradite or prosecute—from the "Grotius formula" to the "triple alternative":

(*a*) Extradite or punish;

(*b*) Extradite or prosecute;

(*c*) Extradite or prosecute or surrender to international court.

3. Secondly, since the *aut dedere aut judicare* principle appears to be assimilated in many internal legislations, it should be necessary to make another systematic collection, i.e. gathering appropriate legal provisions drawn up and adopted in this field by individual States, together with available practice of their application. Similarities and differences existing between such national legislations and practices should be identified, as well as the possible impact of international regulations on national legislations (and vice versa).

4. The third important step, taking into account what has been said before about the sources of the obligation to extradite or prosecute, would be the necessity to establish the actual position of the obligation in contemporary international law, either:

(*a*) As deriving exclusively from international treaties; or

(*b*) As rooted also in customary norms—then taking into account possible consequences of their customary status.

There is also the possibility of a mixed nature of the obligation in question when, for instance, *dedere* derives from conventional commitments, while *judicare* may be based on customary norms (or vice versa).

5. The fourth initial task shall be to establish as precisely as possible the existing mutual relationship and interdependence between the principle of universal jurisdiction and the obligation of *aut dedere aut judicare*.

6. One of the most decisive factors to be established is the extent of the substantive application of the obligation to extradite or prosecute, either:

(*a*) To all offences by which another State is particularly injured (Grotius); or

(*b*) To a limited category or categories of offences/crimes (e.g. to the "crimes against the peace and security of mankind", or to "international offences", or to "crimes under international law", or to "crimes under national law of international concern", etc.).

Identifying the possible criteria of qualifying such offences would be of high importance.

7. The content of the obligation to extradite or prosecute should be identified and analysed, taking into account its complex and alternative nature, including both:

(*a*) Obligations of States (*dedere* or *judicare*):

(i) Extradition: conditions and exceptions,

(ii) Jurisdiction: grounds for establishing, and

(*b*) Rights of States (in case of application, as well as of non-application of the obligation in question).

It has to be decided by the Commission to what extent *dedere* and *judicare* shall be treated as alternative obligations of States, and when they may be considered as rights or competences of States.

8. Mutual relation between the obligation to extradite or prosecute and other rules concerning jurisdictional competences of States in criminal matters should find its place in the analysis conducted by the Commission, including such questions as:

(*a*) "Offence-oriented" approach (e.g. art. 9 of the draft Code of Crimes against the Peace and Security of Mankind;[56] art. 7 of the Convention for the suppression of unlawful seizure of aircraft);

(*b*) "Offender-oriented" approach (e.g. art. 6, para. 2, of the European Convention on Extradition);

(*c*) Principle of universality of jurisdictional competences:

(i) As exercised by States;

(ii) As exercised by international judicial organs.

9. Legal nature of particular obligations deriving under international law from the application of the obligation to extradite or prosecute should be defined, while paying special attention to:

(*a*) Equality of alternative obligations (extradite or prosecute), or a prevailing position of one of them (hierarchy of obligations);

(*b*) Possible limitations or exclusions in fulfilling alternative obligations (e.g. non-extradition of own nationals, political offences exception, limitations deriving from human rights protection, etc.);

(*c*) Possible impact of such limitations or exclusions on another kind of obligation (e.g. impact of extradition exceptions on alternatively exercised prosecution);

(*d*) The obligation in question as a rule of substantive or procedural character, or of a mixed one;

(*e*) Position of the obligation in question in the hierarchy of norms of international law:

(i) Secondary rule;

(ii) Primary rule;

(iii) *Jus cogens* norm (?).

10. Relation between the obligation to extradite or prosecute and other principles of international law (e.g. principle of sovereignty of States, principle of human rights protection, principle of universal suppression of certain crimes, etc.), as well as the impact of these principles on the extent of application of the obligation, also have to be taken into account by the Commission when analysing the topic in question.

---

[56] See paragraph 24 above.

Annex

INTRODUCTORY BIBLIOGRAPHY

(Works not cited in the present report)

CASSESE, Antonio

International Criminal Law. Oxford, Oxford University Press, 2003. 472 p.

COSTELLO, Declan

"International terrorism and the development of the principle *aut dedere aut judicare*", *Journal of International Law and Economics*, vol. 10, 1975, pp. 483–501.

GOODWIN-GILL, Guy S.

"Crime in international law: obligations *erga omnes* and the duty to prosecute", *in* Guy S. Goodwin-Gill and Stefan Talmon, eds., *The Reality of International Law: Essays in Honour of Ian Brownlie*. Oxford, Clarendon Press, 1999, pp. 199–223.

GUILLAUME, Gilbert

"Terrorism and international law", *International and Comparative Law Quarterly*, vol. 53, part 3, July 2004, pp. 537–548.

KELLY, Michael J.

"Cheating justice by cheating death: the doctrinal collision for prosecuting foreign terrorists: passage of *aut dedere aut judicare* into customary law & refusal to extradite based on the death penalty", *Arizona Journal of International and Comparative Law*, vol. 20, No. 3, 2003, pp. 491–532.

PLACHTA, Michael

"Extradition and the principle *aut dedere aut judicare* in the new Polish legislation", *European Journal of Crime, Criminal Law and Criminal Justice*, vol. 6, 1998, pp. 94–105.

STRAPATSAS, Nicolaos

"Universal Jurisdiction and the International Criminal Court", *Manitoba Law Journal*, vol. 29, No. 1, 2002, pp. 1–31.

SUNGA, Lyal S.

The Emerging System of International Criminal Law: Developments in Codification and Implementation. The Hague, Kluwer, 1997. 486 p.

WERLE, Gerhard

Principles of International Criminal Law. The Hague, TMC Asser Press, 2005. 485 p.

WISE, Edward M.

"Extradition: the hypothesis of a *civitas maxima* and the maxim *aut dedere aut judicare*", *International Review of Penal Law*, vol. 62, 1991, pp. 109–134.

"The obligation to extradite or prosecute", *Israel Law Review*, vol. 27, 1993, pp. 268–287.

CHECKLIST OF DOCUMENTS OF THE FIFTY-EIGHTH SESSION

Document	*Title*	*Observations and references*
A/CN.4/559	Provisional agenda	Mimeographed. For agenda as adopted, see *Yearbook ... 2006*, vol. II (Part Two).
A/CN.4/560	Topical summary of the discussion held in the Sixth Committee of the General Assembly during its sixtieth session, prepared by the Secretariat	Mimeographed.
A/CN.4/561 and Add.1–2	Diplomatic protection: comments and observations received from Governments	Reproduced in the present volume.
A/CN.4/562 and Add.1	International liability for injurious consequences arising out of acts not prohibited by international law (international liability in case of loss from transboundary harm arising out of hazardous activities): comments and observations received from Governments	*Idem.*
A/CN.4/563 and Add.1	Filling of casual vacancies in the Commission (article 11 of the statute): note by the Secretariat	A/CN.4/563 reproduced in the present volume. A/CN.4/563/Add.1 mimeographed.
A/CN.4/564 and Add.1–2	Fourth report on responsibility of international organizations, by Mr. Giorgio Gaja, Special Rapporteur	Reproduced in the present volume.
A/CN.4/565 [and Corr.1]	Expulsion of aliens: memorandum by the Secretariat	Mimeographed. Available on the website of the Commission.
A/CN.4/566	Third report on the legal regime for the allocation of loss in case of transboundary harm arising out of hazardous activities, by Mr. Pemmaraju Sreenivasa Rao, Special Rapporteur	Reproduced in the present volume.
A/CN.4/567	Seventh report on diplomatic protection, by Mr. John Dugard, Special Rapporteur	*Idem.*
A/CN.4/568 and Add.1	Responsibility of international organizations: comments and observations received from international organizations	*Idem.*
A/CN.4/569 and Add.1	Ninth report on unilateral acts of States, by Mr. Víctor Rodríguez Cedeño, Special Rapporteur	*Idem.*
A/CN.4/570 [and Corr.1]	Second report on the effects of armed conflicts on treaties, by Mr. Ian Brownlie, Special Rapporteur	*Idem.*
A/CN.4/571	Preliminary report on the obligation to extradite or prosecute (*aut dedere aut judicare*), by Mr. Zdzislaw Galicki, Special Rapporteur	*Idem.*
A/CN.4/572 [and Corr.1]	Reservations to treaties: note on draft guideline 3.1.5 (Definition of the object and purpose of the treaty), by Mr. Alain Pellet, Special Rapporteur	*Idem.*
A/CN.4/573 [and Corr.1]	Second report on the expulsion of aliens, by Mr. Maurice Kamto, Special Rapporteur	*Idem.*
A/CN.4/574	Eleventh report on reservations to treaties, by Mr. Alain Pellet, Special Rapporteur	*Idem.*
A/CN.4/575	Diplomatic protection: comments and observations received from Governments	*Idem.*
A/CN.4/L.682 [and Corr.1] and Add.1	Fragmentation of international law: difficulties arising from the diversification and expansion of international law: report of the Study Group of the Commission finalized by Martti Koskenniemi	Mimeographed. Available on the website of the Commission. The final text will appear as an addendum to the present volume.
A/CN.4/L.683	Working Group on shared natural resources (groundwaters): report of the Working Group	Mimeographed.
A/CN.4/L.684 [and Corr.1–2]	Diplomatic protection: titles and texts of the draft articles on diplomatic protection adopted by the Drafting Committee on second reading	Text reproduced in *Yearbook ... 2006*, vol. I, summary record of the 2881st meeting (para.1).
A/CN.4/L.685 [and Corr.1]	Reservations to treaties: titles and texts of the draft guidelines adopted by the Drafting Committee	Text reproduced in *Yearbook ... 2006*, vol. I, summary record of the 2883rd meeting (para.1).
A/CN.4/L.686 [and Corr.1]	International liability for injurious consequences arising out of acts not prohibited by international law: title and texts of the preamble and the draft principles on the allocation of loss arising out of hazardous activities adopted by the Drafting Committee on second reading	Text reproduced in *Yearbook ... 2006*, vol. I, summary record of the 2882nd meeting (para.1).

Document	Title	Observations and references
A/CN.4/L.687 and Add.1 [and Corr.1]	Responsibility of international organizations: titles and texts of the draft articles adopted by the Drafting Committee	Text reproduced in *Yearbook ... 2006*, vol. I, summary records of the 2884th, 2891st and 2902nd meetings.
A/CN.4/L.688	Shared natural resources: titles and texts of the draft articles adopted by the Drafting Committee on first reading	Text reproduced in *Yearbook ... 2006*, vol. I, summary record of the 2885th meeting (para.1).
A/CN.4/L.689	Draft report of the Commission on the work of its fifty-eighth session: chapter I (Introduction)	Mimeographed. For the adopted text, see *Official Records of the General Assembly, Sixty-first Session, Supplement No. 10* (A/61/10). The final text appears in *Yearbook ... 2006*, vol. II (Part Two).
A/CN.4/L.690	*Idem*: chapter II (Summary of the work of the Commission on the work of its fifty-eighth session)	*Idem.*
A/CN.4/L.691	*Idem*: chapter III (Specific issues on which comments would be of particular interest to the Commission)	*Idem.*
A/CN.4/L.692 and Add.1	*Idem*: chapter IV (Diplomatic protection)	*Idem.*
A/CN.4/L.693 and Add.1	*Idem*: chapter V (International liability for injurious consequences arising out of acts not prohibited by international law (international liability in case of loss from transboundary harm arising out of hazardous activities))	*Idem.*
A/CN.4/L.694 and Add.1 [and Corr.1]	*Idem*: chapter VI (Shared natural resources)	*Idem.*
A/CN.4/L.695 [and Corr.1] and Add.1 [and Corr.1] and Add.2	*Idem*: chapter VII (Responsibility of international organizations)	*Idem.*
A/CN.4/L.696 [and Corr.1] and Add.1 [and Corr.1] and Add.2–3	*Idem*: chapter VIII (Reservations to treaties)	*Idem.*
A/CN.4/L.697 and Add.1 [and Corr.1] and Add.2	*Idem*: chapter IX (Unilateral acts of States)	*Idem.*
A/CN.4/L.698	*Idem*: chapter X (Effects of armed conflicts on treaties)	*Idem.*
A/CN.4/L.699	*Idem*: chapter XI (Obligation to extradite or prosecute (*aut dedere aut judicare*))	*Idem.*
A/CN.4/L.700	*Idem*: chapter XII (Fragmentation of international law: difficulties arising from the diversification and expansion of international law)	*Idem.*
A/CN.4/L.701 and Add.1	*Idem*: chapter XIII (Other decisions and conclusions of the Commission)	*Idem.*
A/CN.4/L.702	Fragmentation of international law: difficulties arising from the diversification and expansion of international law: report of the study group of the Commission	Mimeographed. For the adopted text, see *Official Records of the General Assembly, Sixty-first Session, Supplement No. 10* (A/61/10). The final text appears in *Yearbook ... 2006*, vol. II (Part Two), paras. 241 to 251.
A/CN.4/L.703	Unilateral acts of States—report of the Working Group: conclusions of the Commission	Mimeographed. For the adopted text, see *Official Records of the General Assembly, Sixty-first Session, Supplement No. 10* (A/61/10). The final text appears in *Yearbook ... 2006*, vol. II (Part Two), para. 176.
A/CN.4/L.704	Programme, procedures and working methods of the Commission, and its documentation: report of the Planning Group	Mimeographed. For the adopted text, see *Official Records of the General Assembly, Sixty-first Session, Supplement No. 10* (A/61/10). The final text appears in *Yearbook ... 2006*, vol. II (Part Two), paras. 253 to 270.
A/CN.4/SR.2867–A/CN.4/SR.2913	Provisional summary records of the 2867th to 2913th meetings	*Idem*. The final text appears in *Yearbook ... 2006*, vol. I.